TYPES OF ENGLISH *Drama*

TYPES OF

ENGLISH *Drama*

ⓞ ⓞ

Edited by John W. Ashton

UNIVERSITY OF KANSAS

New York · 1940

THE MACMILLAN COMPANY

PRINTED IN THE UNITED STATES OF AMERICA
AMERICAN BOOK-STRATFORD PRESS, INC., NEW YORK

TYPES OF ENGLISH LITERATURE
Hardin Craig, *General Editor*

❀ ❀

TYPES OF ENGLISH *Poetry*
Edited by Rudolf Kirk *and* Clara Marburg Kirk

TYPES OF ENGLISH *Drama*
Edited by John W. Ashton

TYPES OF ENGLISH *Fiction*
Edited by Hardin Craig *and* John W. Dodds

TYPES OF ENGLISH *Prose*
Edited by Virgil B. Heltzel

PREFACE

THIS VOLUME is designed to present the chief types of English drama to students of English literature, at the same time giving them an opportunity to see in outline something of the historical development of modern English drama. Considerations of expense have made it impossible to include some of the less important types, notably heroic tragedy and some subdivisions of modern realistic drama. No plays by Shakespeare (who tried his hand at most types) are included for the obvious reason that most students will have easy access to his plays in other editions and will wish to know his works more fully than this volume could present them.

Every effort has been made to make the plays readable without endangering the soundness of the texts. Hence the two first plays have been modernized and in the others disturbing or puzzling variations from modern usage in spelling and punctuation have been brought in harmony with modern practice.

The purist may object to the inclusion of an "American" play, O'Neill's *Anna Christie*, in a volume entitled *Types of English Drama*. It should be clear that English is not a provincial term here but is used to designate a literary tradition which the literatures of England and America share. It happens that it seems to the editor that the best examples of one type of drama in English have been produced on this side of the Atlantic. That explains the inclusion of *Anna Christie*.

The reading lists appended to each introduction are designed to be suggestive of the importance of the type and its variations rather than in any sense inclusive. In short, it is hoped that this is a usable volume, without excess baggage but with all the material that the intelligent teacher and student will find necessary for an introduction to the drama.

J. W. A.

To My Wife

CONTENTS

ix

TYPES OF ENGLISH *Drama*

INTRODUCTION

UNLIKE SMALL BOYS of a generation ago, plays should be both seen and heard. Fundamentally there is an element of artificiality in *reading* a play, for any true drama is designed and intended to be put on the stage, to be set out in three dimensions before an audience. It exists not as a lot of words on paper but as a scene with people moving in it, talking about themselves and about other people, playing out the comedy or the tragedy of their lives in crucial moments while we, the audience look on and listen. As Aristotle pointed out centuries ago, the drama is concerned with action and with the sources of action both within and outside human character.

Hence reading plays should never be looked on as a substitute for seeing them. Rather, the reader should try his best to visualize as he reads. He may have the advantage of being less hurried than the viewer often is, may have more time to ponder the intellectual content of the play, but such an advantage is to no purpose if the reader forgets these other aspects of drama. For a play cannot be read as a novel is. It calls for a quite different type of imaginative reconstruction from that necessary for other types of literature. The novelist has at his hand resources of description and narration and straight exposition that are denied to the dramatist, whose story must be told through dialogue. This dialogue, therefore, must carry the burden of giving us all the essential information about both action and character at the same time that it carries forward the story. We who read the play, in turn, must develop the ability to respond to the suggestions of the dramatist, to create in our mind's eye scene and moving character, to hear the proper inflections and intonations of the speeches as we read. The skilful dramatist makes such reconstruction in our imaginations easy by inserting in the dialogue clues as to the stage business which accompanies so many speeches.

It may be something as simple as Hamlet's

> Let us go in together.
> And still your fingers on your lips, I pray. . . .
> Nay, come; let's go together.
>
> (I, v, 187 ff.)

Here Shakespeare says to us, Hamlet motions to Horatio and Marcellus to accompany him out; they stand respectfully aside to let him, their prince, precede them as his rank demands; but Hamlet, the soul of courtesy and friendliness (after all, they have experienced a rendezvous with a ghost together) in spite of his great excitement, rejects the social distinction they would make and takes them off with him as his friends, perhaps with his arm about Horatio's shoulder. Or it may be the more elaborate and thoroughly delightful scene in *Romeo and Juliet* in which we see Romeo first approaching the lovely lady who has attracted him so greatly, his taking her by the hand, his begging a kiss and then tricking her, not unwilling, out of a second kiss—all suggested in the dialogue:

> ROMEO. If I profane with my unworthiest hand
> This holy shrine, the gentle fine is this:
> My lips, two blushing pilgrims, ready stand
> To smooth that rough touch with a tender kiss.
> JULIET. Good pilgrim, you do wrong your hand too much,
> Which mannerly devotion shows in this;
> For saints have hands that pilgrim's hands do touch,
> And palm to palm is holy palmers' kiss.
> ROMEO. Have not saints lips, and holy palmers too?
> JULIET. Ay, pilgrim, lips that they must use in prayer.
> ROMEO. O, then, dear saint, let lips do what hands do;
> They pray, grant thou, lest faith turn to despair.
> JULIET. Saints do not move, though grant for prayers' sake.
> ROMEO. Then move not, while my prayer's effect I take.
> Thus from my lips, by yours, my sin is purged.
> JULIET. Then have my lips the sin that they have took.
> ROMEO. Sin from my lips? O trespass sweetly urged!
> Give me my sin again.
> JULIET. You kiss by the book.
>
> (I, v, 95 ff.)

For such a passage one needs no stage directions for the
dramatist has indicated them fully in the dialogue itself. These
are obvious examples of what is constantly happening in
drama, sometimes on a much more elaborate or more subtle
scale than in these two instances, and they indicate how important it is that the reader should reconstruct the scene in
his mind's eye as he reads. Modern plays are usually specially
prepared for him with elaborate stage directions, even with
discussions of motives and points of view which should come
out in the dialogue. But though such devices serve to inform
us, they do not take the place of the imaginative reconstruction that must be a part of any reading of the drama.

Fierce debate has sometimes raged as to exactly what con-
stitutes drama. Some critics have insisted that conflict is the
essential element; equally vociferously others have called it
crisis. Actually the two terms are not so far apart as their
proponents, in the heat of debate, would imply. In a measure
both parties are right, unless each carries his term (or his
opponent's term) beyond the limits of accuracy or necessity.
That a true drama deals with crisis has been apparent from
the very beginnings of speculation as to its nature. It is that
which Aristotle has in mind when he says that the action of a
play must have a beginning, a middle, and an end. We must
recognize that no story in its entirety has, strictly speaking,
either beginning or end. Always there are antecedent events
that explain what is now happening; always what is now happening results in some later developments. The dramatist like
any other story-teller must draw out of this chain of events
a particular, limited sequence which for one reason or another
may be thought of as significant in itself and as relatively complete in itself. That is, this sequence may be understood without the necessity of too great reference to what has gone
before, and it comes to rest without leaving too many threads
of action incomplete. It is a segment of life which can stand
by itself; it has a beginning and an end. The dramatist, however, must choose with the special conditions of his medium
in mind. His must be a story that lends itself to telling in
dialogue, within the two and a half or three hours possible

on the stage. Hence there must be a moment or series of moments in the succession of circumstances which rises sharply above the level of ordinary experience; that is, there must be a middle, a point to which action leads up and from which it fades away, a climax or turning point.

This rise and fall is usually brought about by conflict, but we must remember that conflict may be of many sorts. It may be, as it always is in melodrama, conflict between external, objective forces; the "hero" is set opposite the "villain" and there ensues a struggle between them for some external end: wealth, the possession of an inheritance, the love of a fair lady, or any other reward. Or the conflict may be internal, within the mind or personality of the main character. He may have to choose between love and honor (the stock situation in the heroic tragedy). He may have to make a compromise between a desire for the balanced, rational life and the idea of a passionate revenge, as Hamlet does. Or in the third place (and this is true of most great tragedies) the conflict may be both internal and external. Hamlet has to bring himself to a bloody, passionate deed, but he also has to outwit and circumvent a clever uncle who has killed the elder Hamlet and seized the throne. The crisis has come as a moment in eternity when these forces, subjective and objective, are in conflict. And when that conflict is ended, in this case by the death of all the principals, the crisis is resolved as far as the dramatist is concerned. We may wonder what the Danes thought of Fortinbras as king, or how Horatio told Hamlet's story, or how Rosencrantz and Guildenstern faced death in England, but these are details outside the particular crisis which Shakespeare has chosen.

What are the dramatist's methods then? First he must make us aware, actually or symbolically, of the general nature of the crisis which he is presenting. That may be done awkwardly, as it often has been, by introducing two subordinate characters who appear at the beginning of the play only to talk about the problems of the principals in the action for the enlightenment of the audience. It is a device burlesqued in *The Critic*. Or even a single speaker may come out and soliloquize, as Richard III does at the beginning of Shakespeare's play about him, telling the audience what it needs to know about the general situation and his place in it. But at their best the greatest dramatists reject such unnatural and clumsy methods. They start the action at once, weaving into it bit by bit, often so unobtrusively that we are not at once aware what is happening, those bits of information that are necessary for our understanding of the story and its significance. Such men realize that the effect of a drama is twofold if the drama is to assume the proportions of true literature. It must arouse in us both an intellectual and an emotional response. But for a maid and a butler to chatter glibly while they perform purposeless and insignificant acts arouses in us no particular response at all. The truly effective dramatist cannot let us sink back into our seats in cold and calm indifference; we must enter into the lives of the characters whose problems are unfolding before us. We do not fool ourselves into thinking even for the moment that the scene is real, but we do understand, if the dramatist is alive to his opportunities and alert to the demands of his art, that the scene is significant. How skilfully the fundamental crisis of the play may be presented is shown in the magnificent artistry of the first scene of *Romeo and Juliet* and of *Hamlet*, where we are not told directly what the crisis is, but all the resources of our imaginations and emotions are drawn into play as we have it suggested indirectly in all its ominous significance.

Having thus provided his beginning and shown its background, the dramatist must sustain our interest in the development of his action by the use of suspense, that is, by indicating the general line of development without making too certain the outcome of each step or the exact means by which that outcome is to be reached. Here he must make a choice. He must decide whether to take his audience completely into his confidence, divulging to them the exact and true significance of all that happens before or as it happens; or whether to keep his audience in the dark, to deceive them or trick them by withholding essential information as Shakespeare does in *The Winters Tale*. In that play he lets us believe that Hermione, the wife of King Leontes, has died until in the last act he divulges the truth, as much to our surprise as Leontes', that she has been hidden away for many years by a faithful servant. On a larger scale Ben Jonson does the same thing in his *Epicene* in which the true sex of one of the characters is not disclosed until the end of the play, to the great confusion of the other characters and to the excited surprise of the audience. Such a method makes for great theatrical effectiveness in the scene in which the secret is disclosed; but the former method results in truer dramatic effectiveness. Instead of a sudden bit of fireworks there is the steady, sustained warmth of a fire that grows more and more brilliant as the action progresses. Our interest is sustained and intensified by the desire to see the response of the characters when they come to be as well informed as we are.

Furthermore, our experience is enriched by the emotional and intellectual satisfaction which comes from the use of dramatic irony (the fact that we have information that is withheld from the characters in the play) made possible by the dramatist's taking us into his confidence. This is a particularly effective device in tragedy (though it is certainly not without its uses in comedy), where the feelings of horror and pity inspired in us by the tragedy may be heightened by our sense of the futility of the characters' striving against opposition which they cannot hope to overcome or against forces with which they should and could be in harmony if they but had a little more knowledge. In *Othello* we know that Desdemona is really innocent of deceit or of infidelity to her husband,—indeed, that she is quite incapable of such things; but Othello cannot judge as we can, since he lacks our sources of information. Because we see Iago alone and with Roderigo, we know that the epithet "honest" applied to him is sheer nonsense, but the other characters cannot know this, and we give them our sympathy because of their very limitations. Before the duel is suggested to Hamlet we know the evil plots that are laid against him and are thus able to watch the duel with an emotional intensity that is heightened by his frank and noble apology to Laertes at the beginning.

In all this it becomes apparent that we must turn our attention to the characters who speak the dialogue and take part in the action, for on them and their development depends in large measure our response to the play. If the characters are inadequate, wooden, insufficiently motivated, the drama is likely to die of pernicious anemia; effective drama must show the warm pulse of humanity. Although there may be momentary satisfaction from a story in which only the plot matters and the characters are only puppets clearly being jerked about by the author (as in a mystery-detective play), permanent pleasure comes only from a work in which we find living human beings whom we recognize as types of men but who have an individual birthright of their own; that is, they are true characters, not merely character parts. The stage Englishman of the comic (or even serious) drama of a generation or two ago may have seemed thoroughly comic on first sight, but he has scarcely stood repetition as has Bottom the Weaver or Hamlet. There is also a further reason than that the stage Englishman was only a caricature. Characters must be sufficiently large in scope; we must feel that there is understandable motivation for what they do; we must find them consistent within the limits of the story and their part in it. Most of all, however, we must feel that the characters are significant for their relationship to life outside the narrow limits of the particular situation in the play. It is only when they have attained to this universality, when they have become involved in basic patterns of human conduct, that we accept the drama as a criticism of life. To put it differently, really effective drama has something to say about life, as all good literature has. And the more profound the commentary, the more necessary it is that the characters shall be able to bear its weight, that they shall be creations sufficiently substantial to impress us with their power (either for good or evil) and their liveliness of perception. If we are to see life through them, they must be alive.

In the presentation of character the dramatist is denied some of the means of the novelist. The dramatist cannot indulge in straight descriptions of any length. He must depend on our forming judgments from the character's own speeches, from his actions, and from what is said about him by other characters in the play. In this connection it is well to remember that each character has his existence only in the play, and

that speculation as to what he was like before the action of
the play (unless the dramatist sees fit to inform us) may be
interesting as guesswork but is pointless as dramatic criticism.
Even Marlowe's Edward II is not the same person as the historical Edward II, and while it may be interesting and profitable to compare the two portraits, they should be kept distinct.

Like any other art the drama has its conventions which
must be understood and accepted if we are to enjoy and appreciate the work. And the conventions change from age to
age and from country to country. Nowadays we are used
to a picture frame stage, set off definitely and finally from the
audience (except in a few experimental plays), and we are
expected to accept the fiction that people in a room on the
stage go about their business blissfully unaware that one side
of their room is gone and that they are being observed by a
great many people. The actors make it seem that they have
no contact with the audience, are not even aware of their
existence.

It has not always been so, however. In earlier times, during
the sixteenth and early seventeenth centuries, there was little
or none of this sharp setting off one from the other of actors
and spectators. In the public theaters in Elizabethan England
a portion of the stage projected into the audience, who stood
close to it. On the stage might be seated young men of fashion,
who were not always too well behaved. Such an arrangement
made for an intimacy between actor and audience that is quite
foreign to our experience. As a result, such devices as the
aside and soliloquy, which seem grotesque and even down-
right silly when shouted across footlights and orchestra well
to a seated audience, would seem perfectly natural when
spoken by an actor thus close to his audience.

Likewise methods of presenting one's subject may change.
The Elizabethan audience was interested in the analysis of
passion by the characters. The modern audience is interested
in the presentation of the passion through the actions of the
character. The Elizabethan method called for long introspec-
tive speeches, at their best rich in rhetorical power, at their

worst mere pieces of rant, the tearing a passion to tatters. The modern method tends to be less loquacious, leaves for the audience the analysis, to be made on the basis of suggestions supplied by action or dialogue. One is not intrinsically better than the other; the two methods simply illustrate the way in which conventions grow out of the physical conditions of the theater and intellectual conditions of the time.

Drama is to be measured, however, not by its conventions but by its more substantial attributes. So we return to the point from which we set out, that drama is an art of movement. We may test a play by the skill with which its author makes it move, breathes life into a story until we grow increasingly aware of it as a significant approach to life, an avenue to adventure it may be or, on a higher level, a rich and satisfying consideration of some or many of the eternal problems of our existence.

SUGGESTED READINGS

Archer, William, *The Old Drama and the New.* NEW YORK, 1923.
——, *Playmaking.* NEW YORK, 1924.
Baker, George P., *Dramatic Technique.* BOSTON, 1919.
Bradbrooke, M. C., *Themes and Conventions of Elizabethan Tragedy.* CAMBRIDGE, 1936.
Brunetière, Ferdinand, *The Law of the Drama.* NEW YORK, 1914.
Chambers, E. K., *The Elizabethan Stage.* OXFORD, 1923.
Cheney, Sheldon, *The Theater.* NEW YORK, 1929.
Clark, Barrett H., *A Study of the Modern Drama.* NEW YORK, 1928.
Cooper, Lane, *An Aristotelian Theory of Comedy.* NEW YORK, 1922.
Drew, Elizabeth, *Discovering Drama.* NEW YORK, 1937.
Eaton, W. P., *The Drama in England.* NEW YORK, 1930.
Freytag, Gustav, *The Technique of the Drama.* NEW YORK, 1894.
Henderson, Archibald, *The Changing Drama.* CINCINNATI, 1919.
Matthews, Brander, *A Study of the Drama.* BOSTON, 1910.
Meredith, George, *Essay on Comedy.* LONDON, 1877.
Nicoll, Allardyce, *Introduction to Dramatic Theory.* NEW YORK, [N.D.].
Thorndike, A. H., *Tragedy.* BOSTON, 1908.
Vaughan, C. E., *Types of Tragic Drama.* LONDON, 1908.
Ward, A. W., *History of English Dramatic Literature to the Death of Queen Anne.* 3 VOLS. LONDON, 1899.

THE MYSTERY PLAY

OUT OF THE SERVICES of the medieval Church developed the drama as we know it today. Said in Latin to congregations which were mostly unlearned, indeed very largely illiterate, the services of the Church could have had little meaning in themselves. Hence, such services were always full of symbolic action. Somewhat more than a thousand years ago (during a period when the church service was undergoing many variations) some clever chorister or priest conceived the idea of acting out the event commemorated in the Easter service to make it more vivid, to give it more meaning for the congregation. In his church on Easter morning something like the following was acted in celebration of an event recorded in the Four Gospels. Three of the clergy representing the three Marys approached the altar, which was guarded by one or two others representing the angels at the tomb. The latter chanted in Latin, "Whom seek ye in the sepulcher, O Christians?" to which the three replied, "Jesus of Nazareth, the Crucified, O Heavenly Ones." Then came the resounding answer from the angels, "He is not here; he is risen, as he foretold. Go and tell that he is risen from the sepulcher."

Simple as it is, this, or something very like it, represents the beginnings of modern drama. There is impersonation; there is dialogue which tells a story; there is even some slight action.

If we may judge from the scattered but very frequent remains, the idea of dramatic representation in the service was picked up rapidly and spread to many religious centers. The simple little play was expanded to give background, even to introduce a touch of comedy to lighten the story and give it new interest, as in a scene between the Marys and an Ointment-Seller, introduced literally but soon expanded purely for comic effect. Furthermore, it was felt that if the crux of the Easter service could be dramatized effectively the same

10

might be done for the services in other important seasons in the Church year. So there grew up Christmas plays and saints plays, a whole mass of dramatic and semi-dramatic literature that grew so elaborate and at times so boisterous and irreligious that it was taken out of the churches, translated into the vernacular, and eventually brought into secular hands.

The Play of Abraham and Isaac is representative of that later, secular development. Instead of a single play for a day of festival, there developed groups or cycles of related plays, or perhaps more accurately, long plays consisting of a large number of episodes, all centered around a single great theme, the fall of man and his redemption and final judgment. Beginning with the Creation of the World, or even going back of that to the Fall of the Evil Angels, these cycles run on through the important narratives of the Old Testament, the stories of patriarchs and prophets, down to the act of Redemption, the Life of Christ, treated as several episodes. But this was not all, for this was the story of the life of Mankind and that could not be concluded without a series of plays or acts dealing with the coming of Antichrist (the last great attempt of Satan to rule the world) and the Last Judgment, in which the good were given their reward and the evil sent howling off to everlasting punishment.

In the thirteenth and fourteenth centuries there grew up under secular auspices, as has been said, cycles of plays in many of the cities of England. Chester and York, Wakefield and Coventry were centers for such entertainments, but cycles long or short appeared in many other places. They were largely in control of craft guilds, which would correspond roughly to our trades unions. Each guild was responsible for one complete part of the cycle. In some cities an attempt was made to give appropriate plays to each of the groups. In Chester the Water Drawers of Dee were responsible for the play of Noah and the flood; the Slaughter of the Innocents was under the direction of the Butchers, and so on. The presentation of a full cycle of plays each year was thus a large scale community enterprise.

Secular responsibility for the plays, however, did not result in a loss of religious significance for them. The material, in spite of the addition of horse-play or profane material, was still thoroughly religious in its implications and interests. Even more than had been true when they were still presented in the church they were used for the inculcation of sound doctrine and for the explanation of important mysteries in the beliefs and practices of the Church. They were presented at the festival seasons of the Church Year, especially on Corpus Christi Day or at Whitsuntide, and they shared in the religious associations of those days.

A word as to the manner of presentation. Such long and diversified plays as these cycles were offered many real problems in staging. As is often the case, the simplest form proved most satisfactory as well as most feasible. In many places, particularly on the continent of Europe but also in England, the component stories of the grand cycle were acted at fixed stations arranged around a central place, or *platea*. In other cities and towns each play was presented on a large "pageant," a wagon with two stories, an upper one on which the play was presented and a lower one which served as dressing room or in appropriate plays could serve as Hell, down into which agonizing souls could be carried or prodded by malicious and leering devils. On the morning of Corpus Christi Day, for instance, the first "pageant," presenting the story of the Fall of Lucifer, would move to a location which had been agreed upon. There the play would be presented, whereupon the wagon would move on to a new station and present its play again, while the second wagon would present the play of the "Creation" at the first station; and so on until all the parts had been played at each of the stations. That some care and expense were taken is indicated by records which have survived and which indicate the use of properties and of rather elaborate costumes. The scene on the stage might be any place that the dramatist wished as long as he gave some clue to the listeners. Thus in the Abraham and Isaac play here presented there are several changes of scene that are indicated only by the dialogue or by some implication that the characters have walked around the stage.

There are more artistically effective plays than the Chester "Abraham and Isaac" in the mystery cycles, but it is safe to

say that there are none which are more representative of the
characteristics of this type of drama. Its connection with the
main theme of the cycle is made abundantly clear at the same
time that the religious and doctrinal elements are being established. As the author saw the story of Abraham and Isaac, it
was the story which showed by anticipation the establishment
of the Eucharist as the great sacrament testifying to the
peculiar relationship between God and Man. You will note
how that is made clear not only in the speeches of the Expositor but also in the obvious symbolism of the bread and
wine in the meeting of Melchizedek and Abraham. Furthermore, tithing, a very important part of ecclesiastical economy
in those days, is given the authority both of antiquity and of
a great personality like Abraham. Then too, the discussion of
the rite of circumcision leads to a distinction between the "Old
Law" of the Old Testament and the "New Law" of the New
Testament.

But a good play needs more than a theme. In the crucial
event of this play, the sacrifice of Isaac, we have the development of emotion which is simple and direct but very effective.
The Brome play on the same subject is perhaps richer in pathos
in this situation, but our Chester dramatist is not unaware of
the possibilities in such a case and uses them with some skill.
The gentle, almost heroic fortitude of the small boy as he
begins to suspect and then learns for certainty the truth as to
the sacrifice still has power to move an audience. The play,
like many other mystery plays, has little real structure, as is
apparent from the succession of rather unrelated episodes, but
we must remember that these episodes are given unity not only
by the character of Abraham but also by the feeling that he is
an instrument of the Divine in the world and that these are
all manifestations of the working of God's purposes. In that
light each episode is truly related to each of the others.

SUGGESTED READINGS

Adams, J. Q., *Chief Pre-Shakespearean Dramas*. NEW YORK, 1924.
Cambridge History of English Literature, VOL. V. NEW YORK, 1910.
Chambers, E. K., *The Mediaeval Stage*. OXFORD, 1903.

Deimling, Hermann, and Dr. Matthews, *The Chester Plays*. EARLY ENGLISH
　　TEXT SOCIETY, EXTRA SERIES. 1893, 1923.
Pollard, A. W., *English Miracle Plays*. OXFORD, 1923.
Spencer, M. L., *Corpus Christi Pageants in England*. NEW YORK, 1911.
Young, Karl, *The Drama of the Medieval Church*. OXFORD, 1933.

Bradford, Roark, and Connelly, Mark, *The Green Pastures*. NEW YORK, 1930.
Marquis, Don, *The Dark Hours*. NEW YORK, 1932.

THE PLAY OF
ABRAHAM AND MELCHIZEDEK AND LOT, WITH THE SACRIFICE OF ISAAC

The Characters

MESSENGER, *or Expositor*	GOD
ABRAHAM	ISAAC
LOT, *His Brother*	TWO ANGELS
MELCHIZEDEK, *King of Salem*	A SOLDIER

This is the fourth pageant of the series. The Fall of Lucifer, the Creation, and the Deluge have already been played. Now a Messenger comes in to announce the new pageant.

MESSENGER. All peace, my Lords, that be present
And hearken now with good intent.
Now Noah away from us is went
And all his company,

And Abraham, through God's grace
He is come into this place
If you will give him room and space
To tell you his story.

This play, in truth, begin shall he
In worship of the Trinity   10
That ye may all hear and see
That shall be done today.

My name is Gobet on the green,
With you no longer I may be seen
Farewell, my good Lords, all by dene
For letting of your play.
> [*He goes out and Abraham and Lot come in, rejoicing over their victory over the four kings, who were carrying Lot into captivity.*

15. *by dene*, together.   16. The story is found in Genesis, XIV–XXII.

15

ABRAHAM. Ah, thou high God, granter of grace,
That neither ending nor beginning has
I thank thee, Lord, that to me has
Today given victory   20

Lot, my brother, that taken was,
I have restored him in this case
And brought him home into his place
Through thy might and mastery.

Worship of thee I will not withstand
That four kings of uncouth land
Today hast sent into my hand,
And of riches great array.

Therefore of all that I can win
To give thee tithe I will begin,   30
As soon as the city I come in,
And share with thee my prey.

Melchizedek, who here king is
And God's priest, also, I wis,
The tithe I will give him of this,
As reason is that I do.

God has sent me victory
Over four kings graciously;
With him my prey share will I
The city when I come to.   40

LOT, *rejoicing in his rescue.*
Abraham, my brother, I thank thee
That this day hast delivered me
From enemy's hands and their postye
And saved me from woe.

Therefore I will give a tithing
Of my goods as long as I am living
And now also of his sending
Tithe I will give also.
    [*Meanwhile Melchizedek has appeared on the other side of
    the stage from Abraham and Lot, and now a soldier rushes
    up to him.*

43. *postye*, power.

SOLDIER. My lord the king, tidings aright
   Your heart to make glad and light: 50
   Abraham hath slain in fight
   Four kings since he went.

   Here he will be this very night
   And riches with him enough in sight.
   I heard him thank God almight
   For grace he had him sent.

MELCHIZEDEK, *raising his hands toward heaven in praise and bless-*
   ing.
   Ah! blessed be God that is but one
   To meet Abraham I will be gone
   Worshipfully, and that at once
   My office to fulfil;   60

   And present him with bread and wine
   For grace of God is him within;
   Hasten away for love mine!
   For this is God's will.

SOLDIER, *bringing a chalice.*
   Sir, here is wine, no doubt or fear,
   And with it bread, both white and clear,
   To present him in good manner
   That so us helped has.·

MELCHIZEDEK. To God, I know, he is most dear,
   For in all things his prayer   70
   He hath, without danger,
   And specially great grace.
     [*So he goes toward Abraham, offering him the chalice with*
       the wine in it and the white bread on the paten, as in the
       Eucharist, and saying.

   Abraham, welcome must thou be,
   God's grace is fully in thee,
   Blessed ever must thou be
   That enemies so makes meek.

   I have brought, as you may see,
   Bread and wine for thy degree;
   Receive this present now from me,
   And that I thee beseech.   80

ABRAHAM. Sir King, welcome in good faith
    Thy present is welcome pleasure today.
    God has helped me today
    Unworthy though I be.

    He shall have part of my prey
    That I won, since I went away.
    Therefore to thee, thou take it may,
    The tenth I offer thee.
      [He gives him a horse laden with gifts.

MELCHIZEDEK. And your present, Sir, take I,
    And honor it devoutly,   90
    For much good it may signify
    In time that is coming.

    Therefore horse, harness, and perye
    As is suitable to my dignity
    The tithe of it I take of thee,
    And receive thy offering.
      [Then Abraham receives the bread and wine and Melchizedek
      takes the gift-laden horse. Lot feels it necessary to play
      his part.

LOT. And I will offer with good intent
    Of such goods as God hath me sent
    To Melchizedek here present,
    As God's will is to be.   100

    Abraham, my brother, offered has
    And so will I through God's grace,
    This royal cup before your face,
    Receive it now from me.
      [Then Lot offers a cup with bread and wine, which Mel-
      chizedek receives.

MELCHIZEDEK. Sir, your offering welcome is,
    And well I know in truth, I wis,
    That fully God's will it is
    What is now done today.

    Go we together to my city,
    And now God heartily thank we   110

93. *perye,* jewelry.

That helps us even through his postye,
For so we very well may.
[*The Expositor rides in to bring this "act" of the play to
a conclusion.*

EXPOSITOR. My Lords, what this may signify
I will expound expertly,
That the unlearned, standing hereby,
May know what this may be.

This offering, a true sacrament,
Signifieth the New Testament
That now is used with good intent
Throughout all Christianity.   120

In the old law, without lying,
When these two good men were living,
Of beasts was all their offering
And, too, their sacrament.

But since Christ died on rood-tree,
With bread and wine him worship we,
At his last supper in his maundy
Was his commandment.

But that these things might used be
Afterward, as now do we,   130
In signification, as you believe me,
Melchizedek did so;

And tithe-makings, as you see here,
By Abraham then begun were.
Therefore he was to God most dear,
And so were they both two.

By Abraham understand I may
The Father of Heaven in good faith,
Melchizedek a priest to his pay
To minister that sacrament   140

That Christ ordained on that said day
In bread and wine to honor him aye:
This signifieth, the truth to say,
Melchizedek's present.
[*He rides off, and God speaks from above; perhaps he does
not appear, but we hear his voice.*

111. *postye*, power.   127. *maundy*, sacrament of the Eucharist.

GOD. Abraham, my servant, I say to thee,
   Thy help and succor I will be,
   For thy good deed much pleaseth me,
   I tell thee surely.

ABRAHAM. Lord, one thing that thou wilt see,
   That I pray after with heart free,   150
   Grant me, Lord, through thy ability:
   Some fruit of my body!

   I have no child, foul or fair,
   Except my nurry, to be my heir,
   That makes me greatly to impair.
   On me, Lord, have mercy.

GOD. My friend, Abraham, believe thou me:
   Thy nurry thine heir shall not be,
   But one son I shall send thee,
   Begotten of thy body.   160

   No more shalt thou, for no need
   Number of thy body the seed
   That thou shalt have, without dread,
   Thou art to me so dear

   Abraham, do as I thee say;
   Look up and tell me, if thou may,
   Stars standing on the straye;
   That impossible were.

   Wherefore, Abraham, servant free,
   See that thou be true to me,   170
   And promise here I make with thee
   Thy seed to multiply.

   So much more further shalt thou be,
   Kings of thy seed men shall see,
   And one Child of great degree
   All mankind shall forbuy.

   I will that from henceforth alway
   Each manchild on the eighth day
   Be circumcised, as I say,
   And thou thyself most soon.   180

---

154. *nurry*, foster-child.   167. *straye*, heavens.   176. *forbuy*, redeem.

And who circumcised ne'er is
Forsaken shall be with me, I wis;
For disobedient that man is.
Therefore look that this be done.

ABRAHAM. Lord, already in good fay
Blessed be thou, ever and ay;
For that men in truth know may
Thy folk from other men,

Circumcised they shall be all
At once, spite of aught that may befall.   190
I thank thee, Lord, thy own thrall,
Kneeling on my knee.

EXPOSITOR, *coming forward again to bring the second "act" to a
    close.*
Good Lords all, take good intent
What betokens this commandment:
- This was some time a sacrament
In th' old law truly ta'en

As followeth now verament,
So was this in the Old Testament;
But when Christ died, away it went,
And baptism then began.   200

Also God commands here
To Abraham, his servant dear,
So much seed that in no manner
Numbered might it be,

And one seed, Mankind to forby,
That was Jesus Christ truly,
For of his stock was our Lady
And so also was he.
    [*He goes away, and we are to imagine the passage of time
     for Isaac to be born and to grow into boyhood. Then the
     voice of God is heard once again.*

GOD. Abraham, my servant Abraham.
ABRAHAM. Lo, Lord, already here I am.   210
GOD. Take Isaac, thy son by name,
    Whom thou lovest best of all

185. *fay,* faith.   197. *verament,* truly.

And in sacrifice offer him to me
Upon that hill, beside thee.
Abraham, I will that it so be,
Spite of aught that may befall.

ABRAHAM. My Lord, to thee is my intent
Ever to be obedient;
That son that thou to me hast sent,
Offer I will to thee   220

And fulfil thy commandment
With hearty will, as I am kent.
High God, Lord omnipotent,
Thy bidding done shall be.

My household and my children each one
Remain at home, both all and one,
Except Isaac shall with me be gone
To a hill here beside.
    [*He goes back to his dwelling and makes ready a bundle of
    wood. Isaac comes to assist him. Abraham covers his emo-
    tion as best he can.*

ABRAHAM. Make thee ready, my darling,
For we must do a little thing.   230
This wood upon thy back thou bring,
We must not long abide.

A sword and fire I will take,
For sacrifice I must make;
God's bidding will I not forsake,
But aye obedient be.

ISAAC. Father I am all ready
To do your bidding meekly.
To bear this wood quite ready am I
As you command me.   240

ABRAHAM, *resting his hand on Isaac's head.*
O Isaac, Isaac, my darling dear,
My blessing now I give thee here.
Take up this faggot with good cheer,
And on thy back it bring,

222. *kent,* known.

And fire with me I will take.

ISAAC. Your bidding I will not forsake,
 Father; I will ne'er be slack
To fulfil your bidding.
 [*So he takes the wood on his back and father and son walk
 around as if they were going up a mountain, talking to-
 gether as they go.*

ABRAHAM. Now, Isaac, son, go we our way
 To yonder mountain, if that we may.   250
ISAAC. My dear father, I will assay
 To follow you full fain.

ABRAHAM [*Aside*]. O! my heart will break in three,
 To hear thy words I have pity.
 As thou wilt, Lord, so must it be:
 To thee I will be bayne.
 [*They come to the mountain top and stop.*

ABRAHAM. Lay down thy faggot, my own son dear.
ISAAC. Already, father, lo it is here.
 But why make you so heavy a cheere?
 Are you of anything adread?   260

Father, if it be your will,
 Where is the beast that we shall kill?
ABRAHAM. There is none, son, upon this hill
 That I see here in this stead.

ISAAC, *beginning to be frightened*.
 Father I am sore afraid
 To see you bear this drawn sword.
 I hope for all middle-earth
 You will not slay your child.

ABRAHAM. Dread thee not, my child, I read
 Our Lord will send, through his Godhead   270
 Some kind of beast into this stead,
 Either tame or wild.

256. *bayne*, ready, willing.
259. *so heavy a cheere*, so sad a countenance.
267. *middle-earth*, this world.

ISAAC, *not yet satisfied.*
　Father, tell me, ere I go,
　Whether I shall have harm or no.
ABRAHAM. Ah, dear God, for me is woe!
　Thou burst my heart in sunder.

ISAAC. Father, tell me of this case,
　Why you your sword drawn has,
　And bear it naked in this place;
　Thereof I have great wonder.　　　　　　　　280

ABRAHAM. Isaac, son, peace, I pray thee!
　Thou breakest my heart, even in three.
ISAAC. I pray you father, keep nothing from me,
　But tell me what you think.

ABRAHAM. O Isaac, Isaac, I must thee kill!
ISAAC. Alas, father, is that your will,
　Your own child here for to spill,
　Upon this hill's brink?

　If I have trespassed in any degree,
　With a stick you may beat me;　　　　　　　290
　Put up your sword, if your will be,
　For I am but a child.

ABRAHAM. O my son, I am sorry
　To do to thee this great annoy:
　God's commandment do must I,
　His works are aye most mild.

ISAAC. Would God my mother were here with me!
　She would kneel upon her knee,
　Praying you, father, if it might be,
　For to save my life.　　　　　　　　　300

ABRAHAM. O comely creature, unless I thee kill,
　I grieve my God, and that most ill;
　I may not work against his will
　But even obedient be.

　O Isaac, son, to thee I say,
　God has commanded me this day
　Sacrifice—this is no nay—
　To make of thy body.

ISAAC. Is it God's will I should be slain?
ABRAHAM. Yea, son, it is not for to layne   310
  To his bidding I will be bayne
  Ever to his pleasing.

  Unless I do this doleful deed,
  My Lord will not pay me my meed.
ISAAC. Mary! father, God forbid
  But that you do your offering.

  Father, at home your sons you shall find
  That you must love by course of kind.
  Be I once out of your mind
  Your sorrow may soon cease,

  But you must do God's bidding.   320
  Father, tell my mother for nothing.
ABRAHAM. For sorrow I may my hands wring,
  Thy mother I cannot please.

  O Isaac, blessed may thou be!
  Almost my wits I lose for thee,
  The blood of thy body so free
  Me thinks most loathe to shed.

ISAAC. Father, since you must needs do so,
  Let it pass lightly and overgo;   330
  Kneeling on my knees two,
  Your blessing on me spread!

ABRAHAM. My blessing, dear son, give I thee
  And thy mother's, with heart so free;
  The blessing of the Trinity,
  My dear son, on thee light.

ISAAC. Father, I pray you hide mine eyes
  That I see not your sword so keen;
  Your stroke, father, would I not have seen
  Lest I before it quake.   340

ABRAHAM. My dear son Isaac, speak no more,
  Thy words make my heart most sore.
ISAAC. O dear father, wherefore? Wherefore?
  Since I must needs be dead?

---

310. *layne*, conceal.   318. *by course of kind*, according to nature.
321. *tell my mother for nothing*, don't let my mother know.

Of one thing I would you pray;
Since I must die the death this day,
As few strokes as you may,
When you smite off my head.

ABRAHAM. Thy meekness, child, makes me afray;
  My song may be, "Well away."   350
ISAAC. O dear father, do away
  Your making so heavy moan!

Now truly father, this long talking
Doth but make long tarrying.
I pray you come and make ending
And let me hence be gone.

ABRAHAM. Come hither, my child, that art so sweet:
  Thou must be bound, both hands and feet.
ISAAC. Ah father, we must no more meet
  By aught that I can see!   360

But do with me just as you will,
I must obey, and that is skill,
God's commandment to fulfil,
For needs so must it be.

Upon the purpose that have set you,
In truth, father, I'll not prevent you,
But ever more unto you bow,
As long as I may.

Father, greet well my brethren young,
And pray my mother of her blessing,   370
I come no more under her wing.
Farewell forever and ay.

But, father, I ask you mercy,
For what I have trespassed to thee,
Forgiven, father, that it may be,
Until Doomsday.

ABRAHAM. My dear son, let be thy moans;
  My child, thou grieved me but once.
Blessed be thou, body and bones,
And I forgive thee here.   380

362. *skill*, proper, right.   377. *let be*, cease.

Lo, my dear son, here shalt thou lie;
Unto my work now must I hie,
I had as lief myself to die
As thou, my darling dear.

ISAAC. Father, if you be to me kind,
About my head a kerchief bind,
And put me lightly out of your mind,
Soon that I may be sped.

ABRAHAM. Farewell, my sweet son of grace!
ISAAC. I pray you, father, turn down my face,   390
A little while, while you have space,
For I am most sore adread.

ABRAHAM. To do this deed I am sorry.
ISAAC. Yea, Lord, to thee I call and cry
On my soul thou have mercy,
Heartily I thee pray.

ABRAHAM. Lord, I would fain work thy will,
This young innocent that lies so still
Most loathe were me him to kill
By any manner of way.   400

ISAAC. My dear father, I you pray,
Let me take my clothes away
For shedding blood on them today
At my last ending.

ABRAHAM. Heart, if thou wouldest break in three
Thou shalt never master me,
I will no longer stay for thee
My God I may not grieve.

ISAAC. Ah mercy, father, why tarry you so?
Smite off my head and let me go!   410
I pray you, rid me of my woe;
For now I take my leave.

ABRAHAM. Ah, son, my heart will break in three
To hear thee speak such words to me.
Jesu, on me thou have pity
That I have most in mind!

ISAAC. Now, father, I see that I shall die,
  Almighty God in majesty   .
My soul I offer unto thee;
Lord, to it be kind.   420

> [*At last having got up his courage, Abraham brandishes the*
> *sword as if to kill Isaac, but at that moment two angels*
> *appear and catch the sword so that the stroke is not com-*
> *pleted.*

ANGEL. Abraham, my servant dear!
ABRAHAM. Lo, Lord, I am already here.
1 ANGEL. Lay not thy sword in no manner
  On Isaac, thy dear darling.

Nay, do thou to him no annoy!
For thou dreadest God, well see I,
That of thy son hast no mercy
In fulfilling his bidding.

2 ANGEL. And since his bidding thou dost ay,
  And spares neither for fear nor fray   430
To do thy son to death today,
Isaac to thee full dear

Therefore God has sent by me, in fay,
A lamb that is both good and gay
Into this place, as thou see may.
Lo, it is right here.

ABRAHAM, *overwhelmed by his good fortune, but not so over-*
  whelmed that he forgets his manners.
Ah, Lord of heaven and King of bliss,
Thy bidding I shall do, I wis.
Sacrifice here to me sent is
And all, Lord, through thy grace.   440

A horned wether here I see,
Among the briars tied is he,
To thee offered it shall be
At once right in this place.

> [*Then he offers the ram, and the approving voice of God*
> *sets His blessing on His faithful servant.*

GOD. Abraham, by myself I swear,
  Since thou hast been obedient ever,
  And spared not thy son so dear,
  To fulfil my bidding,

Thou shalt be blest, thou art worthy,
  Thy seed I shall multiply,   450
  As stars and sand, so many swear I,
  Of thy body coming.

O'er enemies thou shalt have power,
  And thy blood also in fear,
  For thou hast been meek and boneer
  To do as I thee bade.

And all nations, believe thou me,
  Blessed evermore shall be
  Through fruit that shall come of thee,
  And saved through thy seed.   460
    [*Abraham and Isaac and the Angels withdraw and the Ex-*
      positor enters.

EXPOSITOR. Good Lords, this signification
  Of this deed of devotion,
  If you will, you know mon,
  May turn you to much good.

This deed you see done in this place,
  In example of Jesus done it was,
  Who for to win mankind grace
  Was sacrificed on the rood.

By Abraham I may understand
  The Father of Heaven that can fand   470
  With his son's blood to break that band
  The Devil had brought us to.

By Isaac understand I may
  Jesu that was obedient ay,
  His father's will to work alway,
  His death to undergo.
    [*He rides off to make room for the fifth play, the story of*
      Balaam and Balak.

---

455. *boneer*, courteous, gentle.   463. *mon*, may.
468. *rood*, cross.   470. *fand*, put to proof, test.

THE MORAL PLAY

As THE CYCLES of mystery plays attempted to teach by summarizing scriptural story and interpreting it in terms of Christian (particularly Roman Catholic) dogma, so the moral play sought to teach by the use of allegory. It grew out of the same urge to make good doctrine understandable to all classes of people that had been responsible for the earlier attempts at drama. It was an attempt to make moral teaching interesting as well as clear and is thus part of that same spirit that moved Chaucer's Pardoner to tell his story of the three revellers. But in the Moral Play, as has been indicated, interest is not attained by the telling of a lively story that will serve as a good example, but it is secured by bringing abstract qualities to life as persons while their significance as abstractions is retained by such names as Experience, Fame, Discretion, Five Wits, Charity, Confession, etc. As God was the chief figure (though his actual appearances were few) in the cyclic plays, so Man is the central character in these plays, and on him the others make their attacks or to him they bring their support.

There were several types of moral interlude. Many were like *Everyman*, concerned with the transitoriness of life and the multitude of false choices that Mankind may make in his efforts to find security and comfort against the inevitable prospect of death. The most extensive of this sort, indeed the most extensive of all the English moralities, is the *Castle of Perseverance*, which through 3650 lines shows Humanum Genus (Mankind) accompanied by his Good and Evil Angels enduring all manner of experiences until at last he finds Mercy before the throne of the Father, who receives him kindly. The same spirit runs through the shorter *Mankind, Mundus et Infans,* (*The World and the Child*) and *Hyckescorner.*

Another type, however, was less immediately concerned with the salvation of man's soul (though that lies in the background) and more with pedagogical problems, that is, with the development of the rational man rather than simply the moral man. Such plays as Redford's *Wyt and Science*, Medwall's *Nature*, and Rastell's *Nature of the Four Elements* go beyond a concern with the ordinary vices to include such figures as Tediousness and Ignorance as well. In them one may find expositions of the latest scientific theories, as well as general concern for the importance of learning and the utter beastliness of ignorance. One of the most effective scenes occurs in *Wyt and Science* when Idleness tries unsuccessfully to teach Ignorance to spell his own name.

This latter type represented a later development which is often distinguished from the earlier morality by the name interlude, although Tudor Englishmen seem to have had no exact definition for the term. As the century progressed new subjects were treated in these allegorical ways. There were plays dealing with political problems, particularly with the nature of the relationship between ruler and governed. As might be expected in a period of religious reformation, there were plays dealing with religious problems, usually approached with all the vehemence common in such disputes. A transition between the allegorical method of presentation and the introduction of historical characters is to be found in Bishop Bale's play, *King Johan*, which purports to be a presentation of the troubled reign of that unhappy king but also includes such abstractions as Sedition, Civil Order, Private Wealth, Treason, etc.

The chief end of plays of these types was to instruct, as has been said, but the effectiveness of the instruction depended on arousing and maintaining the audience's interest. A debate between personified vices and virtues is not likely in itself to be particularly entertaining, as the authors of the moral plays or interludes saw. So they sought to give liveliness and interest to their often sombre stories by the introduction of a "Vice," who might become so important that he sometimes gave his name to the play, as in *Hyckescorner*. He was a comic figure, though he had usually sinister implications, whose chief pleasure in life consisted in playing practical jokes on all the other characters of the play, both good and bad. He was often a gay figure hardly in harmony with the serious general tone of the piece but certainly, as he was intended to be, a relief from the dead level of didacticism of the play. Testimony to his popularity is found in his frequent appearance, under various names, in the plays and in the fact that the comic element which he represented came to occupy larger and larger space until the serious struggle of Good and Evil for Man's soul became quite dwarfed in comparison.

These moral plays mark the beginnings of a professional theater. Whatever may have been the case with early plays expounding the Pater Noster and the Creed, and other moralities now lost, certainly the later ones were the property of professional companies which toured England, setting up a stage on the village green, in the inn-yard, or if they were fortunate, in the great hall of a manor house, and depending on the "takings" for their livelihood. An amusing indication of the methods of financing the company is given in *Mankind*, where after about 450 lines of the play there is an explosion of gunpowder, and Titivillus, the Vice, shouts within. Then New Guise, one of the evil characters, steps out of character to tell the audience he is going to take up a collection and Now-a-Days chimes in

> Keep your tail, in goodness, I pray you good brother!
> He is a worshipful man, sirs, saving your reverence.
> He loveth no groats, nor pence, nor tuppence;
> Give us red royals, if ye will see his abominable presence.

Everyman, which is sometimes thought to have been brought to England from Holland is in some ways simpler than many examples of this type. In its approach and in its method it is reminiscent of the artistic portrayals of the Dance of Death, of which that by Holbein is perhaps the best known. Death comes to summon Man and leads him to the grave, in spite of all Man's efforts to find help and refuge in all the powers and pleasures of the world. It has a feeling for the tragedy of Man's last adventure, which must be undergone alone, quite foreign to the horseplay and slapstick comedy which characterized the later English moral plays.

The date of *Everyman* is not known, though it comes near

the end of the fifteenth century. There is an early Dutch play, *Elckerlijk*, on the same subject and treated in so much the same way that it seems certain that if the English play was not based on the Dutch, they both must go back to a common source. Testimony to the popularity of the English version is the existence of no less than four separate editions of it shortly after 1500.

SUGGESTED READINGS

Boas, F. S., *Tudor Drama*. OXFORD, 1933.

Brooke, C. F. Tucker, *The Tudor Drama*. NEW YORK, 1911.

Cambridge History of English Literature, VOL. V. NEW YORK, 1905.

Farnham, Willard, *The Medieval Heritage of Elizabethan Tragedy*. BERKE-LEY, CALIF., 1936.

Mackenzie, W. R., *The English Moralities from the Point of View of Allegory*. HARVARD STUDIES IN ENGLISH. VOL. II. CAMBRIDGE, MASS., 1918.

Pollard, A. W., *English Miracle Plays, Moralities, and Interludes*. OXFORD, 1923.

Thompson, E. N. S., "The English Moral Plays," *Transactions of the Connecticut Academy*, XIV (1910), 291-413.

Jerome, Jerome K., *The Passing of the Third Floor Back*. NEW YORK, 1911.

Kennedy, Charles Rann, *A Servant in the House*. NEW YORK, 1908.

THE PLAY OF EVERYMAN

The Characters

MESSENGER	GOOD DEEDS
GOD	KNOWLEDGE
DEATH	CONFESSION
EVERYMAN	DISCRETION
FELLOWSHIP	STRENGTH
KINDRED	FIVE WITS
COUSIN	BEAUTY
GOODS	ANGEL

Here beginneth a treatise how the High Father in Heaven sendeth Death to summon every creature to come and give an account of their lives in this world, and is in manner of a moral play.

PROLOGUE

A Messenger enters, much like the Expositor of Abraham and Isaac.

MESSENGER. I pray you all give your audience,
And hear this matter with reverence,
   In form a moral play.
The Summoning of Everyman it is called so,
That of our lives and ending maketh show
   How transitory we be every day.
This matter is wondrous precious,
But the meaning of it is more gracious
   And sweet to bear away.
The story saith: Man, in the beginning   10
Look well, and take good heed of the ending,
   Be you never so gay!
Ye think sin in the beginning most sweet,
Which, in the end, causeth the soul to weep,
   When the body lieth in clay.
Here shall you see how Fellowship and Jollity,

Both Strength, Pleasure, and Beauty,
   Will fade from thee as flower in May,
For ye shall hear how our Heaven's King
Calleth Everyman to a general reckoning.   20
   Give audience and hear what he doth say.
                    [The Messenger goes out.

GOD SPEAKETH, *probably from above and unseen by the audience.*
I perceive, here in my majesty,
   How that all creatures be to me unkind,
Living, without fear, in worldly prosperity.
   In spiritual vision the people be so blind,
Drowned in sin, they know me not for their God;
   In worldly riches is all their mind.
They fear not my righteousness, the sharp rod.
   My love that I showed, when I for them died,
They clean forget, and shedding of my blood red.   30
   I hung between two it cannot be denied,
To get them life I suffered to be dead,
I healed their feet, with thorns was hurt my head.
   I could do no more than I did, truly,
   And now I see the people do clean forsake me;
They use the seven deadly sins damnable
   So that pride, covetousness, wrath, and lechery
Now in this world be made commendable,
   And thus they leave of angels the heavenly company.
Every man liveth so after his own pleasure,   40
And yet of their lives they be nothing sure.
I see the more that I them forbear
The worse they be from year to year,
All that live groweth evil fast;
Therefore I will, in all haste,
Have a reckoning of every man's person
For, if I leave the people thus alone
In their way of life and wicked tempests,
Verily, they will become much worse than beasts.
Now for envy would one eat up another, and tarry not,   50
Charity is by all clean forgot.
I hoped well that every man
In my glory should make his mansion,
And thereto I made them all elect,
But now I see, like traitors deject,

48. *tempests,* i.e., of passion.

They thank me not for the pleasure that I for them meant,
Nor yet for their being that I them have lent.
I proffered the people great multitude of mercy,
And few there be that ask it heartily.
They be so cumbered with worldly riches,   60
I must needs upon them do justice,—
On every man living without fear.
Where art thou, Death, thou mighty messenger?
    [*Death enters.*

DEATH. Almighty God, I am here at your will,
  Your commandment to fulfil.

GOD. Go thou to Everyman,
  And show him in my name
  A pilgrimage he must on him take,
  Which he in no wise may escape,
  And that he bring with him a sure reckoning   70
  Without delay or any tarrying.

DEATH. Lord, I will in the world go run over all,
  And cruelly search out both great and small.
    [*God goes out, and Death meditates on his plans; walking
      around the stage to indicate his approach to Everyman's
      home.*

Every man will I beset that liveth beastly
Out of God's law, and dreadeth not folly.
He that loveth riches I will strike with my dart
His sight to blind and him from heaven to part—
Except if Alms be his good friend—
In hell for to dwell, world without end.
    [*Everyman enters at the rear, not seeing Death.*
Lo, yonder I see Everyman walking.   80
Full little he thinketh on my coming!
His mind is on fleshly lusts and his treasure, ·
And great pain it shall cause him to endure
Before the Lord, Heaven's King.
Everyman, stand still! Wither art thou going
Thus gayly? Hast thou thy Maker forgot?

EVERYMAN. Why askest thou?
  Wouldest thou know?

DEATH. Yea, sir, I will show you.
  In great haste I am sent to thee   90
  From God, out of his majesty.

EVERYMAN. What, sent to me!

  57. *being*, creation, life.

DEATH. Yea, certainly.
  Though thou hast forgot him here,
  He thinketh on thee in the heavenly sphere,
  As, ere we part, thou shalt know.
EVERYMAN. What desireth God of me?
DEATH. That shall I show thee.
  A reckoning he will needs have
  Without any longer respite.   100
EVERYMAN. To give a reckoning longer leisure I crave.
  This blind matter troubleth my wit.
DEATH. Upon thee thou must take a long journey,
  Therefore, thine accounting-book with thee bring.
  For turn again thou canst not by no way,
  And look thou be sure in thy reckoning,
  For before God thou shalt answer, and show true
  Thy many bad deeds and good but a few,
  How thou hast spent thy life and in what wise
  Before the Chief Lord of Paradise.   110
  Make ready that we may be upon that journey,
  For well thou knowest thou shalt make none attorney.
EVERYMAN. Full unready I am such reckoning to give.
  I know thee not. What messenger art thou?
DEATH. I am Death that no man feareth,
  For every man I arrest and no man spareth;
  For it is God's commandment
  That all to me should be obedient.
EVERYMAN. O Death, thou comest when I had thee least in mind!
  In thy power it lieth me to save;—   120
  Yet of my goods will I give thee, if thou wilt be kind,—
  Yea, a thousand pounds shalt thou have,
  If you defer this matter till another day.
DEATH. Everyman, it may not be in any way.
  I set no store by gold, silver, nor riches,
  Nor by pope, emperor, king, duke, nor princes;
  For, if I would receive gifts great,
  All the world I might get,
  But my custom is clean the contrary.
  I give thee no respite. Come hence, nor tarry!   130
EVERYMAN. Alas, shall I have no longer respite!
  I may say Death giveth no warning!
  To think on thee, it maketh my heart sick,

112. *make none attorney*, find no substitute.
115. *no man feareth*, respects no one.

For all unready is my book of reckoning.
But if I might have twelve years of waiting,
My accounting-book I would make so clear
That my reckoning I should not need to fear.
Wherefore, Death, I pray thee, for God's mercy,
Spare me till I be provided with a remedy!

DEATH. It availeth thee not to cry, weep, and pray,　140
But haste thee lightly, that thou mayest be on thy journey,
And make proof of thy friends, if thou can,
For, know thou well, tide tarrieth for no man,
And in the world each living creature
Because of Adam's sin must die by nature.

EVERYMAN. Death, if I should this pilgrimage take,
And my reckoning surely make,
Show me, for Saint Charity,
Should I not come again shortly?

DEATH. No, Everyman, if once thou art there,　150
Thou mayest nevermore come here,
Trust me, verily.

EVERYMAN. O gracious God, in the high seat celestial,
Have mercy on me in this utmost need!
Shall I have no company from this vale terrestrial
Of mine acquaintance that way me to lead?

DEATH. Yea, if any be so hardy
As to go with thee and bear thee company.
Haste thee that thou mayest be gone to God's magnificence,
Thy reckoning to give before his presence.　160
What, thinkest thou thy life is given thee,
And thy worldly goods also?

EVERYMAN. I had thought so, verily.

DEATH. Nay, nay, it was but lent to thee,
For, as soon as thou dost go,
Another a while shall have it and then go so,
Even as thou hast done.
Everyman, thou art mad! Thou hast thy wits five,
And here on earth will not amend thy life,
For suddenly I do come!　170

EVERYMAN. O wretched caitiff, whither shall I flee
That I may escape this endless sorrow!
Nay, gentle Death, spare me until to-morrow
That I may amend me
With good advisement!

145. *by nature*, i.e., without hope of escape.

DEATH. Nay, thereto I will not consent,
  Nor no man will I respite,
  But to the heart suddenly I shall smite
  Without any advisement.
  And now out of thy sight I will me hie,   180
  See that thou make thee ready shortly,
  For thou mayest say this is the day
  Wherefrom no man living may escape away.
    [*Death leaves the stricken Everyman, who meditates on his
    own sad case.*
EVERYMAN. Alas, I may well weep with sighs deep!
  Now have I no manner of company
To help me on my journey and me to keep,
  And also my writing is all unready.
How shall I do now to excuse me?
  I would to God I had never been begot!
To my soul a full great profit it would be,   190
  For now I fear pains huge and great, God wot!
The time passeth—help, Lord, that all things wrought!
For, though I mourn, it availeth naught.
The day passeth and is almost through,
I wot not well of what I may do.
To whom were it best my plaint to make?
What if to Fellowship I thereof spake,
And showed him about this sudden chance?
For in him is all my trust by chance.
We have in the world so many a day   200
Been good friends in sport and play.
 I see him yonder certainly.
I trust that he will bear me company;
Therefore to him will I speak to ease my sorrow.
Well met, good Fellowship, and a good morrow!
  , [*His friend Fellowship enters, and is touched by his sorrow.*
FELLOWSHIP. Everyman, good morrow, by this day!
  Sir, why lookest thou so piteously?
If anything be amiss, prithee to me it say
  That I may help to remedy.
EVERYMAN. Yea, good Fellowship, yea,   210
  I am in great jeopardy!
FELLOWSHIP. My true friend, show to me your mind.
  I will not forsake thee to my life's end,
  In the way of good company.
  185. *manner*, kind.

EVERYMAN. That was well spoken and lovingly.
FELLOWSHIP. Sir, I must needs know your heaviness.
  I have pity to see you in any distress.
  If any have wronged you, revenged ye shall be,
  Though I upon the ground be slain for thee,
  Even though I know before that I should die.   220
EVERYMAN. Verily, Fellowship, gramercy!
FELLOWSHIP. Tush! By thy thanks I set not a straw.
  Show me your grief and say no more.
EVERYMAN. If I my heart should to you bare,
    And you then should turn your mind from me,
    And no comfort would give when you heard me declare,
    Then should I ten times sorrier be.
FELLOWSHIP. Sir, I say as I will do indeed!
EVERYMAN. Then are you a good friend at need.
  I have found you true heretofore.   230
FELLOWSHIP. And so ye shall evermore,
    For, in faith, if thou goest to hell,
    I will not forsake thee by the way.
EVERYMAN. Ye speak like a good friend—I believe you well.
    I shall deserve it, if so I may!
FELLOWSHIP. I speak of no deserving, by this day,
  For he that will say, and nothing do,
  Is not worthy with good company to go.
  Therefore show me the grief of your mind,
  As to your friend most loving and kind.   240
EVERYMAN. I shall show you how it is:
    Commanded I am to go a journey,
  A long way, hard and dangerous,
    And give a strict account without delay
    Before the High Judge, Adonai.
  Wherefore, I pray you, bear me company,
  As ye have promised, in this journey.
FELLOWSHIP. That is matter, indeed! Promise is duty—
  But if I should take such a voyage on me,
  I know well, it should be to my pain;   250
  Also it maketh me afeard, for certain.
  But let us take counsel here as well as we can,
  For your words would dismay a strong man.
EVERYMAN. Why, if I had need, ye said
    Ye would never forsake me, quick nor dead,
    Though it were to hell truly!

  221. *gramercy*, great thanks.

FELLOWSHIP. So I said certainly,
  But such pleasures be set aside, the truth to say;
  And also, if we took such a journey,
  When should we come again? 260
EVERYMAN. Nay, never again till the day of doom.
FELLOWSHIP. In faith, then, will I not come there.
  Who hath you these tidings brought?
EVERYMAN. Indeed, Death was with me here.
FELLOWSHIP. Now, by God that all hath bought,
  If Death were the messenger,
  For no man that is living today
  I will not go that loathly journey,
  Not for the father that begat me!
EVERYMAN. Ye promised otherwise, pardy! 270
FELLOWSHIP. I know well I said so, truly,
  And yet, if thou wilt eat and drink and make good cheer,
  Or haunt of women the merry company,
  I would not forsake you while the day is clear,
  Trust me, verily.
EVERYMAN. Yea, thereto ye would be ready!
  To go to mirth, solace, and play,
  Your mind will sooner agree
  Than to bear me company on my long journey.
FELLOWSHIP. Now, in good faith, I have no will that way— 280
  But if thou would'st murder, or any man kill,
  In that I will help thee with a good will.
EVERYMAN. Oh, that is simple advice, indeed!
  Gentle Fellowship, help me in my necessity!
  We have loved long, and now I am in need!
  And now, gentle Fellowship, remember me!
FELLOWSHIP. Whether ye have loved me or no,
  By Saint John, I will not with thee go!
EVERYMAN. Yet, I pray thee, take this task on thee and do so much
    for me,
  As to accompany me, for Saint Charity, 290
  And comfort me till I come without the town.
FELLOWSHIP. Nay, if thou wouldest give me a new gown,
  I will not a foot with thee go.
  But, if thou hadst tarried, I would not have left thee so.
  And so now, God speed thee on thy journey,
  For from thee I will depart as fast as I may!
EVERYMAN. Whither away, Fellowship? Will you forsake me?
  265. *bought*, redeemed.

FELLOWSHIP. Yea, by my faith! To God I commit thee.

EVERYMAN. Farewell, good Fellowship,—for thee my heart is sore.
Adieu forever, I shall see thee no more!   300

FELLOWSHIP. In faith, Everyman, farewell now at the ending.
For you I will remember that parting is mourning.
    [*Fellowship hastens off, anxious to escape so dangerous a
      companion.*

EVERYMAN. Alack! Shall we thus part indeed?
    (Ah, Lady, help!) without any more comfort?
Lo, Fellowship forsaketh me in my utmost need.
    For help in this world whither shall I resort?
Fellowship heretofore with me would merry make,
And now little sorrow for me doth he take.
It is said in prosperity men friends may find
Which in adversity be full unkind.   310
Now whither for succor shall I flee,
Since that Fellowship hath forsaken me?
To my kinsmen will I truly,
Praying them to help me in my necessity.
I believe that they will do so,
For "Kind will creep where it may not go."
    [*Kindred and Cousin enter.*
I will go try, for yonder I see them go.
Where be ye now, my friends and kinsmen, lo?

KINDRED. Here we be now at your commandment.
Cousin, I pray you show us your intent   320
In any wise and do not spare.

COUSIN. Yea, Everyman, and to us declare
If ye be disposed to go any whither,
For, wit you well, we will live and die together!

KINDRED. In wealth and woe we will with you hold,
For "with his own kin a man may be bold."

EVERYMAN. Gramercy, my friends and kinsmen kind!
Now shall I show you the grief of my mind.
I was commanded by a messenger
That is a High King's chief officer.   330
He bade me go a pilgrimage to my pain,
And I know well I shall never come again;
Also I must give a reckoning strait,
For I have a great enemy that lieth for me in wait,
Who intendeth me to hinder.

KINDRED. What account is that which you must render?—

324. *wit*, know.   333. *strait*, strict.

That would I know.

EVERYMAN. Of all my works I must show
How I have lived and my days have spent,
   Also of evil deeds which I have used   340
In my time, since life was to me lent,
   And of all virtues that I have refused.
Therefore, I pray you, go thither with me
To help to make my account, for Saint Charity!

COUSIN. What, to go thither? Is that the matter?
Nay, Everyman, I had liefer fast on bread and water
All this five year and more!

EVERYMAN. Alas, that ever I was born!
For now shall I never merry be,
   If that you forsake me!   350

KINDRED. Ah, sir, what! Ye be a merry man!
   Pluck up your heart and make no moan.
But one thing I warn you, by Saint Anne,
   As for me, ye shall go alone!

EVERYMAN. My cousin, will you not with me go?

COUSIN. No, by our Lady! I have the cramp in my toe.
Trust not to me, for, so God me speed,
I will deceive you in your utmost need.

KINDRED, *trying to pass it off with a jest.*
It availeth not us to entice;
   Ye shall have my maid, with all my heart.   360
She loveth to go to feasts, there to be nice,
   And to dance, and in antics to take part.
I will give her leave to help you on that journey,
If so be that you and she may agree.

EVERYMAN. Now show me the very truth within your mind—
Will you go with me or abide behind?

KINDRED. Abide behind? Yea, that I will, if I may—
Therefore farewell till another day!

EVERYMAN. How should I be merry or glad?—
   For fair promises men to me make,   370
   But, when I have most need, they me forsake!
I am deceived—that maketh me sad!

COUSIN. Cousin Everyman, farewell now,
For, verily, I will not go with you.
Also of mine own life an unready reckoning,

361. *be nice,* be gay, sportive.
362. *antics,* mummery, gay sports.

I have to give account of, therefore I make tarrying.
Now God keep thee, for now I go!   [*Kindred and Cousin go.*
    [*Everyman, left alone again, walks around the stage as he*
    meditates, as last coming to the home of Goods.

EVERYMAN. Ah, Jesus, is all to this come so?
Lo, fair words make fools fain,
They promise, and nothing will do, certain.   380
My kinsmen promised me faithfully
For to abide with me stedfastly,
And now fast away do they flee.
Even so Fellowship promised me.
What friend were it best for me to provide?
I am losing my time here longer to abide.
Still in my mind a thing there is,
All my life I have loved riches.
If that my Goods now help me might,
He would make my heart full light.   390
I will speak to him in this distress;
Where art thou my Goods and Riches?
    [*As he comes to the back of the stage, a curtain is drawn,*
    disclosing Goods, surrounded by great chests and heaps of
    money bags.

GOODS. Who calleth me? Everyman? What! Hast thou haste?
    I lie here in corners trussed and piled so high,
And in chests I am locked so fast,
    Also sacked in bags, thou mayest see with thine eye,
I cannot stir; in packs low I lie.
What ye would have, lightly to me say.

EVERYMAN. Come hither, Goods, with all the haste thou may,
For counsel I must ask of thee.   400

GOODS. Sir, if ye in this world have sorrow or adversity,
That can I help you to remedy shortly.

EVERYMAN. It is another disease that grieveth me;
In this world it is not, I tell thee so,
I am sent for another way to go,
To give a strict account general
Before the highest Jupiter of all.
And all my life I have had joy and pleasure in thee,
Therefore I pray thee go with me,
For, peradventure, thou mayest before **God Almighty**   410
My reckoning help to clean and purify,
For it is said ever and anon

403. *disease*, grievance.

That "money maketh all right that is wrong."
GOODS. Nay, Everyman, I sing another song—
  I follow no man on such voyages,
  For, if I went with thee,
  Thou shouldest fare much the worse for me,
  For, because on me thou didst set thy mind,
  Thy reckoning I have made blotted and blind,
  So that thine account thou canst not make truly—   420
  And that hast thou for the love of me.
EVERYMAN. That would grieve me full sore
  When I should come that fearful answer
  Up, let us go thither together!
GOODS. Nay, not so! I am too brittle, I may not endure,
  I will follow no man one foot, be ye sure.
EVERYMAN. Alas! I have thee loved, and had great pleasure
  All the days of my life in goods and treasure.
GOODS. That is to thy damnation, without lying
  For love of me is contrary to the love everlasting.   430
  But if thou hadst the while loved me moderately,
  In such wise as to give the poor a part of me,
  Then would'st thou not in this dolor be,
  Nor in this great sorrow and care.
EVERYMAN. Lo, now was I deceived ere I was ware,
  And all I may blame to misspending of time.
GOODS. What, thinkest thou that I am thine?
EVERYMAN. I had thought so.
GOODS. Nay, Everyman, I say no.
  Just for a while I was lent to thee,   440
  A season thou hast had me in prosperity.
  My nature it is man's soul to kill,
  If I save one, a thousand I do spill.
  Thinkest thou that I will follow thee
  From this world? nay verily!
EVERYMAN. I had thought otherwise.
GOODS. So it is to thy soul Goods is a thief,
  For when thou are dead this is my devise
  Another to deceive in the same wise
    As I have done thee, and all to his soul's grief.   450
EVERYMAN. O false Goods, cursed may thou be!
  Thou traitor to God that hast deceived me,
  And caught me in thy snare.
GOODS. Marry, thou broughtest thyself to this care,—
  423. *answer*, judgment.

Whereof I am right glad!
I must needs laugh, I cannot be sad!
EVERYMAN. Ah, Goods, thou hast had long my hearty love.
I gave thee that which should be the Lord's above.
But wilt thou not go with me, indeed?—
I pray thee truth to say!   460
GOODS. No, so God me speed!
Therefore farewell, and have good-day.
[*As Goods laughs scornfully at him, the curtain falls back
into place and Everyman is left once more alone.*
EVERYMAN. Oh, to whom shall I make my moan
For to go with me on that heavy journey!
First Fellowship, so he said, would have with me gone,
His words were very pleasant and gay,
But afterwards he left me alone;
Then spake I to my kinsmen, all in despair,
And they also gave me words fair,
They lacked no fair speaking   470
But all forsook me in the ending;
Then went I to my Goods that I loved best,
In hope to have comfort, but there had I least,
For my Goods sharply did me tell
That he bringeth many into hell.
Then of myself I was ashamed,
And so I am worthy to be blamed.
Thus may I well myself hate.
Of whom shall I now counsel take?
I think that I shall never speed   480
Till I go to my Good Deeds.
But, alas! she is so weak,
That she can neither move nor speak.
Yet will I venture on her now.
My Good Deeds, where be you?
[*He walks about the stage once more, returning to the rear
to find there Good Deeds, tightly bound with cords.*
GOOD DEEDS. Here I lie, cold in the ground.
Thy sins sorely have me bound
So that I cannot stir.
EVERYMAN. O Good Deeds, I stand in fear!
I must pray you for counsel,   490
For help now would come right well!
GOOD DEEDS. Everyman, I have understanding
That ye be summoned your account to make

Before Messias, of Jerusalem King.
    If you do my counsel, that journey with you will I take.
EVERYMAN. For that I come to you my moan to make.
    I pray you that ye will go with me.
GOOD DEEDS. I would full fain, but I cannot stand, verily.
EVERYMAN. Why, is there anything that did you befall?
GOOD DEEDS. Yea, Sir, I may thank you for all.   500
    If in every wise ye had encouraged me,
    Your book of account full ready would be.
    Look, the books of your works and your deeds thereby.
    Behold how under foot they lie
        Unto your soul's heaviness.
EVERYMAN. Our Lord Jesus help me,
    For one letter here I cannot see.
GOOD DEEDS. There is a blind reckoning in time of distress!
EVERYMAN. Good Deeds, I pray you help me in this need,
    Or else I am forever damned indeed.   510
    Therefore help me to make my reckoning
    Before the Redeemer of everything,
    That is, and was, and shall ever be, King of All.
GOOD DEEDS. Everyman, I am sorry for your fall,
    And fain would I help you, if I were able.
EVERYMAN. Good Deeds, your counsel, I pray you, give me.
GOOD DEEDS. That will I do, verily.
    Though on my feet I may not go,
    I have a sister that shall with you be, also,
    Called Knowledge, who shall with you abide,   520
        To help you to make that dreadful reckoning.
        [*Knowledge enters, bearing a robe.*
KNOWLEDGE. Everyman, I will go with thee and be thy guide,
    In thy utmost need to go by thy side.
EVERYMAN. In good condition I am now in every thing,
    And am wholly content with this good thing,
    Thanks be to God, my creator!
GOOD DEEDS. And when he hath brought thee there,
        Where thou shalt heal thee of thy smart,
    Then go with thy reckoning and thy good deeds together,
        For to make thee joyful at heart   530
    Before the Blessed Trinity.
EVERYMAN. My Good Deeds, gramercy!
    I am well content, certainly,
    With your words sweet.
KNOWLEDGE. Now go we together lovingly

To Confession, that cleansing river.

EVERYMAN. For joy I weep—I would we were there!
But, I pray you, give me cognition,
Where dwelleth that holy man, Confession?

KNOWLEDGE. In the House of Salvation.   540
We shall find him in that place,
That shall us comfort, by God's grace.

   [*They walk about the stage, and Confession enters to them,
   carrying a scourge.*

Lo, this is Confession. Kneel down, and ask mercy,
For he is in good favor with God Almighty.

EVERYMAN [*Kneeling*]. O glorious fountain that all uncleanness
      doth clarify,
Wash from me the spots of vice unclean,
That on me no sin may be seen!
I come with Knowledge for my redemption,
Redeemed with hearty and full contrition,
For I am commanded a pilgrimage to take,   550
And great accounts before God to make.
Now I pray you, Shrift, Mother of Salvation,
Help my good deeds because of my piteous exclamation!

CONFESSION. I know your sorrow well, Everyman,
      Because with Knowledge ye come to me.
I will you comfort as well as I can,
      And a precious jewel will I give thee,
      Called penance, voider of adversity.
      Therewith shall your body chastised be
Through abstinence and perseverance in God's service.   560
   [*He gives Everyman the scourge.*
Here shall you receive that scourge of me
Which is penance strong, that ye must endure,
To remember thy Saviour was scourged for thee
With sharp scourges, and suffered it patiently—
So must thou ere thou escape from that painful pilgrimage.
Knowledge, sustain him on this voyage,
And by that time Good Deeds will be with thee.
But in any case be sure of mercy,
For your time draweth on fast; if ye will saved be,
Ask God mercy, and he will grant it truly.   570
When with the scourge of penance man doth him bind,
The oil of forgiveness then shall he find.
                     [*Confession goes out.*

EVERYMAN. Thanked be God for his gracious work,
  For now will I my penance begin.
This hath rejoiced and lightened my heart,
  Though the knots be painful and hard within.
KNOWLEDGE. Everyman, see that ye your penance fulfil,
  Whatever the pains it to you may be;
And Knowledge shall give you counsel at will,
  How your account ye shall make full clearly.   580
EVERYMAN, *kneeling to pray.*
  O eternal God, O heavenly figure,
  O way of righteousness, O goodly vision,
  Which descended down into a virgin pure
  Because he would for every man redeem
    That which Adam forfeited by his disobedience—
  O blessed Godhead, elect and exalted in thy divinity,
    Forgive me my grievous offence!
  Here I cry thee mercy in this presence.

  O spiritual treasure, O ransomer and redeemer,
  Of all the world the hope and the governor,   590
  Mirror of joy, founder of mercy,
  Who illumineth heaven and earth thereby,
  Hear my clamorous complaint, though late it be,
  Receive my prayers, unworthy of thy benignity,
  Though I be a sinner most abominable,
  Yet let my name be written in Moses' table.

  O Mary, pray to the Maker of everything
  To vouchsafe me help at my ending,
  And save me from the power of my enemy,
  For Death assaileth me strongly!—   600
  And, Lady, that I may, by means of thy prayer,
  In your Son's glory be a partner,
  Through the mediation of his passion I it crave,
  I beseech you, help my soul to save!
    [*He rises.*
  Knowledge, give me the scourge of penance;
  My flesh therewith shall give acquittance.
  I will now begin, if God give me grace.
KNOWLEDGE. Everyman, God give you time and space!
  Thus I bequeath you into the hands of our Saviour,
  Now may you make your reckoning sure.   610
EVERYMAN. In the name of the Holy Trinity,

My body sorely punished shall be.
Take this, body, for the sin of the flesh.
  [*Striking himself.*
As thou delightest to go gay and fresh,
And in the way of damnation thou didst me bring,
Therefore suffer now strokes of punishing.
Now of penance to wade the water clear I desire,
To save me from purgatory, that sharp fire.

GOOD DEEDS, *rising from the floor.*
I thank God now I can walk and go,
And am delivered of my sickness and woe!   620
Therefore with Everyman I will go and not spare;
His good works I will help him to declare.

KNOWLEDGE. Now, Everyman, be merry and glad,
Your Good Deeds cometh now, ye may not be sad.
Now is your Good Deeds whole and sound,
Going upright upon the ground.

EVERYMAN. My heart is light and shall be evermore.
Now will I smite faster than I did before.

GOOD DEEDS. Everyman, pilgrim, my special friend,
Blessed be thou without end!   630
For thee is prepared the eternal glory.
Now thou hast made me whole and sound,
Therefor I will ever with thee be found.

EVERYMAN. Welcome, my Good Deeds! Now I hear thy voice,
I weep for very sweetness of love.

KNOWLEDGE. Be no more sad, but ever rejoice!
God seeth thy manner of life on his throne above.
Put on this garment to thy behoof,
Which wet with the tears of your weeping is,
Or else before God you may it miss,   640
When ye to your journey's end come shall.

EVERYMAN. Gentle Knowledge, what do you it call?

KNOWLEDGE. A garment of sorrow it is by name,
From pain it will you reclaim.
Contrition it is,
That getteth forgiveness,
It pleaseth God passing well.

GOOD DEEDS. Everyman, will you wear it for your soul's health?
  [*Everyman puts on the robe of contrition.*

EVERYMAN. Now blessed be Jesu, Mary's son,
For now have I on true contrition!   650
And let us go now without tarrying.

Good Deeds, have we all clear our reckoning?
GOOD DEEDS. Yea, indeed, I have them here.
EVERYMAN. Then I trust we need not fear.
Now, friends, let us not part in twain!
KNOWLEDGE. Nay, Everyman, that will we not, for certain.
GOOD DEEDS. Yet must thou lead with thee
    Three persons of great might.
EVERYMAN. Who should they be?
GOOD DEEDS. Discretion and Strength they hight.   660
And thy Beauty may not abide behind.
KNOWLEDGE. Also ye must call to mind
Your Five Wits as your counsellors.
GOOD DEEDS. You must have them ready at all hours.
EVERYMAN. How shall I get them hither?
KNOWLEDGE. You must call them all together,
And they will hear you immediately.
EVERYMAN. My friends, come hither and present be,
Discretion, Strength, my Five Wits, and Beauty.
    [*They enter.*]
BEAUTY. Here at your will be we all ready.   670
What will ye that we should do?
GOOD DEEDS. That ye would with Everyman go,
And help him in his pilgrimage.
Advise you—will you with him or not, on that voyage?
STRENGTH. We will all bring him thither,
    To be his help and comfort, believe ye me!
DISCRETION. So will we go with him all together.
EVERYMAN. Almighty God, beloved mayest thou be!
I give thee praise that I have hither brought
Strength, Discretion, Beauty, Five Wits—lack I nought—   680
And my Good Deeds, with Knowledge clear,
All be in company at my will here.
I desire no more in this my business.
STRENGTH. And I, Strength, will stand by you in your distress,
Though thou wouldest in battle fight on the ground.
FIVE WITS. And though it were through the world round,
We will not leave you for sweet or sour.
BEAUTY. No more will I unto Death's hour,
Whatsoever thereof befall.
DISCRETION. Everyman, advise you first of all.   690
    Go with a good advisement and deliberation.
We all give you virtuous monition
    660. *hight*, are called.

That all shall be well.

EVERYMAN. My friends, hearken what I will tell.
I pray God reward you in his heavenly sphere.
Now hearken all that be here,
For I will make my testament
Here before you all present.
  In alms, half my goods will I give with my hands twain,
In the way of charity with good intent,   700
  And the other half still shall remain
In bequest to be returned where it ought to be.
This I do in despite of the fiend of hell,
To escape quite out of his peril
For ever after and this day.

KNOWLEDGE. Everyman, hearken what I say.
Go to Priesthood, I you advise,
And receive of him in any wise
The Holy Sacrament and Unction together,
Then shortly see ye turn again hither.   710
We will all await you here.

FIVE WITS. Yea, Everyman, haste thee that ye may ready be.
There is no emperor, king, duke, nor baron
That from God hath such commission
As doth the least priest in this world here,
For of the Blessed Sacraments, pure and clear,
He beareth the keys, and thereof hath the cure
For man's redemption, it is ever sure,
Which God as medicine for our souls' gain
Gave us out of his heart with great pain,   720
Here in this transitory life for thee and me.
Of the Blessed Sacraments seven there be:
Baptism, Confirmation, with Priesthood good,
And the Sacrament of God's precious Flesh and Blood,
Marriage, the Holy Extreme Unction, and Penance.
These seven are good to have in remembrance,
Gracious Sacraments of high divinity.

EVERYMAN. Fain would I receive that holy body,
And meekly to my spiritual father will I go.

FIVE WITS. Everyman, that is best that ye can do.   730
God will you to salvation bring,
For Priesthood exceedeth every other thing.
To us Holy Scripture they do teach,
And convert men from sin, heaven to reach.
God hath to them more power given

Than to any angel that is in heaven.
With five words he may consecrate
God's body in flesh and blood to make,
And handleth his Maker between his hands.
The priest bindeth and unbindeth all bands   740
Both in earth and in heaven.—
Thou dost administer all the Sacraments seven.
Though we should kiss thy feet, yet thereof thou worthy wert.
Thou art the surgeon that doth cure of mortal sin the hurt.
No remedy do we find under God
Except only in the Priesthood.
Everyman, God gave priests that dignity,
And setteth them in his stead among us to be,
Thus be they above angels in degree.

    [*Everyman goes out as if to the Sacrament.*

KNOWLEDGE. If priests be good, it is so surely;   750
   But when Jesus hung on the cross with grievous smart,
   There he gave out of his blessed heart
   That same Sacrament in great torment.—
   He sold them not to us, that Lord omnipotent.
   Therefore Saint Peter the apostle doth say
   That Jesus' curse have all they
   Which God their Saviour do buy or sell,
   Or if they for any money do take or tell.
   Sinful priests give sinners bad example in deed and word,
   Their children sit by other men's fires, I have heard,   760
   And some haunt of women the company,
   With unclean life as through lustful acts of lechery
   These be with sin made blind.

FIVE WITS. I trust to God no such may we find.
   Therefore let us Priesthood honor,
   And follow their doctrines for our souls' succor.
   We be their sheep, and they shepherds be,
   By whom we all are kept in security.

    [*Everyman returns joyfully, in sharp contrast to his preceding
     despondency.*

   Peace! for yonder I see Everyman come,
   Who hath made true satisfaction.   770

GOOD DEEDS. Methinketh it is he indeed.

EVERYMAN. Now may Jesus all of you comfort and speed!
   I have received the Sacrament for my redemption,
   And also mine extreme unction.
   Blessed be all they that counselled me to take it!

And now, friends, let us go without longer respite.
I thank God ye have tarried so long
Now set each of you on this rood your hand,
And shortly follow me.
I go before where I would be.   780
God be our guide!
STRENGTH. Everyman, we will not from you go,
      Till ye have gone this voyage long.
DISCRETION. I, Discretion, will abide by you also.
KNOWLEDGE. And though this pilgrimage be never so strong,
      I will never depart from you.
Everyman, I will be as sure by thee,
As ever I was by Judas Maccabee.
      [*As they walk about the stage, Everyman grows more and
      more feeble, until he has to be supported by his friends.
      They come to the rear which now represents a grave.*
EVERYMAN. Alas! I am so faint I may not stand,
      My limbs under me do fold.   790
Friends, let us not turn again to this land,
      Not for all the world's gold,
For into this cave must I creep,
And turn to earth, and there to sleep.
BEAUTY. What—into this grave! Alas!
EVERYMAN. Yea, there shall ye consume, more and less.
BEAUTY. And what,—must I smother here?
EVERYMAN. Yea, by my faith, and never more appear!
      In this world we shall live no more at all,
      But in heaven before the highest lord of all.   800
BEAUTY. I cross out all this! Adieu, by Saint John!
      I take "my tap in my lap" and am gone.
EVERYMAN. What, Beauty!—whither go ye?
BEAUTY. Peace! I am deaf, I look not behind me,
      Not if thou wouldest give me all the gold in thy chest.
      [*Beauty goes, followed by the others, as they speak in turn,
      until only the bowed figure of Everyman, supported by
      Good Deeds and Knowledge, remains.*
EVERYMAN. Alas! in whom may I trust!
      Beauty goeth fast away from me.

778. *rood*, cross.   785. *strong*, full of hardships.
787. *Judas Maccabee*, see the apocryphal *I Maccabees*, III.
795. *more and less*, great and small, powerful and weak.
802. *tap in my lap*, proverbial expression, to gather up one's flax in an
apron and hurry away, to go with exaggerated haste.

She promised with me to live and die.

STRENGTH. Everyman, I will thee also forsake and deny,
  Thy game pleaseth me not at all!   810

EVERYMAN. Why, then ye will forsake me all!
  Sweet Strength, tarry a little space.

STRENGTH. Nay, Sir, by the rood of grace,
  I haste me fast my way from thee to take,
  Though thou weep till thy heart do break.

EVERYMAN. Ye would ever abide by me, ye said.

STRENGTH. Yea, I have you far enough conveyed.
  Ye be old enough, I understand,
  Your pilgrimage to take in hand.
  I repent me that I hither came.   820

EVERYMAN. Strength, for displeasing you I am to blame.
  But well you know, "promise is debt."

STRENGTH. In faith, I care not!
  Thou art but a fool to complain,
  You spend your speech and waste your brain.
  Go, thrust thyself into the ground!   [*He goes haughtily.*

EVERYMAN. I had thought more sure I should you have found,
  But I see well, who trusteth in his Strength,
  She him deceiveth at length.
  Both Strength and Beauty have forsaken me,   830
  Yet they promised me fair and lovingly.

DISCRETION. Everyman, I will after Strength be gone—
  As for me, I will leave you alone.

EVERYMAN. Why, Discretion, will ye forsake me!

DISCRETION. Yea, in faith, I will go from thee,
  For when Strength goeth before
  I follow after, evermore.

EVERYMAN. Yet, I pray thee, for love of the Trinity
  Look in my grave once pitifully.

DISCRETION. Nay, so nigh will I not come,   840
  Fare you well, every one.   [*Discretion goes.*

EVERYMAN. Oh, all things fail save God alone—
  Beauty, Strength, and Discretion!
  For when Death bloweth his blast,
  They all run from me full fast.

FIVE WITS. Everyman, my leave now of thee I take.
  I will follow the others, for here I thee forsake.

EVERYMAN. Alas! then may I wail and weep,
    For I took you for my best friend.

813. *rood,* cross on which Jesus was crucified.

FIVE WITS. I will thee no longer keep.   850
    Now farewell, and here's an end!   [*He follows Discretion.*
EVERYMAN. O Jesu, help! All have forsaken me.
GOOD DEEDS. Nay, Everyman, I will abide with thee,
    I will not forsake thee indeed!
    Thou wilt find me a good friend at need.
EVERYMAN. Gramercy, Good Deeds, now may I true friends see.
  They have forsaken me everyone,
  I loved them better than my Good Deeds alone.
  Knowledge, will ye forsake me also?
KNOWLEDGE. Yea, Everyman, when ye to death shall go,   860
  But not yet, for no manner of danger.
EVERYMAN. Gramercy, Knowledge, with all my heart!
KNOWLEDGE. Nay, yet will I not from hence depart,
  Till I see where you shall be come.
EVERYMAN. Methinketh, alas! that I must now go
  To make my reckoning, and my debts pay,
  For I see my time is nigh spent away.
  Take example, all ye that this do hear or see,
  How they that I loved best do forsake me,
  Except my Good Deeds that abideth faithfully.   870
GOOD DEEDS. All earthly things are but vanity.
  Beauty, Strength and Discretion do man forsake,
  Foolish friends and kinsmen that fair spake,
  All flee away save Good Deeds, and that am I!
EVERYMAN. Have mercy on me, God most mighty,
  And stand by me, thou Mother and Maid, holy **Mary**!
GOOD DEEDS. Fear not, I will speak for thee.
EVERYMAN. Here I cry God mercy!
GOOD DEEDS. Shorten our end and minish our pain,
  Let us go and never come again.   880
EVERYMAN. Into thy hands, Lord, my soul I commend—
    Receive it, Lord, that it be not lost!
  As thou didst me buy, so do thou me defend,
    And save me from the fiend's boast
    That I may appear with that blessed host
  That shall be saved at the day of doom.
    In manus tuas, of mights the most,
  Forever *commendo spiritum meum*.
    [*He goes bravely into the grave, accompanied by Good
    Deeds.*

879. *minish*, lessen.
887. *In manus tuas*, into thy hands, a phrase from the service for the dead,
as is *commendo*, etc. I commit my spirit. (l. 888.)

KNOWLEDGE. Now that he hath suffered that we all shall endure,
The Good Deeds shall make all sure;   890
Now he hath made ending,
Methinketh that I hear angels sing,
And make great joy and melody,
Where Everyman's soul shall received be!
    [*An Angel appears above.*
THE ANGEL. Come, excellent elect spouse to Jesu!
    Here above shalt thou go,
Because of thy singular virtue.
    Now thy soul from thy body is taken, lo!
Thy reckoning is crystal clear.
Now shalt thou into the heavenly sphere,   900
    Unto which ye all shall come
    That live well before the day of doom.
    [*The Angel and Knowledge go out, and the Doctor re-enters
    to point the moral.*
DOCTOR. This moral men may have in mind,—
    Ye hearers, take it as of worth, both old and young,
And forsake Pride, for he deceiveth you in the end,
    And remember Beauty, Five Wits, Strength, and Discretion,
They all at the last do Everyman forsake
Save that his Good Deeds there doth he take.
But beware, if they be small,
Before God he hath no help at all,   910
None excuse for Everyman may there be then.
Alas, how shall he do then!
For after death amends may no man make,
For then Mercy and Pity do him forsake.
If his reckoning be not clear when he doth come,
God will say, *Ite, maledicti, in ignem æternum.*
And he that hath his account whole and sound,
High in heaven he shall be crowned,
Unto which place God bring us all thither
That we may live, body and soul, together!   920
Thereto may help the Trinity—
Amen, say ye, for holy Charity!

FINIS

Thus endeth this moral play of Everyman.

916. *Ite,* etc. Go, accursed one, into eternal fire.

ROMANTIC COMEDY

ROMANTIC COMEDY is most easily defined by comparing it to an example of realistic comedy such as Jonson's *Alchemist*. Romantic comedy is not concerned with the immediate but with the far away, either in time or in place. It may be, as in *Friar Bacon and Friar Bungay*, the period of Henry III and his son Edward, i.e., the first half of the thirteenth century. Or it may be, as in *Twelfth Night*, the distant and little known land of Illyria; or as in *Midsummer Night's Dream*, the far off city of Athens in the far off time of King Theseus on the magic eve of Midsummer, when creatures of another world have special powers in our world. Romantic comedy makes no pretentions of dealing with a story that to the cold eye of aloof reason would seem real or even plausible in all its details. Its method is rather one of leading us on by the fertility of the author's invention, the charm of poetic style, the excitement of many incidents, and the liveliness of the emotions. There is little or none of that searching psychological analysis of character that one finds in great tragedy, but the characters are sketched in with bold strokes and our imaginations are left to round out the contours. The question becomes not so much whether the characters are ultimately convincing, then, as whether they are adapted to the spirit of their environment, whether, granting the situations into which they are put, they are satisfying and complete with respect to the demands of those situations.

As the name implies, love is the favorite theme of romantic comedy, particularly love between those who are unequal in rank, like Lacy and Margaret in *Friar Bacon*. Such a situation offers ample opportunity for contrast between the courtly manners of one and the unaffected simplicity of the other. Often to enforce that contrast this mixed love situation is set opposite the more conventional situation of two courtiers in

58

love with each other, and at times two rustics also in love with each other, as in *As You Like It*. For complication, such plays fall back on the old adage that the course of true love never did run smooth. Parental objections, jealousy, the very difference of social station, disguise, the plots of the wicked or of well-intentioned but mistaken meddlers, all may play their part in providing the action of the comedy.

Often there is associated with this type of play a gentle sense of melancholy. Sometimes it is no more than a slight nostalgia for older days when love was more spontaneous and gayer than it is now. Sometimes it is a feeling of apprehension for the fate of young love, set against so many odds. But in a well constructed romantic comedy we are never really in doubt as to the happy outcome of events, for the end of such comedy is that Jack shall have Jill and all shall be well again. Perhaps it is the very case with which the happy event is accomplished that causes our melancholy.

Elizabethan romantic comedy got its inspiration largely from the long prose romances which were enjoying an Indian Summer of popularity in England and on the continent in the sixteenth century. The prose romance tended to be invertebrate in structure, depending on rapid succession of incident, much of it in pastoral settings, the open fields where shepherds tended their flocks or pleasant woods filled like the Forest of Arden with all manner of curious fauna. Because of the multitude of incidents and of a sprawling structure, one would think it the last type of literature that would lend itself to successful dramatization. Yet Greene, who himself tried his hand at prose romances, succeeds in giving unity of tone if not exactly unity of action to the large number of incidents which he chose for his play from a collection of popular stories of Friar Bacon.

Modern romantic comedy, as represented by Eugene O'Neill's *Ah Wilderness!*, has less of the exotic atmosphere than the earlier examples, relies less on professional magic and similar devices, but it has all the delight in young love and its half comic problems and something of that nostalgic looking back to a not too distant time when "youth and blood are warmer."

Paradoxically, in spite of all its apparent superficiality, this type is no less true to human life than is the most realistic of drama. It represents a different method of approach to life rather than, as is sometimes suggested, an escape from life. At its best it has much to say about life, much sound wisdom to offer with respect to fundamental human relationships. Indeed, it is far less of an escape from reality than pieces of the grossest "realism" sometimes are. England in Henry III's time may be far away and long ago, and we may no longer admit any belief in magic; but young love is forever vital, and national pride was never stronger than now, though unfortunately it finds less happy ways of expressing itself than in a relatively harmless contest of magicians. England thinks now in terms of bomb-proof shelters beneath every backyard garden, for walls of bronze can no longer be built high enough to keep out the threat of invasion, but the problem of refuge and security is still essentially the same.

Robert Greene was one of a company of "University Wits," young men just up to London from the Universities, who played so large a part in setting literary fashions in the last two decades of the sixteenth century. He was born probably in 1558, six years before Shakespeare, went up to St. John's College at Cambridge, and travelled on the Continent. After returning to the University for his M.A., he came up to London, perhaps like Jacques in *As You Like It* with empty pockets and a jaundiced view of the world. Certainly he had, if we are to believe the popular accounts of him, all the vices that were supposed to stick to unwary Englishmen on their continental travels. In London he set himself to make his living by his pen and produced a motley array of literary works in the nine or ten years before death stepped in and took him off. He tried his hand at novels, at biting satires, and at pamphlets purporting to expose the rackets and get-rich-quick schemes of the London underworld, as well as at plays. Most of it was hack work, potboilers that scarcely kept the pot simmering; yet much of it, in spite of this fact, has wit and energy and liveliness, even, surprisingly, some flashes of delicate insight. This is particularly true of his handling of the character of women. In general Elizabethan dramtists were likely to be much more successful in the presentation of men than of women. But Greene, though he obviously lacks the great skill of Shakespeare, breathes life and sweetness into many of his women so that they emerge from the shadows as charming if not very complex creations.

Greene died in abject poverty in 1592 having, among other things, given romantic comedy a good start with his *Friar Bacon, George a Greene*, and scenes in his *Scottish History of James IV*.

SUGGESTED READINGS

Brooke, C. F. Tucker, *The Tudor Drama*. NEW YORK, 1911. CHAP. VIII.
Cambridge History of English Literature. VOL. V. NEW YORK, 1905.
Collins, J. C., ed., *The Plays of Robert Greene*. LONDON, 1905.
Dickinson, T. H., *Robert Greene*. NEW YORK, 1909.
Schelling, F. E., *Elizabethan Drama, 1558–1642*. BOSTON, 1908.
Woodberry, G. E., "Greene's Place in Comedy," in C. M. Gayley, *Representative English Comedies*. VOL. I.

Barrie, J. M., *Dear Brutus*. NEW YORK, 1922.
Fletcher, John, *The Faithful Shepherdess*. In *Works of Beaumont and Fletcher*. ED. BY A. R. WALLER, VOL. II. CAMBRIDGE, 1906.
Milne, A. A., *The Ivory Door*. NEW YORK, 1928.
O'Neill, Eugene, *Ah Wilderness!* NEW YORK, 1934.
Shakespeare, William, *As You Like It*.
——, *Merchant of Venice*.
——, *Twelfth Night*.
Sherwood, Robert E., *Reunion in Vienna*. NEW YORK, 1932.
Synge, J. M., *The Playboy of the Western World*. BOSTON, 1911.

FRIAR BACON AND FRIAR BUNGAY
by Robert Greene

Characters

KING HENRY THE THIRD
EDWARD, PRINCE OF WALES, *his son* .
EMPEROR OF GERMANY
KING OF CASTILE
DUKE OF SAXONY
LACY, *Earl of Lincoln*
WARREN, *Earl of Sussex*
ERMSBY, *a Gentleman*
RALPH SIMNELL, *the King's Fool*
FRIAR BACON
MILES, *Friar Bacon's poor scholar*
FRIAR BUNGAY
JAQUES VANDERMAST, *a German scholar and magician*
BURDEN ⎫
MASON ⎬ *Doctors of Oxford*
CLEMENT ⎭

LAMBERT ⎫ *Gentlemen*
SERLSBY ⎭
TWO SCHOLARS, *their sons*
KEEPER
KEEPER'S FRIEND
THOMAS ⎫ *Clowns*
RICHARD ⎭
CONSTABLE
A POST
LORDS, CLOWNS, ETC.
ELINOR, *daughter to the King of Castile*
MARGARET, *the Keeper's daughter*
JOAN, *a country wench*
HOSTESS OF THE BELL AT HENLEY
A DEVIL
SPIRIT IN THE SHAPE OF HERCULES

SCENE I

AT FRAMLINGHAM. *Prince Edward enters, with his hat pulled down over his eyes, the very picture of discontent and unhappiness. He is followed by Lacy, Warren, and Ermsby, all young gentlemen of the court, and by Ralph Simnell, in motley, the King's jester. They have just come from an exciting and successful hunt.*

LACY. Why looks my lord like to a troubled sky,
When heaven's bright shine is shadowed with a fog?

Alate we ran the deer, and through the lawnds
Stripped with our nags the lofty frolic bucks
That scudded 'fore the teasers like the wind:
Ne'er was the deer of merry Fressingfield
So lustily pulled down by jolly mates,
Nor shared the farmers such fat venison,
So frankly dealt, this hundred years before;
Nor have I seen my lord more frolic in the chase,   10
And now changed to a melancholy dump.

WARREN. After the prince got to the keeper's lodge,
And had been jocund in the house awhile,
Tossing off ale and milk in country cans;
Whether it was the country's sweet content,
Or else the bonny damsel filled us drink,
That seem'd so stately in her stammel red,
Or that a qualm did cross his stomach then,
But straight he fell into his passions.

ERMSBY. Sirrah Ralph, what say you to your master,   20
Shall he thus all amort live malcontent?

RALPH. Hearest thou, Ned?—Nay, look if he will speak to me!

PRINCE EDWARD. What say'st thou to me, fool?

RALPH. I prithee, tell me, Ned, art thou in love with the Keeper's
daughter?

PRINCE EDWARD. How if I be, what then?

RALPH. Why then, sirrah, I'll teach thee how to deceive love.

PRINCE EDWARD. How, Ralph?

RALPH. Marry, Sirrah Ned, thou shalt put on my cap and my
coat and my dagger, and I will put on thy clothes and thy   30
sword; and so thou shalt be my fool.

PRINCE EDWARD. And what of this?

RALPH. Why, so thou shalt beguile Love; for Love is such a proud
scab, that he will never meddle with fools nor children. Is not
Ralph's counsel good, Ned?

PRINCE EDWARD. Tell me, Ned Lacy, didst thou mark the maid,
How lively in her country weeds she look'd?
A bonnier wench all Suffolk cannot yield:—
All Suffolk! nay, all England holds none such.

RALPH. Sirrah Will Ermsby, Ned is deceived.   40

3. *Alate*, lately. *Lawnds*, glades.   4. *Stripped*, outstripped.
5. *scudded . . . teasers*, ran before the hunting dogs.
9. *frankly dealt*, freely shared.   11. *dump*, fit of abstraction.
17. *stammel*, coarse woollen cloth.
21. *all amort*, for á la mort, spiritless.

ERMSBY. Why, Ralph?

RALPH. He says all England hath no such, and I say, and I'll stand
to it, there is one better in Warwickshire.

WARREN. How provest thou that, Ralph?

RALPH. Why, is not the abbot a learned man, and hath read many
books, and thinkest thou he hath not more learning than thou
to choose a bonny wench? Yes, I warrant thee, by his whole
grammar.

ERMSBY. A good reason, Ralph.

PRINCE EDWARD. I tell thee, Lacy, that her sparkling eyes   50
  Do lighten forth sweet love's alluring fire;
  And in her tresses she doth fold the looks
  Of such as gaze upon her golden hair:
  Her bashful white, mixed with the morning's red,
  Luna doth boast upon her lovely cheeks;
  Her front is beauty's table, where she paints
  The glories of her gorgeous excellence;
  Her teeth are shelves of precious margarites,
  Richly enclosed with ruddy coral cleeves.
  Tush, Lacy, she is beauty's over-match,   60
  If thou survey'st her curious imagery.

LACY. I grant, my lord, the damsel is as fair
  As simple Suffolk's homely towns can yield;
  But in the court be quainter dames than she,
  Whose faces are enriched with honour's taint,
  Whose beauties stand upon the stage of fame,
  And vaunt their trophies in the courts of love.

PRINCE EDWARD. Ah, Ned, but hadst thou watch'd her as myself,
  And seen the secret beauties of the maid,
  Their courtly coyness were but foolery.   70

ERMSBY. Why, how watched you her, my lord?

PRINCE EDWARD. Whenas she swept like Venus through the
house,—
  And in her shape fast folded up my thoughts,—
  Into the milk-house went I with the maid,
  And there amongst the cream-bowls she did shine
  As Pallas 'mongst her princely huswifery:
  She turned her smock over her lily arms,
  And dived them into milk to run her cheese;

47-48. *by his whole grammar*, by all his learning.
56. *front*, countenance.   58. *margarites*, pearls.   59. *cleeves*, cliffs.
61. *curious imagery*, rare appearance.   64. *quainter*, rarer, daintier.
65. *taint*, tint.

But whiter than the milk her crystal skin,
Checked with lines of azure, made her blush,   . 80
That art or nature durst bring for compare.
Ermsby, if thou hadst seen, as I did note it well,
How beauty played the huswife, how this girl,
Like Lucrece, laid her fingers to the work,
Thou wouldst, with Tarquin, hazard Rome and all
To win the lovely maid of Fressingfield.

RALPH. Sirrah Ned, wouldst fain have her?

PRINCE EDWARD. Ay, Ralph.

RALPH. Why, Ned, I have laid the plot in my head; thou shalt
have her already.   90

PRINCE EDWARD. I'll give thee a new coat, an learn me that.

RALPH. Why, Sirrah Ned, we'll ride to Oxford to Friar Bacon:
O, he is a brave scholar, sirrah; they say he is a brave necromancer, that he can make women of devils, and he can juggle
cats into costermongers.

PRINCE EDWARD. And how then, Ralph?

RALPH. Marry, Sirrah, thou shalt go to him: and because thy father
Harry shall not miss thee, he shall turn me into thee; and I'll
to the court, and I'll prince it out; and he shall make thee either
a silken purse full of gold, or else a fine wrought smock.   100

PRINCE EDWARD. But how shall I have the maid?

RALPH. Marry, sirrah, if thou be'st a silken purse full of gold, then
on Sundays she'll hang thee by her side, and you must not say
a word. Now, sir, when she comes into a great press of people,
for fear of the cutpurse, on a sudden she'll swap thee into her
plackerd; then, sirrah, being there, you may plead for yourself.

ERMSBY. Excellent policy!

PRINCE EDWARD. But how if I be a wrought smock?

RALPH. Then she'll put thee into her chest and lay thee into lav-
ender, and upon some good day she'll put thee on; and at   110
night when you go to bed, then being turned from a smock
to a man, you may make up the match.

LACY. Wonderfully wisely counselled, Ralph.

PRINCE EDWARD. Ralph shall have a new coat.

RALPH. God thank you when I have it on my back, Ned.

PRINCE EDWARD. Lacy, the fool hath laid a perfect plot;
For why our country Margaret is so coy,
And stands so much upon her honest points,

---

80. *made her blush*, i.e., made blush any other woman, that . . .
91. *an learn me*, if you'll teach me.   93. *brave*, excellent.
97. *because*, so that.   106. *plackerd*, placket.   117. *For why*, because.

That marriage or no market with the maid.
Ermsby, it must be necromantic spells　　　　　120
And charms of art that must enchain her love,
Or else shall Edward never win the girl.
Therefore, my wags, we'll horse us in the morn,
And post to Oxford to this jolly friar:
Bacon shall by his magic do this deed.

WARREN. Content, my lord; and that's a speedy way
　　To wean these headstrong puppies from the teat.

PRINCE EDWARD. I am unknown, not taken for the prince;
　　They only deem us frolic courtiers,
　　That revel thus among our liege's game:　　　　130
　　Therefore I have devised a policy.
　Lacy, thou know'st next Friday is Saint James',
　And then the country flocks to Harleston fair:
　Then will the Keeper's daughter frolic there,
　And over-shine the troop of all the maids
　That come to see and to be seen that day.
　Haunt thee disguised among the country-swains,
　Feign thou'rt a farmer's son, not far from thence,
　Espy her loves, and who she liketh best;
　Cote him, and court her to control the clown;　　140
　Say that the courtier 'tired all in green,
　That help'd her handsomely to run her cheese,
　And fill'd her father's lodge with venison,
　Commends him, and sends fairings to herself.
　Buy something worthy of her parentage,
　Not worth her beauty; for, Lacy, then the fair
　Affords no jewel fitting for the maid:
　And when thou talk'st of me, note if she blush:
　O, then she loves; but if her cheeks wax pale,
　Disdain it is. Lacy, send how she fares,　　　　150
　And spare no time nor cost to win her loves.

LACY. I will, my lord, so execute this charge,
　　As if that Lacy were in love with her.

PRINCE EDWARD. Send letters speedily to Oxford of the news.

RALPH. And, Sirrah Lacy, buy me a thousand thousand million of
　　fine bells.

LACY. What wilt thou do with them, Ralph?

RALPH. Marry, every time that Ned sighs for the Keeper's daugh-

---

132. *St. James'*, July 25.
140. *Cote*, pass by, outstrip. *control the clown*, overcome the rustic.
141. *'tired*, attired.　　144. *fairings*, souvenirs from the fair.

ter, I'll tie a bell about him: and so within three or four days
I will send word to his father Harry, that his son, and my   160
master Ned, is become Love's morris-dance.

PRINCE EDWARD. Well, Lacy, look with care unto thy charge,
And I will haste to Oxford to the friar,
That he by art, and thou by secret gifts
Mayst make me lord of merry Fressingfield.

LACY. God send your honour your heart's desire.

        [Edward and his group go out one side, Lacy the other.

SCENE II

OXFORD UNIVERSITY. *Friar Bacon's cell at Brazen-Nose College.
Bacon is at the peak of his career as a necromancer, and is recognized by the authorities of the college as a great ornament
to it. They have come to find out details about his wonderful
studies. He enters, followed by his clownish servant Miles, almost lost beneath a load of books. With him come three learned
doctors of Oxford, Burden, Clement, and Mason.*

BACON. Miles, where are you?

MILES. *Hic sum, doctissime et reverendissime doctor.*

BACON. *Attulisti nos libros meos de necromantia?*

MILES. *Ecce quam bonum et quam jucundum habitare libros in
vnum!*

BACON. Now, masters of our academic state,
That rule in Oxford, viceroys in your place,
Whose heads contain maps of the liberal arts,
Spending your time in depth of learnèd skill,
Why flock you thus to Bacon's secret cell,   10
A friar newly stall'd in Brazen-nose?
Say what's your mind, that I may make reply.

BURDEN. Bacon, we hear, that long we have suspect,
That thou art read in magic's mystery;
In pyromancy, to divine by flames;
To tell, by hydromantic, ebbs and tides;

---

161. *morris-dance*, a rustic dance in which the performers had bells
fastened to their clothing.

2. *Hic sum . . .,* Here I am, most learned and reverend doctor.

3. *Attulisti . . .,* Have you brought us my books of magic?

4. *Ecce quam . . .,* Lo, how good and pleasant it is to dwell together
among books.

11. *stall'd*, installed, located.

By aeromancy to discover doubts,
To plain out questions, as Apollo did.

BACON. Well, Master Burden, what of all this?

MILES. Marry, sir, he doth but fulfil, by rehearsing of these   20
names, the fable of the Fox and the Grapes: that which is above
us pertains nothing to us.

BURDEN. I tell thee, Bacon, Oxford makes report,
Nay, England, and the court of Henry says
Thou'rt making of a brazen head by art,
Which shall unfold strange doubts and aphorisms,
And read a lecture in philosophy;
And, by the help of devils and ghastly fiends,
Thou mean'st, ere many years or days be past,
To compass England with a wall of brass.   30

BACON. And what of this?

MILES. What of this, master! why he doth speak mystically; for
he knows, if your skill fail to make a brazen head, yet Mother
Waters' strong ale will fit his turn to make him have a copper
nose.

CLEMENT. Bacon, we come not grieving at thy skill,
But joying that our academy yields
A man supposed the wonder of the world;
For if thy cunning work these miracles,
England and Europe shall admire thy fame,   40
And Oxford shall in characters of brass,
And statues, such as were built up in Rome,
Eternize Friar Bacon for his art.

MASON. Then, gentle friar, tell us thy intent.

BACON. Seeing you come as friends unto the friar,
Resolve you, doctors, Bacon can by books
Make storming Boreas thunder from his cave,
And dim fair Luna to a dark eclipse.
The great arch-ruler, potentate of hell,
Trembles when Bacon bids him, or his fiends,   50
Bow to the force of his pentageron.
What art can work, the frolic friar knows;
And therefore will I turn my magic books,
And strain out necromancy to the deep.
I have contriv'd and fram'd a head of brass

18. *plain*, explain.   26. *aphorisms*, scientific principles.
46. *Resolve you*, be you certain.
51. *pentageron*, pentagonon a five pointed star used, like a magical circle,
to protect the practitioner from demons.

(I made Belcephon hammer out the stuff),
And that by art shall read philosophy:
And I will strengthen England by my skill,
That if ten Cæsars liv'd and reign'd in Rome,
With all the legions Europe doth contain,   60
They should not touch a grass of English ground:
The work that Ninus rear'd at Babylon,
The brazen walls framed by Semiramis,
Carv'd out like to the portal of the sun,
Shall not be such as rings the English strand
From Dover to the market-place of Rye.

BURDEN. Is this possible?

MILES. I'll bring ye two or three witnesses.

BURDEN. What be those?

MILES. Marry, sir, three or four as honest devils and good   70
companions as any be in hell.

MASON [*Losing interest in witnesses*]. No doubt but magic may
do much in this;
For he that reads but mathematic rules
Shall find conclusions that avail to work
Wonders that pass the common sense of men.

BURDEN. But Bacon roves a bow beyond his reach,
And tells of more than magic can perform;
Thinking to get a fame by fooleries.
Have I not pass'd as far in state of schools,
And read of many secrets? yet to think   80
That heads of brass can utter any voice,
Or more, to tell of deep philosophy,
This is a fable Æsop had forgot.

BACON. Burden, thou wrong'st me in detracting thus;
Bacon loves not to stuff himself with lies:
But tell me 'fore these doctors, if thou dare,
Of certain questions I shall move to thee.

BURDEN. I will: ask what thou can.

MILES. Marry, sir, he'll straight be on your pick-pack, to know
whether the feminine or the masculine gender be most   90
worthy.

56. *Belcephon*, one of the devils.
62. *Ninus*, in Greek legend, the founder of Nineveh.
63. *Semiramis*, wife of Ninus, whom she succeeded on the throne of
Assyria.
76. *roves a bow* . . ., shoots at a target that is out of range.
89. *pick-pack*, pickaback.

BACON. Were you not yesterday Master Burden, at Henley upon
the Thames?

BURDEN. I was: what then?

BACON. What book studied you thereon all night?

BURDEN. I! none at all; I read not there a line.

BACON. Then, doctors, Friar Bacon's art knows naught.

CLEMENT. What say you to this, Master Burden? doth he not
touch you?

BURDEN. I pass not of his frivolous speeches.   100

MILES. Nay, Master Burden, my master, ere he hath done with
you, will turn you from a doctor to a dunce, and shake you so
small, that he will leave no more learning in you than is in
Balaam's ass.

BACON. Masters, for that learn'd Burden's skill is deep,
And sore he doubts of Bacon's cabalism,
I'll show you why he haunts to Henley oft:
Not, doctors, for to taste the fragrant air,
But there to spend the night in alchemy,
To multiply with secret spells of art;   110
Thus private steals he learning from us all.
To prove my sayings true, I'll show you straight
The book he keeps at Henley for himself.

MILES. Nay, now my master goes to conjuration, take heed.

BACON. Masters, stand still, fear not, I'll show you but his book.
    [*Conjures.*
    Per omnes deos infernales, Belcephon!
        [*Enter Hostess with a shoulder of mutton on a spit, and a
        Devil. She looks around in wonder at the company.*

MILES. O, master, cease your conjuration, or you spoil all; for
here's a she-devil come with a shoulder of mutton on a spit:
you have marred the devil's supper; but no doubt he thinks
our college fare is slender, and so hath sent you his cook   120
with a shoulder of mutton, to make it exceed.

HOSTESS. O, where am I, or what's become of me?

BACON. What art thou?

HOSTESS. Hostess at Henley, mistress of the Bell.

BACON. How camest thou here?

HOSTESS. As I was in the kitchen 'mongst the maids,
Spitting the meat against supper for my guess,
A motion mov'd me to look forth of door:

100. *pass not of,* care not for.
116. *Per omnes . . .,* By all the infernal gods, Belcephon!
121. *exceed,* become better.   127. *guess,* guests.   128. *motion,* impulse.

No sooner had I pried into the yard,
But straight a whirlwind hoisted me from thence,   130
And mounted me aloft unto the clouds.
As in a trance I thought nor fearèd naught,
Nor know I where or whither I was ta'en,
Nor where I am, nor what these persons be.
BACON. No? know you not Master Burden?
HOSTESS. O, yes, good sir, he is my daily guest.—
What, Master Burden! 'twas but yesternight
That you and I at Henley play'd at cards.
BURDEN [*Thoroughly embarrassed*]. I know not what we did.—
A pox of all conjuring friars!   140
CLEMENT. Now, jolly friar, tell us, is this the book that Burden
is so careful to look on?
BACON. It is.—But, Burden, tell me now,
Think'st thou that Bacon's necromantic skill
Cannot perform his head and wall of brass,
When he can fetch thine hostess in such post?
MILES. I'll warrant you, master, if Master Burden could conjure
as well as you, he would have his book every night from Hen-
ley to study on at Oxford.
MASON. Burden, what, are you mated by this frolic friar?—   150
Look how he droops; his guilty conscience
Drives him to 'bash and makes his hostess blush.
BACON. Well, mistress, for I will not have you miss'd,
You shall to Henley to cheer up your guests
'Fore supper gin.—Burden, bid her adieu;
Say farewell to your hostess 'fore she goes.—
    [*To the Devil.*
Sirrah, away, and set her safe at home.
HOSTESS. Master Burden, when shall we see you at Henley?
    [*He shrugs away from her and the Devil pushes her out.*
BURDEN. The devil take thee and Henley too.
MILES. Master, shall I make a good motion?   160
BACON. What's that?
MILES. Marry, sir, now that my hostess is gone to provide supper,
conjure up another spirit, and send Doctor Burden flying after.
BACON. Thus, rulers of our academic state,
You have seen the friar frame his art by proof;
And as the college callèd Brazen-nose
Is under him, and he the master there,
So surely shall this head of brass be fram'd,

150. *mated*, confounded.   152. *'bash*, be abashed.

And yield forth strange and uncouth aphorisms;
And hell and Hecate shall fail the friar,   170
But I will circle England round with brass.

MILES. So be it, *et nunc et semper;* amen.   *[Exeunt.*

SCENE III

HARLESTON FAIR. *Lacy has had time to adopt the disguise of coun-*
tryman suggested by the Prince in Scene I, and now he insinu-
ates himself into a group composed of Margaret, the keeper's
daughter, and her friend Joan, and Thomas and Richard and
other country young men.

THOMAS. By my troth, Margaret, here's a weather is able to make
a man call his father "whoreson": if this weather hold, we shall
have hay good cheap, and butter and cheese at Harleston will
bear no price.

MARGARET. Thomas, maids when they come to see the fair
Count not to make a cope for dearth of hay:
When we have turn'd our butter to the salt,
And set our cheese safely upon the racks,
Then let our fathers price it as they please.
We country sluts of merry Fressingfield   10
Come to buy needless naughts to make us fine,
And look that young men should be frank this day,
And court us with such fairings as they can.
Phœbus is blithe, and frolic looks from heaven,
As when he courted lovely Semele,
Swearing the pedlers shall have empty packs,
If that fair weather may make chapmen buy.

LACY. But, lovely Peggy, Semele is dead,
And therefore Phœbus from his palace pries,
And, seeing such a sweet and seemly saint,   20
Shows all his glories for to court yourself.

MARGARET. This is a fairing, gentle sir, indeed,
To soothe me up with such smooth flattery;
But learn of me, your scoff's too broad before.—

172. *et nunc et semper,* now and forever.
  3. *good cheap,* at a bargain.   6. *cope,* bargain.
  10. *sluts,* women (without the evil connotation it now has).
  15. *Semele,* destroyed by Zeus' lightning when she asked to behold him
in all his splendor. She was the mother of Dionysus.
  17. *chapmen,* traders.   24. *too broad before,* too obvious.

Well, Joan, our beauties must abide their jests;
We serve the turn in jolly Fressingfield.

JOAN. Margaret, a farmer's daughter for a farmer's son:
  I warrant you, the meanest of us both
  Shall have a mate to lead us from the church.
    [*Lacy whispers Margaret in the ear.*
  But, Thomas, what's the news? what, in a dump?   30
  Give me your hand, we are near a pedler's shop;
  Out with your purse, we must have fairings now.

THOMAS. Faith, Joan, and shall: I'll bestow a fairing on you, and
  then we will to the tavern, and snap off a pint of wine or two.

MARGARET. Whence are you, sir? of Suffolk? for your terms
  Are finer than the common sort of men.

LACY. Faith, lovely girl, I am of Beccles by,
  Your neighbour, not above six miles from hence,
  A farmer's son, that never was so quaint
  But that he could do courtesy to such dames.   40
  But trust me, Margaret, I am sent in charge,
  From him that revelled in your father's house,
  And fill'd his lodge with cheer and venison,
  'Tirèd in green: he sent you this rich purse,
  His token that he help'd you run your cheese,
  And in the milkhouse chatted with yourself.

MARGARET. To me? You forget yourself.

LACY. Women are often weak in memory.

MARGARET. O, pardon, sir, I call to mind the man:
  'Twere little manners to refuse his gift,   50
  And yet I hope he sends it not for love;
  For we have little leisure to debate of that.

JOAN. What, Margaret! blush not: maids must have their loves.

THOMAS. Nay, by the mass, she looks pale as if she were angry.

RICHARD. Sirrah, are you of Beccles? I pray, how doth Goodman
  Cob? my father bought a horse of him.—I'll tell you, Margaret, 'a were good to be a gentleman's jade, for of all things
  the foul hilding could not abide a dungcart

MARGARET [*Greatly impressed by Lacy's glibness and fine man-*
  ners. Aside]. How different is this farmer from the rest,
  That erst as yet have pleas'd my wandering sight!   60
  His words are witty, quicken'd with a smile,
  His courtesy gentle, smelling of the court;

37. *of Beccles by*, from near Beccles.
47. *You forget yourself*, you must be mistaken.
57. *'a were*, he would have been.   58. *hilding*, good for nothing.

Facile and debonair in all his deeds;
Proportion'd as was Paris, when, in grey,
He courted Œnon in the vale by Troy.
Great lords have come and pleaded for my love:
Who but the Keeper's lass of Fressingfield?
And yet methinks this farmer's jolly son
Passeth the proudest that hath pleas'd mine eye.
But, Peg, disclose not that thou art in love,   70
And show as yet no sign of love to him,
Although thou well wouldst wish him for thy love:
Keep that to thee till time doth serve thy turn,
To show the grief wherein thy heart doth burn.—
Come, Joan and Thomas, shall we to the fair?—
You, Beccles man, will not forsake us now?
LACY. Not whilst I may have such quaint girls as you.
MARGARET. Well, if you chance to come by Fressingfield,
Make but a step into the Keeper's lodge;
And such poor fare as woodmen can afford,   80
Butter and cheese, cream and fat venison,
You shall have store, and welcome therewithal.
LACY. Gramercies, Peggy; look for me ere long.

                            [*They go out happily.*

SCENE IV

HAMPTON COURT PALACE. *King Henry III, the father of Edward, is entertaining the Emperor of Germany and the King of Castile. The latter has brought with him his daughter Elinor as a potential bride for Edward, and the former has brought his most powerful magician, Vandermast, to put down any English pretenders to skill in magic.*

KING HENRY. Great men of Europe, monarchs of the West,
Ringed with the walls of old Oceanus,
Whose lofty surge is like the battlements
That compassed high-built Babel in with towers,—
Welcome, my lords, welcome, brave western kings,
To England's shore, whose promontory-cleeves
Shows Albion is another little world;
Welcome says English Henry to you all;
Chiefly unto the lovely Elinor,

64. *in grey,* the customary color of shepherds' costume.

Who dared for Edward's sake cut through the seas,   10
And venture as Agenor's damsel through the deep,
To get the love of Henry's wanton son.
KING OF CASTILE. England's rich monarch, brave Plantagenet,
  The Pyren Mounts swelling above the clouds,
That ward the wealthy Castile in with walls,
Could not detain the beauteous Elinor;
But hearing of the fame of Edward's youth,
She dared to brook Neptunus' haughty pride,
And bide the brunt of froward Æolus:
Then may fair England welcome her the more.   20
ELINOR. After that English Henry by his lords
Had sent Prince Edward's lovely counterfeit,
A present to the Castile Elinor,
The comely portrait of so brave a man,
The virtuous fame discoursèd of his deeds,
Edward's courageous resolution,
Done at the Holy Land 'fore Damas' walls,
Led both mine eye and thoughts in equal links
To like so of the English monarch's son,
That I attempted perils for his sake.   30
EMPEROR. Where is the prince, my lord?
KING HENRY. He posted down, not long since, from the court,
To Suffolk side, to merry Framlingham,
To sport himself amongst my fallow deer:
From thence, by packets sent to Hampton House,
We hear the prince is ridden, with his lords,
To Oxford, in the academy there
To hear dispute amongst the learnèd men.
But we will send forth letters for my son,
To will him come from Oxford to the court.   40
EMPEROR. Nay, rather, Henry, let us, as we be,
Ride for to visit Oxford with our train.
Fain would I see your universities,
And what learned men your academy yields.
From Hapsburg have I brought a learnèd clerk,
To hold dispute with English orators:
This doctor, surnamed Jaques Vandermast,
A German born, passed into Padua,

11. *Agenor*, son of Neptune and father of Cadmus, hence grandfather of Semele.
22. *counterfeit*, picture.
27. *Damas*, Damascus. Edward did not fight at Damascus.

To Florence and to fair Bologna,
To Paris, Rheims, and stately Orleans,   50
And, talking there with men of art, put down
The chiefest of them all in aphorisms,
In magic, and the mathematic rules:
Now let us, Henry, try him in your schools.
KING HENRY. He shall, my lord; this motion likes me well.
We'll progress straight to Oxford with our trains,
And see what men our academy brings.—
And, wonder Vandermast, welcome to me:
In Oxford shalt thou find a jolly friar,
Called Friar Bacon, England's only flower: 60
Set him but non-plus in his magic spells,
And make him yield in mathematic rules,
And for thy glory I will bind thy brows,
Not with a poet's garland made of bays,
But with a coronet of choicest gold.
Whilst then we set to Oxford with our troops,
Let's in and banquet in our English court.   [*Exeunt.*

SCENE V

While his father is engaged in getting a princess as wife for him,
Edward is still pursuing by devious ways the humble Margaret.
He and his group, except for Lacy, as we have seen, are now
in Oxford, looking for Friar Bacon. Simnel is dressed in the
Prince's clothes, and the Prince, Warren, and Ermsby are dis-
guised.

RALPH. Where be these vacabond knaves, that they attend no
better on their master?

PRINCE EDWARD. If it please your honour, we are all ready at an
inch.

RALPH. Sirrah Ned, I'll have no more post-horse to ride on: I'll
have another fetch.

ERMSBY. I pray you, how is that, my lord?

RALPH. Marry, sir, I'll send to the Isle of Ely for four or five
dozen of geese, and I'll have them tied six and six together with
whip-cord: now upon their backs will I have a fair field-   10
bed with a canopy; and so, when it is my pleasure, I'll flee into
what place I please. This will be easy.

66. *Whilst then*, until.
3-4. *at an inch*, at a moment's notice.   6. *fetch*, trick.
10-11. *field-bed*, folding cot used in military expeditions.

WARREN. Your honour hath said well: but shall we to Brazen-nose
College before we pull off our boots?

ERMSBY. Warren, well motioned; we will to the friar before we
revel it within the town.—Ralph, see you keep your countenance like a prince.

RALPH. Wherefore have I such a company of cutting knaves to
wait upon me, but to keep and defend my countenance against
all mine enemies? have you not good swords and bucklers? 20

[*Enter Friar Bacon and Miles.*

ERMSBY. Stay, who comes here?

WARREN. Some scholar; and we'll ask him where Friar Bacon is.

BACON [*To Miles*]. Why, thou arrant dunce, shall I never make
thee a good scholar? doth not all the town cry out and say,
Friar Bacon's subsizer is the greatest blockhead in all Oxford?
why, thou canst not speak one word of true Latin.

MILES. No, sir? yes! what is this else? *Ego sum tuus homo,* "I am
your man;" I warrant you, sir, as good Tully's phrase as any
is in Oxford.

BACON. Come on, sirrah; what part of speech is *Ego?*   30

MILES. *Ego,* that is "I"; marry, *nomen substantivo.*

BACON. How prove you that?

MILES. Why, sir, let him prove himself an 'a will; I can be heard,
felt and understood.

BACON. O gross dunce!   [*Beats him.*

PRINCE EDWARD. Come, let us break off this dispute between these
two.—Sirrah, where is Brazen-nose College?

MILES. Not far from Coppersmith's Hall.

PRINCE EDWARD. What, dost thou mock me?

MILES. Not I, sir, but what would you at Brazen-nose?   40

ERMSBY. Marry, we would speak with Friar Bacon.

MILES. Whose men be you?

ERMSBY. Marry, scholar, here's our master.

RALPH. Sirrah, I am the master of these good fellows; mayst thou
not know me to be a lord by my reparel?

MILES. Then here's good game for the hawk; for here's the master-
fool, and a covey of coxcombs: one wise man, I think, would
spring you all.

PRINCE EDWARD. Gog's wounds! Warren, kill him.

WARREN [*He tries vainly to draw his dagger*]. Why, Ned, I 50
think the devil be in my sheath; I cannot get out my dagger.

18. *cutting,* swaggering.
25. *subsizer,* student who worked for board and tuition.
48. *spring,* catch in a snare.   49. *Gog's,* euphemism for God's.

ERMSBY. Nor I mine: swones, Ned, I think I am bewitched.

MILES. A company of scabs! the proudest of you all draw your
weapon, if he can.—[*Aside.*] See how boldly I speak, now my
master is by.

PRINCE EDWARD. I strive in vain; but if my sword be shut
And conjured fast by magic in my sheath,
Villain, here is my fist.
[*Strikes Miles a box on the ear.*

MILES. O, I beseech you conjure his hands too, that he may not
lift his arms to his head, for he is light-fingered!   60

RALPH. Ned, strike him; I'll warrant thee by mine honour.

BACON. What! means the English prince to wrong my man?

PRINCE EDWARD. To whom speakest thou?

BACON.   To thee.

PRINCE EDWARD.   Who art thou?

BACON. Could you not judge, when all your swords grew fast,
That Friar Bacon was not far from hence?
Edward, King Henry's son and Prince of Wales,
Thy fool disguised cannot conceal thyself:
I know both Ermsby and the Sussex Earl,
Else Friar Bacon had but little skill.
Thou com'st in post from merry Fressingfield,   70
Fast-fancied to the Keeper's bonny lass,
To crave some succour of the jolly friar:
And Lacy, Earl of Lincoln, hast thou left,
To treat fair Margaret to allow thy loves;
But friends are men, and love can baffle lords;
The earl both woos and courts her for himself.

WARREN. Ned, this is strange; the friar knoweth all.

ERMSBY. Apollo could not utter more than this.

PRINCE EDWARD. I stand amazed to hear this jolly friar,
Tell even the very secrets of my thoughts:—   80
But, learnèd Bacon, since thou know'st the cause
Why I did post so fast from Fressingfield,
Help, friar, at a pinch, that I may have
The love of lovely Margaret to myself,
And, as I am true Prince of Wales, I'll give
Living and lands to strength thy college state.

WARREN. Good friar, help the prince in this.

RALPH. Why, servant Ned, will not the friar do it?—

52. *swones*, another euphemism, God's wounds.
71. *Fast-fancied*, bound by love.   74. *treat*, entreat.

Were not my sword glued to my scabbard by conjuration,
I would cut off his head, and make him do it by force.   90
MILES. In faith, my lord, your manhood and your sword is all
    alike; they are so fast conjured that we shall never see them.
ERMSBY. What, doctor, in a dump! tush, help the prince,
    And thou shalt see how liberal he will prove.
BACON. Crave not such actions greater dumps than these?
    I will, my lord, strain out my magic spells;
    For this day comes the earl to Fressingfield,
    And 'fore that night shuts in the day with dark,
    They'll be betrothèd each to other fast.
    But come with me; we'll to my study straight,   100
    And in a glass prospective I will show
    What's done this day in merry Fressingfield.
PRINCE EDWARD. Gramercies, Bacon; I will quite thy pain.
BACON. But send your train, my lord, into the town:
    My scholar shall go bring them to their inn;
    Meanwhile we'll see the knavery of the earl.
PRINCE EDWARD. Warren, leave me:—and, Ermsby, take the fool:
    Let him be master and go revel it,
    Till I and Friar Bacon talk awhile.
WARREN. We will, my lord.   110
RALPH. Faith, Ned, and I'll lord it out till thou comest;
    I'll be Prince of Wales over all the black-pots in Oxford.
    [*They all go out except Fr. Bacon and the Prince, who walk
      about the stage, go to the rear and open the curtains to
      the inner stage, which we are to understand is Bacon's cell.*

SCENE VI

BACON. Now, frolic Edward, welcome to my cell;
    Here tempers Friar Bacon many toys,
    And holds this place his consistory-court,
    Wherein the devils plead homage to his words.
    Within this glass prospective thou shalt see
    This day what's done in merry Fressingfield
    'Twixt lovely Peggy and the Lincoln Earl.
PRINCE EDWARD. Friar, thou glad'st me: now shall Edward try
    How Lacy meaneth to his sovereign lord.
BACON. Stand there and look directly in the glass.   10

101. *glass prospective*, magic mirror.   103. *quite*, reward.
112. *black-pots*, leather wine jugs.

[Enter Margaret and Friar Bungay, as if in the magic glass.
Edward sees but cannot hear them. Margaret has sought
counsel about this mysterious lover from a local wise man,
Friar Bungay.

What sees my lord?

PRINCE EDWARD. I see the Keeper's lovely lass appear,
As brightsome as the paramour of Mars,
Only attended by a jolly friar.

BACON. Sit still, and keep the crystal in your eye.

MARGARET. But tell me, Friar Bungay, is it true,
That this fair, courteous, country swain,
Who says his father is a farmer nigh,
Can be Lord Lacy, Earl of Lincolnshire?

BUNGAY. Peggy, 'tis true, 'tis Lacy for my life,   20
Or else mine art and cunning both doth fail,
Left by Prince Edward to procure his loves;
For he in green, that holp you run your cheese,
Is son to Henry, and the Prince of Wales.

MARGARET. Be what he will, his lure is but for lust:
But did Lord Lacy like poor Margaret,
Or would he deign to wed a country lass,
Friar, I would his humble handmaid be,
And for great wealth quite him with courtesy.

BUNGAY. Why, Margaret, dost thou love him?   30

MARGARET. His personage, like the pride of vaunting **Troy**,
Might well avouch to shadow Helen's rape:
His wit is quick and ready in conceit,
As Greece afforded in her chiefest prime:
Courteous, ah friar, full of pleasing smiles!
Trust me, I love too much to tell thee more;
Suffice to me he is England's paramour.

BUNGAY. Hath not each eye that viewed thy pleasing **face**
Surnamed thee Fair Maid of Fressingfield?

MARGARET. Yes, Bungay, and would God the lovely earl   40
Had that *in esse*, that so many sought.

BUNGAY. Fear not, the friar will not be behind
To show his cunning to entangle love.

PRINCE EDWARD. I think the friar courts the bonny wench;
Bacon, methinks he is a lusty churl.

BACON. Now look, my lord.

[Enter Lacy disguised as before.

13. *paramour of Mars*, Venus.   32. *shadow*, excuse.
37. *paramour*, darling.

PRINCE EDWARD [*Greatly excited*]. Gog's wounds, Bacon, here
    comes Lacy!

BACON. Sit still, my lord, and mark the comedy.

BUNGAY. Here's Lacy, Margaret, step aside awhile.
    [*They go off to one side while Lacy wrestles with his con-
    science about deceiving his master.*

LACY. Daphne, the damsel that caught Phœbus fast,   50
    And lock'd him in the brightness of her looks,
    Was not so beauteous in Apollo's eyes
    As is fair Margaret to the Lincoln Earl.
    Recant thee, Lacy, thou art put in trust:—
    Edward, thy sovereign's son, hath chosen thee,
    A secret friend, to court her for himself,
    And dar'st thou wrong thy prince with treachery?—
    Lacy, love makes no exception of a friend,
    Nor deems it of a prince but as a man.
    Honour bids thee control him in his lust;   60
    His wooing is not for to wed the girl,
    But to entrap her and beguile the lass.
    Lacy, thou lov'st; then brook not such abuse,
    But wed her, and abide thy prince's frown:
    For better die, than see her live disgraced.

MARGARET. Come, friar, I will shake him from his dumps.—
    [*Comes forward.*
    How cheer you, sir? a penny for your thought:
    You're early up, pray God it be the near.
    What, come from Beccles in a morn so soon?

LACY. Thus watchful are such men as live in love,   70
    Whose eyes brook broken slumbers for their sleep.
    I tell thee, Peggy, since last Harleston fair
    My mind hath felt a heap of passions.

MARGARET. A trusty man, that court it for your friend:
    Woo you still for the courtier all in green?
    I marvel that he sues not for himself.

LACY. Peggy, I pleaded first to get your grace for him;
    But when mine eyes surveyed your beauteous looks,
    Love, like a wag, straight div'd into my heart,
    And there did shrine the idea of yourself.   80
    Pity me, though I be a farmer's son,
    And measure not my riches, but my love.

    68. *You're early up . . .*, the proverb is, "Early up and never the nearer,"
i.e., to your purpose.
    79. *wag*, a tricky boy.

MARGARET. You are very hasty; for to garden well,
　　Seeds must have time to sprout before they spring:
　　Love ought to creep as doth the dial's shade,
　　For timely ripe is rotten too-too soon.
BUNGAY [*Coming forward*]. *Deus hic;* room for a merry friar!
　　What, youth of Beccles, with the Keeper's lass?
　　'Tis well; but tell me, hear you any news.
MARGARET. No, friar: what news?　　　　　　　　　　　　90
BUNGAY. Hear you not how the pursuivants do post
　　With proclamations through each country-town?
LACY. For what, gentle friar? tell the news.
BUNGAY. Dwell'st thou in Beccles, and hear'st not of these news?
　　Lacy, the Earl of Lincoln, is late fled
　　From Windsor court, disguisèd like a swain,
　　And lurks about the country here unknown.
　　Henry suspects him of some treachery,
　　And therefore doth proclaim in every way,
　　That who can take the Lincoln Earl shall have,　　100
　　Paid in the Exchequer, twenty thousand crowns.
LACY. The Earl of Lincoln! friar, thou art mad:
　　It was some other; thou mistak'st the man:
　　The Earl of Lincoln! why, it cannot be.
MARGARET. Yes, very well, my lord, for you are he:
　　The Keeper's daughter took you prisoner:
　　Lord Lacy, yield, I'll be your gaoler once.
PRINCE EDWARD. How familiar they be, Bacon!
BACON. Sit still, and mark the sequel of their loves.
LACY. Then am I double prisoner to thyself:　　　　110
　　Peggy, I yield; but are these news in jest?
MARGARET. In jest with you, but earnest unto me;
　　For why these wrongs do wring me at the heart.
　　Ah, how these earls and noblemen of birth
　　Flatter and feign to forge poor women's ill.
LACY. Believe me, lass, I am the Lincoln Earl:
　　I not deny but, 'tired thus in rags,
　　I lived disguised to win fair Peggy's love.
MARGARET. What love is there where wedding ends not love?
LACY. I meant, fair girl, to make thee Lacy's wife.　　120
MARGARET. I little think that earls will stoop so low.
LACY. Say, shall I make thee countess ere I sleep?
MARGARET. Handmaid unto the earl, so please himself:
　　A wife in name, but servant in obedience.

　　87. *Deus hic,* God is here.

LACY. The Lincoln Countess, for it shall be so:
I'll plight the bands and seal it with a kiss.
PRINCE EDWARD [*Jumping up and drawing his sword*]. Gog's
wounds, Bacon, they kiss! I'll stab them.
BACON. O, hold your hands, my lord; it is the glass.
PRINCE EDWARD. Choler to see the traitors gree so well
Made me think the shadows substances. 130
BACON. 'Twere a long poniard, my lord, to reach between
Oxford and Fressingfield; but sit still and see more.
BUNGAY. Well, Lord of Lincoln, if your loves be knit,
And that your tongues and thoughts do both agree,
To avoid ensuing jars, I'll hamper up the match.
I'll take my portace forth, and wed you here:
Then go to bed and seal up your desires.
LACY. Friar, content.—Peggy, how like you this?
MARGARET. What likes my lord is pleasing unto me.
BUNGAY. Then hand-fast hand, and I will to my book. 140
BACON. What sees my lord now?
PRINCE EDWARD. Bacon, I see the lovers hand in hand,
The friar ready with his portace there
To wed them both: then am I quite undone.
Bacon, help now, if e'er thy magic serv'd;
Help, Bacon; stop the marriage now,
If devils or necromancy may suffice,
And I will give thee forty thousand crowns.
BACON. Fear not, my lord, I'll stop the jolly friar
For mumbling up his orisons this day. 150
LACY. Why speak'st not, Bungay? Friar to thy book.
[*Bungay is mute, crying* "Hud, hud."
MARGARET. How look'st thou, friar, as a man distraught?
Reft of thy senses, Bungay? Show by signs
If thou be dumb, what passions holdeth thee.
LACY. He's dumb indeed. Bacon hath with his devils
Enchanted him, or else some strange disease
Or apoplexy hath possess'd his lungs:
But, Peggy, what he cannot with his book
We'll 'twixt us both unite it up in heart.
MARGARET. Else let me die, my lord, a miscreant. 160
PRINCE EDWARD. Why stands Friar Bungay so amazed?

129. *gree*, agree.   135. *hamper up*, make fast.
136. *portace*, breviary, a prayer book that could be carried around.
140. *hand-fast*, join, the term commonly used for marriage contracts.
150. *For*, from.

BACON. I have struck him dumb, my lord; and, if your honour
     please
  I'll fetch this Bungay straightway from Fressingfield,
  And he shall dine with us in Oxford here.
PRINCE EDWARD. Bacon, do that, and thou contentest me.
LACY. Of courtesy, Margaret, let us lead the friar
  Unto thy father's lodge, to comfort him
  With broths, to bring him from this hapless trance.
MARGARET. Or else, my lord, we were passing unkind
  To leave the friar so in his distress.   170
     [*Enter a Devil, who carries off Bungay on his back.*
  O, help, my lord! a devil, a devil, my lord!
  Look how he carries Bungay on his back!
  Let's hence, for Bacon's spirits be abroad.   [*Exit with Lacy.*
PRINCE EDWARD. Bacon, I laugh to see the jolly friar
  Mounted upon the devil, and how the earl
  Flees with his bonny lass for fear.
  As soon as Bungay is at Brazen-nose,
  And I have chatted with the merry friar,
  I will in post hie me to Fressingfield,
  And quite these wrongs on Lacy ere't be long.   180
BACON. So be it, my lord: but let us to our dinner;
  For ere we have taken our repast awhile,
  We shall have Bungay brought to Brazen-nose.
                         [*They go out together.*

SCENE VII

THE REGENTS' HOUSE AT OXFORD. *Word has come that the King and
his guests are planning to visit the University; Burden, Mason
and Clement are making plans for their entertainment.*

MASON. Now that we are gathered in the Regent House,
  It fits us talk about the king's repair;
  For he, trooped with all the western kings,
  That lie alongst the Dantzic seas by east,
  North by the clime of frosty Germany,
  The Almain monarch and the Saxon duke,
  Castile and lovely Elinor with him,

  2. *repair*, visit.
  3. *trooped with*, accompanied by.
  6. *Almain*, German. The Saxon duke does not appear as the play now
stands.

Have in their jests resolved for Oxford town.

BURDEN. We must lay plots of stately tragedies,
    Strange comic shows, such as proud Roscius   10
    Vaunted before the Roman Emperors,
    To welcome all the western potentates.

CLEMENT. But more; the king by letters hath foretold
    That Frederick, the Almain emperor,
    Hath brought with him a German of esteem,
    Whose surname is Don Jaques Vandermast,
    Skilful in magic and those secret arts.

MASON. Then must we all make suit unto the friar,
    To Friar Bacon, that he vouch this task,
    And undertake to countervail in skill   20
    The German; else there's none in Oxford can
    Match and dispute with learnèd Vandermast.

BURDEN. Bacon, if he will hold the German play,
    Will teach him what an English friar can do:
    The devil, I think, dare not dispute with him.

CLEMENT. Indeed, Mas doctor, he pleasured you,
    In that he brought your hostess, with her spit,
    From Henley, posting unto Brazen-nose.

BURDEN. A vengeance on the friar for his pains!
    But leaving that, let's hie to Bacon straight,   30
    To see if he will take this task in hand.

CLEMENT. Stay, what rumour is this? the town is up in a mutiny:
what hurly-burly is this?

    [*Enter a Constable, with Ralph Simnell, Warren, Ermsby,*
    still disguised as before, and Miles. They have been roister-
    ing in the town, and have been taken up by the Constable.

CONSTABLE. Nay, masters, if you were ne'er so good, you shall
before the doctors to answer your misdemeanour.

BURDEN. What's the matter, fellow?

CONSTABLE. Marry, sir, here's a company of rufflers, that, drinking in the tavern, have made a great brawl, and almost killed
the vintner.

MILES. *Salve*, Doctor Burden!   40
    This lubberly lurden,
    Ill-shaped and ill-faced,
    Disdained and disgraced,
    What he tells unto *vobis*

10. *Roscius*, the most famous of Roman actors.
37. *rufflers*, brawlers.   40. *Salve*, hail.

Mentitur de nobis.

BURDEN. Who is the master and chief of this crew?

MILES. *Ecce asinum mundi*
 Figura rotundi,
 Neat, sheat, and fine,
 As brisk as a cup of wine.   50

BURDEN [*To Ralph*]. What are you?

RALPH. I am, father doctor, as a man would say, the bell-wether
 of this company: these are my lords, and I the Prince of Wales.

CLEMENT. Are you Edward, the king's son?

RALPH. Sirrah Miles, bring hither the tapster that drew the wine,
 and, I warrant, when they see how soundly I have broke his
 head, they'll say 'twas done by no less man than a prince.

MASON. I cannot believe that this is the Prince of Wales.

WARREN. And why so, sir?

MASON. For they say the prince is a brave and a wise gentle-   60
man.

WARREN. Why, and think'st thou, doctor, that he is not so?
 Dar'st thou detract and derogate from him,
 Being so lovely and so brave a youth?

ERMSBY. Whose face, shining with many a sugared smile,
 Bewrays that he is bred of princely race.

MILES. And yet, master doctor,
 To speak like a proctor,
 And tell unto you
 What is veriment and true: 70
 To cease of this quarrel,
 Look but on his apparel;
 Then mark but my talis,
 He is great Prince of Walis,
 The chief of our *gregis,*
 And *filius regis:*
 Then 'ware what is done,
 For he is Henry's white son.

RALPH. Doctors, whose doting night-caps are not capable of my
 ingenious dignity, know that I am Edward Plantagenet,   80
 whom if you displease, will make a ship that shall hold all your
 colleges, and so carry away the Niniversity with a fair wind to

44-45. *vobis mentitur . . .,* whatever he tells you he is lying about us.
47. *Ecce asinum . . .,* Lo, the jackass of the round figured world.
49. *sheat,* trim or lively (?)   66. *bewrays,* betrays, indicates.
70. *veriment,* truth.   75. *gregis,* company.
76. *filius regis,* son of the king.
78. *white,* dear (as in the phrase, the white-headed boy).

the Bankside in Southwark.—How sayest thou, Ned Warren, shall I not do it?

WARREN. Yes, my good lord; and, if it please your lordship, I will gather up all your old pantofles, and with the cork make you a pinnace of five hundred ton, that shall serve the turn marvellous well, my lord.

ERMSBY. And I, my lord, will have pioners to undermine the town, that the very gardens and orchards be carried away 90 for your summer walks.

MILES. And I, with *scientia*
And great *diligentia*,
Will conjure and charm,
To keep you from harm;
That *utrum horum mavis*,
Your very great *navis*,
Like Bartlet's ship,
From Oxford do skip
With colleges and schools,   100
Full-loaden with fools.
Quid dicis ad hoc,
Worshipful *Domine* Dawcock?

CLEMENT. Why, hare-brained courtiers, are you drunk or mad,
To taunt us up with such scurrility?
Deem you us men of base and light esteem,
To bring us such a fop for Henry's son?—
Call out the beadles and convey them hence
Straight to Bocardo: let the roisters lie
Close clapt in bolts, until their wits be tame.   110

ERMSBY. Why, shall we to prison, my lord?

RALPH. What sayest, Miles, shall I honour the prison with my presence?

MILES. No, no: out with your blades,
And hamper these jades;
Have a flirt and a crash,
Now play revel-dash,
And teach these *sacerdos*
That the Bocardos,

86. *pantofles*, slippers.   89. *pioners*, diggers.
96. *utrum* . . . , whichever of these you prefer.   97. *navis*, ship.
98. *Bartlet's*, Miles' mistake for Barclay the English translator of the German *Ship of Fools*.   102. *Quid dicis* . . ., What do you say to this?
103. *Dawcock*, jackdaw, fool.   109. *Bocardo*, a prison in Oxford.
116. *flirt*, quick blow.   117. *revel-dash*, a rowdy game.
118. *sacerdos*, priests.

Like peasants and elves,   120
Are meet for themselves.

MASON. To the prison with them constable.

WARREN. Well, doctors, seeing I have sported me
With laughing at these mad and merry wags,
Know that Prince Edward is at Brazen-nose,
And this, attired like the Prince of Wales,
Is Ralph, King Henry's only loved fool;
I, Earl of Sussex, and this Ermsby,
One of the privy-chamber to the king;
Who, while the prince with Friar Bacon stays,   130
Have revelled it in Oxford as you see.

MASON. My lord, pardon us, we knew not what you were:
But courtiers may make greater scapes than these.
Wilt please your honour dine with me to-day?

WARREN. I will, Master doctor, and satisfy the vintner for his hurt;
only I must desire you to imagine him all this forenoon the
Prince of Wales.

MASON. I will, sir.

RALPH. And upon that I will lead the way; only I will have Miles
go before me, because I have heard Henry say that wisdom   140
must go before majesty.   [*They go out with mock ceremony.*

SCENE VIII

*Prince Edward has kept his threat of the preceding act and has
sought out Lacy and Margaret at Fressingfield. He bursts upon
them angrily, with drawn poniard.*

PRINCE EDWARD. Lacy, thou canst not shroud thy traitorous
thoughts,
Nor cover, as did Cassius, all his wiles;
For Edward hath an eye that looks as far
As Lynceus from the shores of Grecia.
Did I not sit in Oxford by the friar,
And see thee court the maid of Fressingfield,
Sealing thy flattering fancies with a kiss?
Did not proud Bungay draw his portace forth,
And joining hand in hand had married you,

133. *scapes*, escapades.
2. *Cassius*, one of the conspirators who killed Caesar.
4. *Lynceus*, one of the sons of Egyptus. He had eyes so sharp he could
see through the earth, and objects nine miles away.

If Friar Bacon had not struck him dumb,   10
And mounted him upon a spirit's back,
That we might chat at Oxford with the friar?
Traitor, what answer'st? is not all this true?
LACY. Truth all, my lord; and thus I make reply.
At Harleston fair, there courting for your grace,
Whenas mine eye surveyed her curious shape,
And drew the beauteous glory of her looks
To dive into the centre of my heart,
Love taught me that your honour did but jest,
That princes were in fancy but as men;   20
How that the lovely maid of Fressingfield
Was fitter to be Lacy's wedded wife,
Than concubine unto the Prince of Wales.
PRINCE EDWARD [*Shocked that friendship has yielded to love*].
Injurious Lacy, did I love thee more
Than Alexander his Hephestion?
Did I unfold the passions of my love,
And lock them in the closet of thy thoughts?
Wert thou to Edward second to himself,
Sole friend and partner of his secret loves?
And could a glance of fading beauty break   30
Th' enchained fetters of such private friends?
Base coward, false, and too effeminate
To be corrival with a prince in thoughts!
From Oxford have I posted since I dined,
To quite a traitor 'fore that Edward sleep.
MARGARET. 'Twas I, my lord, not Lacy, stept awry:
For oft he su'd and courted for yourself,
And still wooed for the courtier all in green;
But I, whom fancy made but over-fond,
Pleaded myself with looks as if I lov'd;   40
I fed mine eye with gazing on his face,
And still bewitched loved Lacy with my looks;
My heart with sighs, mine eyes pleaded with tears,
My face held pity and content at once;
And more I could not cipher-out by signs
But that I lov'd Lord Lacy with my heart.
Then, worthy Edward, measure with thy mind
If women's favours will not force men fall,
If beauty, and if darts of piercing love,

25. *Hephestion*, Macedonian general, who married sister of Alexander's wife.   33. *corrival*, partner.   45. *cipher-out*, express, demonstrate.

Is not of force to bury thoughts of friends.   50

PRINCE EDWARD. I tell thee, Peggy, I will have thy loves:
  Edward or none shall conquer Margaret.
  In frigates bottomed with rich Sethin planks,
  Topt with the lofty firs of Lebanon,
  Stemmed and encased with burnished ivory,
  And overlaid with plates of Persian wealth,
  Like Thetis shalt thou wanton on the waves,
  And draw the dolphins to thy lovely eyes,
  To dance lavoltas in the purple streams:
  Sirens, with harps and silver psalteries,   60
  Shall wait with music at thy frigate's stem,
  And entertain fair Margaret with their lays.
  England and England's wealth shall wait on thee;
  Britain shall bend unto her prince's love,
  And do due homage to thine excellence,
  If thou wilt be but Edward's Margaret.

MARGARET. Pardon, my lord: if Jove's great royalty
  Sent me such presents as to Danaë;
  If Phœbus tired in Latona's webs,
  Came courting from the beauty of his lodge;   70
  The dulcet tunes of frolic Mercury,—
  Not all the wealth heaven's treasury affords,—
  Should make me leave Lord Lacy or his love.

PRINCE EDWARD. I have learn'd at Oxford, there, this point of
    schools,—
  Ablata causa, tollitur effectus:
  Lacy—the cause that Margaret cannot love
  Nor fix her liking on the English prince—
  Take him away, and then the effects will fail.
  Villain, prepare thyself: for I will bathe
  My poniard in the bosom of an earl.   80

LACY. Rather than live, and miss fair Margaret's love,
  Prince Edward, stop not at the fatal doom,
  But stab it home: end both my loves and life.

MARGARET. Brave Prince of Wales, honoured for royal deeds,
  'Twere sin to stain fair Venus' courts with blood;
  Love's conquest ends, my lord, in courtesy:
  Spare Lacy, gentle Edward; let me die,
  For so both you and he do cease your loves.

53. *Sethin*, Shittim.   57. *Thetis*, a sea nymph, the mother of Achilles.
59. *lavoltas*, lively dances, resembling the polka.   69. *tired*, attired.
75. *Ablata causa* . . ., the cause taken away, the effect is lost.

PRINCE EDWARD. Lacy shall die as traitor to his lord.

LACY. I have deserved it, Edward; act it well.   90

MARGARET. What hopes the prince to gain by Lacy's death?

PRINCE EDWARD. To end the loves 'twixt him and Margaret.

MARGARET. Why, thinks King Henry's son that Margaret's love
    Hangs in th' uncertain balance of proud time?
    That death shall make a discord of our thoughts?
    No, stab the earl, and 'fore the morning sun
    Shall vaunt him thrice over the lofty east,
    Margaret will meet her Lacy in the heavens.

LACY. If aught betides to lovely Margaret
    That wrongs or wrings her honour from content,   100
    Europe's rich wealth nor England's monarchy
    Should not allure Lacy to over-live:
    Then, Edward, short my life and end her loves.

MARGARET. Rid me, and keep a friend worth many loves.

LACY. Nay, Edward, keep a love worth many friends.

MARGARET. An if thy mind be such as fame hath blazed,
    Then, princely Edward, let us both abide
    The fatal resolution of thy rage:
    Banish thou fancy, and embrace revenge,
    And in one tomb knit both our carcases,   110
    Whose hearts were linked in one perfect love.

PRINCE EDWARD [*Aside, impressed by this show of love and logic*].
    Edward, art thou that famous Prince of Wales,
    Who at Damasco beat the Saracens,
    And brought'st home triumph on thy lance's point?
    And shall thy plumes be pull'd by Venus down?
    Is't princely to dissever lover's leagues,
    To part such friends as glory in their loves?
    Leave, Ned, and make a virtue of this fault,
    And further Peg and Lacy in their loves:
    So in subduing fancy's passion,   120
    Conquering thyself, thou gett'st the richest spoil.—
    Lacy, rise up. Fair Peggy, here's my hand:
    The Prince of Wales hath conquered all his thoughts,
    And all his loves he yields unto the earl.
    Lacy, enjoy the maid of Fressingfield;
    Make her thy Lincoln Countess at the church,
    And Ned, as he is true Plantagenet,
    Will give her to thee frankly for thy wife.

LACY. Humbly I take her of my sovereign,

102. *over-live*, outlive, survive.   104. *rid*, get rid of.

As if that Edward gave me England's right, 130
And rich'd me with the Albion diadem.

MARGARET. And doth the English prince mean true?
Will he vouchsafe to cease his former loves,
And yield the title of a country maid
Unto Lord Lacy?

PRINCE EDWARD. I will, fair Peggy, as I am true lord.

MARGARET. Then, lordly sir, whose conquest is as great,
In conquering love, as Cæsar's victories,
Margaret, as mild and humble in her thoughts
As was Aspasia unto Cyrus' self, 140
Yields thanks, and, next Lord Lacy, doth enshrine
Edward the second secret in her heart.

PRINCE EDWARD. Gramercy, Peggy:—now that vows are past,
And that your loves are not to be revolt,
Once, Lacy, friends again. Come, we will post
To Oxford; for this day the king is there,
And brings for Edward Castile Elinor.
Peggy, I must go see and view my wife:
I pray God I like her as I loved thee.
Beside, Lord Lincoln, we shall hear dispute 150
'Twixt Friar Bacon and learned Vandermast.
Peggy, we'll leave you for a week or two.

MARGARET. As it please Lord Lacy: but love's foolish looks
Think footsteps miles, and minutes to be hours.

LACY. I'll hasten, Peggy, to make short return.—
But please your honour go unto the lodge,
We shall have butter, cheese, and venison;
And yesterday I brought for Margaret
A lusty bottle of neat claret-wine:
Thus can we feast and entertain your grace. 160

PRINCE EDWARD. 'Tis cheer, Lord Lacy, for an Emperor,
If he respect the person and the place:
Come, let us in; for I will all this night
Ride post until I come to Bacon's cell. [*Exeunt.*

140. *Aspasia,* the younger Aspasia, so named by her husband, King Cyrus of Persia, because she resembled in beauty and wit the great mistress of the Athenian, Pericles.
144. *revolt,* overturned.

SCENE IX

King Henry enters with his guests, to whom he has been showing Oxford. With him now are the Emperor, the King of Castile, Elinor, Vandermast, and Bacon's compatriot, Bungay.

EMPEROR. Trust me, Plantagenet, these Oxford schools
  Are richly seated near the river-side:
  The mountains full of fat and fallow deer,
  The battling pastures lade with kine and flocks,
  The town gorgeous with high-built colleges,
  And scholars seemly in their grave attire,
  Learnèd in searching principles of art.—
  What is thy judgment, Jaques Vandermast?
VANDERMAST. That lordly are the buildings of the town,
  Spacious the rooms, and full of pleasant walks;   10
  But for the doctors, how that they be learnèd,
  It may be meanly, for aught I can hear,
BUNGAY. I tell thee, German, Hapsburg holds none such
  None read so deep as Oxenford contains:
  There are within our academic state
  Men that may lecture it in Germany
  To all the doctors of your Belgic schools.
KING HENRY. Stand to him, Bungay, charm this Vandermast,
  And I will use thee as a royal king.
VANDERMAST. Wherein dar'st thou dispute with me?   20
BUNGAY. In what a doctor and a friar can.
VANDERMAST. Before rich Europe's worthies put thou forth
  The doubtful question unto Vandermast.
BUNGAY. Let it be this,—Whether the spirits of pyromancy or
  geomancy, be most predominant in magic?
VANDERMAST. I say, of pyromancy.
BUNGAY. And I, of geomancy.
VANDERMAST. The cabalists that write of magic spells,
  As Hermes, Melchie, and Pythagoras,   30
  Affirm that, 'mongst the quadruplicity
  Of elemental essence, *terra* is but thought
  To be a *punctum* squared to the rest;
  And that the compass of ascending elements
  Exceed in bigness as they do in height;

4. *battling*, nourishing. *lade*, laden.   32. *terra*, earth.
33. *a punctum squared to*, an atom compared with.

Judging the concave circle of the sun
To hold the rest in his circumference.
If, then, as Hermes says, the fire be greatest,
Purest, and only giveth shape to spirits,
Then must these *dæmones* that haunt that place 40
Be every way superior to the rest.

BUNGAY. I reason not of elemental shapes,
Nor tell I of the concave latitudes,
Noting their essence nor their quality,
But of the spirits that pyromancy calls,
And of the vigour of the geomantic fiends.
I tell thee, German, magic haunts the ground,
And those strange necromantic spells
That work such shows and wondering in the world
Are acted by those geomantic spirits 50
That Hermes calleth *terræ filii*.
The fiery spirits are but transparent shades,
That lightly pass as heralds to bear news;
But earthly fiends, closed in the lowest deep,
Dissever mountains, if they be but charged,
Being more gross and massy in their power.

VANDERMAST. Rather these earthly geomantic spirits
Are dull and like the place where they remain;
For when proud Lucifer fell from the heavens,
The spirits and angels that did sin with him, 60
Retained their local essence as their faults,
All subject under Luna's continent:
They which offended less hang in the fire,
And second faults did rest within the air;
But Lucifer and his proud-hearted fiends
Were thrown into the centre of the earth,
Having less understanding than the rest,
As having greater sin and lesser grace.
Therefore such gross and earthly spirits do serve
For jugglers, witches, and vile sorcerers; 70
Whereas the pyromantic genii
Are mighty, swift, and of far-reaching power.
But grant that geomancy hath most force;
Bungay, to please these mighty potentates,
Prove by some instance what thy art can do.

BUNGAY. I will.

40. *dæmones*, spirits.　51. *terræ filii*, sons of the earth.

EMPEROR. Now, English Harry, here begins the game;
  We shall see sport between these learnèd men.
VANDERMAST. What wilt thou do?
BUNGAY. Show thee the tree, leaved with refinèd gold,   80
  Whereon the fearful dragon held his seat,
  That watch'd the garden called Hesperides,
  Subdued and won by conquering Hercules.
    [*Here Bungay conjures, and the Tree appears with the
      Dragon shooting fire.*
VANDERMAST. Well done!
KING HENRY. What say you, royal lordings, to my friar?
  Hath he not done a point of cunning skill?
VANDERMAST. Each scholar in the necromantic spells
  Can do as much as Bungay hath perform'd.
  But as Alcmena's bastard razed this tree,
  So will I raise him up as when he liv'd,   90
  And cause him pull the dragon from his seat,
  And tear the branches piecemeal from the root.—
  Hercules! *Prodi, prodi,* Hercules!
    [*Hercules appears in his lion's skin.*
HERCULES. *Quis me vult?*
VANDERMAST. Jove's bastard son, thou Libyan Hercules,
  Pull off the sprigs from off the Hesperian tree,
  As once thou didst to win the golden fruit.
HERCULES. *Fiat.*   [*He begins to break the branches.*
VANDERMAST. Now, Bungay, if thou canst by magic charm
  The fiend, appearing like great Hercules,   100
  From pulling down the branches of the tree,
  Then art thou worthy to be counted learnèd.
BUNGAY. I cannot.
VANDERMAST. Cease, Hercules, until I give thee charge.—
  Mighty commander of this English isle,
  Henry, come from the stout Plantagenets,
  Bungay is learn'd enough to be a friar;
  But to compare with Jaques Vandermast,
  Oxford and Cambridge must go seek their cells
  To find a man to match him in his art.   110
  I have given non-plus to the Paduans,
  To them of Sien, Florence, and Bologna,
  Rheims, Louvain, and fair Rotterdam,

93. *Prodi,* come forth, enter.   94. *Quis me vult,* Who wishes me?
98. *Fiat,* Let it be done.

Frankfort, Lutrech, and Orleans:
And now must Henry, if he do me right,
Crown me with laurel, as they all have done.
 [*Enter Bacon, who feigns ignorance of what has happened.*
  His coming causes a great stir.

BACON. All hail to this royal company,
 That sit to hear and see this strange dispute!—
 Bungay, how stand'st thou as a man amaz'd?
 What, hath the German acted more than thou?   120

VANDERMAST. What art thou that question'st thus?

BACON. Men call me Bacon.

VANDERMAST [*Greatly impressed*]. Lordly thou look'st, as if that
 thou wert learn'd;
 Thy countenance, as if science held her seat
 Between the circled arches of thy brows.

KING HENRY. Now, monarchs, hath the German found his
 match.

EMPEROR. Bestir thee, Jaques, take not now the foil,
 Lest thou dost lose what foretime thou didst gain.

VANDERMAST. Bacon, wilt thou dispute?

BACON. No, unless he were more learn'd than Vandermast; 130
 For yet, tell me, what hast thou done?

VANDERMAST. Rais'd Hercules to ruinate that tree,
 That Bungay mounted by his magic spells.

BACON. Set Hercules to work.

VANDERMAST. Now, Hercules, I charge thee to thy task;
 Pull off the golden branches from the root.

HERCULES. I dare not; see'st thou not great Bacon here,
 Whose frown doth act more than thy magic can?

VANDERMAST. By all the thrones, and dominations,
 Virtues, powers, and mighty hierarchies,   140
 I charge thee to obey to Vandermast.

HERCULES. Bacon, that bridles headstrong Belcephon,
 And rules Asmenoth, guider of the north,
 Binds me from yielding unto Vandermast.

KING HENRY. How now, Vandermast! have you met with your
 match?

VANDERMAST. Never before was't known to Vandermast
 That men held devils in such obedient awe.
 Bacon doth more than art, or else I fail.

114. *Lutrech*, Either Utrecht (not yet a university town) or Lutetia, the
old name for Paris.   127. *foil*, fall, a term borrowed from wrestling.
143. *Asmenoth*, another of Bacon's powerful spirits.

EMPEROR. Why, Vandermast, art thou overcome?—
  Bacon, dispute with him, and try his skill.   150
BACON. I come not, monarchs, for to hold dispute
  With such a novice as is Vandermast;
  I come to have your royalties to dine
  With Friar Bacon here in Brazen-nose:
  And, for this German troubles but the place,
  And holds this audience with a long suspence,
  I'll send him to his academy hence.—
  Thou, Hercules, whom Vandermast did raise,
  Transport the German unto Hapsburg straight,
  That he may learn by travail, 'gainst the spring,   160
  More secret dooms and aphorisms of art.
  Vanish the tree, and thou away with him!
    [*Exit Hercules with Vandermast and the Tree.*
EMPEROR. Why, Bacon, whither dost thou send him?
BACON. To Hapsburg: there your highness at return
  Shall find the German in his study safe.
KING HENRY. Bacon, thou hast honour'd England with thy skill,
  And made fair Oxford famous by thine art:
  I will be English Henry to thyself;—
  But tell me, shall we dine with thee to-day?
BACON. With me, my lord; and while I fit my cheer,   170
  See where Prince Edward comes to welcome you,
  Gracious as the morning-star of heaven.
    [*He goes out as Prince Edward, Lacy, Warren and Ermsby
      enter from the other side. They have just arrived from
      Framlingham.*
EMPEROR. Is this Prince Edward, Henry's royal son?
  How martial is the figure of his face!
  Yet lovely and beset with amorets.
KING HENRY. Ned, where hast thou been?
PRINCE EDWARD. At Framlingham, my lord, to try your bucks
  If they could scape the teasers or the toil.
  But hearing of these lordly potentates
  Landed, and progressed up to Oxford town,   180
  I posted to give entertain to them:
  Chief to the Almain monarch; next to him,
  And joint with him, Castile and Saxony
  Are welcome as they may be to the English court.
  Thus for the men: but see, Venus appears,
  Or one that overmatcheth Venus in her shape!
175. *amorets,* loving looks.

Sweet Elinor, beauty's high-swelling pride,
Rich nature's glory, and her wealth at once,
Fair of all fairs, welcome to *Albion;*
Welcome to me, and welcome to thine own,   190
If that thou deign'st the welcome from myself.

ELINOR. Martial Plantagenet, Henry's high-minded son,
The mark that Elinor did count her aim,
I lik'd thee 'fore I saw thee: now I love,
And so as in so short a time I may;
Yet so as time shall never break that so:
And therefore so accept of Elinor.

KING OF CASTILE. Fear not, my lord, this couple will agree,
If love may creep into their wanton eyes:—
And therefore, Edward, I accept thee here,   200
Without suspence, as my adopted son.

KING HENRY. Let me that joy in these consorting greets,
And glory in these honours done to Ned,
Yield thanks for all these favours to my son,
And rest a true Plantagenet to all.

[*Enter Miles with a cloth and trenchers and salt, bustling
around to set the table for Bacon's guests. He does it very
clumsily.*

MILES. *Salvete, omnes reges,*
That govern your *greges*
In Saxony and Spain,
In England and in Almain!
For all this frolic rabble   210
Must I cover the table
With trenchers, salt, and cloth;
And then look for your broth.

EMPEROR. What pleasant fellow is this?

KING HENRY. 'Tis, my lord, Doctor Bacon's poor scholar.

MILES [*Aside*]. My master hath made me sewer of these great
lords; and, God knows, I am as serviceable at a table as a sow
is under an apple-tree: 'tis no matter; their cheer shall not be
great, and therefore what skills where the salt stand, before or
behind?   [*He hurries comically out.* 220

KING OF CASTILE. These scholars knows more skill in axioms,
How to use quips and sleights of sophistry,

206. *Salvete* . . ., Hail, all you kings.
207. *greges,* peoples.   216. *sewer,* butler.
219. *what skills,* what does it matter. *the salt,* a large salt cellar was the
dividing line between guests of superior and inferior rank.

Than for to cover courtly for a king.

[*Re-enter Miles with a mess of pottage and broth; and, after him, Bacon.*

MILES. Spill, sir? why, do you think I never carried twopenny
    chop before in my life?—
By you leave, *nobile decus,*
For here comes Doctor Bacon's *pecus,*
Being in his full age
To carry a mess of pottage.

BACON. Lordings, admire not if your cheer be this,   230
For we must keep our academic fare;
No riot where philosophy doth reign:
And therefore, Henry, place these potentates,
And bid them fall unto their frugal cates.

EMPEROR [*Highly insulted*]. Presumptuous friar! what, scoff'st
    thou at a king?
What, dost thou taunt us with thy peasant's fare,
And give us cates fit for country swains?—
Henry, proceeds this jest of thy consent,
To twit us with a pittance of such price?
Tell me, and Frederick will not grieve thee long.

KING HENRY. By Henry's honour, and the royal faith   240
The English monarch beareth to his friend,
I knew not of the friar's feeble fare,
Nor am I pleased he entertains you thus.

BACON. Content thee, Frederick, for I showed the cates
To let thee see how scholars use to feed;
How little meat refines our English wits:—
Miles, take away, and let it be thy dinner.

MILES. Marry, sir, I will.
This day shall be a festival-day with me,
For I shall exceed in the highest degree.   250
               [*He joyfully bears the food away.*

BACON. I tell thee, monarch, all the German peers
Could not afford thy entertainment such,
So royal and so full of majesty,
As Bacon will present to Frederick.
The basest waiter that attends thy cups
Shall be in honours greater than thyself;
And for thy cates, rich Alexandria drugs,
Fetched by carvels from Egypt's richest straits,

223. *to cover,* set a table.   225. *nobile decus,* worshipful honor.
226. *pecus,* beast of burden.   229. *admire,* wonder.   257. *drugs,* spices.

Found in the wealthy strand of Africa,
Shall royalize the table of my king;   260
Wines richer than the 'Gyptian courtesan
Quaffed to Augustus' kingly countermatch,
Shall be caroused in English Henry's feasts;
Candy shall yield the richest of her canes;
Persia, down her Volga by canoes,
Send down the secrets of her spicery;
The Afric dates, mirabolans of Spain,
Conserves, and suckets from Tiberias,
Cates from Judæa, choicer that the lamp
That fired Rome with sparks of gluttony,   270
Shall beautify the board for Frederick:
And therefore grudge not at a friar's feast.

[*They parade out.*

SCENE X

BACK AT FRESSINGFIELD. *Two gentlemen of the district, Lambert
and Serlsby have come to ask Margaret's father for her hand,
and each is prepared to outbid the other. They enter with the
Keeper.*

LAMBERT. Come, frolic Keeper of our liege's game,
Whose table spread hath ever venison
And jacks of wines to welcome passengers,
Know I'm in love with jolly Margaret,
That overshines our damsels as the moon
Darkeneth the brightest sparkles of the night.
In Laxfield here my land and living lies:
I'll make thy daughter jointer of it all,
So thou consent to give her to my wife;
And I can spend five-hundred marks a year.   10
SERLSBY. I am the lands-lord, Keeper, of thy holds,
By copy all thy living lies in me;
Laxfield did never see me raise my due:
I will enfeoff fair Margaret in all,
So she will take her to a lusty squire.

261. *'Gyptian courtesan*, Cleopatra, who dissolved pearls in her toasts to
Antony.   264. *Candy*, Candia or Crete, a famous source of sweets.
267. *mirabolans*, dried plums.   268. *suckets*, sweetmeats.
269. *lamp*, lamprey?   8. *jointer*, joint possessor.   9. *to*, for, as.
12. *copy*, copyhold.   14. *enfeoff*, to invest with a "fee" or feudal estate.

KEEPER. Now, courteous gentles, if the Keeper's girl
    Hath pleas'd the liking fancy of you both,
    And with her beauty hath subdu'd your thoughts,
    'Tis doubtful to decide the question.
    It joys me that such men of great esteem   20
    Should lay their liking on this base estate,
    And that her state should grow so fortunate
    To be a wife to meaner men than you:
    But sith such squires will stoop to keeper's fee,
    I will, to avoid displeasure of you both,
    Call Margaret forth, and she shall make her choice.
LAMBERT. Content, Keeper; send her unto us.   [*Exit Keeper.*
    Why, Serlsby, is thy wife so lately dead,
    Are all thy loves so lightly passèd over,
    As thou canst wed before the year be out?   30
SERLSBY. I live not, Lambert, to content the dead,
    Nor was I wedded but for life to her:
    The grave ends and begins a married state.
        [*Enter Margaret.*
LAMBERT. Peggy, the lovely flower of all towns,
    Suffolk's fair Helen, and rich England's star,
    Whose beauty, tempered with her huswifery,
    Makes England talk of merry Fressingfield!
SERLSBY. I cannot trick it up with poesies,
    Nor paint my passions with comparisons,
    Nor tell a tale of Phœbus and his loves: 40
    But this believe me,—Laxfield here is mine,
    Of ancient rent seven-hundred pounds a year;
    And if thou canst but love a country squire,
    I will enfeoff thee, Margaret, in all:
    I cannot flatter; try me, if thou please.
MARGARET. Brave neighbouring squires, the stay of Suffolk's clime,
    A keeper's daughter is too base in gree
    To match with men accounted of such worth:
    But might I not displease, I would reply.
LAMBERT. Say, Peggy; naught shall make us discontent.   50
MARGARET. Then, gentles, note that love hath little stay,
    Nor can the flames that Venus sets on fire
    Be kindled but by fancy's motion:
    Then pardon, gentles, if a maid's reply
    Be doubtful, while I have debated with myself,
    Who, or of whom, love shall constrain me like.
24. *sith,* since.   47. *gree,* degree.

SERLSBY. Let it be me; and trust me, Margaret,
   The meads environ'd with the silver streams,
   Whose battling pastures fatten all my flocks,
   Yielding forth fleeces stapled with such wool,   60
   As Lempster cannot yield more finer stuff,
   And forty kine with fair and burnished heads,
   With strouting dugs that paggle to the ground,
   Shall serve thy dairy, if thou wed with me.

LAMBERT. Let pass the country wealth, as flocks and kine,
   And lands that wave with Ceres' golden sheaves,
   Filling my barns with plenty of the fields;
   But, Peggy, if thou wed thyself to me,
   Thou shalt have garments of embroidered silk,
   Lawns, and rich net-works for thy head-attire: 70
   Costly shall be thy fair habiliments,
   If thou wilt be but Lambert's loving wife.

MARGARET. Content you, gentles, you have proffered fair,
   And more than fits a country maid's degree:
   But give me leave to counsel me a time,
   For fancy blooms not at the first assault;
   Give me but ten days' respite, and I will reply,
   Which or to whom myself affectionates.

SERLSBY. Lambert, I tell thee thou'rt importunate;
   Such beauty fits not such a base esquire: 80
   It is for Serlsby to have Margaret.

LAMBERT. Think'st thou with wealth to overreach me?
   Serlsby, I scorn to brook thy country braves:
   I dare thee, coward, to maintain this wrong,
   At dint of rapier, single in the field.

SERLSBY. I'll answer, Lambert, what I have avouched.—
   Margaret, farewell; another time shall serve.   [*Exit.*

LAMBERT. I'll follow.—Peggy, farewell to thyself;
   Listen how well I'll answer for thy love.   [*Exit.*

MARGARET. How fortune tempers lucky haps with frowns,   90
   And wrongs me with the sweets of my delight!
   Love is my bliss, and love is now my bale.
   Shall I be Helen in my froward fates,
   As I am Helen in my matchless hue,
   And set rich Suffolk with my face afire?
   If lovely Lacy were but with his Peggy,
   The cloudy darkness of his bitter frown

---

60. *stapled*, fibred.   61. *Lempster*, Leominster.
63. *strouting*, swelling. *paggle*, hang loosely.   83. *braves*, insults.

Would check the pride of these aspiring squires.
Before the term of ten days be expir'd,
Whenas they look for answer of their loves,   100
My lord will come to merry Fressingfield,
And end their fancies and their follies both:
Till when, Peggy, be blithe and of good cheer.
    [*Enter a Post with a letter and a bag of gold. Lacy has de-*
      cided to test his lady's love.

POST. Fair, lovely damsel, which way leads this path?
How might I post me unto Fressingfield?
Which footpath leadeth to the Keeper's lodge?
MARGARET. Your way is ready, and this path is right:
Myself do dwell hereby in Fressingfield;
And if the Keeper be the man you seek,
I am his daughter: may I know the cause?   110
POST. Lovely, and once beloved of my lord,—
No marvel if his eye was lodg'd so low,
When brighter beauty is not in the heavens,—
The Lincoln Earl hath sent you letters here,
And, with them, just an hundred pounds in gold.
Sweet, bonny wench, read them, and make reply.
    [*Gives letter and bag.*
MARGARET. The scrolls that Jove sent Danaë,
Wrapt in rich closures of fine burnish'd gold,
Were not more welcome than these lines to me.
Tell me, whilst that I do unrip the seals,   120
Lives Lacy well? how fares my lovely lord?
POST. Well, if that wealth may make men to live well.

MARGARET [*Reads*]. *The blooms of the almond tree grow in a*
night, and vanish in a morn; the flies hæmeræ, fair Peggy, take
life with the sun, and die with the dew: fancy that slippeth in
with a gaze, goeth out with a wink; and too timely loves have
ever the shortest length. I write this as thy grief, and my folly,
who at Fressingfield loved that which time hath taught me to be
but mean dainties: eyes are dissemblers, and fancy is but queasy;
therefore know, Margaret, I have chosen a Spanish lady to   130
be my wife, chief waiting-woman to the Princess Elinor; a lady
fair, and no less fair than thyself, honourable and wealthy. In
that I forsake thee, I leave thee to thine own liking; and for thy
dowry I have sent thee an hundred pounds; and ever assure

---

124. *hæmeræ*, ephemerae. The letter is a good example of the style popu-
larized by Lyly's *Euphues*.

thee of my favour, which shall avail thee and thine much. Fare-
well.

> *Not thine, nor his own,*
>
> *Edward Lacy.*

Fond Ate, doomer of bad-boding fates,
That wraps proud fortune in thy snaky locks,   140
Did'st thou enchant my birthday with such stars
As lighten'd mischief from their infancy?
If heavens had vowed, if stars had made decree,
To show on me their froward influence,
If Lacy had but loved, heavens, hell, and all
Could not have wronged the patience of my mind.

POST. It grieves me, damsel; but the earl is forced
To love the lady by the king's command.

MARGARET. The wealth combined within the English shelves,
Europe's commander, nor the English king,   150
Should not have moved the love of Peggy from her lord.

POST. What answer shall I return to my lord?

MARGARET. First, for thou cam'st from Lacy whom I loved,—
Ah, give me leave to sigh at every thought!—
Take thou, my friend, the hundred pound he sent;
For Margaret's resolution craves no dower:
The world shall be to her as vanity;
Wealth, trash; love, hate; pleasure, despair:
For I will straight to stately Framlingham,
And in the abbey there be shorn a nun,   160
And yield my loves and liberty to God.
Fellow, I give thee this, not for the news,
For those be hateful unto Margaret,
But for thou'rt Lacy's man, once Margaret's love.

POST. What I have heard, what passions I have seen,
I'll make report of them unto the earl.

MARGARET. Say that she joys his fancies be at rest,
And prays that his misfortune may be hers.

> [*They go out, Margaret weeping.*

SCENE XI

FRIAR BACON'S CELL. *He has completed his Brazen Head and is
ready to profit from its wisdom. He is lying on a bed, with a
white stick in one hand, his magic book in the other. Beside*

149. *shelves,* cliffs.

him is a lighted lamp. In full view is the Brazen Head, and
Miles stands by, fully armed.

BACON. Miles, where are you?

MILES. Here, sir.

BACON. How chance you tarry so long?

MILES. Think you that the watching of the Brazen Head craves
no furniture? I warrant you, sir, I have so armed myself that
if all your devils come, I will not fear them an inch.

BACON. Miles, thou know'st that I have dived into hell,
And sought the darkest palaces of fiends;
That with my magic spells great Belcephon
Hath left his lodge and kneeled at my cell;   10
The rafters of the earth rent from the poles,
And three-formed Luna hid her silver looks,
Trembling upon her concave continent,
When Bacon read upon his magic book.
With seven years' tossing necromantic charms,
Poring upon dark Hecat's principles,
I have framed out a monstrous head of brass,
That, by the enchanting forces of the devil,
Shall tell out strange and uncouth aphorisms,
And girt fair England with a wall of brass.   20
Bungay and I have watched these threescore days,
And now our vital spirits crave some rest:
If Argus lived, and had his hundred eyes,
They could not over watch Phobetor's night.
Now, Miles, in thee rests Friar Bacon's weal:
The honour and renown of all his life
Hangs in the watching of this Brazen Head;
Therefore I charge thee by the immortal God,
That holds the souls of men within his fist,
This night thou watch; for ere the morning-star   30
Sends out his glorious glister on the north,
The head will speak: then, Miles, upon thy life,
Wake me; for then by magic art I'll work
To end my seven years' task with excellence.
If that a wink but shut thy watchful eye,
Then farewell Bacon's glory and his fame!
Draw close the curtains, Miles: now, for thy life,
Be watchful, and—   [*Falls asleep.*

MILES. So; I thought you would talk yourself asleep anon; and

24. *Phobetor*, son of Morpheus, god of sleep.

'tis no marvel, for Bungay on the days, and he on the   40
nights, have watched just these ten and fifty days: now this
is the night, and 'tis my task, and no more. Now, Jesus bless
me, what a goodly head it is! and a nose! you talk of *nos autem
glorificare;* but here's a nose that I warrant may be called *nos
autem populare* for the people of the parish. Well, I am furnished with weapons: now, sir, I will set me down by a post,
and make it as good as a watchman to wake me, if I chance to
slumber. I thought, Goodman Head, I would call you out of
your *memento.* [*He sits down, his head nods, and cracks against
the post.*] Passion o' God, I have almost broke my pate!   50
[*A great noise.*] Up, Miles, to your task; take your brown-bill
in your hand; here's some of your master's hobgoblins abroad.

THE BRAZEN HEAD. Time is.

MILES. Time is! Why, Master Brazen-head, have you such a capital nose, and answer you with syllables, "Time is"? Is this all
my master's cunning, to spend seven years' study about "Time
is"? Well, sir, it may be we shall have some better orations of
it anon: well, I'll watch you as narrowly as ever you were
watched, and I'll play with you as the nightingale with the
slowworm; I'll set a prick against my breast. Now rest   60
there, Miles. [*He puts the point of his halberd against his breast,
half dozes off and is nearly transfixed on it.*] Lord have mercy
upon me, I have almost killed myself! [*A great noise.*] Up,
Miles; list how they rumble.

THE BRAZEN HEAD. Time was.

MILES. Well, Friar Bacon, you have spent your seven years' study
well, that can make your head speak but two words at once,
"Time was." Yea, marry, time was when my master was a wise
man, but that was before he began to make the Brazen Head.
You shall lie while your arse ache, an your Head speak no   70
better. Well, I will watch, and walk up and down, and be a
peripatetian and a philosopher of Aristotle's stamp. [*A great
noise. He is startled and fumbles at the pistols stuck in his belt.*]
What, a fresh noise? Take thy pistols in hand, Miles.

THE BRAZEN HEAD. Time is past.

    [*A lightning flashes forth, and a hand appears that breaks
      down the Head with a hammer.*

MILES. Master, master, up! hell's broken loose; your Head speaks;
and there's such a thunder and lightning, that I warrant all

51. *brown-bill,* a watchman's pike or halberd.
60. *slowworm,* a small snake.

Oxford is up in arms. Out of your bed, and take a brown-bill
in your hand; the latter day is come.

BACON. Miles, I come. O passing warily watched!   80
Bacon will make thee next himself in love.
When spake the head?

MILES. When spake the head! did not you say that he should tell
strange principles of philosophy? Why, sir, it speaks but two
words at a time.

BACON. Why, villain, hath it spoken oft?

MILES. Oft! ay, marry, hath it, thrice: but in all those three times
it hath uttered but seven words.

BACON. As how?

MILES. Marry, sir, the first time he said, "Time is," as if Fabius   90
Cumentator should have pronounced a sentence; the second
time he said "Time was"; and the third time with thunder and
lightning, as in great choler, he said, "Time is past."

BACON [Passionately]. 'Tis past indeed. Ah, villain! time is past:
My life, my fame, my glory, all are past.—
Bacon, the turrets of thy hope are ruined down,
Thy seven years' study lieth in the dust:
Thy Brazen Head lies broken through a slave,
That watched, and would not when the Head did will.—
What said the Head first?   100

MILES. Even, sir, "Time is."

BACON. Villain, if thou hadst called to Bacon then,
If thou hadst watched, and waked the sleepy friar,
The Brazen Head had uttered aphorisms,
And England had been circled round with brass:
But proud Asmenoth, ruler of the north,
And Demogorgon, master of the fates,
Grudge that a mortal man should work so much.
Hell trembled at my deep-commanding spells,
Fiends frowned to see a man their over-match;   110
Bacon might boast more than a man might boast:
But now the braves of Bacon have an end,
Europe's conceit of Bacon hath an end,
His seven years' practice sorteth to ill end:
And, villain, sith my glory hath an end,
I will appoint thee to some fatal end.

91. *Cumentator*, his confusion of Commentator and Cunctator.
106. *Asmenoth*, the Astmeroth mentioned earlier.
113. *conceit*, high opinion.   114. *sorteth*, comes out, tends.

Villain, avoid! get thee from Bacon's sight!
Vagrant, go roam and range about the world,
And perish as a vagabond on earth.

MILES. Why, then, sir, you forbid me your service?   120

BACON. My service, villain! with a fatal curse,
That direful plagues and mischief fall on thee.

MILES. 'Tis no matter, I am against you with the old proverb—
"The more the fox is curst the better he fares." God be with
you, sir; I'll take but a book in my hand, a wide-sleeved gown
on my back, and a crowned cap on my head, and see if I can
want promotion.   [*He goes out undismayed.*

BACON. Some fiend or ghost haunt on thy weary steps,
Until they do transport thee quick to hell:
For Bacon shall have never merry day,   130
To lose the fame and honour of his Head.

          [*He goes out greatly dejected.*

SCENE XII

AT COURT *again, a short time after the last court scene. Edward
and Elinor have spent the intervening time in getting acquainted.
They enter together, along with the Emperor, the King of
Castile, King Henry, Lacy, and the jester, Ralph Simnel.*

EMPEROR. Now, lovely prince, the prince of Albion's wealth,
How fare the Lady Elinor and you?
What, have you courted and found Castile fit
To answer England in equivalence?
Will 't be a match 'twixt bonny Nell and thee?

PRINCE EDWARD. Should Paris enter in the courts of Greece,
And not lie fettered in fair Helen's looks?
Or Phœbus scape those piercing amorets,
That Daphne glancèd at his deity?
Can Edward, then, sit by a flame and freeze,   10
Whose heat puts Helen and fair Daphne down?
Now, monarchs, ask the lady if we gree.

KING HENRY. What, madam, hath my son found grace or no?

ELINOR. Seeing, my lord, his lovely counterfeit,
And hearing how his mind and shape agreed,
I come not, trooped with all this warlike train,
Doubting of love, but so affectionate,

121. *fatal* . . ., perhaps should read to some fatal end.
124. *curst,* punning on coursed (chased), and fares (goes).

As Edward hath in England what he won in Spain.

KING OF CASTILE. A match, my lord; these wantons needs must love:

Men must have wives, and women will be wed: 20

Let's haste the day to honour up the rites.

RALPH. Sirrah Harry, shall Ned marry Nell?

KING HENRY. Ay, Ralph; how then?

RALPH. Marry, Harry, follow my counsel: send for Friar Bacon to marry them for he'll so conjure him and her with his necromancy, that they shall love together like pig and lamb whilst they live.

KING OF CASTILE. But hearest thou, Ralph, art thou content to have Elinor to thy lady?

RALPH. Ay, so she will promise me two things.   30

KING OF CASTILE. What's that, Ralph?

RALPH. That she will never scold with Ned, nor fight with me.—
Sirrah Harry, I have put her down with a thing unpossible.

KING HENRY. What's that, Ralph?

RALPH. Why, Harry, didst thou ever see that a woman could both hold her tongue and her hands?   No! but when egg-pies grow on apple-trees, then will thy grey mare prove a bag-piper.

EMPEROR. What says the Lord of Castile and the Earl of Lincoln, that they are in such earnest and secret talk?

KING OF CASTILE. I stand, my lord, amazed at his talk,   40

How he discourseth of the constancy

Of one surnamed, for beauty's excellence,

The Fair Maid of merry Fressingfield.

KING HENRY. 'Tis true, my lord, 'tis wondrous for to hear;

Her beauty passing Mars's paramour,

Her virgin's right as rich as Vesta's was:

Lacy and Ned have told me miracles.

KING OF CASTILE. What says Lord Lacy? shall she be his wife?

LACY. Or else Lord Lacy is unfit to live.—

May it please your highness give me leave to post   50

To Fressingfield, I'll fetch the bonny girl,

And prove in true appearance at the court,

What I have vouched often with my tongue.

KING HENRY. Lacy, go to the 'querry of my stable,

And take such coursers as shall fit thy turn:

Hie thee to Fressingfield, and bring home the lass:

And, for her fame flies through the English coast,

If it may please the Lady Elinor,

18. *As,* that.

One day shall match your excellence and her.

ELINOR. We Castile ladies are not very coy;   60
    Your highness may command a greater boon:
    And glad were I to grace the Lincoln Earl
    With being partner of his marriage-day.

PRINCE EDWARD. Gramercy, Nell, for I do love the lord,
    As he that's second to myself in love.

RALPH. You love her?—Madam Nell, never believe him you,
    though he swears he loves you.

ELINOR. Why, Ralph?

RALPH. Why, his love is like unto a tapster's glass that is broken
    with every touch; for he loved the fair maid of Fressing-   70
    field once out of all ho.—Nay, Ned, never wink upon me: I
    care not, I.

KING HENRY. Ralph tells all; you shall have a good secretary of
    him.—
    But, Lacy, haste thee post to Fressingfield;
    For ere thou hast fitted all things for her state,
    The solemn marriage-day will be at hand.

LACY. I go, my lord.   [*He hurries away.*

EMPEROR. How shall we pass this day, my lord?

KING HENRY. To horse, my lord; the day is passing fair:
    We'll fly the partridge, or go rouse the deer.   80
    Follow, my lords; you shall not want for sport.

                           [*They go out together.*

SCENE XIII

FRIAR BACON'S CELL. *The Friar sits grieving over the destruction
of his Brazen Head. Friar Bungay comes in to him.*

BUNGAY. What means the friar that frolicked it of late,
    To sit as melancholy in his cell,
    As if he had neither lost nor won to-day?

BACON. Ah, Bungay, my Brazen Head is spoiled,
    My glory gone, my seven years' study lost!
    The fame of Bacon, bruited through the world,
    Shall end and perish with this deep disgrace.

BUNGAY. Bacon hath built foundation of his fame
    So surely on the wings of true report,
    With acting strange and uncouth miracles,   10
    As this cannot infringe what he deserves.

71. *out of all ho,* beyond all bounds.

BACON. Bungay, sit down, for by prospective skill
  I find this day shall fall out ominous:
  Some deadly act shall tide me ere I sleep:
  But what and wherein little can I guess,
  My mind is heavy, whatso'er shall hap.   [*Knocking within.*
  Who's that knocks?
BUNGAY. Two scholars that desire to speak with you.
BACON. Bid them come in.—
    [*Enter two Scholars.*
  Now, my youths, what would you have?   20
FIRST SCHOLAR. Sir, we are Suffolkmen and neighbouring friends:
  Our fathers in their countries lusty squires;
  Their lands adjoin: in Crackfield mine doth dwell,
  And his in Laxfield. We are college-mates,
  Sworn brothers, as our fathers live as friends.
BACON. To what end is all this?
SECOND SCHOLAR. Hearing your worship kept within your cell
  A glass prospective, wherein men might see
  Whatso their thoughts or hearts' desire could wish,
  We come to know how that our fathers fare.   30
BACON. My glass is free for every honest man.
  Sit down, and you shall see ere long,
  How or in what state your friendly fathers live.
  Meanwhile, tell me your names.
FIRST SCHOLAR. Mine Lambert.
SECOND SCHOLAR. And mine Serlsby.
BACON. Bungay, I smell there will be a tragedy.
    [*Enter on the upper stage Lambert and Serlsby, with rapiers
    and daggers.*
LAMBERT. Serlsby, thou hast kept thine hour like a man:
  Thou'rt worthy of the title of a squire,
  That durst, for proof of thy affection   40
  And for thy mistress' favour, prize thy blood.
  Thou know'st what words did pass at Fressingfield,
  Such shameless braves as manhood cannot brook:
  Ay, for I scorn to bear such piercing taunts,
  Prepare thee, Serlsby; one of us will die.
SERLSBY. Thou see'st I single [meet] thee [in] the field,
  And what I spake, I'll maintain with my sword:
  Stand on thy guard, I cannot scold it out.
  And if thou kill me, think I have a son,

14. *tide*, betide.   41. *prize*, venture.

That lives in Oxford in the Broadgates-hall,   50
  Who will revenge his father's blood with blood.
LAMBERT. And, Serlsby, I have there a lusty boy,
  That dares at weapon buckle with thy son,
  And lives in Broadgates too, as well as thine:
  But draw thy rapier, for we'll have a bout.
BACON. Now, lusty younkers, look within the glass,
  And tell me if you can discern your sires.
FIRST SCHOLAR. Serlsby, 'tis hard; thy father offers wrong,
  To combat with my father in the field.
SECOND SCHOLAR. Lambert, thou liest, my father's is th' abuse,   60
  And thou shalt find it, if my father harm.
BUNGAY. How goes it, sirs?
FIRST SCHOLAR. Our fathers are in combat hard by Fressingfield.
BACON. Sit still, my friends, and see the event.
LAMBERT. Why stand'st thou, Serlsby? doubt'st thou of thy life?
  A veney, man! fair Margaret craves so much.
SERLSBY. Then this for her.
FIRST SCHOLAR. Ah, well thrust!
SECOND SCHOLAR. But mark the ward.   69
        [*Lambert and Serlsby fight and stab each other.*
LAMBERT. O, I am slain!   [*Dies.*
SERLSBY. And I,—Lord have mercy on me!   [*Dies.*
FIRST SCHOLAR. My father slain! [*He draws his sword.*] Serlsby,
  ward that.
SECOND SCHOLAR. And so is mine! [*He parries the thrust and they
  fence.*] Lambert, I'll quite thee well.
        [*The two Scholars stab each other and die.*
BUNGAY. O strange stratagem!
BACON. See, friar, where the fathers both lie dead!—
  Bacon, thy magic doth effect this massacre:
  This glass prospective worketh many woes;
  And therefore seeing these brave lusty Brutes,   80
  These friendly youths, did perish by thine art,
  End all thy magic and thine art at once.
  The poniard that did end their fatal lives,
  Shall break the cause efficient of their woes.
  So fade the glass, and end with it the shows
  That necromancy did infuse the crystal with.

60. *abuse*, i. e., my father is the offended one.
65. *doubt'st . . . of*, fearest for.
66. *veney*, bout.   77. *fathers*, scholars?
80. *Brutes*, descendants of Brut, mythical founder of Britain.
83. *fatal*, fated.

[*Breaks the glass.*

BUNGAY. What means learned Bacon thus to break his glass?

BACON [*His conscience woefully disturbed*]. I tell thee, Bungay,
    it repents me sore

  That ever Bacon meddled in this art.

  The hours I have spent in pyromantic spells,   90

  The fearful tossing in the latest night

  Of papers full of necromantic charms,

  Conjuring and adjuring devils and fiends,

  With stole and alb and strange pentageron;

  The wresting of the holy name of God,

  As Soter, Eloim, and Adonai,

  Alpha, Manoth, and Tetragrammaton,

  With praying to the five-fold powers of heaven,

  Are instances that Bacon must be damned,

  For using devils to countervail his God.—   100

  Yet, Bacon, cheer thee, drown not in despair:

  Sins have their salves, repentance can do much:

  Think Mercy sits where Justice holds her seat,

  And from those wounds those bloody Jews did **pierce,**

  Which by thy magic oft did bleed afresh,

  From thence for thee the dew of mercy drops,

  To wash the wrath of high Jehovah's ire,

  And make thee as a new-born babe from sin.—

  Bungay, I'll spend the remnant of my life

  In pure devotion, praying to my God   110

  That he would save what Bacon vainly lost.   [*Exeunt.*

SCENE XIV

*Margaret, heartbroken at Lacy's apparent infidelity, has decided
to withdraw from the world and become a nun. She is now
leaving home to go to the nunnery, and is accompanied by the
Keeper and a Friend.*

KEEPER. Margaret, be not so headstrong in these vows:

  O, bury not such beauty in a cell,

  That England hath held famous for the hue!

  Thy father's hair, like to the silver blooms

  That beautify the shrubs of Africa,

  Shall fall before the dated time of death,

  Thus to forgo his lovely Margaret.

  95. *wresting*, misusing.

MARGARET. Ah, father, when the harmony of heaven
  Soundeth the measures of a lively faith,
  The vain illusions of this flattering world   10
  Seem odious to the thoughts of Margaret.
  I loved once,—Lord Lacy was my love;
  And now I hate myself for that I loved,
  And doted more on him than on my God:
  For this I scourge myself with sharp repents.
  But now the touch of such aspiring sins
  Tells me all love is lust but love of heavens;
  That beauty used for love is vanity:
  The world contains naught but alluring baits,
  Pride, flattery, and inconstant thoughts.   20
  To shun the pricks of death, I leave the world,
  And vow to meditate on heavenly bliss,
  To live in Framlingham a holy nun,
  Holy and pure in conscience and in deed;
  And for to wish all maids to learn of me
  To seek heaven's joy before earth's vanity.
FRIEND. And will you then, Margaret, be shorn a nun, and so
  leave us all?
MARGARET. Now farewell, world, the engine of all woe!
  Farewell to friends and father! welcome Christ!   30
  Adieu to dainty robes! this base attire
  Better befits an humble mind to God
  Than all the show of rich habiliments.
  Farewell, O love, and, with fond love, farewell
  Sweet Lacy, whom I loved once so dear!
  Ever be well, but never in my thoughts,
  Lest I offend to think on Lacy's love:
  But even to that, as to the rest, farewell!
     [*Enter Lacy, Warren and Ermsby, booted and spurred.*
LACY. Come on, my wags, we're near the Keeper's lodge.
  Here have I oft walked in the watery meads,   40
  And chatted with my lovely Margaret.
WARREN. Sirrah Ned, is not this the Keeper?
LACY. 'Tis the same.
ERMSBY. The old lecher hath gotten holy mutton to him; a nun,
  my lord.
LACY. Keeper, how far'st thou? holla, man, what cheer?
  How doth Peggy, thy daughter and my love?
KEEPER. Ah, good my lord! O, woe is me for Peggy!

44. *mutton*, a woman of loose morals, slang for prostitute.

See where she stands clad in her nun's attire,
Ready for to be shorn in Framlingham: 50
She leaves the world because she left your love.
O, good my lord, persuade her if you can!
LACY. Why, how now, Margaret! what, a malcontent?
A nun? what holy father taught you this,
To task yourself to such a tedious life
As die a maid? 'twere injury to me
To smother up such beauty in a cell.
MARGARET. Lord Lacy, thinking of my former miss,
How fond the prime of wanton years were spent
In love (O, fie upon that fond conceit,   60
Whose hap and essence hangeth in the eye!),
I leave both love and love's content at once,
Betaking me to him that is true love,
And leaving all the world for love of him.
LACY. Whence, Peggy, comes this metamorphosis?
What, shorn a nun, and I have from the court
 Posted with coursers to convey thee hence
To Windsor, where our marriage shall be kept!
Thy wedding robes are in the tailor's hands.
Come, Peggy, leave these peremptory vows.   70
MARGARET. Did not my lord resign his interest,
And make divorce 'twixt Margaret and him?
LACY. 'Twas but to try sweet Peggy's constancy.
But will fair Margaret leave her love and lord?
MARGARET. Is not heaven's joy before earth's fading bliss,
And life above sweeter than life in love?
LACY. Why, then, Margaret will be shorn a nun?
MARGARET. Margaret hath made a vow which may not be revok'd.
WARREN. We cannot stay, my lord; an if she be so strict,
Our leisure grants us not to woo afresh.   80
ERMSBY. Choose you, fair damsel,—yet the choice is yours,—
Either a solemn nunnery or the court,
God or Lord Lacy: which contents you best,
To be a nun, or else Lord Lacy's wife?
LACY. A good motion.—Peggy, your answer must be short.
MARGARET. The flesh is frail; my lord doth know it well,
That when he comes with his enchanting face,
Whatsoe'er betide I cannot say him nay.
Off goes the habit of a maiden's heart,
And, seeing fortune will, fair Framlingham,   90

58. *miss*, mistake.

And all the show of holy nuns, farewell!
Lacy for me, if he will be my lord.
LACY. Peggy, thy lord, thy love, thy husband.
  Trust me, by truth of knighthood, that the king
  Stays for to marry matchless Elinor,
  Until I bring thee richly to the court,
  That one day may both marry her and thee.—
  How say'st thou, Keeper? art thou glad of this?
KEEPER. As if the English king had given
  The park and deer of Fressingfield to me. 100
ERMSBY. I pray thee, my lord of Sussex, why art thou in a brown
  study?
WARREN. To see the nature of women; that be they never so near
  God, yet they love to die in a man's arms.
LACY. What have you fit for breakfast? We have hied
  And posted all this night to Fressingfield.
MARGARET. Butter and cheese, and umbles of a deer,
  Such as poor keepers have within their lodge.
LACY. And not a bottle of wine?
MARGARET. We'll find one for my lord. 110
LACY. Come, Sussex, let us in: we shall have more,
  For she speaks least, to hold her promise sure.
                  [They go out happily.

SCENE XV

FRIAR BACON'S CELL. *Enter a Devil, hunting around for Miles. Evidently Bacon has not yet lost all associations with the devils.*

DEVIL. How restless are the ghosts of hellish spirits,
  When every charmer with his magic spells,
  Calls us from nine-fold-trenchèd Phlegethon,
  To scud and over-scour the earth in post
  Upon the speedy wings of swiftest winds!
  Now Bacon hath raised me from the darkest deep,
  To search about the world for Miles his man,
  For Miles, and to torment his lazy bones
  For careless watching of his Brazen Head.
  See where he comes: O, he is mine! 10
    [Enter Miles in a gown and a corner-cap.
MILES. A scholar, quoth you! marry, sir, I would I had been
  made a bottle-maker when I was made a scholar; for I can

107. *umbles*, heart, liver, etc. 'umble pie.

get neither to be a deacon, reader, nor schoolmaster, no, not
the clerk of a parish. Some call me dunce; another saith, my
head is as full of Latin as an egg's full of oatmeal: thus I am
tormented, that the devil and Friar Bacon haunt me.—Good
Lord, here's one of my master's devils! I'll go speak to him.
—What, Master Plutus, how cheer you?

DEVIL. Dost thou know me?

MILES. Know you, sir! why, are not you one of my master's   20
devils, that were wont to come to my master, Doctor Bacon,
at Brazen-nose?

DEVIL. Yes, marry, am I.

MILES. Good Lord, Master Plutus, I have seen you a thousand
times at my master's, and yet I had never the manners to make
you drink. But, sir, I am glad to see how comfortable you are
to the statute.—I warrant you, he's as yeomanly a man as you
shall see: mark you, masters, here's a plain, honest man, without welt or guard.—But I pray you, sir, do you come lately
from hell?   30

DEVIL. Ay, marry: how then?

MILES. Faith, 'tis a place I have desired long to see: have you not
good tippling-houses there? may not a man have a lusty fire
there, a pot of good ale, a pair of cards, a swinging piece of
chalk, and a brown toast that will clap a white waistcoat on a
cup of good drink?

DEVIL. All this you may have there.

MILES. You are for me, friend, and I am for you.
But I pray you, may I not have an office there?

DEVIL. Yes, a thousand: what would'st thou be?   40

MILES. By my troth, sir, in a place where I may profit myself. I
know hell is a hot place, and men are marvellous dry, and much
drink is spent there; I would be a tapster.

DEVIL. Thou shalt.

MILES. There's nothing lets me from going with you, but that 'tis
a long journey, and I have never a horse.

DEVIL. Thou shalt ride on my back.

MILES. Now surely here's a courteous devil, that, for to pleasure
his friend, will not stick to make a jade of himself.—But I pray
you, goodman friend, let me move a question to you.   50

DEVIL. What's that?

MILES. I pray you, whether is your pace a trot or an amble?

DEVIL. An amble.

27. *statute*, i.e., that he is dressed according to his station in life.
29. *welt or guard*, facing.   34. *pair*, pack.

MILES. 'Tis well; but take heed it be not a trot: but 'tis no matter,
  I'll prevent it.   [*Puts on spurs.*

DEVIL. What dost?

MILES. Marry, friend, I put on my spurs; for if I find your pace
  either a trot or else uneasy, I'll put you to a false gallop; I'll
  make you feel the benefit of my spurs.

DEVIL. Get up upon my back.   60

  [*Miles mounts on the Devil's back.*

MILES. O Lord, here's even a goodly marvel, when a man rides
  to hell on the devil's back!

  [*Exeunt, the Devil roaring as Miles digs the spurs into him.*

SCENE XVI

AT COURT. *Edward has just married Elinor, and Lacy, Margaret.*

  [*Enter the Emperor with a pointless sword; next the King
    of Castile carrying a sword with a point; Lacy carrying
    the globe; Warren carrying a rod of gold with a dove on
    it; Ermsby with a crown and sceptre; Princess Elinor with
    Margaret, Countess of Lincoln, on her left hand; Prince
    Edward; King Henry; Friar Bacon; and Lords attending.*

PRINCE EDWARD. Great potentates, earth's miracles for state,
  Think that Prince Edward humbles at your feet,
  And, for these favours, on his martial sword
  He vows perpetual homage to yourselves,
  Yielding these honours unto Elinor.

KING HENRY. Gramercies, lordings; old Plantagenet,
  That rules and sways the Albion diadem,
  With tears discovers these conceivèd joys,
  And vows requital, if his men-at-arms,
  The wealth of England, or due honours done   10
  To Elinor, may quite his favourites.
  But all this while what say you to the dames
  That shine like to the crystal lamps of heaven?

EMPEROR. If but a third were added to these two,
  They did surpass those gorgeous images
  That gloried Ida with rich beauty's wealth.

MARGARET. 'Tis I, my lords, who humbly on my knee
  Must yield her orisons to mighty Jove
  For lifting up his handmaid to this state;
  Brought from her homely cottage to the court,   20

And graced with kings, princes, and emperors,
To whom (next to the noble Lincoln Earl)
I vow obedience, and such humble love
As may a handmaid to such mighty men.

PRINCESS ELINOR. Thou martial man that wears the **Almain crown**,
And you the western potentates of might,
The Albion princess, English Edward's wife,
Proud that the lovely star of Fressingfield,
Fair Margaret, Countess to the Lincoln Earl,
Attends on Elinor,—gramercies, lord, for her,—   30
'Tis I give thanks for Margaret to you all,
And rest for her due bounden to yourselves.

KING HENRY. Seeing the marriage is solemnized,
Let's march in triumph to the royal feast.—
But why stands Friar Bacon here so mute?

BACON. Repentant for the follies of my youth,
That magic's secret mysteries misled,
And joyful that this royal marriage
Portends such bliss unto this matchless realm.

KING HENRY. Why, Bacon, what strange event shall happen to
    this land?   40
Or what shall grow from Edward and his Queen?

BACON. I find by deep prescience of mine art,
Which once I tempered in my secret cell,
That here where Brute did build his Troynovant,
From forth the royal garden of a king
Shall flourish out so rich and fair a bud,
Whose brightness shall deface proud Phœbus' **flower**,
And overshadow Albion with her leaves.
Till then Mars shall be master of the field,
But then the stormy threats of wars shall cease: 50
The horse shall stamp as careless of the pike,
Drums shall be turned to timbrels of delight;
With wealthy favours plenty shall enrich
The strand that gladded wandering Brute to see;
And peace from heaven shall harbour in these **leaves**,
That, gorgeous, beautify this matchless flower:
Apollo's heliotropion then shall stoop,
And Venus' hyacinth shall vail her top;
Juno shall shut her gilliflowers up,

44. *Troynovant*, London, supposedly founded by descendants of Trojans.
46. *a bud*, the usual compliment to Queen Elizabeth.
57. *heliotropon*, heliotrope.   58. *vail*, lower, bow.

And Pallas' bay shall 'bash her brightest green;   60
Ceres' carnation, in consort with those,
Shall stoop and wonder at Diana's rose.

KING HENRY. This prophecy is mystical.—
But, glorious commanders of Europa's love,
That make fair England like that wealthy isle
Circled with Gihon and swift Euphrates,
In royalizing Henry's Albion
With presence of your princely mightiness,—
Let's march: the tables all are spread,
And viands, such as England's wealth affords,   70
Are ready set to furnish out the boards.
You shall have welcome, mighty potentates:
It rests to furnish up this royal feast,
Only your hearts be frolic; for the time
Craves that we taste of naught but jouissance.
Thus glories England over all the west.   [*They parade out.*

Omne tulit punctum qui miscuit utile dulci.

75. *jouissance*, pleasure.
77. *Omne tulit . . .*, He wins applause from all who blends the useful
with the agreeable.

THE HISTORY PLAY

A HISTORY PLAY is one which, as its name implies, takes an actual historical situation as its subject and treats it with reasonable regard for documented fact or what seems to the dramatist to be equivalent to documented fact. Though we often speak of dramatic moments in history, we must recognize that a simple historical situation offers definite problems to anyone who would adapt it to effective presentation on the stage. For one thing, the field of action tends to be panoramic; for another, the action is likely to consist of a long series of events from which it may be difficult to select a few closely related ones to fit into the time allotted to a play. Furthermore it is not simply action for its own sake which makes a truly effective play, but the development of character through the action.

Rather early in the dramatic history of the sixteenth century this was discovered through experimentation. As early as the fifth decade of the century John Bale ventured on a departure from the established pattern of the moral play with an interlude that retained much of the machinery of the earlier type, including the personified abstractions, but treated as its titular figure an historical English king, John. It is not a successful drama, but it indicates the way in which the problem of treating historical material might be solved. However much there might be of political or social, economic or religious problem in the play, in the last analysis it had to depend upon the presentation of a significant person to give unity and vigor to the action. That person was not always the titular hero. In the Henry VI plays, wholly or in large part by Shakespeare, this principal person is rather Talbot, the great English general, or the tiger-hearted Queen Margaret than the rather ineffective king. Thus the history play came to be in general an analysis of the development of an historical character in time of crisis rather than an attempt to give a general interpretation of a period such as a professional historian might be expected to produce. .

This is not to say that the approach was always the same. Bale approaches *King Johan* as a religious controversialist, a primitive champion of separation from Rome. Greene romanticized history in *James IV*, so that there is really no history there. Shakespeare concerned himself with the struggle between nobles and king, the last stages of feudalism, in the Henry VI plays and in *Richard II*.

The vogue of the history play has never died, out completely, and in our own day it has experienced a striking renascence of popularity. The great difference in the last century or so, however, has come in the introduction of sentimental touches. Whereas the older history play was concerned with matters of statecraft, the clash of strong personalities with little or no attention to love story, the more recent plays have stressed the part played by love in state affairs, sometimes to the almost total exclusion of the latter. Then too what was a few years ago called the "debunking" of historical figures has cast its shadow on history plays. The Elizabethans saw kings and their courts as a race apart; definitely superior to the race of ordinary men. The modern dramatist is intent on showing that they are after all no whit different from the rest of us.

Christopher Marlowe's career has in it much of the excited turbulence that runs through his plays. Born in Canterbury in 1564, the son of a shoemaker, he went from King's School at Canterbury to Cambridge in 1581. There he got into difficulty with the University authorities, perhaps because he was suspected either of Roman Catholic or atheistic leanings. Color was given to the former view by his trips to the continent, where he was reported to be associating with the Jesuit exiles at Rheims. Actually it may have been that he was even then (as we are sure he was later) in the Queen's secret service, directed by Sir Francis Walsingham. At any rate the University threatened to refuse him his M.A. in 1587, and he received it only on the intervention of powerful friends in the government.

Then Marlowe went up to London, much like Greene, to make a living from his pen, particularly in that increasingly popular medium of the drama, to which all London was flocking. Perhaps he took up with him the manuscript of *Tamberlaine*, his first play, and a great success. He followed part one of the play with a second part which evidently was equally well received. As these two plays deal with the career of a man seeking temporal, political power, so in his next play, *Dr. Faustus*, he took the theme of a man who sought intellectual power, and transgressed beyond the limits of man's legitimate curiosity. This in turn was followed by *The Jew of Malta* (*ca.* 1592), with the Jew serving as a type of colossal greed.

As if satiated with the resounding vigor of all these heroic characters, Marlowe turned in 1593 to a subject drawn from English history, taking as his hero no boisterous king like Richard the Lion Heart or Henry V but the weak and unfortunate Edward II, who has stubbornness instead of strength. Marlowe's dramatic work includes also the less important *The Massacre of Paris*, dramatizing the massacre of St. Bartholomew's Eve, and a play on a classical theme, *The Tragedy of Dido*, in both of which quite certainly others had a part.

Aside from his plays he is known for a not very good translation of Ovid's *Amores* and for two excellent poems, the short "Passionate Shepherd to His Love" and the long fragment (completed by George Chapman) of *Hero and Leander*.

All the while he was writing for the theater, Marlowe seems to have kept his connections with the government and his associations with many other literary men of the time. The most important of his associates, however, were Sir Walter Raleigh and a group of skeptical thinkers who had gathered around him. Marlowe had the reputation of being an atheist, though the term implied less denial of God than it does now. Because of the interrelation of the established religion and the state any kind of dissent or questioning was looked upon by the authorities as dangerous. In May 1593 Marlowe was called before the Privy Council and ordered to appear daily until "licensed to the contrary." Less than two weeks later Marlowe was dead, stabbed in what the witnesses claimed was a quarrel over the tavern bill. Puritan moralists seized on the story, much as tabloid newspapers do now, and perverted it to read as God's judgment on a notorious atheist, with no regard for the actual course of events. That tradition survived down to our own times.

Whatever else may be said of Marlowe's dramas, we should never lose sight of the fact that he was a poet. This is exemplified not only in the blank verse which he adapted to the theater so successfully that it was to be the chief medium for serious dramatic expression for three centuries, but also by the very exuberance and even excess which show something of that fine frenzy that Theseus attributes to the poet in *A Midsummer Night's Dream*. The stress on violent emotion, with not too much care for its motivation, the rich imagery of the language, the analysis of passion, all give that resounding effect that contributed to Ben Jonson's "Marlowe's mighty line." Through it Marlowe evokes a picture of the times. That in *Edward II* he was disturbed by a modern historian's reverence for meticulous detail is less than likely, but he does succeed in giving a sense of the almost anarchic conflict between strong barons and developing central authority which culminated in England in the Wars of the Roses and came to an end only with the coming of the Tudors to the throne after most of the old nobility had been killed off.

SUGGESTED READINGS

Bakeless, John, *Christopher Marlowe*. NEW YORK, 1937.

Boas, F. S. *Marlowe and His Circle*. OXFORD, 1931.

Brooke, C. F. Tucker, *The Tudor Drama*. NEW YORK, 1911.

——, Ed. *The Works of Christopher Marlowe*, OXFORD, 1910.

Cambridge History of English Literature, VOL. V. NEW YORK, 1910.

Chambers, E. K., *Elizabethan Stage*. OXFORD, 1923.

Hotson, J. L., *The Death of Christopher Marlowe*. CAMBRIDGE, MASS., 1925.

Marlowe, Christopher, *The Works and Life of Christopher Marlowe*. R. H. CASE, GEN. EDITOR. LONDON, 1930–1933.

Schelling, F. E., *The English Chronicle Play*. NEW YORK, 1902.

Anderson Maxwell, *Mary of Scotland*. NEW YORK, 1934.

Browning, Robert, *Strafford*. In *Works*. BOSTON, 1888.

Drinkwater, John, *Abraham Lincoln*. BOSTON, 1927.
Housman, Laurance, *Victoria Regina*. NEW YORK, 1935.
Shakespeare, William, *Richard II*.
——, *1 Henry IV*.
——, *2 Henry IV*.
——, *Henry V*.
——, *Richard III*.

EDWARD II

by Christopher Marlowe

Characters

KING EDWARD THE SECOND
PRINCE EDWARD, *his Son, afterwards King Edward the Third*
EARL OF KENT, *Half-brother of King Edward the Second*
PIERS GAVESTON, *the King's favorite*
EARL OF WARWICK
EARL OF LANCASTER
EARL OF PEMBROKE
EARL OF ARUNDEL
EARL OF LEICESTER
SIR THOS. BERKELEY
MORTIMER, *the elder*
MORTIMER, *the younger, his Nephew*
SPENSER, *the elder*
SPENSER, *the younger, his Son, favorite of the King after Gaveston's death*
ARCHBISHOP OF CANTERBURY
BISHOP OF COVENTRY
BISHOP OF WINCHESTER
BALDOCK, *a clerk, tutor to the Duke of Gloucester's daughter*
BEAUMONT
TRUSSEL
GURNEY
MATREVIS } *followers of Young Mortimer*
LIGHTBORN, *a murderer*
SIR JOHN OF HAINAULT
LEVUNE
RICE AP HOWEL
ABBOT, MONKS, HERALD, LORDS, POOR MEN, JAMES, MOWER, CHAMPION, MESSENGERS, SOLDIERS, LADIES, AND ATTENDANTS
QUEEN ISABELLA, *Wife of King Edward the Second*
NIECE TO KING EDWARD THE SECOND, *Daughter of the Duke of Gloucester*

ACT I

SCENE I

A STREET IN LONDON. *Piers Gaveston enters reading a letter from the King, who has summoned him back from France. He is dressed in the most extravagant fashion, and his manners are foppish without being too effeminate.*

GAVESTON. "My father is deceased! Come, Gaveston,
And share the kingdom with thy dearest friend."
Ah! words that make me surfeit with delight!
What greater bliss can hap to Gaveston
Than live and be the favourite of a king!
Sweet prince, I come; these, these thy amorous lines
Might have enforced me to have swum from France,
And, like Leander, gasped upon the sand,
So thou would'st smile, and take me in thy arms.
The sight of London to my exiled eyes   10
Is as Elysium to a new-come soul;
Not that I love the city, or the men,
But that it harbours him I hold so dear—
The king, upon whose bosom let me die,
And with the world be still at enmity.
What need the arctic people love starlight,
To whom the sun shines both by day and night?
Farewell base stooping to the lordly peers!
My knee shall bow to none but to the king.
As for the multitude, that are but sparks,   20
Raked up in embers of their poverty;—
Tanti; I'll fawn first on the wind
That glanceth at my lips, and flieth away.
But how now, what are these?
    [*Enter as suppliants three Men, poorly dressed.*
POOR MEN. Such as desire your worship's service.
GAVESTON. What canst thou do?
1ST POOR MAN. I can ride.
GAVESTON. But I have no horses. What art thou?
2ND POOR MAN. A traveller.
GAVESTON. Let me see. Thou would'st do well   30
    To wait at my trencher and tell me lies at dinner-time;
    And as I like your discoursing, I'll have you.
    And what art thou?

22. *Tanti,* So much for them.

3RD POOR MAN. A soldier, that hath served against the Scot.

GAVESTON. Why, there are hospitals for such as you;
  I have no war, and therefore, sir, begone.

3RD POOR MAN. Farewell, and perish by a soldier's hand,
  That would'st reward them with an hospital.

GAVESTON [*Aside*]. Ay, ay, these words of his move me as much
  As if a goose should play the porpentine,   40
  And dart her plumes, thinking to pierce my breast.
  But yet it is no pain to speak men fair;
  I'll flatter these, and make them live in hope.
  [*Aloud.*] You know that I came lately out of France,
  And yet I have not viewed my lord the king;
  If I speed well, I'll entertain you all.

ALL. We thank your worship.

GAVESTON. I have some business. Leave me to myself.

ALL. We will wait here about the court.   [*Exeunt.*

GAVESTON. Do; these are not men for me: 50
  I must have wanton poets, pleasant wits,
  Musicians, that with touching of a string
  May draw the pliant king which way I please.
  Music and poetry is his delight;
  Therefore I'll have Italian masks by night,
  Sweet speeches, comedies, and pleasing shows:
  And in the day, when he shall walk abroad,
  Like sylvan nymphs my pages shall be clad;
  My men, like satyrs grazing on the lawns,
  Shall with their goat-feet dance an antic hay.   60
  Sometime a lovely boy in Dian's shape,
  With hair that gilds the water as it glides,
  Crownets of pearl about his naked arms,
  And in his sportful hands an olive-tree,
  To hide those parts which men delight to see,
  Shall bathe him in a spring; and there hard by,
  One like Actæon peeping through the grove,
  Shall by the angry goddess be transformed,
  And running in the likeness of an hart
  By yelping hounds pulled down, and seem to die;   70
  Such things as these best please his majesty.
  Here comes my lord the king, and the nobles
  From the parliament. I'll stand aside.
    [*He goes to rear of stage where he is unnoticed.*

40. *porpentine*, porcupine.   60. *antic hay*, a country dance.
63. *crownets*, coronets, garlands.

[Enter King Edward, Lancaster, the Elder Mortimer, young Mortimer, Kent, Warwick, Pembroke, and Attendants.

KING EDWARD. Lancaster!

LANCASTER. My lord.

GAVESTON *[Aside]*. That Earl of Lancaster do I abhor.

KING EDWARD. Will you not grant me this? *[Aside.]* In spite of them

I'll have my will; and these two Mortimers,
That cross me thus, shall know I am displeased.

ELDER MORTIMER. If you love us, my lord, hate Gaveston.   80

GAVESTON *[Aside]*. That villain Mortimer! I'll be his death.

YOUNG MORTIMER. Mine uncle here, this earl, and I myself,
Were sworn to your father at his death,
That he should ne'er return into the realm:
And know, my lord, ere I will break my oath,
This sword of mine, that should offend your foes,
Shall sleep within the scabbard at thy need,
And underneath thy banners march who will,
For Mortimer will hang his armour up.

GAVESTON *[Aside]*. *Mort Dieu!*   90

KING EDWARD. Well, Mortimer, I'll make thee rue these words.
Beseems it thee to contradict thy king?
Frown'st thou thereat, aspiring Lancaster?
The sword shall plane the furrows of thy brows,
And hew these knees that now are grown so stiff.
I will have Gaveston; and you shall know
What danger 'tis to stand against your king.

GAVESTON *[Aside]*. Well done, Ned!

LANCASTER. My lord, why do you thus incense your peers,
That naturally would love and honour you,   100
But for that base and obscure Gaveston?
Four earldoms have I, besides Lancaster—
Derby, Salisbury, Lincoln, Leicester—
These will I sell, to give my soldiers pay,
Ere Gaveston shall stay within the realm;
Therefore, if he be come, expel him straight.

KENT. Barons and earls, your pride hath made me mute;
But now I'll speak, and to the proof, I hope.
I do remember, in my father's days,
Lord Percy of the north, being highly moved,   110

74. *Lancaster*, one of the leaders of the opposition to the king, and Gaveston's chief enemy. At this time he was the most powerful noble in the realm.
90. *Mort Dieu*, God's death.

Braved Mowbery in presence of the king;
For which, had not his highness loved him well,
He should have lost his head; but with his look
The undaunted spirit of Percy was appeased,
And Mowbery and he were reconciled:
Yet dare you brave the king unto his face.—
Brother, revenge it, and let these their heads
Preach upon poles, for trespass of their tongues.

WARWICK. Oh, our heads!

KING EDWARD. Ay, yours; and therefore I would wish you
   grant—   120

WARWICK. Bridle thy anger, gentle Mortimer.

YOUNG MORTIMER. I cannot, nor I will not; I must speak.—
Cousin, our hands I hope shall fence our heads,
And strike off his that makes you threaten us.
Come, uncle, let us leave the brainsick king,
And henceforth parley with our naked swords.

ELDER MORTIMER. Wiltshire hath men enough to save our heads,

WARWICK. All Warwickshire will love him for my sake.

LANCASTER. And northward Gaveston hath many friends.—
Adieu, my lord; and either change your mind,   130
Or look to see the throne, where you should sit,
To float in blood; and at thy wanton head,
The glozing head of thy base minion thrown.

   [*Exeunt all except King Edward, Kent, Gaveston and At-*
   tendants.

KING EDWARD. I cannot brook these haughty menaces;
Am I a king, and must be overruled?—
Brother, display my ensigns in the field;
I'll bandy with the barons and the earls,
And either die or live with Gaveston.

GAVESTON. I can no longer keep me from my lord.

   [*Comes forward, and kneels before the King, who raises him*
   up and embraces him.

KING EDWARD. What, Gaveston! welcome!—Kiss not my
   hand—   140
Embrace me, Gaveston, as I do thee.
Why should'st thou kneel? know'st thou not who I am?
Thy friend, thyself, another Gaveston!

111. *Mowbery,* Mowbray.
117. *heads . . .,* the severed heads of traitors were put upon poles and
displayed on London Bridge and other prominent places.
133. *glozing,* flattering.   137. *bandy,* fight.

Not Hylas was more mourned of Hercules,
Than thou hast been of me since thy exile.

GAVESTON. And since I went from hence, no soul in hell
Hath felt more torment than poor Gaveston.

KING EDWARD. I know it.—Brother, welcome home my friend.
Now let the treacherous Mortimers conspire,
And that high-minded Earl of Lancaster: ·150
I have my wish, in that I joy thy sight;
And sooner shall the sea o'erwhelm my land,
Than bear the ship that shall transport thee hence.
I here create thee Lord High Chamberlain,
Chief Secretary to the state and me,
Earl of Cornwall, King and Lord of Man.

GAVESTON. My lord, these titles far exceed my worth.

KENT [*Startled and disturbed at the unwise loading of honors on*
Gaveston]. Brother, the least of these may well suffice
For one of greater birth than Gaveston.

KING EDWARD. Cease, brother: for I cannot brook these
words.   160
Thy worth, sweet friend, is far above my gifts,
Therefore, to equal it, receive my heart;
If for these dignities thou be envied,
I'll give thee more; for, but to honour thee,
Is Edward pleased with kingly regiment.
Fear'st thou thy person? thou shalt have a guard:
Wantest thou gold? go to my treasury:
Wouldst thou be loved and feared? receive my seal;
Save or condemn, and in our name command
Whatso thy mind affects, or fancy likes.   170

GAVESTON. It shall suffice me to enjoy your love,
Which whiles I have, I think myself as great
As Cæsar riding in the Roman street,
With captive kings at his triumphant car.

[*Enter the Bishop of Coventry, who is of the party of the*
nobles.

KING EDWARD. Whither goes my lord of Coventry so fast?

BISHOP OF COVENTRY. To celebrate your father's exequies.
But is that wicked Gaveston returned?

KING EDWARD. Ay, priest, and lives to be revenged on thee,

---

144. *Hylas,* favorite companion of Hercules on the Argonautic expedition,
during which he was abducted by nymphs at a spring.
150. *high-minded,* arrogant.   156. *Man,* i.e., the Isle of Man.
166. *Fear'st,* Art thou afraid for.   170. *affects,* desires.

That wert the only cause of his exile.

GAVESTON. 'Tis true; and but for reverence of these robes, 180
    Thou should'st not plod one foot beyond this place.

BISHOP OF COVENTRY. I did no more than I was bound to do;
    And, Gaveston, unless thou be reclaimed,
    As then I did incense the parliament,
    So will I now, and thou shalt back to France.

GAVESTON. Saving your reverence, you must pardon me.

KING EDWARD. Throw off his golden mitre, rend his stole,
    And in the channel christen him anew.

KENT. Ah, brother, lay not violent hands on him!
    For he'll complain unto the see of Rome. 190

GAVESTON. Let him complain unto the see of hell;
    I'll be revenged on him for my exile.

KING EDWARD. No, spare his life, but seize upon his goods:
    Be thou lord bishop and receive his rents,
    And make him serve thee as thy chaplain:
    I give him thee—here, use him as thou wilt.

GAVESTON. He shall to prison, and there die in bolts.

KING EDWARD. Ay, to the Tower, the Fleet, or where thou wilt.

BISHOP OF COVENTRY. For this offence, be thou accurst of God!

KING EDWARD. Who's there? Convey this priest to the Tower. 200

BISHOP OF COVENTRY. True, true.

KING EDWARD. But, in the meantime, Gaveston, away,
    And take possession of his house and goods.
    Come, follow me, and thou shalt have my guard
    To see it done, and bring thee safe again.

GAVESTON. What should a priest do with so fair a house?
    A prison may beseem his holiness.

    [*The Bishop is led away and Edward and Gaveston go out
      together.*

SCENE II

AT WESTMINSTER, A SHORT TIME LATER. *The two Mortimers enter
on one side, meeting Warwick and Lancaster, who hurry in
from the other side. They are greatly excited by the news
they have had of the Bishop of Coventry.*

188. *channel*, gutter.
201. *True, true*, The Bishop means that they are using the right word in
convey, which meant to steal.

WARWICK. 'Tis true, the bishop is in the Tower,
  And goods and body given to Gaveston.
LANCASTER. What! will they tyrannize upon the church?
  Ah, wicked king! accursèd Gaveston!
  This ground, which is corrupted with their steps,
  Shall be their timeless sepulchre or mine.
YOUNG MORTIMER. Well, let that peevish Frenchman guard him
    sure;
  Unless his breast be sword-proof he shall die.
ELDER MORTIMER. How now! why droops the Earl of Lancaster?
YOUNG MORTIMER. Wherefore is Guy of Warwick discontent?
LANCASTER. That villain Gaveston is made an earl.   11
ELDER MORTIMER. An earl!
WARWICK. Ay, and besides Lord Chamberlain of the realm,
  And Secretary too, and Lord of Man.
ELDER MORTIMER. We may not, nor we will not suffer this.
YOUNG MORTIMER. Why post we not from hence to levy men?
LANCASTER. "My Lord of Cornwall," now at every word!
  And happy is the man whom he vouchsafes,
  For vailing of his bonnet, one good look.
  Thus, arm in arm, the king and he doth march: 20
  Nay more, the guard upon his lordship waits;
  And all the court begins to flatter him.
WARWICK. Thus leaning on the shoulder of the king,
  He nods and scorns and smiles at those that pass.
ELDER MORTIMER. Doth no man take exceptions at the slave?
LANCASTER. All stomach him, but none dare speak a word.
YOUNG MORTIMER. Ah, that bewrays their baseness, Lancaster!
  Were all the earls and barons of my mind,
  We'd hale him from the bosom of the king,
  And at the court-gate hang the peasant up,   30
  Who, swoln with venom of ambitious pride,
  Will be the ruin of the realm and us.
WARWICK. Here comes my lord of Canterbury's grace.
LANCASTER. His countenance bewrays he is displeased.
  [*Enter the Archbishop of Canterbury and an Attendant. The
    Archbishop, too, has heard the news and is taking steps
    to protect the Bishop.*
ARCHBISHOP OF CANTERBURY. First were his sacred garments rent
    and torn,
  Then laid they violent hands upon him; next

6. *timeless*, untimely.   19. *vailing*, doffing.
26. *stomach*, resent.   34. *bewray*, disclose.

Himself imprisoned, and his goods asseized:
This certify the Pope—away, take horse.   [*Exit Attendant.*

LANCASTER. My lord, will you take arms against the king?

ARCHBISHOP. What need I? God himself is up in arms,   40
When violence is offered to the church.

YOUNG MORTIMER. Then will you join with us, that be his peers,
To banish or behead that Gaveston?

ARCHBISHOP. What else, my lords? for it concerns me near;
The bishopric of Coventry is his.

[*Enter Queen Isabella, in tears because she has been repulsed
by the King.*

YOUNG MORTIMER. Madam, whither walks your majesty so fast?

QUEEN ISABELLA. Unto the forest, gentle Mortimer,
To live in grief and baleful discontent;
For now, my lord, the king regards me not,
But dotes upon the love of Gaveston.   50
He claps his cheeks, and hangs about his neck,
Smiles in his face, and whispers in his ears;
And when I come he frowns, as who should say,
"Go whither thou wilt, seeing I have Gaveston."

ELDER MORTIMER. Is it not strange that he is thus bewitched?

YOUNG MORTIMER. Madam, return unto the court again:
That sly inveigling Frenchman we'll exile,
Or lose our lives; and yet, ere that day come,
The king shall lose his crown; for we have power,
And courage too, to be revenged at full.   60

ARCHBISHOP. But yet lift not your swords against the king.

LANCASTER. No; but we'll lift Gaveston from hence.

WARWICK. And war must be the means, or he'll stay still.

QUEEN ISABELLA. Then let him stay; for rather than my lord
Shall be oppressed by civil mutinies,
I will endure a melancholy life,
And let him frolic with his minion.

ARCHBISHOP. My lords, to ease all this, but hear me speak:
We and the rest, that are his counsellors,
Will meet, and with a general consent   70
Confirm his banishment with our hands and seals.

LANCASTER. What we confirm the king will frustrate.

YOUNG MORTIMER. Then may we lawfully revolt from him.

WARWICK. But say, my lord, where shall this meeting be?

ARCHBISHOP. At the New Temple.

37. *asseized*, seized upon.
47. *unto the forest*, away from the courtly world, in exile.

YOUNG MORTIMER. Content.

ARCHBISHOP. And, in the meantime, I'll entreat you all
  To cross to Lambeth, and there stay with me.

LANCASTER. Come then, let's away.

YOUNG MORTIMER.   Madam, farewell!

QUEEN ISABELLA. Farewell, sweet Mortimer; and, for my sake,   80
  Forbear to levy arms against the king.

YOUNG MORTIMER. Ay, if words will serve; if not, I must.
                                        [*Exeunt.*

SCENE III

THE PALACE, *shortly after the preceding scene. Enter Gaveston
  and Kent.*

GAVESTON. Edmund, the mighty Prince of Lancaster,
  That hath more earldoms than an ass can bear,
  And both the Mortimers, two goodly men,
  With Guy of Warwick, that redoubted knight,
  Are gone towards Lambeth—there let them remain.   [*Exeunt.*

SCENE IV

THE NEW TEMPLE. *Enter Lancaster, Warwick, Pembroke, the
  Elder Mortimer, Young Mortimer, the Archbishop of Canterbury and Attendants. They have drawn up the agreement decided on in* SCENE II.

LANCASTER. Here is the form of Gaveston's exile:
  May it please your lordship to subscribe your name.

ARCHBISHOP. Give me the paper.
      [*He subscribes, as do the others after him.*

LANCASTER. Quick, quick, my lord; I long to write my name.

WARWICK. But I long more to see him banished hence.

YOUNG MORTIMER. The name of Mortimer shall fright the king,
  Unless he be declined from that base peasant.
      [*Enter King Edward, Gaveston, and Kent. The nobles growl
        at Gaveston's place of preferment.*

KING EDWARD. What, are you moved that Gaveston sits here?
  It is our pleasure; we will have it so.

LANCASTER. Your grace doth well to place him by your side,   10
  For nowhere else the new earl is so safe.

  7. *declined from*, separated from.

ELDER MORTIMER. What man of noble birth can brook this sight?
Quam male conveniunt!
See what a scornful look the peasant casts!
PEMBROKE. Can kingly lions fawn on creeping ants?
WARWICK. Ignoble vassal, that like Phaeton
Aspir'st unto the guidance of the sun!
YOUNG MORTIMER. Their downfall is at hand, their forces down:
We will not thus be faced and over-peered.
KING EDWARD. Lay hands on that traitor Mortimer! 20
ELDER MORTIMER. Lay hands on that traitor Gaveston!.
[*They seize him and start to take him out.*
KENT. Is this the duty that you owe your king?
WARWICK. We know our duties—let him know his peers.
KING EDWARD. Whither will you bear him? Stay, or ye shall die.
ELDER MORTIMER. We are no traitors; therefore threaten not.
GAVESTON. No, threaten not, my lord, but pay them home!
Were I a king—
YOUNG MORTIMER. Thou villain, wherefore talk'st thou of a king,
That hardly art a gentleman·by birth?
KING EDWARD. Were he a peasant, being my minion, 30
I'll make the proudest of you stoop to him.
LANCASTER. My lord, you may not thus disparage us.—
Away, I say, with hateful Gaveston!
ELDER MORTIMER. And with the Earl of Kent that favours him.
[*They seize Kent, too, and deliver both to Attendants, who
take them out.*
KING EDWARD. Nay, then, lay violent hands upon your king,
Here, Mortimer, sit thou in Edward's throne:
Warwick and Lancaster, wear you my crown:
Was ever king thus overruled as I?
LANCASTER. Learn then to rule us better, and the realm.
YOUNG MORTIMER. What we have done, our heart-blood shall
maintain. 40
WARWICK. Think you that we can brook this upstart's pride?
KING EDWARD. Anger and wrathful fury stops my speech.
ARCHBISHOP. Why are you moved? be patient, my lord,
And see what we your counsellors have done.
YOUNG MORTIMER. My lords, now let us all be resolute,
And either have our wills, or lose our lives.
KING EDWARD. Meet you for this, proud over-daring peers?
Ere my sweet Gaveston shall part from me,

13. *Quam . . .,* How ill they agree! 19. *over-peered,* looked down on.

This isle shall fleet upon the ocean,
And wander to the unfrequented Inde. 50

ARCHBISHOP. You know that I am legate to the Pope;
On your allegiance to the see of Rome,
Subscribe, as we have done, to his exile.

YOUNG MORTIMER. Curse him, if he refuse; and then may we
Depose·him and elect another king.

KING EDWARD. Ay, there it goes! but yet I will not yield:
Curse me, depose me, do the worst you can.

LANCASTER. Then linger not, my lord, but do it straight.

ARCHBISHOP. Remember how the bishop was abused!
Either banish him that was the cause thereof, 60
Or I will presently discharge these lords
Of duty and allegiance due to thee.

KING EDWARD [*Aside*]. It boots me not to threat—I must speak
fair.
[*Aloud.*] The legate of the Pope will be obeyed.
My lord, you shall be Chancellor of the realm;
Thou, Lancaster, High Admiral of our fleet;
Young Mortimer and his uncle shall be earls;
And you, Lord Warwick, President of the North;
And thou of Wales. If this content you not,
Make several kingdoms of this monarchy, 70
And share it equally amongst you all,
So I may have some nook or corner left,
To frolic with my dearest Gaveston.

ARCHBISHOP. Nothing shall alter us—we are resolved.

LANCASTER. Come, come, subscribe.

YOUNG MORTIMER. Why should you love him whom the world
hates so?

KING EDWARD. Because he loves me more than all the world.
Ah, none but rude and savage-minded men
Would seek the ruin of my Gaveston;
You that be noble-born should pity him. 80

WARWICK. You that are princely-born should shake him off:
For shame subscribe, and let the lown depart.

ELDER MORTIMER. Urge him, my lord.

ARCHBISHOP. Are you content to banish him the realm?

KING EDWARD. I see I must, and therefore am content:
Instead of ink I'll write it with my tears.
[*He signs the decree of banishment.*

YOUNG MORTIMER. The king is lovesick for his minion.

49. *fleet,* float.   61. *presently,* immediately.   82. *lown,* good-for-nothing.

KING EDWARD. 'Tis done—and now, accursèd hand, fall off!
LANCASTER. Give it me—I'll have it published in the streets.
YOUNG MORTIMER. I'll see him presently dispatched away.   90
ARCHBISHOP. Now is my heart at ease.
WARWICK.   And so is mine.
PEMBROKE. This will be good news to the common sort.
ELDER MORTIMER. Be it or no, he shall not linger here.
                    [*Exeunt all except King Edward.*

KING EDWARD. How fast they run to banish him I love!
    They would not stir, were it to do me good.
    Why should a king be subject to a priest?
    Proud Rome! that hatchest such imperial grooms,
    For these thy superstitious taper-lights,
    Wherewith thy antichristian churches blaze,
    I'll fire thy crazèd buildings, and enforce   100
    The papal towers to kiss the lowly ground!
    With slaughtered priests make Tiber's channel swell,
    And banks raised higher with their sepulchres!
    As for the peers, that back the clergy thus,
    If I be king, not one of them shall live.
        [*Re-enter Gaveston.*
GAVESTON. My lord, I hear it whispered everywhere,
    That I am banished, and must fly the land.
KING EDWARD. 'Tis true, sweet Gaveston—Oh! were it false!
    The legate of the Pope will have it so,
    And thou must hence, or I shall be deposed.   110
    But I will reign to be revenged of them;
    And therefore, sweet friend, take it patiently.
    Live where thou wilt, I'll send thee gold enough;
    And long thou shalt not stay, or if thou dost,
    I'll come to thee; my love shall ne'er decline.
GAVESTON. Is all my hope turned to this hell of grief?
KING EDWARD. Rend not my heart with thy too-piercing words:
    Thou from this land, I from myself am banished.
GAVESTON. To go from hence grieves not poor Gaveston;
    But to forsake you, in whose gracious looks   120
    The blessedness of Gaveston remains:
    For nowhere else seeks he felicity.
KING EDWARD. And only this torments my wretched soul,
    That, whether I will or no, thou must depart.
    Be governor of Ireland in my stead,
    And there abide till fortune call thee home.
    Here, take my picture, and let me wear thine;

[They exchange pictures.
  Oh, might I keep thee here as I do this,
  Happy were I! but now most miserable!
GAVESTON. 'Tis something to be pitied of a king.   130
KING EDWARD. Thou shalt not hence—I'll hide thee, Gaveston.
GAVESTON. I shall be found, and then 'twill grieve me more.
KING EDWARD. Kind words and mutual talk makes our grief
    greater:
  Therefore, with dumb embracement, let us part—
  Stay, Gaveston, I cannot leave thee thus.
GAVESTON. For every look, my lord, drops down a tear:
  Seeing I must go, do not renew my sorrow.
KING EDWARD. The time is little that thou hast to stay,
  And, therefore, give me leave to look my fill:
  But come, sweet friend, I'll bear thee on thy way.   140
GAVESTON. The peers will frown.
KING EDWARD. I pass not for their anger.—Come, let's go;
  Oh, that we might as well return as go.
    *[As they start to go out, they meet Queen Isabella, whom
        Edward rejects hatefully.*
QUEEN ISABELLA. Whither goes my lord?
KING EDWARD. Fawn not on me, French strumpet! get thee gone!
QUEEN ISABELLA. On whom but on my husband should I fawn?
GAVESTON. On Mortimer! with whom, ungentle queen—
  I say no more—judge you the rest, my lord.
QUEEN ISABELLA. In saying this, thou wrong'st me, Gaveston;
  Is't not enough that thou corrupt'st my lord,   150
  And art a bawd to his affections,
  But thou must call mine honour thus in question?
GAVESTON. I mean not so; your grace must pardon me.
KING EDWARD. Thou art too familiar with that Mortimer,
  And by thy means is Gaveston exiled;
  But I would wish thee reconcile the lords,
  Or thou shalt ne'er be reconciled to me.
QUEEN ISABELLA. Your highness knows it lies not in my power.
KING EDWARD. Away then! touch me not—Come, Gaveston.
QUEEN ISABELLA. Villain! 'tis thou that robb'st me of my lord. 160
GAVESTON. Madam, 'tis you that rob me of my lord.
KING EDWARD. Speak not unto her; let her droop and pine.
QUEEN ISABELLA. Wherein, my lord, have I deserved these words?
  Witness the tears that Isabella sheds,
  Witness this heart, that sighing for thee, breaks,

142. *pass,* care.

How dear my lord is to poor Isabel.

KING EDWARD. And witness Heaven how dear thou art to me:
There weep: for till my Gaveston be repealed,
Assure thyself thou com'st not in my sight.

[The King and Gaveston go out together.

QUEEN ISABELLA. O miserable and distressèd queen!   170
Would, when I left sweet France and was embarked,
That charming Circe walking on the waves,
Had changed my shape, or at the marriage-day
The cup of Hymen had been full of poison,
Or with those arms that twined about my neck
I had been stifled, and not lived to see
The king my lord thus to abandon me!
Like frantic Juno will I fill the earth
With ghastly murmur of my sighs and cries;
For never doted Jove on Ganymede   180
So much as he on cursèd Gaveston:
But that will more exasperate his wrath;
I must entreat him, I must speak him fair;
And be a means to call home Gaveston:
And yet he'll ever dote on Gaveston;
And so am I for ever miserable.

*[Re-enter Lancaster, Warwick, Pembroke, the Elder Morti-
mer, and Young Mortimer.*

LANCASTER. Look where the sister of the King of France,
Sits wringing of her hands, and beats her breast!

WARWICK. The king, I fear, hath ill-entreated her.

PEMBROKE. Hard is the heart that injures such a saint.   190

YOUNG MORTIMER. I know 'tis 'long of Gaveston she weeps.

ELDER MORTIMER. Why, he is gone.

YOUNG MORTIMER.   Madam, how fares your grace?

QUEEN ISABELLA. Ah, Mortimer! now breaks the king's hate forth,
And he confesseth that he loves me not.

YOUNG MORTIMER. Cry quittance, madam, then; and love not him.

QUEEN ISABELLA. No, rather will I die a thousand deaths:
And yet I love in vain—he'll ne'er love me.

LANCASTER. Fear ye not, madam; now his minion's gone,
His wanton humour will be quickly left.

QUEEN ISABELLA. Oh, never, Lancaster! I am enjoined   200
To sue unto you all for his repeal;
This wills my lord, and this must I perform,

168. *repealed,* called back from exile.   189. *ill-entreated,* ill-used.
191. *'long of,* because of.

Or else be banished from his highness' presence.
LANCASTER. For his repeal, madam! he comes not back,
  Unless the sea cast up his shipwrecked body.
WARWICK. And to behold so sweet a sight as that,
  There's none here but would run his horse to death.
YOUNG MORTIMER. But, madam, would you have us call him home?
QUEEN ISABELLA. Ay, Mortimer, for till he be restored,
  The angry king hath banished me the court;   210
  And, therefore, as thou lov'st and tender'st me,
  Be thou my advocate unto these peers.
YOUNG MORTIMER. What! would you have me plead for Gaveston?
ELDER MORTIMER. Plead for him he that will, I am resolved.
LANCASTER. And so am I, my lord: dissuade the queen.
QUEEN ISABELLA. O Lancaster! let him dissuade the king,
  For 'tis against my will he should return.
WARWICK. Then speak not for him, let the peasant go.
QUEEN ISABELLA. 'Tis for myself I speak, and not for him.
PEMBROKE. No speaking will prevail, and therefore cease.   220
YOUNG MORTIMER. Fair queen, forbear to angle for the fish
  Which, being caught, strikes him that takes it dead;
  I mean that vile torpedo, Gaveston,
  That now, I hope, floats on the Irish seas.
QUEEN ISABELLA. Sweet Mortimer, sit down by me awhile,
  And I will tell thee reasons of such weight
  As thou wilt soon subscribe to his repeal.
YOUNG MORTIMER. It is impossible; but speak your mind.
QUEEN ISABELLA. Then thus, but none shall hear it but ourselves.
    [*Talks to Young Mortimer apart.*
LANCASTER. My lords, albeit the queen win Mortimer,   230
  Will you be resolute, and hold with me?
ELDER MORTIMER. Not I, against my nephew.
PEMBROKE. Fear not, the queen's words cannot alter him.
WARWICK. No? do but mark how earnestly she pleads!
LANCASTER. And see how coldly his looks make denial!
WARWICK. She smiles; now for my life his mind is changed!
LANCASTER. I'll rather lose his friendship, I, than grant.
YOUNG MORTIMER. Well, of necessity it must be so.—
  My lords, that I abhor base Gaveston,
  I hope your honours make no question,   240

211. *tender'st,* carest for.
223. *torpedo,* electric eel that stuns its prey by shocking it.
224. Marlowe here compresses time. Gaveston would in reality scarcely
have had time to get out of London.

And therefore, though I plead for his repeal,
'Tis not for his sake, but for our avail;
Nay, for the realm's behoof, and for the king's.
LANCASTER. Fie, Mortimer, dishonour not thyself!
  Can this be true, 'twas good to banish him?
  And is this true, to call him home again?
  Such reasons make white black, and dark night day.
YOUNG MORTIMER. My lord of Lancaster, mark the respect.
LANCASTER. In no respect can contraries be true.
QUEEN ISABELLA. Yet, good my lord, hear what he can allege.   250
WARWICK. All that he speaks is nothing; we are resolved.
YOUNG MORTIMER. Do you not wish that Gaveston were dead?
PEMBROKE. I would he were!
YOUNG MORTIMER. Why then, my lord, give me but leave to speak.
ELDER MORTIMER. But, nephew, do not play the sophister.
YOUNG MORTIMER. This which I urge is of a burning zeal
  To mend the king, and do our country good.
  Know you not Gaveston hath store of gold,
  Which may in Ireland purchase him such friends,
  As he will front the mightiest of us all?   260
  And whereas he shall live and be beloved,
  'Tis hard for us to work his overthrow.
WARWICK. Mark you but that, my lord of Lancaster.
YOUNG MORTIMER. But were he here, detested as he is,
  How easily might some base slave be suborned
  To greet his lordship with a poniard,
  And none so much as blame the murderer,
  But rather praise him for that brave attempt,
  And in the chronicle enrol his name
  For purging of the realm of such a plague!   270
PEMBROKE. He saith true.
LANCASTER. Ay, but how chance this was not done before?
YOUNG MORTIMER. Because, my lords, it was not thought upon.
  Nay, more, when he shall know it lies in us
  To banish him, and then to call him home,
  'Twill make him vail the top-flag of his pride,
  And fear to offend the meanest nobleman.
ELDER MORTIMER. But how if he do not, nephew?
YOUNG MORTIMER. Then may we with some colour rise in arms;
  For, howsoever we have borne it out,   280
  'Tis treason to be up against the king;

248. *respect*, reason.   260. *front*, confront.
268. *attempt*, enterprise.   279. *colour*, excuse, pretext.

So shall we have the people of our side,
Which for his father's sake lean to the king,
But cannot brook a night-grown mushroom,
Such a one as my lord of Cornwall is,
Should bear us down of the nobility.
And when the commons and the nobles join,
'Tis not the king can buckler Gaveston;
We'll pull him from the strongest hold he hath.
My lords, if to perform this I be slack,   290
Think me as base a groom as Gaveston.
LANCASTER. On that condition, Lancaster will grant.
WARWICK. And so will Pembroke and I.
ELDER MORTIMER.   And I.
YOUNG MORTIMER. In this I count me highly gratified,
And Mortimer will rest at your command.
QUEEN ISABELLA. And when this favour Isabel forgets,
Then let her live abandoned and forlorn.—
But see, in happy time, my lord the king,
Having brought the Earl of Cornwall on his way,
Is new returned; this news will glad him much;   300
Yet not so much as me; I love him more
Than he can Gaveston; would he love me
But half so much, then were I treble-blessed!
    [Re-enter King Edward, *mourning for his lost favorite.*
KING EDWARD. He's gone, and for his absence thus I mourn.
Did never sorrow go so near my heart
As doth the want of my sweet Gaveston;
And could my crown's revenue bring him back,
I would freely give it to his enemies,
And think I gained, having bought so dear a friend.
QUEEN ISABELLA [*Aside, to Mortimer*]. Hark! how he harps upon
    his minion.   310
KING EDWARD. My heart is as an anvil unto sorrow,
Which beats upon it like the Cyclops' hammers,
And with the noise turns up my giddy brain,
And makes me frantic for my Gaveston.
Ah! had some bloodless Fury rose from hell,
And with my kingly sceptre struck me dead,
When I was forced to leave my Gaveston!
LANCASTER. *Diablo!* What passions call you these?
QUEEN ISABELLA. My gracious lord, I come to bring you news.
KING EDWARD. That you have parleyed with your Mortimer!   320

288. *buckler*, shield.   318. *Diablo*, The devil!

QUEEN ISABELLA. That Gaveston, my lord, shall be repealed.

KING EDWARD. Repealed! the news is too sweet to be true.

QUEEN ISABELLA. But will you love me, if you find it so?

KING EDWARD. If it be so, what will not Edward do?

QUEEN ISABELLA. For Gaveston, but not for Isabel.

KING EDWARD. For thee, fair queen, if thou lov'st Gaveston;
  I'll hang a golden tongue about thy neck,
  Seeing thou hast pleaded with so good success.
  [*He takes her in his arms.*

QUEEN ISABELLA. No other jewels hang about my neck
  Than these, my lord; nor let me have more wealth   **330**
  Than I may fetch from this rich treasury—
  Oh, how a kiss revives poor Isabel!

KING EDWARD. Once more receive my hand; and let this be
  A second marriage 'twixt thyself and me.

QUEEN ISABELLA. And may it prove more happy than the first!
  My gentle lord, bespeak these nobles fair,
  That wait attendance for a gracious look,
  And on their knees salute your majesty.

KING EDWARD. Courageous Lancaster, embrace thy king!
  And, as gross vapours perish by the sun,   **340**
  Even so let hatred with thy sovereign's smile.
  Live thou with me as my companion.

LANCASTER. This salutation overjoys my heart.

KING EDWARD. Warwick shall be my chiefest counsellor:
  These silver hairs will more adorn my court
  Than gaudy silks, or rich embroidery.
  Chide me, sweet Warwick, if I go astray.

WARWICK. Slay me, my lord, when I offend your grace.

KING EDWARD. In solemn triumphs, and in public shows,
  Pembroke shall bear the sword before the king.   **350**

PEMBROKE. And with this sword Pembroke will fight for you.

KING EDWARD. But wherefore walks young Mortimer aside?
  Be thou commander of our royal fleet;
  Or, if that lofty office like thee not,
  I make thee here Lord Marshal of the realm.

YOUNG MORTIMER. My lord, I'll marshal so your enemies,
  As England shall be quiet, and you safe.

KING EDWARD. And as for you, Lord Mortimer of Chirke,
  Whose great achievements in our foreign war
  Deserves no common place, nor mean reward;   **360**
  Be you the general of the levied troops,
  That now are ready to assail the Scots.

ELDER MORTIMER. In this your grace hath highly honoured me,
For with my nature war doth best agree.
QUEEN ISABELLA. Now is the King of England rich and strong,
Having the love of his renowned peers.
KING EDWARD. Ay, Isabel, ne'er was my heart so light.—
Clerk of the crown, direct our warrant forth
For Gaveston to Ireland:
    [Enter Beaumont with warrant.
                Beaumont, fly
As fast as Iris or Jove's Mercury.   370
BEAUMONT. It shall be done, my gracious lord.   *[He hurries out.*
KING EDWARD. Lord Mortimer, we leave you to your charge.
Now let us in, and feast it royally.
Against our friend the Earl of Cornwall comes,
We'll have a general tilt and tournament;
And then his marriage shall be solemnized.
For wot you not that I have made him sure
Unto our cousin, the Earl of Gloucester's heir?
LANCASTER. Such news we hear, my lord.
KING EDWARD. That day, if not for him, yet for my sake,   380
Who in the triumph will be challenger,
Spare for no cost; we will requite your love.
WARWICK. In this, or aught your highness shall command us.
KING EDWARD. Thanks, gentle Warwick: come, let's in and revel.
              [Exeunt all except the Mortimers.
ELDER MORTIMER. Nephew, I must go to Scotland; thou stayest
    here.
Leave now t'oppose thyself against the king.
Thou seest by nature he is mild and calm,
And, seeing his mind so dotes on Gaveston,
Let him without controlment have his will.
The mightiest kings have had their minions: 390
Great Alexander loved Hephestion;
The conquering Hercules for Hylas wept;
And for Patroclus stern Achilles drooped.
And not kings only, but the wisest men:
The Roman Tully loved Octavius;
Grave Socrates wild Alcibiades.
Then let his grace, whose youth is flexible,

374. *Against,* until he comes, we will prepare for a general tilt . . .
377. *made him sure,* betrothed him.
378. *cousin,* relative. Margaret de Clare was Edward's niece.
381. *triumph,* tournament.

And promiseth as much as we can wish,
Freely enjoy that vain, light-headed earl;
For riper years will wean him from such toys.　　　400
YOUNG MORTIMER [*Putting his finger on the root of the trouble*].
　　Uncle, his wanton humour grieves not me;
But this I scorn, that one so basely born
Should by his sovereign's favour grow so pert,
And riot it with the treasure of the realm.
While soldiers mutiny for want of pay,
He wears a lord's revenue on his back,
And Midas-like, he jets it in the court,
With base outlandish cullions at his heels,
Whose proud fantastic liveries make such show,
As if that Proteus, god of shapes, appeared.　　　410
I have not seen a dapper Jack so brisk;
He wears a short Italian hooded cloak,
Larded with pearl, and, in his Tuscan cap,
A jewel of more value than the crown.
Whiles others walk below, the king and he
From out a window laugh at such as we,
And flout our train, and jest at our attire.
Uncle, 'tis this that makes me impatient.
ELDER MORTIMER. But, nephew, now you see the king is changed.
YOUNG MORTIMER. Then so am I, and live to do him service:　　　420
But, whiles I have a sword, a hand, a heart,
I will not yield to any such upstart.
You know my mind; come, uncle, let's away.　　　[*They go out.*

ACT II

SCENE I

A ROOM IN GLOUCESTER HOUSE. *The Duke of Gloucester has died,
and Young Spenser and Baldock, who enter, are considering
where they had best turn for patronage and support. It is not
long after the events of the preceding scene.*

BALDOCK. Spenser,
　　Seeing that our lord the Earl of Gloucester's dead,
　　Which of the nobles dost thou mean to serve?
YOUNG SPENSER. Not Mortimer, nor any of his side;
　　Because the king and he are enemies.

407. *jets*, struts.　　　408. *cullions*, scoundrels.　　　411. *Jack*, knave.

Baldock, learn this of me, a factious lord
Shall hardly do himself good, much less us;
But he that hath the favour of a king,
May with one word advance us while we live:
The liberal Earl of Cornwall is the man   10
On whose good fortune Spenser's hope depends.
BALDOCK. What, mean you then to be his follower?
YOUNG SPENSER. No, his companion; for he loves me well,
  And would have once preferred me to the king.
BALDOCK. But he is banished; there's small hope of him.
YOUNG SPENSER. Ay, for a while; but, Baldock, mark the end.
  A friend of mine told me in secrecy
  That he's repealed, and sent for back again;
  And even now a post came from the court
  With letters to our lady from the king;   20
  And as she read she smiled, which makes me think
  It is about her lover Gaveston.
BALDOCK. 'Tis like enough; for, since he was exiled
  She neither walks abroad, nor comes in sight.
  But I had thought the match had been broke off,
  And that his banishment had changed her mind.
YOUNG SPENSER. Our lady's first love is not wavering;
  My life for thine she will have Gaveston.
BALDOCK. Then hope I by her means to be preferred,
  Having read unto her since she was a child.   30
YOUNG SPENSER. Then, Baldock, you must cast the scholar off,
  And learn to court it like a gentleman.
  'Tis not a black coat and a little band,
  A velvet-caped cloak, faced before with serge,
  And smelling to a nosegay all the day,
  Or holding of a napkin in your hand,
  Or saying a long grace at a table's end,
  Or making low legs to a nobleman,
  Or looking downward with your eyelids close,
  And saying, "Truly, an't may please your honour,"   40
  Can get you any favour with great men;
  You must be proud, bold, pleasant, resolute,
  And now and then stab, as occasion serves.
BALDOCK. Spenser, thou know'st I hate such formal toys,
  And use them but of mere hypocrisy.
  Mine old lord whiles he lived was so precise,
  That he would take exceptions at my buttons,

14. *preferred*, recommended.   38. *legs*, bows.   44. *toys*, tricks, manners.

And being like pin's heads, blame me for the bigness;
Which made me curate-like in mine attire,
Though inwardly licentious enough,   50
And apt for any kind of villainy.
I am none of these common pedants, I,
That cannot speak without *propterea quod*.
YOUNG SPENSER. But one of those that saith, *quandoquidem*,
And hath a special gift to form a verb.
BALDOCK. Leave off this jesting, here my lady comes.
     [*Enter King Edward's Niece, the daughter of the Duke of
        Gloucester, with a letter in her hand.*
NIECE. The grief for his exile was not so much,
As is the joy of his returning home.
This letter came from my sweet Gaveston:
What need'st thou, love, thus to excuse thyself?   60
I know thou could'st not come and visit me:
[*Reads.*] "I will not long be from thee, though I die."
This argues the entire love of my lord;
[*Reads.*] "When I forsake thee, death seize on my heart:"
But rest thee here where Gaveston shall sleep.
     [*Puts the letter into her bosom.*
Now to the letter of my lord the king.—
He wills me to repair unto the court,
And meet my Gaveston? Why do I stay,
Seeing that he talks thus of my marriage-day?
Who's there? Baldock!   70
See that my coach be ready, I must hence.
BALDOCK. It shall be done, madam.
NIECE. And meet me at the park-pale presently.   [*Exit Baldock.*
Spenser, stay you and bear me company,
For I have joyful news to tell thee of;
My lord of Cornwall is a-coming over,
And will be at the court as soon as we.
YOUNG SPENSER. I knew the king would have him home again.
NIECE. If all things sort out, as I hope they will,
Thy service, Spenser, shall be thought upon.   80
YOUNG SPENSER. I humbly thank your ladyship.
NIECE. Come, lead the way; I long till I am there.   [*Exeunt.*

53. *propterea quod,* on account of which.
54. *quandoquidem,* seeing that.
55. *to form a verb,* to put a thing neatly.
79. *sort out,* turn out.

SCENE II

AT TYNEMOUTH, *where a ship from Ireland could put in.*

[*Enter King Edward, Queen Isabella, Kent, Lancaster, Young
    Mortimer, Warwick, Pembroke, and Attendants, come to
    welcome Gaveston on his return from exile.*

KING EDWARD. The wind is good, I wonder why he stays;
  I fear me he is wrecked upon the sea.
QUEEN ISABELLA. Look, Lancaster, how passionate he is,
  And still his mind runs on his minion!
LANCASTER. My lord—
KING EDWARD. How now! what news? is Gaveston arrived?
YOUNG MORTIMER. Nothing but Gaveston! what means your
    grace?
  You have matters of more weight to think upon;
  The King of France sets foot in Normandy.
KING EDWARD. A trifle! we'll expel him when we please.   10
  But tell me, Mortimer, what's thy device
  Against the stately triumph we decreed?
YOUNG MORTIMER. A homely one, my lord, not worth the tell-
  ing.
KING EDWARD. Pray thee, let me know it.
YOUNG MORTIMER. But, seeing you are so desirous, thus it is:
  A lofty cedar tree, fair flourishing,
  On whose top-branches kingly eagles perch,
  And by the bark a canker creeps me up,
  And gets into the highest bough of all:
  The motto, *Æque tandem.*   20
KING EDWARD. And what is yours, my lord of Lancaster?
LANCASTER. My lord, mine's more obscure than Mortimer's.
  Pliny reports there is a flying fish
  Which all the other fishes deadly hate,
  And therefore, being pursued, it takes the air:
  No sooner is it up, but there's a fowl
  That seizeth it; this fish, my lord, I bear,
  The motto this: *Undique mors est.*
KENT. Proud Mortimer! ungentle Lancaster!
  Is this the love you bear your sovereign?   30

  3. *passionate*, sorrowful.   4. *still*, always.
  20. *Æque tandem*, justly at length.
  28. *Undique mors est*, Death is everywhere.

Is this the fruit your reconcilement bears?
Can you in words make show of amity,
And in your shields display your rancorous minds!
What call you this but private libelling
Against the Earl of Cornwall and my brother?

QUEEN ISABELLA. Sweet husband, be content, they all love you.

KING EDWARD. They love me not that hate my Gaveston.
I am that cedar, shake me not too much;
And you the eagles; soar ye ne'er so high,
I have the jesses that will pull you down;   40
And *Æque tandem* shall that canker cry
Unto the proudest peer of Britainy.
Though thou compar'st him to a flying fish,
And threatenest death whether he rise or fall,
'Tis not the hugest monster of the sea,
Nor foulest harpy that shall swallow him.

YOUNG MORTIMER [*Aside to Lancaster*]. If in his absence thus he
    favours him,
What will he do whenas he shall be present?

LANCASTER [*Aside*]. That shall we see; look where his lordship
    comes.
        [*Enter Gaveston.*

KING EDWARD. My Gaveston!   50
Welcome to Tynemouth! welcome to thy friend!
Thy absence made me droop and pine away;
For, as the lovers of fair Danae,
When she was locked up in a brazen tower,
Desired her more, and waxed outrageous,
So did it sure with me: and now thy sight
Is sweeter far than was thy parting hence
Bitter and irksome to my sobbing heart.

GAVESTON. Sweet lord and king, your speech preventeth mine,
Yet have I words left to express my joy: 60
The shepherd nipt with biting winter's rage
Frolics not more to see the painted spring,
Than I do to behold your majesty.

KING EDWARD. Will none of you salute my Gaveston?

LANCASTER. Salute him? yes; welcome, Lord Chamberlain!

YOUNG MORTIMER. Welcome is the good Earl of Cornwall!

WARWICK. Welcome, Lord Governor of the Isle of Man!

PEMBROKE. Welcome, Master Secretary!

40. *jesses*, leg-straps used to fasten a hawk to his leash.
59. *preventeth*, anticipateth, with the etymology in mind.

KENT. Brother, do you hear them?

KING EDWARD. Still will these earls and barons use me thus.   70

GAVESTON. My lord, I cannot brook these injuries.

QUEEN ISABELLA [*Aside*]. Ay, me, poor soul, when these begin
    to jar.

KING EDWARD. Return it to their throats, I'll be thy warrant.

GAVESTON. Base, leaden earls, that glory in your birth,
    Go sit at home and eat your tenant's beef;
    And come not here to scoff at Gaveston,
    Whose mounting thoughts did never creep so low
    As to bestow a look on such as you.

LANCASTER. Yet I disdain not to do this for you.
    [*Draws his sword and offers to stab Gaveston. There is a*
    moment of confusion as the nobles close in around Gaves-
    ton while the King tries to protect him.

KING EDWARD. Treason! treason! where's the traitor?   80

PEMBROKE. Here! here!

KING EDWARD. Convey hence Gaveston; they'll murder him.

GAVESTON. The life of thee shall salve this foul disgrace.

YOUNG MORTIMER. Villain! thy life, unless I miss mine aim.
    [*Wounds Gaveston.*

QUEEN ISABELLA. Ah! furious Mortimer, what hast thou done?

YOUNG MORTIMER. No more than I would answer, were he slain.
    [*Attendants finally get Gaveston away and take him off.*

KING EDWARD. Yes, more than thou canst answer, though he live;
    Dear shall you both abide this riotous deed.
    Out of my presence! come not near the court.

YOUNG MORTIMER. I'll not be barred the court for Gaveston.   90

LANCASTER. We'll hale him by the ears unto the block.

KING EDWARD. Look to your own heads; his is sure enough.

WARWICK. Look to your own crown, if you back him thus.

KENT. Warwick, these words do ill beseem thy years.

KING EDWARD. Nay, all of them conspire to cross me thus;
    But if I live, I'll tread upon their heads
    That think with high looks thus to tread me down.
    Come, Edmund, let's away and levy men,
    'Tis war that must abate these barons' pride.
    [*Exeunt King Edward, Queen Isabella, and Kent.*

WARWICK. Let's to our castles, for the king is moved.   100

YOUNG MORTIMER. Moved may he be, and perish in his wrath!

LANCASTER. Cousin, it is no dealing with him now,
    He means to make us stoop by force of arms;
    And therefore let us jointly here protest,

To prosecute that Gaveston to the death.

YOUNG MORTIMER. By heaven, the abject villain shall not live!

WARWICK. I'll have his blood, or die in seeking it.

PEMBROKE. The like oath Pembroke takes.

LANCASTER.   And so doth Lancaster.
   Now send our heralds to defy the king;
   And make the people swear to put him down.   110
     [*Enter a Messenger.*

YOUNG MORTIMER. Letters! from whence?

MESSENGER.   From Scotland, my lord.
     [*Giving letters to Mortimer.*

LANCASTER. Why, how now, cousin, how fares all our friends?

YOUNG MORTIMER. My uncle's taken prisoner by the Scots.

LANCASTER. We'll have him ransomed, man; be of good cheer.

YOUNG MORTIMER. They rate his ransom at five thousand pound.
   Who should defray the money but the king,
   Seeing he is taken prisoner in his wars?
   I'll to the king.

LANCASTER. Do, cousin, and I'll bear thee company.

WARWICK. Meantime, my lord of Pembroke and myself   120
   Will to Newcastle here, and gather head.

YOUNG MORTIMER. About it, then, and we will follow you.

LANCASTER. Be resolute and full of secrecy.

WARWICK. I warrant you.   [*Exit with Pembroke.*

YOUNG MORTIMER. Cousin, and if he will not ransom him,
   I'll thunder such a peal into his ears,
   As never subject did unto his king.

LANCASTER. Content, I'll bear my part—Holla! who's there?
     [*Enter Guard.*

YOUNG MORTIMER. Ay, marry, such a guard as this doth well.

LANCASTER. Lead on the way.   130

GUARD. Whither will your lordships?

YOUNG MORTIMER.   Whither else but to the king.

GUARD. His highness is disposed to be alone.

LANCASTER. Why, so he may, but we will speak to him.

GUARD. You may not in, my lord.

YOUNG MORTIMER.   May we not?
     [*Enter King Edward and Kent.*

KING EDWARD. How now!
   What noise is this? who have we there? is't you?
     [*He starts to leave.*

YOUNG MORTIMER. Nay, stay, my lord, I come to bring you news;

   121. *head*, army, troops.

Mine uncle's taken prisoner by the Scots.

KING EDWARD. Then ransom him.

LANCASTER. 'Twas in your wars; you should ransom him. 140

YOUNG MORTIMER. And you shall ransom him, or else—

KENT. What! Mortimer, you will not threaten him?

KING EDWARD. Quiet yourself, you shall have the broad seal,
To gather for him throughout the realm.

LANCASTER. Your minion Gaveston hath taught you this.

YOUNG MORTIMER. My lord, the family of the Mortimers
Are not so poor, but, would they sell their land,
'Twould levy men enough to anger you.
We never beg, but use such prayers as these.

KING EDWARD. Shall I still be haunted thus? 150

YOUNG MORTIMER. Nay, now you're here alone, I'll speak my
mind.

LANCASTER. And so will I, and then, my lord, farewell.

YOUNG MORTIMER. The idle triumphs, masks, lascivious shows,
And prodigal gifts bestowed on Gaveston,
Have drawn thy treasury dry, and made thee weak;
The murmuring commons overstretchèd hath.

LANCASTER. Look for rebellion, look to be deposed;
Thy garrisons are beaten out of France,
And, lame and poor, lie groaning at the gates.
The wild O'Neill, with swarms of Irish kerns, 160
Lives uncontrolled within the English pale.
Unto the walls of York the Scots make road,
And unresisted drove away rich spoils.

YOUNG MORTIMER. The haughty Dane commands the narrow seas,
While in the harbour ride thy ships unrigged.

LANCASTER. What foreign prince sends thee ambassadors?

YOUNG MORTIMER. Who loves thee, but a sort of flatterers?

LANCASTER. Thy gentle queen, sole sister to Valois,
Complains that thou hast left her all forlorn.

YOUNG MORTIMER. Thy court is naked, being bereft of those 170
That make a king seem glorious to the world;
I mean the peers, whom thou should'st dearly love:
Libels are cast again thee in the street:
Ballads and rhymes made of thy overthrow.

143. *the broad seal*, letters patent under the Great Seal to collect alms throughout the country. Not a tax levy such as might increase the unpopularity of the king.

156. I.e., the shows and triumphs by their extravagance have overstretched the murmuring commons.

160. *kerns*, foot soldiers.   167. *sort*, company.   173. *again*, against.

LANCASTER. The Northern borderers seeing their houses burnt,
    Their wives and children slain, run up and down,
    Cursing the name of thee and Gaveston.

YOUNG MORTIMER. When wert thou in the field with banner
    spread,
    But once? And then thy soldiers marched like players,
    With garish robes, not armour; and thyself,   180
    Bedaubed with gold, rode laughing at the rest,
    Nodding and shaking of thy spangled crest,
    Where women's favours hung like labels down.

LANCASTER. And therefore came it, that the fleering Scots,
    To England's high disgrace, have made this jig:
        Maids of England, sore may you mourn,
        For your lemans you have lost at Bannocksbourn—
            With a heave and a ho!
        What weeneth the King of England,
        So soon to have won Scotland?—   190
            With a rombelow!

YOUNG MORTIMER. Wigmore shall fly, to set my uncle free

LANCASTER. And when 'tis gone, our swords shall purchase more.
    If ye be moved, revenge it as you can;
    Look next to see us with our ensigns spread.
                              [Exit with Young Mortimer.

KING EDWARD. My swelling heart for very anger breaks!
    How oft have I been baited by these peers,
    And dare not be revenged, for their power is great!
    Yet, shall the crowing of these cockerels
    Affright a lion? Edward, unfold thy paws,   200
    And let their lives' blood slake thy fury's hunger.
    If I be cruel and grow tyrannous,
    Now let them thank themselves, and rue too late.

KENT. My lord, I see your love to Gaveston
    Will be the ruin of the realm and you,
    For now the wrathful nobles threaten wars,
    And therefore, brother, banish him for ever.

KING EDWARD. Art thou an enemy to my Gaveston?

KENT. Ay, and it grieves me that I favoured him.

KING EDWARD. Traitor, begone! whine thou with Mortimer.   210

KENT. So will I, rather than with Gaveston.

185. *jig*, a lively song.
187. *lemans*, sweethearts. Bannocksbourn actually was not fought until
1314, after the time of this scene.
189. *weeneth*, imagineth.   192. *fly*, be sold.

KING EDWARD. Out of my sight, and trouble me no more!

KENT. No marvel though thou scorn thy noble peers,
  When I thy brother am rejected thus.

KING EDWARD. Away!   [*Exit Kent.*

  Poor Gaveston, that has no friend but me,
  Do what they can, we'll live in Tynemouth here,
  And, so I walk with him about the walls,
  What care I though the earls begirt us round?—
  Here cometh she that's cause of all these jars.   220

  • [*Enter Queen Isabella with King Edward's Niece, two Ladies,*
    Gaveston, Baldock and Young Spenser.

QUEEN ISABELLA. My lord, 'tis thought the earls are up in arms.

KING EDWARD. Ay, and 'tis likewise thought you favour him.

QUEEN ISABELLA. Thus do you still suspect me without cause?

NIECE. Sweet uncle! speak more kindly to the queen.

GAVESTON. My lord, dissemble with her, speak her fair.

KING EDWARD. Pardon me, sweet, I had forgot myself.

QUEEN ISABELLA. Your pardon is quickly got of Isabel.

KING EDWARD. The younger Mortimer is grown so brave,
  That to my face he threatens civil wars.

GAVESTON. Why do you not commit him to the Tower?   230

KING EDWARD. I dare not, for the people love him well.

GAVESTON. Why, then we'll have him privily made away.

KING EDWARD. Would Lancaster and he had both caroused
  A bowl of poison to each other's health!
  But let them go, and tell me what are these.

NIECE. Two of my father's servants whilst he liv'd—
  May't please your grace to entertain them now.

KING EDWARD. Tell me, where wast thou born? what is thine arms?

BALDOCK. My name is Baldock, and my gentry
  I fetch from Oxford, not from heraldry.   240

KING EDWARD. The fitter art thou, Baldock, for my turn.
  Wait on me, and I'll see thou shall not want.

BALDOCK. I humbly thank your majesty.

KING EDWARD. Knowest thou him, Gaveston?

GAVESTON.   Ay, my lord;
  His name is Spenser, he is well allied;
  For my sake, let him wait upon your grace;
  Scarce shall you find a man of more desert.

KING EDWARD. Then, Spenser, wait upon me; for his sake
  I'll grace thee with a higher style ere long.

YOUNG SPENSER. No greater titles happen unto me,   250

222. *him*, Mortimer.

Than to be favoured of your majesty!

KING EDWARD. Cousin, this day shall be your marriage-feast.
　And, Gaveston, think that I love thee well,
　To wed thee to our niece, the only heir
　Unto the Earl of Gloucester late deceased.

GAVESTON. I know, my lord, many will stomach me,
　But I respect neither their love nor hate.

KING EDWARD. The headstrong barons shall not limit me;
　He that I list to favour shall be great.
　Come, let's away; and when the marriage ends,　·　　260
　Have at the rebels, and their 'complices!

　　　　　　　　　　　　[*They go proudly out.*

SCENE III

NEAR TYNEMOUTH CASTLE. *As Lancaster, Young Mortimer, War-
　wick, Pembroke and their companions go across the stage, they
　are joined by Kent, who has hurried to join them since he has
　deserted the King.*

KENT. My lords, of love to this our native land
　I come to join with you and leave the king;
　And in your quarrel and the realm's behoof
　Will be the first that shall adventure life.

LANCASTER. I fear me, you are sent of policy,
　To undermine us with a show of love.

WARWICK. He is your brother, therefore have we cause
　To cast the worst, and doubt of your revolt.

KENT. Mine honour shall be hostage of my truth:
　If that will not suffice, farewell, my lords.　　　　10

YOUNG MORTIMER. Stay, Edmund; never was Plantagenet
　False of his word, and therefore trust we thee.

PEMBROKE. But what's the reason you should leave him now?

KENT. I have informed the Earl of Lancaster.

LANCASTER. And it sufficeth. Now, my lords, know this,
　That Gaveston is secretly arrived,
　And here in Tynemouth frolics with the king.
　Let us with these our followers scale the walls,
　And suddenly surprise them unawares.

YOUNG MORTIMER. I'll give the onset.

WARWICK.　　　　　　　　　　And I'll follow thee.　20

　　5. *of policy*, in trickery.　　　8. *cast*, suspect.

YOUNG MORTIMER. This tottered ensign of my ancestors,
  Which swept the desert shore of that Dead Sea
  Whereof we got the name of Mortimer,
  Will I advance upon this castle's walls.
  Drums, strike alarum, raise them from their sport,
  And ring aloud the knell of Gaveston!
LANCASTER. None be so hardy as to touch the king;
  But neither spare you Gaveston nor his friends.   [*Exeunt.*

SCENE IV

King Edward hurries in and meets Young Spenser, who comes
in from the other side. There is a sound of fighting.

KING EDWARD. Oh, tell me, Spenser, where is Gaveston?
YOUNG SPENSER. I fear me he is slain, my gracious lord.
KING EDWARD. No, here he comes; now let them spoil and kill.
    [*Enter Queen Isabella, King Edward's Niece, Gaveston, and*
    Nobles.
  Fly, fly, my lords, the earls have got the hold;
  Take shipping and away to Scarborough;
  Spenser and I will post away by land.
GAVESTON. Oh, stay, my lord, they will not injure you.
KING EDWARD. I will not trust them; Gaveston, away!
GAVESTON. Farewell, my lord.
KING EDWARD.   Lady, farewell.
NIECE. Farewell, sweet uncle, till we meet again.   10
KING EDWARD. Farewell, sweet Gaveston; and farewell, niece.
QUEEN ISABELLA. No farewell to poor Isabel thy queen?
KING EDWARD. Yes, yes, for Mortimer, your lover's sake.
QUEEN ISABELLA. Heaven can witness I love none but you:
                    [*Exeunt all but Queen Isabella.*
  From my embracements thus he breaks away.
  Oh, that mine arms could close this isle about,
  That I might pull him to me where I would!
  Or that these tears, that drizzle from mine eyes,
  Had power to mollify his stony heart,
  That when I had him we might never part!   20
    [*Enter Lancaster, Warwick, Young Mortimer, and others.*
    Alarums within.
LANCASTER. I wonder how he 'scaped!
YOUNG MORTIMER.   Who's this? the queen!
  21. *tottered,* tattered.

QUEEN ISABELLA. Ay, Mortimer, the miserable queen,
  Whose pining heart her inward sighs have blasted,
  And body with continual mourning wasted:
  These hands are tired with haling of my lord
  From Gaveston, from wicked Gaveston,
  And all in vain; for, when I speak him fair,
  He turns away, and smiles upon his minion.
YOUNG MORTIMER. Cease to lament, and tell us where's the king?
QUEEN ISABELLA. What would you with the king? is't him you
    seek?   30
LANCASTER. No, madam, but that cursèd Gaveston.
  Far be it from the thought of Lancaster
  To offer violence to his sovereign.
  We would but rid the realm of Gaveston:
  Tell us where he remains, and he shall die.
QUEEN ISABELLA. He's gone by water unto Scarborough;
  Pursue him quickly, and he cannot 'scape;
  The king hath left him, and his train is small.
WARWICK. Forslow no time, sweet Lancaster; let's march.
YOUNG MORTIMER. How comes it that the king and he is parted?
QUEEN ISABELLA. That this your army, going several ways,   41
  Might be of lesser force: and with the power
  That he intendeth presently to raise.
  Be easily suppressed; therefore be gone.
YOUNG MORTIMER. Here in the river rides a Flemish hoy;
  Let's all aboard, and follow him amain.
LANCASTER. The wind that bears him hence will fill our sails:
  Come, come aboard, 'tis but an hour's sailing.
YOUNG MORTIMER. Madam, stay you within this castle here.
QUEEN ISABELLA. No, Mortimer, I'll to my lord the king.   50
YOUNG MORTIMER. Nay, rather sail with us to Scarborough.
QUEEN ISABELLA. You know the king is so suspicious,
  As if he hear I have but talked with you,
  Mine honour will be called in question;
  And therefore, gentle Mortimer, be gone.
YOUNG MORTIMER. Madam, I cannot stay to answer you,
  But think of Mortimer as he deserves.
                         [*Exeunt all except Queen Isabella.*
QUEEN ISABELLA. So well hast thou deserved, sweet Mortimer,
  As Isabel could live with thee for ever.
  In vain I look for love at Edward's hand,   60
  Whose eyes are fixed on none but Gaveston.

  39. *Forslow*, lose.   45. *hoy*, a small ship.

Yet once more I'll importune him with prayers:
If he be strange and not regard my words,
My son and I will over into France,
And to the king my brother there complain,
How Gaveston hath robbed me of his love:
But yet, I hope my sorrows will have end,
And Gaveston this blessèd day be slain.   [*Exit.*

SCENE V

AN OPEN FIELD. *Gaveston runs in as if pursued.*

GAVESTON. Yet, lusty lords, I have escaped your hands,
   Your threats, your larums, and your hot pursuits;
   And though divorcèd from King Edward's eyes,
   Yet liveth Pierce of Gaveston unsurprised,
   Breathing, in hope (malgrado all your beards,
 • That muster rebels thus against your king),
   To see his royal sovereign once again.
      [*Enter Warwick, Lancaster, Pembroke, Young Mortimer,
        Soldiers, James, and other Attendants of Pembroke.*
WARWICK. Upon him, soldiers, take away his weapons.
YOUNG MORTIMER. Thou proud disturber of thy country's peace,   10
   Corrupter of thy king; cause of these broils,   •
   Base flatterer, yield! and, were it not for shame,
   Shame and dishonour to a soldier's name,
   Upon my weapon's point here should'st thou fall,
   And welter in thy gore.
LANCASTER.   Monster of men!
   That, like the Greekish strumpet, trained to arms
   And bloody wars so many valiant knights;
   Look for no other fortune, wretch, than death!
   Kind Edward is not here to buckler thee.
WARWICK. Lancaster, why talk'st thou to the slave?
   Go, soldiers, take him hence, for, by my sword,   20
   His head shall off: Gaveston, short warning
   Shall serve thy turn: it is our country's cause,
   That here severely we will execute
   Upon thy person. Hang him at a bough.
GAVESTON. My lord!—

4. *unsurprised*, untaken.   5. *malgrado*, in spite of.
15. *strumpet*, Helen of Troy.   *trained*, lured.

WARWICK.   Soldiers, have him away—
But for thou wert the favourite of a king,
Thou shalt have so much honour at our hands—
GAVESTON. I thank you all, my lords: then I perceive,
That heading is one, and hanging is the other,
And death is all.
    [*Enter Arundel.*

LANCASTER.   How now, my lord of Arundel?   30
ARUNDEL. My lords, King Edward greets you all by me.
WARWICK. Arundel, say your message.
ARUNDEL.   His majesty,
Hearing that you had taken Gaveston,
Entreateth you by me, yet but he may
See him before he dies; for why, he says,
And sends you word, he knows that die he shall;
And if you gratify his grace so far,
He will be mindful of the courtesy.
WARWICK. How now?
GAVESTON.   Renownèd Edward, how thy name
Revives poor Gaveston!
WARWICK.   No, it needeth not;   40
Arundel, we will gratify the king
In other matters; he must pardon us in this.
Soldiers, away with him!
GAVESTON.   Why, my lord of **Warwick**,
Will not these delays beget my hopes?
I know it, lords, it is this life you aim at,
Yet grant King Edward this.
YOUNG MORTIMER.   Shalt thou appoint
What we shall grant? Soldiers, away with him:
Thus we'll gratify the king,
We'll send his head by thee; let him bestow
His tears on that, for that is all he gets   50
Of Gaveston, or else his senseless trunk.
LANCASTER. Not so, my lords, lest he bestow more cost
In burying him that he hath ever earned.
ARUNDEL. My lords, it is his majesty's request,
And in the honour of a king he swears,
He will but talk with him, and send him back.
WARWICK. When? can you tell? Arundel, no; we wot,
He that the care of his realm remits,

26. *for*, since.
29. I.e., he is to be beheaded like a noble, not hanged like a common felon.

And drives his nobles to these exigents
For Gaveston, will, if he sees him once,   60
Violate any promise to possess him.
ARUNDEL. Then, if you will not trust his grace in keep,
My lords, I will be pledge for his return.
YOUNG MORTIMER. 'Tis honourable in thee to offer this;
But, for we know thou art a noble gentleman,
We will not wrong thee so, to make away
A true man for a thief.
GAVESTON. How mean'st thou, Mortimer? that is over-base.
YOUNG MORTIMER. Away, base groom, robber of king's renown!
Question with thy companions and mates.   70
PEMBROKE. My Lord Mortimer, and you, my lords, each one,
To gratify the king's request therein,
Touching the sending of this Gaveston,
Because his majesty so earnestly
Desires to see the man before his death,
I will upon mine honour undertake
To carry him, and bring him back again;
Provided this, that you my lord of Arundel
Will join with me.
WARWICK.   Pembroke, what wilt thou do?
Cause yet more bloodshed? is it not enough   80
That we have taken him, but must we now
Leave him on "had I wist," and let him go?
PEMBROKE. My lords, I will not over-woo your honours,
But if you dare trust Pembroke with the prisoner,
Upon mine oath, I will return him back.
ARUNDEL. My lord of Lancaster, what say you in this?
LANCASTER. Why, I say, let him go on Pembroke's word.
PEMBROKE. And you, Lord Mortimer?
YOUNG MORTIMER.   How say you, my lord of **Warwick**?
WARWICK. Nay, do your pleasures, I know how 'twill **prove**.
PEMBROKE. Then give him me.
GAVESTON.   Sweet sovereign, yet I come   90
To see thee ere I die.
WARWICK [*Aside*].   Yet not perhaps,
If Warwick's wit and policy prevail.
YOUNG MORTIMER. My lord of Pembroke, we deliver him you;
Return him on your honour. Sound, away!

59. *exigents*, difficulties.   70. *Question*, argue.
82. *had I wist*, had I known what the result would be, I wouldn't have
done it.

[Exeunt all except Pembroke, Arundel, Gaveston, James, and
other Attendants of Pembroke.

PEMBROKE. My lord, you shall go with me.
My house is not far hence; out of the way
A little, but our men shall go along.
We that have pretty wenches to our wives,
Sir, must not come so near to balk their lips.
ARUNDEL. 'Tis very kindly spoke, my lord of Pembroke;   100
Your honour hath an adamant of power
To draw a prince.
PEMBROKE.   So, my lord. Come hither, James:
I do commit this Gaveston to thee,
Be thou this night his keeper; in the morning
We will discharge thee of thy charge: be gone.
GAVESTON. Unhappy Gaveston, whither goest thou now?
                    [He is taken out by Pembroke's men.
HORSE-BOY. My lord, we'll quickly be at Cobham.   *[Exeunt.*

ACT III

SCENE I

A ROAD TO BOROUGHBRIDGE IN YORKSHIRE. *James and other follow-*
ers of Pembroke enter with Gaveston as their prisoner. He is
completely cast down.

GAVESTON. O treacherous Warwick! thus to wrong thy friend.
JAMES. I see it is your life these arms pursue.
GAVESTON. Weaponless must I fall, and die in bands?
Oh! must this day be period of my life?
Centre of all my bliss! An ye be men,
Speed to the king.
          [Enter Warwick and Soldiers.
WARWICK.   My lord of Pembroke's men,
Strive you no longer—I will have that Gaveston.
JAMES. Your lordship does dishonour to yourself,
And wrong our lord, your honourable friend.
WARWICK. No, James, it is my country's cause I follow.   10
Go, take the villain; soldiers, come away.
We'll make quick work. Commend me to your master,
My friend, and tell him that I watched it well.

101. *adamant,* lodestone.

Come, let thy shadow parley with King Edward.
GAVESTON. Treacherous earl, shall I not see the king?
WARWICK. The King of Heaven perhaps, no other king.
    Away!   [*Exeunt Warwick and Soldiers with Gaveston.*
JAMES. Come, fellows, it booted not for us to strive,
    We will in haste go certify our lord.   [*Exeunt.*

SCENE II

NEAR BOROUGHBRIDGE IN YORKSHIRE. *The King has raised an army to put down the rebellious nobles.*

    [*Enter King Edward and Young Spenser, Baldock, and Nobles of the King's side, and Soldiers with drums and fifes.*

KING EDWARD. I long to hear an answer from the barons
  Touching my friend, my dearest Gaveston.
  Ah! Spenser, not the riches of my realm
  Can ransom him! ah, he is marked to die!
  I know the malice of the younger Mortimer,
  Warwick I know is rough, and Lancaster
  Inexorable, and I shall never see
  My lovely Pierce, my Gaveston again!
  The barons overbear me with their pride.
YOUNG SPENSER. Were I King Edward, England's sovereign,   10
  Son to the lovely Eleanor of Spain,
  Great Edward Longshanks' issue, would I bear
  These braves, this rage, and suffer uncontrolled
  These barons thus to beard me in my land,
  In mine own realm? My lord, pardon my speech:
  Did you retain your father's magnanimity,
  Did you regard the honour of your name,
  You would not suffer thus your majesty
  Be counterbuffed of your nobility.
  Strike off their heads, and let them preach on poles!   20
  No doubt, such lessons they will teach the rest,
  As by their preachments they will profit much,
  And learn obedience to their lawful king.

14. *shadow,* ghost.
12. *Edward Longshanks,* Edward I, the Prince Edward of **Friar Bacon.**
19. *counterbuffed,* curbed by.

KING EDWARD. Yea, gentle Spenser, we have been too mild,
  Too kind to them; but now have drawn our sword,
  And if they send me not my Gaveston,
  We'll steel it on their crest, and poll their tops.
BALDOCK. This haught resolve becomes your majesty
  Not to be tied to their affection,
  As though your highness were a schoolboy still,   30
  And must be awed and governed like a child.
    [Enter the Elder Spenser, with his truncheon and Soldiers.
ELDER SPENSER. Long live my sovereign, the noble Edward—
  In peace triumphant, fortunate in wars!
KING EDWARD. Welcome, old man, com'st thou in Edward's aid?
  Then tell thy prince of whence, and what thou art.
ELDER SPENSER. Lo, with a band of bowmen and of pikes,
  Brown bills and targeteers, four hundred strong,
  Sworn to defend King Edward's royal right,
  I come in person to your majesty,
  Spenser, the father of Hugh Spenser there,   40
  Bound to your highness everlastingly,
  For favours done, in him, unto us all.
KING EDWARD. Thy father, Spenser?
YOUNG SPENSER.   True, an it like your grace,
  That pours, in lieu of all your goodness shown,
  His life, my lord, before your princely feet.
KING EDWARD. Welcome ten thousand times, old man, again.
  Spenser, this love, this kindness to thy king,
  Argues thy noble mind and disposition.
  Spenser, I here create thee Earl of Wiltshire,
  And daily will enrich thee with our favour,   50
  That, as the sunshine, shall reflect o'er thee.
  Beside, the more to manifest our love,
  Because we hear Lord Bruce doth sell his land,
  And that the Mortimers are in hand withal,
  Thou shalt have crowns of us t' outbid the barons:
  And, Spenser, spare them not, but lay it on.
  Soldiers, a largess, and thrice welcome all!
YOUNG SPENSER. My lord, here comes the queen.
    [Enter Queen Isabella, Prince Edward, and Levune.
KING EDWARD.   Madam, what news?
QUEEN ISABELLA. News of dishonour, lord, and discontent.
  Our friend Levune, faithful and full of trust,   60

27. *steel it*, try it with our swords. *poll*, crop, cut off.
28. *haught*, bold.   54. *are in hand*, are negotiating for it.

Informeth us, by letters and by words,
That Lord Valois our brother, King of France,
Because your highness hath been slack in homage,
Hath seizèd Normandy into his hands.
These be the letters, this the messenger.
KING EDWARD. Welcome, Levune. Tush, Sib, if this be all,
  Valois and I will soon be friends again.—
  But to my Gaveston; shall I never see,
  Never behold thee now?—Madam, in this matter,
  We will employ you and your little son;   70
  You shall go parley with the King of France.—
  Boy, see you bear you bravely to the king,
  And do your message with a majesty.
PRINCE EDWARD. Commit not to my youth things of more weight
  Than fits a prince so young as I to bear,
  And fear not, lord and father, Heaven's great beams
  On Atlas' shoulder shall not lie more safe,
  Than shall your charge committed to my trust.
QUEEN ISABELLA. Ah, boy! this towardness makes thy mother fear
  Thou art not marked to many days on earth.   80
KING EDWARD. Madam, we will that you with speed be shipped,
  And this our son; Levune shall follow you
  With all the haste we can dispatch him hence.
  Choose of our lords to bear you company;
  And go in peace, leave us in wars at home.
QUEEN ISABELLA. Unnatural wars, where subjects brave their king;
  God end them once! My lord, I take my leave,
  To make my preparation for France.
      [As she goes out with Prince Edward, Arundel hurries in.
KING EDWARD. What, Lord Arundel, dost thou come alone?
ARUNDEL. Yea, my good lord, for Gaveston is dead.   90
KING EDWARD. Ah, traitors! have they put my friend to death?
  Tell me, Arundel, died he ere thou cam'st,
  Or didst thou see my friend to take his death?
ARUNDEL. Neither, my lord; for, as he was surprised,
  Begirt with weapons and with enemies round,
  I did your highness' message to them all;
  Demanding him of them, entreating rather,
  And said, upon the honour of my name,
  That I would undertake to carry him
  Unto your highness, and to bring him back.   100

  66. *Sib*, perhaps a familiar name for Isabella, possibly only an abbreviation of *gossip*, a companion.   79. *towardness*, aptitude.

KING EDWARD. And tell me, would the rebels deny me that?

YOUNG SPENSER. Proud recreants!

KING EDWARD.   Yea, Spenser, traitors all.

ARUNDEL. I found them at the first inexorable;
  The Earl of Warwick would not bide the hearing,
  Mortimer hardly; Pembroke and Lancaster
  Spake least: and, when they flatly had denied,
  Refusing to receive me pledge for him,
  The Earl of Pembroke mildly thus bespake:
  "My lords, because our sovereign sends for him,
  And promiseth he shall be safe returned,   110
  I will this undertake, to have him hence,
  And see him re-delivered to your hands."

KING EDWARD. Well, and how fortunes that he came not?

YOUNG SPENSER. Some treason, or some villainy was the cause.

ARUNDEL. The Earl of Warwick seized him on his way;
  For, being delivered unto Pembroke's men,
  Their lord rode home thinking his prisoner safe;
  But ere he came, Warwick in ambush lay,
  And bare him to his death; and in a trench
  Strake off his head, and marched unto the camp.   120

YOUNG SPENSER. A bloody part, flatly 'gainst law of arms!

KING EDWARD. Oh, shall I speak, or shall I sigh and die!

YOUNG SPENSER. My lord, refer your vengeance to the sword
  Upon these barons; hearten up your men;
  Let them not unrevenged murder your friends!
  Advance your standard, Edward, in the field,
  And march to fire them from their starting holes.

KING EDWARD [*Kneeling*]. By earth, the common mother of us all,
  By Heaven, and all the moving orbs thereof,
  By this right hand, and by my father's sword,   130
  And all the honours 'longing to my crown,
  I will have heads, and lives for him, as many
  As I have manors, castles, towns, and towers!—   [*Rises.*
  Treacherous Warwick! traitorous Mortimer!
  If I be England's king, in lakes of gore
  Your headless trunks, your bodies will I trail,
  That you may drink your fill, and quaff in blood,
  And stain my royal standard with the same,
  That so my bloody colours may suggest
  Remembrance of revenge immortally   140
  On your accursèd traitorous progeny,

120. *strake*, struck.

You villains, that have slain my Gaveston!
And in this place of honour and of trust,
Spenser, sweet Spenser, I adopt thee here:
And merely of our love we do create thee
Earl of Gloucester, and Lord Chamberlain,
Despite of times, despite of enemies.

YOUNG SPENSER. My lord, here's a messenger from the barons
Desires access unto your majesty.

KING EDWARD. Admit him near. 150

[Enter the Herald, with his coat of arms.

HERALD. Long live King Edward, England's lawful lord!

KING EDWARD. So wish not they, I wis, that sent thee hither.
Thou com'st from Mortimer and his 'complices,
A ranker rout of rebels never was.
Well, say thy message.

HERALD. The barons up in arms, by me salute
Your highness with long life and happiness;
And bid me say, as plainer to your grace,
That if without effusion of blood
You will this grief have ease and remedy, 160
That from your princely person you remove
This Spenser, as a putrifying branch,
That deads the royal vine, whose golden leaves
Empale your princely head, your diadem,
Whose brightness such pernicious upstarts dim,
Say they; and lovingly advise your grace,
To cherish virtue and nobility,
And have old servitors in high esteem,
And shake off smooth dissembling flatterers:
This granted, they, their honours, and their lives, 170
Are to your highness vowed and consecrate.

YOUNG SPENSER. Ah, traitors! will they still display their pride?

KING EDWARD. Away, tarry no answer, but be gone!
Rebels, will they appoint their sovereign
His sports, his pleasures, and his company?
Yet, ere thou go, see how I do divorce
[Embraces Spenser.
Spenser from me.—Now get thee to thy lords,
And tell them I will come to chastise them
For murdering Gaveston; hie thee, get thee gone!
Edward with fire and sword follows at thy heels. 180
[Exit Herald.

145. merely, purely.   158. plainer, petitioner.

My lords, perceive you how these rebels swell?
Soldiers, good hearts, defend your sovereign's right,
For now, even now, we march to make them stoop.
Away!

[*Exeunt. Alarums, excursions of groups of soldiers fighting
across the stage, a great fight, and a retreat sounded, within.
Re-enter King Edward, the Elder Spenser, Young Spenser,
and Noblemen of the King's side.*

KING EDWARD. Why do we sound retreat? Upon them, lords!
This day I shall pour vengeance with my sword
On those proud rebels that are up in arms,
And do confront and countermand their king.

YOUNG SPENSER. I doubt it not, my lord, right will prevail.

ELDER SPENSER. 'Tis not amiss, my liege, for either part   190
To breathe awhile; our men, with sweat and dust
All choked well near, begin to faint for heat;
And this retire refresheth horse and man.

YOUNG SPENSER. Here come the rebels.

[*Enter Young Mortimer, Lancaster, Warwick, Pembroke,
and others, ready to use this breathing spell for a parley.*

YOUNG MORTIMER. Look, Lancaster, yonder is Edward
Among his flatterers.

LANCASTER.   And there let him be
Till he pay dearly for their company.

WARWICK. And shall, or Warwick's sword shall smite in vain.

KING EDWARD. What, rebels, do you shrink and sound retreat?

YOUNG MORTIMER. No, Edward, no, thy flatterers faint and fly.   200

LANCASTER. Th'ad best betimes forsake them, and their trains,
For they'll betray thee, traitors as they are.

YOUNG SPENSER. Traitor on thy face, rebellious Lancaster!

PEMBROKE. Away, base upstart, bravest thou nobles thus?

ELDER SPENSER. A noble attempt, and honourable deed,
Is it not, trow ye, to assemble aid,
And levy arms against your lawful king!

KING EDWARD. For which ere long their heads shall satisfy,
To appease the wrath of their offended king.

YOUNG MORTIMER. Then, Edward, thou wilt fight it to the last,
And rather bathe thy sword in subjects' blood,   211
Than banish that pernicious company?

KING EDWARD. Ay, traitors all, rather than thus be braved,

---

188. *countermand*, oppose.
201. *Th'ad*, Thou had. The original text reads *thee* instead of *them*. The
emendation is suggested by Brooke.   *trains*, plots.

Make England's civil towns huge heaps of stones,
And ploughs to go about our palace gates.
WARWICK. A desperate and unnatural resolution!
Alarum!—to the fight!
St. George for England, and the barons' right.
KING EDWARD. Saint George for England, and King Edward's
right.

[*The trumpets sound again. The two parties go out in opposite directions. There is more noise of fighting and groups
of soldiers fight across the stage. The noise dies down and
the King and his followers come in in triumph, leading the
rebellious Barons and Kent captive.*

KING EDWARD. Now, lusty lords, now, not by chance of war,   220
But justice of the quarrel and the cause,
Vailed is your pride; methinks you hang the heads,
But we'll advance them, traitors; now 'tis time
To be avenged on you for all your braves,
And for the murder of my dearest friend,
To whom right well you knew our soul was knit,
Good Pierce of Gaveston, my sweet favourite.
Ah, rebels! recreants! you made him away.
KENT. Brother, in regard of thee, and of thy land,
Did they remove that flatterer from thy throne.   230
KING EDWARD. So, sir, you have spoke; away, avoid our presence!
[*Exit Kent.*

Accursèd wretches, was't in regard of us,
When we had sent our messenger to request
He might be spared to come to speak with us,
And Pembroke undertook for his return,
That thou, proud Warwick, watched the prisoner,
Poor Pierce, and headed him 'gainst law of arms?
For which thy head shall overlook the rest,
As much as thou in rage outwent'st the rest.
WARWICK. Tyrant, I scorn thy threats and menaces;   240
It is but temporal that thou canst inflict.
LANCASTER. The worst is death, and better die to live
Than live in infamy under such a king.
KING EDWARD. Away with them, my lord of Winchester!
These lusty leaders, Warwick and Lancaster,
I charge you roundly—off with both their heads!

223. *advance*, raise, i.e., on the ends of pikes.   224. *braves*, affronts.
229. *in regard of*, in care for.   237. *headed*, beheaded.
241. *temporal*, i.e., temporal punishment.

Away!

WARWICK. Farewell, vain world!

LANCASTER.   Sweet Mortimer, farewell.

YOUNG MORTIMER. England, unkind to thy nobility,
Groan for this grief, behold how thou art maimed!   250

KING EDWARD. Go, take that haughty Mortimer to the Tower,
There see him safe bestowed; and for the rest,
Do speedy execution on them all.
Begone!

YOUNG MORTIMER. What, Mortimer! can ragged stony walls
Immure thy virtue that aspires to Heaven?
No, Edward, England's scourge, it may not be;
Mortimer's hope surmounts his fortune far.

                        [*The captive Barons are led off.*

KING EDWARD. Sound drums and trumpets! March with me, my
        friends,
Edward this day hath crowned him king anew.   260

            [*Exeunt all except Young Spenser, Levune and Baldock.*

YOUNG SPENSER. Levune, the trust that we repose in thee,
Begets the quiet of King Edward's land.
Therefore begone in haste, and with advice
Bestow that treasure on the lords of France,
That, therewith all enchanted, like the guard
That suffered Jove to pass in showers of gold
To Danae, all aid may be denied
To Isabel, the queen, that now in France
Makes friends, to cross the seas with her young son,
And step into his father's regiment.   270

LEVUNE. That's it these barons and the subtle queen
Long levied at.

BALDOCK.   Yea, but, Levune, thou seest
These barons lay their heads on blocks together;
What they intend, the hangman frustrates clean.

LEVUNE. Have you no doubt, my lords, I'll clap so close
Among the lords of France with England's gold,
That Isabel shall make her plaints in vain,
And France shall be obdurate with her tears.

YOUNG SPENSER. Then make for France amain—Levune, away!
Proclaim King Edward's wars and victories.   280

            [*Levune goes out at one side and Spenser and Baldock go
            out at another place to rejoin the King.*

272. *levied*, mistake for *levelled*, aimed at.
275. *clap so close*, contrive so secretly.

ACT IV

SCENE I

NEAR THE TOWER OF LONDON. *Kent appears on his way to exile. He has prepared the escape of Young Mortimer from the Tower.*

KENT. Fair blows the wind for France; blow, gentle gale,
  Till Edmund be arrived for England's good!
  Nature, yield to my country's cause in this.
  A brother? no, a butcher of thy friends!
  Proud Edward, dost thou banish me thy presence?
  But I'll to France, and cheer the wrongèd queen,
  And certify what Edward's looseness is.
  Unnatural king! to slaughter noblemen
  And cherish flatterers! Mortimer, I stay
  Thy sweet escape: stand gracious, gloomy night,   10
  To his device.
    [*Enter Young Mortimer, disguised.*
YOUNG MORTIMER. Holla! who walketh there?
  Is't you, my lord?
KENT.   Mortimer, 'tis I;
  But hath thy potion wrought so happily?
YOUNG MORTIMER. It hath, my lord; the warders all asleep,
  I think them, gave me leave to pass in peace.
  But hath your grace got shipping unto France?
KENT. Fear it not.   [*They hurry away.*

SCENE II

IN PARIS, *where Queen Isabella is seeking aid with little success. Enter Queen Isabella and Prince Edward.*

QUEEN ISABELLA. Ah, boy! our friends do fail us all in France:
  The lords are cruel, and the king unkind;
  What shall we do?
PRINCE EDWARD.   Madam, return to England,
  And please my father well, and then a fig
  For all my uncle's friendship here in France.
  I warrant you, I'll win his highness quickly;

'A loves me better than a thousand Spensers.

QUEEN ISABELLA. Ah, boy, thou art deceived, at least in this,
To think that we can yet be tuned together;
No, no, we jar too far. Unkind Valois!   10
Unhappy Isabel! when France rejects,
Whither, oh! whither dost thou bend thy steps?

    [*Enter Sir John of Hainault, the Queen's chief support and
      advisor.*

SIR JOHN. Madam, what cheer?

QUEEN ISABELLA.   Ah! good Sir John of Hainault,
Never so cheerless, nor so far distrest.

SIR JOHN. I hear, sweet lady, of the king's unkindness;
But droop not, madam; noble minds contemn
Despair; will your grace with me to Hainault,
And there stay time's advantage with your son?
How say you, my lord, will you go with your friends,
And shake off all our fortunes equally?   20

PRINCE EDWARD. So pleaseth the queen, my mother, me it likes:
The King of England, nor the court of France,
Shall have me from my gracious mother's side,
Till I be strong enough to break a staff;
And then have at the proudest Spenser's head.

SIR JOHN. Well said, my lord.

QUEEN ISABELLA. Oh, my sweet heart, how do I moan thy wrongs,
Yet triumph in the hope of thee, my joy!
Ah, sweet Sir John! even to the utmost verge
Of Europe, or the shore of Tanais,   30
Will we with thee to Hainault? So we will.
The marquis is a noble gentleman;
His grace, I dare presume, will welcome me.
But who are these?

    [*Enter Kent and Young Mortimer, just arrived from Eng-
      land.*

KENT.   Madam, long may you live,
Much happier than your friends in England do!

QUEEN ISABELLA. Lord Edmund and Lord Mortimer alive!
Welcome to France! the news was here, my lord,
That you were dead, or very near your death.

YOUNG MORTIMER. Lady, the last was truest of the twain:
But Mortimer, reserved for better hap,   40
Hath shaken off the thraldom of the Tower,
And lives t'advance your standard, good my lord.

PRINCE EDWARD. How mean you? and the king, my father, lives!
  No, my Lord Mortimer, not I, I trow.
QUEEN ISABELLA. Not, son! why not? I would it were no worse.
  But, gentle lords, friendless we are in France.
YOUNG MORTIMER. Monsieur le Grand, a noble friend of yours,
  Told us, at our arrival, all the news—
  How hard the nobles, how unkind the king
  Hath showed himself; but, madam, right makes room   50
  Where weapons want; and, though a many friends
  Are made away, as Warwick, Lancaster,
  And others of our party and faction;
  Yet have we friends, assure your grace, in England
  Would cast up caps, and clap their hands for joy,
  To see us there, appointed for our foes.
KENT. Would all were well, and Edward well reclaimed
  For England's honour, peace, and quietness.
YOUNG MORTIMER. But by the sword, my lord, it must be de-
  served;
  The king will ne'er forsake his flatterers.   60
SIR JOHN. My lords of England, sith the ungentle king
  Of France refuseth to give aid of arms
  To this distressèd queen his sister here,
  Go you with her to Hainault; doubt ye not,
  We will find comfort, money, men and friends
  Ere long, to bid the English king a base.
  How say, young prince? What think you of the match?
PRINCE EDWARD. I think King Edward will outrun us all.
QUEEN ISABELLA. Nay, son, not so; and you must not discourage
  Your friends, that are so forward in your aid.   70
KENT. Sir John of Hainault, pardon us, I pray;
  These comforts that you give our woeful queen
  Bind us in kindness all at your command.
QUEEN ISABELLA. Yea, gentle brother; and the God of Heaven
  Prosper your happy motion, good Sir John.
YOUNG MORTIMER. This noble gentleman, forward in arms,
  Was born, I see, to be our anchor-hold.
  Sir John of Hainault, be it thy renown,
  That England's queen, and nobles in distress,

---

43. *and*, if.   44. *I trow*, I assure you.
56. *appointed*, prepared.   59. *deserved*, earned.
66. *bid . . . a base*, challenge to a game of prisoner's base.
75. *motion*, proposal, suggestion.

Have been by thee restored and comforted.   80
SIR JOHN. Madam, along, and you, my lords, with me,
     That England's peers may Hainault's welcome see.
                   [*They go out together.*

SCENE III

A ROOM IN THE KING'S PALACE AT WESTMINSTER. *The King, Arundel, the two Spensers, and others enter, rejoicing in their success against the rebellious nobles. They do not know of Mortimer's escape to France.*

KING EDWARD. Thus, after many threats of wrathful war,
     Triumpheth England's Edward with his friends;
     And triumph, Edward, with his friends uncontrolled!
     My lord of Gloucester, do you hear the news?
YOUNG SPENSER. What news, my lord?
KING EDWARD. Why, man, they say there is great execution
     Done through the realm; my lord of Arundel,
     You have the note, have you not?
ARUNDEL. From the Lieutenant of the Tower, my lord.
KING EDWARD. I pray let us see it. [*Takes the note.*] What have
     we there?   10
     Read it, Spenser.
       [*Hands the note to Young Spenser, who reads the names.*
     Why, so; they barked apace a month ago:
     Now, on my life, they'll neither bark nor bite.
     Now, sirs, the news from France? Gloucester, I trow
     The lords of France love England's gold so well,
     As Isabella gets no aid from thence.
     What now remains? have you proclaimed, my lord,
     Reward for them can bring in Mortimer?
YOUNG SPENSER. My lord, we have; and if he be in England,
     'A will be had ere long, I doubt it not.   20
KING EDWARD. If, dost thou say? Spenser, as true as death
     He is in England's ground; our portmasters
     Are not so careless of their king's command.
       [*Enter a Messenger.*
     How now, what news with thee? from whence come these?
MESSENGER. Letters, my lord, and tidings forth of France—
     To you, my lord of Gloucester, from Levune.
       [*Gives letters to Young Spenser.*

KING EDWARD. Read.

YOUNG SPENSER [*Reads the letter*].

"*My duty to your honour promised, &c., I have, according
to instructions in that behalf, dealt with the King of France his
lords, and effected, that the queen, all discontented and dis-*   30
*comforted, is gone: whither, if you ask, with Sir John of
Hainault, brother to the marquis, into Flanders. With them
are gone Lord Edmund, and the Lord Mortimer, having in their
company divers of your nation, and others; and, as constant
report goeth, they intend to give King Edward battle in England, sooner than he can look for them. This is all the news of
import.*

> *Your honour's in all service, Levune.*"

KING EDWARD. Ah, villains! hath that Mortimer escaped?
With him is Edmund gone associate?
And will Sir John of Hainault lead the round?   40
Welcome, a God's name, madam, and your son;
England shall welcome you and all your rout.
Gallop apace, bright Phœbus, through the sky,
And dusky night, in rusty iron car,
Between you both shorten the time, I pray,
That I may see that most desirèd day,
When we may meet these traitors in the field.
Ah, nothing grieves me, but my little boy
Is thus misled to countenance their ills.
Come, friends, to Bristow, there to make us strong;   50
And, winds, as equal be to bring them in,
As you injurious were to bear them forth!
> [*They go out to make quick preparations.*

SCENE IV

NEAR HARWICH. *Enter Queen Isabella, Prince Edward, Kent,
Young Mortimer, and Sir John of Hainault, with the army they
have brought over from the continent.*

QUEEN ISABELLA. Now, lords, our loving friends and countrymen,
Welcome to England all, with prosperous winds!
Our kindest friends in Belgia have we left,
To cope with friends at home; a heavy case
When force to force is knit, and sword and glaive,
In civil broils make kin and countrymen

Slaughter themselves in others, and their sides
With their own weapons gore! But what's the help?
Misgoverned kings are cause of all this wreck;
And, Edward, thou art one among them all,   10
Whose looseness hath betrayed thy land to spoil,
And made the channel overflow with blood
Of thine own people; patron shouldst thou be,
But thou—

YOUNG MORTIMER. Nay, madam, if you be a warrior,
You must not grow so passionate in speeches.
Lords,
Sith that we are by sufferance of Heaven
Arrived, and armèd in this prince's right,
Here for our country's cause swear we to him   20
All homage, fealty and forwardness;
And for the open wrongs and injuries
Edward hath done to us, his queen and land,
We come in arms to wreak it with the swords;
That England's queen in peace may repossess
Her dignities and honours: and withal
We may remove these flatterers from the king,
That havoc England's wealth and treasury.

SIR JOHN. Sound trumpets, my lord, and forward let us march.
Edward will think we come to flatter him.   30

KENT. I would he never had been flattered more!
      [*They march out to the sound of drum and trumpet.*

SCENE V

NEAR BRISTOL. *There is the noise of a battle, and King Edward,
    Baldock, and Young Spenser run on as if pursued.*

YOUNG SPENSER. Fly, fly, my lord! the queen is over-strong;
Her friends do multiply, and yours do fail.
Shape we our course to Ireland, there to breathe.

KING EDWARD. What! was I born to fly and run away,
And leave the Mortimers conquerors behind?
Give me my horse, and let's reinforce our troops:
And in this bed of honour die with fame.

BALDOCK. Oh, no, my lord, this princely resolution
Fits not the time; away! we are pursued.   [*They run off.*
      [*Enter Kent, with sword and target. Alone, he has a chance*

      9. stage direction: *target*, shield.

to meditate on the crime he is committing in fighting
against his king and brother.

KENT. This way he fled, but I am come too late. 10
    Edward, alas! my heart relents for thee.
    Proud traitor, Mortimer, why dost thou chase
    Thy lawful king, thy sovereign, with thy sword?
    Vile wretch! and why hast thou, of all unkind,
    Borne arms against thy brother and thy king?
    Rain showers of vengeance on my cursèd head,
    Thou God, to whom in justice it belongs
    To punish this unnatural revolt!
    Edward, this Mortimer aims at thy life!
    Oh, fly him, then! But, Edmund, calm this rage, 20
    Dissemble, or thou diest; for Mortimer
    And Isabel do kiss, while they conspire:
    And yet she bears a face of love forsooth.
    Fie on that love that hatcheth death and hate!
    Edmund, away! Bristow to Longshanks' blood
    Is false; be not found single for suspect.
    Proud Mortimer pries near into thy walks.
      [*Enter Queen Isabella, Prince Edward, **Young Mortimer**,*
        and Sir John of Hainault.

QUEEN ISABELLA. Successful battles gives the God of kings
    To them that fight in right and fear his wrath.
    Since then successfully we have prevailed, 30
    Thanks be Heaven's great architect, and you.
    Ere farther we proceed, my noble lords,
    We here create our well-belovèd son,
    Of love and care unto his royal person,
    Lord Warden of the realm, and sith the fates
    Have made his father so infortunate,
    Deal you, my lords, in this, my loving lords,
    As to your wisdoms fittest seems in all.

KENT. Madam, without offence, if I may ask,
    How will you deal with Edward in his fall? 40

PRINCE EDWARD. Tell me, good uncle, what Edward do you
    mean?

KENT. Nephew, your father: I dare not call him king.

YOUNG MORTIMER. My lord of Kent, what needs these questions?
    'Tis not in her controlment, nor in ours,
    But as the realm and parliament shall please,

14. *of all unkind*, most unnatural of all.
26. *single for suspect*, alone for danger of suspicion.

So shall your brother be disposèd of.—
[*Aside to the Queen.*] I like not this relenting mood in Edmund,
Madam, 'tis good to look to him betimes.

QUEEN ISABELLA. My lord, the Mayor of Bristow knows our mind.

YOUNG MORTIMER. Yea, madam, and they 'scape not easily   50
That fled the field.

QUEEN ISABELLA.   Baldock is with the king.
A goodly chancellor is he not, my lord?

SIR JOHN. So are the Spensers, the father and the son.

KENT. This Edward is the ruin of the realm.

    [*Enter Rice ap Howel, with the Elder Spenser, prisoner, and Attendants.*

RICE. God save Queen Isabel, and her princely son!
Madam, the Mayor and citizens of Bristow,
In sign of love and duty to this presence,
Present by me this traitor to the state,
Spenser, the father to that wanton Spenser,
That, like the lawless Catiline of Rome,   60
Revelled in England's wealth and treasury.

QUEEN ISABELLA. We thank you all.

YOUNG MORTIMER.   Your loving care in this
Deserveth princely favours and rewards.
But where's the king and the other Spenser fled?

RICE. Spenser the son, created Earl of Gloucester,
Is with that smooth-tongued scholar Baldock gone,
And shipped but late for Ireland with the king.

YOUNG MORTIMER [*Aside*]. Some whirlwind fetch them back or
sink them all!—
They shall be started thence, I doubt it not.

PRINCE EDWARD. Shall I not see the king my father yet?   70

KENT [*Aside*]. Unhappy Edward, chased from England's bounds.

SIR JOHN. Madam, what resteth, why stand you in a muse?

QUEEN ISABELLA. I rue my lord's ill-fortune; but alas!
Care of my country called me to this war.

YOUNG MORTIMER. Madam, have done with care and sad complaint;
Your king hath wronged your country and himself,
And we must seek to right it as we may.
Meanwhile, have hence this rebel to the block.
[*To Spenser.*] Your lordship cannot privilege your head.

ELDER SPENSER. Rebel is he that fights against his prince;   80
So fought not they that fought in Edward's right.

    71. *resteth*, remaineth.   79. *privilege*, exempt.

YOUNG MORTIMER. Take him away, he prates; [*Exeunt Attendants
   with the Elder Spenser. You, Rice ap Howel,
Shall do good service to her majesty,
Being of countenance in your country here,
To follow these rebellious runagates.
We in meanwhile, madam, must take advice,
How Baldock, Spenser, and their 'complices,
May in their fall be followed to their end.
    [*Rice goes off in one direction, the Queen and her nobles in
    the other.*

SCENE VI

THE ABBEY OF NEATH, *in which the King has sought refuge. He,
Young Spenser, and Baldock enter, accompanied by the Abbot
and Monks.*

ABBOT. Have you no doubt, my lord; have you no fear;
As silent and as careful will we be,
To keep your royal person safe with us,
Free from suspect, and fell invasion
Of such as have your majesty in chase,
Yourself, and those your chosen company,
As danger of this stormy time requires.
KING EDWARD. Father, thy face should harbour no deceit.
Oh! hadst thou ever been a king, thy heart,
Pierced deeply with a sense of my distress,   10
Could not but take compassion of my state.
Stately and proud, in riches and in train,
Whilom I was, powerful and full of pomp:
But what is he whom rule and empery
Have not in life or death made miserable?
Come, Spenser; come, Baldock, come, sit down by me;
Make trial now of that philosophy,
That in our famous nurseries of arts
Thou suck'dst from Plato and from Aristotle.
Father, this life contemplative is Heaven.   20
Oh, that I might this life in quiet lead!
But we, alas! are chased; and you, my friends,
Your lives and my dishonour they pursue.
Yet, gentle monks, for treasure, gold nor fee,

---

83. *countenance,* authority.   13. *Whilom,* formerly.

Do you betray us and our company.

MONK. Your grace may sit secure, if none but we
Do wot of your abode.

YOUNG SPENSER. Not one alive, but shrewdly I suspect
A gloomy fellow in a mead below.
'A gave a long look after us, my lord;   30
And all the land I know is up in arms,
Arms that pursue our lives with deadly hate.

BALDOCK. We were embarked for Ireland, wretched we!
With awkward winds and sore tempests driven
To fall on shore, and here to pine in fear
Of Mortimer and his confederates.

KING EDWARD. Mortimer! who talks of Mortimer?
Who wounds me with the name of Mortimer,
. That bloody man? Good father, on thy lap
Lay I this head, laden with mickle care.   40
Oh, might I never open these eyes again!
Never again lift up this drooping head!
Oh, never more lift up this dying heart!

YOUNG SPENSER. Look up, my lord.—Baldock, this drowsiness
Betides no good; here even we are betrayed.

　　　[Enter, with Welsh hooks, Rice ap Howel, a Mower, and
　　　　　Leicester.

MOWER. Upon my life, those be the men ye seek.

RICE. Fellow, enough.—My lord, I pray be short,
A fair commission warrants what we do.

LEICESTER. The queen's commission, urged by Mortimer;
What cannot gallant Mortimer with the queen?   50
Alas! see where he sits, and hopes unseen
T' escape their hands that seek to reave his life.
Too true it is, *Quem dies vidit veniens superbum,*
Hunc dies vidit fugiens jacentem.
But, Leicester, leave to grow so passionate.
Spenser and Baldock, by no other names,
I arrest you of high treason here.
Stand not on titles, but obey th' arrest;
'Tis in the name of Isabel the queen.
My lord, why droop you thus?   60

KING EDWARD. O day the last of all my bliss on earth!
Centre of all misfortune! O my stars,

---

33. Note the answer to Young Mortimer's prayer.
53. *Quem dies* . . ., Whom dawning day sees proud, Departing day sees
prostrate. Seneca, *Thyestes* 1.613.

Why do you lour unkindly on a king?
Comes Leicester, then, in Isabella's name
To take my life, my company from me?
Here, man, rip up this panting breast of mine,
And take my heart in rescue of my friends!

RICE. Away with them!

YOUNG SPENSER.   It may become thee yet
To let us take our farewell of his grace.

ABBOT [*Aside*]. My heart with pity earns to see this sight,   70
A king to bear these words and proud commands.

KING EDWARD. Spenser, ah, sweet Spenser, thus then must we part?

YOUNG SPENSER. We must, my lord, so will the angry Heavens.

KING EDWARD. Nay, so will hell and cruel Mortimer;
The gentle Heavens have not to do in this.

BALDOCK. My lord, it is in vain to grieve or storm.
Here humbly of your grace we take our leaves;
Our lots are cast; I fear me, so is thine.

KING EDWARD. In Heaven we may, in earth never shall we meet;
And, Leicester, say, what shall become of us?   80

LEICESTER. Your majesty must go to Killingworth.

KING EDWARD. Must! 'tis somewhat hard, when kings must go.

LEICESTER. Here is a litter ready for your grace,
That waits your pleasure, and the day grows old.

RICE. As good be gone, as stay and be benighted.

KING EDWARD. A litter hast thou? lay me in a hearse,
And to the gates of hell convey me hence;
Let Pluto's bells ring out my fatal knell,
And hags howl for my death at Charon's shore,
For friends hath Edward none but these,   90
And these must die under a tyrant's sword.

RICE. My lord, be going; care not for these,
For we shall see them shorter by the heads.

KING EDWARD. Well, that shall be, shall be: part we must!
Sweet Spenser, gentle Baldock, part we must!
Hence feignèd weeds! unfeignèd are my woes;
          [*Throws off his disguise.*
Father, farewell! Leicester, thou stay'st for me,
And go I must. Life, farewell, with my friends.
                    [*Leicester escorts the King out.*

YOUNG SPENSER. Oh! Is he gone? Is noble Edward gone?
Parted from hence? never to see us more?   100
Rend, sphere of Heaven! and, fire, forsake thy orb!

---

70. *earns*, yearns, feels sorrow.   81. *Killingworth*, Kenilworth.

Earth, melt to air! gone is my sovereign,
Gone, gone, alas! never to make return.

BALDOCK. Spenser, I see our souls are fleeted hence;
We are deprived the sunshine of our life:
Make for a new life, man; throw up thy eyes,
And heart and hands to Heaven's immortal throne;
Pay nature's debt with cheerful countenance;
Reduce we all our lessons unto this,
To die, sweet Spenser, therefore live we all;   110
Spenser, all live to die, and rise to fall.

RICE. Come, come, keep these preachments till you come to the
place appointed. You, and such as you are, have made wise work
in England; will your lordships away?

MOWER. Your worship, I trust, will remember me?

RICE. Remember thee, fellow! what else? Follow me to the town.
                    [*They take Spenser and Baldock out.*

ACT V

SCENE I

A ROOM AT KENILWORTH CASTLE, *to which Leicester has brought
the King since the last scene. Now the party of the nobles is
ready to force him to resign the crown to his son. The King
enters with Leicester, the Bishop of Winchester, and Sir William Trussel, who have come to take his crown from him and
give it to his son.*

LEICESTER. Be patient, good my lord, cease to lament,
Imagine Killingworth Castle were your court,
And that you lay for pleasure here a space,
Not of compulsion or necessity.

KING EDWARD. Leicester, if gentle words might comfort me,
Thy speeches long ago had eased my sorrows;
For kind and loving hast thou always been.
The griefs of private men are soon allayed,
But not of kings. The forest deer, being struck,
Runs to an herb that closeth up the wounds;   10
But, when the imperial lion's flesh is gored,
He rends and tears it with his wrathful paw,
And highly scorning that the lowly earth
Should drink his blood, mounts up into the air.
And so it fares with me, whose dauntless mind

The ambitious Mortimer would seek to curb,
And that unnatural queen, false Isabel,
That thus hath pent and mewed me in a prison;
For such outrageous passions cloy my soul,
As with the wings of rancour and disdain, 20
Full often am I soaring up to Heaven,
To plain me to the gods against them both.
But, when I call to mind I am a king,
Methinks I should revenge me of the wrongs,
That Mortimer and Isabel have done.
But what are kings, when regiment is gone,
But perfect shadows in a sunshine day?
My nobles rule, I bear the name of king;
I wear the crown, but am controlled by them,
By Mortimer, and my unconstant queen, 30
Who spots my nuptial bed with infamy;
Whilst I am lodged within this cave of care,
Where sorrow at my elbow still attends,
To company my heart with sad laments,
That bleeds within me for this strange exchange.
But tell me, must I now resign my crown,
To make usurping Mortimer a king?

BISHOP OF WINCHESTER. Your grace mistakes; it is for England's
good,
And princely Edward's right we crave the crown.

KING EDWARD. No, 'tis for Mortimer, not Edward's head; 40
For he's a lamb, encompassèd by wolves,
Which in a moment will abridge his life.
But if proud Mortimer do wear this crown,
Heavens turn it to a blaze of quenchless fire!
Or like the snaky wreath of Tisiphon,
Engirt the temples of his hateful head;
So shall not England's vine be perishèd,
But Edward's name survives, though Edward dies.

LEICESTER. My lord, why waste you thus the time away?
They stay your answer; will you yield your crown? 50

KING EDWARD. Ah, Leicester, weigh how hardly I can brook
To lose my crown and kingdom without cause;
To give ambitious Mortimer my right,
That like a mountain overwhelms my bliss,
In which extreme my mind here murdered is.
But what the heavens appoint, I must obey!

22. *plain*, complain.   45. *Tisiphon*, one of the Furies.   50. *stay*, await.

Here, take my crown; the life of Edward too;
> [*Taking off the crown, but almost immediately changing his mind.*

Two kings in England cannot reign at once.
But stay awhile, let me be king till night,
That I may gaze upon this glittering crown;   60
So shall my eyes receive their last content,
My head, the latest honour due to it,
And jointly both yield up their wishèd right.
Continue ever thou celestial sun;
Let never silent night possess this clime:
Stand still you watches of the element;
All times and seasons, rest you at a stay,
That Edward may be still fair England's king!
But day's bright beams doth vanish fast away,
And needs I must resign my wishèd crown.   70
Inhuman creatures! nursed with tiger's milk!
Why gape you for your sovereign's overthrow!
My diadem I mean, and guiltless life.
See, monsters, see, I'll wear my crown again!
> [*He puts on the crown.*

What, fear you not the fury of your king?
But, hapless Edward, thou art fondly led;
They pass not for thy frowns as late they did,
But seek to make a new-elected king;
Which fills my mind with strange despairing thoughts,
Which thoughts are martyrèd with endless torments;   80
And in this torment comfort find I none,
But that I feel the crown upon my head;
And therefore let me wear it yet awhile.

TRUSSEL. My lord, the parliament must have present news,
And therefore say, will you resign or no?

KING EDWARD [*Breaking into a rage*]. I'll not resign, but whilst I
live be king.
Traitors, be gone! and join you with Mortimer!
Elect, conspire, install, do what you will—
Their blood and yours shall seal these treacheries!

BISHOP OF WINCHESTER. This answer we'll return, and so fare-   90
well.
> [*Going with Trussel.*

LEICESTER. Call them again, my lord, and speak them fair;

66. *watches of the element*, celestial bodies.
76. *fondly*, foolishly.   77. *pass*, care.

For if they go, the prince shall lose his right.

KING EDWARD [*Overwhelmed and defeated*]. Call thou them back,
    I have no power to speak.

LEICESTER. My lord, the king is willing to resign.

BISHOP OF WINCHESTER. If he be not, let him choose.

KING EDWARD. Oh, would I might! but Heavens and earth con-
    spire
    To make me miserable! Here, receive my crown;
    Receive it? no, these innocent hands of mine
    Shall not be guilty of so foul a crime.
    He of you all that most desires my blood,   100
    And will be called the murderer of a king,
    Take it. What, are you moved? pity you me?
    Then send for unrelenting Mortimer,
    And Isabel, whose eyes, being turned to steel,
    Will sooner sparkle fire than shed a tear.
    Yet stay, for rather than I'll look on them,
    Here, here! [*Gives the crown.*] Now, sweet God of Heaven,
    Make me despise this transitory pomp,
    And sit for aye enthronizèd in Heaven!
    Come, death, and with thy fingers close my eyes,   110
    Or if I live, let me forget myself.

BISHOP OF WINCHESTER. My lord—

KING EDWARD. Call me not lord; away—out of my sight:
    Ah, pardon me: grief makes me lunatic!
    Let not that Mortimer protect my son;
    More safety is there in a tiger's jaws,
    Than his embracements. Bear this to the queen,
    Wet with my tears, and dried again with sighs;
        [*Gives a handkerchief.*
    If with the sight thereof she be not moved,
    Return it back and dip it in my blood.   120
    Commend me to my son, and bid him rule
    Better than I. Yet how have I transgressed,
    Unless it be with too much clemency?

TRUSSEL. And thus most humbly do we take our leave.

KING EDWARD. Farewell;
           [*Exeunt the Bishop of Winchester and Trussel.*
           I know the next news that they bring
    Will be my death; and welcome shall it be;

---

92. *right*, i.e., of succession to the throne.
115. *protect*, be Lord Protector of the realm while the young Edward is
in his minority.

To wretched men, death is felicity.

[*Enter Sir Thomas Berkeley, who gives a paper to Leicester.*

LEICESTER. Another post! what news brings he?

KING EDWARD. Such news as I expect—come, Berkeley, come,
And tell thy message to my naked breast.   130
[*He pulls open his doublet as if to be stabbed.*

BERKELEY. My lord, think not a thought so villainous
Can harbour in a man of noble birth.
To do your highness service and devoir,
And save you from your foes, Berkeley would die.

LEICESTER. My lord, the council of the queen commands
That I resign my charge.

KING EDWARD. And who must keep me now? Must you, my lord?

BERKELEY. Ay, my most gracious lord—so 'tis decreed.

KING EDWARD [*Taking the paper*]. By Mortimer, whose name is
written here!
Well may I rend his name that rends my heart!   140
[*Tears it.*
This poor revenge has something eased my mind.
So may his limbs be torn, as is this paper!
Hear me, immortal Jove, and grant it too!

BERKELEY. Your grace must hence with me to Berkeley straight.

KING EDWARD. Whither you will; all places are alike,
And every earth is fit for burial.

LEICESTER. Favour him, my lord, as much as lieth in you.

BERKELEY. Even so betide my soul as I use him.

KING EDWARD. Mine enemy hath pitied my estate,
And that's the cause that I am now removed.   150

BERKELEY. And thinks your grace that Berkeley will be cruel?

KING EDWARD. I know not; but of this am I assured,
That death ends all, and I can die but once.
Leicester, farewell!

LEICESTER. Not yet, my lord; I'll bear you on your way. [*Exeunt.*

SCENE II

THE PALACE AT WESTMINSTER. *Enter Queen Isabella and Young Mortimer.*

YOUNG MORTIMER. Fair Isabel, now have we our desire;
The proud corrupters of the light-brained king
Have done their homage to the lofty gallows,

133. *devoir*, duty.

And he himself lies in captivity.
Be ruled by me, and we will rule the realm.
In any case take heed of childish fear,
For now we hold an old wolf by the ears,
That, if he slip, will seize upon us both,
And gripe the sorer, being griped himself.
Think therefore, madam, that imports us much   10
To erect your son with all the speed we may,
And that I be protector over him;
For our behoof will bear the greater sway
Whenas a king's name shall be under writ.

QUEEN ISABELLA. Sweet Mortimer, the life of Isabel,
Be thou persuaded that I love thee well,
And therefore, so the prince my son be safe,
Whom I esteem as dear as these mine eyes,
Conclude against his father what thou wilt,
And I myself will willingly subscribe.   20

YOUNG MORTIMER. First would I hear news that he were deposed,
And then let me alone to handle him.
    [*Enter Messenger.*
    Letters! from whence?

MESSENGER.   From Killingworth, my lord.

QUEEN ISABELLA. How fares my lord the king?

MESSENGER. In health, madam, but full of pensiveness.

QUEEN ISABELLA. Alas, poor soul, would I could ease his grief!
    [*Enter the Bishop of Winchester with the crown.*
    Thanks, gentle Winchester. [*To the Messenger.*] Sirrah, be-
        gone.   [*Exit Messenger.*

BISHOP OF WINCHESTER. The king hath willingly resigned his
    crown.

QUEEN ISABELLA. O happy news! send for the prince, my son.

BISHOP OF WINCHESTER. Further, or this letter was sealed, Lord
    Berkeley came,   30
So that he now is gone from Killingworth;
And we have heard that Edmund laid a plot
To set his brother free; no more but so.
The lord of Berkeley is as pitiful
As Leicester that had charge of him before.

QUEEN ISABELLA. Then let some other be his guardian.

YOUNG MORTIMER. Let me alone, here is the privy seal.
    [*Exit the Bishop of Winchester. Mortimer calls to Attend-
    ants within.*

11. *erect*, crown, enthrone.

Who's there?—Call hither Gurney and Matrevis.
To dash the heavy-headed Edmund's drift,
Berkeley shall be discharged, the king removed, 40
And none but we shall know where he lieth.

QUEEN ISABELLA. But, Mortimer, as long as he survives,
What safety rests for us, or for my son?

YOUNG MORTIMER. Speak, shall he presently be dispatched and die?

QUEEN ISABELLA. I would he were, so it were not by my means.

[*Enter Matrevis and Gurney.*

YOUNG MORTIMER. Enough.—
Matrevis, write a letter presently
Unto the lord of Berkeley from ourself
That he resign the king to thee and Gurney;
And when 'tis done, we will subscribe our name. 50

MATREVIS. It shall be done, my lord. [*Writes.*

YOUNG MORTIMER. Gurney.

GURNEY. My lord.

YOUNG MORTIMER. As thou intend'st to rise by Mortimer,
Who now makes Fortune's wheel turn as he please,
Seek all the means thou canst to make him droop,
And neither give him kind word nor good look.

GURNEY. I warrant you, my lord.

YOUNG MORTIMER. And this above the rest: because we hear
That Edmund casts to work his liberty,
Remove him still from place to place by night,
Till at the last he come to Killingworth, 60
And then from thence to Berkeley back again;
And by the way, to make him fret the more,
Speak curstly to him; and in any case
Let no man comfort him if he chance to weep,
But amplify his grief with bitter words.

MATREVIS. Fear not, my lord, we'll do as you command.

YOUNG MORTIMER. So now away; post thitherwards amain.

QUEEN ISABELLA [*Anxious to appear faithful*]. Whither goes this
letter? to my lord the king?
Commend me humbly to his majesty,
And tell him that I labour all in vain 70
To ease his grief, and work his liberty;
And bear him this as witness of my love. [*Gives a ring.*

MATREVIS. I will, madam.

[*He and Gurney go out together.*

YOUNG MORTIMER. Finely dissembled. Do so still, sweet queen.

39. *drift*, scheme.   58. *casts*, plots.

Here comes the young prince with the Earl of Kent.

QUEEN ISABELLA. Something he whispers in his childish ears.

YOUNG MORTIMER. If he have such access unto the prince,
Our plots and stratagems will soon be dashed.

QUEEN ISABELLA. Use Edmund friendly as if all were well.

[*Enter Prince Edward, and Kent talking with him, trying
to persuade him to reject the nobles.*

YOUNG MORTIMER. How fares my honourable lord of Kent?   80

KENT. In health, sweet Mortimer: how fares your grace?

QUEEN ISABELLA. Well, if my lord your brother were enlarged.

KENT. I hear of late he hath deposed himself.

QUEEN ISABELLA. The more my grief.

YOUNG MORTIMER.   And mine.

KENT [*Aside*].   Ah, they do dissemble!

QUEEN ISABELLA. Sweet son, come hither, I must talk with thee.

YOUNG MORTIMER. Thou being his uncle, and the next of blood,
Do look to be protector o'er the prince.

KENT. Not I, my lord; who should protect the son,
But she that gave him life? I mean the queen.

PRINCE EDWARD. Mother, persuade me not to wear the crown: 90
Let him be king—I am too young to reign.

QUEEN ISABELLA. But be content, seeing 'tis his highness' pleasure.

PRINCE EDWARD. Let me but see him first, and then I will.

KENT. Ay, do, sweet nephew.

QUEEN ISABELLA. Brother, you know it is impossible.

PRINCE EDWARD. Why, is he dead?

QUEEN ISABELLA.   No, God forbid.

KENT. I would those words proceeded from your heart.

YOUNG MORTIMER. Inconstant Edmund, dost thou favour him,
That wast a cause of his imprisonment?

KENT. The more cause have I now to make amends.   100

YOUNG MORTIMER [*Aside to Queen Isabella*]. I tell thee, 'tis not
meet that one so false
Should come about the person of a prince.
My lord, he hath betrayed the king his brother,
And therefore trust him not,

PRINCE EDWARD. But he repents, and sorrows for it now.

QUEEN ISABELLA. Come, son, and go with this gentle lord and me.

PRINCE EDWARD. With you I will, but not with Mortimer.

YOUNG MORTIMER. Why, youngling, 'sdain'st thou so of Mortimer?
Then I will carry thee by force away.

PRINCE EDWARD. Help, uncle Kent! Mortimer will wrong me.   110

QUEEN ISABELLA. Brother Edmund, strive not; we are his friends;
    Isabel is nearer than the Earl of Kent.
KENT. Sister, Edward is my charge, redeem him.
QUEEN ISABELLA. Edward is my son, and I will keep him.
KENT. Mortimer shall know that he hath wrongèd me!—
    [*Aside.*] Hence will I haste to Killingworth Castle,
    And rescue agèd Edward from his foes,
    To be revenged on Mortimer and thee.
       [*Exeunt on one side Queen Isabella, Prince Edward, and
       Young Mortimer; on the other Kent.*

SCENE III

NEAR KENILWORTH CASTLE. *Enter Matrevis and Gurney and Soldiers, with King Edward. They have embarked on Mortimer's
plan for wearing the King out.*

MATREVIS. My lord, be not pensive, we are your friends;
    Men are ordained to live in misery,
    Therefore come—dalliance dangereth our lives.
KING EDWARD. Friends, whither must unhappy Edward go?
    Will hateful Mortimer appoint no rest?
    Must I be vexèd like the nightly bird,
    Whose sight is loathsome to all wingèd fowls?
    When will the fury of his mind assuage?
    When will his heart be satisfied with blood?
    If mine will serve, unbowel straight this breast,   10
    And give my heart to Isabel and him;
    It is the chiefest mark they level at.
GURNEY. Not so, my liege, the queen hath given this charge
    To keep your grace in safety;
    Your passions make your dolours to increase.
KING EDWARD. This usage makes my misery increase.
    But can my air of life continue long
    When all my senses are annoyed with stench?
    Within a dungeon England's king is kept,
    Where I am starved for want of sustenance.   20
    My daily diet is heart-breaking sobs,
    That almost rents the closet of my heart;
    Thus lives old Edward not relieved by any,
    And so must die, though pitièd by many.
    Oh, water, gentle friends, to cool my thirst,

And clear my body from foul excrements! ·
MATREVIS. Here's channel water, as our charge is given;
  Sit down, for we'll be barbers to your grace.
KING EDWARD. Traitors, away! what, will you murder me,
  Or choke your sovereign with puddle-water?   30
GURNEY. No; but wash your face, and shave away your beard,
  Lest you be known and so be rescued.
    [*They seize him and he tries to break away.*
MATREVIS. Why strive you thus? your labour is in vain!
KING EDWARD. The wren may strive against the lion's strength,
  But all in vain: so vainly do I strive
  To seek for mercy at a tyrant's hand.
    [*They wash him with puddle-water, and shave off his beard.*
Immortal powers! that know the painful cares
That wait upon my poor distressèd soul,
Oh, level all your looks upon these daring men,
That wrong their liege and sovereign, England's king! 40
O Gaveston, 'tis for thee that I am wronged,
For me, both thou and both the Spensers died!
And for your sakes a thousand wrongs I'll take.
The Spensers' ghosts, wherever they remain,
Wish well to mine; then tush, for them I'll die.
MATREVIS. 'Twixt theirs and yours shall be no enmity.
 Come, come away; now put the torches out,
  We'll enter in by darkness to Killingworth.
    [*Enter Kent.*
GURNEY. How now, who comes there?
MATREVIS. Guard the king sure: it is the Earl of Kent.   50
KING EDWARD. O gentle brother, help to rescue me!
MATREVIS. Keep them asunder; thrust in the king.
KENT. Soldiers, let me but talk to him one word.
GURNEY. Lay hands upon the earl for his assault.
    [*They seize him.*
KENT. Lay down your weapons, traitors! yield the king!
MATREVIS. Edmund, yield thou thyself, or thou shalt die.
KENT. Base villains, wherefore do you gripe me thus?
GURNEY. Bind him and so convey him to the court.
KENT. Where is the court but here? here is the king;
  And I will visit him; why stay you me?   60
MATREVIS. The court is where Lord Mortimer remains;
  Thither shall your honour go; and so farewell.
       [*Exeunt Matrevis and Gurney, with King Edward.*
KENT. Oh, miserable is that commonweal, where lords

Keep courts, and kings are locked in prison!
SOLDIERS. Wherefore stay we? on, sirs, to the court!
KENT. Ay, lead me whither you will, even to my death,
    Seeing that my brother cannot be released.

                                                [They lead him out.

SCENE IV

A ROOM IN THE PALACE. *Enter Young Mortimer, who has been
pushed on by the dangers in the situation.*

YOUNG MORTIMER. The king must die, or Mortimer goes down;
    The commons now begin to pity him:
    Yet he that is the cause of Edward's death,
    Is sure to pay for it when his son is of age;
    And therefore will I do it cunningly.
    This letter, written by a friend of ours,
    Contains his death, yet bids them save his life.   *[Reads.*
    "*Edwardum occidere nolite timere, bonum est.*
    Fear not to kill the king, 'tis good he die."
    But read it thus, and that's another sense: 10
    "*Edwardum occidere nolite, timere bonum est.*
    Kill not the king, 'tis good to fear the worst."
    Unpointed as it is, thus shall it go,
    That, being dead, if it chance to be found,
    Matrevis and the rest may bear the blame,
    And we be quit that caused it to be done.
    Within this room is locked the messenger
    That shall convey it, and perform the rest:
    And by a secret token that he bears,
    Shall he be murdered when the deed is done.—   20
    Lightborn, come forth!
      [Enter Lightborn.
    Art thou so resolute as thou wast?
LIGHTBORN. What else, my lord? and far more resolute.
YOUNG MORTIMER. And hast thou cast how to accomplish it?
LIGHTBORN. Ay, ay, and none shall know which way he died.
YOUNG MORTIMER. But at his looks, Lightborn, thou wilt relent.
LIGHTBORN. Relent! ha, ha! I use much to relent.
YOUNG MORTIMER. Well, do it bravely, and be secret.
LIGHTBORN. You shall not need to give instructions;

---

    13. *unpointed,* unpunctuated.   27. *use much,* am much accustomed.

'Tis not the first time I have killed a man.   30
I learned in Naples how to poison flowers;
To strangle with a lawn thrust through the throat;
To pierce the windpipe with a needle's point;
Or whilst one is asleep, to take a quill
And blow a little powder in his ears:
Or open his mouth and pour quicksilver down.
And yet I have a braver way than these.
YOUNG MORTIMER. What's that?
LIGHTBORN. Nay, you shall pardon me; none shall know my tricks.
YOUNG MORTIMER. I care not how it is, so it be not spied.   40
    Deliver this to Gurney and Matrevis.   [Gives letter.
    At every ten miles end thou hast a horse.
    Take this [Gives money]: away! and never see me more.
LIGHTBORN. No!
YOUNG MORTIMER. No; unless thou bring me news of Edward's
        death.
LIGHTBORN. That will I quickly do. Farewell, my lord.
    [He goes out, and Mortimer meditates on his own situation.
YOUNG MORTIMER. The prince I rule, the queen do I command,
    And with a lowly congé to the ground,
    The proudest lords salute me as I pass;
    I seal, I cancel, I do what I will.   50
    Feared am I more than loved—let me be feared,
    And when I frown, make all the court look pale.
    I view the prince with Aristarchus' eyes,
    Whose looks were as a breeching to a boy.
    They thrust upon me the protectorship,
    And sue to me for that that I desire.
    While at the council-table, grave enough,
    And not unlike a bashful puritan,
    First I complain of imbecility,
    Saying it is onus quam gravissimum;   60
    Till being interrupted by my friends,
    Suscepi that provinciam as they term it;
    And to conclude, I am Protector now.
    Now is all sure: the queen and Mortimer
    Shall rule the realm, the king; and none rules us.

32. *lawn*, handkerchief or strip of linen. *through*, down. The advantage of these methods would be that they would leave no mark to prove that murder had been done.

53. *Aristarchus*, a great Greek scholar of the second century, B.C.
54. *breeching*, flogging.   60. *onus . . .*, a most heavy burden.
62. *Suscepi . . . provinciam*, I have undertaken that office.

Mine enemies will I plague, my friends advance;
And what I list command who dare control?
Major sum quam cui possit fortuna nocere.
And that this be the coronation day,
It pleaseth me, and Isabel the queen.　　[*Trumpets within.*　70
The trumpets sound, I must go take my place.

[*Enter King Edward the Third, who has just been crowned,
Queen Isabella, the Archbishop of Canterbury, Champion
and Nobles.*

ARCHBISHOP. Long live King Edward, by the grace of God,
　King of England and Lord of Ireland!
CHAMPION. If any Christian, Heathen, Turk, or Jew,
　Dares but affirm that Edward's not true king,
　And will avouch his saying with the sword,
　I am the champion that will combat him.
YOUNG MORTIMER. None comes; sound trumpets.
　　[*Trumpets sound.*
KING EDWARD THIRD.　　　　　Champion, here's to thee.
　　[*Gives a purse.*
QUEEN ISABELLA. Lord Mortimer, now take him to your charge.
　　[*Enter Soldiers, with Kent prisoner.*
YOUNG MORTIMER. What traitor have we there with blades and
　bills?　　　　　　　　　　　　　　　　　　　80
SOLDIER. Edmund, the Earl of Kent.
KING EDWARD THIRD.　　　　What hath he done?
SOLDIER. 'A would have taken the king away perforce,
　As we were bringing him to Killingworth.
YOUNG MORTIMER. Did you attempt his rescue, Edmund? speak.
KENT. Mortimer, I did; he is our king,
　And thou compell'st this prince to wear the crown.
YOUNG MORTIMER. Strike off his head! He shall have martial law.
KENT. Strike off my head! base traitor, I defy thee!
KING EDWARD THIRD. My lord, he is my uncle, and shall live.
YOUNG MORTIMER. My lord, he is your enemy, and shall die.　90
KENT. Stay, villains!
KING EDWARD THIRD. Sweet mother, if I cannot pardon him,
　Entreat my Lord Protector for his life.
QUEEN ISABELLA. Son, be content; I dare not speak a word.
KING EDWARD THIRD. Nor I, and yet methinks I should command;
　But, seeing I cannot, I'll entreat for him—
　My lord, if you will let my uncle live,

68. *Major sum* . . ., I am too great for Fortune to harm me. (Ovid,
Metamorphoses, vi, 195.)

I will requite it when I come to age.

YOUNG MORTIMER. 'Tis for your highness' good, and for the
realm's.—

    [*To the attendants.*] How often shall I bid you bear him
hence?   100

KENT. Art thou king? must I die at thy command?

YOUNG MORTIMER. At our command.—Once more away with him.

KENT. Let me but stay and speak; I will not go.

    Either my brother or his son is king,

    And none of both them thirst for Edmund's blood:

    And therefore, soldiers, whither will you hale me?

    [*Soldiers hale Kent away, to be beheaded.*

KING EDWARD THIRD. What safety may I look for at his hands,

    If that my uncle shall be murdered thus?

QUEEN ISABELLA. Fear not, sweet boy, I'll guard thee from thy
foes;

    Had Edmund lived, he would have sought thy death.   110

    Come, son, we'll ride a-hunting in the park.

KING EDWARD THIRD. And shall my uncle Edmund ride with us?

QUEEN ISABELLA. He is a traitor; think not on him; come.

                                         [*Exeunt.*

SCENE V

WITHIN BERKELEY CASTLE. *Enter Matrevis and Gurney. They have
been continuing their ill treatment of the King, and are disturbed that he proves so tough.*

MATREVIS. Gurney, I wonder the king dies not,

    Being in a vault up to the knees in water,

    To which the channels of the castle run,

    From whence a damp continually ariseth,

    That were enough to poison any man,

    Much more a king brought up so tenderly.

GURNEY. And so do I, Matrevis: yesternight

    I opened but the door to throw him meat,

    And I was almost stifled with the savour.

MATREVIS. He hath a body able to endure   10

    More than we can inflict: and therefore now

    Let us assail his mind another while.

GURNEY. Send for him out thence, and I will anger him.

MATREVIS. But stay, who's this?

    [*Enter Lightborn.*

LIGHTBORN.   My Lord Protector greets you.
        [*Gives letter.*
GURNEY. What's here? I know not how to conster it.
MATREVIS. Gurney, it was left unpointed for the nonce;
    "*Edwardum occidere nolite timere,*"
    That's his meaning.
LIGHTBORN. Know you this token? I must have the king.
        [*Gives token.*
MATREVIS. Ay, stay awhile, thou shalt have answer straight.   20
        [*Aside to Gurney.*] This villain's sent to make away the king.
GURNEY [*Aside*]. I thought as much.
MATREVIS [*Aside*].   And when the murder's done,
    See how he must be handled for his labour.
    Pereat iste! Let him have the king.
    What else? Here is the key, this is the lake,
    Do as you are commanded by my lord.
LIGHTBORN. I know what I must do. Get you away.
    Yet be not far off, I shall need your help;
    See that in the next room I have a fire,
    And get me a spit, and let it be red-hot.   30
MATREVIS. Very well.
GURNEY.   Need you anything besides?
LIGHTBORN. What else? A table and a feather-bed.
GURNEY. That's all?
LIGHTBORN. Ay, ay; so, when I call you, bring it in.
MATREVIS. Fear not thou that.
GURNEY. Here's a light, to go into the dungeon.
        [*Gives a light, and then exit with Matrevis.*
LIGHTBORN. So, now must I about this gear; ne'er was there any
    So finely handled as this king shall be.
    Foh, here's a place indeed, with all my heart!
        [*He draws a curtain and King Edward is discovered in the
        dungeon. The feather bed is put on at one side.*
KING EDWARD. Who's there? what light is that? wherefore comes
        thou?   40
LIGHTBORN. To comfort you, and bring you joyful news.
KING EDWARD. Small comfort finds poor Edward in thy looks.
    Villain, I know thou com'st to murder me.
LIGHTBORN. To murder you, my most gracious lord!
    Far is it from my heart to do you harm.

15. *conster*, construe.   16. *for the nonce*, on purpose.
24. *Pereat iste*, Let this man die.   25. *lake*, dungeon.
38. *gear*, affair.

The queen sent me to see how you were used,
For she relents at this your misery:
And what eyes can refrain from shedding tears,
To see a king in this most piteous state?

KING EDWARD. Weep'st thou already? list awhile to me.   50
And then thy heart, were it as Gurney's is,
Or as Matrevis', hewn from the Caucasus,
Yet will it melt, ere I have done my tale.
This dungeon where they keep me is the sink
Wherein the filth of all the castle falls.

LIGHTBORN. O villains!

KING EDWARD. And there in mire and puddle have I stood
This ten days' space; and, lest that I should sleep,
One plays continually upon a drum.
They give me bread and water, being a king;   60
So that, for want of sleep and sustenance,
My mind's distempered, and my body's numbed,
And whether I have limbs or no I know not.
Oh, would my blood dropped out from every vein,
As doth this water from my tattered robes.
Tell Isabel, the queen, I looked not thus,
When for her sake I ran at tilt in France,
And there unhorsed the Duke of Cleremont.

LIGHTBORN. Oh, speak no more, my lord! this breaks my heart.
Lie on this bed, and rest yourself awhile.   70

KING EDWARD. These looks of thine can harbour nought but death:
I see my tragedy written in thy brows.
Yet stay awhile; forbear thy bloody hand,
And let me see the stroke before it comes,
That even then when I shall lose my life,
My mind may be more steadfast on my God.

LIGHTBORN. What means your highness to mistrust me thus?

KING EDWARD. What mean'st thou to dissemble with me thus?

LIGHTBORN. These hands were never stained with innocent blood,
Nor shall they now be tainted with a king's.   80

KING EDWARD. Forgive my thought for having such a thought.
One jewel have I left; receive thou this.   [Giving jewel.
Still fear I, and I know not what's the cause,
But every joint shakes as I give it thee.
Oh, if thou harbourest murder in thy heart,
Let this gift change thy mind, and save thy soul!
Know that I am a king. Oh, at that name
I feel a hell of grief! where is my crown?

Gone, gone! and do I remain alive?

LIGHTBORN. You're overwatched, my lord; lie down and rest. 90

KING EDWARD. But that grief keeps me waking, I should sleep;
For not these ten days have these eyelids closed.
Now as I speak they fall, and yet with fear
Open again. Oh, wherefore sits thou here?

LIGHTBORN. If you mistrust me, I'll begone, my lord.

KING EDWARD. No, no, for if thou mean'st to murder me,
Thou wilt return again, and therefore stay.   [*Sleeps.*

LIGHTBORN. He sleeps.

KING EDWARD [*Waking*]. Oh, let me not die yet! Stay, oh, stay
a while!

LIGHTBORN. How now, my lord?   100

KING EDWARD. Something still buzzeth in mine ears,
And tells me if I sleep I never wake;
This fear is that which makes me tremble thus.
And therefore tell me, wherefore art thou come?

LIGHTBORN. To rid thee of thy life.—Matrevis, come!
          [*Enter Matrevis and Gurney.*

KING EDWARD. I am too weak and feeble to resist—
Assist me, sweet God, and receive my soul!

LIGHTBORN. Run for the table.

KING EDWARD. Oh, spare me, or dispatch me in a trice.
          [*Matrevis brings in a table.*

LIGHTBORN. So, lay the table down, and stamp on it,   110
But not too hard, lest that you bruise his body.
          [*King Edward is murdered.*

MATREVIS. I fear me that this cry will raise the town,
And therefore, let us take horse and away.

LIGHTBORN. Tell me, sirs, was it not bravely done?

GURNEY. Excellent well: take this for thy reward.
          [*Gurney stabs Lightborn, who dies.*
Come, let us cast the body in the moat,
And bear the king's to Mortimer our lord:
Away!   [*They drag out the bodies.*

SCENE VI

THE ROYAL PALACE. *Enter Young Mortimer and Matrevis, who has
just given his report.*

110. Holinshed makes clear what the action is supposed to be here. He
says that the king was murdered by having the hot spit thrust up through
his body while he was held down by heavy featherbeds or a table.

YOUNG MORTIMER. Is't done, Matrevis, and the murderer dead?

MATREVIS. Ay, my good lord; I would it were undone!

YOUNG MORTIMER. Matrevis, if thou now growest penitent
   I'll be thy ghostly father; therefore choose,
   Whether thou wilt be secret in this,
   Or else die by the hand of Mortimer.

MATREVIS. Gurney, my lord, is fled, and will, I fear,
   Betray us both, therefore let me fly.

YOUNG MORTIMER. Fly to the savages!

MATREVIS.   I humbly thank your honour.
                           [*He goes out.*

YOUNG MORTIMER. As for myself, I stand as Jove's huge tree,   10
   And others are but shrubs compared to me.
   All tremble at my name, and I fear none;
   Let's see who dare impeach me for his death!
      [*Enter Queen Isabella.*

QUEEN ISABELLA. Ah, Mortimer, the king my son hath news
   His father's dead, and we have murdered him!

YOUNG MORTIMER. What if he have? the king is yet a child.

QUEEN ISABELLA. Ay, ay, but he tears his hair, and wrings his hands,
   And vows to be revenged upon us both.
   Into the council-chamber he is gone,
   To crave the aid and succour of his peers.   20
   Ay me! see where he comes, and they with him;
   Now, Mortimer, begins our tragedy.
      [*Enter King Edward the Third, in great anger, Lords, and
        Attendants.*

1ST LORD. Fear not, my lord, know that you are a king.

KING EDWARD THIRD [*To Mortimer*]. Villain!—

YOUNG MORTIMER.   How, now, my lord!

KING EDWARD THIRD. Think not that I am frighted with thy words!
   My father's murdered through thy treachery;
   And thou shalt die, and on his mournful hearse
   Thy hateful and accursèd head shall lie.
   To witness to the world, that by thy means
   His kingly body was too soon interred.   30

QUEEN ISABELLA. Weep not, sweet son!

KING EDWARD THIRD. Forbid me not to weep; he was my father;
   And, had you loved him half so well as I,
   You could not bear his death thus patiently.
   But you, I fear, conspired with Mortimer.

1ST LORD. Why speak you not unto my lord the king?

   4. *ghostly father*, confessor.

YOUNG MORTIMER. Because I think it scorn to be accused.
Who is the man dare say I murdered him?
KING EDWARD THIRD. Traitor! in me my loving father speaks,
And plainly saith, 'twas thou that murder'dst him. 40
YOUNG MORTIMER. But has your grace no other proof than this?
KING EDWARD THIRD. Yes, if this be the hand of Mortimer.
[*Showing the letter of Mortimer to Gurney.*
YOUNG MORTIMER [*Aside*]. False Gurney hath betrayed me and
himself.
QUEEN ISABELLA [*Aside*]. I feared as much; murder cannot be hid.
YOUNG MORTIMER. It is my hand; what gather you by this?
KING EDWARD THIRD. That thither thou didst send a murderer.
YOUNG MORTIMER. What murderer? Bring forth the man I sent.
KING EDWARD THIRD. Ah, Mortimer, thou knowest that he is slain;
And so shalt thou be too.—Why stays he here?
Bring him unto a hurdle, drag him forth; 50
Hang him, I say, and set his quarters up;
But bring his head back presently to me.
QUEEN ISABELLA. For my sake, sweet son, pity Mortimer.
YOUNG MORTIMER. Madam, entreat not, I will rather die,
Than sue for life unto a paltry boy.
KING EDWARD THIRD. Hence with the traitor! with the murderer!
YOUNG MORTIMER. Base Fortune, now I see, that in thy wheel
There is a point, to which when men aspire,
They tumble headlong down: that point I touched,
And, seeing there was no place to mount up higher, 60
Why should I grieve at my declining fall?—
Farewell, fair queen; weep not for Mortimer,
That scorns the world, and, as a traveller,
Goes to discover countries yet unknown.
KING EDWARD THIRD. What! suffer you the traitor to delay?
[*Young Mortimer is taken away by First Lord and Attend-
ants.*
QUEEN ISABELLA. As thou receivedest thy life from me,
Spill not the blood of gentle Mortimer!
KING EDWARD THIRD. This argues that you spilt my father's blood,
Else would you not entreat for Mortimer.
QUEEN ISABELLA. I spill his blood? no. 70
KING EDWARD THIRD. Ay, madam, you; for so the rumor runs.
QUEEN ISABELLA. That rumor is untrue; for loving thee,
Is this report raised on poor Isabel.

50. the customary penalty for traitors, to be drawn on a hurdle to the place of execution and there to be hanged, drawn, and quartered.

KING EDWARD THIRD. I do not think her so unnatural.

2ND LORD. My lord, I fear me it will prove too true.

KING EDWARD THIRD. Mother, you are suspected for his death,
And therefore we commit you to the Tower
Till farther trial may be made thereof;
If you be guilty, though I be your son,
Think not to find me slack or pitiful.   80

QUEEN ISABELLA. Nay, to my death, for too long have I lived,
Whenas my son thinks to abridge my days.

KING EDWARD THIRD. Away with her, her words enforce these
tears,
And I shall pity her if she speak again.

QUEEN ISABELLA. Shall I not mourn for my beloved lord,
And with the rest accompany him to his grave?

2ND LORD. Thus, madam, 'tis the king's will you shall hence.

QUEEN ISABELLA. He hath forgotten me; stay, I am his mother.

2ND LORD. That boots not; therefore, gentle madam, go.   89

QUEEN ISABELLA. Then come, sweet death, and rid me of this grief.
[*She is conducted out by the Second Lord. Re-enter First
Lord, with the head of Young Mortimer.*

1ST LORD. My lord, here is the head of Mortimer.

KING EDWARD THIRD. Go fetch my father's hearse, where it shall
lie;
And bring my funeral robes.   [*Exeunt Attendants.*
                    Accursèd head,
Could I have ruled thee then, as I do now,
Thou had'st not hatched this monstrous treachery!—
Here comes the hearse; help me to mourn, my lords.
[*Re-enter Attendants with the hearse and funeral robes.*
Sweet father, here unto thy murdered ghost
I offer up this wicked traitor's head;
And let these tears, distilling from mine eyes,
Be witness of my grief and innocency.   100
[*They all go out to the sound of a funeral march.*

REALISTIC COMEDY

BEN JONSON set forth the requirements for realistic comedy in his prologue to *Every Man in His Humour* in the folio edition of 1616:

> He [the dramatist] rather prays, you will be pleased to see
> One such today as other plays should be;
> Where neither chorus wafts you o'er the seas;
> Nor creaking throne comes down, the boys to please;
> Nor nimble squib is seen, to make afeard
> The gentlewomen; nor rolled bullet heard
> To say, it thunders; nor tempestuous drum
> Rumbles, to tell you when the storm doth come;
> But deeds and language such as men do use:
> And persons, such as comedy would choose,
> When she would show an image of the times,
> And sport with human follies, not with crimes.
> Except we make 'hem such by loving still
> Our popular errors, when we know they're ill.
> I mean, such errors, as you'll all confess,
> By laughing at them, they deserve no less:
> Which when you heartily do, there's hope left then,
> You, that have so graced monsters, may like men.

The realist is always in a way a moralist, but only in the broadest sense of that term. He looks with dispassionate eyes upon the human comedy that unfolds itself before him and because reason keeps his vision clear he is able to laugh rather than weep. If he really wishes to reform society, which the great comic writer seldom openly avows, it is by exposing its follies rather than by preaching at its wickedness and threatening the fate of Sodom and Gomorrah. There is little or none of the comic artist in a Jonah or a Jeremiah.

The creed of the realist in drama is that men are interesting as they are. In the wide view of things, in terms of eternal and immutable reality, they may be insignificant, but in this transient bit of time and space they are important enough to merit study, to be worth vivisection, if you will. So with a surgeon's scalpel the realist goes to work. Such work obviously calls for deftness, a quick, sure skill that is unhampered by too much sympathy for the patient, too much of any emotion on the part of the surgeon. He must remain aloof from his subject, he must cultivate a quality of disinterestedness that he may see clearly and cut cleanly in the right places.

It is not true, as is sometimes implied, that the realist deals only with the sordid—except as folly in the strictest sense is always sordid. He tries to see life in all its aspects. A realist like Erasmus found folly in every walk of life, on every plane of society. But it is true that the dramatist who chooses realistic subject matter often finds his richest subjects in the lower levels of society, rather than in the courts of kings, but that is because there must be a sort of immediacy in realism. It must be concerned with people who are as much like us, the audience, as possible in their general situation. Courts have inevitably something of the romance of distance and inaccessibility about them; the city streets and the people who walk them can be viewed more closely and with fewer illusions.

Ben Jonson is the classicist among the popular dramatists of the Elizabethan period. Rejecting the free structure of the drama developed by his predecessors and used by his contemporaries, Jonson adapted to the English public stage in his plays the unified patterns of the classical theater as it was understood by the critics of the Renaissance. Perhaps priding himself on his classical training (he had been educated at Westminster School under the famous scholar, William Camden) he followed the patterns of such classical writers of comedy as Plautus and Terence. The time of the action must not be more than twenty-four hours; there must be no real change of scene, and there must be only a single action. If one compares such comedies as Greene's *Friar Bacon*, Shakespeare's *Twelfth Night*, or Shaw's *Candida* (to take examples at random) with the *Alchemist*, one sees the great difference in effect which results from differing points of view as to dramatic structure. Coleridge listed the plot of the *Alchemist* as one of the finest in all literature, and unquestionably much of its effectiveness comes from the compression of the story, the skilful building up of climaxes, and the rich use of irony both in character and situation. The author makes his medium appropriate to his subject and his method.

Jonson was somewhat younger than Shakespeare and Marlowe. Born in 1573, he was educated, as was said, at Westminster School. For a time he worked as a bricklayer, a trade he learned from his step-father. Tiring of that he went off with an English force to fight in the Low Countries. Back in London by 1592 he turned to the theater, probably first as an actor, then as a playwright. According to tradition he was assisted in his early efforts by Shakespeare.

He led a vigorous if not violent life. In 1598 he escaped hanging for the murder of Gabriel Spencer only by pleading benefit of clergy. At the turn of the century he was involved in the "War of the Theaters", the details of which are not now fully known, but which was in part concerned with that antagonism between adult and child companies that the Player King refers to in *Hamlet*. With the coming of James I to the throne and the developing popularity of the masque as a court entertainment, Jonson developed into one of the most popular of all writers of masques, but squabbled continually with the scene designer, Inigo Jones, and with others with whom he was associated. High in the royal favor, the recipient of pensions and honors, he none the less outlived his popularity and lost the royal patronage. Gathered around him, however, were a group of young poets, "The Tribe of Ben" as they liked to call themselves, who looked upon him as their great master and whose work, as in the case of Herrick, was greatly influenced by him. Jonson died in 1637.

He made his first and most substantial name in the public theater with a special type of realistic comedy, the comedy of humours, which he did not originate but which he brought to a high point of perfection. It was a type of comedy that made capital of the flaws or aberrations in personality which resulted from a superabundance of one of the four "humours" which made up an individual's character.

He never departed completely from his interest in humours, but in the years from 1601 to 1616 he devoted himself to true realistic comedy, producing such plays as *Volpone* and the *Alchemist;* and to tragedy on classical models, *Sejanus* and *Catiline.* In his last years his satiric spirit developed more and more strongly in such plays as the *Staple of the News* and the *Tale of a Tub.* Yet when he died he left a fragment, one of his most charming pieces, *The Sad Shepherd; a Tale of Robin Hood.* It is well to remember, however, that his greatest popularity from about 1600 on came from his masques and courtly entertainments.

He was a great realist because his was a critical mind, not only with respect to society but also with respect to the literary art. He was a thoughtful and discerning observer of life and art, less genial in his acceptance of it as material for comedy than was his great contemporary, Shakespeare.

In the notes to this text no attempt is made to explain all the alchemical terms. Part of the humor for Jonson's audience undoubtedly came from the glib rattling off of technical terms which only experts in the "science" would be expected to know.

SUGGESTED READINGS

Davies, Hugh S., *Realism in the Drama.* CAMBRIDGE, 1934.

Eliot, T. S., *Elizabethan Essays.* LONDON, 1934.

Herford, C. H., and Percy Simpson, *The Works of Ben Jonson.* VOL. I. LONDON, 1925.

Jonson, Ben, *The Complete Plays.* EVERYMAN'S LIBRARY. NEW YORK, 1910.

Palmer, John, *Ben Jonson.* NEW YORK, 1934.

Welsford, Enid, *The Court Masque.* CAMBRIDGE, 1927.

Middleton, Thomas, *A New Way to Pay Old Debts.* MERMAID SERIES. NEW YORK, 1904.

Shaw, George Bernard, *Widowers' Houses.* NEW YORK, 1913.

Kaufmann, G. S., and Edna Ferber, *Dinner at Eight.* NEW YORK, 1922.

Hecht, Ben and Charles MacArthur, *The Front Page.* NEW YORK, 1929.

THE ALCHEMIST

by Ben Jonson

Characters

SUBTLE, *the Alchemist, temporarily staying in Lovewit's house. He corresponds to the modern confidence man*

FACE, *the House-Keeper. During his master's absence, he has brought Subtle and Doll in to work their tricks. He is the brains of the combination*

DAPPER, *a Lawyer's clerk, anxious to get rich quickly, not concerned about the means used*

DRUGGER, *owner of a tobacco shop, a simple soul but anxious to get on in the world*

LOVEWIT, *the Master of the house, an older man, with a sense of humor*

SIR EPICURE MAMMON, *a thoroughly worldly fop without any principles at all*

PERTINAX SURLY, *a Gamester and a cynical observer of life*

TRIBULATION WHOLESOME, *Pastor of a congregation of English Puritans, exiled to Amsterdam*

ANANIAS, *a deacon there and the assistant of Tribulation*

KASTRIL, *a young man who has just come into his inheritance and who wants to learn all the city fashions and vices*

OFFICER, ATTENDANTS, *and* NEIGHBORS

DOLL COMMON, *a Prostitute in league with Subtle and Face*

DAME PLIANT, *Kastril's sister, a widow, with not many brains but of great pliability*

To the Lady Most Deserving Her Name and Blood,

LADY MARY WROTH

Madam,

In the age of sacrifices, the truth of religion was not in the greatness and fat of the offerings, but in the devotion and zeal of the sacrificers: else what could a handful of gums have done in the sight of a hecatomb? or how might I appear at this altar, except with those affections that no less love the light and witness, than they have the conscience of your virtue? If what I offer bear an acceptable odour, and hold the first strength, it is your value of it, which remembers where, when, and to whom it was kindled. Otherwise, as the times are, there comes rarely forth that thing so full of authority or example, but by assiduity and   10 custom grows less and loses. This yet, safe in your judgement (which is a Sidney's) is forbidden to speak more, lest it talk or look like one of the ambitious faces of the time, who the more they paint are the less themselves.

Your Ladyship's true Honourer,

BEN JONSON.

To the Reader

If thou beest more, thou art an understander, and then I trust thee. If thou art one that tak'st up, and but a pretender, beware of what hands thou receivest thy commodity; for thou wert never more fair in the way to be cozened, than in this age, in Poetry, especially in Plays: wherein now the concupiscence of dances and of antics so reigneth, as to run away from nature, and be afraid of her, is the only point of art that tickles the spectators. But how out of purpose, and place, do I name art? When the professors are grown so obstinate contemners of it, and presumers on their own naturals, as they are deriders of all diligence   10 that way, and, by simple mocking at the terms, when they understand not the things, think to get off wittily with their ignorance. Nay, they are esteemed the more learned, and sufficient for this, by the many, through their excellent vice of judgement. For they commend writers as they do fencers or wrestlers; who

2. *one that tak'st up*, one who accepts others' judgments on faith.
4. *cozened*, cheated.   10. *naturals*, natural abilities.
14. *excellent vice*, great deficiency.

if they come in robustuously, and put for it with a great deal of
violence, are received for the braver fellows: when many times
their own rudeness is the cause of their disgrace, and a little touch
of their adversary gives all that boisterous force the foil. I deny
not but that these men, who always seek to do more than   10
enough, may some time happen on some thing that is good and
great; but very seldom: and when it comes it doth not recompense the rest of their ill. It sticks out perhaps, and is more emi-
nent, because all is sordid and vile about it: as lights are more
discerned in a thick darkness than a faint shadow. I speak not this
out of a hope to do good on any man against his will; for I know
if it were put to the question of theirs and mine, the worst would
find more suffrages: because the most favour common errors.
But I give thee this warning, that there is a great difference between those that, to gain the opinion of copy, utter all they   30
can, however unfitly; and those that use election and a mean. For
it is only the disease of the unskilful to think rude things greater
than polished: or scattered more numerous than composed.

ARGUMENT

T he sickness hot, a master quit, for fear,
H is house in town, and left one servant there;
E ase him corrupted, and gave means to know
A Cheater and his punk; who now brought low,
L eaving their narrow practice, were become
C ozeners at large; and only wanting some
H ouse to set up, with him they here contract,
E ach for a share, and all begin to act.
M uch company they draw, and much abuse,
I n casting figures, telling fortunes, news,   10
S elling of flies, flat bawdry with the stone,
T ill it, and they, and all in fume are gone.

19. *foil*, an incomplete fall in wrestling.
30. *copy*, plentiful wit. *utter*, publish.
31. *election and a mean*, selection and moderation.
 4. *punk*, mistress.   9. *abuse*, deceive.
10. *casting figures*, telling fortunes by horoscopes.
11. *flies*, familiar spirits. *stone*, philosopher's stone.

PROLOGUE

Fortune, that favours fools, these two short hours
  We wish away, both for your sakes and ours,
Judging spectators; and desire, in place,
  To th' author justice, to ourselves but grace.
Our scene is London, 'cause we would make known,
  No country's mirth is better than our own:
No clime breeds better matter for your whore,
  Bawd, squire, impostor, many persons more,
Whose manners, now called humours, feed the stage;
  And which have still been subject for the rage   10
Or spleen of comic writers. Though this pen
  Did never aim to grieve, but better men;
Howe'er the age he lives in doth endure.
  The vices that she breeds, above their cure.
But when the wholesome remedies are sweet,
  And in their working gain and profit meet,
He hopes to find no spirit so much diseased,
  But will with such fair correctives be pleased:
For here he doth not fear who can apply.
  If there be any that will sit so nigh   20
Unto the stream, to look what it doth run,
  They shall find things, they'd think or wish were done;
They are so natural follies, but so shown,
  As even the doers may see, and yet not own.

ACT I

SCENE I

A ROOM IN LOVEWIT'S HOUSE. *During the absence of the owner, the house has been taken over by a group of swindlers who use it as the center of their operations to give them an aura of respectability. Subtle, an Alchemist, is the center of the group, but Face, Lovewit's housekeeper, is the brains of the gang. But thieves fall out, and so have these two. They enter now, Face dressed as a captain, brandishing his sword at Subtle, who is carrying a vial. Doll Common, a prostitute who is part of the gang, brings up the rear, careful to keep out of harm's way.*

FACE. Believe't, I will.
SUBTLE.   Thy worst. I fart at thee.

DOLL. Have you your wits? why, gentlemen! for love—
FACE. Sirrah, I'll strip you—
SUBTLE.   What to do? lick figs
   Out at my—
FACE.   Rogue, rogue!—out of all your sleights.
DOLL. Nay, look ye, sovereign, general, are you madmen?
SUBTLE. O, let the wild sheep loose. I'll gum your silks
   With good strong water, an you come.
      [*He threatens to throw on him the liquid in the vial in his
      hand.*
DOLL.   Will you have
   The neighbours hear you? will you betray all?
   Hark! I hear somebody.
FACE.   Sirrah—
SUBTLE.   I shall mar   10
   All that the tailor has made if you approach.
FACE. You most notorious whelp, you insolent slave,
   Dare you do this?
SUBTLE.   Yes, faith; yes, faith.
FACE.   Why, who
   Am I, my mongrel, who am I?
SUBTLE.   I'll tell you,
   Since you know not yourself.
FACE.   Speak lower, rogue.
SUBTLE. Yes, you were once (time's not long past) the good,
   Honest, plain, livery-three-pound-thrum that kept
   Your master's worship's house here in the Friars,
   For the vacations—
FACE.   Will you be so loud?
SUBTLE. Since, by my means, translated suburb-captain.
FACE. By your means, doctor dog!
SUBTLE.   Within man's memory,   20
   All this I speak of.
FACE.   Why, I pray you, have I

3. *lick figs*, the point of this scurvy allusion is made clear in *Rabelais*,
Bk. IV, Chap. 45.
   4. *out of all your sleights*, quit your tricks.
   7. *an*, if.
   16. *thrum*, base servant, dressed in livery made of odd ends of a weaver's
warp.
   17. *Friar's*, Blackfriar's, a district in London.
   18. *vacations*, i.e., between terms of court.
   19. *suburb-captain*, a pander, so called because most of the brothels were
located in the suburbs.

Been countenanced by you, or you by me?
Do but collect, sir, where I met you first.

SUBTLE. I do not hear well.

FACE.   Not of this, I think it.
But I shall put you in mind, sir;—at Pie-corner,
Taking your meal of steam in, from cooks' stalls
Where, like the father of hunger, you did walk
Piteously costive, with your pinched-horn-nose,
And your complexion of the Roman wash,
Stuck full of black and melancholic worms,   30
Like powder-corns shot at the artillery-yard.

SUBTLE. I wish you could advance your voice a little.

FACE. When you went pinned up in the several rags
You had raked and picked from dunghills, before day;
Your feet in mouldy slippers, for your kibes;
A felt of rug, and a thin threaden cloak;
That scarce would cover your no-buttocks—

SUBTLE.   So, sir!

FACE. When all your alchemy, and your algebra,
Your minerals, vegetals, and animals,
Your conjuring, cozening, and your dozen of trades,   40
Could not relieve your corpse with so much linen
Would make you tinder, but to see a fire;
I gave you countenance, credit for your coals,
Your stills, your glasses, your materials;
Built you a furnace, drew you customers,
Advanced all your black arts; lent you, beside,
A house to practise in—

SUBTLE.   Your master's house!

FACE. Where you have studied the more thriving skill
Of bawdry since.

SUBTLE.   Yes, in your master's house,
You and the rats here kept possession.   50
Make it not strange. I know you were one could keep

23. *collect*, recollect.
25. *Pie-corner*, in Smithfield, noted for its cook shops and as a place
where pigs were butchered.
29. *Roman wash*, probably swarthy.
31. *powder corns*, grains of powder. artillery Yard, the drilling ground of
the Honorable Artillery, to which belonged wealthy citizens and members
of the upper classes.
35. *kibes*, chilblains.   36. *felt of rug*, hat of coarse, cheap cloth.
42. *would make you tinder*, would give you enough tinder to start a little
fire.
51. *Make it not strange*, Don't pretend ignorance.

The buttery-hatch still locked, and save the chippings,
Sell the dole beer to aqua-vitæ men,
The which, together with your Christmas vails
At post-and-pair, your letting out of counters,
Made you a pretty stock, some twenty marks,
And gave you credit to converse with cobwebs,
Here, since your mistress' death hath broke up house.

FACE. You might talk softlier, rascal.

SUBTLE.   No, you scarab,
I'll thunder you in pieces: I will teach you   60
How to beware to tempt a Fury again
That carries tempest in his hand and voice.

FACE. The place has made you valiant.

SUBTLE.   No, your clothes.—
Thou vermin, have I ta'en thee out of dung,
So poor, so wretched, when no living thing
Would keep thee company, but a spider, or worse?
Raised thee from brooms, and dust, and watering-pots,
Sublimed thee, and exalted thee, and fixed thee
I' the third region, called our state of grace?
Wrought thee to spirit, to quintessence, with pains   70
Would twice have won me the philosopher's work?
Put thee in words and fashion, made thee fit
For more than ordinary fellowships?
Given thee thy oaths, thy quarrelling dimensions,
Thy rules to cheat at horse-race, cock-pit, cards,
Dice, or whatever gallant tincture else?
Made thee a second in mine own great art?
And have I this for thank! Do you rebel,
Do you fly out in the projection?
Would you be gone now?

DOLL.   Gentlemen, what mean you?   80
Will you mar all?

SUBTLE.   Slave, thou hadst had no name—

DOLL. Will you undo yourselves with civil war?

SUBTLE. Never been known, past *equi clibanum*,

52. *chippings*, bread scraps.
53. *dole beer*, designed for the poor. *aqua-vitae men*, dealers in strong spirits.
54. *vails*, tips.
55. *post-and-pair*, a game of cards putting a premium on bidding on the excellence of one's hand. *Letting out of counters*, i.e., to gamesters.
74. *quarrelling dimensions*, instruction in quarrelling "by the book."
76. *gallant tincture*, inclination to gallantry.
79. *in the projection*, just as the experiment is completed.

The heat of horse-dung, under ground, in cellars,
Or an ale-house darker than deaf John's; been lost
To all mankind, but laundresses and tapsters,
Had not I been.

DOLL.   Do you know who hears you, sovereign?

FACE. Sirrah—

DOLL.   Nay, general, I thought you were civil.

FACE. I shall turn desperate, if you grow thus loud.

SUBTLE. And hang thyself, I care not.

FACE.   Hang thee, collier,   90
And all thy pots and pans, in pictures, I will,
Since thou hast moved me—

DOLL.   O, this will o'erthrow all.

FACE. Write thee up bawd in Paul's, have all thy tricks
Of cozening with a hollow coal, dust, scrapings,
Searching for things lost, with a sieve and sheers,
Erecting figures in your rows of houses,
And taking in of shadows with a glass,
‛Told in red letters; and a face cut for thee,
Worse than Gamaliel Ratsey's.

DOLL.   Are you sound?
Have you your senses, masters?

FACE.   I will have   100
A book, but barely reckoning thy impostures,
Shall prove a true philosopher's stone to printers.

SUBTLE. Away, you trencher-rascal!

FACE.   Out, you dog-leech!
The vomit of all prisons—

DOLL.   Will you be
Your own destructions, gentlemen?

FACE.   Still spewed out
For lying too heavy on the basket.

SUBTLE.   Cheater!

FACE. Bawd!

93. *Write thee . . .,* set up a notice proclaiming you a bawd in St. Paul's
cathedral, where all London met.
94. *Cozening with a hollow coal,* hollowing out a piece of beech coal,
filling the hollow with scrapings of gold or silver, and stopping it up with
wax, so that the victim would think transmutation had occurred.
96. *Erecting figures,* taking horoscopes.
97. *taking in . . .,* crystal gazing.   98. *told,* written.
99. *Ratsey,* a highwayman hanged in 1605.
106. *lying too heavy . . .,* taking more than his share of food for the
prisoners.

SUBTLE.   Cow-herd!

FACE.   Conjurer!

SUBTLE.   Cutpurse!

FACE.   Witch!

DOLL.   O me!

We are ruined, lost! have you no more regard
To your reputations? where's your judgement? 'slight,
Have yet some care of me, of your republic—   110

FACE. Away, this brach! I'll bring thee, rogue, within
The statute of sorcery, *tricesimo tertio*
Of Harry the Eighth: ay, and perhaps thy neck
Within a noose, for laundring gold and barbing it.

DOLL [*Snatches Face's sword*]. You'll bring your head within a
cockscomb, will you?
And you, sir, with your menstrue [*Dashes Subtle's vial out of
his hand.*]—gather it up.
'Sdeath, you abominable pair of stinkards,
Leave off your barking, and grow one again,
Or, by the light that shines, I'll cut your throats.
I'll not be made a prey unto the marshal   120
For ne'er a snarling dog-bolt of you both.
Have you together cozened all this while,
And all the world, and shall it now be said,
You have made most courteous shift to cozen **yourselves?**
You will accuse him! you will "bring him in   [*To Face.*
Within the statute!" Who shall take your **word?**
A whoreson, upstart, apocryphal captain,
Whom not a Puritan in Blackfriars will trust
So much as for a feather: and you, too,   [*To Subtle.*
Will give the cause, forsooth! you will insult,   130
And claim a primacy in the divisions!
You must be chief! as if you only had
The powder to project with, and the work
Were not begun out of equality!
The venture tripartite? all things in common?
Without priority? 'Sdeath! you perpetual curs,
Fall to your couples again, and cozen kindly,
And heartily, and lovingly, as you should

109. *'slight*, God's light, a mild oath.   111. *brach*, bitch.
112. *statute* . . ., which forbade attempts at multiplying gold or silver, the
thirty-third year of Henry VIII, i.e., 1541.
114. *laundring* . . . *and barbing*, washing coins in acid and clipping them.
118. *grow one*, be reconciled.
121. *dog-bolt*, useless arrow, good-for-nothing.

And lose not the beginning of a term,
Or, by this hand, I shall grow factious too,   ·140
And take my part, and quit you.
FACE.   'Tis his fault;
He ever murmurs, and objects his pains,
And says, the weight of all lies upon him. .
SUBTLE. Why, so it does.
DOLL.   How does it? do not we
Sustain our parts?
SUBTLE.   Yes, but they are not equal.
DOLL. Why, if your part exceed to-day, I hope
Ours may to-morrow match it.
SUBTLE.   Ay, they *may*.
DOLL. May, murmuring mastiff! ay, and do. Death on me!
Help me to throttle him.   [*Seizes Subtle by the throat.*
SUBTLE.   Dorothy! Mistress Dorothy!
'Ods precious, I'll do anything. What do you mean?   150
DOLL. Because o' your fermentation and cibation?
SUBTLE. Not I, by Heaven—
DOLL.   Your Sol and Luna—help me.   [*To Face.*
SUBTLE. Would I were hanged then! I'll conform myself.
DOLL. Will you, sir? do so then, and quickly: swear.
SUBTLE. What should I swear?
DOLL.   To leave your fraction, sir,
And labour kindly in the common work.
SUBTLE. Let me not breathe if I meant aught beside.
I only used those speeches as a spur
To him.
DOLL. I hope we need no spurs, sir. Do we?
FACE. 'Slid, prove to-day who shall shark best.
SUBTLE.   Agreed.   160
DOLL. Yes, and work close and friendly.
SUBTLE.   'Slight, the knot
Shall grow the stronger for this breach, with me.
      [*They shake hands.*
DOLL. Why, so, my good baboons! Shall we go make
A sort of sober, scurvy, precise neighbours,
That scarce have smiled twice since the king came in,
A feast of laughter at our follies? Rascals,
Would run themselves from breath, to see me ride,

139. *beginning . . .,* when country people came to town and were easy
marks for sharpers.
160. *shark,* swindle.   164. *sort,* crowd. He refers to the Puritans.
165. *since the king came in,* 1603, seven years before the play.

Or you t' have but a hole to thrust your heads in,
For which you should pay ear-rent? No, agree.
And may Don Provost ride a feasting, long,   170
In his old velvet jerkin and stained scarfs,
My noble sovereign, and worthy general,
Ere we contribute a new crewel garter
To his most worsted worship.

SUBTLE.   Royal Doll!
Spoken like Claridiana, and thyself.

FACE. For which at supper, thou shalt sit in triumph,
And not be styled Doll Common, but Doll Proper,
Doll Singular: the longest cut at night
Shall draw thee for his Doll Particular.
    [*Bell rings without.*

SUBTLE. Who's that? one rings. To the window, Doll:—pray
   Heaven,   180
The master do not trouble us this quarter.

FACE. O, fear not him. While there dies one a week
O' the plague, he's safe from thinking toward London:
Beside, he's busy at his hop-yards now;
I had a letter from him. If he do,
He'll send such word, for airing of the house,
As you shall have sufficient time to quit it:
Though we break up a fortnight, 'tis no matter.

SUBTLE. Who is it, Doll?

DOLL.   A fine young quodling.

FACE.   O,   190
My lawyer's clerk, I lighted on last night,
In Holborn, at the Dagger. He would have
(I told you of him) a familiar,
To rifle with at horses, and win cups.

DOLL. O, let him in.

SUBTLE.   Stay. Who shall do't?

FACE.   Get you
Your robes on: I will meet him, as going out.

---

169. *ear-rent*, i.e., lose your ears in the pillory.
174. *worship*, the hangman, who received the clothes of his victims.
175. *Claridiana*, heroine in the lengthy romance of chivalry, *The Mirrour of Princely Deeds and Knighthood.*
189. *quodling*, codling, a green apple, an immature young man.
191. *Dagger*, a disreputable gambling house, much frequented by apprentices and clerks.
192. *familiar*, familiar spirit.
193. *rifle*, raffle, to dispose of horses by lottery.

DOLL. And what shall I do?

FACE.   Not be seen; away!   [*Exit Doll.*
   Seem you very reserved.

SUBTLE.   Enough.   [*Exit.*

FACE [*Aloud and retiring*]. God be wi' you, sir,
   I pray you let him know that I was here:
   His name is Dapper. I would gladly have stayed, but—

SCENE II

*Dapper, a lawyer's clerk, the first of the victims of the gang, en-
ters after first announcing his presence from outside. Face
meets him at the door as if hurrying away. Their method is to
feign great unwillingness to deal with anyone and so run up
the price.*

DAPPER [*Within*]. Captain, I am here.

FACE.   Who's that?—He's come,
   I think, doctor.
      [*Enter Dapper.*
   Good faith, sir, I was going away.

DAPPER.   In truth,
   I am very sorry, captain.

FACE.   But I thought
   Sure I should meet you.

DAPPER.   Ay, I am very glad.
   I had a scurvy writ or two to make
   And I had lent my watch last night to one
   That dines to-day at the sheriff's, and so was robbed
   Of my pastime.
      [*Re-enter Subtle in his velvet cap and gown.*
                  Is this the cunning-man?

FACE. This is his worship.

DAPPER.   Is he a doctor?

FACE.   Yes.

DAPPER. And have you broke with him, captain?

FACE.   Ay.

DAPPER.   And how?

FACE. Faith, he does make the matter, sir, so dainty,   11
   I know not what to say.

DAPPER.   Not so, good captain.

   8. *cunning,* learned.   10. *broke,* broached the matter.
   11. *make . . . dainty,* is so scrupulous in the matter.

FACE. Would I were fairly rid of it, believe me.

DAPPER. Nay, now you grieve me, sir. Why should you wish so?
    I dare assure you, I'll not be ungrateful.

FACE. I cannot think you will, sir. But the law
    Is such a thing—and then he says, Read's matter
    Falling so lately.

DAPPER.   Read! he was an ass,
    And dealt, sir, with a fool.

FACE.   It was a clerk, sir.

DAPPER. A clerk!

FACE.   Nay, hear me, sir, you know the law   **20**
    Better, I think—

DAPPER.   I should, sir, and the danger:
    You know, I showed the statute to you.

FACE.   You did so.

DAPPER. And will I tell then! By this hand of flesh,
    Would it might never write good court-hand more,
    If I discover. What do you think of me,
    That I am a chiaus?

FACE.   What's that?

DAPPER.   The Turk was here.
    As one would say, do you think I am a Turk?

FACE. I'll tell the doctor so.

DAPPER.   Do, good sweet captain.

FACE. Come, noble doctor, pray thee let's prevail;
    This is the gentleman, and he is no chiaus.   **30**

SUBTLE. Captain, I have returned you all my answer.
    I would do much, sir, for your love— But this
    I neither may, nor can.

FACE.   Tut, do not say so.
    You deal now with a noble fellow, doctor,
    One that will thank you richly; and he is no chiaus:
    Let that, sir, move you.

SUBTLE.   Pray you, forbear—

FACE.   He has
    Four angels here.

SUBTLE.   You do me wrong, good sir.

FACE. Doctor, wherein? To tempt you with these spirits?

SUBTLE. To tempt my art and love, sir, to my peril.

17. *Read*, recently convicted as a magician.

25. *discover*, reveal, "blab."

26. *chiaus*, a Turkish messenger. One had recently swindled some London merchants.

37. *angels*, gold coins.

'Fore Heaven, I scarce can think you are my friend,　　40
That so would draw me to apparent danger.

FACE. I draw you! a horse draw you, and a halter,
You, and your flies together—

DAPPER.　　　　　　　　　　Nay, good captain.

FACE. That know no difference of men.

SUBTLE.　　　　　　　　　　Good words, sir.

FACE. Good deeds, sir, doctor dogs'-meat. 'Slight, I bring you
No cheating Clim-o'-the-Cloughs, or Claribels,
That look as big as five-and-fifty and flush;
And spit out secrets like hot custard—

DAPPER.　　　　　　　　　　Captain!

FACE. Nor any melancholic underscribe,
Shall tell the vicar; but a special gentle,　　　　　　50
That is the heir to forty marks a year,
Consorts with the small poets of the time,
Is the sole hope of his old grandmother;
That knows the law, and writes you six fair hands,
Is a fine clerk, and has his ciphering perfect,
Will take his oath o' the Greek Xenophon,
If need be, in his pocket; and can court
His mistress out of Ovid.

DAPPER. -　　　　　　　Nay, dear captain—

FACE. Did you not tell me so?

DAPPER.　　　　　　　　Yes; but I'd have you
Use master doctor with some more respect.　　　　60

FACE. Hang him, proud stag, with his broad velvet head!—
But for your sake, I'd choke ere I would change
An article of breath with such a puck-fist!
Come, let's be gone.　　　　　　　[*Starting to leave.*

SUBTLE.　　　　　　Pray you let me speak with you.

DAPPER. His worship calls you, captain.

FACE.　　　　　　　　　　I am sorry
I e'er embarked myself in such a business.

DAPPER. Nay, good sir; he did call you.

FACE.　　　　　　　　Will he take, then?

SUBTLE. First, hear me—

FACE.　　　　　　Not a syllable, 'less you take.

SUBTLE. Pray you, sir—

46. *Clim*, a ballad hero. *Claribel*, a hero of romance.
47. *five-and-fifty*, the highest hand at primero. 50. *gentle*, gentleman.
61. *proud stag*, Subtle's astrologer's hat of velvet makes Face think of a stag's velvety horns.
63. *puck-fist*, worthless fellow.

FACE.   Upon no terms but an *assumpsit*.

SUBTLE. Your humour must be law.

    [*He takes the four angels.*

FACE.   Why now, sir, talk.   70
    Now I dare hear you with mine honour. Speak.
    So may this gentleman too.

SUBTLE.   Why, sir—

    [*Offering to whisper Face.*

FACE.   No whispering.

SUBTLE. 'Fore Heaven, you do not apprehend the loss
    You do yourself in this.

FACE.   Wherein? for what?

SUBTLE. Marry, to be so importunate for one
    That, when he has it, will undo you all:
    He'll win up all the money in the town.

FACE. How?

SUBTLE.   Yes, and blow up gamester after gamester,
    As they do crackers in a puppet-play.
    If I do give him a familiar,   80
    Give you him all you play for; never set him,
    For he will have it.

FACE.   You are mistaken, doctor.
    Why, he does ask one but for cups and horses,
    A rifling fly; none of your great familiars.

DAPPER. Yes, captain, I would have it for all games.

SUBTLE. I told you so.

FACE [*Taking Dapper aside*]. 'Slight, that is a new business!
    I understood you, a tame bird, to fly
    Twice in a term, or so, on Friday nights,
    When you had left the office, for a nag
    Of forty or fifty shillings.

DAPPER.   Ay, 'tis true, sir;   90
    But I do think now I shall leave the law,
    And therefore—

FACE.   Why, this changes quite the case.
    Do you think that I dare move him?

DAPPER.   If you please, sir;
    All's one to him, I see.

FACE.   What! for that money?
    I cannot with my conscience; nor should you
    Make the request, methinks.

    69. *assumpsit*, term used of a contract calling for an initial payment.
    81. *set*, bet against.   87. *tame bird*, familiar spirit.

DAPPER.   No, sir, I mean
  To add consideration.
FACE.   Why then, sir,
  I'll try. [*Goes to Subtle.*] Say that it were for all games, doctor?
SUBTLE. I say then, not a mouth shall eat for him
  At any ordinary, but on the score,   100
  That is a gaming mouth, conceive me.
FACE.   Indeed!
SUBTLE. He'll draw you all the treasure of the realm,
  If it be set him.
FACE.   Speak you this from art?
SUBTLE. Ay, sir, and reason too, the ground of art.
  He is of the only best complexion,
  The Queen of Fairy loves.
FACE.   What! is he?
SUBTLE.   Peace.
  He'll overhear you. Sir, should she but see him—
FACE. What?
SUBTLE.   Do not you tell him.
FACE.   Will he win at cards too?
SUBTLE. The spirits of dead Holland, living Isaac,
  You'd swear were in him; such as a vigorous luck   110
  As cannot be resisted. 'Slight, he'll put
  Six of your gallants to a cloak, indeed.
FACE. A strange success, that some man shall be born to!
SUBTLE. He hears you, man—
DAPPER.   Sir, I'll not be ingrateful.
FACE. Faith, I have confidence in his good nature:
  You hear, he says he will not be ingrateful.
SUBTLE. Why, as you please; my venture follows yours.
FACE. Troth, do it, doctor; think him trusty, and make him.
  He may make us both happy in an hour;
  Win some five thousand pound, and send us two on't.   120
DAPPER. Believe it, and I will, sir.
FACE.   And you shall, sir.
    [*Takes him aside.*
  You have heard all?
DAPPER.   No, what was't? Nothing, I, sir.
FACE. Nothing!
DAPPER.   A little, sir.

---

99. *for*, because of.   100. *but on the score*, except on credit.
109. *Holland, Isaac*, perhaps famous gamblers of the time.
112. *to a cloak*, i.e., leave only one cloak for all six.

FACE.   Well, a rare star
  Reigned at your birth.
DAPPER.   At mine, sir! No.
FACE.   The doctor
  Swears that you are—
SUBTLE.   Nay, captain, you'll tell all now.
FACE. Allied to the Queen of Fairy.
DAPPER.   Who? that I am?
  Believe it, no such matter—
FACE.   Yes, and that
  You were born with a caul o' your head.
DAPPER.   Who says so?
FACE.   Come,
  You know it well enough, though you dissemble it.
DAPPER. I' fac, I do not; you are mistaken.
FACE.   How!   130
  Swear by your fac, and in a thing so known
  Unto the doctor? How shall we, sir, trust you
  In the other matter; can we ever think,
  When you have won five or six thousand pound,
  You'll send us shares in't by this rate?
DAPPER.   By Jove, sir,
  I'll win ten thousand pound, and send you half.
  I' fac's no oath.
SUBTLE.   No, no, he did but jest.
FACE. Go to. Go thank the doctor: he's your friend
  To take it so.
DAPPER.   I thank his worship.
FACE.   So!
  Another angel.
DAPPER.   Must I?
FACE.   Must you! 'slight,   140
  What else is thanks? will you be trivial?—Doctor,
      [Dapper gives him the money.
  When must he come for his familiar?
DAPPER. Shall I not have it with me?
SUBTLE.   O, good sir!
  There must be a world of ceremonies pass;
  You must be bathed and fumigated first:
  Besides, the Queen of Fairy does not rise
  Till it be noon.

128. *born with a caul*, long considered a sign of good luck.
130. *I' fac*, In faith.

FACE.   Not, if she danced, to-night.

SUBTLE. And she must bless it.

FACE.   Did you never see
Her royal grace yet?

DAPPER.   Whom?

FACE.   Your aunt of Fairy?

SUBTLE. Not since she kissed him in the cradle, captain;   150
I can resolve you that.

FACE.   Well, see her grace,
Whate'er it cost you, for a thing that I know.
It will be somewhat hard to compass; but
However, see her. You are made, believe it,
If you can see her. Her grace is a lone woman,
And very rich; and if she takes a fancy,
She will do strange things. See her, at any hand.
'Slid, she may hap to leave you all she has:
It is the doctor's fear.

DAPPER.   How will't be done, then?

FACE. Let me alone, take you no thought. Do you   160
But say to me, captain, I'll see her grace.

DAPPER. "Captain, I'll see her grace."

FACE.   Enough.
        [*Knocking within.*

SUBTLE.   Who's there?
Anon.—[*Aside to Face.*] Conduct him forth by the back
    way.—
Sir, against one o'clock prepare yourself;
Till when you must be fasting; only take
Three drops of vinegar in at your nose,
Two at your mouth, and one at either ear;
Then bathe your fingers' ends and wash your eyes,
To sharpen your five senses, and cry *hum*
Thrice, and then *buz* as often; and then come. . [*He goes out.*

FACE. Can you remember this?

DAPPER.   I warrant you.   171

FACE. Well then, away. It is but your bestowing
Some twenty nobles 'mong her grace's servants,
And put on a clean shirt: you do not know
What grace her grace may do you in clean linen.
                            [*Exeunt Face and Dapper.*

153. *compass*, bring about.
168. *hum, buz*, supposed to have secret meanings in incantations.

SCENE III

Subtle is heard talking within to Abel Drugger, their second victim, who also has come for magic help.

SUBTLE. Come in. Good wives, I pray you forbear me now;
  Troth, I can do you no good till afternoon—
    [*Subtle re-enters, followed by Drugger.*
  What is your name, say you; Abel Drugger?
DRUGGER.   Yes, sir.
SUBTLE. A seller of tobacco?
DRUGGER.   Yes, sir.
SUBTLE.   Umph!
  Free of the grocers?
DRUGGER.   Ay, an't please you.
SUBTLE.   Well—
  Your business, Abel?
DRUGGER.   This, an't please your worship;
  I am a young beginner, and am building
  Of a new shop, an't like your worship, just
  At corner of a street:—Here is the plot on't—
  And I would know by art, sir, of your worship,   10
  Which way I should make my door, by necromancy,
  And where my shelves; and which should be for boxes,
  And which for pots. I would be glad to thrive, sir:
  And I was wished to your worship by a gentleman,
  One Captain Face, that says you know men's planets,
  And their good angels, and their bad.
SUBTLE.   I do,
  If I do see them—
    [*Re-enter Face.*
FACE.   What! my honest Abel?
  Thou art well met here.
DRUGGER.   Troth, sir, I was speaking,
  Just as your worship came here, of your worship:
  I pray you speak for me to master doctor.   20
FACE. He shall do anything. Doctor, do you hear?
  This is my friend, Abel, an honest fellow;
  He lets me have good tobacco, and he does not
  Sophisticate it with sack-lees or oil,

  5. *free . . .*, a member of the grocer's guild.   9. *plot*, diagram.
  14. *wished*, recommended.   24. *sophisticate*, adulterate.

Nor washes it in muscadel and grains,
Nor buries it in gravel, under ground,
Wrapped up in greasy leather, or pissed clouts:
But keeps it in fine lily pots, that, opened,
Smell like conserve of roses, or French beans.
He has his maple block, his silver tongs,
Winchester pipes, and fire of juniper: 30
A neat, spruce, honest fellow, and no goldsmith.
SUBTLE. He is a fortunate fellow, that I am sure on.
FACE. Already, sir, have you found it? Lo thee, Abel!
SUBTLE. And in right way toward riches—
FACE.   Sir!
SUBTLE.   This summer
He will be of the clothing of his company,
And next spring called to the scarlet; spend what he can.
FACE. What, and so little beard?
SUBTLE.   Sir, you must think,
He may have a receipt to make hair come:
But he'll be wise, preserve his youth, and find for't;   40
His fortune looks for him another way.
FACE. 'Slid, doctor, how canst thou know this so soon?
I am amused at that.
SUBTLE.   By a rule, captain,
In metoposcopy, which I do work by;
A certain star in the forehead, which you see not.
Your chestnut or your olive-coloured face
Does never fail: and your long ear doth promise.
I knew't, by certain spots, too, in his teeth,
And on the nail of his mercurial finger.
FACE. Which finger's that?
SUBTLE.   His little finger. Look.   50
You were born upon a Wednesday?
DRUGGER.   Yes, indeed, sir.
SUBTLE. The thumb, in chiromancy, we give Venus;
The forefinger to Jove; the midst to Saturn;
The ring to Sol; the least to Mercury,

25. *grains*, of paradise, a spice, used to flavor inferior tobacco.
28. *lily pots*, ornamental jars.
30. *maple block*, for shredding tobacco.
31. *fire*, at which customers could light their pipes.
32. *goldsmith*, usurer.   36. *clothing*, livery.
37. *called to the scarlet*, made an alderman.   43. *amused*, amazed.
44. *metoposcopy*, system of divination based on observation of the subject's forehead.

Who was the lord, sir, of his horoscope,
His house of life being Libra; which foreshowed
He should be a merchant, and should trade with **balance.**
FACE. Why, this is strange! Is it not, honest Nab?
SUBTLE. There is a ship now coming from Ormus,
    That shall yield him such a commodity   60
Of drugs—This is the west, and this the south?
    [*Pointing to the plan of Drugger's shop.*
DRUGGER. Yes, sir.
SUBTLE.   And those are your two sides?
DRUGGER.   Ay, sir.
SUBTLE. Make me your door then, south; your broad side, **west:**
    And on the east side of your shop, aloft,
    Write Mathlai, Tarmiel, and Baraborat;
    Upon the north part, Rael, Velel, Thiel.
    They are the names of those Mercurial spirits
    That do fright flies from boxes.
DRUGGER.   Yes, sir.
SUBTLE.   And
    Beneath your threshold, bury me a loadstone
    To draw in gallants that wear spurs: the rest,   70
    They'll seem to follow.
FACE.   That's a secret, Nab!
SUBTLE. And, on your stall, a puppet, with a vice
    And a court-fucus, to call city-dames:
    You shall deal much with minerals.
DRUGGER.   Sir, I have
    At home, already—
SUBTLE.   Ay, I know you have arsenic,
    Vitriol, sal-tartar, argaile, alkali,
    Cinoper: I know all.—This fellow, captain,
    Will come, in time, to be a great distiller,
    And give a say—I will not say directly,
    But very fair—at the philosopher's stone.   80
FACE. Why, how now, Abel! is this true?
DRUGGER [*Aside to Face*].   Good captain,
    What must I give?
FACE.   Nay, I'll not counsel thee.

65. *Mathlai*, etc., mercurial spirits governing **Wednesday.**
71. *seem*, be seen.   72. *vice*, clamp.
73. *court-fucus*, cosmetic favored by the court.
76. *argaile*, argol, tartar deposited by wine.
77. *Cinoper*, cinnabar.   79. *say*, try, attempt.

Thou hear'st what wealth (he says, spend what thou canst),
Thou'rt like to come to.

DRUGGER.   I would gi' him a crown.

FACE. A crown! and toward such a fortune? Heart,
Thou shalt rather gi' him thy shop. No gold about thee?

DRUGGER. Yes, I have a portague, I have kept this half-year.

FACE. Out on thee, Nab! 'Slight, there was such an offer—
Shalt keep't no longer, I'll give't him for thee. Doctor,
Nab prays your worship to drink this, and swears   90
He will appear more grateful, as your skill
Does raise him in the world.

DRUGGER.   I would entreat
Another favour of his worship.

FACE.   What is't, Nab?

DRUGGER. But to look over, sir, my almanac,
And cross out my ill-days, that I may neither
Bargain, nor trust upon them.

FACE.   That he shall, Nab:
Leave it, it shall be done, 'gainst afternoon.

SUBTLE. And a direction for his shelves.

FACE.   Now, Nab,
Art thou well pleased, Nab?

DRUGGER.   'Thank, sir, both your worships.

FACE.   Away.

[*Drugger goes out, and Face doesn't refrain from saying, "I
told you so."*]

Why, now, you smoky persecutor of nature!   100
Now do you see, that something's to be done,
Beside your beech-coal, and your corsive waters,
Your crosslets, crucibles, and cucurbites?
You must have stuff brought home to you, to work on:
And yet you think, I am at no expense
In searching out these veins, then following them,
Then trying them out. 'Fore God, my intelligence
Costs me more money than my share oft comes to,
In these rare works.

SUBTLE.   You are pleasant, sir. How, now!

87. *portague*, a gold coin.
102. *corsive*, corrosive.
103. *crosslets*, vessels. *cucurbites*, retorts.

SCENE IV

Doll enters in haste, greatly excited.

SUBTLE. What says my dainty Dolkin?

DOLL.   Yonder fish-wife
  Will not away. And there's your giantess,
  The bawd of Lambeth.

SUBTLE.   Heart, I cannot speak with them.

DOLL. Not afore night, I have told them in a voice,
  Thorough the trunk, like one of your familiars.
  But I have spied Sir Epicure Mammon—

SUBTLE.   Where?

DOLL. Coming along, at far end of the lane,
  Slow of his feet, but earnest of his tongue
  To one that's with him.

SUBTLE.   Face, go you and shift.

                                    [*Face hurries away.*

  Doll, you must presently make ready too.   10

DOLL. Why, what's the matter?

SUBTLE.   O, I did look for him
  With the sun's rising: marvel he could sleep.
  This is the day I am to perfect for him
  The magisterium, our great work, the stone;
  And yield it, made, into his hands: of which
  He has, this month, talked as he were possessed.
  And now he's dealing pieces on't away.
  Methinks I see him entering ordinaries,
  Dispensing for the pox, and plaguy houses,
  Reaching his dose, walking Moorfields for lepers,   20
  And offering citizen's wives pomander-bracelets,
  As his preservative, made of the elixir;
  Searching the spital, to make old bawds young;
  And the highways, for beggars, to make rich:
  I see no end of his labours. He will make
  Nature ashamed of her long sleep: when art,
  Who's but a step-dame, shall do more then she,

5. *trunk*, a speaking tube.   9. *shift*, change costume.
19. *plaguy houses*, houses infected with the plague.
20. *reaching*, offering.
21. *pomander bracelets*, a popular remedy against disease.
23. *spital*, hospital.

In her best love to mankind, ever could:
If his dream last, he'll turn the age to gold.

[*Subtle and Doll go out.*]

ACT II

SCENE I

AN OUTER ROOM IN LOVEWIT'S HOUSE, *immediately after the last scene. Sir Epicure Mammon and his friend Surly enter. Sir Epicure is a fop and a fool; Surly is suspicious without being intelligent. Sir Epicure is engaged in the amiable pastime of counting his eggs before they are hatched.*

MAMMON. Come on, sir. Now you set your foot on shore
In *Novo Orbe;* here's the rich Peru:
And there within, sir, are the golden mines,
Great Solomon's Ophir! he was sailing to't,
Three years, but we have reached it in ten months.
This is the day wherein, to all my friends, .
I will pronounce the happy word, "Be rich;
This day you shall be *spectatissimi.*"
You shall no more deal with the hollow die,
Or the frail card. No more be at charge of keeping   10
The livery-punk for the young heir, that must
Seal, at all hours, in his shirt: no more,
If he deny, have him beaten to't, as he is
That brings him the commodity. No more
Shall thirst of satin, or the covetous hunger
Of velvet entrails for a rude-spun cloak,
To be displayed at Madam Augusta's, make
The sons of Sword and Hazard fall before
The golden calf, and on their knees, whole nights,
Commit idolatry with wine and trumpets: 20
Or go a feasting after drum and ensign.

2. *Novo Orbe*, New World.   8. *spectatissimi*, cynosures.
9. *hollow*, loaded.
11. *livery-punk*, a prostitute in league with a swindler who tricked young heirs into lending money with worthless goods as security, or who loaned extravagant young men worthless goods instead of money. The latter is implied by what follows.
12. *seal*, sign away (his inheritance).   16. *entrails*, lining.
17. *Madam Augusta's*, probably a brothel.
18. *Sword and Hazard*, to which order Surly belongs.

No more of this. You shall start up young viceroys,
And have your punks and punkettees, my Surly.
And unto thee I speak it first, "Be rich."
Where is my Subtle, there? Within, ho!

FACE [*Within*]. Sir. He'll come to you by and by.

MAMMON.　　　　　　　　　　That's his fire-drake,
His lungs, his Zephyrus, he that puffs his coals,
Till he firk nature up, in her own centre.
You are not faithful, sir. This night I'll change
All that is metal in my house to gold:　　　　　　30
And, early in the morning, will I send
To all the plumbers and the pewterers,
And buy their tin and lead up; and to Lothbury
For all the copper.

SURLY.　　　　　　What, and turn that, too?

MAMMON. Yes, and I'll purchase Devonshire and Cornwall,
And make them perfect Indies! you admire now?

SURLY. No, faith.

MAMMON.　　But when you see th' effects of the Great Medicine,
Of which one part projected on a hundred
Of Mercury, or Venus, or the moon,
Shall turn it to as many of the sun;　　　　　　40
Nay, to a thousand, so *ad infinitum:*
You will believe me.

SURLY.　　　　　　Yes, when I see't, I will.
But if my eyes do cozen me so, and I
Giving them no occasion, sure I'll have
A whore shall piss them out next day.

MAMMON.　　　　　　　　Ha! why?
Do you think I fable with you? I assure you,
He that has once the flower of the sun,
The perfect ruby, which we call elixir,
Not only can do that, but by its virtue,
Can confer honour, love, respect, long life;　　　　50
Give safety, valour, yea, and victory,
To whom he will. In eight and twenty days,
I'll make an old man of fourscore, a child.

SURLY. No doubt; he's that already.

23. *punkettees*, young prostitutes.　　26. *fire-drake*, dragon.
27. *Lungs*, bellows.　　　　　　　　28. *firk*, stir.
29. *faithful*, full of faith, believing.
33. *Lothbury*, district where most of the metal founders worked.
36. *Indies*, i.e., as rich as the Indies in supplying gold.　*admire*, wonder.
39-40. Turn Mercury, copper, and silver into gold.

MAMMON.   Nay, I mean,
　Restore his years, renew him, like an eagle,
　To the fifth age; make him get sons and daughters,
　Young giants; as our philosophers have done,
　The ancient patriarchs, afore the flood,
　But taking, once a week, on a knife's point,
　The quantity of a grain of mustard of it;   60
　Become stout Marses, and beget young Cupids.
SURLY. The decayed vestals of Pict-hatch would thank you,
　That keep the fire alive there.
MAMMON.   'Tis the secret
　Of nature naturized 'gainst all infections,
　Cures all diseases coming of all causes;
　A month's grief in a day, a year's in twelve;
　And, of what age soever, in a month:
　Past all the doses of your drugging doctors.
　I'll undertake, withal, to fright the plague
　Out of the kingdom in three months.
SURLY.   And I'll   70
　Be bound, the players shall sing your praises then,
　Without their poets.
MAMMON.   Sir, I'll do't. Meantime,
　I'll give away so much unto my man,
　Shall serve the whole city with preservative
　Weekly; each house his dose, and at the rate—
SURLY. As he that built the Water-work does with water?
MAMMON. You are incredulous.
SURLY.   Faith, I have a humour,
　I would not willingly be gulled. Your stone
　Cannot transmute me.
MAMMON.   Pertinax, my Surly,
　Will you believe antiquity? records?   80
　I'll show you a book where Moses and his sister,
　And Solomon have written of the art;
　Ay, and a treatise penned by Adam—
SURLY.   How!
MAMMON. Of the philosopher's stone, and in High Dutch.
SURLY. Did Adam write, sir, in High Dutch?

　　56. *fifth age,* cf. Jaques' Seven Ages of Man, *As You Like It,* II, vii, 139 ff.
　　62. *decayed vestals . . .,* prostitutes of a bad district of London.
　　71. *praises,* presentation of plays was forbidden in London when deaths
from the plague reached forty or more a day.
　　76. *water-work,* built in 1595 to carry water from the Thames to the central and western part of the city.

MAMMON.   He did;
   Which proves it was the primitive tongue.
SURLY.   What paper?
MAMMON. On cedar board.
SURLY.   O that, indeed, they say,
   Will last 'gainst worms.
MAMMON.   'Tis like your Irish wood,
   'Gainst cobwebs. I have a piece of Jason's fleece, too,
   Which was no other than a book of alchemy,   90
   Writ in large sheepskin, a good fat ram-vellum.
   Such was Pythagoras' thigh, Pandora's tub,
   And all that fable of Medea's charms,
   The manner of our work; the bulls, our furnace,
   Still breathing fire; our argent-vive, the dragon:
   The dragon's teeth, mercury sublimate,
   That keeps the whiteness, hardness, and the biting;
   And they are gathered into Jason's helm,
   The alembic, and then sowed in Mars his field,
   And thence sublimed so often, till they are fixed,   100
   Both this, the Hesperian garden, Cadmus' story,
   Jove's shower, the boon of Midas, Argus' eyes,
   Boccace his Demogorgon, thousands more,
   All abstract riddles of our stone.—How now!

SCENE II

Enter Face, dressed as a Servant. Mammon rushes anxiously to him.

MAMMON. Do we succeed? Is our day come? and holds it?
FACE. The evening will set red upon you, sir;
   You have colour for it, crimson: the red ferment
   Has done his office; three hours hence prepare you
   To see projection.
MAMMON.   Pertinax, my Surly,
   Again I say to thee, aloud, "Be rich."
   This day thou shalt have ingots; and to-morrow
   Give lords th' affront.—Is it, my Zephyrus, right?

   88. *Irish wood*, there was a tradition that spiders and the like would never
breed about bog-oak.
   91. *ram-vellum*, vellum made from the skin of a ram.
   95. *argent-vive*, quicksilver.
   5. *projection*, the last process in transmutation.

Blushes the bolt's-head?

FACE. Like a wench with child, sir, 10
That were but now discovered to her master.

MAMMON. Excellent witty Lungs!—my only care is
Where to get stuff enough now, to project on;
This town will not half serve me.

FACE. No, sir! buy
The covering off o' churches.

MAMMON. That's true.

FACE. Yes.
Let 'hem stand bare, as do their auditory;
Or cap 'hem new with shingles.

MAMMON. No, good thatch:
Thatch will lie light upon the rafters, Lungs.—
Lungs, I will manumit thee from the furnace;
I will restore thee thy complexion, Puffe,
Lost in the embers; and repair this brain, 20
Hurt with the fume o' the metals.

FACE. I have blown, sir,
Hard, for your worship; thrown by many a coal,
When 'twas not beech, weighed those I put in, just
To keep your heat still even; these bleared eyes
Have waked to read your several colours, sir,
Of the pale citron, the green lion, the crow,
The peacock's tail, the plumèd swan.

MAMMON. And lastly,
Thou hast descried the flower, the *sanguis agni?*

FACE. Yes, sir.

MAMMON. Where's master?

FACE. At his prayers, sir, he;
Good man, he's doing his devotions 30
For the success.

MAMMON. Lungs, I will set a period
To all thy labours; thou shalt be the master
Of my seraglio.

FACE. Good, sir.

MAMMON. But do you hear?
I'll geld you, Lungs.

FACE. Yes, sir.

MAMMON. For I do mean

---

9. *bolt's-head,* flask.   15. *auditory,* congregation.   18. *manumit,* free.
23. *beech,* since alchemists used only beech coal. *just,* exactly.
28. *sanguis agni,* blood of the lamb.

To have a list of wives and concubines
Equal with Solomon, who had the stone
Alike with me; and I will make me a back
With the elixir, that shall be as tough
As Hercules, to encounter fifty a night.—
Thou art sure thou saw'st it blood?

FACE.   Both blood and spirit, sir. 40

MAMMON. I will have all my beds blown up, not stuffed:
Down is too hard: and then, mine oval room
Filled with such pictures as Tiberius took
From Elephantis, and dull Aretine
But coldly imitated. Then, my glasses
Cut in more subtle angles, to disperse
And multiply the figures, as I walk
Naked between my *succubæ*. My mists
I'll have of perfume, vapoured 'bout the room,
To lose ourselves in; and my baths, like pits   50
To fall into; from whence we will come forth,
And roll us dry in gossamer and roses.—
Is it arrived at ruby?—Where I spy
A wealthy citizen, or rich lawyer,
Have a sublimed pure wife, unto that fellow
I'll send a thousand pound to be my cuckold.

FACE. And I shall carry it?

MAMMON.   No. I'll have no bawds
But fathers and mothers: they will do it best,
Best of all others. And my flatterers
Shall be the pure and gravest of divines   60
That I can get for money. My mere fools,
Eloquent burgesses, and then my poets
The same that writ so subtly of the fart,
Whom I will entertain still for that subject.
The few that would give out themselves to be
Court and town-stallions, and, each-where, bely
Ladies, who are known most innocent, for them;
Those will I beg, to make me eunuchs of:
And they shall fan me with ten estrich tails
A-piece, made in a plume to gather wind.   70
We will be brave, Puffe, now we have the med'cine.
My meat shall all come in, in Indian shells,

48. *succubæ*, concubines.   61. *fools*, supply "shall be."

Dishes of agate set in gold, and studded
With emeralds, sapphires, hyacinths, and rubies.
The tongues of carps, dormice, and camel's heels,
Boiled in the spirit of sol, and dissolved pearl,
Apicius' diet, 'gainst the epilepsy:
And I will eat these broths with spoons of amber,
Headed with diamond and carbuncle.
My foot-boy shall eat pheasants, calvered salmons,   80
Knots, godwits, lampreys: I myself will have
The beards of barbels served instead of salads;
Oiled mushrooms; and the swelling unctuous paps
Of a fat pregnant sow, newly cut off,
Dressed with an exquisite and poignant sauce;
For which, I'll say unto my cook, *There's gold,*
Go forth, and be a knight.

FACE.   Sir, I'll go look
   A little, how it heightens.   [*He goes out.*

MAMMON.   Do.—My shirts
I'll have of taffeta-sarsnet, soft and light
As cobwebs; and for all my other raiment,   90
It shall be such as might provoke the Persian,
Were he to teach the world riot anew.
My gloves of fishes' and birds' skins, perfumed
With gums of paradise, and Eastern air—

SURLY. And do you think to have the stone with this?

MAMMON. No, I do think t' have all this with the stone.

SURLY. Why, I have heard he must be *homo frugi,*
   A pious, holy, and religious man,
   One free from mortal sin, a very virgin.

MAMMON. That makes it, sir; he is so: but I buy it;   100
   My venture brings it me. He, honest wretch,
   A notable, superstitious, good soul,
   Has worn his knees bare, and his slippers bald,
   With prayer and fasting for it; and, sir, let him
   Do it alone, for me, still. Here he comes.
   Not a profane word afore him; 'tis poison.—

74. *hyacinth*, a precious stone.
77. *Apicius*, a famous Roman gourmand.
81. *Knots*, a kind of sandpiper; *godwits*, wading birds of snipe family.
82. *barbels*, fresh-water fish.
87. *Go forth . . .*, a hit at King James's practice of selling knighthoods.
97. *homo frugi*, a man of virtue.

SCENE III

Enter to them Subtle, looking as sanctimonious as he can.

MAMMON. Good morrow, father.

SUBTLE.   Gentle son, good morrow,
    And to your friend there. What is he, is with you?

MAMMON. An heretic, that I did bring along,
    In hope, sir, to convert him.

SUBTLE.   Son, I doubt
    You are covetous, that thus you meet your time
    In the just point; prevent your day at morning.
    This argues something worthy of a fear
    Of importune and carnal appetite.
    Take heed you do not cause the blessing leave you,
    With your ungoverned haste. I should be sorry   10
    To see my labours, now even at perfection,
    Got by long watching and large patience,
    Not prosper where my love and zeal hath placed them.
    Which (Heaven I call to witness, with yourself
    To whom I have poured my thoughts) in all my ends,
    Have looked no way, but into public good,
    To pious uses, and dear charity
    Now grown a prodigy with men. Wherein
    If you, my son, should now prevaricate,
    And to your own particular lusts employ   20
    So great and catholic a bliss, be sure
    A curse will follow, yea and overtake
    Your subtle and most secret ways.

MAMMON.   I know, sir;
    You shall not need to fear me; I but come
    To have you confute this gentleman.

SURLY.   Who is,
    Indeed, sir, somewhat costive of belief
    Toward your stone; would not be gulled.

SUBTLE.   Well, son,
    All that I can convince him in, is this,
    The work is done, bright Sol is in his robe.
    We have a medicine of the triple soul,   30
    The glorified spirit. Thanks be to Heaven,

---

4. *doubt*, fear.   6. *prevent your day*, come before your time.

And make us worthy of it!—Ulen Spiegel!

FACE [*Within*]. Anon, sir.

SUBTLE.   Look well to the register.
And let your heat still lessen by degrees,
To the aludels.

FACE [*Within*]. Yes, sir.

SUBTLE.   Did you look
O' the bolt's-head yet?

FACE [*Within*].   Which? on D, sir?

SUBTLE.   Ay;
What's the complexion?

FACE [*Within*].   Whitish.

SUBTLE.   Infuse vinegar,
To draw his volatile substance and his tincture:
And let the water in glass E be filtered,
And put into the gripe's egg. Lute him well;   40
And leave him closed in balneo.

FACE [*Within*].   I will, sir.

SURLY. What a brave language here is! next to canting.

SUBTLE. I have another work you never saw, son,
That three days since passed the philosopher's wheel,
In the lent heat of Athanor; and's become
Sulphur o' Nature.

MAMMON.   But 'tis for me?

SUBTLE.   What need you?
You have enough in that is perfect.

MAMMON.   O, but—

SUBTLE. Why, this is covetise!

MAMMON.   No, I assure you,
I shall employ it all in pious uses,
Founding of colleges and grammar schools,   50
Marrying young virgins, building hospitals,
And now and then a church.

    [*Re-enter Face, excitedly.*

32. *Ulen Spiegel*, Owl Glass, the hero of a series of German stories of
trickery and rascality.

35. *aludels*, alchemical vessels.   40. *Lute*, Seal.

41. *balneo*, bath (of water or possibly sand).   42. *canting*, thieves' talk.

44. *philosopher's wheel*, the elements were taken in rotation, so that the
substance changed from water to earth to air to fire.

45. *lent*, slow, gentle.

46. *Sulphur o' Nature*, red sulphur, never actually produced.

48. *covetise*, covetousness.

SUBTLE.   How now!

FACE.   Sir, please you,
   Shall I not change the filter?

SUBTLE.   Marry, yes;
   And bring me the complexion of glass B.   [*Face hurries out.*

MAMMON. Have you another?

SUBTLE.   Yes, son; were I assured
   Your piety were firm, we would not want
   The means to glorify it: but I hope the best.
   I mean to tinct C in sand-heat to-morrow,
   And give him imbibition.

MAMMON.   Of white oil?

SUBTLE. No, sir, of red. F is come over the helm too,   60
   I thank my maker, in St. Mary's bath,
   And shows *lac virginis*. Blessed be Heaven!
   I sent you of his fæces there calcined;
   Out of that calx, I have won the salt of mercury.

MAMMON. By pouring on your rectified water?

SUBTLE. Yes, and reverberating in Athanor.

     [*Re-enter Face.*

   How now! what colour says it?

FACE.   The ground black, sir.

MAMMON. That's your crow's head.

SURLY.   Your cock's-comb's, is it not?

SUBTLE. No, 'tis not perfect. Would it were the crow!
   That work wants something.

SURLY [*Aside*].   O, I looked for this,   70
   The hay is a pitching.

SUBTLE.   Are you sure you loosed them
   In their own menstrue?

FACE.   Yes, sir, and then married them.
   And put them in a bolt's-head nipped to digestion,
   According as you bade me, when I set
   The liquor of Mars to circulation
   In the same heat.

SUBTLE.   The process then was right.

FACE. Yes, by the token, sir, the retort brake,
   And what was saved was put into the pelican,
   And signed with Hermes' seal.

---

61. *St. Mary's bath*, a double boiler.   62. *lac virginis*, milk of the virgin.
63. *fæces*, dregs.
71. *hay*, net for catching rabbits. Sharpers called their victims *conies*,
rabbits.   79. *Hermes' seal*, or, as we should say, hermetically sealed.

SUBTLE.   I think 'twas so.
  We should have a new amalgama.
SURLY [*Aside*].   O, this ferret   80
  Is rank as any polecat.
SUBTLE.   But I care not;
  Let him e'en die; we have enough beside,
  In embrion. H has his white shirt on?
FACE.   Yes, sir,
  He's ripe for inceration, he stands warm,
  In his ash-fire. I would not you should let
  Any die now, if I might counsel, sir,
  For luck's sake to the rest: it is not good.
MAMMON. He says right.
SURLY [*Aside*].   Ay, are you bolted?
FACE.   Nay, I know't, sir,
  I have seen the ill fortune. What is some three ounces
  Of fresh materials?
MAMMON.   Is't no more?
FACE.   No more, sir,   90
  Of gold, t' amalgame with some six of mercury.
MAMMON. Away, here's money. What will serve?
FACE.   Ask him, sir.
MAMMON. How much?
SUBTLE.   Give him nine pound; you may give him ten.
SURLY. Yes, twenty, and be cozened, do.
MAMMON.   There 'tis. [*Gives Face the money.*
SUBTLE. This needs not; but that you will have it so.
  To see conclusions of all: for two
  Of our inferior works are at fixation,
  A third is in ascension. Go your ways.
  Have you set the oil of luna in kemia?
FACE. Yes, sir.
SUBTLE.   And the philosopher's vinegar?
FACE.   Ay.   [*Exit.* 100
SURLY. We shall have a salad!
MAMMON.   When do you make projection?
SUBTLE. Son, be not hasty, I exalt our med'cine,
  By hanging him *in balneo vaporoso;*
  And giving him solution; then congeal him;
  And then dissolve him; then again congeal him;

80. *ferret,* i.e., coney catcher.
88. *bolted,* driven out.
103. *in balneo vaporoso,* in vapor bath.

For look, how oft I iterate the work,
So many times I add unto his virtue.
As if at first one ounce convert a hundred,
After his second loose, he'll turn a thousand;
His third solution, ten; his fourth, a hundred;   **110**
After his fifth, a thousand thousand ounces
Of any imperfect metal, into pure
Silver or gold, in all examinations,
As good as any of the natural mine.
Get you your stuff here against afternoon,
Your brass, your pewter, and your andirons.

MAMMON. Not those of iron?

SUBTLE.   Yes, you may bring them too;
We'll change all metals.

SURLY.   I believe you in that.

MAMMON. Then I may send my spits?

SUBTLE.   Yes, and your racks.

SURLY. And dripping-pans, and pot-hangers, and hooks?   **120**
Shall he not?

SUBTLE.   If he please.

SURLY.   —To be an ass.

SUBTLE. How, sir!

MAMMON.   This gentleman you must bear withal:
I told you he had no faith.

SURLY.   And little hope, sir;
But much less charity, should I gull myself.

SUBTLE. Why, what have you observed, sir, in our art,
Seems so impossible?

SURLY.   But your whole work, no more.
That you should hatch gold in a furnace, sir,
As they do eggs in Egypt!

SUBTLE.   Sir, do you
Believe that eggs are hatched so?

SURLY.   If I should?

SUBTLE. Why, I think that the greater miracle.   **130**
No egg but differs from a chicken more
Than metals in themselves.

SURLY.   That cannot be.
The egg's ordained by nature to that end,
And is a chicken *in potentia.*

SUBTLE. The same we say of lead and other metals,
Which would be gold if they had time.

134. *in potentia,* potentially.

MAMMON.   And that
    Our art doth further.

SUBTLE.   Ay, for 'twere absurd
    To think that nature in the earth bred gold
    Perfect in the instant: something went before.
    There must be remote matter.

SURLY.   Ay, what is that?   140
SUBTLE. Marry, we say—

MAMMON.   Ay, now it heats: stand, father,
    Pound him to dust.

SUBTLE.   It is, of the one part,
    A humid exhalation, which we call
    Materia liquida, or the unctuous water;
    On t' other part, a certain crass and viscous
    Portion of earth; both which, concorporate,
    Do make the elementary matter of gold;
    Which is not yet *propria materia,*
    But common to all metals and all stones;
    For, where it is forsaken of that moisture,   150
    And hath more dryness, it becomes a stone:
    Where it retains more of the humid fatness,
    It turns to sulphur, or to quicksilver,
    Who are the parents of all other metals.
    Nor can this remote matter suddenly
    Progress so from extreme unto extreme,
    As to grow gold, and leap o'er all the means.
    Nature doth first beget the imperfect, then
    Proceeds she to the perfect. Of that airy
    And oily water, mercury is engendered;   160
    Sulphur of the fat and earthy part; the one,
    Which is the last, supplying the place of male,
    The other, of the female, in all metals.
    Some do believe hermaphrodeity,
    That both do act and suffer. But these two
    Make the rest ductile, malleable, extensive.
    And even in gold they are; for we do find
    Seeds of them by our fire, and gold in them;
    And can produce the species of each metal
    More perfect thence, than nature doth in earth.   170
    Beside, who doth not see in daily practice
    Art can beget bees, hornets, beetles, wasps,

147. *propria materia,* particular matter.
157. *means,* the intermediate stages.

Out of the carcasses and dung of creatures;
Yea, scorpions of an herb, being rightly placed?
And these are living creatures, far more perfect
And excellent than metals.

MAMMON.   Well said, father!
Nay, if he take you in hand, sir, with an argument,
He'll bray you in a mortar.

SURLY.   Pray you, sir, stay.
Rather than I'll be brayed, sir, I'll believe
That Alchemy is a pretty kind of game,   180
Somewhat like tricks o' the cards, to cheat a man
With charming.

SUBTLE.   Sir?

SURLY.   What else are all your terms,
Whereon no one of your writers 'grees with other?
Of your elixir, your *lac virginis*,
Your stone, your med'cine, and your chrysosperme,
Your sal, your sulphur, and your mercury,
Your oil of height, your tree of life, your blood,
Your marchesite, your tutie, your magnesia,
Your toad, your crow, your dragon, and your panther;
Your sun, your moon, your firmament, your adrop,   190
Your lato, azoch, zernich, chibrit, heautarit,
And then your red man, and your white woman,
With all your broths, your menstrues, and materials
Of piss and egg-shells, women's terms, man's blood,
Hair o' the head, burnt clouts, chalk, merds, and clay,
Powder of bones, scalings of iron, glass,
And worlds of other strange ingredients,
Would burst a man to name?

SUBTLE.   And all these named,
Intending but one thing; which art our writers
Used to obscure their art.

MAMMON.   Sir, so I told him—   200
Because the simple idiot should not learn it,
And make it vulgar.

SUBTLE.   Was not all the knowledge
Of the Egyptians writ in mystic symbols?
Speak not the scriptures oft in parables?
Are not the choicest fables of the poets,
That were the fountains and first springs of wisdom,

179. *bray*, pulverize.
195. *merds*, faeces.

Wrapped in perplexed allegories?

MAMMON.   I urged that,
And cleared to him, that Sisyphus was damned
To roll the ceaseless stone, only because
He would have made ours common. [*Doll appears at the door.*]
—Who is this?   210

SUBTLE. God's precious!—What do you mean? go in, good lady,
Let me entreat you. [*Doll retires.*]—Where's this varlet?
. [*Re-enter Face.*

FACE.   Sir.

SUBTLE. You very knave! do you use me thus?

FACE.   Wherein, sir?

SUBTLE. Go in and see, you traitor. Go!   [*Face runs out.*

MAMMON.   Who is it, sir?

SUBTLE. Nothing, sir; nothing.

MAMMON.   What's the matter, good sir?
I have not seen you thus distempered: who is't?

SUBTLE. All arts have still had, sir, their adversaries;
But ours the most ignorant.—
[*Re-enter Face.*

What now?

FACE. 'Twas not my fault, sir; she would speak with you.

SUBTLE. Would she, sir! Follow me.   [*He goes out angrily.*

MAMMON [*Stopping him*].   Stay, Lungs.

FACE.   I dare not, sir.   220

MAMMON. Stay, man; what is she?

FACE.   A lord's sister, sir.

MAMMON. How! pray thee, stay.

FACE.   She's mad, sir, and sent hither—
He'll be mad too.—

MAMMON.   I warrant thee.—Why sent hither?

FACE. Sir, to be cured.

SUBTLE [*Within*].   Why, rascal!

FACE.   Lo you.—Here, sir!
[*He leaves.*

MAMMON. 'Fore God, a Bradamante, a brave piece.

SURLY. Heart, this is a bawdy house! I will be burnt else.

MAMMON. O, by this light, no: do not wrong him. He's
Too scrupulous that way: it is his vice.
No, he's a rare physician, do him right,

223. *I warrant thee*, I promise to protect thee against the effects of his displeasure.
225. *Bradamante*, heroine of Ariosto's *Orlando Furioso*.

An excellent Paracelsian, and has done   230
Strange cures with mineral physic. He deals all
With spirits, he; he will not hear a word
Of Galen or his tedious recipes.
  [Re-enter Face.
How now, Lungs!

FACE.   Softly, sir; speak softly. I meant
  To have told your worship all. This must not hear.
                                        [Indicating Surly.

MAMMON [*Sarcastically*]. No, he will not be "gulled;" let him
  alone.

FACE. You are very right, sir; she is a most rare scholar,
  And is gone mad with studying Broughton's works.
  If you but name a word touching the Hebrew,
  She falls into her fit, and will discourse   240
  So learnedly of genealogies,
  As you would run mad too, to hear her, sir.

MAMMON. How might one do t' have conference with her, Lungs?

FACE. O, divers have run mad upon the conference:
  I do not know, sir. I am sent in haste
  To fetch a vial.

SURLY.   Be not gulled, Sir Mammon.

MAMMON. Wherein? pray ye, be patient.

SURLY.   Yes, as you are.
  And trust confederate knaves and bawds and whores.

MAMMON. You are too foul, believe it.—Come here, Ulen,
  One word.

FACE.   I dare not, in good faith.   [*Going.*

MAMMON.   Stay, knave.   250

FACE. He is extreme angry that you saw her, sir.

MAMMON. Drink that. [*Gives him money.*] What is she when
  she's out of her fit?

FACE. O, the most affablest creature, sir! so merry!
  So pleasant! she'll mount you up, like quicksilver,
  Over the helm; and circulate like oil,
  A very vegetal: discourse of state,
  Of mathematics, bawdry, anything—

231. *mineral physic*, instead of the vegetable compounds of the followers
of Galen.
238. *Broughton*, a pugnacious English divine and Hebrew scholar, whose
attempts at clarifying Hebrew ecclesiastical terms resulted only in greater
obscurity.

MAMMON. Is she no way accessible? no means,
　　No trick to give a man a taste of her—wit—
　　Or so?
SUBTLE [*Within*]. Ulen!
FACE.　　　　　　　　I'll come to you again, sir. 　[*Exit.* 260
MAMMON. Surly, I did not think one of your breeding
　　Would traduce personages of worth.
SURLY.　　　　　　　　　　　　　Sir Epicure,
　　Your friend to use; yet still loath to be gulled:
　　I do not like your philosophical bawds.
　　Their stone is lechery enough to pay for,
　　Without this bait.
MAMMON.　　　　　'Heart, you abuse yourself.
　　I know the lady, and her friends, and means,
　　The original of this disaster. Her brother
　　Has told me all.
SURLY.　　　　　And yet you never saw her
　　Till now!
MAMMON.　　O yes, but I forgot. I have, believe it,   270
　　One of the treacherousest memories, I do think,
　　Of all mankind.
SURLY.　　　　　What call you her brother?
MAMMON.　　　　　　　　　　　　My lord—
　　He will not have his name known, now I think on't.
SURLY. A very treacherous memory!
MAMMON.　　　　　　　　O' my faith—
SURLY. Tut, if you have it not about you, pass it,
　　Till we meet next.
MAMMON.　　　　　Nay, by this hand, 'tis true.
　　He's one I honour, and my noble friend;
　　And I respect his house.
SURLY.　　　　　　Heart! can it be
　　That a grave sir, a rich, that has no need,
　　A wise sir, too, at other times, should thus,   280
　　With his own oaths, and arguments, make hard means
　　To gull himself? And this be your elixir,
　　Your *lapis mineralis*, and your lunary,
　　Give me your honest trick yet at primero,
　　Or gleek; and take your *lutum sapientis*,

283. *lapis mineralis*, stone. *lunary*, moonwart, the plant called honesty.
284-5. *primero*, *gleek*, card games, *lutum sapientis*, clay for sealing vessels.

Your *menstruum simplex!* I'll have gold before you,
And with less danger of the quicksilver,
Or the hot sulphur.

    [*Re-enter Face, resolved to get rid of Surly, who is too dan-
       gerous to have around.*

FACE.   Here's one from Captain Face, sir,
  [*To Surly.*] Desires you meet him in the Temple-church,
  Some half-hour hence, and upon earnest business.   290
  Sir, [*Whispers Mammon.*] if you please to quit us now; and
    come
  Again within two hours, you shall have
  My master busy examining o' the works;
  And I will steal you in unto the party,
  That you may see her converse.—Sir, shall I say
  You'll meet the captain's worship?

SURLY.   Sir, I will—   [*Walks aside.*
  But by attorney, and to a second purpose.
  Now, I am sure it is a bawdy-house;
  I'll swear it, were the marshal here to thank me:
  The naming this commander doth confirm it.   300
  Don Face! why, he's the most authentic dealer
  In these commodities, the superintendent
  To all the quainter traffickers in town!
  He is their visitor, and does appoint
  Who lies with whom, and at what hour; what price;
  Which gown, and in what smock; what fall; what tire.
  Him will I prove, by a third person, to find
  The subtleties of this dark labyrinth:
  Which if I do discover, dear Sir Mammon,
  You'll give your poor friend leave, though no philosopher,
  To laugh: for you that are, 'tis thought, shall weep.   311

FACE. Sir, he does pray you'll not forget.

SURLY.   I will not, sir.
  Sir Epicure, I shall leave you.   [*Exit.*

MAMMON.   I follow you straight.

FACE. But do so, good sir, to avoid suspicion.
  This gentman has a parlous head.

286. *menstruum simplex*, simple solvent.
287. *with less danger, etc.*, of syphilis, for which quicksilver was used as a
remedy, or the itch, which was treated with hot sulphur.
288. *one*, i.e., a messenger.
297. *But by attorney, etc.*, someone else will act in my stead.
303. *quainter*, cleverer. 306. *fall*, ruff or possibly veil. *tire*, headdress.
315. *has a parlous head*, is dangerously shrewd.

MAMMON. But wilt thou, Ulen,
Be constant to thy promise?

FACE. As my life, sir.

MAMMON. And wilt thou insinuate what I am, and praise me,
And say I am a noble fellow?

FACE. O, what else, sir.
And that you'll make her royal with the stone,
An empress; and yourself King of Bantam. 320

MAMMON. Wilt thou do this?

FACE. Will I, sir.

MAMMON. Lungs, my Lungs!
I love thee.

FACE. Send your stuff, sir, that my master
May busy himself about projection.

MAMMON. Thou hast witched me, rogue: take, go.
[*Gives him money.*

FACE. Your jack, and all, sir.

MAMMON. Thou art a villain—I will send my jack,
And the weights too. Slave, I could bite thine ear.
Away, thou dost not care for me.

FACE. Not I, sir!

MAMMON. Come, I was born to make thee, my good weasel,
Set thee on a bench, and have thee twirl a chain
With the best lord's vermin of 'em all.

FACE. Away, sir. 330

MAMMON. A count, nay, a count palatine—

FACE. Good sir, go.

MAMMON. Shall not advance thee better: no, nor faster.
[*He goes out at one door and Subtle and Doll enter from
the opposite side.*

SCENE IV

SUBTLE. Has he bit? has he bit?

FACE. And swallowed, too, my Subtle.
I have given him line, and now he plays, i' faith.

SUBTLE. And shall we twitch him?

FACE. Thorough both the gills.
A wench is a rare bait, with which a man
No sooner's taken, but he straight firks mad.

5, *firks*, runs jerkily.

SUBTLE. Doll, my Lord What's-hum's sister, you must now
    Bear yourself *statelich*.
DOLL.   O, let me alone.
    I'll not forget my race, I warrant you.
    I'll keep my distance, laugh and talk aloud;
    Have all the tricks of a proud scurvy lady,   10
    And be as rude as her woman.
FACE.   Well said, sanguine!
SUBTLE. But will he send his andirons?
FACE.   His jack too;
    And 's iron shoeing-horn: I have spoke to him. Well,
    I must not lose my wary gamester yonder.
SUBTLE. O, Monsieur Caution, that *will not be gulled.*
FACE. Ay, if I can strike a fine hook into him, now!—
    The Temple-church, there I have cast mine angle.
    Well, pray for me. I'll about it.   [*Knocking without.*
SUBTLE.   What, more gudgeons!
    Doll, scout, scout! [*Doll goes to the window.*] Stay, Face, you
      must go to the door:
    'Pray God it be my Anabaptist—Who is't, Doll?   20
DOLL. I know him not: he looks like a gold-end-man.
SUBTLE. Ods so! 'tis he, he said he would send. What call you him?
    The sanctified elder, that should deal
    For Mammon's jack and andirons. Let him in.
    Stay, help me off, first, with my gown. [*He slips out of the*
      gown, which Face takes away.] Away,
    Madam, to your withdrawing chamber. [*Doll goes out.*] Now,
    In a new tune, new gesture, but old language.—
    This fellow is sent from one negotiates with me
    About the stone too; for the holy brethren
    Of Amsterdam, the exiled saints; that hope   30
    To raise their discipline by it. I must use him
    In some strange fashion now, to make him admire me.

---

   7. *statelich*, stately.
  11. *sanguine*, red face or possibly red head.
  21. *gold-end man*, one who buys odds and ends of gold.
  22. *Ods so*, another of the mild oaths of the time.
  29. *holy brethren*, non-conformists who went to live in the Low Countries.
  31. *discipline*, form of church government.

SCENE V

Ananias enters. He is a caricature of the Puritans, generally hated
by dramatists and actors for their opposition to the theater.
Subtle feigns not to notice him.

SUBTLE [*Aloud*]. Where is my drudge?
    [*Re-enter Face.*

FACE.   Sir!

SUBTLE.   Take away the recipient,
  And rectify your menstrue from the phlegma.
  Then pour it o' the Sol, in the cucurbite,
  And let 'hem macerate together.

FACE.   Yes, sir.
  And save the ground?

SUBTLE.   No: *terra damnata*
  Must not have entrance in the work.—Who are you?

ANANIAS. A faithful brother, if it please you.

SUBTLE.   What's that?
  A Lullianist? a Ripley? *Filius artis?*
  Can you sublime and dulcify? calcine?
  Know you the sapor pontic? sapor stiptic?
  Or what is homogene, or heterogene?   10

ANANIAS. I understand no heathen language, truly.

SUBTLE. Heathen! you Knipperdoling? is *Ars sacra,*
  Or chrysopœia, or spagyrica,
  Or the pamphysic, or panarchic knowledge,
  A heathen language?

ANANIAS.   Heathen Greek, I take it.

SUBTLE. How! heathen Greek?

ANANIAS.   All's heathen but the Hebrew.

SUBTLE. Sirrah my varlet, stand you forth and speak to him,
  Like a philosopher: answer, in the language.
  Name the vexations, and the martyrizations   20
  Of metals in the work.

---

   5. *terra damnata*, grounds condemned as unfit for alchemical purposes.
   8. *Lullianist*, Lully and Ripley were two famous early alchemists. *Filius artis*, son of the art.
   13. *Knipperdoling*, an Anabaptist leader who had made great disturbance in the Low Countries in 1534, associated with John of Leyden.
   17. *Hebrew*, the Puritans, drawing largely on the Old Testament, thought Hebrew was superior to Greek or other languages, unaware that much of the Bible was written in Greek.

FACE.   Sir, putrefaction,
Solution, ablution, sublimation,
Cohobation, calcination, ceration and
Fixation.
SUBTLE.   This is heathen Greek to you, now!—
And when comes vivification?
FACE.   After mortification.
SUBTLE. What's cohobation?
FACE.   'Tis the pouring on
Your *aqua regis*, and then drawing him off,
To the trine circle of the seven spheres.
SUBTLE. What's the proper passion of metals?
FACE.   Malleation.
SUBTLE. What's your *ultimum supplicium auri?*
FACE.   Antimonium.   30
SUBTLE. This is heathen Greek to you!—And what's your mer-
      cury?
FACE. A very fugitive, he will be gone, sir.
SUBTLE. How know you him?
FACE.   By his viscosity,
His oleosity, and his suscitability.
SUBTLE. How do you sublime him?
FACE.   With the calce of egg-shells,
White marble, talc.
SUBTLE.   Your magisterium now,
What's that?
FACE.   Shifting, sir, your elements,
Dry into cold, cold into moist, moist into hot,
Hot into dry.
SUBTLE.   This is heathen Greek to you still!
Your *lapis philosophicus?*
FACE.   'Tis a stone,   40
And not a stone; a spirit, a soul, and a body:
Which if you do dissolve, it is dissolved.
If you coagulate, it is coagulated;
If you make it to fly, it flieth.
SUBTLE.   Enough.   [*Exit Face.*
This is heathen Greek to you! What are you, sir?
ANANIAS, Please you, a servant of the exiled brethren,
That deal with widows' and with orphans' goods,

27. *aqua regis*, king's water.
30. *ultimum . . .,* last punishment of gold, the alchemical process.
40. *lapis*, philosopher's stone.

And make a just account unto the saints:
A deacon.

SUBTLE. O, you are sent from Master Wholesome,
Your teacher?

ANANIAS. From Tribulation Wholesome, 50
Our very zealous pastor.

SUBTLE. Good! I have
Some orphans' goods to come here.

ANANIAS. Of what kind, sir?

SUBTLE. Pewter and brass, andirons and kitchenware.
Metals, that we must use our medicine on:
Wherein the brethren may have a pennyworth
For ready money.

ANANIAS. Were the orphans' parents
Sincere professors?

SUBTLE. Why do you ask?

ANANIAS. Because
We then are to deal justly, and give, in truth,
Their utmost value.

SUBTLE. 'Slid, you'd cozen else,
And if their parents were not of the faithful!— 60
I will not trust you, now I think on it,
Till I have talked with your pastor. Have you brought money
To buy more coals?

ANANIAS. No, surely.

SUBTLE. No! how so?

ANANIAS. The brethren bid me say unto you, sir,
Surely, they will not venture any more
Till they may see projection.

SUBTLE. How!

ANANIAS. You have had,
For the instruments, as bricks, and loam, and glasses,
Already thirty pound; and for materials,
They say, some ninety more: and they have heard since,
That one, at Heidelberg, made it of an egg, 70
And a small paper of pin-dust.

SUBTLE. What's your name?

ANANIAS. My name is Ananias.

SUBTLE. Out, the varlet
That cozened the apostles! Hence, away!
Flee, mischief! had your holy consistory
No name to send me, of another sound,

71. *pin-dust,* dust from the manufacture of pins.

Than wicked Ananias? send your elders
Hither, to make atonement for you, quickly,
And give me satisfaction; or out goes
The fire; and down th' alembics, and the furnace,
Piger Henricus, or what not. Thou wretch!   80
Both *sericon* and *bufo* shall be lost,
Tell them. All hope of rooting out the bishops,
Or the antichristian hierarchy shall perish,
If they stay threescore minutes: the aqueity,
Terreity, and sulphureity
Shall run together again, and all be annulled,
Thou wicked Ananias! [*Ananias leaves in great confusion.*]
   This will fetch 'em,
And make them haste towards their gulling more.
A man must deal like a rough nurse, and fright
Those that are froward, to an appetite.   90

SCENE VI

Re-enter Face in his uniform, followed by Drugger.

FACE. He is busy with his spirits, but we'll upon him.
SUBTLE [*Feigning great anger*]. How now! what mates, what
   Baiards have we here?
FACE. I told you he would be furious.—Sir, here's Nab
   Has brought you another piece of gold to look on:
   [*To Nab.*] We must appease him. Give it me,—and prays you,
   You would devise—what is it, Nab?
DRUGGER.   A sign, sir.
FACE. Ay, a good lucky one, a thriving sign, doctor.
SUBTLE. I was devising now.
FACE.   'Slight, do not say so,
   He will repent he gave you any more—
   What say you to his constellation, doctor?   10
   The Balance?
SUBTLE.   No, that way is stale and common.
   A townsman born in Taurus, gives the bull,
   Or the bull's head: in Aries, the ram,
   A poor device! No, I will have his name

80. *piger Henricus*, a kind of slow furnace.
81. *sericon and bufo*, probably a black and red tincture.
2. *Baiards*, blind fools, or bold ones. Baiard was a blind horse in the *Orlando Furioso*.

Formed in some mystic character; whose radii,
Striking the senses of the passers by,
Shall, by a virtual influence, breed affections,
That may result upon the party owns it:
And thus—

FACE. Nab!

SUBTLE. He shall have *a bell*, that's *Abel;* 20
And by it standing one whose name is *Dee,*
In a *rug* gown, there's *D*, and *Rug*, that's *drug:*
And right anenst him a dog snarling *er;*
There's *Drugger, Abel Drugger*. That's his sign.
And here's now mystery and hieroglyphic!

FACE. Abel, thou art made.

DRUGGER. Sir, I do thank his worship.

FACE. Six o' thy legs more will not do it, Nab.
He has brought you a pipe of tobacco, doctor.

DRUGGER. Yes, sir;
I have another thing I would impart—

FACE. Out with it, Nab.

DRUGGER. Sir, there is lodged, hard by me,
A rich young widow—

FACE. Good! a bona roba? 30

DRUGGER. But nineteen at the most.

FACE. Very good, Abel.

DRUGGER. Marry, she's not in the fashion yet; she wears
A hood, but it stands a cop.

FACE. No matter, Abel.

DRUGGER. And I do now and then give her a fucus—

FACE. What! dost thou deal, Nab?

SUBTLE. I did tell you, captain.

DRUGGER. And physic too, sometime, sir; for which she trusts me
With all her mind. She's come up here of purpose
To learn the fashion.

FACE. Good (his match too!)—On, Nab.

DRUGGER. And she does strangely long to know her fortune.

FACE. God's lid, Nab, send her to the doctor, hither. 40

DRUGGER. Yes, I have spoke to her of his worship already;

---

20. *Dee*, Dr. John Dee was a famous mathematician and astrologer of Elizabeth's reign, consulted by the Queen herself, but enjoying a reputation for dangerous magic among the common people.
21. *rug*, a coarse fabric.   22. *anenst*, beside.   26. *legs*, bows.
30. *bona roba*, pretty girl.
33. *a cop*, probably square on the top of her head, not tilted on the side.

But she's afraid it will be blown abroad,
And hurt her marriage.

FACE.   Hurt it! 'tis the way
To heal it, if 'twere hurt; to make it more
Followed and sought. Nab, thou shalt tell her this.
She'll be more known, more talked of; and your widows
Are ne'er of any price till they be famous;
Their honour is their multitude of suitors:
Send her, it may be thy good fortune. What!
Thou dost not know.

DRUGGER.   No, sir, she'll never marry   50
Under a knight: her brother has made a vow.

FACE. What! and dost thou despair, my little Nab,
Knowing what the doctor has set down for thee,
And seeing so many of the city dubbed?
One glass o' thy water, with a madam I know,
Will have it done, Nab: what's her brother, a knight?

DRUGGER. No, sir, a gentleman newly warm in his land, sir,
Scarce cold in his one and twenty, that does govern
His sister here; and is a man himself
Of some three thousand a year, and is come up   60
To learn to quarrel, and to live by his wits,
And will go down again, and die in the country.

FACE. How, to quarrel?

DRUGGER.   Yes, sir, to carry quarrels,
As gallants do; and manage them by line.

FACE. 'Slid, Nab, the doctor is the only man
In Christendom for him. He has made a table,
With mathematical demonstrations,
Touching the art of quarrels: he will give him
An instrument to quarrel by. Go, bring them both,
Him and his sister. And, for thee, with her   70
The doctor happ'ly may persuade. Go to:
'Shalt give his worship a new damask suit
Upon the premises.

SUBTLE.   O, good captain!

FACE.   He shall;
He is the honestest fellow, doctor. Stay not,

54. *dubbed*, knighted.
57. *newly warm*, recently come into his patrimony.
61. *quarrel*, i.e., the fashionable way of duelling. Cf. Touchstone's comments in *As You Like It*, V, iv, 71 ff.
64. *line*, rule.

No offers; bring the damask, and the parties.
DRUGGER. I'll try my power, sir.
FACE.   And thy will too, Nab.
SUBTLE. 'Tis good tobacco, this! what is't an ounce?
FACE. He'll send you a pound, doctor.
SUBTLE.   O no.
FACE.   He will do't.
  It is the goodest soul!—Abel, about it.
  Thou shalt know more anon. Away, be gone.   80
          [*Abel goes off rejoicing and in all haste.*
  A miserable rogue, and lives with cheese,
  And has the worms. That was the cause, indeed,
  Why he came now: he dealt with me in private,
  To get a med'cine for them.
SUBTLE.   And shall, sir. This works.
FACE. A wife, a wife for one of us, my dear Subtle!
  We'll e'en draw lots, and he that fails, shall have
  The more in goods, the other has in tail.
SUBTLE. Rather the less: for she may be so light
  She may want grains.
FACE.   Ay, or be such a burden,
  A man would scarce endure her for the whole.   90
SUBTLE. Faith, best let's see her first, and then determine.
FACE. Content: but Doll must have no breath on't.
SUBTLE.   Mum.
  Away you, to your Surly yonder, catch him.
FACE. Pray God I have not stayed too long.
SUBTLE.   I fear it.
          [*They go out in different directions.*

ACT III

SCENE I

IT IS THE STREET IN FRONT OF LOVEWIT'S HOUSE. *Ananias has brought the leader of the congregation, Tribulation Wholesome, who represents the characteristics most frequently satirized in attacks on the Puritan movement. At present they are both torn between avarice and fear for their safety if they employ what is obviously evil means toward their ends.*

89. *want grains*, be underweight. But the point is the pun on *light*.

TRIBULATION. These chastisements are common to the saints,
  And such rebukes we of the separation
  Must bear with willing shoulders, as the trials
  Sent forth to tempt our frailties.

ANANIAS.   In pure zeal,
  I do not like the man; he is a heathen,
  And speaks the language of Canaan, truly.

TRIBULATION. I think him a profane person indeed.

ANANIAS.   He bears
  The visible mark of the beast in his forehead.
  And for his stone, it is a work of darkness,
  And with philosophy blinds the eyes of man.   10

TRIBULATION. Good brother, we must bend unto all means,
  That may give furtherance to the holy cause.

ANANIAS. Which his cannot: the sanctified cause
  Should have a sanctified course.

TRIBULATION.   Not always necessary:
  The children of perdition are ofttimes
  Made instruments even of the greatest works:
  Beside, we should give somewhat to man's nature,
  The place he lives in, still about the fire,
  And fume of metals, that intoxicate
  The brain of man, and make him prone to passion.   20
  Where have you greater atheists than your cooks?
  Or more profane, or choleric, than your glass-men?
  More antichristian than your bell-founders?
  What makes the devil so devilish, I would ask you,
  Sathan, our common enemy, but his being
  Perpetually about the fire, and boiling
  Brimstone and arsenic? We must give, I say,
  Unto the motives, and the stirrers up
  Of humours in the blood. It may be so,
  When as the work is done, the stone is made,   30
  This heat of his may turn into a zeal,
  And stand up for the beauteous discipline,
  Against the menstruous cloth and rag of Rome.
  We must await his calling, and the coming
  Of the good spirit. You did fault, t' upbraid him
  With the brethren's blessing of Heidelberg, weighing
  What need we have to hasten on the work,
  For the restoring of the silenced saints,
  Which ne'er will be but by the philosopher's stone.
  And so a learned elder, one of Scotland,   40

Assured me; *aurum potabile* being
The only med'cine, for the civil magistrate,
T' incline him to a feeling of the cause;
And must be daily used in the disease.
ANANIAS. I have not edified more, truly, by man;
Not since the beautiful light first shone on me;
And I am sad my zeal hath so offended.
TRIBULATION. Let us call on him then.
ANANIAS.   The motion's good,
And of the spirit; I will knock first. [*Knocks.*] Peace be within!
[*The door is opened, and they enter.*

SCENE II

A ROOM IN LOVEWIT'S HOUSE. *Enter Subtle, followed by Tribulation and Ananias.*

SUBTLE. O, are you come? 'twas time. Your threescore minutes
Were at last thread, you see; and down had gone
Furnus acediæ, turris circulatorius:
Lembec, bolt's-head, retort, and pelican
Had all been cinders. Wicked Ananias!
Art thou returned? nay, then it goes down yet.
TRIBULATION. Sir, be appeased; he is come to humble
Himself in spirit, and to ask your patience,
If too much zeal hath carried him aside
From the due path.
SUBTLE.   Why, this doth qualify!   10
TRIBULATION. The brethren had no purpose, verily,
To give you the least grievance: but are ready
To lend their willing hands to any project
The spirit and you direct.
SUBTLE.   This qualifies more!
TRIBULATION. And for the orphans' goods, let them be valued.
Or what is needful else to the holy work,
It shall be numbered; here, by me, the saints
Throw down their purse before you.
SUBTLE.   This qualifies most!

41. *aurum potabile*, drinkable gold, here a bribe.
45. *edified*, been edified.
  3. *Furnus acediæ*, an oven that keeps hot with little attention, *turris
circulatorius*, a glass vessel for mixing liquids with a circulatory motion.
  10. *qualify*, put matters in a new light.

Why, thus it should be, now you understand.
Have I discoursed so unto you of our stone,   20
And of the good that it shall bring your cause?
Showed you (beside the main of hiring forces
Abroad, drawing the Hollanders, your friends,
From the Indies, to serve you, with all their fleet)
That even the med'cinal use shall make you a faction,
And party in the realm? As, put the case,
That some great man in state, he have the gout,
Why, you but send three drops of your elixir,
You help him straight: there you have made a friend.
Another has the palsy or the dropsy,   30
He takes of your incombustible stuff,
He's young again: there you have made a friend.
A lady that is past the feat of body,
Though not of mind, and hath her face decayed
Beyond all cure of paintings, you restore,
With the oil of talc: there you have made a friend;
And all her friends. A lord that is a leper,
A knight that has the bone-ache, or a squire
That hath both these, you make them smooth and sound,
With a bare fricace of your med'cine: still   40
You increase your friends.

TRIBULATION.   Ay, it is very pregnant.
SUBTLE. And then the turning of this lawyer's pewter
  To plate at Christmas—
ANANIAS.   Christ-tide, I pray you.
SUBTLE. Yet, Ananias!
ANANIAS.   I have done.
SUBTLE.   Or changing
  His parcel gilt to massy gold. You cannot
  But raise your friends. Withal, to be of power
  To pay an army in the field, to buy
  The King of France out of his realms, or Spain
  Out of his Indies. What can you not do
  Against lords spiritual or temporal,   50
  That shall oppone you?
TRIBULATION.   Verily, 'tis true.
  We may be temporal lords ourselves, I take it.
SUBTLE. You may be anything, and leave off to make
  Long-winded exercises; or suck up

40. *fricace*, rubbing.   45. *parcel gilt*, gold plate to solid gold.
51. *oppone*, oppose.

Your *ha!* and *hum!* in a tune. I not deny,
But such as are not graced in a state,
May, for their ends, be adverse in religion,
And get a tune to call the flock together:
For, to say sooth, a tune does much with women
And other phlegmatic people; it is your bell. 60
ANANIAS. Bells are profane; a tune may be religious.
SUBTLE. No warning with you! then farewell my patience.
　　　[*He starts away.*
'Slight, it shall down; I will not be thus tortured.
TRIBULATION. I pray you, sir.
SUBTLE. 　　　　　　　　All shall perish. I have spoke it.
TRIBULATION. Let me find grace, sir, in your eyes; the man
He stands corrected: neither did his zeal,
But as your self, allow a tune somewhere.
Which now, being toward the stone, we shall not need.
SUBTLE. No, nor your holy vizard, to win widows
To give you legacies; or make zealous wives 70
To rob their husbands for the common cause:
Nor take the start of bonds broke but one day,
And say they were forfeited by providence.
Nor shall you need o'er night to eat huge meals,
To celebrate your next day's fast the better;
The whilst the brethren and the sisters humbled,
Abate the stiffness of the flesh. Nor cast
Before your hungry hearers scrupulous bones;
As whether a Christian may hawk or hunt,
Or whether matrons of the holy assembly 80
May lay their hair out, or wear doublets,
Or have that idol, starch, about their linen.
ANANIAS. It is indeed an idol.
TRIBULATION [*Hurriedly*]. Mind him not, sir.
I do command thee, spirit of zeal, but trouble,
To peace within him! Pray you, sir, go on.
SUBTLE. Nor shall you need to libel 'gainst the prelates,
And shorten so your ears against the hearing
Of the next wire-drawn grace. Nor of necessity
Rail against plays, to please the alderman
Whose daily custard you devour: nor lie 90

---

68. *toward*, almost in possession of. 69. *vizard*, mask.
79. *hawk or hunt*, these are actual samples of scruples that the Puritans
had.
87. *ears*, lose your ears in the pillory.

With zealous rage till you are hoarse. Not one
Of these so singular arts. Nor call yourselves
By names of Tribulation, Persecution,
Restraint, Long-patience, and such like, affected
By the whole family or wood of you,
Only for glory, and to catch the ear
Of the disciple.
TRIBULATION.   Truly, sir, they are
Ways that the godly brethren have invented,
For propagation of the glorious cause,
As very notable means, and whereby also   100
Themselves grow soon, and profitably famous.
SUBTLE. O, but the stone, all's idle to it! nothing!
The art of angels, nature's miracle,
The divine secret that doth fly in clouds
From east to west: and whose tradition
Is not from men, but spirits.
ANANIAS.   I hate traditions;
I do not trust them—
TRIBULATION.   Peace!
ANANIAS.   They are popish all.
I will not peace: I will not—
TRIBULATION.   Ananias!
ANANIAS. Please the profane, to grieve the godly; I may not.
SUBTLE. Well, Ananias, thou shalt overcome.   110
TRIBULATION. It is an ignorant zeal that haunts him, sir:
But truly else a very faithful brother,
A botcher, and a man by revelation,
That hath a competent knowledge of the truth.
SUBTLE. Has he a competent sum there in the bag
To buy the goods within? I am made guardian,
And must, for charity and conscience' sake,
Now see the most be made for my poor orphan;
Though I desire the brethren, too, good gainers:
There they are within. When you have viewed and bought
    'em,   120
And ta'en the inventory of what they are,
They are ready for projection; there's no more
To do: cast on the med'cine, so much silver
As there is tin there, so much gold as brass,
I'll give't you in by weight.

95. *wood*, crowd.   102. *nothing* (equals it)!
113. *botcher*, tailor. It was a slang term for Puritan.

TRIBULATION.   But how long time,
  Sir, must the saints expect yet?
SUBTLE.   Let me see,
  How's the moon now? Eight, nine, ten days hence,
  He will be silver potate; then three days
  Before he citronize. Some fifteen days,
  The magisterium will be perfected.   130
ANANIAS. About the second day of the third week,
  In the ninth month?
SUBTLE.   Yes, my good Ananias.
TRIBULATION. What will the orphans' goods arise to, think you?
SUBTLE. Some hundred marks, as much as filled three cars,
  Unladed now: you'll make six millions of them—
  But I must have more coals laid in.
TRIBULATION.   How?
SUBTLE.   Another load,
  And then we have finished. We must now increase
  Our fire to *ignis ardens*, we are past
  Fimus equinus, balnei, cineris,
  And all those lenter heats. If the holy purse   140
  Should with this draught fall low, and that the saints
  Do need a present sum, I have a trick
  To melt the pewter, you shall buy now instantly,
  And with a tincture make you as good Dutch dollars
  As any are in Holland.
TRIBULATION.   Can you so?
SUBTLE. Ay, and shall bide the third examination.
ANANIAS. It will be joyful tidings to the brethren.
SUBTLE. But you must carry it secret.
TRIBULATION.   Ay; but stay,
  This act of coining, is it lawful?
ANANIAS.   Lawful!
  We know no magistrate: or, if we did,   150
  This is foreign coin.
SUBTLE.   It is no coining, sir.
  It is but casting.

126. *expect*, wait.
131. Puritans rejected the names of days, and months as heathenish.
138. *ignis ardens*, hot fire.
139. *Fimus equinus*, horse dung. *balnei*, baths. *cineris*, ashes.
146. *third examination*, i.e., very close scrutiny.
150. *know*, acknowledge. The Puritans rejected human forms of government as too worldly.

TRIBULATION. Ha! you distinguish well:
Casting of money may be lawful.

ANANIAS. 'Tis, sir.

TRIBULATION. Truly, I take it so.

SUBTLE. There is no scruple,
Sir, to be made of it; believe Ananias:
This case of conscience he is studied in.

TRIBULATION. I'll make a question of it to the brethren.

ANANIAS. The brethren shall approve it lawful, doubt not.
Where shall it be done? [*Knocking without.*

SUBTLE. For that we'll talk anon.
There's some to speak with me. Go in, I pray you, 160
And view the parcels. That's the inventory.
I'll come to you straight.

[*Exeunt Tribulation and Ananias to look over the utensils
brought by Sir Epicure.*

Who is it?—Face! appear.

SCENE III

*Enter Face in his uniform, jubilant over the prospect of a new
victim.*

SUBTLE. How now! good prize?

FACE. Good pox! yond' costive cheater
Never came on.

SUBTLE. How then?

FACE. I have walked the round
Till now, and no such thing.

SUBTLE. And have you quit him?

FACE. Quit him! an hell would quit him too, he were happy.
'Slight! would you have me stalk like a mill-jade,
All day, for one that will not yield us grains?
I know him of old.

SUBTLE. O, but to have gulled him,
Had been a mastery.

FACE Let him go, black boy!
And turn thee, that some fresh news may possess thee.
A noble count, a don of Spain, my dear 10
Delicious compeer, and my party-bawd,

3. *quit*, given him up.
8. *mastery*, great achievement. *black boy*, rascal.
11. *party*, associate, partner.

Who is come hither private for his conscience,
And brought munition with him, six great slops,
Bigger than three Dutch hoys, beside round trunks,
Furnished with pistolets, and pieces of eight,
Will straight be here, my rogue, to have thy bath,
(That is the colour,) and to make his battery
Upon our Doll, our castle, our cinque-port,
Our Dover pier, our what thou wilt. Where is she?
She must prepare perfumes, delicate linen,   20
The bath in chief, a banquet, and her wit,
For she must milk his epididymis.
Where is the doxy?

SUBTLE.   I'll send her to thee:
And but dispatch my brace of little John Leydens,
And come again myself.

FACE.   Are they within then?

SUBTLE. Numbering the sum.

FACE.   How much?

SUBTLE.   A hundred marks, boy.
                      [He goes out.

FACE. Why, this is a lucky day. Ten pounds of Mammon!
Three of my clerk! a portague of my grocer!
This of the brethren! beside reversions,
And states to come in the widow, and my count!   30
My share to-day will not be bought for forty—
    [Enter Doll.

DOLL.   What?

FACE. Pounds, dainty Dorothy! art thou so near?

DOLL. Yes; say, lord general, how fares our camp?

FACE. As with the few that had entrenched themselves
Safe, by their discipline, against a world, Doll,
And laughed within those trenches, and grew fat
With thinking on the booties, Doll, brought in
Daily by their small parties. This dear hour,
A doughty don is taken with my Doll;
And thou mayst make his ransom what thou wilt,   .   40

13. *slops*, loose breeches, a common subject for satire.
14. *hoys*, cargo ships. *trunks*, trunk hose.
15. *pistolets and pieces of eight*, gold coins.   17. *colour*, pretext.
18. *cinque port*, stronghold. The five ports on the southern coast of England opposite France: Dover, Sandwich, Romney, Hastings, and Hithe.
23. *doxy*, wench, whore.
24. *Leydens*, John of Leyden, a great leader of Anabaptists on the continent was executed in 1536.

My Dousabel; he shall be brought here fettered
With thy fair looks, before he sees thee; and thrown
In a down-bed, as dark as any dungeon;
Where thou shalt keep him waking with thy drum;
Thy drum, my Doll, thy drum; till he be tame
As the poor blackbirds were in the great frost,
Or bees are with a basin; and so hive him·
In the swan-skin coverlid and cambric sheets,
Till he work honey and wax, my little God's-gift.

DOLL. What is he, general?

FACE.   An adelantado,   50
A grandee, girl. Was not my Dapper here yet?

DOLL. No.

FACE.   Nor my Drugger?

DOLL.   Neither.

FACE.   A pox on 'em,
They are so long a furnishing! such stinkards
Would not be seen upon these festive days.—
    [*Re-enter Subtle, having put through the deal of selling
    Mammon's goods to the Puritans.*
How now! have you done?

SUBTLE.   Done. They are gone: the sum
Is here in bank, my Face. I would we knew
Another chapman now would buy 'em outright.

FACE. 'Slid, Nab shall do't against he have the widow,
To furnish household.

SUBTLE.   Excellent, well thought on:
Pray God he come.

FACE.   I pray he keep away   60
Till our new business be o'erpast.

SUBTLE.   But, Face,
How cam'st thou by this secret don?

FACE.   A spirit
Brought me th' intelligence in a paper here,
As I was conjuring yonder in my circle
For Surly; I have my flies abroad. Your bath
Is famous, Subtle, by my means. Sweet Doll,
You must go tune your virginal, no losing
O' the least time: and, do you hear? good action.
Firk, like a flounder; kiss, like a scallop; close;
And tickle him with thy mother tongue. His great   70

49. *God's-gift,* Dorothea is a Greek compound meaning **God's gift.**
50. *adelantado,* Spanish governor.   57. *chapman,* dealer.

Verdugoship has not a jot of language;
So much the easier to be cozened, my Dolly.
He will come here in a hired coach, obscure,
And our own coachman, whom I have sent as guide,
No creature else. [*Knocking without.*] Who's that?

SUBTLE.   It is not he?
                                                    [*Doll runs off.*

FACE. O no, not yet this hour.
     [*Re-enter Doll.*

SUBTLE.   Who is't?
DOLL.   Dapper,
     Your clerk.
FACE.   God's will then, Queen of Fairy,
     On with your tire; [*Exit Doll.*] and, doctor, with your robes.
     Let's dispatch him for God's sake.
SUBTLE.   'Twill be long.
FACE. I warrant you, take but the cues I give you,   80
     It shall be brief enough. [*Goes to the window.*] 'Slight, here are
          more!
     Abel, and I think the angry boy, the heir,
     That fain would quarrel.
SUBTLE.   And the widow?
FACE.   No,
     Not that I see. Away!   [*Subtle goes out.*
          [*Enter Dapper.*
                    O, sir, you are welcome.

                    SCENE IV

FACE. The doctor is within a moving for you;
     I have had the most ado to win him to it!—
     He swears you'll be the darling of the dice:
     He never heard her highness dote till now.
     Your aunt has given you the most gracious words
     That can be thought on.
DAPPER.   Shall I see her grace?
FACE. See her, and kiss her too.—
          [*Enter Abel, followed by Kastril, who wants to be a gay
          young blade, but who has neither the knowledge nor the
          convictions.*
                    What, honest Nab!
     Hast brought the damask?

71. *not a jot*, knows no English.   79. *dispatch*, get rid of.

DRUGGER.   No, sir; here's tobacco.

FACE. 'Tis well done, Nab: thou'lt bring the damask too?

DRUGGER. Yes: here's the gentleman, captain, Master Kastril,   10
    I have brought to see the doctor.

FACE.   Where's the widow?

DRUGGER. Sir, as he likes, his sister, he says, shall come.

FACE. O, is it so? good time. Is your name Kastril, sir?

KASTRIL. Ay, and the best of the Kastrils, I'd be sorry else,
    By fifteen hundred a year. Where is this doctor?
    My mad tobacco-boy here tells me of one
    That can do things: has he any skill?

FACE.   Wherein, sir?

KASTRIL. To carry a business, manage a quarrel fairly,
    Upon fit terms.

FACE.   It seems, sir, you are but young
    About the town, that can make that question.   20

KASTRIL. Sir, not so young but I have heard some speech
    Of the angry boys, and seen 'em take tobacco;
    And in his shop; and I can take it too.
    And I would fain be one of 'em, and go down
    And practise in the country.

FACE.   Sir, for the duello,
    The doctor, I assure you, shall inform you,
    To the least shadow of a hair; and show you
    An instrument he has of his own making,
    Wherewith no sooner shall you make report
    Of any quarrel, but he will take the height on't   30
    Most instantly, and tell in what degree
    Of safety it lies in, or mortality.
    And how it may be borne, whether in a right line,
    Or a half circle; or may else be cast
    Into an angle blunt, if not acute:
    All this he will demonstrate. And then, rules
    To give and take the lie by.

KASTRIL.   How! to take it?

FACE. Yes, in oblique he'll show you, or in circle;
    But never in diameter. The whole town
    Study his theorems, and dispute them ordinarily   40
    At the eating academies.

KASTRIL.   But does he teach
    Living by the wits too?

22. *angry boys*, roisterers.   38. *oblique*, Touchstone's lie circumstantial.
39. *diameter*, the lie direct.

FACE.   Anything whatever.
You cannot think that subtlety but he reads it,
He made me a captain. I was a stark pimp,
Just of your standing, 'fore I met with him;
It is not two months since. I'll tell you his method:
First, he will enter you at some ordinary.
KASTRIL. No, I'll not come there: you shall pardon me.
FACE.   For why, sir?
KASTRIL. There's gaming there, and tricks.
FACE.   Why, would you be
A gallant, and not game?
KASTRIL.   Ay, 'twill spend a man.   50
FACE. Spend you! it will repair you when you are spent.
How do they live by their wits there, that have vented
Six times your fortunes?
KASTRIL.   What, three thousand a year!
FACE. Ay, forty thousand.
KASTRIL.   Are there such?
FACE.   Ay, sir,
And gallants yet. Here's a young gentleman
Is born to nothing—[*Points to Dapper.*] forty marks a year
Which I count nothing:—he is to be initiated,
And have a fly of the doctor. He will win you
By unresistible luck, within this fortnight,
Enough to buy a barony. They will set him   60
Upmost, at the groom porters, all the Christmas:
And for the whole year through at every place
Where there is play, present him with the chair;
The best attendance, the best drink, sometimes
Two glasses of Canary, and pay nothing;
The purest linen and the sharpest knife,
The partridge next his trencher: and somewhere
The dainty bed, in private, with the dainty.
You shall have your ordinaries bid for him,
As playhouses for a poet; and the master   70
Pray him aloud to name what dish he affects,
Which must be buttered shrimps: and those that drink
To no mouth else, will drink to his, as being
The goodly president mouth of all the board.
KASTRIL. Do you not gull one?
FACE.   Ods my life! do you think it?

61. *groom porter*, an official who supervised the gambling house.

You shall have a cast commander, (can but get
In credit with a glover, or a spurrier,
For some two pair of either's ware aforehand,)
Will, by most swift posts, dealing with him,
Arrive at competent means to keep himself,   80
His punk, and naked boy, in excellent fashion,
And be admired for't.

KASTRIL.   Will the doctor teach this?

FACE. He will do more, sir: when your land is gone,
As men of spirit hate to keep earth long
In a vacation, when small money is stirring,
And ordinaries suspended till the term,
He'll show a perspective, where on one side
You shall behold the faces and the persons
Of all sufficient young heirs in town,
Whose bonds are current for commodity;   90
On th' other side, the merchants' forms, and others,
That without help of any second broker,
Who would expect a share, will trust such parcels:
In the third square, the very street and sign
Where the commodity dwells, and does but wait
To be delivered, be it pepper, soap,
Hops, or tobacco, oatmeal, woad, or cheeses.
All which you may so handle, to enjoy
To your own use, and never stand obliged.

KASTRIL. I' faith! is he such a fellow?

FACE.   Why, Nab here knows him.   100
And then for making matches for rich widows,
Young gentlewomen, heirs, the fortunat'st man!
He's sent to, far and near, all over England,
To have his counsel, and to know their fortunes.

KASTRIL. God's will, my suster shall see him.

FACE.   I'll tell you, sir,
What he did tell me of Nab. It's a strange thing:—
By the way, you must eat no cheese, Nab, it breeds melancholy,
And that same melancholy breeds worms; but pass it:—
He told me, honest Nab here was ne'er at tavern
But once in's life.

76. *cast*, one dismissed from the service, cashiered.

90. *current for commodity*, money-lenders sometimes compelled young spendthrifts to take part of a loan in worthless goods, for which the lender got as high a price as he pleased. The theory was that the borrower would be able to sell for a good price, but of course that didn't work out.

97. *woad*, a plant used in making blue dye.

DRUGGER.   Truth, and no more I was not.   110
FACE. And then he was so sick—
DRUGGER.   Could he tell you that too?
FACE. How should I know it?
DRUGGER.   In troth, we had been a shooting,
  And had a piece of fat ram-mutton to supper,
  That lay so heavy o' my stomach—
FACE.   And he has no head
  To bear any wine; for what with the noise of the fiddlers,
  And care of his shop, for he dares keep no servants—
DRUGGER. My head did so ache—
FACE.   As he was fain to be brought home,
  The doctor told me: and then a good old woman—
DRUGGER. Yes, faith, she dwells in Sea-coal-lane,—did cure me,
  With sodden ale, and pellitory of the wall—   120
  Cost me but twopence. I had another sickness
  Was worse than that.
FACE.   Ay, that was with the grief
  Thou took'st for being cessed at eighteenpence,
  For the water-work.
DRUGGER.   In truth, and it was like
  T' have cost me almost my life.
FACE.   Thy hair went off?
DRUGGER. Yes, sir; 'twas done for spite.
FACE.   Nay, so says the doctor.
KASTRIL. Pray thee, tobacco-boy, go fetch my suster;
  I'll see this learnèd boy before I go;
  And so shall she.
FACE.   Sir, he is busy now:
  But if you have a sister to fetch hither,   130
  Perhaps your own pains may command her sooner:
  And he by that time will be free.
KASTRIL.   I go.   [He hurries out.
FACE. Drugger, she's thine: the damask!

        [Abel, delighted, goes out.
        [Aside.] Subtle and I
  Must wrestle for her.—Come on, Master Dapper,
  You see how I turn clients here away,
  To give your cause dispatch; have you performed
  The ceremonies were enjoined you?
DAPPER.   Yes, of the vinegar,
  And the clean shirt.

120. *sodden*, warmed. *pellitory*, an herb.   123. *cessed*, assessed, taxed.

FACE. 'Tis well: that shirt may do you
  More worship than you think. Your aunt's a-fire,
  But that she will not show it, t' have a sight on you. 140
  Have you provided for her grace's servants?
DAPPER. Yes, here are six score Edward shillings.
FACE. Good!
DAPPER. And an old Harry's sovereign.
FACE. Very good!
DAPPER. And three James shillings, and an Elizabeth groat,
  Just twenty nobles.
FACE. O, you are too just.
  I would you had had the other noble in Maries.
DAPPER. I have some Philip and Maries.
FACE. Ay, those same
  Are best of all: where are they? Hark, the doctor.

SCENE V

Enter Subtle, disguised like a Priest of Fairy, with a strip of cloth.

SUBTLE [*In a feigned voice*]. Is yet her grace's cousin come?
FACE. He is come.
SUBTLE. And is he fasting?
FACE. Yes.
SUBTLE. And hath cried *hum*?
FACE. Thrice, you must answer.
DAPPER. Thrice.
SUBTLE. And as oft *buz*?
FACE. If you have, say.
DAPPER. I have.
SUBTLE. Then, to her cuz,
  Hoping that he hath vinegared his senses,
  As he was bid, the Fairy queen dispenses,
  By me, this robe, the petticoat of fortune;
  Which that he straight put on, she doth importune.
  And though to fortune near be her petticoat,
  Yet nearer is her smock, the queen doth note: 10
  And therefore, even of that a piece she has sent,

---

142. *Edward shillings*, shillings coined during the reign of Edward VI.
Face wants a Mary noble to have the series complete from Henry VIII to
James I. The value of a coin might vary from coinage to coinage under
different sovereigns.

Which, being a child, to wrap him in was rent;
And prays him for a scarf he now will wear it,
With as much love as then her grace did tear it,
About his eyes, [*They blind him with the rag.*] to show he is
  fortunate.
And, trusting unto her to make his state,
He'll throw away all worldly pelf about him;
Which that he will perform, she doth not doubt him.

FACE. She need not doubt him, sir. Alas, he has nothing
  But what he will part withal as willingly,   20
  Upon her grace's word—throw away your purse—
  As she would ask it:—handkerchiefs and all—
    [*He throws away, as they bid him.*
  She cannot bid that thing but he'll obey.—
  If you have a ring about you, cast it off,
  Or a silver seal at your wrist; her grace will **send**
  Her fairies here to search you, therefore deal
  Directly with her highness: if they find
  That you conceal a mite, you are undone.

DAPPER. Truly, there's all.

FACE.   All what?

DAPPER.   My money; truly.

FACE. Keep nothing that is transitory about you.—   30
  [*Aside to Subtle.*] Bid Doll play music.—Look, **the elves are**
    come
    [*Doll plays on the cittern within.*
  To pinch you, if you tell not truth. Advise you.
    [*They pinch him.*

DAPPER. O! I have a paper with a spur-ryal in't.

FACE.   *Ti, ti.*
  They knew't, they say.

SUBTLE.   *Ti, ti, ti, ti.* He has more yet.

FACE. *Ti, ti-ti-ti.*—[*Aside to Subtle.*] I' the t'other pocket?

SUBTLE.   *Titi, titi, titi, titi.*
  They must pinch him or he will never confess, they say.
    [*They pinch him again.*

DAPPER. O, O!

FACE.   Nay, pray you hold: he is her grace's nephew,
  Ti, ti, ti? What care you? good faith, you shall care.—
  Deal plainly, sir, and shame the fairies. Show
  You are an innocent.

DAPPER.   By this good light, I have nothing.   40

27. *directly,* honestly.

SUBTLE. *Ti, ti, ti, ti, to, ta.* He does equivocate she says:
  Ti, ti do ti, ti ti do, ti da; and swears by the *light* when he is
  blinded.
DAPPER. By this good *dark*, I have nothing but a half-crown
  Of gold about my wrist, that my love gave me;
  And a leaden heart I wore since she forsook me.
FACE. I thought 'twas something. And would you incur
  Your aunt's displeasure for these trifles? Come,
  I had rather you had thrown away twenty half-crowns.
    [*Takes it off.*
  You may wear your leaden heart still.—
    [*Enter Doll, hastily.*
                                How now!
SUBTLE [*Aside, so that Nab cannot hear*]. What news, Doll?
DOLL.   Yonder's your knight, Sir Mammon.   50
FACE. Gods lid, we never thought of him till now!
  Where is he?
DOLL.   Here hard by: he is at the door.
SUBTLE. And you are not ready now! Doll, get his suit.
                                [*Doll hurries off.*
  He must not be sent back.
FACE.   O, by no means.
  What shall we do with this same puffin here,
  Now he's o' the spit?
SUBTLE.   Why, lay him back awhile,
  With some device.
    [*Re-enter Doll with Face's clothes.*
                    —*Ti, titi, tititi.* Would her grace speak with
  me?
  I come.—Help, Doll!   [*Knocking without.*
FACE [*Speaks through the keyhole while Subtle takes Dapper to
  one side*]. Who's there? Sir Epicure,
  My master's i' the way. Please you to walk
  Three or four turns, but till his back be turned,   60
  And I am for you.—Quickly, Doll!
SUBTLE.   Her grace
  Commends her kindly to you, Master Dapper.
DAPPER. I long to see her grace.
SUBTLE.   She now is set
  At dinner in her bed, and she has sent you
  From her own private trencher, a dead mouse,
  And a piece of gingerbread, to be merry withal,
  And stay your stomach, lest you faint with fasting:

Yet if you could hold out till she saw you, she says,
It would be better for you.

FACE.   Sir, he shall

Hold out, an 'twere this two hours, for her highness,   70
I can assure you that. We will not lose
All we have done—

SUBTLE.   He must not see, nor speak
To anybody, till then.

FACE.   For that we'll put, sir,
A stay in's mouth.

SUBTLE.   Of what?

FACE.   Of gingerbread.
Make you it fit. He that hath pleased her grace
Thus far, shall not now crinkle for a little.—
Gape, sir, and let him fit you.

    [*They thrust a gag of gingerbread in his mouth.*

SUBTLE.   Where shall we now
Bestow him?

DOLL.   In the privy.

SUBTLE.   Come along, sir,
I must now show you Fortune's privy lodgings.

FACE. Are they perfumed, and his bath ready?

SUBTLE.   All: 80
Only the fumigation's somewhat strong.

FACE [*Speaking through the keyhole*]. Sir Epicure, I am yours,
    sir, by and by.

    [*Subtle takes Dapper off, and Face follows after his last word
    to Sir Epicure.*

ACT IV

SCENE I

ANOTHER ROOM IN LOVEWIT'S HOUSE. *Subtle and Face have disposed
    of Dapper; Subtle has gone off, and Face has admitted Sir
    Epicure, who is on tenterhooks until he gets the wealth and the
    lady.*

FACE. O, sir, you are come in the only finest time—

MAMMON. Where's master?

FACE.   Now preparing for projection, sir.
Your stuff will be all changed shortly.

MAMMON.   Into gold?

FACE. To gold and silver, sir.

MAMMON.   Silver I care not for.

FACE. Yes, sir, a little to give beggars.

MAMMON.   Where's the lady?

FACE. At hand here. I have told her such brave things of you,
    Touching your bounty and your noble spirit—

MAMMON.   Hast thou?

FACE. As she is almost in her fit to see you.
    But, good sir, no divinity in your conference,
    For fear of putting her in rage.—

MAMMON.   I warrant thee.   10

FACE. Six men will not hold her down: and then,
    If the old man should hear or see you—

MAMMON.   Fear not.

FACE. The very house, sir, would run mad. You know it,
    How scrupulous he is, and violent,
    'Gainst the least act of sin. Physic or mathematics,
    Poetry, state, or bawdry, as I told you,
    She will endure, and never startle; but
    No word of controversy.

MAMMON.   I am schooled, good Ulen.

FACE. And you must praise her house, remember that,
    And her nobility.

MAMMON.   Let me alone: 20
    No herald, no, nor antiquary, Lungs,
    Shall do it better. Go.

FACE [Aside].   Why, this is yet
    A kind of modern happiness, to have
    Doll Common for a great lady.   [He goes off.

MAMMON.   Now, Epicure,
    Heighten thyself, talk to her all in gold;
    Rain her as many showers as Jove did drops
    Unto his Danäe; show the god a miser,
    Compared with Mammon. What! the stone will do't.
    She shall feel gold, taste gold, hear gold, sleep gold;
    Nay, we will concumbere gold: I will be puissant,   30
    And mighty in my talk to her.—
        [Re-enter Face, with Doll richly dressed.
                              Here she comes.

19. house, family.
23. modern, also meant common.   happiness, fitness, appropriateness.
30. concumbere, lie with.

FACE. To him, Doll, suckle him.—This is the noble knight
    I told your ladyship—

MAMMON.   Madam, with your pardon,
    I kiss your vesture.

DOLL.   Sir, I were uncivil
    If I would suffer that; my lip to you, sir.

MAMMON. I hope my lord your brother be in health, lady.

DOLL. My lord, my brother is, though I no lady, sir.

FACE [*Aside*]. Well said, my Guinea bird.

MAMMON.   Right noble madam—

FACE [*Aside*]. O, we shall have most fierce idolatry.

MAMMON. 'Tis your prerogative.

DOLL.   Rather your courtesy.   40

MAMMON. Were there nought else t' enlarge your virtues to me,
    These answers speak your breeding and your blood.

DOLL. Blood we boast none, sir, a poor baron's daughter.

MAMMON. Poor! and gat you? profane not. Had your father
    Slept all the happy remnant of his life
    After the act, lien but there still, and panted,
    He had done enough to make himself, his issue,
    And his posterity noble.

DOLL.   Sir, although
    We may be said to want the gilt and trappings,
    The dress of honour, yet we strive to keep   50
    The seeds and the materials.

MAMMON.   I do see
    The old ingredient, virtue, was not lost,
    Nor the drug money used to make your compound.
    There is a strange nobility in your eye,
    This lip, that chin! methinks you do resemble
    One of the Austriac princes.

FACE [*Aside*].   Very like!
    Her father was an Irish costermonger.

MAMMON. The house of Valois just had such a nose,
    And such a forehead yet the Medici
    Of Florence boast.

DOLL.   Troth, and I have been likened   60
    To all these princes.

FACE.   I'll be sworn, I heard it.

MAMMON. I know not how! it is not any one,
    But e'en the very choice of all their features.

38. *Guinea bird*, prostitute.   46. *lien*, lain.
57. *costermonger*, apple-seller.

FACE [*Aside*]. I'll in, and laugh.   [*He goes off.*

MAMMON.   A certain touch, or air,
  That sparkles a divinity beyond
  An earthly beauty!
DOLL.   O, you play the courtier.
MAMMON. Good lady, give me leave—
DOLL.   In faith, I may not,
  To mock me, sir.
MAMMON.   To burn in this sweet flame;
  The phœnix never knew a nobler death.
DOLL. Nay, now you court the courtier, and destroy   70
  What you would build: this art, sir, in your words,
  Calls your whole faith in question.
MAMMON.   By my soul—
DOLL. Nay, oaths are made of the same air, sir.
MAMMON.   Nature
  Never bestowed upon mortality
  A more unblamed, a more harmonious feature;
  She played the step-dame in all faces else:
  Sweet madam, let me be particular—
DOLL. Particular, sir! I pray you know your distance.
MAMMON. In no ill sense, sweet lady; but to ask
  How your fair graces pass the hours? I see   80
  You are lodged here, in the house of a rare man,
  An excellent artist; but what's that to you?
DOLL. Yes, sir; I study here the mathematics,
  And distillation.
MAMMON.   O, I cry your pardon.
  He's a divine instructor! can extract
  The souls of all things by his art; call all
  The virtues, and the miracles of the sun,
  Into a temperate furnace; teach dull nature
  What her own forces are. A man, the emperor
  Has courted above Kelly; sent his medals   90
  And chains, to invite him.
DOLL.   Ay, and for his physic, sir—
MAMMON. Above the art of Æsculapius,
  That drew the envy of the thunderer!

77. *particular*, personal, intimate.
90. *Kelly*, a rascally associate of Dr. John Dee. He was detected trying to cheat the Emperor Rudolph II at Prague, and was imprisoned and died.
92. *Aesculapius*, legendary founder of science of medicine, killed by Jupiter for bringing the dead back to life.

I know all this, and more.
DOLL.   Troth, I am taken, sir,
  Whole with these studies, that contemplate nature.
MAMMON. It is a noble humour; but this form
  Was not intended to so dark a use.
  Had you been crooked, foul, of some coarse mould,
  A cloister had done well; but such a feature
  That might stand up the glory of a kingdom,   100
  To live recluse! is a mere solecism,
  Though in a nunnery. It must not be.
  I muse, my lord your brother will permit it:
  You should spend half my land first, were I he.
  Does not this diamond better on my finger
  Than in the quarry?
DOLL.   Yes.
MAMMON.   Why, you are like it.
  You were created, lady, for the light.
  Here, you shall wear it; take it, the first pledge
  Of what I speak, to bind you to believe me.
DOLL. In chains of adamant?
MAMMON.   Yes, the strongest bands.   110
  And take a secret too—here, by your side,
  Doth stand this hour the happiest man in Europe.
DOLL. You are contented, sir?
MAMMON,   Nay, in true being,
  The envy of princes and the fear of states.
DOLL. Say you so, Sir Epicure?
MAMMON.   Yes, and thou shalt prove it,
  Daughter of honour. I have cast mine eye
  Upon thy form, and I will rear this beauty
  Above all styles.
DOLL.   You mean no treason, sir?
MAMMON. No, I will take away that jealousy.
  I am the lord of the philosopher's stone,   120
  And thou the lady.
DOLL.   How, sir! have you that?
MAMMON. I am the master of the mastery.
  This day the good old wretch here o' the house
  Has made it for us: now he's at projection.
  Think therefore thy first wish now, let me hear it:
  And it shall rain into thy lap, no shower,

103. *muse*, wonder, am astonished.   119. *jealousy*, suspicion.
122. *mastery*, magisterium, the task of discovering the philosopher's stone.

But floods of gold, whole cataracts, a deluge,
To get a nation on thee.

DOLL.   You are pleased, sir,
To work on the ambition of our sex.

MAMMON. I am pleased the glory of her sex should know,   130
  This nook here of the Friars is no climate
  For her to live obscurely in, to learn
  Physic and surgery, for the constable's wife
  Of some odd hundred in Essex; but come forth,
  And taste the air of palaces; eat, drink
  The toils of emp'rics, and their boasted practice;
  Tincture of pearl, and coral, gold, and amber;
  Be seen at feasts and triumphs; have it asked
  What miracle she is? set all the eyes
  Of court a-fire, like a burning glass,   140
  And work 'em into cinders, when the jewels
  Of twenty states adorn thee, and the light
  Strikes out the stars! that, when thy name is mentioned,
  Queens may look pale; and we but showing our love,
  Nero's Poppæa may be lost in story!
  Thus will we have it.

DOLL.   I could well consent, sir.
  But in a monarchy, how will this be?
  The prince will soon take notice, and both seize
  You and your stone, it being a wealth unfit
  For any private subject.

MAMMON.   If he knew it.   150

DOLL. Yourself do boast it, sir.

MAMMON.   To thee, my life.

DOLL. O, but beware, sir! you may come to end
  The remnant of your days in a loathed prison,
  By speaking of it.

MAMMON.   'Tis no idle fear:
  We'll therefore go withal, my girl, and live
  In a free state, where we will eat our mullets,
  Soused in high-country wines, sup pheasants' eggs
  And have our cockles boiled in silver shells;
  Our shrimps to swim again, as when they lived,
  In a rare butter made of dolphins' milk,   160
  Whose cream does look like opals; and with these
  Delicate meats set ourselves high for pleasure,

134. *hundred*, district in a county.
136. *toils of emp'rics*, work of experimenters.

And take us down again, and then renew
Our youth and strength with drinking the elixir,
And so enjoy a perpetuity
Of life and lust! And thou shalt have thy wardrobe
Richer than nature's, still to change thyself,
And vary oftener, for thy pride, than she,
Or art, her wise and almost-equal servant.

[*Re-enter Face.*

FACE. Sir, you are too loud. I hear you every word   170
Into the laboratory. Some fitter place;
The garden, or great chamber above. How like you her?
MAMMON. Excellent! Lungs. There's for thee.

[*Gives him money.*

FACE.   But do you hear?
Good sir, beware, no mention of the rabbins.
MAMMON. We think not on 'em.

[*Mammon and Doll go out with a great show of affection.*

FACE.   O, it is well, sir.—Subtle!

SCENE II

Subtle enters.

FACE. Dost thou not laugh?
SUBTLE.   Yes; are they gone?
FACE.   All's clear.
SUBTLE. The widow is come.
FACE.   And your quarrelling disciple?
SUBTLE. Ay.
FACE.   I must to my captainship again then.
SUBTLE. Stay, bring 'em in first.
FACE.   So I meant. What is she?
A bonnibel?
SUBTLE.   I know not.
FACE.   We'll draw lots:
You'll stand to that?
SUBTLE.   What else?
FACE.   O, for a suit,
To fall now like a curtain, flap!

5. *bonnibel*, pretty girl.
6. *suit*, his captain's uniform, which might be draped around him like a
curtain; so that he would not need to leave Subtle alone with the lady.

SUBTLE.   To the door, man.

FACE. You'll have the first kiss, 'cause I am not ready.   [*Exit.*

SUBTLE. Yes, and perhaps hit you through both the nostrils.

FACE [*Within*]. Who would you speak with?

KASTRIL [*Within*].   Where's the captain?

FACE [*Within*].   Gone, sir,   10

    About some business.

KASTRIL [*Within*].   Gone!

FACE [*Within*].   He'll return straight.

    But master doctor, his lieutenant, is here.

    [*Enter Kastril, followed by Dame Pliant.*

SUBTLE. Come near, my worshipful boy, my *terræ fili*,

    That is, my boy of land; make thy approaches:

    Welcome; I know thy lusts, and thy desires,

    And I will serve and satisfy 'em. Begin,

    Charge me from thence, or thence, or in this line;

    Here is my centre: ground thy quarrel.

KASTRIL.   You lie.

SUBTLE. How, child of wrath and anger! the loud lie?

    For what, my sudden boy?

KASTRIL.   Nay, that look you to,   20

    I am aforehand.

SUBTLE.   O, this is no true grammar,

    And as ill logic! You must render causes, child,

    Your first and second intentions, know your canons

    And your divisions, moods, degrees, and differences,

    Your predicaments, substance, and accident,

    Series extern and intern, with their causes,

    Efficient, material, formal, final,

    And have your elements perfect.

KASTRIL [*Aside*].   What is this!

    The angry tongue he talks in?

SUBTLE.   That false precept,

    Of being aforehand, has deceived a number,   30

    And made 'em enter quarrels oftentimes

    Before they were aware; and afterward,

    Against their wills.

KASTRIL.   How must I do then, sir?

   9. *nostrils*, put your nose out of joint.

  22. *You must render causes . . .*, Subtle proceeds to overwhelm Kastril
with technical terms of scholastic logic as he had used alchemical terms to
the same end on the puritans.

SUBTLE. I cry this lady mercy: she should first
  Have been saluted. [*Kisses her.*] I do call you lady,
  Because you are to be one ere 't be long,
  My soft and buxom widow.

KASTRIL.   Is she, i' faith?

SUBTLE. Yes, or my art is an egregious liar.

KASTRIL. How know you?

SUBTLE.   By inspection on her forehead,
  And subtlety of her lip, which must be tasted   40
  Often to make a judgement. [*Kisses her again.*] 'Slight, she melts
  Like a myrobolane: here is yet a line,
  In *rivo frontis*, tells me he is no knight.

DAME PLIANT. What is he then, sir?

SUBTLE.   Let me see your hand.
  O, your *linea fortunæ* makes it plain;
  And *stella* here *in monte Veneris:*
  But, most of all, *junctura annularis.*
  He is a soldier, or a man of art, lady,
  But shall have some great honour shortly.

DAME PLIANT.   Brother,
  He's a rare man, believe me!
    [*Re-enter Face, in his uniform.*

KASTRIL.   Hold your peace.   50
  Here comes the t' other rare man.—'Save you, captain.

FACE. Good Master Kastril! Is this your sister?

KASTRIL.   Ay, sir.
  Please you to kuss her, and be proud to know her.

FACE. I shall be proud to know you, lady.   [*Kisses her.*

DAME PLIANT.   Brother,
  He calls me lady, too.

KASTRIL.   Ay, peace: I heard it.   [*Takes her aside.*

FACE. The count is come.

SUBTLE.   Where is he?

FACE.   At the door.

SUBTLE. Why, you must entertain him.

FACE.   What will you do
  With these the while?

---

42. *myrobolane*, dried plum.   43. *rivo frontis*, frontal vein.
45. *linea fortunæ*, line of fortune.
46. *stella, etc.*, star in the Mount of Venus.
47. *junctura*, the ring joint.

SUBTLE.   Why, have 'em up, and show 'em
  Some fustian book, or the dark glass.

FACE.   'Fore God,
  She is a delicate dabchick! I must have her.   60
                                                 [*Exit.*

SUBTLE. Must you? ay, if your fortune will, you must.—
  Come, sir, the captain will come to us presently:
  I'll have you to my chamber of demonstrations,
  Where I will show you both the grammar and logic,
  And rhetoric of quarrelling: my whole method
  Drawn out in tables; and my instrument,
  That hath the several scales upon't, shall make you
  Able to quarrel at a straw's-breadth by moonlight.
  And, lady, I'll have you look in a glass,
  Some half an hour, but to clear your eyesight,   70
  Against you see your fortune; which is greater
  Than I may judge upon the sudden, trust me.
            [*Exit, followed by Kastril and Dame Pliant.*

SCENE III

Re-enter Face.

FACE. Where are you, doctor?
SUBTLE [*Within*].   I'll come to you presently.
FACE. I will have this same widow, now I have seen her,
  On any composition.
     [*Re-enter Subtle.*
SUBTLE.   What do you say?
FACE. Have you disposed of them?
SUBTLE.   I have sent 'em up.
FACE. Subtle, in troth, I needs must have this widow.
SUBTLE. Is that the matter?
FACE.   Nay, but hear me.
SUBTLE.   Go to.
  If you rebel once, Doll shall know it all:
  Therefore be quiet, and obey your chance.

---

   58. *fustian book*, book full of high sounding trash. *dark glass,* polished
black stone, in which they gazed.
   60. *dabchick,* water hen.   71. *against,* in preparation to.
   3. *composition,* terms.

FACE. Nay, thou art so violent now. Do but conceive,
  Thou art old, and canst not serve—
SUBTLE.   Who cannot? I?   10
  'Slight, I will serve her with thee, for a—
FACE.   Nay,
  But understand: I'll give you composition.
SUBTLE. I will not treat with thee; what! sell my fortune?
  'Tis better than my birthright. Do not murmur:
  Win her, and carry her. If you grumble, Doll
  Knows it directly.
FACE.   Well, sir, I am silent.
  Will you go help to fetch in Don in state?
SUBTLE. I follow you, sir. [*Face goes out.*] We must keep Face
  in awe,
  Or he will overlook us like a tyrant.

  [*Face re-enters, introducing Surly disguised as a Spaniard,
    and intent on exposing the trickery of Face and Subtle.
    His costume exaggerates all the eccentricities of Spanish
    dress: his ruff is extra large, his cloak extra short, and his
    "slops" or breeches cut extra full. He is supposed to be able
    to speak and understand only Spanish.*

  Brain of a tailor! who comes here? Don John!   20
SURLY. *Señores, beso las manos a vuestras mercedes.*
SUBTLE. Would you had stooped a little, and kissed our *anos!*
FACE. Peace, Subtle.
SUBTLE.   Stab me; I shall never hold, man,
  He looks in that deep ruff like a head in a platter,
  Served in by a short cloak upon two trestles.
FACE. Or what do you say to a collar of brawn, cut down
  Beneath the souse, and wriggled with a knife?
SUBTLE. 'Slud, he does look too fat to be a Spaniard.
FACE. Perhaps some Fleming or some Hollander got him
  In d'Alva's time; Count Egmont's bastard.

19. *overlook*, despise.
20. *Don John*, of Austria the Spaniard who commanded the fleet in the
defeat of the Turks at Lepanto, Oct. 7, 1571.
21. *Señores . . .*, Gentlemen, I kiss your honors' hands.
25. *trestles*, stilts.
26. *collar of brawn*, a neck or roll of pork.
27. *souse*, ear. *wriggled*, slashed into a pattern that looks like a ruff.
28. *'Slud*, God's Lord, another mild oath.
30. *d'Alva*, the Spaniard who governed the Low Countries from 1567–73.
Egmont, a Flemish leader.

SUBTLE.   Don,
Your scurvy, yellow, Madrïd face is welcome.

SURLY. *Gratia.*

SUBTLE.   He speaks out of a fortification.
Pray God he have no squibs in those deep sets.

SURLY. *Por dios, señores, muy linda casa!*

SUBTLE. What says he?

FACE.   Praises the house, I think;
I know no more but's action.

SUBTLE.   Yes, the *casa*,
My precious Diego, will prove fair enough
To cozen you in. Do you mark? you shall
Be cozened, Diego.

FACE.   Cozened, do you see,
My worthy Donzel, cozened.

SURLY.   *Entiendo.*   40

SUBTLE. Do you intend it? so do we, dear Don.
Have you brought pistolets, or portagues,
My solemn Don? Dost thou feel any?

FACE *[Feels his pockets].*   Full.

SUBTLE. You shall be emptied, Don, pumped and drawn
Dry, as they say.

FACE.   Milked, in troth, sweet Don.

SUBTLE. See all the monsters; the great lion of all, **Don.**

SURLY. *Con licencia, se puede ver a esta señora?*

SUBTLE. What talks he now?

FACE.   Of the *señora.*

SUBTLE.   O, Don,
This is the lioness, which you shall see
Also, my Don.

FACE.   'Slid, Subtle, how shall we do?   50

SUBTLE. For what?

FACE.   Why, Doll's employed, you know.

SUBTLE.   That's true.
'Fore Heaven I know not: he must stay, that's all.

FACE. Stay! that he must not by no means.

SUBTLE.   No! why?

---

32. *Gratia,* Thanks.   33. *sets,* plaits of his ruff.
34. *Por dios . . .,* By Jove, gentlemen, a very fine house.
40. *Donzel,* little Don. *Entiendo,* I understand.
46. *monsters,* i.e., see all the sights.
47. *Con licencia . . .,* By your leave, may I see this lady?

FACE. Unless you'll mar all. 'Slight, he will suspect it:
And then he will not pay, not half so well.
This is a travelled punk-master, and does know
All the delays; a notable hot rascal,
And looks already rampant.
SUBTLE.   'Sdeath, and Mammon
Must not be troubled.
FACE.   Mammon! in no case.
SUBTLE. What shall we do then?
FACE.   Think: you must be sudden.   60
SURLY. *Entiendo, que la señora es tan hermosa, que codicio tan*
    A verla, como la bien aventuranza de mi vida.
FACE. *Mi vida!* 'Slid, Subtle, he puts me in mind o' the widow.
What dost thou say to draw her to it, ha!
And tell her 'tis her fortune? all our venture
Now lies upon't. It is but one man more,
Which on's chance to have her: and beside,
There is no maidenhead to be feared or lost.
What dost thou think on't, Subtle?
SUBTLE [*Hesitant*].   Who, I? why—
FACE. The credit of our house, too, is engaged.   70
SUBTLE. You made me an offer for my share erewhile.
What wilt thou give me, i' faith?
FACE.   O, by that light
I'll not buy now. You know your doom to me.
E'en take your lot, obey your chance, sir; win her,
And wear her out for me.
SUBTLE.   'Slight, I'll not work her then.
FACE. It is the common cause; therefore bethink you.
Doll else must know it, as you said.
SUBTLE.   I care not.
SURLY. *Señores, porque se tarda tanto?*
SUBTLE. Faith, I am not fit, I am old.
FACE.   That's now no reason, sir.
SURLY. *Puede ser de hacer burla de mi amor?*   80
FACE. You hear the Don too? by this air I call,
And loose the hinges. Doll!
SUBTLE.   A plague of hell—

61. *Entiendo* . . ., I understand that the lady is so handsome that I am as
anxious to see her as the good fortune of my life.
73. *doom*, decree.
78. *Señores* . . ., Gentlemen, why so much delay?
80. *Puede ser* . . ., Can it be you make sport of my love?

FACE. Will you then do?

SUBTLE.　　　　　　You are a terrible rogue!
　　I'll think of this: will you, sir, call the widow?

FACE. Yes, and I'll take her too with all her faults,
　　Now I do think on't better.

SUBTLE.　　　　　　With all my heart, sir;
　　Am I discharged o' the lot?

FACE.　　　　　As you please.

SUBTLE.　　　　　　　　Hands. [*They shake hands.*

FACE. Remember now, that upon any change,
　　You never claim her.

SUBTLE.　　　　Much good joy and health to you, sir.
　　Marry a whore! fate, let me wed a witch first.　　　　90

SURLY. *Por estas honradas barbas—*

SUBTLE.　　　　　　He swears by his beard.
　　Dispatch, and call the brother too.
　　　　　　　　[*Face hurries off to bring in Dame Pliant.*

SURLY.　　　　　　*Tengo duda, señores,*
　　Que no me hagan alguna traición.

SUBTLE. How, issue on? yes, *præsto, señor.* Please you
　　Enthratha the *chambratha*, worthy Don:
　　Where if you please the fates, in your *bathada,*
　　You shall be soaked, and stroked, and tubbed, and rubbed,
　　And scrubbed, and fubbed, dear Don, before you go.
　　You shall in faith, my scurvy baboon Don,
　　Be curried, clawed, and flawed, and tawed, indeed.　　　100
　　I will the heartlier go about it now,
　　And make the widow a punk so much the sooner,
　　To be revenged on this impetuous Face:
　　The quickly doing of it is the grace.
　　　　[*He takes the "Don" off to prepare him to meet the lady.*

SCENE IV

ANOTHER ROOM IN THE HOUSE. *Face has been telling Dame Pliant and her brother of the good fortune that has come to her: she is loved by a Spanish count who wants to marry her.*

91. *Por estas . . . ,* By this honored beard.
92. *Tengo duda . . .,* I fear, gentlemen, you are playing some trick on me.
94. *præsto,* quickly, at once.　　98. *fubbed,* cheated, tricked.
100. *flawed,* cracked. *tawed,* soaked, as hides were in the tanning.

FACE. Come, lady: I knew the doctor would not leave
  Till he had found the very nick of her fortune.
KASTRIL. To be a countess, say you?
FACE.   A Spanish countess, sir.
DAME PLIANT. Why, is that better than an English countess?
FACE. Better! 'Slight, make you that a question, lady?
KASTRIL. Nay, she is a fool, captain, you must pardon her.
FACE. Ask from your courtier, to your inns-of-court-man,
  To your mere milliner; they will tell you all,
  Your Spanish jennet is the best horse; your Spanish
  Stoup is the best garb; your Spanish beard   10
  Is the best cut; your Spanish ruffs are the best
  Wear; your Spanish pavin the best dance;
  Your Spanish titillation in a glove
  The best perfume: and for your Spanish pike,
  And Spanish blade, let your poor captain speak—
  Here comes the doctor.
    [*Enter Subtle with a paper, pretending to read from it her*
      good fortune.
SUBTLE.   My most honoured lady,
  For so I am now to style you, having found
  By this my scheme, you are to undergo
  An honourable fortune very shortly.
  What will you say now, if some—
FACE.   I have told her all, sir;   20
  And her right worshipful brother here, that she shall be
  A countess; do not delay 'em, sir: a Spanish countess.
SUBTLE. Still, my scarce-worshipful captain, you can keep
  No secret! Well, since he has told you, madam,
  Do you forgive him, and I do.
KASTRIL.   She shall do that, sir;
  I'll look to it, 'tis my charge.
SUBTLE.   Well then: nought rests
  But that she fit her love now to her fortune.
DAME PLIANT. Truly I shall never brook a Spaniard.
SUBTLE.   No!
DAME PLIANT. Never since eighty-eight, could I abide 'em,
  And that was some three year afore I was born, in truth.   30

10. *Stoup*, probably bow, perhaps bearing. *garb*, mode.
18. *scheme*, horoscope.
29. *eighty-eight*, i.e., the year of the defeat of the Armada.

SUBTLE. Come, you must love him, or be miserable;
   Choose which you will.

FACE.   By this good rush, persuade her,
   She will cry strawberries else within this twelve month.

SUBTLE. Nay, shads and mackerel, which is worse.

FACE.   Indeed, sir!

KASTRIL. God's lid, you shall love him, or I'll kick you.

DAME PLIANT.   Why,
   I'll do as you will have me, brother.

KASTRIL.   Do,
   Or by this hand I'll maul you.

FACE.   Nay, good sir,
   Be not so fierce.

SUBTLE.   No, my enragèd child;
   She will be ruled. What, when she comes to taste
   The pleasures of a countess! to be courted—   40

FACE. And kissed, and ruffled!

SUBTLE.   Ay, behind the hangings.

FACE. And then come forth in pomp!

SUBTLE.   And know her state!

FACE. Of keeping all the idolaters of the chamber
   Barer to her, than at their prayers!

SUBTLE.   Is served
   Upon the knee!

FACE.   And has her pages, ushers,
   Footmen, and coaches—

SUBTLE.   Her six mares—

FACE.   Nay, eight!

SUBTLE. To hurry her through London, to the Exchange,
   Bethlem, the china-houses—

FACE.   Yes, and have
   The citizens gape at her, and praise her tires,
   And my lord's goose-turd bands, that rides with her!   50

KASTRIL. Most brave! By this hand, you are not my suster
   If you refuse.

---

   33. *cry*, hawk.

   47. *Exchange*, the chief shopping district.

   48. *Bethlem*, Bethlehem Hospital, where the fine world went to watch the
insane for an afternoon's amusement. *china-houses*, where goods from the
Orient were sold.

   50. *goose-turd bands*, green collars.

DAME PLIANT. I will not refuse, brother.
　[*Enter Surly.*
SURLY. *Qué es esto, señores, que no se venga?*
　Esta tardanza me mata!
FACE.　　　　　　　　It is the count come:
　The doctor knew he would be here, by his art.
SUBTLE [*Presenting Dame Pliant with a flourish*]. *En gallanta*
　madama, Don! gallantissima!
SURLY. *Por todos los dioses, la mas acabada*
　Hermosura, que he visto en mi vida!
FACE. Is't not a gallant language that they speak?
KASTRIL. An admirable language! Is't not French?　　　　60
FACE. No, Spanish, sir.
KASTRIL.　　　　　　It goes like law-French,
　And that, they say, is the courtliest language.
FACE. List, sir.
SURLY.　　　*El sol ha perdido su lumbre, con el*
　Resplandor que trae esta dama! Válgame dios!
FACE. He admires your sister.
KASTRIL.　　　　　　　Must not she make curt'sy?
SUBTLE. Ods will, she must go to him, man, and kiss him!
　It is the Spanish fashion, for the women
　To make first court.
FACE.　　　　'Tis true he tells you, sir:
　His art knows all.
SURLY.　　　　*Por qué no se acude?*
KASTRIL. He speaks to her, I think.
FACE.　　　　　　That he does, sir.　　　　70
SURLY. *Por el amor de dios, qué es esto que se tarda?*
KASTRIL. Nay, see: she will not understand him! Gull.
　Noddy.
DAME PLIANT. What say you, brother?
·KASTRIL.　　　　　　　Ass, my suster,
　Go kuss him, as the cunning-man would have you;
　I'll thrust a pin in your buttocks else.

53. *Que es* . . ., What's the matter, gentlemen, that she doesn't come?
This delay is killing me.
57. *Por todos* . . ., By all the gods the most perfect beauty I have seen in
my life.
63. *El sol* . . ., The sun has lost his light with the splendor this lady
brings! So help me God.
69. *Por qué* . . . , Why don't you draw near?
71. *Por el amor* . . ., For the love of God, why this delay?

FACE.   O no, sir.

SURLY. *Señora mía, mi persona muy indigna está*
   A llegar á tanta hermosura.

FACE. Does he not use her bravely?

KASTRIL.   Bravely, i' faith!

FACE. Nay, he will use her better.

KASTRIL.   Do you think so?

SURLY. *Señora, si será servida, entrémos.*   80
   [*He takes her out with a great show of affection.*

KASTRIL. Where does he carry her?

FACE.   Into the garden, sir;
   Take you no thought: I must interpret for her.

SUBTLE [*Aside to Face who goes out*]. Give Doll the word.—
   Come, my fierce child, advance,
   We'll to our quarrelling lesson again.

KASTRIL.   Agreed.
   I love a Spanish boy with all my heart.

SUBTLE. Nay, and by this means, sir, you shall be brother
   To a great count.

KASTRIL.   Ay, I knew that at first.
   This match will advance the house of the Kastrils.

SUBTLE. 'Pray God your sister prove but pliant!

KASTRIL.   Why,
   Her name is so, by her other husband.

SUBTLE.   How!   90

KASTRIL. The Widow Pliant. Knew you not that?

SUBTLE.   No, faith, sir;
   Yet, by erection of her figure, I guessed it.
   Come, let's go practise.

KASTRIL.   Yes, but do you think, doctor,
   I e'er shall quarrel well?

SUBTLE.   I warrant you.   [*They go out together.*

SCENE V

ANOTHER ROOM IN THE HOUSE. *The gulling of Sir Epicure is nearly
complete. Doll is feigning a fit of madness brought on by
Mammon's chatter. She rushes around the room, followed by
Mammon, trying his best to quiet her.*

76. *Senora mia . . .,* My Lady, my person is quite unworthy to draw near
to such beauty.

80. *Senora, si . . .,* Madam, if you please, let us go in.

92. *erection of her figure,* casting of her horoscope, with an obvious pun.

DOLL. For after Alexander's death . . .

MAMMON. Good lady—

DOLL. That Perdiccas and Antigonus were slain,
  The two that stood, Seleuc and Ptolomee—

MAMMON. Madam—

DOLL. Make up the two legs, and the fourth beast,
  That was Gog-north and Egypt-south: which after
  Was called Gog-iron-leg and South-iron-leg.

MAMMON. Lady—

DOLL. And then Gog-hornèd. So was Egypt, too:
  Then Egypt-clay-leg, and Gog-clay-leg—

MAMMON. Sweet madam—

DOLL. And last Gog-dust, and Egypt-dust, which fall
  In the last link of the fourth chain. And these   10
  Be stars in story, which none see, or look at—

MAMMON. What shall I do?

DOLL. For, as he says, except
  We call the rabbins, and the heathen Greeks—

MAMMON. Dear lady—

DOLL. To come from Salem, and from Athens,
  And teach the people of Great Britain—

    [*Enter Face hastily, in his servant's dress, as if aroused by the
    racket.*

FACE. What's the matter, sir?

DOLL. To speak the tongue of Eber and Javan—

MAMMON. O,
  She's in her fit.

DOLL. We shall know nothing—

FACE. Death, sir,
  We are undone!

DOLL. Where then a learned linguist
  Shall see the ancient used communion
  Of vowels and consonants—

FACE. My master will hear!   20

DOLL. A wisdom, which Pythagoras held most high—

MAMMON. Sweet honourable lady!

DOLL. To comprise
  All sounds of voices, in few marks of letters.

FACE. Nay, you must never hope to lay her now.

  1. *Alexander's death*, Doll's ravings are unconnected passages from the *Concent of Scripture* by Hugh Broughton, 1590.
  14. *Salem*, Jerusalem.
  16. *Eber and Javan*, Hebrew and Greek, so named from the greatgrandson of Shem and the son of Japheth respectively.

[They all speak together.

DOLL. And so we may arrive by
    Talmud skill,
And profane Greek, to raise
    the building up
Of Helen's house against the
    Ismaelite,
King of Thogarma, and his
    habergions
Brimstony, blue, and fiery;
    and the force
Of king Abaddon, and the
    beast of Cittim,   30
Which Rabbi David Kimchi,
    Onkelos,
And Aben-Ezra do interpret
    Rome.

FACE. How did you put her
    into't?
MAMMON.   Alas, I talked
    Of a fifth monarchy I would
        erect,
With the philosopher's stone,
    by chance, and she
Falls on the other four
    straight.
FACE. Out of Broughton!
    I told you so. 'Slid, stop her
    mouth.
MAMMON.   Is't best?
FACE. She'll never leave else. If
    the old man hear her,
We are but fæces, ashes.
SUBTLE [*Within*]. What's to do
    there?
FACE. O, we are lost! Now she
    hears him, she is quiet.   40

*[Enter Subtle; they run different ways, making grotesque
    efforts to hide; Face slips out just as Subtle enters.*

MAMMON. Where shall I hide me!
SUBTLE.   How! what sight is here?
    Close deeds of darkness, and that shun the light!
    Bring him again. Who is he? What, my son!
    O, I have lived too long!
MAMMON.   Nay, good, dear father,
    There was no unchaste purpose.
SUBTLE.   Not! and flee me,
    When I come in?
MAMMON.   That was my error.
SUBTLE.   Error!
    Guilt, guilt, my son: give it the right name. No marvel,
    If I found check in your great work within,
    When such affairs as these were managing!
MAMMON. Why, have you so?
SUBTLE.   It has stood still this half hour: 50
    And all the rest of our less works gone back.
    Where is the instrument of wickedness,
    My lewd false drudge?

MAMMON.   Nay, good sir, blame not him;
Believe me, 'twas against his will or knowledge:
I saw her by chance.
SUBTLE.   Will you commit more sin,
To excuse a varlet?
MAMMON.   By my hope, 'tis true, sir.
SUBTLE. Nay, then I wonder less, if you, for whom
The blessing was prepared, would so tempt Heaven,
And lose your fortunes.
MAMMON.   Why, sir?
SUBTLE.   This will retard
The work a month at least.
MAMMON.   Why, if it do,   60
What remedy? But think it not, good father:
Our purposes were honest.
SUBTLE.   As they were,
So the reward will prove. [*A loud explosion within.*]—How
now! ah me!
 *God and all saints be good to us.—
[*Face rushes blindly in, covered with soot and roaring as if
with pain and mortification.*
What's that?
FACE. O, sir, we are defeated! all the works
Are flown *in fumo*, every glass is burst:
Furnace, and all rent down! as if a bolt
Of thunder had been driven through the house.
Retorts, receivers, pelicans, bolt-heads,
All struck in shivers! [*Subtle falls down as in a swoon.*] Help,
good sir! alas,   70
Coldness and death invades him. Nay, Sir Mammon,
Do the fair offices of a man! you stand,
As you were readier to depart than he.   [*Knocking within.*
Who's there? my lord her brother is come.
[*He runs to the window.*
MAMMON.   Ha, Lungs!
FACE. His coach is at the door. Avoid his sight,
For he's as furious as his sister's mad.
MAMMON. Alas!
FACE.   My brain is quite undone with the fume, sir,
I ne'er must hope to be mine own man again.
MAMMON. Is all lost, Lungs? will nothing be preserved
Of all our cost?

62. *honest*, chaste.

FACE. Faith, very little, sir;
A peck of coals or so, which is cold comfort, sir.

MAMMON. O, my voluptuous mind! I am justly punished.

FACE. And so am I, sir.

MAMMON. Cast from all my hopes—

FACE. Nay, certainties, sir.

MAMMON. By mine own base affections.

SUBTLE [*Seeming to come to himself*]. O, the cursed fruits of vice
and lust!

MAMMON. Good father,
It was my sin. Forgive it.

SUBTLE. Hangs my roof
Over us still, and will not fall, O justice,
Upon us, for this wicked man!

FACE. Nay, look, sir,
You grieve him now with staying in his sight:
Good sir, the nobleman will come too, and take you, 90
And that may breed a tragedy.

MAMMON. I'll go.

FACE. Ay, and repent at home, sir. It may be,
For some good penance you may have it yet;
A hundred pound to the box at Bethlem—

MAMMON. Yes.

FACE. For the restoring such as—have their wits.

MAMMON. I'll do't.

FACE. I'll send one to you to receive it.

MAMMON. Do.
Is no projection left?

FACE. All flown, or stinks, sir.

MAMMON. Will nought be saved that's good for med'cine, think'st
thou?

FACE. I cannot tell, sir. There will be perhaps
Something about the scraping of the shards, 100
Will cure the itch—[*Aside.*] though not your itch of mind,
sir.—
It shall be saved for you, and sent home. Good sir,
This way, for fear the lord should meet you.   [*Exit Mammon.*

SUBTLE [*Raising his head*]. Face!

FACE. Ay.

SUBTLE. Is he gone?

FACE. Yes, and as heavily
As all the gold he hoped for were in's blood.
Let us be light though.

SUBTLE [*Leaping up*].   Ay, as balls, and bound
　　And hit our heads against the roof for joy:
　　There's so much of our care now cast away.
FACE. Now to our Don.
SUBTLE.　　　　　　　Yes, your young widow by this time
　　Is made a countess, Face; she has been in travail　　　　110
　　Of a young heir for you.
FACE.　　　　　　　Good, sir.
SUBTLE.　　　　　　　　　Off with your case,
　　And greet her kindly, as a bridegroom should,
　　After these common hazards.
FACE.　　　　　　　Very well, sir.
　　Will you go fetch Don Diego off the while?
SUBTLE. And fetch him over too, if you'll be pleased, sir:
　　Would Doll were in her place, to pick his pockets now!
FACE. Why, you can do't as well, if you would set to't.
　　I pray you prove your virtue.
SUBTLE.　　　　　　　For your sake, sir.   [*They hurry out.*

SCENE VI

A ROOM TO WHICH SURLY AND DAME PLIANT HAVE WITHDRAWN. *Instead of having tried to seduce her, however, as the tricksters
had expected, Surly has used the time to tell her of the rascality of the others and to plead his own cause as an honest
man. She is on the way to being convinced.*

SURLY. Lady, you see into what hands you are fallen;
　　'Mongst what a nest of villains! and how near
　　Your honour was t' have catched a certain clap,
　　Through your credulity, had I but been
　　So punctually forward, as place, time,
　　And other circumstances would have made a man;
　　For you're a handsome woman; would you were wise too!
　　I am a gentleman come here disguised,
　　Only to find the knaveries of this citadel;
　　And where I might have wronged your honour, and have not,
　　I claim some interest in your love. You are,　　　　11
　　They say, a widow, rich; and I'm a bachelor,
　　Worth nought; your fortunes may make me a man,
　　As mine have preserved you a woman. Think upon it,

111. *case*, disguise.

And whether I have deserved you or no.

DAME PLIANT.   I will, sir.

SURLY. And for these household-rogues, let me alone
To treat with them.

   [*Enter Subtle, anxious to trick the "Don" as neatly as he has*
   Sir Epicure.

SUBTLE.   How doth my noble Diego,
And my dear madam countess? hath the count
Been courteous, lady? liberal and open?
Donzel, methinks you look melancholic,   20
After your coitum, and scurvy: truly,
I do not like the dullness of your eye;
It hath a heavy cast, 'tis upsee Dutch,
And says you are a lumpish whoremaster.
Be lighter, I will make your pockets so.
   [*Attempts to pick them.*

SURLY [*Throws open his cloak*]. Will you, Don bawd and pick-
   purse? [*Strikes him down.*] How now! reel you?
Stand up, sir, you shall find, since I am so heavy,
I'll give you equal weight.

SUBTLE.   Help! murder!

SURLY [*Continuing to beat him*].   No, sir.
There's no such thing intended: a good cart
And a clean whip shall ease you of that fear.   30
I am the Spanish Don *that should be cozened,*
Do you see, cozened! Where's your Captain Face,
That parcel-broker, and whole-bawd, all rascal?
   [*Enter Face in his uniform.*

FACE. How, Surly!

SURLY [*Intent on disclosing the tricks of the sharpers*]. O, make
   your approach, good captain.
I have found from whence your copper rings and spoons
Come now, wherewith you cheat abroad in taverns.
'Twas here you learned t'anoint your boot with brimstone,
Then rub men's gold on't for a kind of touch,
And say 'twas naught, when you had changed the colour,
That you might have't for nothing. And this doctor,   40
Your sooty, smoky-bearded compeer, he

---

23. *upsee Dutch*, in the Dutch fashion (op zijn Dutch).

29. *a good cart . . .*, a common punishment for bawds and whores was to
tie them to the tail of a cart and whip them through town, roughly equivalent to riding on a rail.

33. *parcel*, part.

Will close you so much gold, in a bolt's-head,
And, on a turn, convey in the stead another
With sublimed mercury, that shall burst in the heat,
And fly out all *in fumo!* Then weeps Mammon;
Then swoons his worship. [*Face slips out.*] Or, he is the
    Faustus,
That casteth figures and can conjure, cures
Plagues, piles, and pox, by the ephemerides,
And holds intelligence with all the bawds
And midwives of three shires: while you send in—   50
Captain!—what! is he gone?—damsels with child,
Wives that are barren, or the waiting-maid
With the green sickness. [*Subtle tries to run off, but Surly
seizes him.*]—Nay sir, you must tarry,
Though he be scaped; and answer by the ears, sir.

SCENE VII

*Face has been trying to save the situation. He has rushed to Kas-
tril and persuaded him that Surly is a rascal and now brings
Kastril in to help them get rid of Surly.*

FACE. Why, now's the time, if ever you will quarrel
Well, as they say, and be a true-born child:
The doctor and your sister both are abused.
KASTRIL. Where is he? which is he? he is a slave,
Whate'er he is, and the son of a whore.—Are you
The man, sir, I would know?
SURLY.   I should be loath, sir,
To confess so much.
KASTRIL.   Then you lie in your throat.
SURLY.   How!
FACE. [*To Kastril*]. A very errant rogue, sir, and a cheater,
Employed here by another conjurer
That does not love the doctor, and would cross him   10
If he knew how.
SURLY.   Sir, you are abused.
KASTRIL.   You lie:
And 'tis no matter.
FACE.   Well said, sir! He is
The impudent'st rascal—

48. *epheremides,* astrological almanacs.
53. *green-sickness,* chlorosis, an anemic disorder.

SURLY.   You are indeed. Will you hear me, sir?
FACE. By no means: bid him be gone.
KASTRIL.   Be gone, sir, quickly.
SURLY. This is strange!—Lady, do you inform your brother.
FACE [*Determined not to let her speak*]. There is not such a foist
    in all the town,
  'The doctor had him presently; and finds yet
  The Spanish count will come here.—[*Aside.*] Bear up, Subtle.
SUBTLE. Yes, sir, he must appear within this hour.
FACE. And yet this rogue would come in a disguise,   20
  By the temptation of another spirit,
  To trouble our art, though he could not hurt it!
KASTRIL [*As his sister tries to speak*].   Ay,
  I know—Away, [*To his sister.*] you talk like a foolish mauther.
SURLY. Sir, all is truth she says.
FACE.   Do not believe him, sir.
  He is the lying'st swabber! Come your ways, sir.
SURLY. You are valiant out of company!
KASTRIL.   Yes, how then, sir?
  [*Enter Drugger with a piece of damask. Face seizes the op-*
    portunity to discredit Surly.
FACE. Nay, here's an honest fellow too that knows him,
  And all his tricks.—[*Aside to Drugger.*] Make good what I say,
    Abel,
  This cheater would have cozened thee o' the widow.—
  He owes this honest Drugger here seven pound,   30
  He has had on him in two-penny'orths of tobacco.
DRUGGER. Yes, sir. And he has damned himself three terms to
  pay me.
FACE. And what does he owe for lotium?
DRUGGER.   Thirty shillings, sir;
  And for six syringes.
SURLY.   Hydra of villainy!
FACE. Nay, sir, you must quarrel him out o' the house.
KASTRIL.   I will.
  —Sir, if you get not out o' doors, you lie;
  And you are a pimp.
SURLY.   Why, this is madness, sir,
  Not valour in you; I must laugh at this.
KASTRIL. It is my humour; you are a pimp and a trig,
  And an Amadis de Gaul, or a Don Quixote.   40

16. *foist*, rogue.   23. *mauther*, wench.   39. *trig*, coxcomb.

DRUGGER. Or a knight o' the curious coxcomb, do you see?

[*Enter Ananias, exulting in the result of the Congregation's meditations.*

ANANIAS. Peace to the household!

KASTRIL.   I'll keep peace for no man.

ANANIAS. Casting of dollars is concluded lawful.

KASTRIL. Is he the constable?

SUBTLE.   Peace, Ananias.

FACE.   No, sir.

KASTRIL. Then you are an otter, and a shad, a whit,
    A very tim.

SURLY.   You'll hear me, sir?

KASTRIL.   I will not.

ANANIAS. What is the motive?

SUBTLE [*Ready to use all things to gain his ends*]. Zeal in the
    young gentleman,
    Against his Spanish slops.

ANANIAS.   They are profane,
    Lewd, superstitious, and idolatrous breeches.

SURLY. New rascals!

KASTRIL.   Will you be gone, sir?

ANANIAS.   Avoid, Sathan!   50
    Thou art not of the light! That ruff of pride
    About thy neck betrays thee; and is the same
    With that which the unclean birds, in seventy-seven,
    Were seen to prank it with on divers coasts:
    Thou look'st like Antichrist, in that lewd hat.

SURLY. I must give way.

KASTRIL.   Be gone, sir.

SURLY.   But I'll take
    A course with you—

ANANIAS.   Depart, proud Spanish fiend!

SURLY. Captain and doctor—

ANANIAS.   Child of perdition!

KASTRIL.   Hence, sir!—
    [*They all threaten him; so Surly goes off.*
    Did I not quarrel bravely?

FACE.   Yes, indeed, sir.

KASTRIL. Nay, an I give my mind to't, I shall do't.   60

---

46. *tim*, a mere particle.

53. *seventy-seven*, an occurrence that has not been explained. Spencer suggests a migration of birds with ruffled necks, in such great numbers as to make foul nuisances of themselves.

FACE. O, you must follow sir, and threaten him tame:
  He'll turn again else:
KASTRIL.   I'll re-turn him then.
    [*Exit. Subtle takes Ananias aside, and Face engages Drugger.*
FACE. Drugger, this rogue prevented us, for thee:
  We had determined that thou should'st have come
  In a Spanish suit, and have carried her so; and he,
  A brokerly slave! goes, puts it on himself.
  Hast brought the damask?
DRUGGER.   Yes, sir.
FACE.   Thou must borrow
  A Spanish suit; hast thou no credit with the players?
DRUGGER. Yes, sir; did you never see me play the Fool?
FACE. I know not, Nab.—[*Aside.*] thou shalt, if I can help it.—
  Hieronimo's old cloak, ruff, and hat will serve;   71
  I'll tell thee more when thou bring'st 'em.
    [*Drugger hurries anxiously away.*
ANANIAS.   Sir, I know
  The Spaniard hates the brethren, and hath spies
  Upon their actions: and that this was one
  I make no scruple.—But the holy synod
  Have been in prayer and meditation for it;
  And 'tis revealed no less to them than me,
  That casting of money is most lawful.
SUBTLE.   True.
  But here I cannot do it: if the house
  Should chance to be suspected, all would out,   80
  And we be locked up in the Tower for ever,
  To make gold there for the state, never come out;
  And then are you defeated.
ANANIAS.   I will tell
  This to the elders and the weaker brethren,
  That the whole company of the separation
  May join in humble prayer again.
SUBTLE.   And fasting.
ANANIAS. Yea, for some fitter place. The peace of mind
  Rest with these walls!   [*He goes out.*
SUBTLE.   Thanks, courteous Ananias.
FACE. What did he come for?
SUBTLE.   About casting dollars,
  Presently, out of hand. And so I told him,   90
  A Spanish minister came here to spy,

  71. *Hieronimo*, one of the principals in Kyd's *Spanish Tragedy.*

Against the faithful—

FACE.   I conceive. Come, Subtle,
Thou art so down upon the least disaster!
How wouldst thou ha' done, if I had not helped thee out?

SUBTLE. I thank thee, Face, for the angry boy, i' faith.

FACE. Who would have looked it should have been that rascal
Surly? He has dyed his beard and all. Well, sir,
Here's damask come to make you a suit.

SUBTLE.   Where's Drugger?

FACE. He is gone to borrow me a Spanish habit;
I'll be the count now.

SUBTLE.   But where's the widow?   100

FACE. Within, with my lord's sister; Madam Doll
Is entertaining her.

SUBTLE.   By your favour, Face,
Now she is honest, I will stand again.

FACE. You will not offer it?

SUBTLE.   Why?

FACE.   Stand to your word,
Or—here comes Doll, she knows—

SUBTLE.   You are tyrannous still.
    [*Enter Doll hastily.*

FACE.—Strict for my right.—How now, Doll! Hast told her,
The Spanish count will come?

DOLL.   Yes; but another is come,
You little looked for!

FACE.   Who is that?

DOLL.   Your master;
The master of the house.

SUBTLE.   How, Doll!

FACE.   She lies,
This is some trick. Come, leave your quiblins, Dorothy.

DOLL. Look out and see.   [*Face goes to the window.*

SUBTLE.   Art thou in earnest?

DOLL.   'Slight,   111
Forty o' the neighbours are about him, talking.

FACE. 'Tis he, by this good day.

DOLL.   'Twill prove ill day
For some on us.

FACE.   We are undone, and taken.

DOLL. Lost, I'm afraid.

SUBTLE.   You said he would not come,

110. *quiblins*, quibbles, tricks.

While there died one a week within the liberties.

FACE. No: 'twas within the walls.

SUBTLE. Was't so! cry you mercy.
I thought the liberties. What shall we do now, Face?

FACE. Be silent: not a word, if he call or knock.
I'll into mine old shape again, and meet him,   120
Of Jeremy, the butler. In the mean time,
Do you two pack up all the goods and purchase,
That we can carry in the two trunks. I'll keep him
Off for to-day, if I cannot longer: and then
At night, I'll ship you both away to Ratcliff
Where we will meet to-morrow, and there we'll share.
Let Mammon's brass and pewter keep the cellar;
We'll have another time for that. But, Doll,
Prithee go heat a little water quickly;
Subtle must shave me: all my captain's beard   130
Must off, to make me appear smooth Jeremy.
You'll do it?

SUBTLE. Yes, I'll shave you as well as I can.

FACE. And not cut my throat, but trim me?

SUBTLE. You shall see, sir.
[They go out anxiously.

ACT V

SCENE I

OUTSIDE THE HOUSE. *Lovewit stands on the doorstep, surrounded by a group of his neighbors who have been telling him excitedly of all the strange doings that have been going on in his house during his absence. Lovewit is puzzled.*

LOVEWIT. Has there been such resort, say you?

1 NEIGHBOR. Daily, sir.

2 NEIGHBOR. And nightly, too.

3 NEIGHBOR. Ay, some as brave as lords.

4 NEIGHBOR. Ladies and gentlewomen.

5 NEIGHBOR. Citizens' wives.

1 NEIGHBOR. And knights.

116. *liberties*, the sections outside the city walls but within the control of the city.

122. *purchase*, plunder.

6 NEIGHBOR.   In coaches.

2 NEIGHBOR.   Yes, and oyster-women.

1 NEIGHBOR. Beside other gallants.

3 NEIGHBOR.   Sailors' wives.

4 NEIGHBOR.   Tobacco-men.

5 NEIGHBOR. Another Pimlico!

LOVEWIT.   What should my knave advance,
To draw this company? he hung out no banners
Of a strange calf with five legs to be seen,
Or a huge lobster with six claws?

6 NEIGHBOR.   No, sir.

3 NEIGHBOR. We had gone in then, sir.

LOVEWIT.   He has no gift   10
Of teaching in the nose that e'er I knew of.
You saw no bills set up that promised cure
Of agues, or the toothache?

2 NEIGHBOR.   No such thing, sir!

LOVEWIT. Nor heard a drum struck for baboons or puppets?

5 NEIGHBOR. Neither, sir.

LOVEWIT.   What device should he bring forth now?
I love a teeming wit as I love my nourishment:
'Pray God he have not kept such open house,
That he hath sold my hangings, and my bedding!
I left him nothing else. If he have eat 'em,
A plague o' the moth, say I! Sure he has got   20
Some bawdy pictures to call all this ging;
The friar and the nun; or the new motion
Of the knight's courser covering the parson's mare;
The boy of six year old with the great thing;
Or't may be, he has the fleas that run a tilt
Upon a table, or some dog to dance.
When saw you him?

1 NEIGHBOR.   Who, sir, Jeremy?

2 NEIGHBOR.   Jeremy butler?
We saw him not this month.

LOVEWIT.   How!

4 NEIGHBOR.   Not these five weeks, sir.

6 NEIGHBOR. These six weeks at the least.

LOVEWIT.   You amaze me, neighbours!

5 NEIGHBOR. Sure, if your worship know not where he is,   30

6. *Pimlico,* a popular resort.
11. *nose,* as if he had turned Puritan preacher.
21. *ging,* gang, crowd.   22. *motion,* puppet show.

He's slipped away.

6 NEIGHBOR.   Pray God he be not made away.

LOVEWIT. Ha! it's no time to question, then.

    [*Knocks at the door.*

6 NEIGHBOR.   About

    Some three weeks since I heard a doleful cry,

    As I sat up a mending my wife's stockings.

LOVEWIT. 'Tis strange that none will answer! Did'st thou hear

    A cry, sayst thou?

6 NEIGHBOR.   Yes, sir, like unto a man

    That had been strangled an hour, and could not speak.

2 NEIGHBOR. I heard it too, just this day three weeks, at two

    o'clock

    Next morning.

LOVEWIT.   These be miracles, or you make them so!

    A man an hour strangled, and could not speak,   40

    And both you heard him cry?

3 NEIGHBOR.   Yes, downward, sir.

LOVEWIT. Thou art a wise fellow. Give me thy hand, I pray thee,

    What trade art thou on?

3 NEIGHBOR.   A smith, an't please your worship.

LOVEWIT. A smith! then lend me thy help to get this door open.

3 NEIGHBOR. That I will presently, sir, but fetch my tools—

                                     [*Exit.*

1 NEIGHBOR. Sir, best to knock again afore you break it.

SCENE II

LOVEWIT [*Knocks again*]. I will.

    [*Enter Face in his butler's livery, his beard shaved off, and
    far more innocent looking than the Capt. Face or the Lungs
    of the preceding scenes.*

FACE.   What mean you, sir?

1, 2, 4, NEIGHBORS.   O, here's Jeremy!

FACE. Good sir, come from the door.

LOVEWIT.   Why, what's the matter?

FACE. Yet farther, you are too near yet.

LOVEWIT.   In the name of wonder,

    What means the fellow!

FACE.   The house, sir, has been visited.

LOVEWIT. What, with the plague? stand thou then farther.

FACE.   No, sir,
    I had it not.

LOVEWIT.   Who had it then? I left
    None else but thee in the house.

FACE.   Yes, sir, my fellow,
    The cat that kept the buttery, had it on her
    A week before I spied it; but I got her
    Conveyed away in the night: and so I shut   10
    The house up for a month—

LOVEWIT.   How!

FACE. .   Purposing then, sir,
    To have burnt rose-vinegar, treacle, and tar,
    And have made it sweet, that you should ne'er have known it;
    Because I knew the news would but afflict you, sir.

LOVEWIT. Breathe less, and farther off! Why this is stranger:
    The neighbours tell me all here that the doors
    Have still been open—

FACE.   How, sir!

LOVEWIT.   Gallants, men and women,
    And of all sorts, tag-rag, been seen to flock here
    In threaves, these ten weeks, as to a second Hogsden,
    In days of Pimlico and Eye-bright.

FACE.   Sir,   20
    Their wisdoms will not say so.

LOVEWIT.   To-day they speak
    Of coaches and gallants; one in a French hood
    Went in, they tell me; and another was seen
    In a velvet gown at the window: divers more
    Pass in and out.

FACE.   They did pass through the doors then,
    Or walls, I assure their eyesights, and their spectacles;
    For here, sir, are the keys, and here have been,
    In this my pocket, now above twenty days:
    And for before, I kept the fort alone there.
    But that 'tis yet not deep in the afternoon,   30
    I should believe my neighbours had seen double
    Through the black-pot, and made these apparitions!
    For, on my faith to your worship, for these three weeks
    And upwards, the door has not been opened.

LOVEWIT.   Strange!

8. *kept*, guarded.   19. *threaves*, droves.
20. *Eye-bright*, probably either a tavern or a popular drink.
31. *seen double*, i.e., had been drunk.

1 NEIGHBOR. Good faith, I think I saw a coach.

2 NEIGHBOR.   And I too,
 I'd have been sworn.

LOVEWIT.   Do you but think it now?
 And but one coach?

4 NEIGHBOR.   We cannot tell, sir; Jeremy
 Is a very honest fellow.

FACE.   Did you see me at all?

1 NEIGHBOR. No; that we are sure on.

2 NEIGHBOR.   I'll be sworn o' that.

LOVEWIT. Fine rogues to have your testimonies built on!

 [*Re-enter third Neighbour, with his tools.*

3 NEIGHBOR. Is Jeremy come!

1 NEIGHBOR.   O yes; you may leave your tools;
 We were deceived, he says.

2 NEIGHBOR.   He has had the keys;
 And the door has been shut these three weeks.

3 NEIGHBOR.   Like enough.

LOVEWIT. Peace, and get hence, you changelings.

FACE [*Aside. He sees Surly and Mammon approaching in the dis-
 tance*].   Surly come!
 And Mammon made acquainted! they'll tell all.
 How shall I beat them off? what shall I do?
 Nothing's more wretched than a guilty conscience.

SCENE III

*Surly and Mammon come in. The former is still trying to con-
vince Sir Epicure that he has been tricked, but it is hard to make
a fool realize his folly. Surly is sarcastic as usual.*

SURLY. No, sir, he was a great physician. This,
 It was no bawdy house, but a mere chancel!
 You knew the lord and his sister.

MAMMON.   Nay, good Surly.—

SURLY. The happy word, "Be rich"—

MAMMON.   Play not the tyrant.—

SURLY. Should be to-day pronounced to all your friends.
 And where be your andirons now? and your brass pots,
 That should have been golden flagons, and great wedges?

MAMMON. Let me but breathe. What, they have shut their doors,

 2. *mere*, real, actual.

[The others draw off to one side as they enter.
Methinks!

SURLY. Ay, now 'tis holiday with them.

MAMMON. Rogues, *[He and Surly knock.*
Cozeners, impostors, bawds!

FACE. What mean you, sir? 10

MAMMON. To enter if we can.

FACE. Another man's house?
Here is the owner, sir; turn you to him,
And speak your business.

MAMMON. Are you, sir, the owner?

LOVEWIT. Yes, sir.

MAMMON. And are those knaves within your cheaters!

LOVEWIT. What knaves, what cheaters?

MAMMON. Subtle and his Lungs.

FACE. The gentleman is distracted, sir! No lungs,
Nor lights have been seen here these three weeks, sir,
Within these doors, upon my word.

SURLY. Your word,
Groom arrogant!

FACE. Yes, sir, I am the housekeeper,
And know the keys have not been out of my hands. 20

SURLY. This is a new Face.

FACE. You do mistake the house, sir:
What sign was't at?

SURLY. You rascal! this is one
Of the confederacy. Come, let's get officers,
And force the door.

LOVEWIT. Pray you stay, gentlemen.

SURLY. No, sir, we'll come with warrant.

MAMMON. Ay, and then
We shall have your doors open.

[Mammon and Surly go away in great anger.

LOVEWIT. What means this?

FACE. I cannot tell, sir.

1 NEIGHBOR. These are two of the gallants
That we do think we saw.

FACE. Two of the fools!
You talk as idly as they. Good faith, sir,
I think the moon has crazed 'em all.—*[Aside.]* O me, 30

---

22. *sign*, signs were hung out before private houses as well as places of
business to identify them to an illiterate populace.

[*Enter Kastril, who has begun to come to his senses.*
The angry boy come too! He'll make a noise,
And ne'er away till he have betrayed us all.

KASTRIL [*Knocking*]. What rogues, bawds, slaves, you'll open the
　　door, anon!
Punk, cockatrice, my suster! By this light
I'll fetch the marshal to you. You are a whore
To keep your castle—

FACE.　　　　　　　Who would you speak with, sir?

KASTRIL. The bawdy doctor, and the cozening captain,
　And puss my suster.

LOVEWIT.　　　　This is something, sure.

FACE. Upon my trust, the doors were never open, sir.

KASTRIL. I have heard all their tricks told me twice over,　　40
　By the fat knight and the lean gentleman.

LOVEWIT. Here comes another.

　　[*Enter Ananias and Tribulation, likewise so lost in contem-
　　plation of their wrong that they pay no attention to the
　　group gathered there.*

FACE.　　　　　　　Ananias, too!
　And his pastor!

TRIBULATION [*Beating at the door*]. The doors are shut against us.

ANANIAS. Come forth, you seed of sulphur, sons of fire!
　Your stench it is broke forth; abomination
　Is in the house.

KASTRIL.　　　Ay, my suster's there.

ANANIAS.　　　　　　　The place,
　It is become a cage of unclean birds.

KASTRIL. Yes, I will fetch the scavenger, and the constable.

TRIBULATION. You shall do well.

ANANIAS.　　　　　We'll join to weed them out.

KASTRIL. You will not come then, punk devise, my suster!　　50

ANANIAS. Call her not sister; she's a harlot verily.

KASTRIL. I'll raise the street.

LOVEWIT.　　　Good gentlemen, a word.

ANANIAS. Satan avoid, and hinder not our zeal!

　　[*Exeunt Ananias, Tribulation, and Kastril.*

LOVEWIT. The world's turned Bethlem.

FACE.　　　　　　These are all broke loose,
　Out of St. Katherine's, where they use to keep
　The better sort of mad-folks.

1 NEIGHBOR.　　　All these persons

50. *punk devise*, perfect whore.

We saw go in and out there.

2 NEIGHBOR. Yes, indeed, sir.

3 NEIGHBOR. These were the parties.

FACE. Peace, you drunkards! Sir,
I wonder at it: please you to give me leave
To touch the door, I'll try an the lock be changed. 60

LOVEWIT. It amazes me!

FACE [*Goes to the door*]. Good faith, sir, I believe
There's no such thing: 'tis all *deceptio visus*.—
[*Aside.*] Would I could get him away.

DAPPER [*Within*]. Master captain! master doctor!

LOVEWIT. Who's that?

FACE [*Aside*]. Our clerk within, that I forgot!—[*To Lovewit.*] I know not, sir.

DAPPER [*Within*]. For God's sake, when will her grace be at leisure?

FACE. Ha!
Illusions, some spirit o' the air!—[*Aside*]. His gag is melted,
And now he sets out the throat.

DAPPER [*Within*]. I am almost stifled—

FACE [*Aside*]. Would you were altogether.

LOVEWIT. 'Tis in the house.
Ha! list.

FACE. Believe it, sir, in the air.

LOVEWIT. Peace, you.

DAPPER [*Within*]. Mine aunt's grace does not use me well.

SUBTLE [*Within*]. You fool, 70
Peace, you'll mar all.

FACE [*Speaks through the keyhole, while Lovewit advances to the
door unobserved*]. Or you will else, you rogue.

LOVEWIT. O, is it so? then you converse with spirits!—
Come, sir. No more of your tricks, good Jeremy,
The truth, the shortest way.

FACE. Dismiss this rabble, sir.—
[*Aside.*] What shall I do? I am catched.

LOVEWIT. Good neighbours,
I thank you all. You may depart. [*Exeunt Neighbours.*]—
Come, sir,
You know that I am an indulgent master;
And therefore conceal nothing. What's your medicine,
To draw so many several sorts of wild fowl?

FACE. Sir, you were wont to affect mirth and wit— 80

61. *deceptio visus*, optical illusion.

But here's no place to talk on't in the street.
Give me but leave to make the best of my fortune,
And only pardon me the abuse of your house:
It's all I beg. I'll help you to a widow,
In recompense, that you shall give me thanks for,
Will make you seven years younger, and a rich one.
'Tis but your putting on a Spanish cloak:
I have her within. You need not fear the house:
It was not visited.

LOVEWIT.   But by me, who came
Sooner than you expected.

FACE.   It is true, sir.   90
Pray you forgive me.

LOVEWIT.   Well: let's see your widow.

> [*They enter the house.*

SCENE IV

Subtle is anxious to let no chance slip, even in these last dangerous moments. He leads in Dapper, still blindfolded, and more anxious than ever. Meanwhile Face and Doll have presumably been packing up all their goods. Face has refrained from telling them the details of his conversation with his master.

SUBTLE. How! have you eaten your gag?

DAPPER.   Yes, faith, it crumbled
Away in my mouth.

SUBTLE.   You have spoiled all then.

DAPPER.   No!
I hope my aunt of Fairy will forgive me.

SUBTLE. Your aunt's a gracious lady; but in troth
You were to blame.

DAPPER.   The fume did overcome me,
And I did do't to stay my stomach. Pray you
So satisfy her grace.

> [*Enter Face in his uniform.*

                    Here comes the captain.

FACE. How now! is his mouth down?

SUBTLE.   Ay, he has spoken!

FACE. A pox, I heard him, and you too. He's undone then.—
[*Aside to Subtle.*] I have been fain to say, the house is haunted
With spirits, to keep churl back.

89. *visited*, i.e., by the plague.

SUBTLE.   And hast thou done it?   11

FACE. Sure, for this night.

SUBTLE.   Why, then triumph, and sing
   Of Face so famous, the precious king
   Of present wits.

FACE.   Did you not hear the coil
   About the door?

SUBTLE.   Yes, and I dwindled with it.

FACE. Show him his aunt, and let him be dispatched:
   I'll send her to you.   *[Exit Face.*

SUBTLE.   Well, sir, your aunt her grace
   Will give you audience presently, on my suit,
   And the captain's word that you did not eat your gag
   In any contempt of her highness.   *[Unbinds his eyes.*

DAPPER.   Not I, in troth, sir.   20
   [Enter Doll like the Queen of Fairy.

SUBTLE. Here she is come. Down o' your knees and wriggle:
   She has a stately presence. *[Dapper kneels and shuffles towards
   her.]* Good! Yet nearer,
   And bid, God save you!

DAPPER.   Madam!

SUBTLE.   And your aunt.

DAPPER. And my most gracious aunt, God save your grace.

DOLL. Nephew, we thought to have been angry with you;
   But that sweet face of yours hath turned the tide,
   And made it flow with joy, that ebbed of love.
   Arise, and touch our velvet gown.

SUBTLE.   The skirts,
   And kiss 'em. So!

DOLL.   Let me now stroke that head.
   Much, nephew, shalt thou win, much shalt thou spend;   30
   Much shalt thou give away, much shalt thou lend.

SUBTLE *[Aside].* Ay, much! indeed.—Why do you not thank her
   grace?

DAPPER. I cannot speak for joy.

SUBTLE.   See, the kind wretch!
   Your grace's kinsman right.

DOLL.   Give me the bird.
   Here is your fly in a purse, about your neck, cousin;
   Wear it, and feed it about this day sev'n-night
   On your right wrist—

SUBTLE.   Open a vein with a pin,

14. *coil,* disturbance.

And let it suck but once a week; till then,
You must not look on't.
DOLL.   No: and, kinsman,
Bear yourself worthy of the blood you come on.   40
SUBTLE. Her grace would have you eat no more Woolsack pies,
Nor Dagger frume'ty.
DOLL.   Nor break his fast
In Heaven and Hell.
SUBTLE.   She's with you everywhere!
Nor play with costermongers, at mum-chance, tray-trip,
God make you rich; (when as your aunt has done it;) but keep
The gallant'st company, and the best games—
DAPPER.   Yes, sir.
SUBTLE. Gleek and primero: and what you get, be true to us.
DAPPER. By this hand, I will.
SUBTLE.   You may bring's a thousand pound
Before to-morrow night, (if but three thousand
Be stirring) an you will.
DAPPER.   I swear I will then.   50
SUBTLE. Your fly will learn you all games.
FACE [Within].   Have you done there?
SUBTLE. Your grace will command him no more duties?
DOLL.   No:
But come, and see me often. I may chance
To leave him three or four hundred chests of treasure,
And some twelve thousand acres of fairy land,
If he game well and comely with good gamesters.
SUBTLE. There's a kind aunt: kiss her departing part.—
But you must sell your forty mark a year now.
DAPPER. Ay, sir, I mean.
SUBTLE.   Or, give 't away; pox on't!
DAPPER. I'll give 't mine aunt: I'll go and fetch the writings.   60
                    [He goes out joyfully.
SUBTLE. 'Tis well, away.
        [Re-enter Face.
FACE.   Where's Subtle?
SUBTLE.   Here: what news?
FACE. Drugger is at the door, go take his suit,

38. *suck*, the common belief was that familiar spirits fed on the blood of those whom they served.
42. *frume'ty*, frumenty, wheat boiled in milk.
43. *Woolsack*, *Dagger*, *Heaven*, and *Hell*, popular taverns.
44. *mumchance*, etc., gambling games; gleek and primero were more popular with the upper classes.

And bid him fetch a parson presently:
Say he shall marry the widow. Thou shalt spend
A hundred pound by the service! [*Exit Subtle.*] Now, Queen
  Doll,
Have you packed up all?

DOLL.   Yes.

FACE.   And how do you like
  The Lady Pliant?

DOLL.   A good dull innocent.
    [*Re-enter Subtle with a Spanish cloak and hat.*

SUBTLE. Here's your Hieronimo's cloak and hat.

FACE.   Give me 'em.

SUBTLE. And the ruff too?

FACE.   Yes; I'll come to you presently.   [*Exit.*

SUBTLE. Now he is gone about his project, Doll,   70
  I told you of, for the widow.

DOLL.   'Tis direct
  Against our articles.

SUBTLE.   Well, we will fit him, wench.
  Hast thou gulled her of her jewels or her bracelets?

DOLL. No; but I will do't.

SUBTLE.   Soon at night, my Dolly,
  When we are shipped, and all our goods aboard,
  Eastward for Ratcliff; we will turn our course
  To Brainford, westward, if thou sayst the word,
  And take our leaves of this o'erweening rascal,
  This peremptory Face.

DOLL.   Content, I'm weary of him.

SUBTLE. Thou'st cause, when the slave will run a wiving, Doll,   80
  Against the instrument that was drawn between us.

DOLL. I'll pluck his bird as bare as I can.

SUBTLE.   Yes, tell her
  She must by any means address some present
  To the cunning-man, make him amend for wronging
  His art with her suspicion; send a ring,
  Or chain of pearl; she will be tortured else
  Extremely in her sleep, say, and have strange things
  Come to her. Wilt thou?

DOLL.   Yes.

SUBTLE.   My fine flitter-mouse,
  My bird o' the night! we'll tickle it at the Pigeons,

---

88. *flitter-mouse*, bat.   89. *Pigeons*, an inn at Brainford or Brentford.

When we have all, and may unlock the trunks,   90
And say, this's mine, and thine; and thine, and mine.
                                        [*They kiss.*

  [*Re-enter Face.*
FACE. What now! a billing?
SUBTLE.   Yes, a little exalted
  In the good passage of our stock-affairs.
FACE. Drugger has brought his parson; take him in, Subtle,
  And send Nab back again to wash his face.
SUBTLE. I will: and shave himself?   [*Exit.*
FACE.   If you can get him.
DOLL. You are hot upon it, Face, whate'er it is!
FACE. A trick that Doll shall spend ten pound a month by.
      [*Re-enter Subtle.*
  Is he gone?
SUBTLE.   The chaplain waits you in the hall, sir.
FACE. I'll go bestow him.   [*Exit.*
DOLL.   He'll now marry her instantly.   100
SUBTLE. He cannot yet, he is not ready. Dear Doll,
  Cozen her of all thou canst. To deceive him
  Is no deceit, but justice, that would break
  Such an inextricable tie as ours was.
DOLL. Let me alone to fit him.
      [*Re-enter Face.*
FACE.   Come, my venturers,
  You have packed up all? where be the trunks? bring forth.
SUBTLE. Here.
FACE.   Let us see 'em. Where's the money?
SUBTLE.   Here,
  In this.
FACE. Mammon's ten pound; eight score before:
  The brethren's money this. Drugger's and Dapper's.
  What paper's that?
DOLL.   The jewel of the waiting maid's,   110
  That stole it from her lady, to know certain—
FACE. If she should have precedence of her mistress?
DOLL.   Yes.
FACE. What box is that?
SUBTLE.   The fish-wives' rings, I think,
  And the ale-wives' single money. Is't not, Doll?
DOLL. Yes; and the whistle that the sailor's wife

  114. *single money*, small change, pin money.

Brought you to know an her husband were with Ward.

FACE. We'll wet it to-morrow; and our silver beakers
    And tavern cups. Where be the French petticoats.
    And girdles and hangers?

SUBTLE.   Here, in the trunk,
    And the bolts of lawn.

FACE.   Is Drugger's damask there,   120
    And the tobacco?

SUBTLE.   Yes.

FACE.   Give me the keys.

DOLL. Why you the keys?

SUBTLE.   No matter, Doll; because
    We shall not open 'em before he comes.

FACE. 'Tis true, you shall not open them, indeed,
    Nor have 'em forth, do you see? not forth, Doll.

DOLL [In consternation].   No!
    [Subtle stares at him as if unable to comprehend.

FACE. No, my smock-rampant. The right is, my master
    Knows all, has pardoned me, and he will keep 'em;
    Doctor, 'tis true—you look—for all your figures:
    I sent for him, indeed. Wherefore, good partners,
    Both he and she be satisfied; for here   130
    Determines the indenture tripartite
    'Twixt Subtle, Doll, and Face. All I can do
    Is to help you over the wall, o' the back-side,
    Or lend you a sheet to save your velvet gown, Doll.
    Here will be officers presently, bethink you
    Of some course suddenly to scape the dock;
    For thither you'll come else. [Loud knocking.] Hark you,
        thunder.

SUBTLE. You are a precious fiend!

OFFICER [Without].   Open the door.

FACE. Doll, I am sorry for thee i' faith; but hearst thou?
    It shall go hard but I will place thee somewhere: 140
    Thou shalt have my letter to Mistress Amo—

DOLL.   Hang you!

FACE. Or Madam Cæsarean.

DOLL.   Pox upon you, rogue,
    Would I had but time to beat thee!

FACE.   Subtle,
    Let's know where you set up next; I will send you

116. *Ward*, a famous pirate. A ballad was sung about him.
128. *look*, stare.   131. *determines*, comes to an end.

A customer now and then, for old acquaintance:
What new course have you?
SUBTLE.　　　　　　　　　　　　Rogue, I'll hang myself;
That I may walk a greater devil than thou,
And haunt thee in the flock-bed and the buttery.
　　　　　　　　　　　　　　[*In great anger they go out.*

SCENE V

*Another room in the house. Lovewit enters in the Spanish dress
which Face has procured for him. He is accompanied by a
parson. As they enter, the loud knocking which we heard in
the preceding scene is renewed. Lovewit calls through the door.*

LOVEWIT. What do you mean, my masters?
MAMMON [*Without*].　　　　　　　　　Open your door,
Cheaters, bawds, conjurers.
OFFICER. [*Without*].　　　　Or we will break it open.
LOVEWIT. What warrant have you?
OFFICER. [*Without*].　　　　Warrant enough, sir, doubt not,
If you'll not open it.
LOVEWIT.　　　　　　　Is there an officer there?
OFFICER [*Without*]. Yes, two or three for failing.
LOVEWIT.　　　　　　　　　　　　　　Have but patience,
And I will open it straight.
　　　　[*Enter Face, as butler.*
FACE.　　　　　　　　　Sir, have you done?
Is it a marriage? perfect?
LOVEWIT.　　　　　　　　Yes, my brain.
FACE. Off with your ruff and cloak then: be yourself, sir.
SURLY [*Without*]. Down with the door.
KASTRIL [*Without*].　　　　　'Slight, ding it open.
LOVEWIT [*Opening the door*].　　　　　　　　Hold.
Hold, gentlemen, what means this violence?　　　　　10
　　　[*Mammon, Surly, Kastril, Ananias, Tribulation, and Officers
　　　rush in.*
MAMMON. Where is this collier?
SURLY.　　　　　　　　And my Captain Face?
MAMMON. These day-owls.
SURLY.　　　　　　That are birding in men's purses.

148. *flock-bed*, mattress stuffed with rags.
5. *for*, for fear of.　9. *ding*, break.　12. *birding*, stealing.

MAMMON. Madam Suppository.

KASTRIL. Doxy, my suster.

ANANIAS. Locusts
Of the foul pit.

TRIBULATION. Profane as Bel and the Dragon.

ANANIAS. Worse than the grasshoppers, or the lice of Egypt.

LOVEWIT. Good gentlemen, hear me. Are you officers,
And cannot stay this violence?

1 OFFICER. Keep the peace.

LOVEWIT. Gentlemen, what is the matter? whom do you seek?

MAMMON. The chemical cozener.

SURLY. And the captain pander.

KASTRIL. The nun my suster.

MAMMON. Madam Rabbi.

ANANIAS. Scorpions,   20
And caterpillars.

LOVEWIT. Fewer at once,. I pray you.

2 OFFICER. One after another, gentlemen, I charge you,
By virtue of my staff.

ANANIAS. They are the vessels
Of pride, lust, and the cart.

LOVEWIT. Good zeal, lie still
A little while.

TRIBULATION. Peace, Deacon Ananias.

LOVEWIT [*At last making himself heard*]. The house is mine here,
and the doors are open;
If there be any such persons as you seek for,
Use your authority, search on o' God's name.
I am but newly come to town, and finding
This tumult 'bout my door, to tell you true,   30
It somewhat mazed me; till my man here, fearing
My more displeasure, told me he had done
Somewhat an insolent part, let out my house
(Belike presuming on my known aversion
From any air o' the town while there was sickness),
To a doctor and a captain: who, what they are,
Or where they be, he knows not.

MAMMON. Are they gone?

LOVEWIT. You may go in and search, sir. [*Mammon, Ananias and
Tribulation go in.*] Here, I find
The empty walls worse than I left 'em, smoked,
A few cracked pots, and glasses, and a furnace;   40
The ceiling filled with poesies of the candle,

And "madam with a dildo" writ o' the walls:
Only one gentlewoman I met here,
That is within, that said she was a widow—

KASTRIL. Ay, that's my suster; I'll go thump her. Where is she?
    [*Goes in.*

LOVEWIT. And should have married a Spanish count, but he,
  When he came to't, neglected her so grossly,
  That I, a widower, am gone through with her.

SURLY. How! have I lost her then?

LOVEWIT.   Were you the Don, sir?
  Good faith, now she does blame you extremely, and says   50
  You swore, and told her you had taken the pains
  To dye your beard, and umber o'er your face,
  Borrowed a suit, and ruff, all for her love:
  And then did nothing. What an oversight,
  And want of putting forward, sir, was this!
  Well fare an old harquebusier yet,
  Could prime his powder, and give fire, and hit,
  All in a twinkling!
    [*Re-enter Mammon, disconsolate.*

MAMMON.   The whole nest are fled!

LOVEWIT. What sort of birds were they?

MAMMON.   A kind of choughs,   60
  Or thievish daws, sir, that have picked my purse
  Of eight score and ten pounds within these five weeks,
  Beside my first materials; and my goods,
  That lie in the cellar, which I am glad they have left,
  I may have home yet.

LOVEWIT.   Think you so, sir?

MAMMON.   Ay.

LOVEWIT. By order of law, sir, but not otherwise.

MAMMON. Not mine own stuff!

LOVEWIT.   Sir, I can take no knowledge
  That they are yours, but by public means.
  If you can bring certificate that you were gulled of them,
  Or any formal writ out of a court,
  That you did cozen yourself, I will not hold them.   70

MAMMON. I'll rather lose them.

LOVEWIT.   That you shall not, sir,
  By me, in troth: upon these terms, they are yours.
  What should they have been, sir, turned into gold, all?

42. *madame . . .*, probably a fragment of a jocose ballad.
56. *harquebusier*, musketeer.

MAMMON [*Hopelessly embarrassed*]. **No.**
    I cannot tell—It may be they should—What then?
LOVEWIT. What a great loss in hope have you sustained!
MAMMON. Not I, the commonwealth has.
FACE.   Ay, he would have built
    The city new; and made a ditch about it
    Of silver, should have run with cream from Hogsden;
    That every Sunday in Moorfields the younkers,
    And tits and tom-boys should have fed on, gratis.   80
MAMMON. I will go mount a turnip-cart, and preach
    The end of the world within these two months. Surly,
    What! in a dream?
SURLY.   Must I needs cheat myself,
    With that same foolish vice of honesty!
    Come, let us go and hearken out the rogues:
    That Face I'll mark for mine, if e'er I meet him.
FACE. If I can hear of him, sir, I'll bring you word
    Unto your lodging; for in troth, they were strangers
    To me, I thought them honest as myself, sir.
    [*Thoroughly downcast, Mammon and Surly go out. Re-
    enter Ananias and Tribulation, finding some shreds of com-
    fort in the hope of getting the goods they had bought.*
TRIBULATION. 'Tis well, the saints shall not lose all yet. Go 90
    And get some carts—
LOVEWIT.   For what, my zealous friends?
ANANIAS. To bear away the portion of the righteous,
    Out of this den of thieves.
LOVEWIT.   What is that portion?
ANANIAS. The goods, sometimes the orphans', that the brethren
    Bought with their silver pence.
LOVEWIT.   What, those in the cellar,
    The knight Sir Mammon claims?
ANANIAS.   I do defy
    The wicked Mammon, so do all the brethren,
    Thou profane man! I ask thee with what conscience
    Thou canst advance that idol against us,
    That have the seal? were not the shillings numbered   100
    That made the pounds; were not the pounds told out
    Upon the second day of the fourth week,
    In the eighth month, upon the table dormant,
    The year of the last patience of the saints,

---

80. *tits*, wenches.   94. *sometimes*, formerly.
100. *seal*, are chosen of God.

Six hundred and ten?

LOVEWIT.   Mine earnest vehement botcher,
And deacon also, I cannot dispute with you;
But if you get you not away the sooner,
I shall confute you with a cudgel.

ANANIAS.   Sir!

TRIBULATION. Be patient, Ananias.

ANANIAS.   I am strong,
And will stand up, well girt, against an host   110
That threaten Gad in exile.

LOVEWIT.   I shall send you
To Amsterdam, to your cellar.

ANANIAS.   I will pray there,
Against thy house: may dogs defile thy walls,
And wasps and hornets breed beneath thy roof,
This seat of falsehood, and this cave of cozenage!

[*Snorting execrations he and Tribulation leave. Enter Drugger.*

LOVEWIT. Another too?

DRUGGER.   Not I, sir, I am no brother.

LOVEWIT [*Beats him*]. Away, you Harry Nicholas! do you talk?

[*Drugger runs out to escape more beating.*

FACE. No, this was Abel Drugger. Good sir, go,
[*To the Parson.*
And satisfy him; tell him all is done:
He stayed too long a washing of his face.   120
The doctor, he shall hear of him at Westchester;
And of the captain, tell him, at Yarmouth, or
Some good port-town else, lying for a wind.
[*The Parson goes out mystified.*
If you can get off the angry child now, sir—
[*Enter Kastril, dragging in his sister, from whom he has got
the story of her marriage.*

KASTRIL. Come on, you ewe, you have matched most sweetly,
have you not?
Did not I say, I would never have you tupped
But by a dubbed boy, to make you a lady-tom?
'Slight, you are a mammet! O, I could touse you now.

117. *Harry Nicholas*, a religious fanatic, known chiefly as the founder
of a sect called the "Family of Love."
127. *dubbed boy*, knight.
128. *mammet*, doll, puppet. (From Mohamet, since Mohametans were er-
roneously supposed to be idolators)

Death, mun' you marry with a pox!

LOVEWIT.   You lie, boy!
As sound as you; and I'm aforehand with you.

KASTRIL.   Anon!   130

LOVEWIT [*He draws his sword*]. Come, will you quarrel? I will
    feize you, sirrah;
Why do you not buckle to your tools?

KASTRIL [*Wide-eyed in admiration*]. God's light,
This is a fine old boy as e'er I saw!

LOVEWIT. What, do you change your copy now? proceed,
Here stands my dove: stoop at her if you dare.

KASTRIL. 'Slight, I must love him! I cannot choose, i' faith,
An I should be hanged for't! Suster, I protest,
I honour thee for this match.

LOVEWIT.   O, do you so, sir?

KASTRIL. Yes, and thou canst take tobacco and drink, old boy,
I'll give her five hundred pound more to her marriage,   140
Than her own state.

LOVEWIT.   Fill a pipe full, Jeremy.

FACE. Yes; but go in and take it, sir.

LOVEWIT.   We will—
I will be ruled by thee in anything, Jeremy.

KASTRIL. 'Slight, thou art not hide-bound, thou art a jovy boy!
Come, let's in, I pray thee, and take our whiffs.

LOVEWIT. Whiff in with your sister, brother boy. [*Kastril and
    Dame Pliant go.*] That master
That had received such happiness by a servant,
In such a widow, and with so much wealth,
Were very ungrateful, if he would not be
A little indulgent to that servant's wit,   150
And help his fortune, though with some small strain
Of his own candour. [*Advancing.*] Therefore, gentlemen,
And kind spectators, if I have outstripped
An old man's gravity, or strict canon, think
What a young wife and a good brain may do;
Stretch age's truth sometimes, and crack it too.
Speak for thyself, knave.

FACE.   So I will, sir. [*Advancing to the front
    of the stage.*] Gentlemen,

129. *mun*, must. *with a pox*, with one infected with venereal disease.
131. *feize*, beat, flog.
135. *stoop*, pounce upon. A term in falconry, appropriate since Kastril
means hawk.
144. *jovy*, jovial.   152. *candour*, integrity.

My part a little fell in this last scene,
Yet 'twas decorum. And though I am clean
Got off from Subtle, Surly, Mammon, Doll,
Hot Ananias, Dapper, Drugger, all
With whom I traded; yet I put myself
On you, that are my country: and this pelf,
Which I have got, if you do quit me, rests
To feast you often, and invite new guests.

> [*They go off happily together.*

159. *decorum*, according to dramatic propriety.
163. *country*, jury.   164. *quit*, acquit.

DOMESTIC TRAGEDY

It is a far cry from the trumpet blare and courtly talk of *Edward II* to the quiet if not tranquil love of Mr. Frankford. By one of the changes in taste that are so common in literary fashions, the domestic drama has in our own time achieved a popularity equal to that of courtly tragedy in the sixteenth century. Indeed, it has come to be one of the chief types of serious play now on the stage. A domestic drama might conceivably concern itself with almost any aspect of home life, but in practice it is almost always concerned with some phase of the age old problem of the relation of the sexes in marriage, very often, as here, the case of a wife who is tempted and either falls or, as in the case of Desdemona in *Othello*, is supposed by her husband to have fallen. Such material is likely to call forth a quite different emotional response from that of the heroic tragedy, done in the grand style. It often evokes pathos rather than the true tragic spirit, impressing us with the personal emotions of the characters without giving their emotions that relationship to great times and events that one finds, for instance, in the historical drama. It tends to be particular rather than universal, to put the stress on personal pain rather than its more general implications.

Historically the most important aspect of domestic tragedy, however, was the fact that it represented a middle class point of view both as to character and as to moral patterns. As a result, there is far less of the heavy "passioning," the speculative analysis of emotion in grandiloquent terms that one finds in tragedy on a higher social level. Though much is said of the husband's honor, the dramatist emphasizes for us the moral delinquency of the wife as well, and from the latter extracts a feeling of tragic fulfilment.

Thomas Heywood, the author of *A Woman Killed with Kindness*, boasted that in his long life (from about 1572 to about 1650) he had "either an entire hand, or at least a main finger" in 220 plays. That would be a sufficient life work for almost any ordinary man, but Heywood also wrote pageants, poems, and even among other works made a translation of Sallust. He tells us that he had been a resident member of Cambridge University. He came up to London to write for the theater a decade too late to be numbered among the talented but mad and roistering crew of "University Wits," who, it will be remembered, included Greene and Marlowe in their numbers. In 1598 he became a member of the Lord Admiral's acting company (at a time when the Admiral's Men were one of the best companies in the London theaters) and later joined the Queen's Servants. As late as 1634 he was still associated with the theater, joining the company of Charles I in that year. In addition to the large number of plays he composed or tinkered with, he took part in the controversy between puritans and the stage with a pamphlet, *An Apology for Actors*, published in 1612, which is exceptional in that controversy in its mildness of tone and relatively calm impersonality.

His attitude toward his plays, however, seems to have been much like that of other dramatists of the time, except for Ben Jonson. They were to Heywood what their name implies, light trifles, not particularly worth the preserving; though on one occasion he did, with an author's natural self-respect, object to the mangled form in which one of his plays was printed by a literary pirate who had presumably taken the play down in shorthand in the theater.

He tried his hand at all manner of subjects, and a survey of his plays is a good means of seeing the steady changes of taste that occurred in the first third of the seventeenth century. *A Woman Killed* fitted a rather short-lived vogue (though the type never died out completely) in the first decade of that century, though *Arden of Feversham*, an early example of this type with a particularly bloody and infamous murder as its central incident had appeared as early as 1592. The sub-plot, too, which to many a modern reader seems an excrescence, was witness to the dramatist's effort to offer his audience all that they had come by this time to expect in the way of variety and complication. One of the most charming features of the play is found in the pictures of country sports, from the hawking scene, which ends so disastrously, to the rustic jigs and reels with which Frankford's marriage is celebrated.

In his picture of middle class moral standards, in the free nobility of Frankford's character who refrains from even an Othello's bloody thoughts of mutilation and execution, in Mrs. Frankford's own sense of guilt and her willing death when honor is lost, in the temptations and trials to which love is subjected we see Heywood working out skilfully the themes that in one form or another have long been the richest ones in domestic drama.

SUGGESTED READINGS

Cambridge History of English Literature, VOL. VI. NEW YORK, 1910.

Clark, A. M., *Thomas Heywood: Playwright and Miscellanist*. OXFORD, 1931.

Heywood, Thomas, *Selected Plays*. MERMAID SERIES. NEW YORK [n.d.].

Schelling, F. E., *Elizabethan Playwrights*. NEW YORK, 1928.

Wright, L. B., *Middle-Class Culture in Elizabethan England*. CHAPEL HILL, N. C., 1935.

Booth, Clare, *The Women*. NEW YORK, 1937.

Davis, Owen, and Donald Davis, *Ethan Frome*. NEW YORK, 1935.

Lillo, George, *The London Merchant*. NEW YORK, 1906.

Masefield, John, *The Tragedy of Nan*. NEW YORK, 1909.

O'Neill, Eugene, *The First Man*. NEW YORK, 1922.

——, *Mourning Becomes Electra*. NEW YORK, 1931.

Shakespeare, William, *Othello*

——, *Winters Tale*

A WOMAN KILLED WITH KINDNESS
by Thomas Heywood

Characters

SIR FRANCIS ACTON, *Brother of Mistress Frankford*
SIR CHARLES MOUNTFORD
MASTER FRANKFORD
MASTER WENDOLL, *Friend to Frankford*
MASTER MALBY, *Friend to Sir Francis*
MASTER CRANWELL
SHAFTON, *a False Friend to Sir Charles*
OLD MOUNTFORD, *Uncle to Sir Charles*
TIDY, *Cousin to Sir Charles*
SANDY
RODER
NICHOLAS,
JENKIN,
ROGER BRICKBAT, } *Servants to Frankford*
JACK SLIME,
SPIGOT, *a Butler,*
SHERIFF
A SERJEANT, A KEEPER, OFFICERS, FALCONERS, HUNTSMEN, A COACH-
  MAN, CARTERS, SERVANTS, MUSICIANS

MISTRESS FRANKFORD
SUSAN, *Sister of Sir Charles*
CICELY, *Maid to Mistress Frankford*
WOMEN SERVANTS

SCENE—*The North of England*

THE PROLOGUE

I come but as a harbinger, being sent
  To tell you what these preparations mean:
Look for no glorious state; our Muse is bent
  Upon a barren subject, a bare scene.
We could afford this twig a timber tree,
  Whose strength might boldly on your favours build;
Our russet, tissue; drone, a honey-bee;
  Our barren plot, a large and spacious field;
Our coarse fare, banquets; our thin water, wine;
  Our brook, a sea; our bat's eyes, eagle's sight;   10
Our poet's dull and earthy Muse, divine;
  Our ravens, doves; our crow's black feathers, white
But gentle thoughts, when they may give the foil,
Save them that yield, and spare where they may spoil.

ACT I

SCENE I

A ROOM IN FRANKFORD'S HOUSE. *Frankford has just been married to the sister of Sir Francis Acton, and the wedding party enters gaily. Master Frankford and Mistress Frankford come first, followed by Sir Francis Acton, Sir Charles Mountford, Master Malby, Master Wendoll, and Master Cranwell.*

SIR FRANCIS. Some music there: none lead the bride a dance?
SIR CHARLES. Yes, would she dance "The Shaking of the Sheets";
  But that's the dance her husband means to lead her.
WENDOLL. That's not the dance that every man must dance,
  According to the ballad.

> "Make ready then your winding sheet
> And see how you can bestir your feet,
> For death is the man that all must meet."

SIR FRANCIS.   Music, ho!
By your leave, sister;—by your husband's leave,
I should have said: the hand that but this day
Was given you in the church I'll borrow. [*To the musicians.*]
  Sound!
This marriage music hoists me from the ground.

2. *The Shaking of the Sheets*, a popular song and dance tune.

FRANKFORD. Ay, you may caper, you are light and free: 10
    Marriage hath yoked my heels; pray pardon me.
SIR FRANCIS. I'll have you dance too, brother.
SIR CHARLES.   Master Frankford,
    You are a happy man, sir; and much joy
    Succeed your marriage mirth! you have a wife
    So qualified, and with such ornaments
    Both of the mind and body. First, her birth
    Is noble, and her education such
    As might become the daughter of a prince:
    Her own tongue speaks all tongues, and her own hand
    Can teach all strings to speak in their best grace,   20
    From the shrillest treble to the hoarsest base.
    To end her many praises in one word,
    She's beauty and perfection's eldest daughter,
    Only found by yours, though many a heart hath sought her.
FRANKFORD. But that I know your virtues and chaste thoughts,
    I should be jealous of your praise, Sir Charles.
CRANWELL. He speaks no more than you approve.
MALBY. Nor flatters he that gives to her her due.
MISTRESS FRANKFORD. I would your praise could find a fitter theme
    Than my imperfect beauty to speak on: 30
    Such as they be, if they my husband please,
    They suffice me now I am married:
    His sweet content is like a flattering glass,
    To make my face seem fairer to mine eye;
    But the least wrinkle from his stormy brow
    Will blast the roses in my cheeks that grow.
SIR FRANCIS. A perfect wife already, meek and patient:
    How strangely the word "husband" fits your mouth,
    Not married three hours since! Sister, 'tis good;
    You, that begin betimes thus, must needs prove   40
    Pliant and duteous in your husband's love.—
    Gramercies, brother, wrought her to't already:
    "Sweet husband," and a curtsey, the first day!
    Mark this, mark this, you that are bachelors,
    And never took the grace of honest man;
    Mark this, against you marry, this one phrase:
    "In a good time that man both wins and woos,
    That takes his wife down in her wedding shoes."

46. *against*, in preparation for the time when.
47. *In a good time*, etc., That husband is happiest who asserts his authority over his wife at once.

FRANKFORD. Your sister takes not after you, Sir Francis;
    All his wild blood your father spent on you: 50
    He got her in his age, when he grew civil:
    All his mad tricks were to his land entailed,
    And you are heir to all; your sister, she
    Hath to her dower her mother's modesty.
SIR CHARLES. Lord, sir, in what a happy state live you!
    This morning, which to many seems a burden
    Too heavy to bear, is unto you a pleasure.
    This lady is no clog, as many are:
    She doth become you like a well-made suit,
    In which the tailor hath used all his art; 60
    Not like a thick coat of unseasoned frieze,
    Forced on your back in summer. She's no chain
    To tie your neck, and curb you to the yoke;
    But she's a chain of gold to adorn your neck.
    You both adorn each other, and your hands,
    Methinks, are matches: there's equality
    In this fair combination; you are both
    Scholars, both young, both being descended nobly.
    There's music in this sympathy; it carries
    Consort, and expectation of much joy, 70
    Which God bestow on you, from this first day
    Until your dissolution; that's for aye.
SIR FRANCIS. We keep you here too long, good brother Frankford.
    Into the hall; away! go cheer your guests.
    What, bride and bridegroom both withdrawn at once?
    If you be missed, the guests will doubt their welcome,
    And charge you with unkindness.
FRANKFORD.   To prevent it,
    I'll leave you here, to see the dance within.
MISTRESS FRANKFORD. And so will I.
            [*Exeunt Frankford and Mistress Frankford.*
SIR FRANCIS.   To part you, it were sin.
    Now, gallants, while the town-musicians 80
    Finger their frets within; and the mad lads
    And country-lasses, every mother's child,
    With nosegays and bridelaces in their hats,
    Dance all their country measures, rounds, and jigs,
    What shall we do? Hark, they are all on the hoigh;

51. *got*, begot.   70. *Consort*, it implies harmony.
83. *bridelaces*, ribbons, streamers.
85. *on the hoigh*, all excited, "steamed up."

They toil like mill-horses, and turn as round,—
Marry, not on the toe. Ay, and they caper,
Not without cutting; you shall see, to-morrow,
The hall-floor pecked and dinted like a mill-stone,
Made with their high shoes: though their skill be small,   90
Yet they tread heavy where their hob-nails fall.

SIR CHARLES. Well, leave them to their sports. Sir Francis Acton,
   I'll make a match with you; meet to-morrow
At Chevy-chase, I'll fly my hawk with yours.

SIR FRANCIS. For what? For what?

SIR CHARLES.   Why, for a hundred pound.

SIR FRANCIS. Pawn me some gold of that.

SIR CHARLES.   Here are ten angels;
   I'll make them good a hundred pound to-morrow
Upon my hawk's wing.

SIR FRANCIS.   'Tis a match, 'tis done.
   Another hundred pound upon your dogs;
Dare ye, Sir Charles?

SIR CHARLES.   I dare: were I sure to lose,   100
   I durst do more than that: here is my hand,
The first course for a hundred pound.

SIR FRANCIS.   A match.

WENDOLL. Ten angels on Sir Francis Acton's hawk;
   As much upon his dogs.

CRANWELL. I am for Sir Charles Mountford; I have seen
   His hawk and dog both tried. What, clap you hands?
Or is't no bargain?

WENDOLL.   Yes, and stake them down:
   Were they five hundred, they were all my own.

SIR FRANCIS. Be stirring early with the lark to-morrow;
   I'll rise into my saddle ere the sun   110
Rise from his bed.

SIR CHARLES.   If there you miss me, say
   I am no gentleman: I'll hold my day.

SIR FRANCIS. It holds on all sides. Come, to-night let's dance,
   Early to-morrow let's prepare to ride;
We had need be three hours up before the bride.

                  [*They go out to dance.*

---

96. *Pawn*, pledge.   *angels*, gold coins.   106. *clap*, shake.

SCENE II

THE YARD OF FRANKFORD'S HOUSE. *The servants are gathering for a country dance to match the courtly dances of the gentle folk.*

[*Enter Nicholas, Jenkin, Jack Slime, and Roger Brickbat, with Country Wenches, and two or three Musicians.*

JENKIN. Come, Nick, take you Joan Miniver to trace withal; Jack Slime, traverse you with Cicely Milk-pail: I will take Jane Trubkin, and Roger Brickbat shall have Isbel Motley; and now that they are busy in the parlour, come, strike up; we'll have a crash here in the yard.

NICHOLAS. My humour is not compendious; dancing I possess not, though I can foot it; yet, since I am fallen into the hands of Cicely Milk-pail, I consent.

SLIME. Truly Nick, though we were never brought up like serving courtiers, yet we have been brought up with serving crea- 10
tures, ay, and God's creatures too; for we have been brought up to serve sheep, oxen, horses, hogs, and such like: and, though we be but country fellows, it may be in the way of dancing we can do the horse-trick as well as the serving-men.

BRICKBAT. Ay, and the cross-point too.

JENKIN. O Slime, O Brickbat, do not you know that comparisons are odious? now we are odious ourselves too, therefore there are no comparisons to be made betwixt us.

NICHOLAS. I am sudden, and not superfluous;
 I am quarrelsome, and not seditious;   20
 I am peaceable, and not contentious;
 I am brief, and not compendious.

SLIME. Foot it quickly: if the music overcome not my melancholy, I shall quarrel; and if they suddenly do not strike up, I shall presently strike thee down.

JENKIN. No quarrelling, for God's sake: truly, if you do, I shall set a knave between ye.

SLIME. I come to dance, not to quarrel. Come, what shall it be? "Rogero?"

JENKIN. "Rogero!" no; we will dance "The Beginning of the   30
World."

1-2. *trace, traverse,* dance.   5. *crash,* merry bout, brawl.
14-15. *horse-trick; cross-point,* vigorous and complicated steps in the dance.

30. *Rogero,* this and the other names that follow were well known dance tunes of the time.

CICELY. I love no dance so well as "John come kiss me now."

NICHOLAS. I, that have ere now deserved a cushion, call for the "Cushion-dance."

BRICKBAT. For my part, I like nothing so well as "Tom Tyler."

JENKIN. No; we'll have "The Hunting of the Fox."

SLIME. "The Hay," "The Hay;" there's nothing like "The Hay."

NICHOLAS. I have said, do say, and will say again—

JENKIN. Every man agree to have it as Nick says.

ALL. Content.   40

NICHOLAS. It hath been, it now is, and it shall be—

CICELY. What, Master Nicholas, what?

NICHOLAS. "Put on your smock a' Monday."

JENKIN. So the dance will come cleanly off. Come, for God's sake agree of something: if you like not that, put it to the musicians; or let me speak for all, and we'll have "Sellenger's round."

ALL. That, that, that.

NICHOLAS. No, I am resolved, thus it shall be:
First take hands, then take ye to your heels.

JENKIN. Why, would ye have us run away?   50

NICHOLAS. No; but I would have you shake your heels.
Music, strike up!

> [*They dance. Nicholas whilst dancing speaks stately and scurvily, the rest after the country fashion.*

JENKIN. Hey! lively, my lasses! here's a turn for thee!

> [*They dance out.*

SCENE III

THE OPEN COUNTRY *on the next morning. The sound of horns is followed by the entrance of Sir Charles Mountford, Sir Francis Acton, Malby, Cranwell, Wendoll, Falconers, and Huntsmen. They are carrying out the wager made the day before.*

SIR CHARLES. So; well cast off: aloft, aloft! well flown!
Oh, now she takes her at the sowse, and strikes her
Down to th' earth, like a swift thunder-clap.

WENDOLL. She hath struck ten angels out of my way.

SIR FRANCIS. A hundred pound from me.

SIR CHARLES.   What, falconer!

---

54. *scurvily*, sourly.

2. *sowse*, swoop. This and the following are technical terms borrowed from falconry, the hunting of other birds with hawks.

FALCONER.   At hand, sir.

SIR CHARLES. Now she hath seized the fowl, and 'gins to plume her,
    Rebeck her not: rather stand still and check her.
    So, seize her gets, her jesses, and her bells:
    Away!

SIR FRANCIS. My hawk killed too.

SIR CHARLES.   Ay, but 'twas at the querre,
    Not at the mount, like mine.

SIR FRANCIS.   Judgment, my masters.   10

CRANWELL. Yours missed her at the ferre.

WENDOLL. Ay, but our merlin first had plumed the fowl,
    And twice renewed her from the river too;
    Her bells, Sir Francis, had not both one weight,
    Nor was one semi-tune above the other:
    Methinks these Milan bells do sound too full,
    And spoil the mounting of your hawk.

SIR CHARLES.   .   .   'Tis lost.

SIR FRANCIS. I grant it not. Mine likewise seized a fowl
    Within her talons; and you saw her paws
    Full of the feathers: both her petty singles,   20
    And her long singles gripped her more than other;
    The terrials of her legs were stained with blood:
    Not of the fowl only, she did discomfit
    Some of her feathers; but she brake away.
    Come, come, your hawk is but a rifler.

SIR CHARLES.   How!

SIR FRANCIS. Ay, and your dogs are trindle-tails and curs.

SIR CHARLES. You stir my blood.
    You keep not one good hound in all your kennel,
    Nor one good hawk upon your perch.

SIR FRANCIS.   How, knight!

SIR CHARLES. So, knight: you will not swagger, sir?   30

SIR FRANCIS. Why, say I did?

SIR CHARLES.   Why, sir,

6. 'gins to plume, begins to pluck.
7. Rebeck, recall. check, whistle to, so as not to alarm her and make her
fly off with her booty.
8. gets, perhaps parts of the harness of the hawk. jesses, leg-straps.
9. querre, before the bird rose from the ground.
11. ferre, higher or farther point.   13. renewed, driven her back.
20. singles, claws.
22. terrials, perhaps a misprint for terriets, loops that tied the bells to the
hawk's legs.
25. rifler, bungler.   26. trindle-tails, curly tails.

I say you would gain as much by swaggering,
As you have got by wagers on your dogs:
You will come short in all things.

SIR FRANCIS.   Not in this:
  Now I'll strike home.

SIR CHARLES.   Thou shalt to thy long home,
  Or I will want my will.

SIR FRANCIS. All they that love Sir Francis, follow me.

SIR CHARLES. All that affect Sir Charles, draw on my part.

CRANWELL. On this side heaves my hand.

WENDOLL.   Here goes my heart.
  [*They divide themselves. Sir Charles Mountford, Cranwell,
    Falconer, and Huntsman, fight against Sir Francis Acton,
    Wendoll, his Falconer, and Huntsman; and Sir Charles's
    side gets the better, beating the others away, and killing
    both of Sir Francis's men. Exeunt all except Sir Charles.*

SIR CHARLES. My God! what have I done? what have I done?   40
  My rage hath plunged into a sea of blood,
  In which my soul lies drowned. Poor innocents,
  For whom we are to answer! Well, 'tis done,
  And I remain the victor. A great conquest,
  When I would give this right hand, nay, this head,
  To breathe in them new life whom I have slain.
  Forgive me, God! 'twas in the heat of blood,
  And anger quite removes me from myself:
  It was not I, but rage, did this vile murder;
  Yet I, and not my rage, must answer it.   50
  Sir Francis Acton he is fled the field;
  With him all those that did partake his quarrel,
  And I am left alone with sorrow dumb,
  And in my height of conquest overcome.
  [*Enter Susan, the sister of Sir Charles.*

SUSAN. O God! my brother wounded 'mong the dead!
  Unhappy jest, that in such earnest ends:
  The rumour of this fear stretched to my ears,
  And I am come to know if you be wounded.

SIR CHARLES. Oh! sister, sister, wounded at the heart.

SUSAN. My God forbid!

SIR CHARLES.   In doing that thing which He forbad,   60
  I am wounded, sister.

SUSAN.   I hope not at the heart.

SIR CHARLES. Yes, at the heart.

SUSAN.   O God! a surgeon there!

SIR CHARLES. Call me a surgeon, sister, for my soul;
   The sin of murder it hath pierced my heart,
   And made a wide wound there: but for these scratches,
   They are nothing, nothing.
SUSAN.   Charles, what have you done?
   Sir Francis hath great friends, and will pursue you
   Unto the utmost danger of the law.
SIR CHARLES. My conscience is become mine enemy,
   And will pursue me more than Acton can.   70
SUSAN. Oh, fly, sweet brother.
SIR CHARLES.   Shall I fly from thee?
   Why, Sue, art weary of my company?
SUSAN. Fly from your foe.
SIR CHARLES.   You, sister, are my friend;
   And, flying you, I shall pursue my end.
SUSAN. Your company is as my eye-ball dear;
   Being far from you, no comfort can be near;
   Yet fly to save your life: what would I care
   To spend my future age in black despair,
   So you were safe? and yet to live one week
   Without my brother Charles, through every cheek   80
   My streaming tears would downwards run so rank,
   Till they could set on either side a bank,
   And in the midst a channel; so my face
   For two salt-water brooks shall still find place.
SIR CHARLES. Thou shalt not weep so much, for I will stay
   In spite of danger's teeth; I'll live with thee,
   Or I'll not live at all. I will not sell
   My country and my father's patrimony,
   Nor thy sweet sight, for a vain hope of life.
     [*Enter Sheriff, with Officers. They have been sent by Sir
     Francis.*
SHERIFF. Sir Charles, I am made the unwilling instrument   90
   Of your attach and apprehension:
   I'm sorry that the blood of innocent men
   Should be of you exacted. It was told me
   That you were guarded with a troop of friends,
   And therefore came thus armed.
SIR CHARLES.   O, Master Sheriff,
   I came into the field with many friends,
   But see, they all have left me: only one
   Clings to my sad misfortune, my dear sister.

68. *danger*, penalty.

I know you for an honest gentleman;
I yield my weapons, and submit to you;
Convey me where you please.

SHERIFF. To prison then, 100
To answer for the lives of these dead men.

SUSAN. O God! O God!

SIR CHARLES. Sweet sister, every strain
Of sorrow from your heart augments my pain;
Your grief abounds, and hits against my breast.

SHERIFF. Sir, will you go?

SIR CHARLES. Even where it likes you best.

[They go out, Sir Charles in the Sheriff's custody and Susan
trying to comfort him.

ACT II

SCENE I

A ROOM IN FRANKFORD'S HOUSE, shortly after the time of the preceding scene. Frankford enters, meditating on his good fortune.

FRANKFORD. How happy am I amongst other men,
That in my mean estate embrace content!
I am a gentleman, and by my birth,
Companion with a king; a king's no more.
I am possessed of many fair revenues,
Sufficient to maintain a gentleman.
Touching my mind, I am studied in all arts;
The riches of my thoughts, and of my time,
Have been a good proficient; but the chief
Of all the sweet felicities on earth, 10
I have a fair, a chaste, and loving wife;
Perfection all, all truth, all ornament;
If man on earth may truly happy be,
Of these at once possessed, sure I am he.

[Enter Nicholas.

NICHOLAS. Sir, there's a gentleman attends without
To speak with you.

FRANKFORD. On horseback?

NICHOLAS. Yes, on horseback.

FRANKFORD. Entreat him to alight, and I'll attend him.
Know'st thou him, Nick?

9. *have been a good proficient*, have made good use of.

NICHOLAS. Know him! yes, his name's Wendoll:
It seems he comes in haste: his horse is booted
Up to the flank in mire, himself all spotted 20
And stained with plashing. Sure he rid in fear,
Or for a wager: horse and man both sweat;
I ne'er saw two in such a smoking heat.

FRANKFORD. Entreat him in: about it instantly. [*Exit Nicholas.*
This Wendoll I have noted, and his carriage
Hath pleased me much: by observation
I have noted many good deserts in him:
He's affable, and seen in many things,
Discourses well, a good companion;
And though of small means, yet a gentleman 30
Of a good house, somewhat pressed by want:
I have preferred him to a second place
In my opinion, and my best regard.

[*Enter Wendoll, Mistress Frankford, and Nicholas. Wendoll
has already had time to tell Mrs. Frankford of the tragic
events of the preceding scene.*

MISTRESS FRANKFORD. O Master Frankford, Master Wendoll here
Brings you the strangest news that e'er you heard.

FRANKFORD. What news, sweet wife? What news, good Master
Wendoll?

WENDOLL. You knew the match made 'twixt Sir Francis Acton
And Sir Charles Mountford.

FRANKFORD. True, with their hounds and hawks.

WENDOLL. The matches were both played.

FRANKFORD. Ha! and which won?

WENDOLL. Sir Francis, your wife's brother, had the worst, 40
And lost the wager.

FRANKFORD. Why, the worse his chance:
Perhaps the fortune of some other day
Will change his luck.

MISTRESS FRANKFORD. Oh, but you hear not all.
Sir Francis lost, and yet was loth to yield:
At length the two knights grew to difference,
From words to blows, and so to banding sides;
Where valorous Sir Charles slew in his spleen
Two of your brother's men; his falconer,
And his good huntsman, whom he loved so well:
More men were wounded, no more slain outright. 50

FRANKFORD. Now, trust me, I am sorry for the knight;

19. *booted,* covered.   28. *seen,* skilled.

But is my brother safe?

WENDOLL.   All whole and sound,
His body not being blemished with one wound:
But poor Sir Charles is to the prison led,
To answer at the assize for them that's dead.

FRANKFORD. I thank your pains, sir; had the news been better
Your will was to have brought it, Master Wendoll.
Sir Charles will find hard friends; his case is heinous,
And will be most severely censured on:
I'm sorry for him. Sir, a word with you   60
I know you, sir, to be a gentleman
In all things; your possibility but mean:
Please you to use my table and my purse,
They are yours.

WENDOLL.   O Lord, sir, I shall never deserve it.

FRANKFORD. O sir, disparage not your worth too much:
You are full of quality and fair desert:
Choose of my men which shall attend you, sir,
And he is yours. I will allow you, sir,
Your man, your gelding, and your table, all
At my own charge; be my companion.   70

WENDOLL. Master Frankford, I have oft been bound to you
By many favours; this exceeds them all,
That I shall never merit your least favour:
But, when your last remembrance I forget,
Heaven at my soul exact that weighty debt!

FRANKFORD. There needs no protestation; for I know you
Virtuous, and therefore grateful. Pr'ythee, Nan,
Use him with all thy loving'st courtesy.

MISTRESS FRANKFORD. As far as modesty may well extend,
It is my duty to receive your friend.   80

FRANKFORD. To dinner, come, sir; from this present day,
Welcome to me for ever: come, away.
    [*Frankford, Mistress Frankford, and Wendoll go out pleas-
        antly.*

NICHOLAS. I do not like this fellow by no means:
I never see him but my heart still yearns:
Zounds! I could fight with him, yet know not why:
The devil and he are all one in my eye.
    [*Enter Jenkin.*

JENKIN. O Nick, what gentleman is that comes to lie at our house?

59. *censured on*, judged.   61. *possibility*, resources.
84. *yearns*, grieves.

my master allows him one to wait on him, and I believe it will
fall to thy lot.

NICHOLAS. I love my master; by these hilts I do!   90
But rather than I'll ever come to serve him,
I'll turn away my master.
  [*Enter Cicely.*

CICELY. Nich'las, where are you, Nich'las? you must come in,
Nich'las, and help the young gentleman off with his boots.

NICHOLAS. If I pluck off his boots, I'll eat the spurs,
And they shall stick fast in my throat like burs.

CICELY. Then, Jenkin, come you.

JENKIN. Nay, 'tis no boot for me to deny it. My master hath
given me a coat here, but he takes pains himself to brush it once
or twice a day with a holly-wand.   100

CICELY. Come, come, make haste, that you may wash your hands
again, and help to serve in dinner.

JENKIN [*Turning to the audience*]. You may see, my masters,
though it be afternoon with you, 'tis but early days with us,
for we have not dined yet: stay a little, I'll but go in and help
to bear up the first course, and come to you again presently.
                                    [*They go out separately.*

SCENE II

A ROOM IN THE JAIL. *Enter Malby and Cranwell.*

MALBY. This is the sessions-day; pray can you tell me
How young Sir Charles hath sped? Is he acquit,
Or must he try the law's strict penalty?

CRANWELL. He's cleared of all, spite of his enemies,
Whose earnest labour was to take his life:
But in this suit of pardon he hath spent
All the revenues that his father left him;
And he is now turned a plain countryman,
Reformed in all things. See, sir, here he comes.
  [*Enter Sir Charles and Keeper.*

KEEPER. Discharge your fees, and you are then at freedom.   10

SIR CHARLES. Here, Master Keeper, take the poor remainder
Of all the wealth I have: my heavy foes
Have made my purse light; but, alas! to me
'Tis wealth enough that you have set me free.

98. *boot*, use.   9. *Reformed*, transformed.

MALBY. God give you joy of your delivery!
  I am glad to see you abroad, Sir Charles.
SIR CHARLES. The poorest knight in England, Master Malby:
  My life hath cost me all my patrimony
  My father left his son: well, God forgive them
  That are the authors of my penury.   20
    [*Enter Shafton. He greets Sir Charles with great effusive-*
        ness, for he has an axe to grind.

SHAFTON. Sir Charles! a hand, a hand! at liberty?
  Now, by the faith I owe, I am glad to see it.
  What want you? wherein may I pleasure you?
SIR CHARLES. O me! O most unhappy gentleman!
  I am not worthy to have friends stirred up,
  Whose hands may help me in this plunge of want.
  I would I were in Heaven, to inherit there
  The immortal birth-right which my Saviour keeps,
  And by no unthrift can be bought and sold;
  For here on earth what pleasures should we trust?   30
SHAFTON. To rid you from these contemplations,
  Three hundred pounds you shall receive of me;
  Nay, five for fail. Come, sir; the sight of gold
  Is the most sweet receipt for melancholy,
  And will revive your spirits: you shall hold law
  With your proud adversaries. Tush, let Frank Acton
  Wage with his knighthood like expense with me,
  And he will sink, he will. Nay, good Sir Charles,
  Applaud your fortune, and your fair escape
  From all these perils.
SIR CHARLES.   O sir, they have undone me.   40
  Two thousand and five hundred pound a year
  My father, at his death, possessed me of;
  All which the envious Acton made me spend.
  And, notwithstanding all this large expense,
  I had much ado to gain my liberty:
  And I have only now a house of pleasure,
  With some five hundred pounds, reserved
  Both to maintain me and my loving sister.
SHAFTON [*Aside*]. That must I have, it lies convenient for me:
  If I can fasten but one finger on him,   50
  With my full hand I'll gripe him to the heart.
  'Tis not for love I proffered him this coin,
  But for my gain and pleasure. [*Aloud*.] Come, Sir Charles,

33. *for fail*, to prevent failure.

I know you have need of money; take my offer.

SIR CHARLES. Sir, I accept it, and remain indebted
   Even to the best of my unable power.
   Come, gentlemen, and see it tendered down.

                              [*They go out together.*

SCENE III

A ROOM IN FRANKFORD'S HOUSE *some time later. The fears of Nicholas have been in a measure justified, for Wendoll has fallen in love with the wife of his benefactor. But he is not yet ready to bow to that passion. He enters brooding over his problem.*

WENDOLL. I am a villain if I apprehend
   But such a thought: then, to attempt the deed,—
   Slave, thou art damned without redemption.
   I'll drive away this passion with a song.
   A song! ha, ha: a song! as if, fond man,
   Thy eyes could swim in laughter, when thy soul
   Lies drenched and drowned in red tears of blood.
   I'll pray, and see if God within my heart
   Plant better thoughts. Why, prayers are meditations;
   And when I meditate (O God, forgive me!)   10
   It is on her divine perfections.
   I will forget her; I will arm myself
   Not to entertain a thought of love to her:
   And, when I come by chance into her presence,
   I'll hale these balls until my eye-strings crack,
   From being pulled and drawn to look that way.
      [*Frankford, Mistress Frankford, and Nicholas* cross over the
        *upper stage as if walking along a gallery. They do not see
        Wendoll, but he sees them.*
   O God! O God! with what a violence
   I'm hurried to mine own destruction.
   There goest thou, the most perfectest man
   That ever England bred a gentleman;   20
   And shall I wrong his bed? Thou God of thunder!
   Stay in thy thoughts of vengeance and of wrath,
   Thy great, almighty, and all-judging hand
   From speedy execution on a villain:
   A villain, and a traitor to his friend.

15. *hale . . . balls,* turn my eyes away.

*[Enter Jenkin. Wendoll is so immersed in his thoughts that
    he does not see his man.*

JENKIN. Did your worship call?

WENDOLL. He doth maintain me, he allows me largely
    Money to spend—

JENKIN. By my faith, so do not you me; I cannot get a cross of
    you.   30

WENDOLL. My gelding, and my man—

JENKIN.   That's Sorrell and I.

WENDOLL. This kindness grows of no alliance 'twixt us—

JENKIN. Nor is my service of any great acquaintance.

WENDOLL. I never bound him to me by desert:
    Of a mere stranger, a poor gentleman,
    A man by whom in no kind he could gain,
    And he hath placed me in his highest thoughts,
    Made me companion with the best and chiefest
    In Yorkshire. He cannot eat without me,
    Nor laugh without me: I am to his body   40
    As necessary as his digestion,
    And equally do make him whole or sick:
    And shall I wrong this man? Base man! ingrate
    Hast thou the power straight with thy gory hands
    To rip thy image from his bleeding heart?
    To scratch thy name from out the holy book
    Of his remembrance; and to wound his name
    That holds thy name so dear? or rend his heart
    To whom thy heart was knit and joined together?
    And yet I must: then, Wendoll, be content;   50
    Thus villains, when they would, cannot repent.

JENKIN. What a strange humour is my new master in! pray God
    he be not mad: if he should be so, I should never have any
    mind to serve him in Bedlam. It may be he's mad for missing
    of me.

WENDOLL [*Seeing Jenkin*]. What, Jenkin, where's your mistress?

JENKIN. Is your worship married?

WENDOLL.   Why dost thou ask?

JENKIN. Because you are my master; and if I have a mistress, I
    would be glad, like a good servant, to do my duty to her.   60

WENDOLL. I mean Mistress Frankford.

JENKIN. Marry, sir, her husband is riding out of town, and she
    went very lovingly to bring him on his way to horse. Do you
    see, sir? here she comes, and here I go.

    29. *cross,* a coin.

WENDOLL. Vanish.   [*Jenkin trots out.*

[*Re-enter Mistress Frankford.*

MISTRESS FRANKFORD. You are well met, sir; now, in ·troth, my
    husband,
    Before he took horse, had a great desire
    To speak with you: we sought about the house,
    Hollaed into the fields, sent every way,
    But could not meet you: therefore he enjoined me   70
    To do unto you his most kind commends.
    Nay, more; he wills you, as you prize his love,
    Or hold in estimation his kind friendship,
    To make bold in his absence, and command
    Even as himself were present in the house:
    For you must keep his table, use his servants,
    And be a present Frankford in his absence.

WENDOLL. I thank him for his love.
    [*Aside.*] Give me a name, you whose infectious tongues
    Are tipped with gall and poison: as you would   80
    Think on a man that had your father slain,
    Murdered your children, made your wives base strumpets,
    So call me, call me so: print in my face
    The most stigmatic title of a villain,
    For hatching treason to so true a friend.

MISTRESS FRANKFORD. Sir, you are much beholding to my husband;
    You are a man most dear in his regard.

WENDOLL [*Aside*]. I am bound unto your husband, and you too.
    I will not speak to wrong a gentleman
    Of that good estimation, my kind friend: 90
    I will not; zounds! I will not. I may choose,
    And I will choose. Shall I be so misled?
    Or shall I purchase to my father's crest
    The motto of a villain? If I say
    I will not do it, what thing can enforce me?
    What can compel me? What sad destiny
    Hath such command upon my yielding thoughts?
    I will not—Ha! some fury pricks me on,
    The swift Fates drag me at their chariot-wheel,
    And hurry me to mischief. Speak I must;   100
    Injure myself, wrong her, deceive his trust.

MISTRESS FRANKFORD. Are you not well, sir, that you seem thus
    troubled?
    There is sedition in your countenance.

93. *purchase*, acquire, add.

WENDOLL. And in my heart, fair angel, chaste and wise.
  I love you: start not, speak not, answer not.
  I love you: nay, let me speak the rest:
  Bid me to swear, and I will call to record
  The host of Heaven.

MISTRESS FRANKFORD.   The host of Heaven forbid
  Wendoll should hatch such a disloyal thought!

WENDOLL. Such is my fate; to this suit I was born,   110
  To wear rich pleasure's crown, or fortune's scorn.

MISTRESS FRANKFORD. My husband loves you.

WENDOLL.   I know it.

MISTRESS FRANKFORD.   He esteems you
  Even as his brain, his eye-ball, or his heart.

WENDOLL. I have tried it.

MISTRESS FRANKFORD. His purse is your exchequer, and his table
  Doth freely serve you.

WENDOLL.   So I have found it.

MISTRESS FRANKFORD. O! with what face of brass, what brow of
    steel,
  Can you, unblushing, speak this to the face
  Of the espoused wife of so dear a friend?
  It is my husband that maintains your state;   120
  Will you dishonour him that in your power
  Hath left his whole affairs? I am his wife,
  It is to me you speak.

WENDOLL.   O speak no more!
  For more than this I know, and have recorded
  Within the red-leaved table of my heart.
  Fair, and of all beloved, I was not fearful
  Bluntly to give my life into your hand,
  And at one hazard all my earthly means.
  Go, tell your husband; he will turn me off,
  And I am then undone. I care not, I;   130
  'Twas for your sake. Perchance in rage he'll kill me:
  I care not, 'twas for you. Say I incur
  The general name of villain through the world,
  Of traitor to my friend; I care not, I.
  Beggary, shame, death, scandal, and reproach,
  For you I'll hazard all: why, what care I?
  For you I'll live, and in your love I'll die.

MISTRESS FRANKFORD. You move me, sir, to passion and to pity.
  The love I bear my husband is as precious

    125. *table*, tablet.

As my soul's health. 140

WENDOLL. I love your husband too,
And for his love I will engage my life:
Mistake me not, the augmentation
Of my sincere affection borne to you
Doth no whit lessen my regard of him.
I will be secret, lady, close as night;
And not the light of one small glorious star
Shall shine here in my forehead, to bewray
That act of night.

MISTRESS FRANKFORD. What shall I say?
My soul is wandering, and hath lost her way.
Oh, Master Wendoll! Oh! 150

WENDOLL [*Embracing her*]. Sigh not, sweet saint;
For every sigh you breathe draws from my heart
A drop of blood.

MISTRESS FRANKFORD. I ne'er offended yet:
My fault, I fear, will in my brow be writ.
Women that fall, not quite bereft of grace,
Have their offences noted in their face.
I blush and am ashamed. Oh, Master Wendoll,
Pray God I be not born to curse your tongue,
That hath enchanted me! This maze I am in
I fear will prove the labyrinth of sin.
[*Re-enter Nicholas behind.*

WENDOLL. The path of pleasure, and the gate to bliss, 160
Which on your lips I knock at with a kiss.

NICHOLAS [*Aside*]. I'll kill the rogue.

WENDOLL. Your husband is from home, your bed's no blab.
Nay, look not down and blush.
[*Wendoll and Mrs. Frankford go out lovingly.*

NICHOLAS. Zounds! I'll stab.
Ay, Nick, was it thy chance to come just in the nick?
I love my master, and I hate that slave:
I love my mistress, but these tricks I like not.
My master shall not pocket up this wrong;
I'll eat my fingers first. [*He draws his sword.*] What say'st
thou, metal?
Does not the rascal Wendoll go on legs 170
That thou must cut off? Hath he not ham-strings

151. *sigh*, lovers were supposed to lose a drop of blood each time they sighed. Wendoll implies that his heart has been taken by Mrs. Frankford.

That thou must hough? Nay, metal, thou shalt stand
To all I say. I'll henceforth turn a spy,
And watch them in their close conveyances.
I never looked for better of that rascal,
Since he came miching first into our house:
It is that Satan hath corrupted her,
For she was fair and chaste. I'll have an eye
In all their gestures. Thus I think of them,
If they proceed as they have done before: 180
Wendoll's a knave, my mistress is a—

       [*He goes out threatening.*

ACT III

SCENE I

A ROOM IN SIR CHARLES MOUNTFORD'S HOUSE. *Some time has elapsed
since he was freed from prison. He enters with his sister.*

SIR CHARLES. Sister, you see we are driven to hard shift
 To keep this poor house we have left unsold;
 I am now enforced to follow husbandry,
 And you to milk; and do we not live well?
 Well, I thank God.
SUSAN.   O brother, here's a change,
 Since old Sir Charles died, in our father's house!
SIR CHARLES. All things on earth thus change, some up, some down;
 Content's a kingdom, and I wear that crown.
  [*Enter Shafton with a Serjeant.*
SHAFTON. Good morrow, morrow, Sir Charles: what, with your
  sister,
 Plying your husbandry? [*Aside.*] Serjeant, stand off.— 10
 You have a pretty house here, and a garden,
 And goodly ground about it. Since it lies
 So near a lordship that I lately bought,
 I would fain buy it of you. I will give you—
SIR CHARLES. O, pardon me: this house successively
 Hath 'longed to me and my progenitors
 Three hundred years. My great-great-grandfather,
 He in whom first our gentle style began,

---

172. *hough,* cut.   174. *close conveyances,* secret trickery.
176. *miching,* sneaking.   18. *gentle style,* title of gentleman.

Dwelt here; and in this ground, increased this mole-hill
Unto that mountain which my father left me.   20
Where he the first of all our house began,
I now the last will end, and keep this house,
This virgin title, never yet deflowered
By any unthrift of the Mountfords' line.
In brief, I will not sell it for more gold
Than you could hide or pave the ground withal.

SHAFTON. Ha, ha! a proud mind and a beggar's purse!
  Where's my three hundred pounds, besides the use?
  I have brought it to execution
  By course of law: what, is my moneys ready?   30

SIR CHARLES. An execution, sir, and never tell me
  You put my bond in suit! you deal extremely.

SHAFTON. Sell me the land, and I'll acquit you straight.

SIR CHARLES. Alas, alas! 'tis all trouble hath left me
  To cherish me and my poor sister's life.
  If this were sold, our names should then be quite
  Razed from the bead-roll of gentility.
  You see what hard shift we have made to keep it
  Allied still to our own name. This palm, you see,
  Labour hath glowed within: her silver brow,   40
  That never tasted a rough winter's blast
  Without a mask or fan, doth with a grace
  Defy cold winter, and his storms outface.

SUSAN. Sir, we feed sparing, and we labour hard,
  We lie uneasy, to reserve to us
  And our succession this small plot of ground.

SIR CHARLES. I have so bent my thoughts to husbandry,
  That I protest I scarcely can remember
  What a new fashion is; how silk or satin
  Feels in my hand: why, pride is grown to us   50
  A mere, mere stranger. I have quite forgot
  The names of all that ever waited on me;
  I cannot name ye any of my hounds,
  Once from whose echoing mouths I heard all music
  That e'er my heart desired. What should I say?
  To keep this place I have changed myself away.

SHAFTON [*To the Serjeant*]. Arrest him at my suit. Actions and
    actions
  Shall keep thee in continual bondage fast:
  Nay, more, I'll sue thee by a late appeal,

28. *use*, interest.   37. *Razed*, Erased.   *bead-roll*, official list.

  And call thy former life in question.
  The keeper is my friend, thou shalt have irons,
  And usage such as I'll deny to dogs:
  Away with him!

SIR CHARLES. You are too timorous:
  But trouble is my master,
  And I will serve him truly.—My kind sister,
  Thy tears are of no force to mollify
  This flinty man. Go to my father's brother,
  My kinsmen and allies; entreat them for me,
  To ransom me from this injurious man,
  That seeks my ruin.   70

SHAFTON. Come, irons, irons! come away;
  I'll see thee lodged far from the sight of day.
             [*Exeunt Shafton and Serjeant with Sir Charles.*

SUSAN. My heart's so hardened with the frost of grief,
  Death cannot pierce it through. Tyrant too fell!
  So lead the fiends condemnèd souls to hell.
      [*Enter Sir Francis Acton and Malby at the back of the stage.*

SIR FRANCIS. Again to prison! Malby, hast thou seen
  A poor slave better tortured? Shall we hear
  The music of his voice cry from the grate,
  "Meat for the Lord's sake"? No, no, yet I am not
  Throughly revenged. They say he hath a pretty wench
  To his sister: shall I, in my mercy-sake   80
  To him and to his kindred, bribe the fool
  To shame herself by lewd dishonest lust?
  I'll proffer largely; but, the deed being done,
  I'll smile to see her base confusion.

MALBY [*Disturbed by Acton's callousness*]. Methinks, Sir Francis,
    you are full revenged
  For greater wrongs than he can proffer you.
  See where the poor sad gentlewoman stands.

SIR FRANCIS. Ha, ha! now will I flout her poverty,
  Deride her fortunes, scoff her base estate;
  My very soul the name of Mountford hates.   90
  But stay, my heart! oh, what a look did fly
  To strike my soul through with thy piercing eye!
  I am enchanted; all my spirits are fled,
  And with one glance my envious spleen struck dead.

---

63. *timorous*, threatening, i.e., *causing* fear.
77. *from the grate*, the grating of the debtor's prison, where the prisoners collected to cry for alms.

SUSAN. Acton! that seeks our blood.   [*She runs away.*

SIR FRANCIS.   O chaste and fair!

MALBY. Sir Francis, why, Sir Francis, in a trance?
   Sir Francis, what cheer, man? Come, come, how is't?

SIR FRANCIS. Was she not fair? Or else this judging eye
   Cannot distinguish beauty.

MALBY.   She was fair.

SIR FRANCIS [*Greatly impressed*]. She was an angel in a mortal's
   shape,   100
And ne'er descended from old Mountford's line.
But soft, soft, let me call my wits together.
A poor, poor wench, to my great adversary
Sister, whose very souls denounce stern war,
One against other. How now, Frank? turned **fool**
Or madman, whether? But no; master of
My perfect senses and directest wits.
Then why should I be in this violent humour
Of passion and of love; and with a person
So different every way, and so opposed   110
In all contractions, and still-warring actions?
Fie, fie; how I dispute against my soul!
Come, come; I'll gain her, or in her fair quest
Purchase my soul free and immortal rest.
    [*They go out together, Sir Francis in meditative mood.*

SCENE II

A SITTING-ROOM IN FRANKFORD'S HOUSE. *Enter Serving-Men, one
with a voider* * *and a wooden knife to take away; another with
the salt and bread; another with the table-cloth and napkins;
another with the carpet:* † *Jenkin follows them with two lights.*

JENKIN. So, march in order, and retire in battle array. My master
   and the guests have supped already, all's taken away: here, now
   spread for the serving-men in the hall. Butler, it belongs to your
   office.

BUTLER. I know it, Jenkin. What d'ye call the gentleman that
   supped there to-night?

JENKIN. Who, my master?

BUTLER. No, no; Master Wendoll, he's a daily guest: I mean the
   gentleman that came but this afternoon.

111. *contractions*, dealings, with special reference to lawsuits here.
 * *voider*, a basket or tray into which scraps were scraped with the wooden
knife.   † *carpet*, table cover.

JENKIN. His name's Master Cranwell. God's light, hark, within   10
there, my master calls to lay more billets upon the fire. Come,
come! Lord, how we that are in office here in the house are
troubled! One spread the carpet in the parlour, and stand ready
to snuff the lights; the rest be ready to prepare their stomachs.
More lights in the hall there. Come, Nich'las.

[*Exeunt all but Nicholas.*

NICHOLAS. I cannot eat, but had I Wendoll's heart
I would eat that; the rogue grows impudent.
Oh, I have seen such vile notorious tricks,
Ready to make my eyes dart from my head.
I'll tell my master, by this air I will!   20
Fall what may fall, I'll tell him. Here he comes.

[*Enter Frankford, brushing the crumbs from his clothes
with a napkin, as newly risen from supper.*

FRANKFORD. Nicholas, what make you here? why are not you
At supper in the hall among your fellows?
NICHOLAS. Master, I stayed your rising from the board,
To speak with you.
FRANKFORD.   Be brief, then, gentle Nicholas;
My wife and guests attend me in the parlour.
Why dost thou pause? Now, Nicholas, you want money,
And, unthrift-like, would eat into your wages
Ere you have earned it: here, sir, 's half a crown;
Play the good husband, and away to supper.   30
NICHOLAS. By this hand, an honourable gentleman! I will not see
him wronged.—Sir, I have served you long; you entertained
me seven years before your beard. You knew me, sir, before
you knew my mistress.
FRANKFORD. What of this, good Nicholas?
NICHOLAS. I never was a make-bate or a knave;
I have no fault but one: I'm given to quarrel,
But not with women. I will tell you, master,
That which will make your heart leap from your breast,
Your hair to startle from your head, your ears to tingle.   40
FRANKFORD. What preparation's this to dismal news?
NICHOLAS. 'Sblood, sir! I love you better than your wife;
I'll make it good.

24. *stayed*, awaited.   30. *play . . . husband*, be frugal.
32-33. *entertained . . . beard*, took me into service seven years before
you were old enough to grow a beard.
36. *make-bate*, trouble-maker.

FRANKFORD. You are a knave, and I have much ado
  With wonted patience to contain my rage,
  And not to break thy pate. Thou art a knave:
  I'll turn you, with your base comparisons,
  Out of my doors.

NICHOLAS. Do, do: there is not room
  For Wendoll and me, too, both in one house.
  Oh master, master, that Wendoll is a villain.

FRANKFORD [*Threatening to strike him*]. Ay, saucy! 50

NICHOLAS. Strike, strike; do, strike; yet hear me: I am no fool,
  I know a villain, when I see him act
  Deeds of a villain. Master, master, that base slave
  Enjoys my mistress, and dishonours you.

FRANKFORD. Thou hast killed me with a weapon whose sharp point
  Hath pricked quite through and through my shivering heart:
  Drops of cold sweat sit dangling on my hairs,
  Like morning's dew upon the golden flowers,
  And I am plunged into strange agonies.
  What didst thou say? If any word that touched 60
  His credit or her reputation,
  It is as hard to enter my belief
  As Dives into heaven.

NICHOLAS. I can gain nothing;
  They are two that never wronged me. I knew before
  'Twas but a thankless office, and perhaps
  As much as is my service, or my life
  Is worth. All this I know; but this and more,
  More by a thousand dangers, could not hire me
  To smother such a heinous wrong from you.
  I saw, and I have said. 70

FRANKFORD [*Aside*]. 'Tis probable; though blunt, yet he is honest:
  Though I durst pawn my life, and on their faith
  Hazard the dear salvation of my soul,
  Yet in my trust I may be too secure.
  May this be true? O, may it, can it be?
  Is it by any wonder possible?
  Man, woman, what thing mortal can we trust,
  When friends and bosom wives prove so unjust?—
  [*To Nicholas.*] What instance hast thou of this strange report?

NICHOLAS. Eyes, master, eyes. 80

FRANKFORD. Thy eyes may be deceived, I tell thee:

63. *Dives*, the parable of Dives and Lazarus, *Luke XVI*, 19 ff. It was a popular subject on tapestries.

For, should an angel from the heavens drop down,
And preach this to me that thyself hast told,
He should have much ado to win belief;
In both their loves I am so confident.

NICHOLAS. Shall I discourse the same by circumstance?

FRANKFORD. No more! to supper, and command your fellows
To attend us and the strangers. Not a word,
I charge thee on thy life: be secret then,
For I know nothing.   90

NICHOLAS. I am dumb; and, now that I have eased my stomach,
I will go fill my stomach.

FRANKFORD.   Away; be gone.   [*Exit Nicholas.*
She is well born, descended nobly;
Virtuous her education, her repute
Is in the general voice of all the country
Honest and fair; her carriage, her demeanour,
In all her actions that concern the love
To me her husband, modest, chaste, and godly.
Is all this seeming gold plain copper?
But he, that Judas that hath borne my purse,   100
And sold me for a sin!—O God! O God!
Shall I put up these wrongs? No. Shall I trust
The bare report of this suspicious groom,
Before the double-gilt, the well-hatched ore
Of their two hearts? No, I will lose these thoughts:
Distraction I will banish from my brow,
And from my looks exile sad discontent,
Their wonted favours· in my tongue shall flow;
Till I know all, I'll nothing seem to know.
Lights and a table there! Wife, Master Wendoll,   110
And gentle Master Cranwell.

> [*Enter Mistress Frankford, Wendoll, Cranwell, Nicholas,
> and Jenkin, with cards, carpets, stools, and other neces-
> saries.*

FRANKFORD. O Master Cranwell, you are a stranger here,
And often baulk my house: faith, y'are a churl:
Now we have supped, a table, and to cards.

JENKIN. A pair of cards, Nicholas, and a carpet to cover the table.
Where's Cicely with her counters and her box? Candles and

91. *stomach,* anger.
104. *double-gilt,* true gold, with the obvious pun on guilt.   *well-hatched,*
of noble origin.
113. *baulk,* avoid.   115. *pair,* pack.

candlesticks there! Fie, we have such a household of serving.
creatures! unless it be Nick and I, there's not one amongst them
all can say bo to a goose. Well said, Nick.

[They spread a carpet, set down lights and cards.

MISTRESS FRANKFORD. Come, Master Frankford, who shall take my
    part?   120

FRANKFORD. Marry, that will I, sweet wife.

WENDOLL. No, by my faith; when you are together I sit out: it
    must be Mistress Frankford and I, or else it is no match.

FRANKFORD. I do not like that match.

NICHOLAS [*Aside*]. You have no reason, marry, knowing all.

FRANKFORD. 'Tis no great matter neither. Come, Master Cranwell,
    shall you and I take them up?

CRANWELL. At your pleasure, sir.

FRANKFORD. I must look to you, Master Wendoll, for you will be
    playing false; nay, so will my wife too.   130

NICHOLAS [*Aside*]. Ay, I will be sworn she will.

MISTRESS FRANKFORD. Let them that are taken false, forfeit the set.

FRANKFORD. Content; it shall go hard but I'll take you.

CRANWELL. Gentlemen, what shall our game be?

WENDOLL. Master Frankford, you play best at noddy.

FRANKFORD. You shall not find it so; indeed you shall not.

MISTRESS FRANKFORD. I can play at nothing so well as double ruff.

FRANKFORD. If Master Wendoll and my wife be together, there's
    no playing against them at double hand.

NICHOLAS. I can tell you, sir, the game that Master Wendoll 140
    is best at.

WENDOLL. What game is that, Nick?

NICHOLAS. Marry, sir, knave out of doors.

WENDOLL. She and I will take you at lodam.

MISTRESS FRANKFORD. Husband, shall we play at saint?

FRANKFORD. My saint's turned devil. No, we'll none of saint:
    You are best at new-cut, wife; you'll play at that.

WENDOLL. If you play at new-cut, I am soonest hitter of any here,
    for a wager.

FRANKFORD. 'Tis me they play on. Well, you may draw out. 150
    For all your cunning, 'twill be to your shame;
    I'll teach you, at your new-cut, a new game.
    Come, come.

119. *Well said*, Well done.

135. *noddy*, a game much like cribbage, but *noddy* also means fool.

137. *double-ruff*, a predecessor of whist. The other games mentioned are
not so well-known, but the point, of course, in each case is on the play on
the name rather than on the nature of the game.

CRANWELL. If you cannot agree upon the game, to post and pair.
WENDOLL. We shall be soonest pairs; and my good host,
  When he comes late home, he must kiss the post.
FRANKFORD. Whoever wins, it shall be thy cost.
CRANWELL. Faith, let it be vide-ruff, and let's make honours.
FRANKFORD. If you make honours, one thing let me crave:
  Honour the king and queen; except the knave.   160
WENDOLL. Well, as you please for that. Lift who shall deal.
MISTRESS FRANKFORD. The least in sight: what are you, Master
  Wendoll?
WENDOLL. I am a knave.
NICHOLAS [Aside].   I'll swear it.
MISTRESS FRANKFORD.   I a queen.
FRANKFORD [Aside]. A quean thou shouldst say. [Aloud.] Well,
  the cards are mine;
  They are the grossest pair that e'er I felt.
MISTRESS FRANKFORD. Shuffle, I'll cut: would I had never dealt.
FRANKFORD. I have lost my dealing.
WENDOLL.   Sir, the fault's in me:
  This queen I have more than mine own, you see.
  Give me the stock.
FRANKFORD.   My mind's not on my game.   170
  Many a deal I have lost; the more's your shame.
  You have served me a bad trick, Master Wendoll.
WENDOLL. Sir, you must take your lot. To end this strife,
  I know I have dealt better with your wife.
FRANKFORD. Thou hast dealt falsely, then.
MISTRESS FRANKFORD.   What's trumps?
WENDOLL. Hearts: partner, I rub.
FRANKFORD [Aside]. Thou robb'st me of my soul, of her chaste
  love;
  In thy false dealing thou hast robbed my heart.
  [Aloud.] Booty you play; I like a loser stand,
  Having no heart, or here or in my hand.   180
  I will give o'er the set; I am not well.
  Come, who will hold my cards?
MISTRESS FRANKFORD. Not well, sweet Master Frankford!
  Alas, what ail you? 'Tis some sudden qualm.
WENDOLL. How long have you been so, Master Frankford?
FRANKFORD. Sir, I was lusty, and I had my health,

---

156. *kiss the post*, be locked out.   160. *except*, exclude, discard.
161. *Lift*, cut.   165. *quean*, whore.
179. *Booty you play*, you are in league with another player to trick me.

But I grew ill when you began to deal.
Take hence this table. Gentle Master Cranwell,
You are welcome; see your chamber at your pleasure.
I'm sorry that this meagrim takes me so,   190
I cannot sit and bear you company.
Jenkin, some lights, and show him to his chamber.

                    [Exeunt Cranwell and Jenkin.

MISTRESS FRANKFORD. A night-gown for my husband; quickly
    there:
    It is some rheum or cold.

WENDOLL. Now, in good faith, this illness you have got
    By sitting late without your gown.

FRANKFORD.   I know it, Master Wendoll.
    Go, go to bed, lest you complain like me.
    Wife, prythee, wife, into my bed-chamber;
    The night is raw and cold, and rheumatic:
    Leave me my gown and light; I'll walk away my fit.   200

WENDOLL. Sweet sir, good night.

FRANKFORD.   Myself, good night.

                         [Exit Wendoll.

MISTRESS FRANKFORD. Shall I attend you, husband?

FRANKFORD. No, gentle wife, thou'lt catch cold in thy head;
    Prythee, be gone, sweet; I'll make haste to bed.

MISTRESS FRANKFORD. No sleep will fasten on mine eyes, you
    know,
    Until you come.

FRANKFORD.   Sweet Nan, I prythee go.—

    [Exit Mistress Frankford. As soon as she is out, he turns to
      Nicholas.

I have bethought me: get me, by degrees,
The keys of all my doors, which I will mould
In wax, and take their fair impression,
To have by them new keys. This being compassed,   210
At a set hour a letter shall be brought me,
And, when they think they may securely play,
They nearest are to danger. Nick, I must rely
Upon thy trust and faithful secrecy.

NICHOLAS. Build on my faith.

FRANKFORD.   To bed then, not to rest:
    Care lodges in my brain, grief in my breast.

        [Nick hurries away and Frankford sadly goes out.

   192. *night-gown,* dressing gown.

ACT IV

SCENE I

*In her efforts to help her brother, Susan has come to her uncle,
who thinks much more of his money than he does of his
nephew. Susan and Old Mountford enter, followed by her
cousin Tidy and by Sandy and Roder.*

OLD MOUNTFORD. You say my nephew is in great distress:
  Who brought it to him, but his own lewd life?
  I cannot spare a cross. I must confess
  He was my brother's son: why, niece, what then?
  This is no world in which to pity men.

SUSAN. I was not born a beggar, though his extremes
  Enforce this language from me: I protest
  No fortune of mine own could lead my tongue
  To this base key. I do beseech you, uncle,
  For the name's sake, for Christianity,   10
  Nay, for God's sake, to pity his distress:
  He is denied the freedom of the prison,
  And in the hole is laid with men condemned;
  Plenty he hath of nothing but of irons,
  And it remains in you to free him thence.

OLD MOUNTFORD. Money I cannot spare; men should take heed;
  He lost my kindred when he fell to need.
                 [He goes out before she can say more.

SUSAN. Gold is but earth, thou earth enough shalt have,
  When thou hast once took measure of thy grave.
  You know me, Master Sandy, and my suit.   20

SANDY. I knew you, lady, when the old man lived;
  I knew you ere your brother sold his land;
  Then you were Mistress Sue, trick'd up in jewels:
  Then you sung well, played sweetly on the lute;
  But now I neither know you nor your suit.
                 [He follows Old Mountford.

SUSAN. You, Master Roder, was my brother's tenant,
  Rent-free he placed you in that wealthy farm,
  Of which you are possessed.

RODER.   True, he did;
  And have I not there dwelt still for his sake?
  I have some business now; but, without doubt,   30

They that have hurled him in will help him out.

         [He too goes out.

SUSAN. Cold comfort still: what say you, cousin Tidy?

TIDY. I say this comes of roysting, swaggering.
 Call me not cousin: each man for himself.
 Some men are born to mirth, and some to sorrow,
 I am no cousin unto them that borrow.

     [He leaves her standing wretchedly alone.

SUSAN. O charity! why art thou fled to heaven,
 And left all things on this earth uneven?
 Their scoffing answers I will ne'er return;
 But to myself his grief in silence mourn.   40

  [As she stands in despair, Sir Francis Acton and Malby enter.
   Sir Francis cannot rid his mind of her beauty and goodness
   so seeks to win her by offering money.

SIR FRANCIS. She is poor, I'll therefore tempt her with this gold.
 Go, Malby, in my name deliver it,
 And I will stay thy answer.

MALBY. Fair mistress, as I understand, your grief
 Doth grow from want, so I have here in store
 A means to furnish you, a bag of gold,
 Which to your hands I freely tender you.

SUSAN. I thank you, Heavens! I thank you, gentle sir:
 God make me able to requite this favour!

MALBY. This gold Sir Francis Acton sends by me,   50
 And prays you—

SUSAN. Acton! O God! that name I am born to curse:
 Hence, bawd! hence, broker! see, I spurn his gold;
 My honour never shall for gain be sold.

SIR FRANCIS. Stay, lady, stay.

SUSAN.   From you I'll posting hie,
 Even as the doves from feathered eagles fly.

          [She goes proudly off.

SIR FRANCIS. She hates my name, my face: how should I woo?
 I am disgraced in every thing I do.
 The more she hates me, and disdains my love,
 The more I am rapt in admiration   60
 Of her divine and chaste perfections.
 Woo her with gifts I cannot, for all gifts
 Sent in my name she spurns: with looks I cannot,
 For she abhors my sight; nor yet with letters,
 For none she will receive. How then, how then?

33. **roysting**, rioting. 53. **broker**, go-between, pandar.

Well, I will fasten such a kindness on her
As shall o'ercome her hate and conquer it.
Sir Charles, her brother, lies in execution
For a great sum of money; and, besides,
The appeal is sued still for my huntsman's death,   70
Which only I have power to reverse:
In her I'll bury all my hate of him.
Go seek the keeper, Malby, bring him to me:
To save his body, I his debts will pay;
To save his life, I his appeal will stay.   *[They go out.*

· SCENE II ·

A PRISON CELL IN YORK CASTLE. *Enter Sir Charles Mountford, with
irons, his feet bare, his garments all ragged and torn.*

SIR CHARLES. Of all on the earth's face most miserable,
  Breathe in this hellish dungeon thy laments,
  Thus like a slave ragged, like a felon gyved.
  What hurls thee headlong to this base estate?
  O unkind uncle! O my friends ingrate!
  Unthankful kinsmen! Mountford's all too base,
  To let thy name be fettered in disgrace!
  A thousand deaths here in this grave I die;
  Fear, hunger, sorrow, cold, all threat my death,
  And join together to deprive my breath.   10
  But that which most torments me, my dear sister
  Hath left to visit me, and from my friends
  Hath brought no hopeful answer: therefore I
  Divine they will not help my misery.
  If it be so, shame, scandal, and contempt
  Attend their covetous thoughts; need make their graves!
  Usurers they live, and may they die like slaves!
      [Enter Keeper.
KEEPER. Knight, be of comfort, for I bring thee freedom
  From all thy troubles.
SIR CHARLES.   Then I am doomed to die?
  Death is the end of all calamity.   20
KEEPER. Live: your appeal is stayed; the execution
  Of all your debts discharged; your creditors .
  Even to the utmost penny satisfied.

12. *left*, ceased.

In sign whereof, your shackles I knock off.
You are not left so much indebted to us
As for your fees; all is discharged, all paid.
Go freely to your house, or where you please,
After long miseries, embrace your ease.

SIR CHARLES. Thou grumblest out the sweetest music to me
That ever organ played. Is this a dream 30
Or do my waking senses apprehend
The pleasing taste of these applausive news?
Slave that I was, to wrong such honest friends,
My loving kinsmen, and my near allies.
Tongue, I will bite thee for the scandal breath
Against such faithful kinsmen: they are all
Composed of pity and compassion,
Of melting charity, and of moving ruth.
That which I spake before was in my rage; 40
They are my friends, the mirrors of this age,
Bounteous and free. The noble Mountford's race,
Ne'er bred a covetous thought, or humour base.
[Enter Susan.

SUSAN. I can no longer stay from visiting
My woful brother: while I could, I kept
My hapless tidings from his hopeful ear.

SIR CHARLES. Sister, how much am I indebted to thee,
And to thy travel!

SUSAN. What, at liberty?

SIR CHARLES. Thou seest I am, thanks to thy industry:
Oh! unto which of all my courteous friends
Am I thus bound? My uncle Mountford, he 50
Even of an infant loved me: was it he?
So did my cousin Tidy; was it he?
So Master Roder, Master Sandy too:
Which of all these did this high kindness do?

SUSAN. Charles, can you mock me in your poverty,
Knowing your friends deride your misery?
Now, I protest I stand so much amazed
To see your bonds free, and your irons knocked off,
That I am rapt into a maze of wonder:
The rather for I know not by what means 60
This happiness hath chanced.

SIR CHARLES. Why, by my uncle,
My cousins, and my friends: who else, I pray,

32. *applausive*, worthy to be applauded.

Would take upon them all my debts to pay?

SUSAN. O brother, they are men all of flint,
　Pictures of marble, and as void of pity
　As chased bears. I begged, I sued, I kneeled,
　Laid open all your griefs and miseries,
　Which they derided; more than that, denied us
　A part in their alliance; but, in pride,
　Said that our kindred with our plenty died.　　　70

SIR CHARLES. Drudges too much—what did they? oh, known evil!
　Rich fly the poor, as good men shun the devil.
　Whence should my freedom come? of whom alive,
　Saving of those, have I deserved so well?
　Guess, sister, call to mind, remember me:
　These I have raised; they follow the world's guise;
　Whom rich in honour, they in woe despise.

SUSAN. My wits have lost themselves, let's ask the keeper.

SIR CHARLES. Jailer!

KEEPER.　　　　At hand, sir.

SIR CHARLES. Of courtesy resolve me one demand.　　　80
　What was he took the burden of my debts
　From off my back, stayed my appeal to death,
　Discharged my fees, and brought me liberty?

KEEPER. A courteous knight, and called Sir Francis Acton.

SIR CHARLES. Ha! Acton! O me, more distressed in this
　Than all my troubles! hale me back,
　Double my irons, and my sparing meals
　Put into halves, and lodge me in a dungeon
　More deep, more dark, more cold, more comfortless.
　By Acton freed! not all thy manacles　　　90
　Could fetter so my heels as this one word
　Hath thralled my heart; and it must now lie bound
　In more strict prison than thy stony jail.
　I am not free; I go but under bail.

KEEPER. My charge is done, sir, now I have my fees;
　As we get little, we will nothing leese.　　　[He goes out.

SIR CHARLES. By Acton freed, my dangerous opposite!
　Why, to what end? or what occasion? ha!
　Let me forget the name of enemy,
　And with indifference balance this high favour:　　　100
　Ha!

SUSAN [Aside]. His love to me? upon my soul 'tis so:

---

71. *Drudges too much*, too thoroughly base.　　　76. *raised*, thought of.
80. *resolve . . .*, answer one question.　　　97. *leese*, lose.

That is the root from whence these strange things grow.
SIR CHARLES. Had this proceeded from my father, he
  That by the law of nature is most bound
  In offices of love, it had deserved
  My best employment to requite that grace:
  Had it proceeded from my friends or him,
  From them this action had deserved my life:
  And from a stranger more; because from such   110
  There is less execution of good deeds.
  But he, nor father, nor ally, nor friend,
  More than a stranger, both remote in blood
  And in his heart opposed my enemy,—
  That this high bounty should proceed from him,—
  Oh, there I lose myself! What should I say,
  What think, what do, his bounty to repay?
SUSAN. You, wonder, I am sure, whence this strange kindness
  Proceeds in Acton. I will tell you, brother:
  He dotes on me, and oft hath sent me gifts,   120
  Letters and tokens: I refused them all.
SIR CHARLES. I have enough, though poor; my heart is set,
  In one rich gift to pay back all my debt.

                        [They go out together.

SCENE III

A ROOM IN FRANKFORD'S HOUSE. *Frankford has had time to perfect his plans. He enters with Nicholas, who has the duplicate keys.*

FRANKFORD. This is the night that I must play my part
  To try two seeming angels. Where's my keys?
NICHOLAS. They are made according to your mould in wax:
  I bade the smith be secret, gave him money,
  And here they are. The letter, sir.
FRANKFORD. True, take it, there it is;   *[Gives him the letter.*
  And when thou seest me in my pleasant'st vein,
  Ready to sit to supper, bring it me.
NICHOLAS. I'll do't, make no more question but I'll do't.
    *[He goes out. Enter Mistress Frankford, Cranwell, Wendoll,
    and Jenkin.*
MISTRESS FRANKFORD. Sirrah, 'tis six o'clock already struck!   10
  Go bid them spread the cloth and serve in supper.
JENKIN. It shall be done, forsooth, mistress. Where's

Spigot, the butler, to give us our salt and trenchers?

[He hurries out.

WENDOLL. We that have been a-hunting all the day
Come with prepared stomachs. Master Frankford,
We wished you at our sport.

FRANKFORD. My heart was with you, and my mind was on you.
Fie, Master Cranwell! you are still thus sad?
A stool, a stool. Where's Jenkin, and where's Nick?
'Tis supper-time at least an hour ago.   20
What's the best news abroad?

WENDOLL. I know none good.

FRANKFORD [*Aside*].   But I know too much bad.
[Enter Jenkin and Butler with a table-cloth, bread, trench-
ers, and salt.

CRANWELL. Methinks, sir, you might have that interest
In your wife's brother, to be more remiss
In his hard dealing against poor Sir Charles,
Who, as I hear, lies in York Castle, needy,
And in great want.   *[Exeunt Jenkin and Butler.*

FRANKFORD. Did not more weighty business of my own
Hold me away, I would have laboured peace   30
Betwixt them, with all care; indeed I would, sir.

MISTRESS FRANKFORD. I'll write unto my brother earnestly
In that behalf.

WENDOLL.   A charitable deed,
And will beget the good opinion
Of all your friends that love you, Mistress Frankford.

FRANKFORD. That's you for one; I know you love Sir Charles,
And my wife too, well.

WENDOLL.   He deserves the love
Of all true gentlemen; be yourselves judge.

FRANKFORD. But supper, ho! Now as thou lov'st me, Wendoll,
Which I am sure thou dost, be merry, pleasant,   40
And frolic it to-night. Sweet Master Cranwell,
Do you the like. Wife, I protest my heart
Was ne'er more bent on sweet alacrity.
Where be those lazy knaves to serve in supper?
[Re-enter Nicholas.

NICHOLAS. Here's a letter, sir.

FRANKFORD. Whence comes it? and who brought it?

NICHOLAS. A stripling that below attends your answer,
And, as he tells me, it is sent from York.

24. *remiss,* lenient.

FRANKFORD. Have him into the cellar; let him taste
  A cup of our March beer: go, make him drink.   50
  [*Reads the letter.*

NICHOLAS. I'll make him drunk, if he be a Trojan.

FRANKFORD. My boots and spurs! where's Jenkin? **God forgive**
  me,
  How I neglect my business! Wife, look here;
  I have a matter to be tried to-morrow
  By eight o'clock, and my attorney writes me,
  I must be there betimes with evidence,
  Or it will go against me. Where's my boots?
  [*Re-enter Jenkin with boots and spurs.*

MISTRESS FRANKFORD. I hope your business craves **no such despatch**
  That you must ride to-night.

WENDOLL [*Aside*].   I hope it doth.

FRANKFORD. God's me! no such despatch!   60
  Jenkin, my boots. Where's Nick? Saddle my **roan**,
  And the grey dapple for himself. Content ye,
  It much concerns me. Gentle Master Cranwell,
  And Master Wendoll, in my absence use
  The very ripest pleasures of my house.

WENDOLL. Lord! Master Frankford, will you ride **to-night**?
  The ways are dangerous.

FRANKFORD.   Therefore will I ride
  Appointed well; and so shall Nick my man.

MISTRESS FRANKFORD. I'll call you up by five o'clock to-morrow.

FRANKFORD. No, by my faith, wife, I'll not trust to that;   70
  'Tis not such easy rising in a morning
  From one I love so dearly: no, by my faith,
  I shall not leave so sweet a bedfellow,
  But with much pain. You have made me a sluggard
  Since I first knew you.

MISTRESS FRANKFORD.   Then, if you needs will go
  This dangerous evening, Master Wendoll,
  Let me entreat you bear him company.

WENDOLL. With all my heart, sweet mistress. My boots there!

FRANKFORD. Fie, fie, that for my private business
  I should disease my friend, and be a trouble   80
  To the whole house! Nick!

NICHOLAS.   Anon, sir.

FRANKFORD. Bring forth my gelding.—[*Exit Nicholas.*]—As you
  love me, sir,

80. *disease*, discomfort.

Use no more words: a hand, good Master Cranwell.

CRANWELL. Sir, God be your good speed!

FRANKFORD. Good night, sweet Nan; nay, nay, a kiss and part.

[*Aside.*] Dissembling lips, you suit not with my heart.

[*He goes out with a great show of haste.*

WENDOLL. How business, time, and hours, all gracious prove,
And are the furtherers to my new-born love!
I am husband now in Master Frankford's place,
And must command the house. My pleasure is   90
We will not sup abroad so publicly,
But in your private chamber, Mistress Frankford.

MISTRESS FRANKFORD. O, sir, you are too public in your love,
And Master Frankford's wife—

CRANWELL.   Might I crave favour,
I would entreat you I might see my chamber;
I am on the sudden grown exceeding ill,
And would be spared from supper.

WENDOLL.   Light there, ho!
See you want nothing, sir; for, if you do,
You injure that good man, and wrong me too.   100

CRANWELL. I will make bold: good night.   [*He goes out.*

WENDOLL.   How all conspire
To make our bosom sweet, and full entire!
Come, Nan, I pr'ythee let us sup within.

MISTRESS FRANKFORD. Oh, what a clog unto the soul is sin!
We pale offenders are still full of fear;
Every suspicious eye brings danger near,
When they whose clear heart from offence are free
Despise report, base scandals do outface,
And stand at mere defiance with disgrace.

WENDOLL. Fie, fie! you talk too like a puritan.   110

MISTRESS FRANKFORD. You have tempted me to mischief, Master
Wendoll:
I have done I know not what. Well, you plead custom;
That which for want of wit I granted erst,
I now must yield through fear. Come, come, let's in;
Once o'er shoes, we are straight o'er head in sin.

WENDOLL. My jocund soul is joyful above measure;
I'll be profuse in Frankford's richest treasure.

[*They go out together.*

103. *bosom*, intimacy.
109. *mere*, absolute.
113. *erst*, in the first place.

SCENE IV

ANOTHER PART OF THE HOUSE, *immediately afterwards. Enter Cicely, Jenkin, and Butler.*

JENKIN. My mistress and Master Wendoll, my master, sup in her chamber to-night. Cicely, you are preferred from being the cook to be chambermaid: of all the loves betwixt thee and me, tell me what thou thinkest of this?

CICELY. Mum; there's an old proverb,—when the cat's away, the mouse may play.

JENKIN. Now you talk of a cat, Cicely, I smell a rat.

CICELY. Good words, Jenkin, lest you be called to answer them.

JENKIN. Why, God make my mistress an honest woman! are not these good words? Pray God my new master play not the 10 knave with my old master! is there any hurt in this? God send no villainy intended! and, if they do sup together, pray God they do not lie together! God make my mistress chaste, and make us all His servants! What harm is there in all this? Nay, more; here is my hand, thou shalt never have my heart unless thou say Amen.

CICELY. Amen, I pray God, I say.

  [*Enter Serving-man.*

SERVING-MAN. My mistress sends that you should make less noise, to lock up the doors, and see the household all got to bed: you, Jenkin, for this night are made the porter to see the gates 20 shut in.

JENKIN. Thus, by little and little, I creep into office. Come, to kennel, my masters, to kennel; tis eleven o'clock, already.

SERVING-MAN. When you have locked the gates in, you must send up the keys to my mistress.

CICELY. Quickly, for God's sake, Jenkin, for I must carry them. I am neither pillow nor bolster, but I know more than both.

JENKIN. To bed, good Spigot; to bed, good honest serving-creatures; and let us sleep as snug as pigs in pease-straw.

  [*They go out.*

SCENE V

OUTSIDE FRANKFORD'S HOUSE, *later that night. He and Nicholas have ridden a little way away and then returned quietly. As the*

2. *preferred*, promoted.

scene progresses, the location changes from outside the gate
to the hall outside Mrs. Frankford's room.

FRANKFORD. Soft, soft; we have tied our geldings to a tree,
  Two flight-shoot off, lest by their thundering hoofs
  They blab our coming back. Hear'st thou no noise?
NICHOLAS. I hear nothing but the owl and you.
FRANKFORD. So; now my watch's hand points upon twelve,
  And it is just midnight. Where are my keys?
NICHOLAS. Here, sir.
FRANKFORD. This is the key that opes my outward gate;
  This is the hall-door; this the withdrawing chamber;
  But this, that door that's bawd unto my shame,   10
  Fountain and spring of all my bleeding thoughts,
  Where the most hallowed order and true knot
  Of nuptial sanctity hath been profaned;
  It leads to my polluted bed-chamber,
  Once my terrestrial heaven, now my earth's hell,
  The place where sins in all their ripeness dwell.
  But I forget myself: now to my gate.
NICHOLAS. It must ope with far less noise than Cripple-gate, or
  your plot's dashed.
FRANKFORD. So, reach me my dark lanthorn to the rest;   20
  Tread softly, softly.
NICHOLAS.   I will walk on eggs this pace.
      [*They walk to the door at the rear of the stage.*
FRANKFORD. A general silence hath surprised the house,
  And this is the last door. Astonishment,
  Fear, and amazement beat upon my heart,
  Even as a madman beats upon a drum.
  Oh, keep my eyes, you Heavens, before I enter,
  From any sight that may transfix my soul;
  Or, if there be so black a spectacle,
  Oh, strike mine eyes stark blind; or, if not so,
  Lend me such patience to digest my grief   30
  That I may keep this white and virgin hand
  From any violent outrage or red murder!
  And with that prayer I enter.   [*He goes in.*
NICHOLAS.   Here's a circumstance, indeed.
  A man may be made cuckold in the time
  That he's about it. An the case were mine,
  As 'tis my master's,—'sblood that he makes me swear!—

---

2. *flight-shoot,* bow shot.   20. *rest,* besides our other equipment.

I would have placed his action, entered there;
I would, I would!
    [*Re-enter Frankford.*

FRANKFORD.   Oh! oh!

NICHOLAS. Master, 'sblood! master! master!

FRANKFORD. O me unhappy! I have found them lying   40
Close in each other's arms, and fast asleep.
But that I would not damn two precious souls,
Bought with my Saviour's blood, and send them, laden
With all their scarlet sins upon their backs,
Unto a fearful judgment, their two lives
Had met upon my rapier.

NICHOLAS. Master, what, have you left them sleeping still?
Let me go wake 'em.

FRANKFORD.   Stay, let me pause a while.
O God! O God! that it were possible
To undo things done; to call back yesterday!   50
That Time could turn up his swift sandy glass,
To untell the days, and to redeem these hours!
Or that the sun
Could, rising from the west, draw his coach backward,
Take from the account of time so many minutes,
Till he had all these seasons called again,
Those minutes, and those actions done in them,
Even from her first offence; that I might take her
As spotless as an angel in my arms!
But, oh! I talk of things impossible,   60
And cast beyond the moon. God give me patience!
For I will in and wake them.   [*He rushes into the room again.*

NICHOLAS.   Here's patience perforce;
He needs must trot afoot that tires his horse.
    [*Enter Wendoll, running over the stage in a night-gown,
      Frankford after him with a sword drawn; a Maid-servant
      in her smock stays his hand, and clasps hold on him. Frank-
      ford pauses for a while.*

FRANKFORD. I thank thee, maid; thou, like an angel's hand,
Hast stayed me from a bloody sacrifice.   [*Exit Maid-servant.*
Go, villain, and my wrongs sit on thy soul
As heavy as this grief doth upon mine!
When thou record'st my many courtesies,
And shalt compare them with thy treacherous heart,
Lay them together, weigh them equally,   70

37. *placed his action*, established his case.

'Twill be revenge enough. Go, to thy friend
A Judas: pray, pray, lest I live to see
Thee, Judas-like, hanged on an elder-tree.
[Enter Mistress Frankford in her night attire.

MISTRESS FRANKFORD. Oh, by what word, what title, or what name,
Shall I entreat your pardon? Pardon! oh!
I am as far from hoping such sweet grace
As Lucifer from heaven. To call you husband—
O me, most wretched! I have lost that name,
I am no more your wife.

NICHOLAS.   'Sblood, sir, she swoons.

FRANKFORD. Spare thou thy tears, for I will weep for thee: 80
And keep thy countenance, for I'll blush for thee.
Now, I protest, I think 'tis I am tainted,
For I am most ashamed; and 'tis more hard
For me to look upon thy guilty face,
Than on the sun's clear brow. What wouldst thou speak?

MISTRESS FRANKFORD. I would I had no tongue, no ears, no eyes,
No apprehension, no capacity.
When do you spurn me like a dog? when tread me
Under your feet? when drag me by the hair?
Though I deserve a thousand thousand fold   90
More than you can inflict: yet, once my husband,
For womanhood, to which I am a shame,
Though once an ornament—even for His sake
That hath redeemed our souls, mark not my face
Nor hack me with your sword; but let me go
Perfect and undeformed to my tomb.
I am not worthy that I should prevail
In the least suit; no, not to speak to you,
Nor look on you, nor to be in your presence.
Yet, as an abject, this one suit I crave;   100
This granted, I am ready for my grave.   *[Kneels.*

FRANKFORD. My God, with patience arm me! Rise, nay, rise,
And I'll debate with thee. Was it for want
Thou playedst the strumpet? Wast thou not supplied
With every pleasure, fashion, and new toy
Nay, even beyond my calling?

MISTRESS FRANKFORD.   I was.

FRANKFORD. Was it then disability in me;
Or in thine eye seemed he a properer man?

94. *mark not my face,* a punishment for adultery.
106. *calling,* station in life.   108. *properer,* handsomer.

MISTRESS FRANKFORD. Oh, no.

FRANKFORD.   Did not I lodge thee in my bosom?
   Wear thee in my heart?

MISTRESS FRANKFORD.   You did.   .   110

FRANKFORD. I did, indeed; witness my tears I did.
   Go, bring my infants hither.
     [*Enter Servant with two Children.*

                O Nan! O Nan!
   If neither fear of shame, regard of honour,
   The blemish of my house, nor my dear love
   Could have withheld thee from so lewd a fact,
   Yet for these infants, these young harmless souls,
   On whose white brows thy shame is charactered,
   And grows in greatness as they wax in years,—
   Look but on them, and melt away in tears.
   Away with them! lest, as her spotted body   120
   Hath stained their names with stripe of bastardy,
   So her adulterous breath may blast their spirits
   With her infectious thoughts. Away with them!
                [*Exeunt Servant and Children.*

MISTRESS FRANKFORD. In this one life I die ten thousand deaths.

FRANKFORD. Stand up, stand up; I will do nothing rashly;
   I will retire a while into my study,
   And thou shalt hear thy sentence presently.   [*He leaves her.*

MISTRESS FRANKFORD. 'Tis welcome, be it death. O me, base
     strumpet,
   That, having such a husband, such sweet children,
   Must enjoy neither! Oh, to redeem my honour,   130
   I would have this hand cut off, these my breasts seared,
   Be racked, strappadoed, put to any torment:
   Nay, to whip but this scandal out, I would hazard
   The rich and dear redemption of my soul.
   He cannot be so base as to forgive me;
   Nor I so shameless to accept his pardon.
   O women, women, you that yet have kept
   Your holy matrimonial vow unstained,
   Make me your instance: when you tread awry,
   Your sins, like mine, will on your conscience lie.   140
     [*Enter Cicely, Jenkin, and all the serving-men as newly come
     out of bed.*

ALL. O mistress, mistress, what have you done, mistress?

NICHOLAS. What a caterwauling keep you here!

JENKIN. O Lord, mistress, how comes this to pass? My master is

run away in his shirt, and never so much as called me to bring
his clothes after him.

MISTRESS FRANKFORD. See what guilt is! here stand I in this place,
Ashamed to look my servants in the face.

[*Enter Frankford and Cranwell, whom seeing, she falls on
her knees.*

FRANKFORD. My words are registered in Heaven already,
With patience hear me. I'll not martyr thee,
Nor mark thee for a strumpet; but with usage   150
Of more humility torment thy soul,
And kill thee even with kindness.

CRANWELL [*Trying to quiet Frankford*]. Master Frankford—

FRANKFORD [*Putting him aside*]. Good Master Cranwell. Woman,
hear thy judgment.
Go make thee ready in thy best attire;
Take with thee all thy gowns, all thy apparel;
Leave nothing that did ever call thee mistress,
Or by whose sight, being left here in the house,
I may remember such a woman by.
Choose thee a bed and hangings for thy chamber;
Take with thee every thing that hath thy mark,   160
And get thee to my manor seven mile off,
Where live; 'tis thine; I freely give it thee.
My tenants by shall furnish thee with wains
To carry all thy stuff, within two hours,—
No longer will I limit thee my sight.
Choose which of all my servants thou likest best,
And they are thine to attend thee.

MISTRESS FRANKFORD.   A mild sentence.

FRANKFORD. But, as thou hopest for Heaven, as thou believest
Thy name's recorded in the book of life,
I charge thee never, after this sad day,   170
To see me, or to meet me, or to send
By word or writing, gift, or otherwise,
To move me, by thyself, or by thy friends;
Nor challenge any part in my two children.
So, farewell, Nan! for we will henceforth be
As we had never seen, ne'er more shall see.

MISTRESS FRANKFORD. How full my heart is, in mine eyes appears;
What wants in words, I will supply in tears.

FRANKFORD. Come, take your coach, your stuff; all must along;
Servants and all, make ready; all be gone.   180

163. *by,* near.   165. *limit,* allot.

It was thy hand cut two hearts out of one.
> [*They go out in different directions.*

ACT V

SCENE I

JUST OUTSIDE SIR FRANCIS ACTON'S HOUSE. *Sir Charles Mountford and Susan enter, both well dressed. Sir Charles is disturbed at the thought of the proposal he has to make to his sister.*

SUSAN. Brother, why have you tricked me like a bride,
  Bought me this gay attire, these ornaments?
  Forget you our estate, our poverty?
SIR CHARLES. Call me not brother, but imagine me
  Some barbarous outlaw, or uncivil kern;
  For if thou shutt'st thy eye, and only hearest
  The words that I shall utter, thou shalt judge me
  Some staring ruffian, not thy brother Charles.
  O sister!—
SUSAN. O brother, what doth this strange language mean?   10
SIR CHARLES. Dost love me, sister? wouldst thou see me live
  A bankrupt beggar in the world's disgrace,
  And die indebted to mine enemies?
  Wouldst thou behold me stand like a huge beam
  In the world's eye, a bye-word and a scorn?
  It lies in thee of these to acquit me free,
  And all my debt I may out-strip by thee.
SUSAN. By me! why, I have nothing, nothing left;
  I owe even for the clothes upon my back;
  I am not worth—
SIR CHARLES. O sister, say not so;   20
  It lies in you my downcast state to raise,
  To make me stand on even points with the world.
  Come, sister, you are rich; indeed you are;
  And in your power you have, without delay,
  Acton's five hundred pound back to repay.
SUSAN. Till now I had thought y' had loved me. By my honour
  (Which I have kept as spotless as the moon),
  I ne'er was mistress of that single doit
  Which I reserved not to supply your wants;

---

1. *tricked*, dressed, tricked out.   5. *kern*, peasant.
28. *doit*, a very small Dutch coin, a cent.

And do you think that I would hoard from you?
Now, by my hopes in Heaven, knew I the means
To buy you from the slavery of your debts
(Especially from Acton, whom I hate),
I would redeem it with my life or blood.

SIR CHARLES. I challenge it; and, kindred set apart,
Thus, ruffian-like, I lay siege to thy heart.
What do I owe to Acton?

SUSAN. Why some five hundred pounds; towards which, I swear,
In all the world I have not one denier.

SIR CHARLES. It will not prove so. Sister, now resolve me: 40
What do you think (and speak your conscience)
Would Acton give, might he enjoy your bed?

SUSAN. He would not shrink to spend a thousand pound,
To give the Mountfords' name so deep a wound.

SIR CHARLES. A thousand pound! I but five hundred owe;
Grant him your bed, he's paid with interest so.

SUSAN [Horrified]. O brother!

SIR CHARLES.   O sister! only this one way,
With that rich jewel you my debts may pay.
In speaking this my cold heart shakes with shame;
Nor do I woo you in a brother's name,   50
But in a stranger's. Shall I die in debt
To Acton, my grand foe, and you still wear
The precious jewel that he holds so dear?

SUSAN. My honour I esteem as dear and precious
As my redemption.

SIR CHARLES.   I esteem you, sister,
As dear, for so dear prizing it.

SUSAN.   Will Charles
Have me cut off my hands, and send them Acton?
Rip up my breast, and with my bleeding heart
Present him as a token?

SIR CHARLES.   Neither, sister: 60
But hear me in my strange assertion.
Thy honour and my soul are equal in my regard;
Nor will thy brother Charles survive thy shame.
His kindness, like a burthen hath surcharged me,
And under his good deeds I stooping go,
Not with an upright soul. Had I remained
In prison still, there doubtless I had died:
Then, unto him that freed me from that prison,

39. *denier*, penny.   40. *resolve*, satisfy.

Still do I owe this life. What moved my foe
To enfranchise me? 'Twas, sister, for your love.
With full five hundred pounds he bought your love,   70
And shall he not enjoy it? Shall the weight
Of all this heavy burthen lean on me,
And will not you bear part? You did partake
The joy of my release; will you not stand
In joint-bond bound to satisfy the debt?
Shall I be only charged?

SUSAN.   But that I know
These arguments come from an honoured mind,
As in your most extremity of need
Scorning to stand in debt to one you hate,—
Nay, rather would engage your unstained honour   80
Than to be held ingrate,—I should condemn you.
I see your resolution, and assent;
So Charles will have me, and I am content.

SIR CHARLES. For this I tricked you up.

SUSAN.   But here's a knife,
To save mine honour, shall slice out my life.

SIR CHARLES. Ay! know thou pleasest me a thousand times
More in that resolution than thy grant.—
Observe her love; to soothe it to my suit,
Her honour she will hazard, though not lose:
To bring me out of debt, her rigorous hand   90
Will pierce her heart. O wonder! that will choose,
Rather than stain her blood, her life to lose.—
Come, you sad sister to a woful brother,
This is the gate: I'll bear him such a present,
Such an acquittance for the knight to seal,
As will amaze his senses, and surprise
With admiration all his fantasies.

SUSAN. Before his unchaste thoughts shall seize on me,
'Tis here shall my imprisoned soul set free.
    [Enter Sir Francis Acton and Malby.

SIR FRANCIS. How! Mountford with his sister, hand in hand!   100
What miracle's afoot?

MALBY.   It is a sight
Begets in me much admiration.

SIR CHARLES. Stand not amazed to see me thus attended;
Acton, I owe thee money, and being unable
To bring thee the full sum in ready coin,

102. *admiration*, wonder.

Lo! for thy more assurance, here's a pawn,—
My sister, my dear sister, whose chaste honour
I prize above a million: here, nay, take her;
She's worth your money, man; do not forsake her.

SIR FRANCIS. I would he were in earnest!   110
SUSAN. Impute it not to my immodesty:
My brother being rich in nothing else
But in his interest that he hath in me,
According to his poverty hath brought you
Me, all his store; whom howsoe'er you prize
As forfeit to your hand, he values highly,
And would not sell, but to acquit your debt,
For any emperor's ransom.

SIR FRANCIS [*Aside*]. Stern heart, relent;
Thy former cruelty at length repent.
Was ever known, in any former age,   120
Such honourable wrested courtesy?
Lands, honours, life, and all the world forego,
Rather than stand engaged to such a foe.

SIR CHARLES. Acton, she is too poor to be thy bride,
And I too much opposed to be thy brother.
There, take her to thee: if thou hast the heart
To seize her as a rape, or lustful prey;
To blur our house, that never yet was stained;
To murder her that never meant thee harm;
To kill me now, whom once thou savedst from death,   130
Do them at once: on her all these rely,
And perish with her spotted chastity.

SIR FRANCIS [*Greatly moved*]. You overcome me in your love, Sir
    Charles;
I cannot be so cruel to a lady
I love so dearly. Since you have not spared
To engage your reputation to the world,
Your sister's honour, which you prize so dear,
Nay, all the comforts which you hold on earth,
To grow out of my debt, being your foe,
Your honoured thoughts, lo! thus I recompense: 140
Your metamorphosed foe receives your gift
In satisfaction of all former wrongs.
This jewel I will wear here in my heart;
And, where before I thought her for her wants
Too base to be my bride, to end all strife,

144. *for her wants*, because she was so poor.

I seal you my dear brother, her my wife.
SUSAN. You still exceed us: I will yield to fate,
   And learn to love, where I till now did hate.
SIR CHARLES. With that enchantment you have charmed my soul,
   And made me rich even in those very words.   150
   I pay no debt, but am indebted more;
   Rich in your love, I never can be poor.
SIR FRANCIS. All's mine is yours; we are alike in state,
   Let's knit in love what was opposed in hate.
   Come! for our nuptials we will straight provide,
   Blest only in our brother and fair bride.

                              [*They go out joyfully.*

                    SCENE II

A ROOM IN FRANKFORD'S HOUSE. *Frankford, accompanied by Cran-*
   well and Nicholas, enters as if searching for something. Mrs.
   Frankford has been sent away.

CRANWELL. Why do you search each room about your house,
   Now that you have despatched your wife away?
FRANKFORD. O sir, to see that nothing may be left
   That ever was my wife's. I loved her dearly,
   And when I do but think of her unkindness,
   My thoughts are all in hell; to avoid which torment,
   I would not have a bodkin or a cuff,
   A bracelet, necklace, or rebato wire;
   Nor any thing that ever was called hers,
   Left me, by which I might remember her.   10
   Seek round about.
NICHOLAS. 'Sblood, master! here's her lute flung in a corner.
FRANKFORD. Her lute! O God! upon this instrument
   Her fingers have run quick division,
   Sweeter than that which now divides our hearts.
   These frets have made me pleasant, that have now
   Frets of my heart-strings made. O Master Cranwell,
   Oft hath she made this melancholy wood,
   Now mute and dumb for her disastrous chance,
   Speak sweetly many a note, sound many a strain   20
   To her own ravishing voice, which being well strung,

   8. *rebato*, ruff, the wire was used for stiffening.
   14. *division*, variation.   19. *for . . . chance*, because of her ill fortune.

What pleasant strange airs have they jointly rung!
Post with it after her. Now nothing's left;
Of her and hers, I am at once bereft.
NICHOLAS. I'll ride and overtake her; do my message,
And come back again.   [*He goes out.*
CRANWELL.   Mean time, sir, if you please,
I'll to Sir Francis Acton, and inform him
Of what hath passed betwixt you and his sister.
FRANKFORD. Do as you please. How ill am I bested,
To be a widower ere my wife be dead!   [*They go out.*

SCENE III

A COUNTRY ROAD. *Enter Mistress Frankford, on her way to seclusion, with Jenkin, Cicely, a Coachman, and three Carters.*

MISTRESS FRANKFORD. Bid my coach stay: why should I ride in state,
Being hurled so low down by the hand of fate?
A seat like to my fortunes let me have;
Earth for my chair, and for my bed a grave.
JENKIN. Comfort, good mistress; you have watered your coach
with tears already: you have but two mile now to go to your
manor. A man cannot say by my old master Frankford as he
may say by me, that he wants manors; for he hath three or
four, of which this is one that we are going to now.
CICELY. Good mistress, be of good cheer; sorrow, you see,   10
hurts you, but helps you not; we all mourn to see you so sad.
CARTER. Mistress, I spy one of my landlord's men
Come riding post: 'tis like he brings some news.
MISTRESS FRANKFORD. Comes he from Master Frankford, he is
welcome;
So is his news because they come from him.
     [*Enter Nicholas.*
NICHOLAS [*Presenting lute*]. There.
MISTRESS FRANKFORD. I know the lute; oft have I sung to thee:
We both are out of tune, both out of time.
NICHOLAS [*Rudely*]. Would that had been the worst instru-   20
ment that e'er you played on. My master commends him unto
ye; there's all he can find that was ever yours: he hath nothing
left that ever you could lay claim to but his own heart, and he
could afford you that. All that I have to deliver you is this:
he prays you to forget him, and so he bids you farewell.

MISTRESS FRANKFORD. I thank him: he is kind, and ever was.
  All you that have true feeling of my grief,
  That know my loss, and have relenting hearts,
  Gird me about, and help me with your tears
  To wash my spotted sins: my lute shall groan;   30
  It cannot weep, but shall lament my moan.
    [*Enter Wendoll, unnoticed by the group near the front of
    the stage. They do not become aware of his presence until
    later, when he addresses Mrs. Frankford.*

WENDOLL. Pursued with horror of a guilty soul,
  And with the sharp scourge of repentance lashed,
  I fly from my own shadow. O my stars!
  What have my parents in their lives deserved,
  That you should lay this penance on their son?
  When I but think of Master Frankford's love,
  And lay it to my treason, or compare
  My murdering him for his relieving me,
  It strikes a terror like a lightning's flash   40
  To scorch my blood up. Thus I, like the owl,
  Ashamed of day, live in these shadowy woods,
  Afraid of every leaf or murmuring blast,
  Yet longing to receive some perfect knowledge
  How he hath dealt with her. [*Sees Mistress Frankford.*] O my
    sad fate!
  Here, and so far from home, and thus attended!
  O God! I have divorced the truest turtles
  That ever lived together; and, being divided
  In several places, make their several moan;
  She in the fields laments, and he at home.   50
  So poets write that Orpheus made the trees
  And stones to dance to his melodious harp,
  Meaning the rustic and the barbarous hinds,
  That had no understanding part in them:
  So she from these rude carters tears extracts,
  Making their flinty hearts with grief to rise,
  And draw down rivers from their rocky eyes.

MISTRESS FRANKFORD [*To Nicholas*]. If you return unto your
    master, say
  (Though not from me; for I am all unworthy
  To blast his name so with a strumpet's tongue)   60
  That you have seen me weep, wish myself dead:
  Nay, you may say too, for my vow is passed,

47. *turtles*, doves.

Last night you saw me eat and drink my last.
This to your master you may say and swear;
For it is writ in Heaven, and decreed here.

NICHOLAS [*Softened by her grief*]. I'll say you wept: I'll swear
   you made me sad.
Why how now, eyes? what now? what's here to do?
I'm gone, or I shall straight turn baby too.

WENDOLL. I cannot weep, my heart is all on fire:
Curst be the fruits of my unchaste desire!   70

MISTRESS FRANKFORD. Go, break this lute upon my coach's wheel,
As the last music that I e'er shall make;
Not as my husband's gift, but my farewell
To all earth's joy; and so your master tell.

NICHOLAS. If I can for crying.

WENDOLL.   Grief, have done,
Or like a madman I shall frantic run.

MISTRESS FRANKFORD. You have beheld the wofullest wretch on
   earth;
A woman made of tears: would you had words
To express but what you see! My inward grief
No tongue can utter; yet unto your power   80
You may describe my sorrow, and disclose
To thy sad master my abundant woes.

NICHOLAS. I'll do your commendations.

MISTRESS FRANKFORD.   Oh no:
I dare not so presume; nor to my children:
I am disclaimed in both; alas, I am.
Oh, never teach them, when they come to speak,
To name the name of mother; chide their tongue,
If they by chance light on that hated word;
Tell them 'tis naught; for, when that word they name,
Poor pretty souls! they harp on their own shame.   90

WENDOLL. To recompense her wrongs, what canst thou do?
Thou hast made her husbandless and childless too.

MISTRESS FRANKFORD. I have no more to say. Speak not for me;
Yet you may tell your master what you see.

NICHOLAS. I'll do't.   [*He goes out.*

WENDOLL. I'll speak to her, and comfort her in grief.
Oh! but her wound cannot be cured with words.
No matter though, I'll do my best good-will
To work a cure on her whom I did kill.

MISTRESS FRANKFORD. So, now unto my coach, then to my
   home,   100

So to my death-bed; for from this sad hour
I never will nor eat, nor drink, nor taste
Of any cates that may preserve my life:
I never will nor smile, nor sleep, nor rest;
But when my tears have washed my black soul white,
Sweet Saviour, to Thy hands I yield my sprite.

WENDOLL. O Mistress Frankford—

[*He approaches her, but she starts back in horror.*

MISTRESS FRANKFORD.　　　　　Oh, for God's sake fly!
The devil doth come to tempt me ere I die.
My coach! this sin, that with an angel's face
Conjured mine honour, till he sought my wrack,　　110
In my repentant eyes seems ugly black.

[*Exeunt all, except Wendoll and Jenkin; the Carters whistling.*

JENKIN. What, my young master that fled in his shirt! How come
you by your clothes again? You have made our house in a
sweet pickle, ha' ye not, think you? What, shall I serve you
still, or cleave to the old house?

WENDOLL. Hence, slave! away with thy unseasoned mirth!
Unless thou canst shed tears, and sigh, and howl,
Curse thy sad fortunes, and exclaim on fate,
Thou art not for my turn.

JENKIN. Marry, an you will not, another will: farewell, and　120
be hanged! Would you had never come to have kept this coil
within our doors; we shall ha' you run away like a sprite again.

[*He goes out, threatening.*

WENDOLL. She's gone to death; I live to want and woe;
Her life, her sins, and all upon my head.
And I must now go wander, like a Cain,
In foreign countries and remoted climes,
Where the report of my ingratitude
Cannot be heard. I'll over first to France,
And so to Germany and Italy;
Where when I have recovered, and by travel　　130
Gotten those perfect tongues, and that these rumours
May in their height abate, I will return:
And I divine (however now dejected)
My worth and parts being by some great man praised,
At my return I may in court be raised.　　[*He goes out.*

121. *kept coil*, made this disturbance.
131. *Gotten . . . tongues*, learned their languages perfectly.

SCENE IV

BEFORE THE MANOR HOUSE *in which Mrs. Frankford has been
confined. Some time has elapsed since the last scene. Enter Sir
Francis Acton, Susan, Sir Charles Mountford, Cranwell, and
Malby.*

SIR FRANCIS. Brother, and now my wife, I think these troubles
　　Fall on my head by justice of the Heavens,
　　For being so strict to you in your extremities:
　　But we are now atoned. I would my sister
　　Could with like happiness o'ercome her griefs,
　　As we have ours.
SUSAN. You tell us, Master Cranwell, wondrous things,
　　Touching the patience of that gentleman,
　　With what strange virtue he demeans his grief.
CRANWELL. I told you what I was witness of;
　　It was my fortune to lodge there that night.　　　　　　10
SIR FRANCIS. O that same villain Wendoll! 'twas his tongue
　　That did corrupt her; she was of herself
　　Chaste, and devoted well. Is this the house?
CRANWELL. Yes, sir, I take it here your sister lies.
SIR FRANCIS. My brother Frankford showed too mild a spirit
　　In the revenge of such a loathèd crime;
　　Less than he did, no man of spirit could do:
　　I am so far from blaming his revenge,
　　That I commend it. Had it been my case,
　　Their souls at once had from their breasts been freed:　　20
　　Death to such deeds of shame is the due meed.
　　　　[*Jenkin and Cicely enter most mournfully.*
JENKIN. O my mistress, my mistress, my poor mistress.
CICELY. Alas that ever I was born! what shall I do for my poor
　　mistress?
SIR CHARLES. Why, what of her?
JENKIN. O Lord, sir, she no sooner heard that her brother and her
　　friends were come to see how she did, but she, for very shame
　　of her guilty conscience, fell into such a swoon, that we had
　　much ado to get life into her.
SUSAN. Alas that she should bear so hard a fate!　　　　　　30
　　Pity it is repentance comes too late.
SIR FRANCIS. Is she so weak in body?
JENKIN. O sir, I can assure you there's no hope of life in her, for

　　4. *atoned,* made at one, reconciled.

she will take no sustenance: she hath plainly starved herself,
and now she is as lean as a lath. She ever looks for the good
hour. Many gentlemen and gentlewomen of the country are
come to comfort her.

> [*The curtains are drawn and Mrs. Frankford is disclosed in
> bed. The group approach her.*

MALBY. How fare you, Mistress Frankford?

MISTRESS FRANKFORD. Sick, sick, oh, sick. Give me some air, I pray
you.

    Tell me, oh, tell me where is Master Frankford?   40
    Will not he deign to see me ere I die?

MALBY. Yes, Mistress Frankford: divers gentlemen,
    Your loving neighbours, with that just request
    Have moved, and told him of your weak estate:
    Who, though with much ado to get belief,
    Examining of the general circumstance,
    Seeing your sorrow and your penitence,
    And hearing therewithal the great desire
    You have to see him ere you left the world,
    He gave to us his faith to follow us,   50
    And sure he will be here immediately.

MISTRESS FRANKFORD. You have half revived me with those pleasing news:
    Raise me a little higher in my bed.
    Blush I not, brother Acton? Blush I not, Sir Charles?
    Can you not read my fault writ in my cheek?
    Is not my crime there? tell me, gentlemen.

SIR CHARLES. Alas! good mistress, sickness hath not left you
    Blood in your face enough to make you blush.

MISTRESS FRANKFORD. Then sickness, like a friend, my fault would
hide.
    Is my husband come? My soul but tarries   60
    His arrive, then I am fit for Heaven.

SIR FRANCIS. I came to chide you; but my words of hate
    Are turned to pity and compassionate grief.
    I came to rate you; but my brawls, you see,
    Melt into tears, and I must weep by thee.
    Here's Master Frankford now.

> [*Enter Frankford.*

FRANKFORD. Good-morrow, brother; morrow, gentlemen:
    God, that hath laid this cross upon our heads,
    Might (had He pleased) have made our cause of meeting
    On a more fair and more contented ground;   70

But He that made us, made us to this woe.

MISTRESS FRANKFORD. And is he come? Methinks that voice I
know.

FRANKFORD. How do you, woman?

MISTRESS FRANKFORD. Well, Master Frankford, well; but shall be
better,
I hope, within this hour. Will you vouchsafe,
Out of your grace and your humanity,
To take a spotted strumpet by the hand?

FRANKFORD. This hand once held my heart in faster bonds
Than now 'tis gripped by me. God pardon them
That made us first break hold!   80

MISTRESS FRANKFORD.   Amen, amen.
Out of my zeal to Heaven, whither I'm now bound,
I was so impudent to wish you here;
And once more beg your pardon. O good man,
And father to my children, pardon me,
Pardon, oh, pardon me! My fault so heinous is,
That if you in this world forgive it not,
Heaven will not clear it in the world to come.
Faintness hath so usurped upon my knees
That kneel I cannot, but on my heart's knees
My prostrate soul lies thrown down at your feet   90
To beg your gracious pardon. Pardon, oh, pardon me!

FRANKFORD. As freely, from the low depth of my soul,
As my Redeemer hath forgiven His death,
I pardon thee. I will shed tears for thee, pray with thee;
And, in mere pity of thy weak estate,
I'll wish to die with thee.

ALL.   So do we all.

NICHOLAS. So will not I;
I'll sigh and sob, but, by my faith, not die.

SIR FRANCIS. O Master Frankford, all the near alliance
I lose by her shall be supplied in thee: 100
You are my brother by the nearest way;
Her kindred hath fallen off, but yours doth stay.

FRANKFORD. Even as I hope for pardon at that day
When the great Judge of Heaven in scarlet sits,
So be thou pardoned. Though thy rash offence
Divorced our bodies, thy repentant tears
Unite our souls.

SIR CHARLES. Then comfort, Mistress Frankford;
You see your husband hath forgiven your fall;

Then rouse your spirits, and cheer your fainting soul. 110
SUSAN. How is it with you?
SIR FRANCIS. How do ye feel yourself?
MISTRESS FRANKFORD. Not of this world.
FRANKFORD. I see you are not, and I weep to see it.
My wife, the mother to my pretty babes!
Both those lost names I do restore thee back,
And with this kiss I wed thee once again:
Though thou art wounded in thy honoured name,
And with that grief upon thy death-bed liest,
Honest in heart, upon my soul, thou diest.
MISTRESS FRANKFORD. Pardoned on earth, soul, thou in Heaven
    art free. 120
Once more thy wife dies, thus embracing thee. [Dies.
FRANKFORD. New married, and new widowed. Oh! she's dead,
And a cold grave must be her nuptial bed.
SIR CHARLES. Sir, be of good comfort; and your heavy sorrow
Part equally amongst us: storms divided
Abate their force, and with less rage are guided.
CRANWELL. Do, Master Frankford: he that hath least part
Will find enough to drown one troubled heart.
SIR FRANCIS. Peace with thee, Nan. Brothers, and gentlemen,
All we that can plead interest in her grief, 130
Bestow upon her body funeral tears.
Brother, had you with threats and usage bad
Punished her sin, the grief of her offence
Had not with such true sorrow touched her heart.
FRANKFORD. I see it had not: therefore on her grave
Will I bestow this funeral epitaph,
Which on her marble tomb shall be engraved.
In golden letters shall these words be filled,
"Here lies she whom her husband's kindness killed."

EPILOGUE

An honest crew, disposèd to be merry,
    Come to a tavern by, and called for wine:
The drawer brought it, smiling like a cherry,
    And told them it was pleasant, neat, and fine.
"Taste it," quoth one. He did so. "Fie!" quoth he;
    "This wine was good; now't runs too near the lee."

138. *filled*, i.e. the engraving shall be filled with gold.
  6. *lee*, lees.

Another sipped, to give the wine his due,
 And said unto the rest it drunk too flat;
The third said, it was old; the fourth, too new;
 Nay, quoth the fifth, the sharpness likes me not. 10
Thus, gentlemen, you see how, in one hour,
The wine was new, old, flat, sharp, sweet, and sour.

Unto this wine we do allude our play;
 Which some will judge too trivial, some too grave:
You as our guests we entertain this day,
 And bid you welcome to the best we have.
Excuse us, then: good wine may be disgraced,
When every several mouth hath sundry taste.

13. *allude*, compare.

THE COMEDY OF MANNERS

THE COMEDY OF MANNERS has its roots in the same soil as the Comedy of Humours. Both stem from the same critical impulse toward society, a feeling for the inadequacies, the superficialities and follies of the accepted modes of social life and manners. Both hold up to laughter those aberrations from the ideal of which society has been unconscious or by which it has been undisturbed. The great difference between the two, however, is indicated by their names. Humours are elements inherent in the constitution of the individual, basic traits of character; Manners are the externalities, the acquired characteristics. Nominally they are more superficial than Humours, but actually through long use they may become so deep-seated that it is hard to distinguish between the two.

Then, too, the Comedy of Manners usually deals with the genteel world, the world which is presumed to set the fashion in the social graces and in charm of living, the world which is likely to be most satisfied with and least critical of itself. In the hands of a skilful dramatist like Congreve or Wycherley that complacency offers one of the most subtle and effective points of attack. Out of the very unawareness of the characters he is able to create the most delightful comic effects, for what seems so natural and acceptable to them is lighted up by the dramatist's irony, so that we, the audience, perhaps enjoying a sense of superiority to the characters, come to see the great gap between what they think they are with all their appearance of polish and wit, and what they really are in all their folly and affectation. It is, of course, a type which degenerates easily into burlesque on the one hand or ranting preachment on the other unless the dramatist keeps a wise sense of balance and avoids committing himself to partisanship among his characters.

The society pictured in *The Way of the World* was one which had developed in revolt against the bare and suppres-

sive life of Puritan England in the days of Cromwell and his
Roundheads. It was, as Dobrée has so clearly shown, as frankly
experimental in its attitude as our own time has been. It put its
stress on polish and cleverness and poise in the associations of
people of quality, on skepticism about love and on a freely experimental attitude toward the relations of the sexes that is
not only strikingly modern but also came into sharp conflict
with long accepted and thoroughly conventionalized attitudes.
The Comedy of Manners is not, as Charles Lamb suggested a
century or so ago, a picture of a society that never was on
land or sea, "out of Christendom into cuckoldry"; for it is a
type of realistic comedy concerned with the criticism of
social life.

By 1700, when this play was produced, however, new
tendencies were beginning to make themselves felt. The rabid
Puritan antagonism to the theater had once more found a
champion, this time in the person of Jeremy Collier, whose
*Short View of the Immorality and Profaneness of the English
Stage* had appeared two years previously. Collier and his ilk
objected vigorously to the type of play that Wycherley, Vanbrugh, and Congreve were writing, but Steele's commendatory verses prefixed to the published play give us a better idea
of the nature of the change in the audience's attitude:

> No sense of wit when dull spectators know
> But in distorted gesture, farce and show;
> How could, great author, your aspiring mind
> Dare to write only to the few refined?

Steele was trying to remove from his friend the sting of a
poorly received play, but he also indicated something of the
nature of an English theatrical audience in 1700. The play
failed partly because its story is too confused in details for it
to be easily followed on the stage unless one knew the out-
lines in advance, but more important, if Steele is to be believed, was the fact that the audience was no longer capable
of appreciating a play which depended, as the Comedy of
Manners should, on sprightly, witty dialogue and on scintillat-
ing characterization, both carried along in a majestically im-
personal amiability that presents without judging too severely.

William Congreve was born in England in 1670, but not long thereafter his officer father was sent to Ireland to command the garrison at Youghal. In Ireland young Congreve grew up in much the same educational pattern as one of the other great satirists of the time. Three years after Swift Congreve entered the famous Kilkenny School and went from there to Dublin University. Like many another literary man he had some training in law at the Inner Temple in London but deserted that profession for letters under the guardianship of Dryden, then (1692) at the height of his literary fame. His plays, *The Old Bachelor, The Double Dealer, Love for Love, The Mourning Bride,* and *The Way of the World* were all written in the seven years between 1693 and 1700. The cold reception afforded the last of the plays evidently frightened him off from the stage, for he tried his luck no more. He had little need to, for government positions were showered upon him so that he became a man of considerable wealth. As early as 1694 he had been given a commission as licenser of hackney and stage coaches (shades of Apollo!); was made commissioner of wine licenses in 1705; Secretary for Jamaica and an Under-searcher of the Customs in the Port of London from 1714 till his death in 1729.

He did not originate the Comedy of Manners, but he brought to it a gift for speech that was of higher quality than any of his associates possessed. No other dramatist of the Restoration had so fine a sense of dramatic speech, its possibilities both for characterization and for delight in itself, its varied rhythms and inflections, as did Congreve. Hazlitt very ably summarized it in his essay on the *English Comic Writers:*

"Congreve is the most distinct from the others, and the most easily defined, both from what he possessed and from what he wanted. He had by far the most wit and elegance, with less of other things, of humor, character, incident, &c. His style is inimitable, nay perfect. It is the highest model of comic dialogue. Every sentence is replete with sense and satire, conveyed in the most polished and brilliant terms. . . . [His style] bears every mark of being what he himself in the dedication of one of his plays tells us that it was, a spirited copy taken off and carefully revised from the most select society of his time, exhibiting all the sprightliness, ease, and animation of familiar conversation with the correctness and delicacy of the most finished composition."

SUGGESTED READINGS

Dobrée, Bonamy, *Restoration Comedy, 1660–1720*. OXFORD, 1924.

Cambridge History of English Literature, VOL. VIII. NEW YORK, 1912.

Hazlitt, W. C., *Lectures on the English Comic Writers*. OXFORD, 1907.

Lamb, Charles, "On the Artificial Comedy of the Last Century," *Essays of Elia*. NEW YORK, 1927.

Macaulay, T. B., *Comic Dramatists of the Restoration*. BOSTON, 1925.

Meredith, George, *Essay on Comedy*. NEW YORK, 1918.

Nicoll, Allardyce, *Restoration Drama*. NEW YORK, 1923.

Palmer, John, *The Comedy of Manners*. LONDON, 1913.

Coward, Noel, *Private Lives*. NEW YORK, 1931.

Farquhar, George, *The Beaux Stratagem*. In *Complete Works*. ED. BY CHAS. STONEHILLS, VOL. II. LONDON, 1930.

Jones, Henry Arthur, *Mary Goes First*. NEW YORK, 1913.

Pinero, Arthur W., *The Gay Lord Quex*. BOSTON [n. d.].

Shaw, G. B., *Pygmalion*. NEW YORK, 1916.

Sheridan, R. B., *The School for Scandal*. NEW YORK, 1930.

Vanbrugh, Sir John, *The Relapse* in *Complete Works*. ED. BY BONAMY DOBRÉE AND GEOFFREY WEBB. LONDON AND NEW YORK, 1927–28.

Wycherley, William, *The Country Wife* and *The Plain Dealer*. In *Complete Works*, ED. BY MONTAGUE SUMMERS, VOL. II. WESTMINSTER, 1924.

THE WAY OF THE WORLD

A COMEDY

by William Congreve

Characters

FAINALL, *In Love with Mrs. Marwood*

MIRABELL, *In Love with Mrs. Millamant*

WITWOUD,
PETULANT, } *Followers of Mrs. Millamant*

SIR WILFULL WITWOUD, *Half Brother to Witwoud, and Nephew to Lady Wishfort*

WAITWELL, *Servant to Mirabell*

LADY WISHFORT, *Enemy to Mirabell, for having falsly pretended Love to her*

MRS. MILLAMANT, *A fine Lady, Niece to Lady Wishfort, and loves Mirabell*

MRS. MARWOOD, *Friend to Mr. Fainall, and likes Mirabell*

MRS. FAINALL, *Daughter to Lady Wishfort, and Wife to Fainall, formerly Friend to Mirabell*

FOIBLE, *Woman to Lady Wishfort*

MINCING, *Woman to Mrs. Millamant*

DANCERS, FOOTMEN, *and* ATTENDANTS

SCENE—*London*

THE TIME *equal to that of the Presentation*

To MR. CONGREVE,

Occasion'd by his Comedy called

The Way of the World

When pleasure's falling to the low delight,
In the vain joys of the uncertain sight,
No sense of wit when rude spectators know,
But in distorted gesture, farce and show;
How could, great author, your aspiring mind
Dare to write only to the few refined!
Yet tho' that nice ambition you pursue,
'Tis not in Congreve's power to please but few.
Implicitly devoted to his fame,
Well-dressed barbarians know his awful name;   10
Tho' senseless they're of mirth, but when they laugh,
As they feel wine, but when, 'till drunk, they quaff.

On you, from Fate, a lavish portion fell
In ev'ry way of writing to excell.
Your muse applause to Arabella brings,
In notes as sweet as Arabella sings.
When e'er you draw an undissembled woe,
With sweet distress your rural numbers flow
Pastora's the complaint of ev'ry swain,
Pastora still the eccho of the plain!   20
Or if your muse describe, with warming force,
The wounded Frenchman falling from his horse;
And her own William glorious in the strife,
Bestowing on the prostrate foe his life:
You the great act as gen'rously rehearse,
And all the English fury's in your verse.
By your selected scenes, and handsome choice,
Ennobled comedy exalts her voice;
You check unjust esteem and fond desire,
And teach to scorn, what else we should admire;   30
The just impression taught by you we bear,
The player acts the world, the world the player,

---

11. *Tho' senseless* . . ., i.e., they understand comedy only when it makes
them laugh, just as they enjoy wine only in drinking till they are intoxicated.

Whom still that world unjustly disesteems,
Tho' he, alone, professes what he seems:
But when your muse assumes her tragick part,
She conquers and she reigns in ev'ry heart;
To mourn with her men cheat their private woe,
And gen'rous pity's all the grief they know;
The widow, who impatient of delay,
From the town-joys must mask it to the play,   40
Joins with your Mourning-Bride's resistless moan,
And weeps a loss she slighted, when her own;
You give us torment, and you give us ease,
And vary our afflictions as you please;
Is not a heart so kind as yours in pain,
To load your friends with cares you only feign;
Your friends in grief, composed your self, to leave?
But 'tis the only way you'll e'er deceive.
Then still, great sir, your moving power employ,
To lull our sorrow, and correct our joy.   50

                                        R. STEELE.

To the Right Honourable RALPH, Earl of Mountague,* &c.

My Lord,

Whether the world will arraign me of vanity, or not, that I have presum'd to dedicate this comedy to your Lordship, I am yet in doubt: tho' it may be it is some degree of vanity even to doubt of it. One who has at any time had the honour of your Lordship's conversation, cannot be supposed to think very meanly of that which he would prefer to your perusal: yet it were to incur the imputation of too much sufficiency, to pretend to such a merit as might abide the test of your Lordship's censure.

Whatever value may be wanting to this play while yet it is mine, will be sufficiently made up to it, when it is once become   10
your Lordship's; and it is my security, that I cannot have over-rated it more by my dedication, than your Lordship will dignify it by your patronage.

---

* *Mountague*, one of the typical members of the court party during the reigns of Charles II, James II, and William. He represents the pleasure loving society which made a pose of patronizing letters, without being greatly interested in literature.

That it succeeded on the stage, was almost beyond my expectation; for but little of it was prepared for that general taste which seems now to be predominant in the palates of our audience.

Those characters which are meant to be ridiculed in most of our comedies, are of fools so gross, that in my humble opinion, they should rather disturb than divert the well-natured and re- 20 flecting part of an audience; they are rather objects of charity than contempt; and instead of moving our mirth, they ought very often to excite our compassion.

This reflection moved me to design some characters, which should appear ridiculous not so much thro' a natural folly (which is incorrigible, and therefore not proper for the stage) as thro' an affected wit; a wit, which at the same time that it is affected, is also false. As there is some difficulty in the formation of a character of this nature, so there is some hazard which attends the progress of its success, upon the stage: for many come to 30 a play, so over-charged with criticism, that they very often let fly their censure, when thro' their rashness they have mistaken their aim. This I had occasion lately to observe: for this play had been acted two or three days, before some of these hasty judges could find the leisure to distinguish betwixt the character of a Witwoud and a Truewit.

I must beg your Lordship's pardon for this digression from the true course of this epistle; but that it may not seem altogether impertinent, I beg, that I may plead the occasion of it, in part of that excuse of which I stand in need, for recommending this 40 comedy to your protection. It is only by the countenance of your Lordship, and the few so qualified, that such who write with care and pains can hope to be distinguished: for the prostituted name of poet promiscuously levels all that bear it.

Terence, the most correct writer in the world, had a Scipio and a Lelius, if not to assist him, at least to support him in his reputation: and notwithstanding his extraordinary merit, it may be, their countenance was not more than necessary.

The purity of his style, the delicacy of his turns, and the justness of his characters, were all of them beauties, which the 50 greater part of his audience were incapable of tasting: some of

45. *Terence*, Roman writer of comedy in the second century, B.C. *Scipio*, a Roman general, patron of Terence.

46. *Lelius*, C. Laelius Sapiens, intimate friend of Scipio Africanus, general and prominent citizen and statesman of Rome in the second century, B.C.

the coarsest strokes of Plautus, so severely censured by Horace, were more likely to affect the multitude; such, who come with expectation to laugh at the last act of a play, and are better entertained with two or three unseasonable jests, than with the artful solution of the Fable.

As Terence excelled in his performances, so had he great advantages to encourage his undertakings; for he built most on the foundations of Menander: his plots were generally modelled, and his characters ready drawn to his hand. He copied Menander; 60 and Menander had no less light in the formation of his characters, from the observations of Theophrastus, of whom he was a disciple; and Theophrastus it is known was not only the disciple, but the immediate successor of Aristotle, the first and greatest judge of poetry. These were great models to design by; and the further advantage which Terence possessed, towards giving his plays the due ornaments of purity of style, and justness of manners, was not less considerable, from the freedom of conversation, which was permitted him with Lelius and Scipio, two of the greatest and most polite men of his age. And indeed, the privilege of such 70 a conversation, is the only certain means of attaining to the perfection of dialogue.

If it has happened in any part of this comedy, that I have gained a turn of style, or expression more correct, or at least more corrigible than in those which I have formerly written, I must, with equal pride and gratitude, ascribe it to the honour of your Lordship's admitting me into your conversation, and that of a society where every body else was so well worthy of you, in your retirement last summer from the town: for it was immediately after, that this comedy was written. If I have failed in my perform- 80 ance, it is only to be regretted, where there were so many, not inferior either to a Scipio or a Lelius, that there should be one wanting, equal in capacity to a Terence.

If I am not mistaken, poetry is almost the only art, which has not yet laid claim to your Lordship's patronage. Architecture, and painting, to the great honour of our country, have flourished under your influence and protection. In the mean time, poetry, the eldest

52. *Plautus*, another great Roman composer of comedies, 254?-184, B.C. *Horace*, Roman poet and critic of the time of Augustus.

56. *Fable*, Plot.

59. *Menander*, the master of late Greek comedy, 343-291, B.C.

62. *Theophrastus*, noted chiefly for his "characters," a third century B.C. philosopher.

64. *Aristotle*, his *Poetics* the critical Bible for centuries.

sister of all arts, and parent of most, seems to have resigned her
birth-right, by having neglected to pay her duty to your Lordship; and by permitting others of a later extraction, to pre-   90
possess that place in your esteem, to which none can pretend a
better title. Poetry, in its nature, is sacred to the good and great;
the relation between them is reciprocal, and they are ever propitious to it. It is the privilege of poetry to address to them, and
it is their prerogative alone to give it protection.

This received maxim is a general apology for all writers who
consecrate their labours to great men: but I could wish, at this
time, that this address were exempted from the common pretence
of all dedications; and that as I can distinguish your Lordship even
among the most deserving, so this offering might become re-   100
markable by some particular instance of respect, which should
assure your Lordship, that I am, with all due sense of your extreme worthiness and humanity,

My LORD,

Your Lordship's most Obedient
and most Obliged Humble Servant,

WILL. CONGREVE.

PROLOGUE

Spoken by Mr. Betterton

Of those few fools, who with ill stars are curst,
Sure scribbling fools, called poets, fare the worst:
For they're a sort of fools which Fortune makes,
And after she has made 'em fools, forsakes.
With Nature's oafs 'tis quite a diff'rent case,
For Fortune favours all her idiot-race:
In her own nest the cuckow-eggs we find,
O'er which she broods to hatch the changling-kind.
No portion for her own she has to spare,
So much she dotes on her adopted care.   10
    Poets are bubbles, by the town drawn in,
Suffered at first some trifling stakes to win:

92-94. *Poetry . . . propitious to it*, Congreve is thinking of the attacks on
the stage and on his plays by Jeremy Collier, who damned the drama as a
source of corruption and an offence to good morals in his *Short View of
the Immorality and Profaneness of the English Stage*. 1698.

But what unequal hazards do they run!
Each time they write they venture all they've won:
The squire that's buttered still, is sure to be undone.
This author, heretofore, has found your favour,
But pleads no merit from his past behaviour;
To build on that might prove a vain presumption,
Should grants to poets made, admit resumption:
And in Parnassus he must lose his seat,   20
If that be found a forfeited estate.

He owns, with toil, he wrought the following scenes,
But if they're naught ne'er spare him for his pains:
Damn him the more; have no commiseration
For dulness on mature deliberation.
He swears he'll not resent one hissed-off scene
Nor, like those peevish wits, his play maintain,
Who, to assert their sense, your taste arraign.
Some plot we think he has, and some new thought;
Some humour too, no farce; but that's a fault.   30
Satire, he thinks, you ought not to expect;
For so reformed a town, who dares correct?
To please, this time, has been his sole pretence,
He'll not instruct, lest it should give offence.
Should he by chance a knave or fool expose,
That hurts none here, sure here are none of those.
In short, our play shall (with your leave to show it)
Give you one instance of a passive poet.
Who to your judgments yields all resignation;
So save or damn, after your own discretion.   40

ACT I

SCENE I

A CHOCOLATE HOUSE.* *Mirabell and Fainall are finishing a game of
cards to which the former has given so little of his attention
that Fainall has won easily.*

MIRABELL. You are a fortunate man, Mr. Fainall.
FAINALL. Have we done?
MIRABELL. What you please. I'll play on to entertain you.

* *Chocolate House,* the chocolate houses of the time were common meeting places for the gay society, who met not only to drink chocolate but
to gossip and gamble.

FAINALL. No, I'll give you your revenge another time, when you are not so indifferent; you are thinking of something else now, and play too negligently; the coldness of a losing gamester lessens the pleasure of the winner. I'd no more play with a man that slighted his ill fortune, than I'd make love to a woman who undervalued the loss of her reputation.

MIRABELL. You have a taste extreamly delicate, and are for 10 refining on your pleasures.

FAINALL. Prithee, why so reserved? Something has put you out of humour.

MIRABELL. Not at all: I happen to be grave today; and you are gay; that's all.

FAINALL. Confess, Millamant and you quarrelled last night, after I left you; my fair cousin has some humours that wou'd tempt the patience of a Stoic. What, some coxcomb came in, and was well receiv'd by her, while you were by.

MIRABELL. Witwoud and Petulant; and what was worse, her 20 aunt, your wife's mother, my evil genius; or to sum up all in her own name, my old Lady Wishfort came in.—

FAINALL. O there it is then—she has a lasting passion for you, and with reason.—What, then my wife was there?

MIRABELL. Yes, and Mrs. Marwood and three or four more, whom I never saw before; seeing me, they all put on their grave faces, whispered one another; then complained aloud of the vapours, and after fell into a profound silence.

FAINALL. They had a mind to be rid of you.

MIRABELL. For which good reason I resolved not to stir. At 30 last the good old lady broke thro' her painful taciturnity, with an invective against long visits. I would not have understood her, but Millamant joining in the argument, I rose and with a constrained smile told her, I thought nothing was so easie as to know when a visit began to be troublesome; she reddened and I withdrew, without expecting her reply.

FAINALL. You were to blame to resent what she spoke only in compliance with her aunt.

MIRABELL. She is more mistress of her self, than to be under the necessity of such a resignation. 40

FAINALL. What? tho' half her fortune depends upon her marrying with my lady's approbation?

MIRABELL. I was then in such a humour, that I should have been better pleased if she had been less discreet.

FAINALL. Now I remember, I wonder not they were weary of

36. *expecting*, awaiting.

you; last night was one of their cabal-nights; they have 'em three times a week, and meet by turns, at one another's apartments, where they come together like the coroner's inquest, to sit upon the murdered reputations of the week. You and I are excluded; and it was once proposed that all the male sex should be ex- 50 cepted; but some body moved that to avoid scandal there might be one man of the community; upon which Witwoud and Petulant were enrolled members.

MIRABELL. And who may have been the foundress of this sect? My Lady Wishfort, I warrant, who publishes her detestation of mankind; and full of the vigour of fifty five, declares for a friend and ratafia; and let posterity shift for it self, she'll breed no more.

FAINALL. The discovery of your sham addresses to her, to conceal your love to her niece, has provoked this separation: had you dissembled better, things might have continued in the state of 60 nature.

MIRABELL. I did as much as man could, with any reasonable conscience; I proceeded to the very last act of flattery with her, and was guilty of a song in her commendation. Nay, I got a friend to put her into a lampoon, and compliment her with the imputation of an affair with a young fellow, which I carried so far, that I told her the malicious town took notice that she was grown fat of a sudden; and when she lay in of a dropsie, persuaded her she was reported to be in labour. The devil's in't, if an old woman is to be flattered further, unless a man should en- 70 deavour downright personally to debauch her; and that my vertue forbad me. But for the discovery of this amour, I am indebted to your friend, or your wife's friend, Mrs. Marwood.

FAINALL [*Curious, since he is courting Mrs. Marwood*]. What should provoke her to be your enemy, unless she has made you advances, which you have slighted? Women do not easily forgive omissions of that nature.

MIRABELL. She was always civil to me, 'till of late; I confess I am not one of those coxcombs who are apt to interpret a woman's good manners to her prejudice; and think that she who does 80 not refuse 'em everything, can refuse 'em nothing.

FAINALL. You are a gallant man, Mirabell; and tho' you may have cruelty enough, not to satisfy a lady's longing; you have too much generosity, not to be tender of her honour. Yet you speak with an indifference which seems to be affected; and confesses you are conscious of a negligence.

57. *ratafia*, a popular drink of the time, a liqueur flavored with fruit kernels.

MIRABELL. You pursue the argument with a distrust that seems to be unaffected, and confesses you are conscious of a concern for which the lady is more indebted to you, than is your wife.

FAINALL. Fie, fie friend, if you grow censorious I must leave 90 you;—I'll look upon the gamesters in the next room.

MIRABELL. Who are they?

FAINALL. Petulant and Witwoud—Bring me some chocolate.

MIRABELL. Betty, what says your clock?

BETTY. Turn'd of the last canonical hour, sir.

MIRABELL. How pertinently the jade answers me! Ha? almost one a clock! [*Looking on his watch.*] O, y'are come—

[*Mirabell's Footman enters from assisting at a wedding engineered by his master.*

MIRABELL. Well; is the grand affair over? You have been something tedious.

SERVANT. Sir, there's such coupling at Pancras, that they 100 stand behind one another, as 'twere in a country dance. Ours was the last couple to lead up; and no hopes appearing of dispatch, besides, the parson growing hoarse, we were afraid his lungs would have failed before it came to our turn; so we drove round to Duke's-Place; and there they were rivetted in a trice.

MIRABELL. So, so, you are sure they are married.

SERVANT. Married and bedded, sir: I am witness.

MIRABELL. Have you the certificate.

SERVANT. Here it is, sir.

MIRABELL. Has the tailor brought Waitwell's clothes home, 110 and the new liveries?

SERVANT. Yes, sir.

MIRABELL. That's well. Do you go home again, d'ye hear, and adjourn the consummation 'till farther order; bid Waitwell shake his ears, and Dame Partlet rustle up her feathers, and meet me at one a clock by Rosamond's pond; that I may see her before she returns to her lady: and as you tender your ears be secret.

[*The Footman goes out, and Mirabell and Fainall return to their former subject.*

95. *canonical hour*, certain hours of the day set aside for prayer and special devotions, beginning with prime, originally at midnight and going through compline, said after nightfall.
96. *pertinently*, saucily.   100. *Pancras*, St. Pancras' Church in the Fields.
105. *Duke's-Place*, St. James' Church, in Aldgate.
115. *Partlet*, traditionally a name for a hen; cf. Chaucer's *Nunne's Priestes Tale*.
116. *Rosamond's Pond*, in St. James' Park, a popular resort of mournful lovers.

FAINALL. Joy of your success, Mirabell; you look pleas'd.

MIRABELL. Ay; I have been engag'd in a matter of some sort of mirth, which is not yet ripe for discovery. I am glad this is 120 not a cabal-night. I wonder, Fainall, that you who are married, and of consequence should be discreet, will suffer your wife to be of such a party.

FAINALL. Faith, I am not jealous. Besides, most who are engaged are women and relations; and for the men, they are of a kind too contemptible to give scandal.

MIRABELL. I am of another opinion. The greater the coxcomb, always the more the scandal: for a woman who is not a fool, can have but one reason for associating with a man who is one.

FAINALL. Are you jealous as often as you see Witwoud en- 130 tertained by Millamant?

MIRABELL. Of her understanding I am, if not of her person.

FAINALL. You do her wrong; for to give her her due, she has wit.

MIRABELL. She has beauty enough to make any man think so; and complaisance enough not to contradict him who shall tell her so.

FAINALL. For a passionate lover, methinks you are a man some-what too discerning in the failings of your mistress.

MIRABELL. And for a discerning man, somewhat too pas- 140 sionate a lover; for I like her with all her faults; nay, like her for her faults. Her follies are so natural, or so artful, that they become her; and those affectations which in another woman would be odious, serve but to make her more agreeable. I'll tell thee, Fainall, she once used me with that insolence, that in revenge I took her to pieces; sifted her, and separated her failings; I studied 'em, and got 'em by rote. The catalogue was so large, that I was not with-out hopes, one day or other to hate her heartily: to which end I so used my self to think of 'em, that at length, contrary to my design and expectation, they gave me every hour less and less 150 disturbance; 'till in a few days it became habitual to me, to re-member 'em without being displeased. They are now grown as familiar to me as my own frailties; and in all probability in a little time longer I shall like 'em as well.

FAINALL. Marry her, marry her; be half as well acquainted with her charms, as you are with her defects, and my life on't, you are your own man again.

MIRABELL. Say you so?

FAINALL. Ay, ay, I have experience: I have a wife, and so forth.

[*A Messenger enters with a letter.*]

MESSENGER. Is one Squire Witwoud here?

BETTY. Yes; what's your business?

MESSENGER. I have a letter for him, from his brother Sir Wilfull, which I am charg'd to deliver into his own hands.

BETTY. He's in the next room, friend—That way.

[The Messenger goes out.

MIRABELL. What, is the chief of that noble family in town, Sir Wilfull Witwoud?

FAINALL. He is expected today. Do you know him?

MIRABELL. I have seen him, he promises to be an extraordinary person; I think you have the honour to be related to him.

FAINALL. Yes; he is half brother to this Witwoud by a for- 170
mer wife, who was sister to my lady Wishfort, my wife's mother. If you marry Millamant, you must call cousins too.

MIRABELL. I had rather be his relation than his acquaintance.

FAINALL. He comes to town in order to equip himself for travel.

MIRABELL. For travel! Why the man that I mean is above forty.

FAINALL. No matter for that; 'tis for the honour of England, that all Europe should know that we have blockheads of all ages.

MIRABELL. I wonder there is not an act of parliament to save the credit of the nation, and prohibit the exportation of fools.

FAINALL. By no means, 'tis better as 'tis; 'tis better to trade 180
with a little loss, than to be quite eaten up, with being over-stocked.

MIRABELL. Pray, are the follies of this knight-errant, and those of the squire his brother, any thing related?

FAINALL. Not at all: Witwoud grows by the knight, like a medlar grafted on a crab. One will melt in your mouth, and t'other set your teeth on edge; one is all pulp, and the other all core.

MIRABELL. So one will be rotten before he be ripe, and the other will be rotten without ever being ripe at all.   190

FAINALL. Sir Wilfull is an odd mixture of bashfulness and obstinacy.—But when he's drunk, he's as loving as the monster in the *Tempest;* and much after the same manner. To give t'other his due; he has something of good nature, and does not always want wit.

MIRABELL. Not always; but as often as his memory fails him, and his common place of comparisons. He is a fool with a good memory, and some few scraps of other folks wit. He is one

186. *medlar,* a fruit somewhat the size and shape of a crab apple, but eaten when it was dead ripe.
192. *monster,* Caliban in Shakespeare's *Tempest.*

whose conversation can never be approv'd, yet it is now and then to be endur'd. He has indeed one good quality, he is not exceptious; for he so passionately affects the reputation of understanding raillery, that he will construe an affront into a jest; and call downright rudeness and ill language, satire and fire. 200

FAINALL. If you have a mind to finish his picture, you have an opportunity to do it at full length. Behold the original.

[*Witwoud comes in from the other room. He is a vacuous young man-about-town with affected and effeminate manners.*

WITWOUD. Afford me your compassion, my dears; pity me, Fainall, Mirabell, pity me.

MIRABELL. I do from my soul.

FAINALL. Why, what's the matter?

WITWOUD. No letters for me, Betty? 210

BETTY. Did not a messenger bring you one but now, sir?

WITWOUD. Ay, but no other? ·

BETTY. No, sir.

WITWOUD. That's hard, that's very hard;—a messenger, a mule, a beast of burden, he has brought me a letter from the fool my brother, as heavy as a panegyrick in a funeral sermon, or a copy of commendatory verses from one poet to another. And what's worse, 'tis as sure a forerunner of the author, as an epistle dedicatory.

MIRABELL. A fool, and your brother, Witwoud! 220

WITWOUD. Ay, ay, my half brother. My half brother he is, no nearer upon honour.

MIRABELL. Then 'tis possible he may be but half a fool.

WITWOUD. Good, good, Mirabell, *le Drole!* Good, good, hang him, don't let's talk of him;—Fainall, how does your Lady? Gad. I say any thing in the world to get this fellow out of my head. I beg pardon that I should ask a man of pleasure, and the town, a question at once so foreign and domestick. But I talk like an old maid at a marriage, I don't know what I say: But she's the best woman in the world.· 230

FAINALL. 'Tis well you don't know what you say, or else your commendation would go near to make me either vain or jealous.

WITWOUD. No man in town lives well with a wife but Fainall. Your judgment, Mirabell?

MIRABELL. You had better step and ask his wife; if you would be credibly inform'd.

WITWOUD. Mirabell.

MIRABELL. Ay.

WITWOUD. My dear, I ask ten thousand pardons;—Gad I have forgot what I was going to say to you.   240

MIRABELL. I thank you heartily, heartily.

WITWOUD. No, but prithee excuse me,—my memory is such a memory.

MIRABELL. Have a care of such apologies, Witwoud;—for I never knew a fool but he affected to complain, either of the spleen or his memory.

FAINALL. What have you done with Petulant?

WITWOUD. He's reckoning his money,—my money it was—I have no luck to day.

FAINALL. You may allow him to win of you at play;—for 250 you are sure to be too hard for him at repartee: Since you monopolize the wit that is between you, the fortune must be his of course.

MIRABELL. I don't find that Petulant confesses the superiority of wit to be your talent, Witwoud.

WITWOUD [*Condescendingly*]. Come, come, you are malicious now, and would breed debates—Petulant's my friend, and a very honest fellow, and a very pretty fellow, and has a smattering— faith and troth a pretty deal of an odd sort of a small wit: nay, I'll do him justice. I'm his friend, I won't wrong him.—And if 260 he had any judgment in the world,—he would not be altogether contemptible. Come, come, don't detract from the merits of my friend.

FAINALL. You don't take your friend to be overnicely bred.

WITWOUD. No, no, hang him, the rogue has no manners at all, that I must own—no more breeding than a bum-bailey, that I grant you,—'Tis pity; the fellow has fire and life.

MIRABELL. What, courage?

WITWOUD. Hum, faith I don't know as to that,—I can't say as to that.—Yes, faith, in a controversie he'll contradict any 270 body.

MIRABELL. Tho' 'twere a man whom he feared, or a woman whom he loved?

WITWOUD. Well, well, he does not always think before he speaks;—we have all our failings; you are too hard upon him, you are faith. Let me excuse him,—I can defend most of his faults, except one or two; one he has, that's the truth on't, if he were my brother, I could not acquit him—That indeed I could wish were otherwise.

MIRABELL. Ay marry, what's that, Witwoud?   280

266. *bum-bailey*, a stupid bailiff, of Dogberry's kind.

WITWOUD. O pardon me—expose the infirmities of my friend.
—No, my dear, excuse me there.

FAINALL. What I warrant he's unsincere, or 'tis some such trifle.

WITWOUD. No, no, what if he be? 'Tis no matter for that, his
wit will excuse that: A wit should no more be sincere, than a
woman constant; one argues a decay of parts, as t'other of beauty.

MIRABELL. May be you think him too positive?

WITWOUD. No, no, his being positive is an incentive to argument, and keeps up conversation.

FAINALL. Too illiterate.   290

WITWOUD. That! that's his happiness—his want of learning
gives him the more opportunities to shew his natural parts.

MIRABELL. He wants words.

WITWOUD. Ay; but I like him for that now; for his want of
words gives me the pleasure very often to explain his meaning.

FAINALL. He's impudent.

WITWOUD. No, that's not it.

MIRABELL. Vain.

WITWOUD. No.

MIRABELL. What, he speaks unseasonable truths sometimes,   300
because he has not wit enough to invent an evasion.

WITWOUD. Truths! Ha, ha, ha! No, no, since you will have it,
—I mean, he never speaks truth at all,—that's all. He will lie like
a chambermaid, or a woman of quality's porter. Now that is a
fault.

[*A Coachman enters.*

COACHMAN [*To Betty*]. Is Master Petulant here, mistress?

BETTY. Yes.

COACHMAN. Three gentlewomen in a coach would speak with
him.

FAINALL. O brave Petulant, three!   310

BETTY. I'll tell him. [*She goes out.*]

COACHMAN. You must bring two dishes of chocolate and a glass
of cinnamon-water. [*He goes out.*]

WITWOUD. That should be for two fasting strumpets, and a
bawd troubled with wind. Now you may know what the three
are.

MIRABELL. You are free with your friend's acquaintance.

WITWOUD. Ay, ay, friendship without freedom is as dull as love
without enjoyment, or wine without toasting; but to tell you a
secret, these are trulls whom he allows coach-hire, and some-   320
thing more by the week, to call on him once a day at publick
places.

MIRABELL. How!

WITWOUD. You shall see he won't go to 'em because there's no
more company here to take notice of him.—why this is nothing
to what he us'd to do;—before he found out this way, I have
known him call for himself—

FAINALL. Call for himself? What dost thou mean?

WITWOUD. Mean, why he would slip you out of this chocolate-
house, just when you had been talking to him.—As soon as 330
your back was turned—whip he was gone;—then trip to his lodg-
ing, clap on a hood and scarf, and a mask, slap into a hackney-
coach, and drive hither to the door again in a trice; where he
would send in for himself, that I mean, call for himself, wait for
himself, nay and what's more, not finding himself, sometimes
leave a letter for himself.

MIRABELL. I confess this is something extraordinary.—I believe
he waits for himself now, he is so long a coming; O, I ask his
pardon.

[*Betty shows in Petulant, who pauses to talk with the others.*
He is cut from the same pattern as Witwoud. Betty tries
to hurry him along.

BETTY. Sir, the Coach stays. 340

PETULANT. Well, well; I come—'sbud a man had as good be a
professed midwife, as a professed whoremaster, at this rate;
to be knocked up and raised at all hours, and in all places. Pox on
'em, I won't come—d'ye hear, tell 'em I won't come.—Let 'em
snivel and cry their hearts out. [*She goes out to deliver the mes-*
sage.]

FAINALL. You are very cruel, Petulant.

PETULANT. All's one, let it pass—I have a humour to be cruel.

MIRABELL. I hope they are not persons of condition that you
use at this rate. 350

PETULANT. Condition, condition's a dried fig, if I am not in
humour—by this hand, if they were your—a—a—your what-dee-
call-'ems themselves, they must wait or rub off, if I want appetite.

MIRABELL. What-dee-call-'ems! What are they, Witwoud?

WITWOUD. Empresses, my dear—By your what-dee-call-'ems he
means sultana queens.

PETULANT. Ay, Roxolana's.

MIRABELL. Cry you mercy.

FAINALL. Witwoud says they are—

PETULANT. What does he say th'are? 360

357. *Roxolana*, the queen of Solyman in *The Siege of Rhodes*, Davenant's
"opera."

WITWOUD. I? Fine ladies I say.

PETULANT. Pass on, Witwoud—harkee, by this light, his relations—two co-heiresses his cousins, and an old aunt, who loves catterwauling better than a conventicle.

WITWOUD. Ha, ha, ha; I had a mind to see how the rogue would come off—ha, ha, ha; gad I can't be angry with him; if he had said they were my mother and my sisters.

MIRABELL. No!

WITWOUD. No; the rogue's wit and readiness of invention charm me, dear Petulant.   370

[Betty re-enters.

BETTY. They are gone, sir, in great anger.

PETULANT. Enough, let 'em trundle. Anger helps complexion, saves paint.

FAINALL. This continence is all dissembled; this is in order to have something to brag of the next time he makes court to Millamant, and swear he has abandoned the whole sex for her sake.

MIRABELL. Have you not left off your impudent pretensions there yet? I shall cut your throat, sometime or other, Petulant, about that business.

PETULANT. Ay, ay, let that pass.—There are other throats   380
to be cut.—

MIRABELL. Meaning mine, Sir?

PETULANT. Not I—I mean no body—I know nothing.—But there are uncles and nephews in the world—and they may be rivals—what then? All's one for that—

MIRABELL. How! Harkee Petulant, come hither—explain, or I shall call your interpreter.

PETULANT. Explain; I know nothing.—Why you have an uncle, have you not, lately come to town, and lodges by my Lady Wishfort's?   390

MIRABELL. True.

PETULANT. Why that's enough.—You and he are not friends; and if he should marry and have a child, you may be disinherited, ha?

MIRABELL. Where hast thou stumbled upon all this truth?

PETULANT. All's one for that; why then say I know something.

MIRABELL. Come, thou art an honest fellow Petulant, and shalt make love to my mistress, thou shalt, Faith. What hast thou heard of my uncle?

PETULANT. I, nothing I. If throats are to be cut, let swords   400
clash; snug's the word, I shrug and am silent.

372-373. *Anger . . . paint*, i.e., by making the lady red in the face.

MIRABELL. O raillery, raillery. Come, I know thou art in the women's secrets—what, you're a cabalist, I know you staid at Millamant's last night, after I went. Was there any mention made of my uncle, or me? Tell me; if thou hadst but good nature equal to thy wit Petulant, Tony Witwoud, who is now thy competitor in fame, would shew as dim by thee as a dead whiting's eye by a pearl of orient; he would no more be seen by thee, than Mercury is by the sun: Come, I'm sure thou wo't tell me.

PETULANT. If I do, will you grant me common sense then, 410 for the future?

MIRABELL. Faith I'll do what I can for thee, and I'll pray that heav'n may grant it thee in the mean time.

PETULANT. Well, harkee.

FAINALL. Petulant and you both will find Mirabell as warm a rival as a lover.

WITWOUD. Pshaw, pshaw, that she laughs at Petulant is plain. And for my part—but that it is almost a fashion to admire her, I should—harkee—to tell you a secret, but let it go no further—between friends, I shall never break my heart for 420 her.

FAINALL. How!

WITWOUD. She's handsome; but she's a sort of an uncertain woman.

FAINALL. I thought you had died for her.

WITWOUD. Umh—no—

FAINALL. She has wit.

WITWOUD. 'Tis what she will hardly allow any body else—Now, demme, I should hate that, if she were as handsome as Cleopatra. Mirabell is not so sure of her as he thinks for. 430

FAINALL. Why do you think so?

WITWOUD. We staid pretty late there last night; and heard something of an uncle to Mirabell, who is lately come to town—and is between him and the best part of his estate; Mirabell and he are at some distance, as my Lady Wishfort has been told; and you know she hates Mirabell, worse than a Quaker hates a parrot, or than a fishmonger hates a hard frost. Whether this uncle has seen Mrs. Millamant or not, I cannot say; but there were items of such a treaty being in embryo; and if it should come to life, poor Mirabell would be in some sort unfortunately fobbed 440 i'faith.

436. *Quaker* . . . , because it is too talkative.
437. *fishmonger* . . . , because cold weather makes fishing and handling fish uncomfortable.

FAINALL. 'Tis impossible Millamant should harken to it.

WITWOUD. Faith, my dear, I can't tell; she's a woman and a kind of a humorist.

MIRABELL. And this is the sum of what you could collect last night?

PETULANT. The quintessence. May be Witwoud knows more, he stayed longer—besides they never mind him; they say any thing before him.

MIRABELL. I thought you had been the greatest favourite. 450

PETULANT. Ay *tête a tête;* But not in public, because I make remarks.

MIRABELL. You do?

PETULANT. Ay, ay, pox I'm malicious, man. Now he's soft, you know, they are not in awe of him—the fellow's well bred, he's what you call a—what-d'ye-call-'em. A fine gentleman, but he's silly withal.

MIRABELL. I thank you, I know as much as my curiosity requires. Fainall, are you for the Mall?

FAINALL. Ay, I'll take a turn before dinner. 460

WITWOUD. Ay, we'll all walk in the park; the ladies talked of being there.

MIRABELL. I thought you were obliged to watch for your brother Sir Wilfull's arrival.

WITWOUD. No, no, he's come to his aunt's, my Lady Wishfort; pox on him, I shall be troubled with him too; what shall I do with the fool?

PETULANT. Beg him for his estate; that I may beg you afterwards; and so have but one Trouble with you both.

WITWOUD. O rare Petulant; thou art as quick as fire in a 470 frosty morning; thou shalt to the Mall with us; and we'll be very severe.

PETULANT. Enough, I'm in a humour to be severe.

MIRABELL. Are you? Pray then walk by your selves;—let not us be accessary to your putting the ladies out of countenance, with your senseless ribaldry; which you roar out aloud as often as they pass by you; and when you have made a handsome woman blush, then you think you have been severe.

PETULANT. What, what? Then let 'em either show their innocence by not understanding what they hear, or else show 480 their discretion by not hearing what they would not be thought to understand.

451. *tête a tête*, in private conversation.
471. *Mall*, a famous promenade, once a part of St. James' Park.

MIRABELL. But hast not thou then sense enough to know that thou ought'st to be most ashamed thy self, when thou hast put another out of countenance.

PETULANT. Not I, by this hand—I always take blushing either for a sign of guilt, or ill breeding.

MIRABELL. I confess you ought to think so. You are in the right, that you may plead the error of your judgment in defence of your practice.   490

> *Where modesty's ill manners, 'tis but fit*
> *That impudence and malice pass for wit.*

[*They go out together.*]

END OF THE FIRST ACT

ACT II

SCENE I

ST. JAMES'S PARK *at about the same time as the end of the preceding scene. Mrs. Fainall and Mrs. Marwood are promenading, discussing the ever popular subject of Men and their ways.*

MRS. FAINALL. Ay, ay, dear Marwood, if we will be happy, we must find the means in our selves, and among our selves. Men are ever in extreams; either doting or averse. While they are lovers, if they have fire and sense, their jealousies are insupportable: And when they cease to love, (we ought to think at least) they loathe; they look upon us with horror and distaste; they meet us like the ghosts of what we were, and as from such, fly from us.

MRS. MARWOOD. True, 'tis an unhappy circumstance of life, that love should ever die before us; and that the man so often should out-live the lover. But say what you will, 'tis better to be   10 left, than never to have been loved. To pass our youth in dull indifference, to refuse the sweets of life because they once must leave us, is as preposterous, as to wish to have been born old, because we one day must be old. For my part, my youth may wear and waste, but it shall never rust in my possession.

MRS. FAINALL. Then it seems you dissemble an aversion to mankind, only in compliance to my mother's humour.

MRS. MARWOOD. Certainly. To be free; I have no taste of those insipid dry discourses, with which our sex of force must enter-

tain themselves, apart from men. We may affect endearments 20
to each other, profess eternal friendships, and seem to dote like
lovers; but 'tis not in our natures long to persevere. Love will
resume his empire in our breasts, and every heart, or soon or late,
receive and readmit him as its lawful tyrant.

MRS. FAINALL. Bless me, how have I been deceived! Why you
profess a libertine.

MRS. MARWOOD. You see my friendship by my freedom. Come,
be as sincere, acknowledge that your sentiments agree with mine.

MRS. FAINALL. Never.

MRS. MARWOOD. You hate mankind?   30

MRS. FAINALL. Heartily, inveterately.

MRS. MARWOOD. Your husband?

MRS. FAINALL. Most transcendently; ay, tho' I say it, meritori-
ously.

MRS. MARWOOD. Give me your hand upon it.

MRS. FAINALL. There.

MRS. MARWOOD. I join with you; what I have said has been to
try you.

MRS. FAINALL. Is it possible? Dost thou hate those vipers, men?

MRS. MARWOOD. I have done hating 'em, and am now come 40
to despise 'em; the next thing I have to do, is eternally to forget
'em.

MRS. FAINALL. There spoke the spirit of an Amazon, a Penthesilea.

MRS. MARWOOD. And yet I am thinking sometimes to carry my
aversion further.

MRS. FAINALL. How?

MRS. MARWOOD. Faith by marrying; if I could but find one that
loved me very well, and would be thoroughly sensible of ill usage,
I think I should do my self the violence of undergoing the 50
ceremony.

MRS. FAINALL. You would not make him a cuckold?

MRS. MARWOOD. No; but I'd make him believe I did, and that's
as bad.

MRS. FAINALL. Why had not you as good do it?

MRS. MARWOOD. O if he should ever discover it, he would then
know the worst, and be out of his pain; but I would have him
ever to continue upon the rack of fear and jealousie.

MRS. FAINALL. Ingenious Mischief! Would thou wert married
to Mirabell.   60

MRS. MARWOOD. Would I were.

43-44. *Penthesilea*, the Queen of the Amazons.

MRS. FAINALL. You change colour.

MRS. MARWOOD. Because I hate him.

MRS. FAINALL. So do I; but I can hear him named. But what reason have you to hate him in particular?

MRS. MARWOOD. I never loved him; he is, and always was insufferably proud.

MRS. FAINALL. By the reason you give for your aversion, one would think it dissembled; for you have laid a fault to his charge, of which his enemies must acquit him.   70

MRS. MARWOOD. O then it seems you are one of his favourable enemies. Methinks you look a little pale, and now you flush again.

MRS. FAINALL. Do I? I think I am a little sick o' the sudden.

MRS. MARWOOD. What ails you?

MRS. FAINALL. My husband. Don't you see him? He turn'd short upon me unawares, and has almost overcome me.

[*Fainall and Mirabell come in from the coffee house, where we last saw them.*

MRS. MARWOOD. Ha, ha, ha; he comes opportunely for you.

MRS. FAINALL. For you, for he has brought Mirabell with him.

FAINALL. My dear.

MRS. FAINALL. My soul.   80

FAINALL. You don't look well today, child.

MRS. FAINALL. D'ye think so?

MIRABELL. He is the only man that does, madam.

MRS. FAINALL. The only man that would tell me so at least; and the only man from whom I could hear it without mortification.

FAINALL. O my dear I am satisfied of your tenderness; I know you cannot resent any thing from me; especially what is an effect of my concern.

MRS. FAINALL. Mr. Mirabell, my mother interrupted you in   90 a pleasant relation last night: I would fain hear it out.

MIRABELL. The persons concerned in that affair, have yet a tolerable reputation.—I am afraid Mr. Fainall will be censorious.

MRS. FAINALL. He has a humour more prevailing than his curiosity, and will willingly dispense with the hearing of one scandalous story, to avoid giving an occasion to make another by being seen to walk with his wife. This way Mr. Mirabell, and I dare promise you will oblige us both.

[*She and Mirabell go out, and Fainall uses the time to push his flirtation with Mrs. Marwood.*

FAINALL. Excellent creature! Well, sure if I should live to be rid of my wife, I should be a miserable man.   100

MRS. MARWOOD. Ay!

FAINALL. For having only that one hope, the accomplishment of it, of consequence must put an end to all my hopes; and what a wretch is he who must survive his hopes! Nothing remains when that day comes, but to sit down and weep like Alexander, when he wanted other worlds to conquer.

MRS. MARWOOD. Will you not follow 'em?

FAINALL. Faith, I think not.

MRS. MARWOOD. Pray let us; I have a reason.

FAINALL. You are not jealous?   110

MRS. MARWOOD. Of whom?

FAINALL. Of Mirabell.

MRS. MARWOOD. If I am, is it inconsistent with my love to you that I am tender of your honour?

FAINALL. You would intimate then, as if there were a fellow-feeling between my wife and him.

MRS. MARWOOD. I think she does not hate him to that degree she would be thought.

FAINALL. But he, I fear, is too insensible.

MRS. MARWOOD. It may be you are deceived.   120

FAINALL. It may be so. I do not now begin to apprehend it.

MRS. MARWOOD. What?

FAINALL. That I have been deceived, madam, and you are false.

MRS. MARWOOD. That I am false! What mean you?

FAINALL. To let you know I see through all your little arts.—Come, you both love him; and both have equally dissembl'd your aversion. Your mutual jealousies of one another, have made you clash 'till you have both struck fire. I have seen the warm confession red'ning on your cheeks, and sparkling from your eyes.

MRS. MARWOOD. You do me wrong.   130

FAINALL. I do not.—'Twas for my ease to oversee and wilfully neglect the gross advances made him by my wife; that by permitting her to be engaged, I might continue unsuspected in my pleasures; and take you oftner to my arms in full security. But could you think, because the nodding husband would not wake, that e'er the watchful lover slept?

MRS. MARWOOD. And wherewithal can you reproach me?

FAINALL. With infidelity, with loving another, with love of Mirabell.

MRS. MARWOOD. 'Tis false. I challenge you to show an in-   140 stance that can confirm your groundless accusation. I hate him.

FAINALL. And wherefore do you hate him? He is insensible,

106. *wanted*, lacked.

and your resentment follows his neglect. An instance! The injuries you have done him are a proof: your interposing in his
love. What cause had you to make discoveries of his pretended
passion? To undeceive the credulous aunt, and be the officious
obstacle of his match with Millamant?

MRS. MARWOOD. My obligations to my lady urged me: I had
professed a friendship to her; and could not see her easy nature
so abused by that dissembler.   150

FAINALL. What, was it conscience then? Professed a friendship!
O the pious friendships of the female sex!

MRS. MARWOOD. More tender, more sincere, and more enduring,
than all the vain and empty vows of men, whether professing
love to us, or mutual faith to one another.

FAINALL. Ha, ha, ha; you are my wife's friend too.

MRS. MARWOOD. Shame and ingratitude! Do you reproach me?
You, you upbraid me! Have I been false to her, thro' strict fidelity
to you, and sacrificed my friendship to keep my love inviolate?
And have you the baseness to charge me with the guilt, un-   160
mindful of the merit! To you it should be meritorious, that I have
been vicious: And do you reflect that guilt upon me, which
should lie buried in your bosom?

FAINALL. You misinterpret my reproof. I meant but to remind
you of the slight account you once could make of strictest ties,
when set in competition with your love to me.

MRS. MARWOOD. 'Tis false, you urged it with deliberate malice.
—'Twas spoke in scorn, and I never will forgive it.

FAINALL. Your guilt, not your resentment, begets your rage.
If yet you lov'd, you could forgive a jealousy: But you are   170
stung to find you are discovered.

MRS. MARWOOD. It shall be all discovered. You too shall be discovered; be sure you shall. I can but be exposed.—If I do it my
self I shall prevent your baseness.

FAINALL. Why, what will you do?

MRS. MARWOOD. Disclose it to your wife; own what has past
between us.

FAINALL. Frenzy!

MRS. MARWOOD. By all my wrongs I'll do't.—I'll publish to the
world the injuries you have done me, both in my fame and   180
fortune: With both I trusted you, you bankrupt in honour, as
indigent of wealth.

FAINALL. Your fame I have preserved. Your fortune has been
bestowed as the prodigality of your love would have it, in pleas-

174. *prevent*, anticipate.

ures which we both have shared. Yet, had not you been false, I
had e'er this repaid it—'Tis true—had you permitted Mirabell
with Millamant to have stolen their marriage, my lady had been
incensed beyond all means of reconcilement: Millamant had forfeited the moiety of her fortune; which then would have descended to my wife;—And wherefore did I marry, but to   190
make lawful prize of a rich widow's wealth, and squander it on
love and you?

MRS. MARWOOD. Deceit and frivolous pretence.

FAINALL. Death, am I not married? What's pretence? Am I not
imprisoned, fettered? Have I not a wife? Nay a wife that was a
widow, a young widow, a handsome widow; and would be again
a widow, but that I have a heart of proof, and something of a
constitution to bustle thro' the ways of wedlock and this world.
Will you yet be reconciled to truth and me?

MRS. MARWOOD. Impossible. Truth and you are inconsistent   200
—I hate you, and shall for ever.

FAINALL. For loving you?

MRS. MARWOOD. I loath the name of love after such usage; and
next to the guilt with which you would asperse me, I scorn you
most. Farewell.

FAINALL [Seizing her hands]. Nay, we must not part thus.

MRS. MARWOOD. Let me go.

FAINALL. Come, I'm sorry.

MRS. MARWOOD. I care not!—Let me go!—Break my hands, do!
—I'd leave 'em to get loose.   210

FAINALL. I would not hurt you for the world. Have I no other
hold to keep you here?

MRS. MARWOOD. Well, I have deserv'd it all.

FAINALL. You know I love you.

MRS. MARWOOD. Poor dissembling!—O that—well, it is not
yet—

FAINALL. What? What is it not? What is it not yet? It is not
yet too late—

MRS. MARWOOD. No, it is not yet too late—I have that comfort.

FAINALL. It is, to love another.   220

MRS. MARWOOD [weeping]. But not to loath, detest, abhor mankind, my self and the whole treacherous world.

FAINALL. Nay, this is extravagance.—Come, I ask your pardon—
no tears—I was to blame, I could not love you and be easy in my
doubts.—Pray forbear—I believe you; I'm convinced I've done
you wrong; and any way, ev'ry way will make amends;—I'll hate
my wife yet more, damn her, I'll part with her, rob her of all

she's worth, and we'll retire somewhere, any where, to another
world, I'll marry thee.—Be pacified—'sdeath they come, hide
your face, your tears—You have a mask, wear it a moment.   230
This way, this way, be persuaded.

> [*She puts on her mask, and they hurry out as Mirabell and
> Mrs. Fainall re-enter from the other side of the stage. They
> have been discussing her husband and her attitude toward
> him.*

MRS. FAINALL. They are here yet.

MIRABELL. They are turning into the other walk.

MRS. FAINALL. While I only hated my husband, I could bear to
see him; but since I have despised him, he's too offensive.

MIRABELL. O you should hate with prudence.

MRS. FAINALL. Yes, for I have loved with indiscretion.

MIRABELL. You should have just so much disgust for your husband, as may be sufficient to make you relish your lover.

MRS. FAINALL. You have been the cause that I have loved   240
without bounds, and would you set limits to that aversion, of
which you have been the occasion? Why did you make me marry
this man?

MIRABELL. Why do we daily commit disagreeable and dangerous actions? To save that idol, reputation. If the familiarities of
our loves had produced that consequence, of which you were
apprehensive, where could you have fixed a father's name with
credit, but on a husband? I knew Fainall to be a man lavish of his
morals, an interested and professing friend, a false and a design-
ing lover; yet one whose wit and outward fair behavior   250
have gained a reputation with the town, enough to make that
woman stand excus'd, who has suffered her self to be won by his
addresses. A better man ought not to have been sacrificed to the
occasion; a worse had not answered to the purpose. When you
are weary of him, you know your remedy.

MRS. FAINALL. I ought to stand in some degree of credit with
you, Mirabell.

MIRABELL. In justice to you, I have made you privy to my
whole design, and put it in your power to ruin or advance my
fortune.   260

MRS. FAINALL. Whom have you instructed to represent your
pretended uncle?

MIRABELL. Waitwell, my servant.

230. *mask*, ladies of the time carried masks which were used freely to
keep them from being recognized.

MRS. FAINALL. He is an humble servant to Foible my mother's woman, and may win her to your interest.

MIRABELL. Care is taken for that—she is won and worn by this time. They were married this morning.

MRS. FAINALL. Who?

MIRABELL. Waitwell and Foible. I would not tempt my servant to betray me by trusting him too far. If your mother, in 270 hopes to ruin me, should consent to marry my pretended uncle, he might, like Mosca in the *Fox*, stand upon terms; so I made him sure before-hand.

MRS. FAINALL. So, if my poor mother is caught in a contract, you will discover the imposture betimes; and release her by producing a certificate of her gallant's former marriage.

MIRABELL. Yes, upon condition that she consent to my marriage with her niece, and surrender the moiety of her fortune in her possession.

MRS. FAINALL. She talked last night of endeavouring at a 280 match between Millamant and your uncle.

MIRABELL. That was by Foible's direction, and my instruction, that she might seem to carry it more privately.

MRS. FAINALL. Well, I have an opinion of your success; for I believe my Lady will do any thing to get an husband; and when she has this, which you have provided for her, I suppose she will submit to any thing to get rid of him.

MIRABELL. Yes, I think the good lady would marry any thing that resembled a man, though 'twere no more than what a butler could pinch out of a napkin.

MRS. FAINALL. Female frailty! We must all come to it, if 290 we live to be old, and feel the craving of a false appetite when the true is decayed.

MIRABELL. An old woman's appetite is depraved like that of a girl—'tis the green-sickness of a second childhood; and like the faint offer of a latter spring, serves but to usher in the fall; and withers in an affected bloom.

MRS. FAINALL. Here's your mistress.

[*Mrs. Millamant hurries in to them, followed by her maid, Mincing, and by Witwoud, who is puffing at the unaccustomed speed he has had to assume.*

264. *servant*, suitor.

272. *Mosca in the Fox*, In Jonson's play, Mosca, the servant of Volpone (the Fox), tricked a group of dupes by promising that they would be Volpone's heirs if they would make satisfactory terms with Volpone and himself.

MIRABELL. Here she comes i'faith full sail, with her fan spread and streamers out, and a shoal of fools for tenders—ha, no, I cry her mercy. 300

MRS. FAINALL. I see but one poor empty sculler; and he tows her woman after him.

MIRABELL. [*Bowing ceremoniously to Millamant*]. You seem to be unattended, madam,—You us'd to have the *beau-mond* throng after you; and a flock of gay fine perukes hovering round you.

WITWOUD. Like moths about a candle—I had like to have lost my comparison for want of breath.

MILLAMANT. O, I have denied my self airs today. I have walked as fast through the crowd—

WITWOUD. As a favourite just disgraced; and with as few 310 followers.

MILLAMANT. Dear Mr. Witwoud, truce with your similitudes: For I am as sick of 'em—

WITWOUD. As a physician of a good air.—I cannot help it, madam, tho' 'tis against my self.

MILLAMANT. Yet again! Mincing, stand between me and his wit.

WITWOUD. Do, Mrs. Mincing, like a screen before a great fire. I confess I do blaze today, I am too bright.

MRS. FAINALL. But dear Millamant, why were you so long?

MILLAMANT. Long! Lord, have I not made violent haste? I 320 have asked every living thing I met for you; I have enquired after you, as after a new fashion.

WITWOUD. Madam, truce with your similitudes.—No, you met her husband, and did not ask him for her.

MIRABELL. By your leave Witwoud, that were like enquiring after an old fashion, to ask a husband for his wife.

WITWOUD. Hum, a hit, a hit, a palpable hit, I confess it.

MRS. FAINALL. You were dressed before I came abroad.

MILLAMANT. Ay, that's true—O but then I had—Mincing, what had I? Why was I so long? 330

MINCING. O mem, your laship staid to peruse a packet of letters.

MILLAMANT. O ay, letters—I had letters—I am persecuted with letters—I hate letters—no body knows how to write letters; and yet one has 'em, one does not know why.—They serve one to pin up one's hair.

WITWOUD. Is that the way? Pray, madam, do you pin up your hair with all your letters; I find I must keep copies.

MILLAMANT. Only with those in verse, Mr. Witwoud. I never pin up my hair with prose. I think I tried once, Mincing.

305. *perukes*, wigs, i.e., dandies.

MINCING. O mem, I shall never forget it.　340

MILLAMANT. Ay, poor Mincing tift and tift all the morning.

MINCING. 'Till I had the cramp in my fingers, I'll vow mem. And all to no purpose. But when your laship pins it up with poetry, it sits so pleasant the next day as any thing, and is so pure and so crips.

WITWOUD. Indeed, so crips?

MINCING. You're such a critic, Mr. Witwoud.

MILLAMANT. Mirabell, did you take exceptions last night? O ay, and went away—now I think on't I'm angry—no, now I think on't I'm pleased—for I believe I gave you some pain.　350

MIRABELL. Does that please you?

MILLAMANT. Infinitely; I love to give pain.

MIRABELL. You would affect a cruelty which is not in your nature; your true vanity is in the power of pleasing.

MILLAMANT. O I ask your pardon for that—one's cruelty is one's power, and when one parts with one's cruelty, one parts with one's power; and when one has parted with that, I fancy one's old and ugly.

MIRABELL. Ay, ay, suffer your cruelty to ruin the object of your power, to destroy your lover—and then how vain, how　360 lost a thing you'll be? Nay, 'tis true: You are no longer handsome when you've lost your lover; your beauty dies upon the instant: For beauty is the lover's gift; 'tis he bestows your charms—your glass is all a cheat. The ugly and the old, whom the looking-glass mortifies, yet after commendation can be flattered by it, and discover beauties in it: for that reflects our praises, rather than your face.

MILLAMANT. O the vanity of these men! Fainall, d'ye hear him? If they did not commend us, we were not handsome! Now you must know they could not commend one, if one was not　370 handsome. Beauty the lover's gift—Lord, what is a lover, that it can give? Why one makes lovers as fast as one pleases, and they live as long as one pleases, and they die as soon as one pleases: And then if one pleases one makes more.

WITWOUD. Very pretty. Why you make no more of making of lovers, madam, than of making so many card-matches.

MILLAMANT. One no more owes ones beauty to a lover, than ones wit to an echo: They can but reflect what we look and say; vain empty things if we are silent or unseen, and want a being.

MIRABELL. Yet, to those two vain empty things, you owe　380 two of the greatest pleasures of your life.

341. *tift*, prinked, dressed (the hair).　346. *crips*, curly.

MILLAMANT. How so?

MIRABELL. To your lover you owe the pleasure of hearing your selves praised; and to an echo the pleasure of hearing your selves talk.

WITWOUD. But I know a lady that loves talking so incessantly, she won't give an echo fair play; she has that everlasting rotation of tongue, that an echo must wait 'till she dies, before it can catch her last words.

MILLAMANT. O fiction; Fainall, let us leave these men.   390

MIRABELL [*Aside to Mrs. Fainall*]. Draw off Witwoud.

MRS. FAINALL. Immediately; I have a word or two for Mr. Witwoud.

[*Mrs. Fainall and Witwoud go out. Mirabell detains Millamant; he is very serious now, for he really loves Millamant.*

MIRABELL. I would beg a little private audience too.—You had the tyranny to deny me last night; tho' you knew I came to impart a secret to you that concerned my love.

MILLAMANT. You saw I was engaged.

MIRABELL. Unkind. You had the leisure to entertain a herd   400 of fools; Things who visit you from their excessive idleness; bestowing on your easiness that time, which is the incumbrance of their lives. How can you find delight in such society? It is impossible they should admire you, they are not capable: Or if they were, it should be to you as a mortification; for sure to please a fool is some degree of folly.

MILLAMANT. I please my self—besides, sometimes to converse with fools is for my health.

MIRABELL. Your health! Is there a worse disease than the conversation of fools?   410

MILLAMANT. Yes, the vapours; fools are physick for it, next to Asafœtida.

MIRABELL. You are not in a course of fools?

MILLAMANT. Mirabell, if you persist in this offensive freedom—you'll displease me—I think I must resolve after all, not to have you.—We shan't agree.

MIRABELL. Not in our physick it may be.

MILLAMANT. And yet our distemper in all likelihood will be the same; for we shall be sick of one another. I shan't endure to be reprimanded, nor instructed; 'tis so dull to act always by   420 advice, and so tedious to be told of ones faults—I can't bear it. Well, I won't have you Mirabell—I'm resolved—I think—you may go.—Ha, ha, ha. What would you give, that you could help loving me?

MIRABELL. I would give something that you did not know, I could not help it.

MILLAMANT. Come, don't look grave then. Well, what do you say to me?

MIRABELL. I say that a man may as soon make a friend by his wit, or a fortune by his honesty, as win a woman with plain- 430 dealing and sincerity.

MILLAMANT. Sententious Mirabell! Prithee don't look with that violent and inflexible wise face, like Solomon at the dividing of the child in an old tapestry hanging.

MIRABELL. You are merry, madam, but I would persuade you for a moment to be serious.

MILLAMANT. What, with that face? No, if you keep your countenance, 'tis impossible I should hold mine. Well, after all, there is something very moving in a lovesick face. Ha, ha, ha!—Well I won't laugh, don't be peevish—heigho! Now I'll be mel- 440 ancholy, as melancholy as a watchlight. Well, Mirabell, if ever you will win me, woo me now—nay, if you are so tedious, fare you well;—I see they are walking away.

MIRABELL. Can you not find in the variety of your disposition one moment—

MILLAMANT. To hear you tell me Foible's married, and your plot like to speed?—No.

MIRABELL. But how you came to know it—

MILLAMANT. Without the help of the devil, you can't imagine; unless she should tell me her self. Which of the two it may 450 have been, I will leave you to consider; and when you have done thinking of that, think of me. [*She goes saucily and triumphantly out, leaving Mirabell gasping.*]

MIRABELL. I have something more—gone!—Think of you! To think of a whirlwind, tho' 'twere in a whirlwind, were a case of more steady contemplation; a very tranquility of mind and mansion. A fellow that lives in a windmill, has not a more whimsical dwelling than the heart of a man that is lodged in a woman. There is no point of the compass to which they cannot turn, and by which they are not turned; and by one as well as another; for 460 motion not method is their occupation. To know this, and yet continue to be in love, is to be made wise from the dictates of reason, and yet persevere to play the fool by the force of instinct. —O here come my pair of turtles,—

[*Waitwell and Foible, the newlyweds, enter with great show of affection for each other.*]

—What, billing so sweetly!

Is not Valentine's Day over with you yet? Sirrah, Waitwell, why sure you think you were married for your own recreation, and not for my conveniency.

WAITWELL. Your pardon, sir. With submission, we have indeed been solacing in lawful delights; but still with an eye to business, sir. I have instructed her as well as I could. If she can take 470 your directions as readily as my instructions, sir, your affairs are in a prosperous way.

MIRABELL. Give you joy, Mrs. Foible.

FOIBLE. O-las, sir, I'm so asham'd—I'm afraid my lady has been in a thousand inquietudes for me. But I protest, sir, I made as · much haste as I could.

WAITWELL. That she did indeed, sir. It was my fault that she did not make more.

MIRABELL. That I believe.

FOIBLE. But I told my Lady as you instructed me, sir. That 480 I had a prospect of seeing Sir Rowland your uncle; and that I would put her Ladyship's picture in my pocket to show him; which I'll be sure to say has made him so enamoured of her beauty, that he burns with impatience to lie at her Ladyship's feet and worship the original.

MIRABELL. Excellent Foible! Matrimony has made you eloquent in love.

WAITWELL. I think she has profited, sir. I think so.

FOIBLE. You have seen madam Millamant, sir?

MIRABELL. Yes.   490

FOIBLE. I told her, sir, because I did not know that you might find an opportunity; she had so much company last night.

MIRABELL. Your diligence will merit more.—In the mean time—
                                                    [*Gives Money.*

FOIBLE. O dear sir, your humble servant.

WAITWELL. Spouse. [*Moves to take the money from her.*]

MIRABELL. Stand off sir, not a penny.—Go on and prosper, Foible.—The lease shall be made good and the farm stocked, if we succeed.

FOIBLE. I don't question your generosity, sir: And you 500 need not doubt of success. If you have no more commands, sir, I'll be gone; I'm sure my Lady is at her toilet, and can't dress 'till I come.—O dear, I'm sure that [*Looking out.*] was Mrs. Marwood that went by in a mask; if she has seen me with you I'm sure she'll tell my Lady. I'll make haste home and prevent her. Your servant sir. B'w'y Waitwell. [*She hurries off.*]

WAITWELL. Sir Rowland if you please. The jade's so pert upon her preferment she forgets her self.

MIRABELL. Come sir, will you endeavour to forget your self—and transform into Sir Rowland. 510

WAITWELL. Why sir; it will be impossible I should remember my self!—married, knighted and attended all in one day! 'Tis enough to make any man forget himself. The difficulty will be how to recover my acquaintance and familiarity with my former self; and fall from my transformation to a reformation into Waitwell. Nay, I shan't be quite the same Waitwell neither—for now I remember me, I'm married, and can't be my own man again.

> *Ay there's my grief; that's the sad change*
> *of life;*
> *To lose my title, and yet keep my wife.*

> [*Master and man go out together.*

END OF THE SECOND ACT

ACT III

SCENE I

LADY WISHFORT'S DRESSING ROOM *at about the time of the preceding scene. She is a fidgety, excitable woman, now engaged before the mirror in the final primping with the not too intelligent help of her maid, Peg, whose stupidity grates on her mistress' nerves.*

LADY WISHFORT. Merciful, no news of Foible yet?

PEG. No, madam.

LADY WISHFORT. I have no more patience—if I have not fretted my self 'till I am pale again, there's no veracity in me. Fetch me the red—the red, do you hear, sweet-heart? An errant ash colour, as I'm a person. Look you how this wench stirs! Why dost thou not fetch me a little red? Didst thou not hear me, Mopus?

PEG. The red ratafia does your Ladyship mean, or the cherry-brandy?

LADY WISHFORT. Ratafia, fool. No, fool. Not the ratafia, fool 10 —grant me patience! I mean the Spanish paper, idiot, complexion,

7. *mopus*, a dull person.   11. *Spanish paper*, a cosmetic.

darling. Paint, paint, paint, dost thou understand that, changeling, dangling thy hands like bobbins before thee? Why dost thou not stir, puppet? thou wooden thing upon wires!

PEG. Lord, madam, your Ladyship is so impatient—I cannot come at the paint, madam, Mrs. Foible has lock'd it up, and carried the key with her.

LADY WISHFORT. A pox take you both.—Fetch me the cherry-brandy then.

[*Peg goes out and Lady Wishfort continues to examine her appearance in the mirror.*

LADY WISHFORT. I'm as pale and as faint, I look like Mrs.   20 Qualmsick the curate's wife, that's always breeding.—Wench, come, come, wench, what art thou doing, sipping? tasting? Save thee, dost thou not know the bottle?

[*Peg returns with a bottle of brandy and a tiny china cup.*

PEG. Madam, I was looking for a cup.

LADY WISHFORT. A cup, save thee, and what a cup hast thou brought! Dost thou take me for a fairy, to drink out of an acorn? Why didst thou not bring thy thimble? Hast thou ne'er a brass-thimble clinking in thy pocket with a bit of nutmeg? I warrant thee. Come, fill, fill.—So—again. See who that is—[*One knocks.*] Set down the bottle first. Here, here, under the table.—What,   30 wouldst thou go with the bottle in thy hand like a tapster. As I'm a person, this wench has lived in an inn upon the road, before she came to me, like Maritornes the Asturian in *Don Quixote*. No Foible yet?

PEG. No, madam, Mrs. Marwood.

LADY WISHFORT. O Marwood, let her come in. Come in good Marwood.

[*Mrs. Marwood enters, ready for a rich session of gossip.*

MRS. MARWOOD. I'm surprised to find your Ladyship in dis-habillé at this time of day.

LADY WISHFORT. Foible's a lost thing; has been abroad since   40 morning, and never heard of since.

MRS. MARWOOD. I saw her but now, as I came mask'd through the park, in conference with Mirabell.

LADY WISHFORT. With Mirabell! You call my blood into my face, with mentioning that traitor. She durst not have the confidence. I sent her to negotiate an affair, in which if I'm detected I'm un-done. If that wheedling villain has wrought upon Foible to detect me, I'm ruined. Oh my dear friend, I'm a wretch of wretches if I'm detected.

33. *Maritornes*, a homely, deformed girl at an inn visited by Don Quixote.

MRS. MARWOOD. O madam, you cannot suspect Mrs. Foible's 50
integrity.

LADY WISHFORT. O, he carries poison in his tongue that would
corrupt integrity it self. If she has given him an opportunity, she
has as good as put her integrity into his hands. Ah dear Marwood,
what's integrity to an opportunity?—Hark! I hear her.—Dear
friend retire into my closet, that I may examine her with more
freedom.—You'll pardon me, dear friend, I can make bold with
you.—There are books over the chimney—Quarles and Prynne,
and the *Short View of the Stage*, with Bunyan's works to entertain you.—[*To Peg.*] Go, you thing, and send her in.   60
> [*Peg goes out one door to admit Foible, and Mrs. Marwood
> another. Foible hurries in, hoping Mrs. Marwood has not
> yet arrived.*

LADY WISHFORT. O Foible, where hast thou been? what hast
thou been doing?

FOIBLE. Madam, I have seen the party.

LADY WISHFORT. But what hast thou done?

FOIBLE. Nay, 'tis your Ladyship has done, and are to do; I have
only promised. But a man so enamoured—so transported! Well,
if worshipping of pictures be a sin—poor Sir Rowland, I say.

LADY WISHFORT. The miniature has been counted like—but hast
thou not betrayed me, Foible? Hast thou not detected me to that
faithless Mirabell?—What hadst thou to do with him in the 70
park? Answer me, has he got nothing out of thee?

FOIBLE. So, the devil has been beforehand with me, what shall
I say?—Alas, madam, could I help it, if I met that confident thing?
Was I in fault? If you had heard how he used me, and all upon
your Ladyship's account, I'm sure you would not suspect my
fidelity. Nay, if that had been the worst I could have born: But
he had a fling at your Ladyship too; and then I could not hold:
But i'faith, I gave him his own.

LADY WISHFORT. Me? What did the filthy fellow say?

FOIBLE. O madam; 'tis a shame to say what he said—with his 80
taunts and his fleers, tossing up his nose. Humh (says he) what
you are a hatching some plot (says he) you are so early abroad,
or catering (says he) ferreting for some disbanded officer, I warrant.—Half pay is but thin subsistance (says he).—Well, what

58. *Quarles*, a prominent sacred poet of the times. *Prynne*, one of the
most vicious attackers of the stage. His *Histriomastix* uses the dramatic
method to present his charges.

59. *Short View* . . . , Jeremy Collier's work, in which Congreve was at-
tacked as one whose work contributed to the general immorality of the
stage.   *Bunyan*, John Bunyan, the author of *Pilgrim's Progress*, etc.

pension does your Lady propose? Let me see (says he) what she must come down pretty deep now, she's superannuated (says he) and—

LADY WISHFORT. Ods my life, I'll have him, I'll have him murdered. I'll have him poisoned. Where does he eat? I'll marry a drawer to have him poison'd in his wine. I'll send for Robin 90 from Lockets—immediately.

FOIBLE. Poison him? Poisoning's too good for him. Starve him, madam, starve him; marry Sir Rowland, and get him disinherited. O you would bless your self, to hear what he said.

LADY WISHFORT. A villain, superannuated!

FOIBLE. Humh (says he) I hear you are laying designs against me too (says he) and Mrs. Millamant is to marry my uncle; (he does not suspect a word of your Ladyship;) but (says he) I'll fit you for that, I warrant you (says he) I'll hamper you for that (says he) you and your old frippery too (says he) I'll handle 100 you—

LADY WISHFORT. Audacious villain! handle me, would he durst! —frippery? old frippery! Was there ever such a foul-mouthed fellow? I'll be married to morrow, I'll be contracted to-night.

FOIBLE. The sooner the better, madam.

LADY WISHFORT. Will Sir Rowland be here, sayest thou? when, Foible?

FOIBLE. Incontinently, madam. No new sheriff's wife expects the return of her husband after knighthood, with that impatience in which Sir Rowland burns for the dear hour of kissing 110 your Ladyship's hand after dinner.

LADY WISHFORT. Frippery! superannuated frippery! I'll frippery the villain; I'll reduce him to frippery and rags: A tatterdemallion —I hope to see him hung with tatters, like a Long-Lane penthouse, or a gibbet-thief. A slander-mouthed railer: I warrant the spendthrift prodigal's in debt as much as the million lottery, or the whole court upon a birth-day. I'll spoil his credit with his tailor. Yes, he shall have my niece with her fortune, he shall.

FOIBLE. He! I hope to see him lodge in Ludgate first, and angle into Black-Fryars for brass farthings, with an old mitten. 120

90-91. *Robin from Lockets*, a waiter in Locket's tavern.
114. *Long-Lane*, where old clothes were sold.
116. *million lottery*, a lottery with a million pounds as prizes.
117. *court upon a birth day*, with all the courtiers penniless because they have spent all their money for presents.
119. *Ludgate*, where a debtor's prison was located, and debtors might beg for coins by angling mittens from the windows into the street.

LADY WISHFORT. Ay dear Foible; thank thee for that, dear Foible.
He has put me out of all patience. I shall never recompose my
features, to receive Sir Rowland with any economy of face. This
wretch has fretted me that I am absolutely decayed. Look Foible.

FOIBLE. Your Ladyship has frown'd a little too rashly, indeed
madam. There are some cracks discernable in the white varnish.

LADY WISHFORT. Let me see the glass—cracks, say'st thou? Why
I am arrantly flea'd—I look like an old peeled wall. Thou must
repair me, Foible, before Sir Rowland comes; or I shall never keep
up to my picture.   130

FOIBLE. I warrant you, madam; a little art once made your picture like you; and now a little of the same art must make you
like your picture. Your picture must sit for you, madam.

LADY WISHFORT. But art thou sure Sir Rowland will not fail to
come? Or will a not fail when he does come? Will he be importunate, Foible, and push? For if he should not be importunate
—I shall never break decorums—I shall die with confusion, if
I am forced to advance.—Oh no, I can never advance—I shall
swoon if he should expect advances. No, I hope Sir Rowland is
better bred, than to put a Lady to the necessity of breaking her
forms. I won't be too coy neither.—I won't give him despair   140
—but a little disdain is not amiss; a little scorn is alluring.

FOIBLE. A little scorn becomes your Ladyship.

LADY WISHFORT. Yes, but tenderness becomes me best—A sort
of dyingness—you see that picture has a sort of a—ha Foible? A
swimmingness in the eyes—yes, I'll look so—my niece affects it;
but she wants features. Is Sir Rowland handsome? Let my toilet
be removed—I'll dress above. I'll receive Sir Rowland here. Is he
handsome? Don't answer me. I won't know: I'll be surprised. I'll
be taken by surprise.

FOIBLE. By storm, madam. Sir Rowland's a brisk man.   150

LADY WISHFORT. Is he! O then he'll importune, if he's a brisk
man. I shall save decorums if Sir Rowland importunes. I have a
mortal terror at the apprehension of offending against decorums.
O I'm glad he's a brisk man. Let my things be removed, good
Foible.

[*She goes out and Foible starts to gather up her things, but
Mrs. Fainall hurries in and interrupts her.*

123. *economy*, good order. Cosmetics of the time were put on like enamel,
and the lady had to settle upon an expression for the day and keep it, lest
she crack the finish.

146. *wants*, lacks.

MRS. FAINALL. O Foible, I have been in a fright, lest I should come too late. That devil, Marwood, saw you in the park with Mirabell, and I'm afraid will discover it to my Lady.

FOIBLE. Discover what, madam?

MRS. FAINALL. Nay, nay, put not on that strange face. I am   160 privy to the whole design, and know Waitwell, to whom thou wert this morning married, is to personate Mirabell's uncle, and as such, winning my Lady, to involve her in those difficulties from which Mirabell only must release her, by his making his conditions to have my cousin and her fortune left to her own disposal.

FOIBLE. O dear madam, I beg your pardon. It was not my confidence in your Ladyship that was deficient; but I thought the former good correspondence between your Ladyship and Mr. Mirabell, might have hindered his communicating this secret.

MRS. FAINALL. Dear Foible, forget that.   170

FOIBLE. O dear madam, Mr. Mirabell is such a sweet winning gentleman—but your Ladyship is the pattern of generosity.— Sweet lady, to be so good! Mr. Mirabell cannot choose but to be grateful. I find your Ladyship has his heart still. Now, madam, I can safely tell your Ladyship our success, Mrs. Marwood had told my Lady; but I warrant I managed my self. I turned it all for the better. I told my Lady that Mr. Mirabell railed at her. I laid horrid things to his charge, I'll vow; and my Lady is so incensed, that she'll be contracted to Sir Rowland to night, she says;—I warrant I worked her up, that he may have her for asking for, as they   180 say of a Welsh maidenhead.

MRS. FAINALL. O rare Foible!

FOIBLE. Madam, I beg your Ladyship to acquaint Mr. Mirabell of his success. I would be seen as little as possible to speak to him—besides, I believe Madam Marwood watches me.—She has a month's mind; but I know Mr. Mirabell can't abide her.— [Calls.] John—remove my Lady's toilet. Madam, your servant. My Lady is so impatient, I fear she'll come for me, if I stay.

MRS. FAINALL. I'll go with you up the back stairs, lest I should meet her.   190

[*They go out together, and Mrs. Marwood emerges from the closet, where she has overheard the whole conversation.*

MRS. MARWOOD. Indeed, Mrs. Engine, is it thus with you? Are you become a go-between of this importance? Yes, I shall watch you. Why this wench is the *Pass-par-toute*, a very master-key to every body's strong box. My friend Fainall, have you carried it so

186. *month's mind*, an inclination toward, a longing.

swimmingly? I thought there was something in it; but it seems
it's over with you. Your loathing is not from a want of appetite
then, but from a surfeit. Else you could never be so cool to fall
from a principal to be an assistant; to procure for him! A pattern
of generosity, that I confess. Well, Mr. Fainall, you have met with
your match.—O man, man! woman, woman! The devil's an   200
ass: If I were a painter, I would draw him like an idiot, a driveler
with a bib and bells. Man should have his head and horns, and
woman the rest of him. Poor simple fiend! Madam Marwood has
a month's mind, but he can't abide her.—'Twere better for him
you had not been his confessor in that affair; without you could
have kept his counsel closer. I shall not prove another pattern of
generosity—he has not obliged me to that with those excesses of
himself; and now I'll have none of him. Here comes the good
Lady, panting ripe; with a heart full of hope, and a head full of
care, like any chemist upon the day of projection.   210

[*Lady Wishfort re-enters.*

LADY WISHFORT. O dear Marwood, what shall I say for this rude
forgetfulness—but my dear friend is all goodness.

MRS. MARWOOD. No apologies, dear madam. I have been very
well entertained.

LADY WISHFORT. As I'm a person I am in a very chaos to think
I should so forget my self—but I have such an olio of affairs
really I know not what to do—[*Calls.*]—Foible—I expect my
nephew Sir Wilfull ev'ry moment too:—Why Foible!—He
means to travel for improvement.

MRS. MARWOOD. Methinks Sir Wilfull should rather think   220
of marrying than travelling at his years. I hear he is turned of
forty.

LADY WISHFORT. O he's in less danger of being spoiled by his
travels.—I am against my nephew's marrying too young. It will
be time enough when he comes back, and has acquired discretion
to choose for himself.

MRS. MARWOOD. Methinks Mrs. Millamant and he would make
a very fit match. He may travel afterwards. 'Tis a thing very
usual with young gentlemen.

LADY WISHFORT. I promise you I have thought on't—and   230
since 'tis your judgment, I'll think on't again. I assure you I will;
I value your judgment extremely. On my word I'll propose it.

[*Foible returns.*

210. *chemist*, alchemist, on day when baser metals are to be changed to
gold. *day of projection*, the day when gold is to be obtained from baser
metals. Cf. the *Alchemist.*

LADY WISHFORT. Come, come Foible—I had forgot my nephew will be here before dinner—I must make haste.

FOIBLE. Mr. Witwoud and Mr. Petulant are come to dine with your Ladyship.

LADY WISHFORT. O Dear, I can't appear 'till I am dressed. Dear Marwood shall I be free with you again, and beg you to entertain 'em. I'll make all imaginable haste. Dear friend excuse me.

[As she hurries out, Mrs. Millamant enters angrily with her maid, Mincing.

MILLAMANT. Sure never any thing was so unbred as that   240 odious man.—Marwood, your servant.

MRS. MARWOOD. You have a colour, what's the matter?

MILLAMANT. That horrid fellow Petulant has provok'd me into a flame—I have broke my fan—Mincing, lend me yours;—is not all the powder out of my hair?

MRS. MARWOOD. No. What has he done?

MILLAMANT. Nay, he has done nothing; he has only talked— Nay, he has said nothing neither; but he has contradicted ev'ry thing that has been said. For my part, I thought Witwoud and he would have quarrell'd.   250

MINCING. I vow, mem, I thought once they would have fitt.

MILLAMANT. Well, 'tis a lamentable thing I swear, that one has not the liberty of choosing one's acquaintance as one does ones clothes.

MRS. MARWOOD. If we had that liberty, we should be as weary of one set of acquaintance, tho' never so good, as we are of one suit, tho' never so fine. A fool and a doily stuff would now and then find days of grace, and be worn for variety.

MILLAMANT. I could consent to wear 'em, if they would wear alike; but fools never wear out—they are such *Drap-de-*   260 *berry* things! Without one could give 'em to ones chamber-maid after a day or two.

MRS. MARWOOD. 'Twere better so indeed. Or what think you of the play-house? A fine gay glossy Fool should be given there, like a new masking habit, after the masquerade is over, and we have done with the disguise. For a fool's visit is always a disguise; and never admitted by a woman of wit, but to blind her affair with a lover of sense. If you would but appear bare-faced now, and own Mirabell; you might as easily put off Petulant and Witwoud, as your hood and scarf. And indeed 'tis time, for   270 the town has found it: the secret is grown too big for the pre-

251. *fitt,* fought.
260-261. *Drap-de-berry,* a woollen cloth imported from France.

tence: 'tis like Mrs. Primly's great belly; she may lace it down before, but it burnishes on her hips. Indeed, Millamant, you can no more conceal it, than my Lady Strammel can her face, that goodly face, which in defiance of her Rhenish-wine tea, will not be comprehended in a mask.

MILLAMANT. I'll take my death, Marwood, you are more censorious than a decayed beauty, or a discarded toast; Mincing, tell the men they may come up. My aunt is not dressing here; their folly is less provoking than your malice.   280

[*Mincing goes out.*

MILLAMANT. The town has found it. What has it found? That Mirabell loves me is no more a secret, than it is a secret that you discovered it to my aunt, or than the reason why you discovered it is a secret.

MRS. MARWOOD. You are nettled.

MILLAMANT. You're mistaken. Ridiculous!

MRS. MARWOOD. Indeed, my dear, you'll tear another fan, if you don't mitigate those violent airs.

MILLAMANT. O silly! Ha, ha, ha. I could laugh immoderately. Poor Mirabell! His constancy to me has quite destroyed his   290 complaisance for all the world beside. I swear, I never enjoined it him, to be so coy.—If I had the vanity to think he would obey me; I would command him to show more gallantry—'tis hardly well bred to be so particular on one hand, and so insensible on the other. But I despair to prevail, and so let him follow his own way. Ha, ha, ha. Pardon me, dear creature, I must laugh, ha, ha, ha; tho' I grant you 'tis a little barbarous, ha, ha, ha.

MRS. MARWOOD. What pity 'tis, so much fine Railery, and deliver'd with so significant gesture, should be so unhappily directed to miscarry.   300

MILLAMANT. Hæ? Dear creature I ask your pardon—I swear I did not mind you.

MRS. MARWOOD. Mr. Mirabell and you both may think it a thing impossible, when I shall tell him by telling you—

MILLAMANT. O dear, what? for it is the same thing, if I hear it— ha, ha, ha.

MRS. MARWOOD. That I detest him, hate him, madam.

MILLAMANT. O madam, why so do I—and yet the creature loves me, ha, ha, ha. How can one forbear laughing to think of it—I am a sybil if I am not amazed to think what he can see in me.   310 I'll take my death, I think you are handsomer—and within a year or two as young.—If you could but stay for me, I should over-

275. *Rhenish-wine tea*, used in reducing.

take you—but that cannot be—well, that thought makes me melancholic—now I'll be sad.

MRS. MARWOOD. Your merry note may be changed sooner than you think.

MILLAMANT. D'ye say so? Then I'm resolved I'll have a song to keep up my spirits.

[*Mincing returns.*

MINCING. The gentlemen stay but to comb, madam; and will wait on you.   320

MILLAMANT. Desire Mrs.—— that is in the next room to sing the song I would have learnt yesterday. You shall hear it, madam —not that there's any great matter in it—but 'tis agreeable to my humour.

SONG

Set by Mr. John Eccles.

I.

Love's but the frailty of the mind,
When 'tis not with ambition join'd;
A sickly flame, which if not fed expires;
And feeding, wastes in self-consuming fires.

II.

'Tis not to wound a wanton boy   330
Or am'rous youth, that gives the joy;
But 'tis the glory to have pierced a swain,
For whom inferior beauties sighed in vain.

III.

Then I alone the conquest prize,
When I insult a rival's eyes:
If there's delight in love, 'tis when I see
That heart which others bleed for, bleed for me.

[*Petulant and Witwoud enter.*

MILLAMANT. Is your animosity composed, gentlemen?

WITWOUD. Raillery, raillery, madam, we have no animosity—

319. *to comb*, i.e., their wigs.

we hit off a little wit now and then, but no animosity.—The   340
falling out of wits is like the falling out of lovers—we agree in
the main, like treble and base. Ha, Petulant!

PETULANT. Ay in the main—but when I have a humour to contradict—

WITWOUD. Ay, when he has a humour to contradict, then I
contradict too. What, I know my cue. Then we contradict one
another like two battledores; for contradictions beget one another like Jews.

PETULANT. If he says black's black—if I have a humour to say
'tis blue—let that pass—all's one for that. If I have a humour   350
to prove it, it must be granted.

WITWOUD. Not positively must—but it may—it may.

PETULANT. Yes, it positively must, upon proof positive.

WITWOUD. Ay, upon proof positive it must; but upon proof
presumptive it only may. That's a logical distinction now, madam.

MRS. MARWOOD. I perceive your debates are of importance, and
very learnedly handled.

PETULANT. Importance is one thing, and learning's another; but
a debate's a debate, that I assert.

WITWOUD. Petulant's an enemy to learning; he relies alto-   360
gether on his parts.

PETULANT. No, I'm no enemy to learning; it hurts not me.

MRS. MARWOOD. That's a sign indeed its no enemy to you.

PETULANT. No, no, it's no enemy to any body, but them that
have it.

MILLAMANT. Well, an illiterate man's my aversion; I wonder
at the impudence of any illiterate man, to offer to make love.

WITWOUD. That I confess I wonder at too.

MILLAMANT. Ah! to marry an ignorant! that can hardly read or
write.   370

PETULANT. Why should a man be any further from being married tho' he can't read, than he is from being hanged. The ordinary's paid for setting the Psalm, and the parish-priest for reading
the ceremony. And for the rest which is to follow in both cases,
a man may do it without book—so all's one for that.

MILLAMANT. D'ye hear the creature? Lord, here's company, I'll
be gone.

[*She goes out, and from the opposite side Sir Wilfull Wit-*

372-373. *ordinary*, the chaplain at Newgate, who read a passage from the
Bible to the condemned.

woud is ushered in by a Footman. Sir Wilfull is a blunt, outspoken country squire, scornful of city ways and manners. He is still dressed in his riding clothes and is in sharp contrast to the foppishly dressed young men in the room.

WITWOUD. In the name of Bartlemew and his fair, what have we here?

MRS. MARWOOD. 'Tis your brother, I fancy. Don't you 380 know him?

WITWOUD. Not I—yes, I think it is he—I've almost forgot him; I have not seen him since the revolution.

FOOTMAN. Sir, my Lady's dressing. Here's company; if you please to walk in, in the mean time.

SIR WILFULL. Dressing! What, it's but morning here I warrant with you in London; we should count it towards afternoon in our parts, down in Shropshire—why then belike my aunt han't dined yet—ha, friend?

FOOTMAN [*Astonished and supercilious*]. Your Aunt, sir? 390

SIR WILFULL. My aunt, sir, yes my aunt, sir, and your lady, sir; your lady is my aunt, sir—why, what do'st thou not know me, friend? Why then send some body hither that does. How long hast thou lived with thy Lady, fellow, ha?

FOOTMAN. A week, sir; longer than any body in the house, except my Lady's woman.

SIR WILFULL. Why then belike thou dost not know thy Lady, if thou seest her, ha friend?

FOOTMAN. Why truly sir, I cannot safely swear to her face in a morning, before she is dressed. 'Tis like I may give a 400 shrewd guess at her by this time.

SIR WILFULL. Well, prithee try what thou canst do; if thou canst not guess, enquire her out, do'st hear, fellow? And tell her, her nephew, sir Wilfull Witwoud, is in the house.

FOOTMAN. I shall, sir.

SIR WILFULL. Hold ye, hear me, friend; a word with you in your ear, prithee who are these gallants?

FOOTMAN. Really, sir, I can't tell; here come so many here, 'tis hard to know 'em all. [*He goes out.*]

378. *Bartlemew*, Bartholomew's Fair was held at Smithfield down to 1855. There were all kinds of entertainments as well as exhibits of various sorts. See Ben Jonson's play, *Bartholomew Fair*.

383. *the revolution*, the "Bloodless Revolution of 1688," in which James II was driven from the throne and succeeded by his daughter, Mary and her husband, William of Orange.

SIR WILFULL. Oons! This fellow knows less than a starling; 410
I don't think a'knows his own name.

MRS. MARWOOD. Mr. Witwoud, your brother is not behind hand
in forgetfulness.—I fancy he has forgot you too.

WITWOUD. I hope so—The devil take him that remembers first,
I say.

SIR WILFULL. Save you gentlemen and lady.

MRS. MARWOOD. For shame, Mr. Witwoud; why don't you
speak to him?—[*To Sir Wilfull.*] And you, sir.

WITWOUD. Petulant, speak.

PETULANT. And you, sir. 420

SIR WILFULL. No offence, I hope. [*Salutes Marwood in the
country fashion, instead of kissing her hand.*]

MRS. MARWOOD. No sure, sir.

WITWOUD. This is a vile dog, I see that already. No offence!
Ha, ha, ha, to him; to him, Petulant, smoke him.

PETULANT [*Surveying him round*]. It seems as if you had come
a journey, sir; hem, hem.

SIR WILFULL. Very likely, sir, that it may seem so.

PETULANT. No offence, I hope, sir. 430

WITWOUD. Smoke the boots, the boots; Petulant, the boots; Ha,
ha, ha.

SIR WILFULL. May be not, sir; thereafter as 'tis meant, sir.

PETULANT. Sir, I presume upon the information of your boots.

SIR WILFULL. Why, 'tis like you may, sir: If you are not satisfied
with the information of my boots, sir, if you will step to the stable,
you may enquire further of my horse, sir.

PETULANT. Your horse, sir! Your horse is an ass, sir!

SIR WILFULL. Do you speak by way of offence, sir?

MRS. MARWOOD. The gentleman's merry, that's all, sir— 440
[*Aside.*] S'life, we shall have a quarrel betwixt an horse and an
ass, before they find one another out. [*To Sir Wilfull.*] You must
not take any thing amiss from your friends, sir. You are among
your friends, here, tho' it may be you don't know it—if I am
not mistaken, you are Sir Wilfull Witwoud.

SIR WILFULL. Right lady; I am Sir Wilfull Witwoud, so I write
my self; no offence to anybody, I hope; and nephew to the Lady
Wishfort of this mansion.

MRS. MARWOOD. Don't you know this gentleman, sir?

SIR WILFULL. Hum! What, sure 'tis not—yea by'r Lady, 450
but 'tis—'sheart I know not whether 'tis or no—yea but 'tis, by the

410. *Oons,* God's wounds.

Wrekin. Brother Antony! What Tony, i'faith! What! do'st thou
not know me? By'r Lady nor I thee, thou art so becravated, and
so beperriwig'd—'sheart why do'st not speak? Art thou o'erjoy'd?

WITWOUD. Odso brother, is it you? Your servant, brother.

SIR WILFULL [*So excited he stammers and puffs*]. Your servant!
Why yours, sir. Your servant again—'sheart, and your friend and
servant to that—and a—and a flap dragon for your service, sir:
And a hare's foot, and a hare's scut for your service, sir; an you
be so cold and so courtly!   460

WITWOUD. No offence, I hope, brother.

SIR WILFULL. 'Sheart, sir, but there is, and much offence.—A
pox, is this your Inns o'.Court breeding, not to know your friends
and your relations, your elders, and your betters?

WITWOUD. Why, brother Wilfull of Salop, you may be as short
as a Shrewsbury cake, if you please. But I tell you 'tis not modish
to know relations in town. You think you're in the country,
where great lubberly brothers slabber and kiss one another when
they meet, like a call of serjeants—'tis not the fashion here; 'tis
not indeed, dear brother.   470

SIR WILFULL. The fashion's a fool; and you're a fop, dear brother.
'Sheart, I've suspected this—by'r Lady, I conjectured you were a
fop, since you began to change the style of your letters, and
write in a scrap of paper gilt round the edges, no bigger than a
subpœna. I might expect this when you left off hououred brother;
and hoping you are in good health, and so forth.—To begin with
a rat me, knight, I'm so sick of a last night's debauch.—'Ods heart,
and then tell a familiar tale of a cock and a bull, and a whore and
a bottle, and so conclude.—You could write news before you
were out of your time, when you lived with honest Pumple-   480
nose the attorney of Furnival's inn.—You could intreat to be remembered then to your friends round the Wrekin. We could have
gazettes then, and Dawks's letter, and the weekly bill, 'till of late
days.

PETULANT. 'Slife, Witwoud, were you ever an attorney's clerk?
Of the family of the Furnivals. Ha, ha, ha!

WITWOUD [*Ashamed*]. Ay, ay, but that was but for a while.

452. *Wrekin*, a high hill near Shrewsbury.

458. *flap dragon*, originally a raisin burning in brandy and caught in the
mouth and eaten. Here anything worthless.

465. *Salop*, Shropshire.

481. *Furnivall's Inn*, one of the inns of chancery, where lawyers resided.

483. *Dawks's letter*, a news letter, founded by one Dawks in 1696, one of
the precursors of the newspaper. *weekly bill*, Bills of Mortality, published
in London.

Not long, not long; pshaw, I was not in my own power then. An
orphan, and this fellow was my guardian; ay, ay, I was glad to
consent to that man to come to London. He had the disposal   490
of me then. If I had not agreed to that, I might have been bound
prentice to a felt-maker in Shrewsbury; this fellow would have
bound me to a maker of felts.

SIR WILFULL. 'Sheart, and better than to be bound to a maker
of fops; where, I suppose, you have served your time; and now
you may set up for your self.

MRS. MARWOOD. You intend to travel, sir, as I'm informed.

SIR WILFULL. Belike I may, madam. I may chance to sail upon
the salt seas, if my mind hold.

PETULANT. And the wind serve.   500

SIR WILFULL. Serve or not serve, I shan't ask license of you, sir;
nor the weather-cock your companion. I direct my discourse to
the lady, sir; 'tis like my aunt may have told you, madam—yes,
I have settled my concerns, I may say now, and am minded to see
foreign parts. If an how that the peace holds, whereby that is,
taxes abate.

MRS. MARWOOD. I thought you had designed for France at all
adventures.

SIR WILFULL. I can't tell that; 'tis like I may, and 'tis like I may
not. I am somewhat dainty in making a resolution,—because   510
when I make it I keep it. I don't stand shill I, shall I, then; if I
say't, I'll do't: But I have thoughts to tarry a small matter in town,
to learn somewhat of your lingo first, before I cross the seas. I'd
gladly have a spice of your French as they say, whereby to hold
discourse in foreign countries.

MRS. MARWOOD. Here's an academy in town for that use.

SIR WILFULL. There is? 'Tis like there may.

MRS. MARWOOD. No doubt you will return very much improv'd.

WITWOUD. Yes, refined like a Dutch skipper from a whale-
fishing.   520

[Lady Wishfort and Fainall enter.

LADY WISHFORT. Nephew, you are welcome.

SIR WILFULL. Aunt, your servant.

FAINALL. Sir Wilfull, your most faithful servant.

SIR WILFULL. Cousin Fainall, give me your hand.

LADY WISHFORT. Cousin Witwoud, your servant; Mr. Petulant,
your servant—nephew, you are welcome again. Will you drink
any thing after your journey, nephew, before you eat? Dinner's
almost ready.

SIR WILFULL. I'm very well I thank you, aunt—however, I   530

thank you for your courteous offer. 'Sheart I was afraid you
would have been in the fashion too, and have remembered to
have forgot your relations. Here's your cousin Tony, belike, I
mayn't call him brother for fear of offence.

LADY WISHFORT. O he's a rallier, nephew—my cousin's a wit:
And your great wits always rally their best friends to choose.
When you have been abroad, nephew, you'll understand raillery
better.

[*Fainall and Mrs. Marwood talk apart; she tells him of what
she has overheard.*

SIR WILFULL. Why then let him hold his tongue in the 540
mean time; and rail when that day comes.

[*Mincing enters.*

MINCING. Mem, I come to acquaint your Laship that dinner is
impatient.

SIR WILFULL. Impatient? Why then belike it won't stay 'till I
pull off my boots. Sweet-heart, can you help me to a pair of
slippers?—My man's with his horses, I warrant. [*He starts to kick
off his muddy riding boots.*]

LADY WISHFORT. Fie, fie, nephew, you would not pull off your
boots here—go down into the hall—dinner shall stay for 550
you—my nephew's a little unbred, you'll pardon him, madam,—
gentlemen will you walk? Marwood?

MRS. MARWOOD. I'll follow you, madam,—before Sir Wilfull
is ready.

[*All go out except Mrs. Marwood and Fainall, who resume
the conversation they have been holding privately during
the last scene. Fainall exclaims indignantly at the way in
which he has been tricked by his wife and Mirabell.*

FAINALL. Why then Foible's a bawd, an errant, rank, match-
making bawd. And I it seems am a husband, a rank-husband; and
my wife a very errant, rank-wife,—all in *The Way of the World*.
'Sdeath to be a cuckold by anticipation, a cuckold in embryo?
Sure I was born with budding antlers like a young satyr, or a
citizen's child. 'Sdeath! to be out-witted, to be out-jilted— 560
out-matrimonied,—if I had kept my speed like a stag, 'twere somewhat,—but to crawl after, with my horns like a snail, and be outstripped by my wife—'tis scurvy wedlock.

MRS. MARWOOD. Then shake it off, you have often wished for an
opportunity to part;—and now you have it. But first prevent
their plot,—the half of Millamant's fortune is too considerable to
be parted with, to a foe, to Mirabell.

FAINALL. Damn him, that had been mine—had you not made
that fond discovery—that had been forfeited, had they been married. My wife had added lustre to my horns, by that encrease 570
of fortune, I could have worn 'em tipt with gold, tho' my forehead had been furnished like a deputy-lieutenant's-hall.

MRS. MARWOOD. They may prove a cap of maintenance to you
still, if you can away with your wife. And she's no worse than
when you had her—I dare swear she had given up her game, before she was married.

FAINALL. Hum! That may be—

MRS. MARWOOD. You married her to keep you; and if you can
contrive to have her keep you better than you expected; why
should you not keep her longer than you intended? 580

FAINALL. The means, the means.

MRS. MARWOOD. Discover to my Lady your wife's conduct;
threaten to part with her.—My Lady loves her, and will come to
any composition to save her reputation. Take the opportunity of
breaking it, just upon the discovery of this imposture. My Lady
will be enraged beyond bounds, and sacrifice niece, and fortune,
and all at that conjuncture. And let me alone to keep her warm;
if she should flag in her part, I will not fail to prompt her.

FAINALL. Faith, this has an appearance.

MRS. MARWOOD. I'm sorry I hinted to my Lady to endeavor 590
a match between Millamant and Sir Wilfull, that may be an
obstacle.

FAINALL. O for that matter leave me to manage him; I'll disable
him for that, he will drink like a Dane: after dinner, I'll set his
hand in.

MRS. MARWOOD. Well, how do you stand affected towards your
Lady?

FAINALL. Why faith I'm thinking of it.—Let me see—I am
married already; so that's over—my wife has plaid the jade with
me—well, that's over too—I never loved her, or if I had, why 600
that would have been over too by this time—jealous of her I
cannot be, for I am certain; so there's an end of jealousie. Weary
of her, I am and shall be—no, there's no end of that; no, no, that
were too much to hope. Thus far concerning my repose. Now
for my reputation,—as to my own, I married not for it; so that's
out of the question.—And as to my part in my wife's—why she
had parted with hers before; so bringing none to me, she can take

572. *Deputy-Lieutenant's Hall,* decorated with antlers.
574. *away with,* endure.

none from me; 'tis against all rule of play, that I should lose to
one, who has not wherewithal to stake.

MRS. MARWOOD. Besides you forget, marriage is honour- 610
able.

FAINALL. Hum! Faith and that's well thought on; marriage is
honourable, as you say; and if so, wherefore should cuckoldom
be a discredit, being derived from so honourable a root?

MRS. MARWOOD. Nay I know not; if the root be honourable,
why not the branches?

FAINALL. So, so, why this point's clear.—Well, how do we
proceed?

MRS. MARWOOD. I will contrive a letter which shall be delivered
to my Lady at the time when that rascal who is to act Sir 620
Rowland is with her. It shall come as from an unknown hand—
for the less I appear to know of the truth, the better I can play
the incendiary. Besides, I would not have Foible provoked if I
could help it,—because you know she knows some passages—
nay I expect all will come out—but let the mine be sprung first,
and then I care not if I am discovered.

FAINALL. If the worst come to the worst,—I'll turn my wife to
grass—I have already a deed of settlement of the best part of her
estate; which I wheedled out of her; and that you shall partake
at least.   630

MRS. MARWOOD. I hope you are convinced that I hate Mirabell
now: You'll be no more jealous?

FAINALL. Jealous, no,—by this kiss—let husbands be jealous;
but let the lover still believe: or if he doubt, let it be only to
endear his pleasure, and prepare the joy that follows, when he
proves his mistress true. But let husbands doubts convert to endless jealousy; or if they have belief, let it corrupt to superstition,
and blind credulity. I am single, and will herd no more with 'em.
True, I wear the badge, but I'll disown the order. And since I
take my leave of 'em, I care not if I leave 'em a common 640
motto to their common crest.

> *All husbands must, or pain, or shame, endure;*
> *The wise too jealous are, fools too secure.*

> [*They go out to dinner.*

END OF THE THIRD ACT

ACT IV

SCENE I

IT IS THE SAME ROOM, *after dinner. Lady Wishfort, all excited at the prospect of seeing "Sir Rowland," enters, followed by, Foible.*

LADY WISHFORT. Is Sir Rowland coming say'st thou, Foible? and are things in order?

FOIBLE. Yes, madam. I have put wax-lights in the sconces; and placed the footmen in a row in the hall, in their best liveries, with the coachman and postilion to fill up the equipage.

LADY WISHFORT. Have you pullvilled the coachman and postilion, that they may not stink of the stable, when Sir Rowland comes by?

FOIBLE. Yes, madam.

LADY WISHFORT. And are the dancers and the musick ready, 10 that he may be entertained in all points with correspondence to his passion?

FOIBLE. All is ready, madam.

LADY WISHFORT. And—well—and how do I look, Foible?

FOIBLE. Most killing well, madam.

LADY WISHFORT. Well, and how shall I receive him? In what figure shall I give his heart the first impression? There is a great deal in the first impression. Shall I sit?—No, I won't sit—I'll walk —ay I'll walk from the door upon his entrance; and then turn full upon him—no, that will be too sudden. I'll lie—ay, I'll lie 20 down—I'll receive him in my little dressing-room, there's a couch —yes, yes, I'll give the first impression on a couch—I won't lie neither, but loll and lean upon one elbow; with one foot a little dangling off, jogging in a thoughtful way—yes—and then as soon as he appears, start, ay, start and be surprised, and rise to meet him in a pretty disorder—yes—O, nothing is more alluring than a levee from a couch in some confusion—it shews the foot to advantage, and furnishes with blushes, and recomposing airs beyond comparison. Hark! there's a coach.

FOIBLE. 'Tis he, madam. 30

LADY WISHFORT. O dear, has my nephew made his addresses to Millamant? I ordered him.

FOIBLE. Sir Wilfull is set in to drinking, madam, in the parlour.

LADY WISHFORT. Ods my life, I'll send him to her. Call her down,

6. *pullvilled,* perfumed with powder.

Foible; bring her hither. I'll send him as I go—when they are
together, then come to me Foible, that I may not be too long
alone with Sir Rowland.

[*She goes out in one direction; Foible in the other, returning
in a moment with Mrs. Millamant and Mrs. Fainall.*

FOIBLE. Madam, I stayed here, to tell your Ladyship that Mr.
Mirabell has waited this half hour for an opportunity to talk
with you. Tho' my Lady's orders were to leave you and Sir   40
Wilfull together. Shall I tell Mr. Mirabell that you are at leisure?

MILLAMANT [*Still aloof, but curious*]. No.—What would the
dear man have? I am thoughtful, and would amuse my self,—bid
him come another time. [*Walking about and quoting Suckling's
verse.*]

> There never yet was woman made,
> Nor shall, but to be curs'd.

That's hard!

MRS. FAINALL. You are very fond of Sir John Suckling to day,
Millamant, and the poets.   50

MILLAMANT. He? Ay, and filthy verses—so I am.

FOIBLE. Sir Wilfull is coming, madam. Shall I send Mr. Mirabell
away?

MILLAMANT. Ay, if you please, Foible, send him away,—or send
him hither,—just as you will, dear Foible.—I think I'll see him—
Shall I? Ay, let the wretch come. [*Repeating a bit from Waller.*]

> Thyrsis, a Youth of the Inspir'd Train.

Dear Fainall, entertain Sir Wilfull—thou hast philosophy to undergo a fool, thou art married and hast patience—I would confer
with my own thoughts.   60

MRS. FAINALL. I am obliged to you, that you would make me
your proxy in this affair; but I have business of my own.

[*Sir Wilfull enters rather diffidently.*

MRS. FAINALL. O Sir Wilfull; you are come at the critical instant.
There's your mistress up to the ears in love and contemplation,
pursue your point, now or never.

SIR WILFULL [*Standing nervously aloof while Millamant walks
about, repeating to herself, as if unaware of his presence*]. Yes;
my aunt will have it so,—I would gladly have been encouraged
with a bottle or two, because I'm somewhat wary at first, before
I am acquainted;—but I hope, after a time, I shall break my   70
mind—that is upon further acquaintance—so for the present,

cousin, I'll take my leave—if so be you'll be so kind to make my excuse, I'll return to my company—

MRS. FAINALL. O fie, Sir Wilfull! What, you must not be daunted.

SIR WILFULL. Daunted, no, that's not it, it is not so much for that—for if so be that I set on't, I'll do't. But only for the present, 'tis sufficient 'till further acquaintance, that's all—your servant.

MRS. FAINALL. Nay, I'll swear you shall never lose so favourable an opportunity, if I can help it. I'll leave you together, and 80 lock the door.

[*With a smirk she leaves them. Sir Wilfull runs after her as soon as he realizes that he is alone with Millamant.*

SIR WILFULL. Nay, nay, cousin,—I have forgot my gloves,— what d'ye do? 'Sheart a'has locked the door indeed, I think.— Nay, cousin Fainall, open the door—pshaw, what a vixen trick is this?—Nay, now a'has seen me too.—[*Bowing and trying the door once again.*] Cousin, I-made bold to pass thro's as it were—I think this door's enchanted—

MILLAMANT [*Repeating, still from Suckling*].

> *I prithee spare me, gentle boy,*
> *Press me no more for that slight toy.* 90

SIR WILFULL. Anan? Cousin, your servant.

MILLAMANT.—*That foolish trifle of a heart*—Sir Wilfull!

SIR WILFULL. Yes—your servant. No offence I hope, cousin.

MILLAMANT [*Repeating*].

> *I swear it will not do its part,*
> *Tho' thou dost thine, employ'st thy power and art.*

Natural, easy Suckling!

SIR WILFULL. Anan? Suckling? No such suckling neither, cousin, nor stripling: I thank heaven I'm no minor.

MILLAMANT. Ah rustic, ruder than Gothick. 100

SIR WILFULL. Well, well, I shall understand your lingo one of these days, cousin, in the mean while I must answer in plain English.

MILLAMANT. Have you any business with me, Sir Wilfull?

SIR WILFULL. Not at present, cousin,—yes, I made bold to see, to come and know if that how you were disposed to fetch a walk this evening, if so be that I might not be troublesome, I would have sought a walk with you.

MILLAMANT. A walk? What then?

91. *Anan*, what did you say?

SIR WILFULL. Nay nothing—only for the walk's sake, that's   110
all—

MILLAMANT. I nauseate walking; 'tis a country diversion, I
loath the country and every thing that relates to it.

SIR WILFULL. Indeed! Hah! Look ye, look ye, you do? nay, 'tis
like you may—here are choice of pastimes here in town, as plays
and the like, that must be confessed indeed.—

MILLAMANT. Ah l'etourdie! I hate the town too.

SIR WILFULL. Dear heart, that's much—hah! that you should
hate 'em both! Hah! 'tis like you may; there are some can't relish
the town, and others can't away with the country,—'tis like   120
you may be one of those, cousin.

MILLAMANT. Ha, ha, ha. Yes, 'tis like I may.—[A pause.] You
have nothing further to say to me?

SIR WILFULL. Not at present, cousin.—'Tis like when I have an
opportunity to be more private,—I may break my mind in some
measure—I conjecture you partly guess—however, that's as time
shall try,—but spare to speak and spare to speed, as they say.

MILLAMANT. If it is of no great importance, Sir Wilfull, you
will oblige me to leave me: I have just now a little business.—

SIR WILFULL [Greatly relieved]. Enough, enough, cousin: 130
yes, yes, all a case—when you're disposed, when you're disposed.
Now's as well as another time; and another time as well as now.
All's one for that,—yes; yes, if your concerns call you, there's no
haste; it will keep cold as they say—cousin, your servant.—I think
this door's locked. [He tries the door again.]

MILLAMANT [At the other door]. You may go this way, sir.

SIR WILFULL. Your servant, then with your leave I'll return to
my company.

MILLAMANT. Ay, ay; ha, ha, ha.

Like Phœbus sung the no less am'rous Boy.   140

[Sir Wilfull goes out the door indicated by Millamant just
as the other door is unlocked and Mirabell enters.

MIRABELL.—Like Daphne she, as Lovely and as Coy. Do you
lock your self up from me, to make my search more curious?
Or is this pretty artifice contrived, to signify that here the chase
must end, and my pursuit be crowned, for you can fly no further?—

MILLAMANT. Vanity! No—I'll fly and be followed to the last
moment, tho' I am upon the very verge of matrimony, I expect

117. *l'etourdie,* such dulness!

you should solicit me as much as if I were wavering at the grate
of a monastery, with one foot over the threshold. I'll be solicited
to the very last, nay and afterwards.   150

MIRABELL. What, after the last?

MILLAMANT. O, I should think I was poor and had nothing to
bestow, if I were reduced to an inglorious ease; and freed from
the agreeable fatigues of solicitation.

MIRABELL. But do not you know, that when favours are con-
ferred upon instant and tedious solicitation, that they diminish in
their value, and that both the giver loses the grace, and the receiver
lessens his pleasure?

MILLAMANT. It may be in things of common application; but
never sure in love. O, I hate a lover, that can dare to think he   160
draws a moment's air, independent on the bounty of his mistress.
There is not so impudent a thing in nature, as the sawcy look
of an assured man, confident of success. The pedantic arrogance
of a very husband, has not so pragmatical an air. Ah! I'll never
marry, unless I am first made sure of my will and pleasure.

MIRABELL. Would you have 'em both before marriage? Or will
you be contented with the first now, and stay for the other 'till
after grace?

MILLAMANT. Ah don't be impertinent.—My dear liberty, shall
I leave thee? My faithful solitude, my darling contemplation,   170
must I bid you then adieu? Ay-h adieu—my morning thoughts,
agreeable wakings, indolent slumbers, all ye *douceurs*, ye *Someils
du Matin*, adieu.—I can't do't, 'tis more than impossible—positively Mirabell, I'll lie a-bed in a morning as long as I please.

MIRABELL. Then I'll get up in a morning as early as I please.

MILLAMANT. Ah! Idle creature, get up when you will—and
d'ye hear, I won't be called names after I'm married; positively
I won't be called names.

MIRABELL. Names!

MILLAMANT. Ay, as wife, spouse, my dear, joy, jewel, love,   180
sweetheart, and the rest of that nauseous cant, in which men and
their wives are so fulsomly familiar,—I shall never bear that.—
Good Mirabell don't let us be familiar or fond, nor kiss before
folks, like my Lady Fadler and Sir Francis: Nor go to Hyde-Park
together the first Sunday in a new chariot, to provoke eyes and
whispers; and then never be seen there together again; as if we
were proud of one another the first week, and ashamed of one
another ever after. Let us never visit together, nor go to a play

172. *douceurs, etc.,* ye sweets, ye morning naps.

together, but let us be very strange and well bred: let us be as
strange as if we had been married a great while; and as well   190
bred as if we were not married at all.

MIRABELL. Have you any more conditions to offer? Hitherto
your demands are pretty reasonable.

MILLAMANT. Trifles,—as liberty to pay and receive visits to and
from whom I please; to write and receive letters, without interrogatories or wry faces on your part; to wear what I please; and
choose conversation with regard only to my own taste; to have
no obligation upon me to converse with wits that I don't like, because they are your acquaintance; or to be intimate with fools,
because they may be your relations. Come to dinner when I   200
please, dine in my dressing-room when I'm out of humour, without giving a reason. To have my closet inviolate; to be sole empress
of my tea-table, which you must never presume to approach
without first asking leave. And lastly wherever I am, you shall
always knock at the door before you come in. These articles
subscribed, if I continue to endure you a little longer, I may by
degrees dwindle into a wife.

MIRABELL. Your bill of fare is something advanced in this latter
account. Well, have I liberty to offer conditions:—that when you
are dwindled into a wife, I may not be beyond measure en-   210
larged into a husband.

MILLAMANT. You have free leave, propose your utmost, speak
and spare not.

MIRABELL. I thank you. *Inprimis* then, I covenant that your
acquaintance be general; that you admit no sworn confident, or
intimate of your own sex; no she friend to screen her affairs under
your countenance, and tempt you to make trial of a mutual
secresy. No decoy-duck to wheedle you a fop—scrambling to the
play in a mask—then bring you home in a pretended fright, when
you think you shall be found out—and rail at me for missing   220
the play, and disappointing the frolic which you had to pick me
up and prove my constancy.

MILLAMANT. Detestable *inprimis!* I go to the play in a mask!

MIRABELL. *Item,* I article, that you continue to like your own
face, as long as I shall: and while it passes current with me, that
you endeavour not to new coin it. To which end, together with
all vizards for the day, I prohibit all masks for the night, made of
oiled-skins and I know not what—hog's bones, hare's gall, pig
water, and the marrow of a roasted cat. In short, I forbid all
commerce with the gentlewoman in what-d'ye-call-it court.   230
Item, I shut my doors against all bawds with baskets, and penny-

worths of Muslin, China, Fans, Atlasses, &c.—*Item*, when you shall be breeding—

MILLAMANT. Ah! name it not.

MIRABELL. Which may be presumed, with a blessing on our endeavours—

MILLAMANT. Odious endeavours!

MIRABELL. I denounce against all strait lacing, squeezing for a shape, 'till you mould my boy's head like a sugar-loaf; and instead of a man-child, make me father to a crooked-billet. Lastly, to 240 the dominion of the tea-table I submit.—But with proviso, that you exceed not in your province; but restrain your self to native and simple tea-table drinks, as tea, chocolate, and coffee. As likewise to genuine and authorized tea-table talk—such as mending of fashions, spoiling reputations, railing at absent friends, and so forth—but that on no account you encroach upon the men's prerogative, and presume to drink healths, or toast fellows; for prevention of which, I banish all foreign forces, all auxiliaries to the tea-table, as orange-brandy, all anniseed, cinamon, citron and Barbadoes-waters, together with ratafia and the most noble 250 spirit of clary.—But for couslip-wine, poppy-water, and all dormitives, those I allow.—These proviso's admitted, in other things I may prove a tractable and complying husband.

MILLAMANT. O horrid provisos! filthy strong waters! I toast fellows, odious men! I hate your odious provisos.

MIRABELL. Then we're agreed. Shall I kiss your hand upon the contract? and here comes one to be a witness to the sealing of the deed.

[*Mrs. Fainall enters.*

MILLAMANT. Fainall, what shall I do? Shall I have him? I think I must have him. 260

MRS. FAINALL. Ay, ay, take him, take him, what should you do?

MILLAMANT. Well then—I'll take my death I'm in a horrid fright—Fainall, I shall never say it—Well—I think—I'll endure you.

MRS. FAINALL. Fy, fy, have him, have him, and tell him so in plain terms: for I am sure you have a mind to him.

MILLAMANT. Are you? I think I have—and the horrid man looks as if he thought so too.—Well, you ridiculous thing you, I'll have you—I won't be kissed, nor I won't be thanked.—Here kiss my hand tho'—so, hold your tongue now, don't say a word. 270

250. *Barbadoes-waters*, a cordial flavored with orange or lemon peel.
251. *clary*, a liquor made from wine and honey flavored with cinnamon and other spices.

MRS. FAINALL. Mirabell, there's a necessity for your obedience;
—you have neither time to talk nor stay. My mother is coming;
and in my conscience if she should see you, would fall into fits,
and may be not recover, time enough to return to Sir Rowland;
who, as Foible tells me, is in a fair way to succeed. Therefore spare
your ecstasies for another occasion, and slip down the back stairs,
where Foible waits to consult you.

MILLAMANT. Ay, go, go. In the mean time I suppose you have
said something to please me.

MIRABELL. I am all obedience.   [*He goes out.* 280

MRS. FAINALL. Yonder Sir Wilfull's drunk; and so noisy that
my mother has been forced to leave Sir Rowland to appease him;
but he answers her only with singing and drinking.—What they
may have done by this time I know not; but Petulant and he were
upon quarrelling as I came by.

MILLAMANT. Well, if Mirabell should not make a good husband,
I am a lost thing;—for I find I love him violently.

MRS. FAINALL. So it seems; for you mind not what's said to you.
—If you doubt him, you had best take up with Sir Wilfull.

MILLAMANT. How can you name that superannuated lub- 290
ber? foh!

[*Enter Witwoud who has been drinking.*

MRS. FAINALL. So, is the fray made up, that you have left 'em?

WITWOUD. Left 'em? I could stay no longer—I have laughed
like ten Christnings—I am tipsy with laughing—if I had staid any
longer I should have burst,—I must have been let out and pieced
in the sides like an unsized camlet—yes, yes, the fray is composed;
my Lady came in like a *noli prosequi*, and stopt the proceedings.

MILLAMANT. What was the dispute?

WITWOUD. That's the jest; there was no dispute. They could
neither of 'em speak for rage; and so fell a sputt'ring at one 300
another like two roasting apples.

[*Petulant staggers in, drunk.*

WITWOUD. Now Petulant? all's over, all's well? Gad my head
begins to whim it about—why dost thou not speak? thou art both
as drunk and as mute as a fish.

PETULANT. Look you, Mrs. Millamant—if you can love me,
dear nymph—say it—and that's the conclusion—pass on, or pass
off,—that's all.

WITWOUD. Thou hast utter'd volumes, folio's, in less than

297. *noli prosequi*, notice of unwillingness to prosecute a case in court.

decimo sexto, my dear Lacedemonian. Sirrah, Petulant, thou art
an epitomizer of words.   310

PETULANT. Witwoud—You are an annihilator of sense.

WITWOUD. Thou art a retailer of phrases; and dost deal in remnants of remnants, like a maker of pincushions—thou art in truth
(metaphorically speaking) a speaker of short-hand.

PETULANT. Thou art (without a figure) just one half of an ass,
and Baldwin yonder, thy half brother, is the rest—a Gemini of
asses split, would make just four of you.

WITWOUD. Thou dost bite, my dear mustard-seed; kiss me for
that.

PETULANT. Stand off—I'll kiss no more males,—I have   320
kiss'd your twin yonder in a humour of reconciliation, 'till he
[*hiccup*] rises upon my stomach like a radish.

MILLAMANT. Eh! filthy creature—what was the quarrel?

PETULANT. There was no quarrel—there might have been a
quarrel.

WITWOUD. If there had been words enow between 'em to have
expressed provocation, they had gone together by the ears like
a pair of castanets.

PETULANT. You were the quarrel.

MILLAMANT. Me!   330

PETULANT. If I have a humour to quarrel, I can make less matters conclude premises,—if you are not handsome, what then; if
I have a humour to prove it?—If I shall have my reward, say so;
if not, fight for your face the next time your self—I'll go sleep.

WITWOUD. Do, wrap thy self up like a woodlouse, and dream
revenge—and hear me, if thou canst learn to write by to morrow
morning, pen me a challenge—I'll carry it for thee.

PETULANT. Carry your mistress's monkey a spider,—go flea
Dogs, and read romances—I'll go to bed to my maid.

MRS. FAINALL. He's horridly drunk—how came you all in   340
this pickle?

WITWOUD. A plot, a plot, to get rid of the knight,—your husband's advice; but he sneaked off.

[*Enter Sir Wilfull, even drunker than Sir Petulant, Lady
Wishfort is with him.*

LADY WISHFORT. Out upon't, out upon't, at years of discretion,
and comport your self at this rantipole rate.

309. *Lacedemonian*, one who speaks curtly, as the Spartans did.
316. *Baldwin*, the ass in the medieval beast epic of Reynard the Fox.
Gemini, twins, Castor and Pollux, but here, as often, simply pair.

SIR WILFULL. No offence, aunt.

LADY WISHFORT. Offence? As I'm a person, I'm ashamed of you—fogh! how you stink of wine! D'ye think my niece will ever endure such a Borachio! you're an absolute Borachio.

SIR WILFULL. Borachio!   350

LADY WISHFORT. At a time when you should commence an amour, and put your best foot foremost—

SIR WILFULL. 'Sheart, an you grutch me your liquor, make a bill—give me more drink, and take my purse.

[*Sings.*]   *Prithee fill me the glass*
'Till it laugh in my face,
With ale that is potent and mellow;
He that whines for a lass
Is an ignorant ass,
For a Bumper has not its fellow.   360

But if you would have me marry my cousin,—say the word, and I'll do't—Wilfull will do't, that's the word—Wilfull will do't, that's my crest—my motto I have forgot.

LADY WISHFORT [*Apologetically to Millamant*]. My nephew's a little overtaken, cousin—but 'tis with drinking your health.—O' my word you are obliged to him—

SIR WILFULL. *In vino veritas*, Aunt:—if I drunk your health to day, cousin,—I am a Borachio. But if you have a mind to be married, say the word, and send for the piper, Wilfull will do't. If not, dust it away, and let's have t'other round.—Tony,   370 ods-heart where's Tony—Tony's an honest fellow, but he spits after a bumper, and that's a fault,

[*Sings.*]   *We'll drink and we'll never ha' done boys,*
Put the glass then around with the sun boys,
Let Apollo's example invite us;
For he's drunk ev'ry night,
And that makes him so bright,
That he's able next morning to light us.

The sun's a good pimple, an honest soaker, he has a cellar at your Antipodes. If I travel, aunt, I touch at your Antipodes—   380 your Antipodes are a good rascally sort of topsie turvy fellows —if I had a Bumper I'd stand upon my head and drink a health to 'em—a match or no match, cousin, with the hard name—aunt,

349. *Borachio*, drunkard, lit., wine-skin.
367. *In vino veritas*, There is truth in wine.
379. *good pimple*, jolly companion.

Wilfull will do't. If she has her maidenhead let her look to't; if she has not, let her keep her own counsel in the mean time, and cry out at the nine months end.

MILLAMANT. Your pardon, madam, I can stay no longer—Sir Wilfull grows very powerful, egh! how he smells! I shall be overcome if I stay. Come, cousin. [*She and Mrs. Fainall go out with show of great distress.*]   390

LADY WISHFORT. Smells! he would poison a tallow-chandler and his family. Beastly creature, I know not what to do with him.— Travel quoth a; ay travel, travel, get thee gone, get thee but far enough, to the Saracens, or the Tartars, or the Turks—for thou art not fit to live in a christian commonwealth, thou beastly pagan.

SIR WILFULL. Turks, no; no Turks, aunt: your Turks are Infidels, and believe not in the grape. Your Mahometan, your Mussulman is a dry stinkard—no offence, aunt. My map says that your Turk is not so honest a man as your Christian—I cannot find   400 by the map that your Mufti is orthodox—whereby it is a plain case, that orthodox is a hard word, aunt, and (*hiccup*) Greek for claret.

[*Sings.*]   *To drink is a Christian diversion.*
           Unknown to the Turk or the Persian:
              Let Mahometan fools
              Live by heathenish rules,
           And be damn'd over tea-cups and coffee.
              But let British lads sing,
              Crown a health to the king,   410
           And a fig for your Sultan and Sophy.

Ah, Tony!
      [*Foible enters and whispers to Lady Wishfort. The conspirators are anxious to prosecute "Sir Rowland's" wooing.*

LADY WISHFORT [*Aside*]. Sir Rowland impatient? Good lack! what shall I do with this beastly tumbril?—Go lie down and sleep, you sot—or as I'm a person, I'll have you bastinadoed with broom-sticks. Call up the wenches with broom-sticks.

SIR WILFULL. Ahay? Wenches, where are the wenches?

LADY WISHFORT. Dear cousin Witwoud get him away, and you will bind me to you inviolably. I have an affair of moment that invades me with some precipitation.—You will oblige me to   420 all futurity.

WITWOUD. Come, knight—pox on him, I don't know what to say to him—will you go to a cockmatch?

SIR WILFULL. With a wench, Tony? Is she a shakebag, sirrah? Let me bite your cheek for that.

WITWOUD. Horrible! He has a breath like a bagpipe.—Ay, ay, come will you march, my Salopian?

SIR WILFULL. Lead on, little Tony—I'll follow thee my Anthony, my Tantony, sirrah thou shalt be my Tantony, and I'll be thy Pig. 430

—*And a Fig for your Sultan and Sophy.*

LADY WISHFORT. This will never do. It will never make a match. —At least before he has been abroad.

[*But her regret at the loss of a match between Millamant and Sir Wilfull is lost in her excitement at the entrance of Waitwell disguised as Sir Rowland. She musters all the dignity she can.*

LADY WISHFORT. Dear Sir Rowland, I am confounded with confusion at the retrospection of my own rudeness,—I have more pardons to ask than the Pope distributes in the year of Jubilee. But I hope where there is likely to be so near an alliance,—we may unbend the severity of decorum—and dispense with a little ceremony.

WAITWELL. My impatience, madam, is the effect of my 440 transport;—and 'till I have the possession of your adorable person, I am tantalized on the rack; and do but hang, madam, on the tenter of expectation.

LADY WISHFORT. You have excess of gallantry, Sir Rowland; and press things to a conclusion, with a most prevailing vehemence. —But a day or two for decency of marriage.—

WAITWELL. For decency of funeral, madam. The delay will break my heart—or if that should fail, I shall be poisoned. My nephew will get an inkling of my designs, and poison me,—and I would willingly starve him before I die—I would gladly 450 go out of the world with that satisfaction.—That would be some comfort to me, if I could but live so long as to be revenged on that unnatural viper.

LADY WISHFORT. Is he so unnatural, say you? Truly I would contribute much both to the saving of your life, and the accomplishment of your revenge—not that I respect my self; tho' he has been a perfidious wretch to me.

WAITWELL. Perfidious to you!

LADY WISHFORT. O Sir Rowland, the hours that he has died

---

427. *Salopian*, resident of Shropshire.

away at my feet, the tears that he has shed, the oaths that he 460
has sworn, the palpitations that he has felt, the trances and the
tremblings, the ardors and the ecstasies, the kneelings, and the
risings, the heart-heavings and the hand-gripings, the pangs and
the pathetic regards of his protesting eyes! Oh no memory can
register.

WAITWELL. What, my rival! Is the rebel my rival? a'dies.

LADY WISHFORT. No, don't kill him at once, Sir Rowland, starve
him gradually inch by inch.

WAITWELL. I'll do't. In three weeks he shall be bare-foot; in a
month out at knees with begging an alms,—he shall starve 470
upward and upward, 'till he has nothing living but his head, and
then go out in a stink like a candle's end upon a saveall.

LADY WISHFORT. Well, Sir Rowland, you have the way,—you
are no novice in the labyrinth of love—you have the clue.—But
as I am a person, Sir Rowland, you must not attribute my yielding
to any sinister appetite, or indigestion of widowhood; nor impute
my complacency to any lethargy of continence—I hope you do
not think me prone to any iteration of nuptials.—

WAITWELL. Far be it from me—

LADY WISHFORT. If you do, I protest I must recede—or 480
think that I have made a prostitution of decorums, but in the
vehemence of compassion, and to save the life of a person of so
much importance—

WAITWELL. I esteem it so—

LADY WISHFORT. Or else you wrong my condescension—

WAITWELL. I do not, I do not—

LADY WISHFORT. Indeed you do.

WAITWELL. I do not, fair shrine of virtue.

LADY WISHFORT. If you think the least scruple of carnality was
an ingredient— 490

WAITWELL. Dear madam, no. You are all camphire and frankin-
cense, all chastity and odour.

LADY WISHFORT. Or that—

[*Foible enters.*

FOIBLE. Madam, the dancers are ready, and there's one with a
letter, who must deliver it into your own hands.

LADY WISHFORT. Sir Rowland, will you give me leave? Think
favourably, judge candidly, and conclude you have found a person who would suffer racks in honour's cause, dear Sir Rowland,

---

472. *saveall,* a candle-holder with a spike for holding butts of candles.
491. *camphire,* popularly supposed to cause impotence.

and will wait on you incessantly. [*She goes out, and Waitwell turns with relief to his wife, Foible.*]   500

WAITWELL. Fie, fie!—What a slavery have I undergone; spouse, hast thou any cordial, I want spirits.

FOIBLE. What a washy rogue art thou, to pant thus for a quarter of an hours lying and swearing to a fine lady?

WAITWELL. O, she is the antidote to desire. Spouse, thou wilt fare the worse for't—I shall have no appetite to iteration of nuptials—this eight and forty hours.—By this hand I'd rather be a chairman in the dog-days—than act Sir Rowland 'till this time to morrow.

[*Lady Wishfort returns with a Letter.*]

LADY WISHFORT [*To Foible*]. Call in the dancers;—Sir   510 Rowland, we'll sit, if you please, and see the entertainment.

[*Dance.*]

Now with your permission, Sir Rowland, I will peruse my letter—I would open it in your presence, because I would not make you uneasy. If it should make you uneasy I would burn it— speak if it does—but you may see, the superscription is like a woman's hand.

FOIBLE [*Aside to Waitwell*]. By heav'n! Mrs. Marwood's, I know it,—my heart aches—get it from her—

WAITWELL. A woman's hand? No, madam, that's no woman's hand, I see that already. That's some body whose throat   520 must be cut.

LADY WISHFORT. Nay, Sir Rowland, since you give me a proof of your passion by your jealousy, I promise you I'll make a return, by a frank communication—you shall see it—we'll open it together—look you here.

[*Reads.*] *Madam, though unknown to you,* (Look you there, 'tis from no body that I know.)—*I have that honour for your character, that I think my self oblig'd to let you know you are abused. He who pretends to be Sir Rowland is a cheat and a rascal—*   530

Oh heav'ns! what's this?

FOIBLE [*Aside*]. Unfortunate, all's ruin'd.

WAITWELL. How, how, let me see, let me see—[*Reading.*] *A rascal and disguised, and suborned for that imposture,*—O villainy! O villainy!—*by the contrivance of*—

LADY WISHFORT. I shall faint, I shall die, oh!

---

508. *chairman,* i.e., a bearer of a sedan chair in which people rode instead of in carriages.

FOIBLE [*Aside to Waitwell*]. Say, 'tis your nephew's hand.—
Quickly, his plot, swear, swear it.—

WAITWELL. Here's a villain! Madam, don't you perceive it,
don't you see it? 540

LADY WISHFORT. Too well, too well. I have seen too much.

WAITWELL. I told you at first I knew the hand—a woman's
hand? The rascal writes a sort of a large hand; your Roman hand
—I saw there was a throat to be cut presently. If he were my
son, as he is my nephew, I'd pistol him—

FOIBLE. O treachery! But are you sure, Sir Rowland, it is his
writing?

WAITWELL. Sure? Am I here? do I live? do I love this pearl
of India? I have twenty letters in my pocket from him, in the
same character. 550

LADY WISHFORT. How!

FOIBLE. O what luck it is, Sir Rowland, that you were present
at this juncture! This was the business that brought Mr. Mirabell
disguised to Madam Millamant this afternoon. I thought something was contriving, when he stole by me and would have hid
his face.

LADY WISHFORT. How, how!—I heard the villain was in the
house indeed; and now I remember, my niece went away abruptly, when Sir Wilfull was to have made his addresses.

FOIBLE. Then, then madam, Mr. Mirabell waited for her in 560
her chamber; but I would not tell your ladyship to discompose
you when you were to receive Sir Rowland.

WAITWELL. Enough, his date is short.

FOIBLE. No, good Sir Rowland, don't incur the law.

WAITWELL. Law! I care not for law. I can but die, and 'tis in a
good cause—my Lady shall be satisfied of my truth and innocence, tho' it cost me my life.

LADY WISHFORT. No, dear Sir Rowland, don't fight, if you
should be killed I must never show my face; or hanged,—O consider my reputation, Sir Rowland—no you shan't fight,—I'll 570
go and examine my niece; I'll make her confess. I conjure you
Sir Rowland by all your love not to fight.

WAITWELL. I am charmed madam, I obey. But some proof you
must let me give you;—I'll go for a black box, which contains the
writings of my whole estate, and deliver that into your hands.

LADY WISHFORT. Ay dear Sir Rowland, that will be some comfort, bring the black box.

WAITWELL. And may I presume to bring a contract to be signed
this night? May I hope so far?

LADY WISHFORT. Bring what you will; but come alive,   580
pray come alive. O this is a happy discovery.

WAITWELL. Dead or alive I'll come—and married we will be
in spite of treachery; ay and get an heir that shall defeat the last
remaining glimpse of hope in my abandoned nephew. Come, my
buxom widow:

> *E'er long you shall substantial proof receive*
> *That I'm an arrant knight—*

FOIBLE.   *Or arrant knave.*

[*He goes out one door while Foible supports her excited
mistress out the other.*

END OF THE FOURTH ACT

ACT V

SCENE I

*Lady Wishfort has discovered the plot against her and is venting
her rage on Foible.*

LADY WISHFORT. Out of my house, out of my house, thou viper,
thou serpent, that I have fostered; thou bosom traitress, that I
raised from nothing.—Begone, begone, begone, go, go,—that I
took from washing of old gauze and weaving of dead hair, with
a bleak blue nose, over a chafing-dish of starved embers, and dining behind a traverse rag, in a shop no bigger than a bird-cage,—
go, go, starve again, do, do.

FOIBLE. Dear madam, I'll beg pardon on my knees.

LADY WISHFORT. Away, out, out, go set up for your self again
—do, drive a trade, do, with your three-penny-worth of small   10
ware, flaunting upon a packthread, under a brandy-sellers bulk,
or against a dead wall by a ballad-monger. Go, hang out an old
Frisoneer-gorget, with a yard of yellow colberteen again; do; an
old gnawed mask, two rows of pins and a child's fiddle; a glass
necklace with the beads broken, and a quilted night-cap with one
ear. Go, go, drive a trade,—these were your commodities, you

11. *Bulk*, stall.

13. *Frisoneer-gorget*, a woollen scarf to protect the throat. *colberteen*, a
kind of lace.

treacherous trull, this was the merchandize you dealt in, when I took you into my house, placed you next my self, and made you governante of my whole family. You have forgot this, have you, now you have feathered your nest? 20

FOIBLE. No, no, dear madam. Do but hear me, have but a moment's patience—I'll confess all. Mr. Mirabell seduced me; I am not the first that he has wheedled with his dissembling tongue; your ladyship's own wisdom has been deluded by him, then how should I, a poor ignorant, defend my self? O madam, if you knew but what he promised me, and how he assured me your Ladyship should come to no damage—or else the wealth of the Indies should not have bribed me to conspire against so good, so sweet, so kind a lady as you have been to me.

LADY WISHFORT. No damage? What, to betray me, to marry 30 me to a cast-serving-man; to make me a receptacle, an hospital for a decayed pimp? No damage? O thou frontless impudence, more than a big-bellied actress.

FOIBLE. Pray do but hear me madam, he could not marry your Ladyship, madam—no indeed, his marriage was to have been void in law; for he was married to me first, to secure your Ladyship. He could not have bedded your Ladyship; for if he had consummated with your Ladyship, he must have run the risk of the law, and been put upon his clergy.—Yes indeed, I enquired of the law in that case before I would meddle or make. 40

LADY WISHFORT. What, then I have been your property, have I? I have been convenient to you, it seems,—while you were catering for Mirabell; I have been broker for you? What, have you made a passive bawd of me?—this exceeds all precedent; I am brought to fine uses, to become a botcher of second-hand marriages between Abigails and Andrews! I'll couple you. Yes, I'll baste you together, you and your Philander. I'll Duke's-Place you, as I'm a person. Your turtle is in custody already: you shall coo in the same cage, if there be constable or warrant in the parish. [She goes out.] 50

FOIBLE. O that ever I was born, O that I was ever married,—a bride, ay I shall be a Bridewell-bride. Oh!

[Mrs. Fainall enters.

MRS. FAINALL. Poor Foible, what's the matter?

FOIBLE. O madam, my Lady's gone for a constable; I shall be

39. *put upon his clergy*, forced to plead benefit of clergy to escape from punishment by civil law.
46. *Abigails and Andrews*, names for servants.
52. *Bridewell*, the jail where prostitutes were confined.

had to a justice, and put to Bridewell to beat hemp; poor Waitwell's gone to prison already.

MRS. FAINALL. Have a good heart, Foible, Mirabell's gone to
give security for him. This is all Marwood's and my husband's
doing.

FOIBLE. Yes, yes, I know it, madam; she was in my Lady's 60
closet, and overheard all that you said to me before dinner. She
sent the letter to my lady; and that missing effect, Mr. Fainall
laid this plot to arrest Waitwell, when he pretended to go for
the papers; and in the mean time Mrs. Marwood declared all to
my lady.

MRS. FAINALL. Was there no mention made of me in the letter?
—My mother does not suspect my being in the confederacy? I
fancy Marwood has not told her, tho' she has told my husband.

FOIBLE. Yes, madam; but my lady did not see that part: we
stifled the letter before she read so far. Has that mischievous 70
devil told Mr. Fainall of your Ladyship then?

MRS. FAINALL. Ay, all's out, my affair with Mirabell, every thing
discovered. This is the last day of our living together, that's my
comfort.

FOIBLE. Indeed madam, and so 'tis a comfort if you knew all,—
he has been even with your Ladyship; which I could have told
you long enough since, but I love to keep peace and quietness by
my good will: I had rather bring friends together, than set 'em
at distance. But Mrs. Marwood and he are nearer related than ever
their parents thought for. 80

MRS. FAINALL. Say'st thou so, Foible? Canst thou prove this?

FOIBLE. I can take my oath of it, madam, so can Mrs. Mincing;
we have had many a fair word from Madam Marwood, to conceal
something that passed in our chamber one evening when you
were at Hyde-Park;—and we were thought to have gone a walking: But we went up unawares,—tho' we were sworn to secresy
too; Madam Marwood took a book and swore us upon it: but it
was but a book of poems,—so long as it was not a bible-oath, we
may break it with a safe conscience.

MRS. FAINALL. This discovery is the most opportune thing 90
I could wish. Now Mincing?

[Mincing enters.

MINCING. My lady would speak with Mrs. Foible, mem. Mr.
Mirabell is with her; he has set your spouse at liberty, Mrs. Foible,
and would have you hide your self in my Lady's closet, 'till my
old Lady's anger is abated. O, my old Lady is in a perilous pas-

sion, at something Mr. Fainall has said; he swears, and my old
Lady cries. There's a fearful hurricane I vow. He says, mem, how
that he'll have my Lady's fortune made over to him, or he'll be
divorced.

MRS. FAINALL. Does your Lady or Mirabell know that? 100

MINCING. Yes mem, they have sent me to see if Sir Wilfull be
sober, and to bring him to them. My Lady is resolved to have him
I think, rather than lose such a vast sum as six thousand pound.
O, come Mrs. Foible, I hear my old Lady.

MRS. FAINALL. Foible, you must tell Mincing, that she must prepare to vouch when I call her.

FOIBLE. Yes, yes, madam.

MINCING. O yes, mem, I'll vouch any thing for your Ladyship's
service, be what it will.

[The two maids go out, and Lady Wishfort and Marwood
enter, not at first noticing Mrs. Fainall.

LADY WISHFORT. O my dear friend, how can I enumerate 110
the benefits that I have received from your goodness? To you I
owe the timely discovery of the false vows of Mirabell; to you I
owe the detection of the impostor Sir Rowland. And now you are
become an intercessor with my son-in-law, to save the honour of
my house, and compound for the frailties of my daughter. Well
friend, you are enough to reconcile me to the bad world, or else
I would retire to desarts and solitudes; and feed harmless sheep
by groves and purling streams. Dear Marwood, let us leave the
world, and retire by our selves and be shepherdesses.

MRS. MARWOOD. Let us first dispatch the affair in hand, 120
madam. We shall have leisure to think of retirement afterwards.
Here is one who is concerned in the treaty.

LADY WISHFORT [Discovering Mrs. Fainall]. O daughter, daughter, is it possible thou should'st be my child, bone of my bone, and
flesh of my flesh, and as I may say, another me, and yet trangress
the most minute particle of severe virtue? Is it possible you should
lean aside to iniquity, who have been cast in the direct mold of
virtue? I have not only been a mold but a pattern for you, and a
model for you, after you were brought into the world.

MRS. FAINALL. I don't understand your Ladyship. 130

LADY WISHFORT. Not understand? Why have you not been
naught? Have you not been sophisticated? Not understand? Here
I am ruined to compound for your caprices and your cuckoldoms.
I must pawn my plate and my jewels, and ruin my niece, and all
little enough—

MRS. FAINALL. I am wronged and abused, and so are you. 'Tis a false accusation, as false as hell, as false as your friend there, ay or your friend's friend, my false husband.

MRS. MARWOOD. My friend, Mrs. Fainall? Your husband my friend, what do you mean?   140

MRS. FAINALL. I know what I mean, madam, and so do you; and so shall the world at a time convenient.

MRS. MARWOOD. I am sorry to see you so passionate, madam. More temper would look more like innocence. But I have done. I am sorry my zeal to serve your Ladyship and family, should admit of misconstruction, or make me liable to affront. You will pardon me, madam, if I meddle no more with an affair, in which I am not personally concerned.

LADY WISHFORT. O dear friend, I am so ashamed that you should meet with such returns;—you ought to ask pardon on your   150 knees, ungrateful creature; she deserves more from you, than all your life can accomplish.—O don't leave me destitute in this perplexity;—no, stick to me, my good genius.

MRS. FAINALL. I tell you, madam, you're abused—stick to you? ay, like a leech, to suck your best blood—she'll drop off when she's full. Madam, you shan't pawn a bodkin, nor part with a brass counter, in composition for me. I defie 'em all. Let 'em prove their aspersions: I know my own innocence, and dare stand a trial. [*She swishes out.*]

LADY WISHFORT. Why, if she should be innocent, if she   160 should be wronged after all, ha? I don't know what to think,— and I promise you, her education has been unexceptionable—I may say it; for I chiefly made it my own care to initiate her very infancy in the rudiments of virtue, and to impress upon her tender years a young odium and aversion to the very sight of men,—ay friend, she would have shrieked if she had but seen a man, 'till she was in her teens. As I'm a person 'tis true—she was never suffered to play with a male-child, tho' but in coats; nay her very babies were of the feminine gender,—O, she never looked a man in the face but her own father, or the chaplain, and him we   170 made a shift to put upon her for a woman, by the help of his long garments, and his sleek face; 'till she was going in her fifteen.

MRS. MARWOOD. 'Twas much she should be deceived so long.

LADY WISHFORT. I warrant you, or she would never have born to have been catechized by him; and have heard his long lectures against singing and dancing, and such debaucheries; and going to

144. *temper,* moderation.

filthy plays; and prophane musick-meetings, where the lewd
trebles squeek nothing but bawdy, and the bases roar blasphemy.
O, she would have swooned at the sight or name of an obscene
play-book—and can I think after all this, that my daughter 180
can be naught? What, a whore? And thought it excommunication
to set her foot within the door of a play-house. O dear friend, I
can't believe it, no, no; as she says, let him prove it, let him
prove it.

MRS. MARWOOD [*Intent on preventing any such move*]. Prove it,
madam? What, and have your name prostituted in a publick
court; yours and your daughter's reputation worried at the bar
by a pack of bawling lawyers? To be ushered in with an *O yes*
of scandal; and have your case opened by an old fumbler leacher
in a quoif like a man midwife, to bring your daughter's in- 190
famy to light; to be a theme for legal punsters, and quiblers by
the statute; and become a jest, against a rule of court, where there
is no precedent for a jest in any record; not even in Dooms-day-
book: to discompose the gravity of the bench, and provoke
naughty interrogatories in more naughty law Latin; while the
good Judge, tickled with the proceeding, simpers under a grey
beard, and fidgets off and on his cushion as if he had swallowed
cantharides, or sate upon cow-itch.

LADY WISHFORT. O, 'tis very hard!

MRS. MARWOOD. And then to have my young revellers of the 200
Temple take notes, like prentices at a conventicle; and after talk
it over again in commons, or before drawers in an eating-house.

LADY WISHFORT. Worse and worse.

MRS. MARWOOD. Nay this is nothing; if it would end here 'twere
well. But it must after this be consigned by the short-hand writers
to the public press; and from thence be transferred to the hands,
nay into the throats and lungs of hawkers, with voices more licentious than the loud flounder-man's: And this you must hear 'till
you are stunned; nay, you must hear nothing else for some days.

LADY WISHFORT. O, 'tis insupportable. No, no, dear friend, 210
make it up, make it up; ay, ay, I'll compound. I'll give up all, my
self and my all, my niece and her all—any thing, every thing for
composition.

MRS. MARWOOD. Nay, madam, I advise nothing, I only lay before

188. *o yes,* fr. Oyez, hear ye.
190. *quoif,* a white cap worn by lawyers.
197. *cantharides,* an aphrodisiac when taken internally. *cow-itch,* cowage,
a tropical plant bearing pods with barbed hairs which cause an intolerable
itching.

you, as a friend, the inconveniencies which perhaps you have overseen. Here comes Mr. Fainall; if he will be satisfied to huddle up all in silence, I shall be glad. You must think I would rather congratulate than condole with you.

[*Fainall enters, thoroughly self-assured since his counter-plot is working so well.*

LADY WISHFORT. Ay, ay, I do not doubt it, dear Marwood: no, no, I do not doubt it.   220

FAINALL. Well, madam; I have suffered my self to be overcome by the importunity of this lady your friend; and am content you shall enjoy your own proper estate during life; on condition you oblige your self never to marry, under such penalty as I think convenient.

LADY WISHFORT. Never to marry?

FAINALL. No more Sir Rowlands,—the next imposture may not be so timely detected.

MRS. MARWOOD. That condition, I dare answer, my Lady will consent to, without difficulty; she has already but too much   230 experienced the perfidiousness of men. Besides, madam, when we retire to our pastoral solitude we shall bid adieu to all other thoughts.

LADY WISHFORT. Ay, that's true; but in case of necessity; as of health, or some such emergency—

FAINALL. O, if you are prescribed marriage, you shall be considered; I will only reserve to my self the power to choose for you. If your physic be wholesome, it matters not who is your apothecary. Next, my wife shall settle on me the remainder of her fortune, not made over already; and for her maintenance   240 depend entirely on my discretion.

LADY WISHFORT. This is most inhumanly savage; exceeding the barbarity of a Muscovite husband.

FAINALL. I learned it from his Czarish majesty's retinue, in a winter evening's conference over brandy and pepper, amongst other secrets of matrimony and policy, as they are at present practised in the northern hemisphere. But this must be agreed unto, and that positively. Lastly, I will be endowed, in right of my wife, with that six thousand pound, which is the moiety of Mrs. Millamant's fortune in your possession; and which she has   250 forfeited (as will appear by the last will and testament of your deceased husband, Sir Jonathan Wishfort) by her disobedience in contracting her self against your consent or knowledge; and by refusing the offered match with Sir Wilfull Witwoud, which you, like a careful aunt, had provided for her.

LADY WISHFORT. My nephew was *non compos;* and could not make his addresses.

FAINALL. I come to make demands—I'll hear no objections.

LADY WISHFORT. You will grant me time to consider?

FAINALL. Yes, while the instrument is drawing, to which 260 you must set your hand 'till more sufficient deeds can be perfected: which I will take care shall be done with all possible speed. In the mean while I will go for the said instrument, and 'till my return you may balance this matter in your own discretion. [*He goes out.*]

LADY WISHFORT. This insolence is beyond all precedent, all parallel; must I be subject to this merciless villain?

MRS. MARWOOD. 'Tis severe indeed, madam, that you should smart for your daughter's wantonness.

LADY WISHFORT. 'Twas against my consent that she married 270 this barbarian, but she would have him, tho' her year was not out. —Ah! her first husband, my son Languish, would not have carried it thus. Well, that was my choice, this is hers; she is matched now with a witness—I shall be mad, dear friend; is there no comfort for me? Must I live to be confiscated at this rebel-rate?— Here comes two more of my Egyptian plagues too.

[*Millamant and Sir Wilfull enter.*]

SIR WILFULL. Aunt, your servant.

LADY WISHFORT. Out Caterpillar, call not me aunt; I know thee not.

SIR WILFULL. I confess I have been a little in disguise, as 280 they say,—'sheart! and I'm sorry for't. What would you have? I hope I committed no offence, Aunt—and if I did I am willing to make satisfaction; and what can a man say fairer? If I have broke any thing I'll pay for't, an it cost a pound. And so let that content for what's past, and make no more words. For what's to come, to pleasure you I'm willing to marry my cousin. So pray let's all be friends, she and I are agreed upon the matter before a witness.

LADY WISHFORT. How's this, dear niece? Have I any comfort? Can this be true? 290

MILLAMANT. I am content to be a sacrifice to your repose, madam; and to convince you that I had no hand in the plot, as you were misinformed, I have laid my commands on Mirabell to come in person, and be a witness that I give my hand to this flower of knighthood; and for the contract that passed between Mirabell and me, I have obliged him to make a resignation of it

271. *year,* i.e., her year of mourning after her first husband's death.

in your Ladyship's presence;—he is without, and waits your leave for admittance.

LADY WISHFORT. Well, I'll swear I am something revived at this testimony of your obedience; but I cannot admit that traitor, 300 —I fear I cannot fortify my self to support his appearance. He is as terrible to me as a Gorgon; if I see him I fear I shall turn to stone, petrify incessantly.

MILLAMANT. If you disoblige him he may resent your refusal, and insist upon the contract still. Then 'tis the last time he will be offensive to you.

LADY WISHFORT. Are you sure it will be the last time?—If I were sure of that—shall I never see him again?

MILLAMANT. Sir Wilfull, you and he are to travel together, are you not? 310

SIR WILFULL. 'Sheart the gentleman's a civil gentleman, aunt, let him come in; why we are sworn brothers and fellow-travellers.— We are to be Pylades and Orestes, he and I.—He is to be my interpreter in foreign parts. He has been overseas once already; and with proviso that I marry my cousin, will cross 'em once again, only to bear me company.—'Sheart, I'll call him in,—an I set on't once, he shall come in; and see who'll hinder him. [*Goes to the door and hems.*]

MRS. MARWOOD. This is precious fooling, if it would pass; but I'll know the bottom of it. 320

LADY WISHFORT. O dear Marwood, you are not going?

MRS. MARWOOD. Not far, madam; I'll return immediately.

[*She goes out, as Mirabell enters despondently.*]

SIR WILFULL. Look up, man, I'll stand by you, 'sbud an she do frown, she can't kill you;—besides—harkee she dare not frown desperately, because her face is none of her own; 'sheart, and she should her forehead would wrinkle like the coat of a cream-cheese; but mum for that, fellow-traveller.

MIRABELL. If a deep sense of the many injuries I have offered to so good a Lady, with a sincere remorse, and a hearty contrition, can but obtain the least glance of compassion, I am too 330 happy,—ah madam, there was a time—but let it be forgotten— I confess I have deservedly forfeited the high place I once held, of sighing at your feet; nay kill me not, by turning from me in disdain—I come not to plead for favour;—nay not for pardon; I

313. *Pylades and Orestes,* one of the most famous pairs of classical friends. Orestes, having slain his mother, is pursued by her Furies, but is accompanied and comforted by Pylades.

am a suppliant only for pity.—I am going where I never shall behold you more—

SIR WILFULL. How, fellow-traveller!—You shall go by your self then.

MIRABELL. Let me be pitied first; and afterwards forgotten—I ask no more.   340

SIR WILFULL. By'r Lady a very reasonable request, and will cost you nothing, aunt,—come, come, forgive and forget aunt, why you must an you are a Christian.

MIRABELL. Consider madam, in reality, you could not receive much prejudice; it was an innocent device; tho' I confess it had a face of guiltiness,—it was at most an artifice which love contrived—and errors which love produces have ever been accounted venial. At least think it is punishment enough, that I have lost what in my heart I hold most dear, that to your cruel indignation, I have offered up this beauty, and with her my peace   350 and quiet; nay all my hopes of future comfort.

SIR WILFULL. An he does not move me, would I may never be o' the quorum,—An it were not as good a deed as to drink, to give her to him again,—I would I might never take shipping.—Aunt, if you don't forgive quickly, I shall melt, I can tell you that. My contract went no farther than a little mouth-glew, and that's hardly dry;—one doleful sigh more from my fellow-traveller and 'tis dissolved.

LADY WISHFORT. Well nephew, upon your account—ah, he has a false insinuating tongue—well sir, I will stifle my just   360 resentment at my nephew's request.—I will endeavour what I can to forget,—but on proviso that you resign the contract with my niece immediately.

MIRABELL. It is in writing and with papers of concern; but I have sent my servant for it, and will deliver it to you, with all acknowledgments for your transcendent goodness.

LADY WISHFORT [Aside]. Oh, he has witchcraft in his eyes and tongue;—when I did not see him I could have bribed a villain to his assassination; but his appearance rakes the embers which have so long lain smothered in my breast.—   370

[Mrs. Marwood and Fainall enter, still gloating over their success and expecting to clinch it now.

FAINALL. Your date of deliberation, Madam, is expired. Here is the instrument, are you prepared to sign?

353. quorum, certain justices of the peace, some of whom, because of great ability, were required to be present at the court sessions.

LADY WISHFORT. If I were prepared, I am not impowered. My niece exerts a lawful claim, having matched her self by my direction to Sir Wilfull.

FAINALL. That sham is too gross to pass on me—tho' 'tis imposed on you, madam.

MILLAMANT. Sir, I have given my consent.

MIRABELL. And, sir, I have resigned my pretensions.

SIR WILFULL. And, sir, I assert my right; and will main-   380
tain it in defiance of you, sir, and of your instrument. S'heart an you talk of an instrument sir, I have an old fox by my thigh shall hack your instrument of ram vellum to shreds, sir. It shall not be sufficient for a mittimus or a tailor's measure; therefore withdraw your instrument sir, or by'r Lady I shall draw mine.

LADY WISHFORT. Hold, nephew, hold.

MILLAMANT. Good Sir Wilfull, respite your valour.

FAINALL. Indeed? Are you provided of your guard, with your single beef-eater there? But I'm prepared for you; and insist upon my first proposal. You shall submit your own estate to my   390
management, and absolutely make over my wife's to my sole use; as pursuant to the purport and tenor of this other covenant.—I suppose, madam, your consent is not requisite in this case; nor, Mr. Mirabell, your resignation; nor, Sir Wilfull, your right.—You may draw your fox if you please sir, and make a bear-garden flourish somewhere else: for here it will not avail. This, my Lady Wishfort, must be subscribed, or your darling daughter's turned a-drift, like a leaky hulk to sink or swim, as she and the current of this lewd town can agree.

LADY WISHFORT. Is there no means, no remedy, to stop my   400
ruin? Ungrateful wretch! dost thou not owe thy being, thy subsistance to my daughter's fortune?

FAINALL. I'll answer you when I have the rest of it in my possession.

MIRABELL. But that you would not accept of a remedy from my hands—I own I have not deserved you should owe any obligation to me; or else perhaps I could advise,—

LADY WISHFORT. O what? what? to save me and my child from ruin, from want, I'll forgive all that's past; nay I'll consent to any thing to come, to be deliver'd from this tyranny.   410

MIRABELL. Ay madam; but that is too late, my reward is intercepted. You have disposed of her, who only could have made me

382. *fox*, sword.
384. *mittimus*, a writ commanding a jailer to guard a prisoner especially well.

a compensation for all my services;—but be it as it may, I am resolved I'll serve you, you shall not be wronged in this savage
manner.

LADY WISHFORT. How! Dear Mr. Mirabell, can you be so generous at last! But it is not possible. Harkee, I'll break my nephew's
match, you shall have my niece yet, and all her fortune; if you
can but save me from this imminent danger.

MIRABELL. Will you? I take you at your word. I ask no   420
more. I must have leave for two criminals to appear.

LADY WISHFORT. Ay, ay, any body, any body.

MIRABELL. Foible is one, and a penitent.

[*Mrs. Fainall, Foible, and Mincing enter and Mirabell and
Lady Wishfort go to meet them. They talk together, while
Fainall and Marwood are disturbed.*

MRS. MARWOOD. O my shame! these corrupt things are brought
hither to expose me.

FAINALL. If it must all come out, why let 'em know it, 'tis but
the *Way of the World*. That shall not urge me to relinquish or
abate one tittle of my terms, no, I will insist the more.

FOIBLE. Yes indeed madam, I'll take my bible-oath of it.

MINCING. And so will I, mem.   430

LADY WISHFORT. O Marwood, Marwood, art thou false? my
friend deceive me? Hast thou been a wicked accomplice with that
profligate man?

MRS. MARWOOD. Have you so much ingratitude and injustice,
to give credit against your friend, to the aspersions of two such
mercenary trulls?

MINCING. Mercenary, mem? I scorn your words. 'Tis true we
found you and Mr. Fainall in the blue garret; by the same token,
you swore us to secrecy upon Messalinas's poems. Mercenary?
No, if we would have been mercenary, we should have held   440
our tongues; you would have bribed us sufficiently.

FAINALL. Go, you are an insignificant thing.—Well, what are
you the better for this! Is this Mr. Mirabell's expedient? I'll be
put off no longer—you, thing, that was a wife, shall smart for
this. I will not leave thee wherewithal to hide thy shame: your
body shall be naked as your reputation.

MRS. FAINALL. I despise you, and defie your malice.—You have
aspersed me wrongfully.—I have proved your falsehood—go you
and your treacherous—I will not name it, but starve together—
perish.   450

FAINALL. Not while you are worth a groat, indeed my dear.
Madam, I'll be fooled no longer.

LADY WISHFORT. Ah Mr. Mirabell, this is small comfort, the detection of this affair.

MIRABELL. O in good time—your leave for the other offender and penitent to appear, madam.

[*Waitwell enters with a Box of Writings.*

LADY WISHFORT [*Caught for a moment by her memory*]. O Sir Rowland—[*Sharply, to hide her confusion.*] Well, rascal.

WAITWELL. What your Ladyship pleases.—I have brought the black-box at last, madam.   460

MIRABELL. Give it me. Madam, you remember your promise.

LADY WISHFORT. Ay, dear sir.

MIRABELL. Where are the gentlemen?

WAITWELL. At hand sir, rubbing their eyes,—just risen from sleep.

FAINALL. S'death what's this to me? I'll not wait your private concerns.

[*Petulant and Witwoud enter sleepily.*

PETULANT. How now? What's the matter? who's hand's out?

WITWOUD. Hey day! what are you all got together, like players at the end of the last act?   470

MIRABELL. You may remember, gentlemen, I once requested your hands as witnesses to a certain parchment.

WITWOUD. Ay I do, my hand I remember—Petulant set his mark.

MIRABELL. You wrong him, his name is fairly written, as shall appear.—You do not remember, gentlemen, any thing of what that parchment contained—[*Undoing the Box.*]

WITWOUD. No.

PETULANT. Not I. I writ, I read nothing.

MIRABELL. Very well, now you shall know—madam, your   480 promise.

LADY WISHFORT. Ay, ay, sir, upon my honour.

MIRABELL. Mr. Fainall, it is now time that you should know, that your Lady, while she was at her own disposal, and before you had by your insinuations wheedled her out of a pretended settlement of the greatest part of her fortune—

FAINALL. Sir! pretended!

MIRABELL. Yes, sir. I say that this Lady while a widow, having it seems received some cautions respecting your inconstancy and tyranny of temper, which from her own partial opinion and   490 fondness of you she could never have suspected—she did, I say, by the wholesome advice of friends and of sages learned in the laws of this land, deliver this same as her act and deed to me in trust, and to the uses within mentioned. You may read if you please—[*Holding out the parchment.*] tho' perhaps what is written on the back may serve your occasions.

FAINALL. Very likely, sir. What's here? Damnation?

[*Reads.*] *A deed of conveyance of the whole estate real of Arabella Languish, widow, in trust to Edward Mirabell.* Confusion! 500

MIRABELL. Even so, sir, 'tis *The Way of the World*, sir; of the widows of the world. I suppose this deed may bear an elder date than what you have obtained from your Lady.

FAINALL. Perfidious fiend! then thus I'll be revenged.—[*Offers to run at Mrs. Fainall.*]

SIR WILFULL [*Holding him*]. Hold, sir, now you may make your bear-garden flourish somewhere else, sir.

FAINALL. Mirabell, you shall hear of this, sir, be sure you shall. —Let me pass, oaf. [*He stamps off.*]

MRS. FAINALL. Madam, you seem to stifle your resentment: 510 you had better give it vent.

MRS. MARWOOD. Yes, it shall have vent—and to your confusion, or I'll perish in the attempt. [*She goes out trying to collect some shreds of dignity about her.*]

LADY WISHFORT. O daughter, daughter, 'tis plain thou has inherited thy mother's prudence.

MRS. FAINALL. Thank Mr. Mirabell, a cautious friend, to whose advice all is owing.

LADY WISHFORT. Well Mr. Mirabell, you have kept your promise —and I must perform mine.—First I pardon for your sake 520 Sir Rowland there and Foible—the next thing is to break the matter to my nephew—and how to do that—

MIRABELL. For that, madam, give your self no trouble,—let me have your consent—Sir Wilfull is my friend; he has had compassion upon lovers, and generously engaged a volunteer in this action, for our service; and now designs to prosecute his travels.

SIR WILFULL [*With hearty good-nature*]. 'Sheart, aunt, I have no mind to marry. My cousin's a fine Lady, and the gentleman loves her, and she loves him, and they deserve one another; my resolution is to see foreign parts—I have set on't—and when 530 I'm set on't, I must do't. And if these two gentlemen would travel too, I think they may be spared.

PETULANT. For my part, I say little—I think things are best off or on.

WITWOUD. Igad, I understand nothing of the matter,—I'm in a maze yet, like a dog in a dancing-school.

LADY WISHFORT. Well sir, take her, and with her all the joy I can give you.

MILLAMANT. Why does not the man take me? Would you have me give my self to you over again? , 540

MIRABELL. Ay, and over and over again; [*Kisses her hand.*] I would have you as often as possibly I can. Well, Heav'n grant I love you not too well, that's all my fear.

SIR WILFULL. 'Sheart you'll have time enough to toy after you're married; or if you will toy now, let us have a dance in the mean time; that we who are not lovers may have some other employment, besides looking on.

MIRABELL. With all my heart, dear Sir Wilfull. What shall we do for musick?

FOIBLE. O sir, some that were provided for Sir Rowland's 550 entertainment are yet within call. [*A Dance.*

LADY WISHFORT. As I am a person I can hold out no longer;—I have wasted my spirits so today already, that I am ready to sink under the fatigue; and I cannot but have some fears upon me yet, that my Son Fainall will pursue some desperate course.

MIRABELL. Madam, disquiet not your self on that account; to my knowledge his circumstances are such, he must of force comply. For my part I will contribute all that in me lives to a reunion: in the meantime, madam, [*To Mrs. Fainall.*] let me before these witnesses restore to you this deed of trust; it may be a means, 560 well managed, to make you live easily together.

> *From hence let those be warned, who mean to wed;*
> *Lest mutual falshood stain the bridal-bed:*
> *For each deceiver to his cost may find,*
> *That marriage frauds too oft are paid in kind.*

[*They all promenade joyfully out.*

EPILOGUE
Spoken by Mrs. Bracegirdle

After our *epilogue* this crowd dismisses,
I'm thinking how this play'll be pulled to pieces.
But pray consider, e'er you doom its fall,
How hard a thing 'twould be, to please you all.
There are some critics so with spleen diseased,
They scarcely come inclining to be pleased;

And sure he must have more than mortal skill,
Who pleases any one against his will.
Then, all bad poets we are sure are foes,
And how their number's swelled the town well knows: 10
In shoals, I've marked 'em judging in the pit;   ⎫
Tho' they're on no pretence for judgment fit,   ⎬
But that they have been damned for want of wit.   ⎭
Since when, they by their own offences taught,
Set up for spies on plays, and finding fault.
Others there are, whose malice we'd prevent;   ⎫
Such, who watch plays, with scurrilous intent   ⎬
To mark out who by *characters* are meant.   ⎭
And tho' no perfect likeness they can trace;
Yet each pretends to know the *copied face*.   20
These, with false glosses feed their own ill-nature,
And turn to *libel*, what was meant a *satire*.
May such malicious *fops* this fortune find,
To think themselves alone the *fools* designed:
If any are so arrogantly vain,   ⎫
To think they *singly* can support a *scene*,   ⎬
And furnish *fool* enough to entertain.   ⎭
For well the learned and the judicious know,   ⎫
That *satire* scorns to stoop so meanly low,   ⎬
As any one abstracted *fop* to show.   ⎭   30
For, as when painters form a matchless face,
They from each *fair* one catch some diff'rent grace:
And shining features in one portrait blend,
To which no single beauty must pretend:
So poets oft, do in one piece expose
Whole *belles assemblées* of *cocquets* and *beaux*.

SONG DRAMA

Music in the theater was no new thing when John Gay wrote his *Beggar's Opera* in 1728. Even the casual reader of Shakespeare is struck by the frequent introduction of lyrics in his plays, and his practice is indicative of the fashion in his time. Evidently the dramatic companies prided themselves on having a few singing boys in their ranks. More dramatic were the song and dance afterpieces which were used to fill out an afternoon's entertainment in the theater. The masques, too, had made much of the union between drama, dancing, and music. That interest continued through the seventeenth century.

But the eighteenth century saw the rapid development of a type of dramatic entertainment which seemed to threaten for a time to do away with true drama. That was the Italian opera, which combined music and acting, and which occasioned a veritable foreign invasion of actor-singers, whose popularity threatened quite to eclipse the English actors.

It may well be that Gay was not consciously attempting to satirize the form (which he himself was to try in his *Achilles*), but the *Beggar's Opera* does nonetheless stand in its sturdy realism in sharp contrast to the artificialities of the imported opera. Gay's work differs sharply from the Italian mode, in that in his play the stress is still on spoken dialogue, with the songs supplementary to the speeches. His is song drama, or ballad opera, somewhat akin to musical comedy in our own day. Many of his tunes he took from the popular music of the time as it was found in such a popular work as Thomas Durfey's *Pills to Purge Melancholy*. These he weaves in at appropriate moments to set or maintain a mood rather than to advance the action.

In many ways John Gay was a good example of the popular conception (or misconception) of what a poet is like. Careless, improvident, almost completely dependent on his friends and patrons, able to work only when hard-pressed by friends or creditors, he was still able to impress his generation with his genius. His geniality and serene undependability, though irritating, made for him friends where a stronger practical sense might have failed.

He was born in Devonshire in 1685 of a then poor but long established family. After a grammar school education at Barnstaple he was apprenticed to a silk mercer of London. That proved to be no trade for him, however; so he turned to letters and was soon moving in intimate companionship with the leading literary lights of the day, Pope, Swift, Arbuthnot, and their circle. With their assistance he received many good appointments that left him much time free for composing poetry. He became secretary to the Duchess of Monmouth in 1712, and two years later was taken under the wing of the Earl of Clarendon. In 1713 he wrote a serious pastoral poem, *Rural Sports*, and in the next year he burlesqued the type especially as it appeared in the work of Pope's enemy, Ambrose Philips. *The Shepherds' Week* does more than burlesque the work of an inferior poet, however, for in it there are already some of the touches of realistic observation of humble life that give variety and liveliness to the *Beggar's Opera*. Something of the same quality, and in a poem more closely related to the subject matter of the *Opera*, was his *Trivia, or the Art of Walking the Streets of London*, which appeared in 1717.

By 1720 he had become prominent enough as a poet to warrant the publishing of his *Collected Poems* in two volumes, for which he received a thousand pounds, which he promptly lost by investing it in the South Sea Company. He thereafter held a succession of sinecures in the government and with individuals until his death in 1732. In 1727 he was offered a post as Gentleman Usher to the three-year old Princess Louise, but so staunch was his opposition to the policies of King George II and his advisor, Walpole, that Gay refused.

Swift seems to have been responsible for the idea of an opera dealing with Newgate life. He suggested a Newgate Pastoral to Pope in a letter in August of 1716. Gay had already shown interest enough in common life to find the suggestion attrac-

tive when it was passed on to him, but he soon gave up the
idea of treating the material in the manner of a pastoral and,
perhaps with an eye to the artificialities of Italian opera, invented the form which we have here.

There were hazards in such an attempt. The form was an
innovation. The subject was "low," and so might be hissed
off the stage by a fashionable audience. Gay's friends, however, counselled him to try it, and the play met with very great
success, enjoying a run of sixty-two performances, quite unusual for those days. Whether or not it was designed definitely
to burlesque the Italian opera, there is little question that for
a time it did substantially impair the popularity of that type.

Gay's method is interesting. Far from depending simply on
the unusual aspects of his story and its treatment—the presentation of a group of outlaws and their associates, all of whom
are likely to burst into song at a moment's notice,—he gave
the relatively simple story vigor and point by making the play
an incisive commentary on contemporary political and social
characteristics. It is in this respect that song drama differs from
the method of musical comedy or comic opera, as they usually
appear. The chief object of political satire is Sir Robert Walpole, the unscrupulous but very capable Prime Minister, who
as leader of the Whigs was thoroughly despised by Gay's
circle. So Gay refers to him as Bob Booty, and it is believed
that the scene of the quarrel between Peachum and Lockit in
II, x was an allusion to a notorius quarrel between Walpole
and Lord Townshend, an allusion noticed with great glee by
the audience. Walpole was diplomatic (or thick-skinned)
enough to applaud the play at its first performance, but was
probably instrumental in prohibiting on the grounds of immorality the sequel, *Polly*, from appearing on the stage.

The mere political reference, however, is insignificant in
comparison with the social and moral commentary in the play.
Gay is attacking something more than the evils of prison ad-
ministration and the dangers of organized crime as it had been
exemplified in England in the careers of Jack Shepherd and
Jonathan Wild, hanged only a short time before the play was
written. He is looking with disillusioned eyes on the state of
society, so degenerate that he feels it represents the antithesis

of all the values that people assume and talk about glibly. So the ironic tone of the play becomes especially striking as the underworld characters make no pretensions to holding to the virtue of loyalty or honesty with each other or disinterested love, and insist that they are but imitating the courtly world of fashion in all their moral anarchy. The miracle is that the play does not descend as a result to the level of dull and heavy preaching but maintains a lightness of tone that emphasizes for us Swift's insistence that the purpose of his friend's play was to delight not to reform.

SUGGESTED READINGS

Baskerville, C. R., *The Elizabethan Jig and Related Song Drama*. CHICAGO, 1929.

Cambridge History of English Literature, VOL. X. NEW YORK, 1913.

Gagey, Edmond M., *Ballad Opera*. NEW YORK, 1937.

Hazlitt, W. C., *Lectures on the English Poets*. OXFORD, 1925.

McLeod, G. H., *The Beggar's Opera* (WITH THE MUSIC FOR THE SONGS). LONDON, 1905.

Nettleton, G. H., *English Drama of the Restoration and Eighteenth Century*. NEW YORK, 1928.

Nicoll, Allardyce, *History of Early Eighteenth Century Drama*. NEW YORK, 1925.

Pearce, Charles, *"Polly Peachum" and "The Beggar's Opera."* LONDON, 1913.

Cummings, E. E., *Him.* NEW YORK, 1929.

Gilbert, Sir William and Sir Arthur Sullivan, *The Mikado, H. M. S. Pinafore, The Pirates of Penzance, Patience*. In *The Savoy Operas*. LONDON, 1926.

Sheridan, Richard B., *The Duenna*. OXFORD, 1936.

THE BEGGAR'S OPERA
by John Gay

Characters

PEACHUM, *a disposer of stolen goods, who sells thieves out to the law when they no longer steal enough*

LOCKIT, *the Newgate jailer, in league with Peachum*

MACHEATH, *a famous and most capable highwayman, in love with Polly—and others*

FILCH, *Peachum's servant*

JEREMY TWITCHER
CROOK-FINGERED JACK
WAT DREARY
ROBIN OF BAGSHOT
NIMMING NED   } *Gangsters under Macheath's leadership*
HARRY PADDINGTON
MATT OF THE MINT
BEN BUDGE

MRS. PEACHUM, *mistress of Peachum and a business woman in her own right*

POLLY PEACHUM, *their daughter, her head filled with romantic notions from reading sentimental stories*

LUCY LOCKIT, *the jailer's daughter, a cast-off sweetheart of Macheath's*

DIANA TRAPES, *an outfitter of prostitutes*

MRS. COAXER
DOLLY TRULL
MRS. VIXEN
BETTY DOXY   } *Women of the town, many of them Mac-*
JENNY DIVER   *heath's sometime mistresses*
MRS. SLAMMEKIN
SUKY TAWDRY
MOLLY BRAZEN

474

PROLOGUE

Enter a Beggar, who is the Presenter of the play, and a Player.

BEGGAR. If poverty be a title to poetry, I am sure nobody can dispute mine. I own myself of the company of beggars; and I make one at their weekly festivals at St. Giles's. I have a small yearly salary for my catches, and am welcome to a dinner there whenever I please, which is more than most poets can say.

PLAYER. As we live by the muses, it is but gratitude in us to encourage poetical merit wherever we find it. The muses, contrary to all other ladies, pay no distinction to dress, and never partially mistake the pertness of embroidery for wit, nor the modesty of want for dulness. Be the author who he will, we 10 push his play as far as it will go. So (though you are in want) I wish you success heartily.

BEGGAR. This piece I own was originally writ for the celebrating the marriage of James Chanter and Moll Lay, two most excellent ballad-singers. I have introduced the similes that are in all your celebrated operas: The swallow, the moth, the bee, the ship, the flower, &c. Besides, I have a prison scene, which the ladies always reckon charmingly pathetick. As to the parts, I have observed such a nice impartiality to our two ladies, that it is impossible for either of them to take offence. I hope I may be 20 forgiven, that I have not made my opera throughout unnatural, like those in vogue; for I have no recitative: excepting this, as I have consented to have neither prologue nor epilogue, it must be allowed an opera in all its forms. The piece indeed hath been heretofore frequently presented by ourselves in our great Room at St. Giles's, so that I cannot too often acknowledge your charity in bringing it now on the stage.

PLAYER. But I see 'tis time for us to withdraw; the actors are preparing to begin. [*To the orchestra.*] Play away the overture.

[*They go out.*]

4. *catches,* brief, lively songs, originally rounds for three or more singers.
15. *similes,* Gay makes fun of the stereotyped devices of Italian opera, which was enjoying a considerable vogue in London at the time.
26. *St. Giles's,* one of the slums of London.

ACT I

SCENE I

A ROOM IN PEACHUM'S HOUSE. *Peachum is a Master Thief, the head of a gang of journeymen and apprentices in the profession. Now he is seated at a table with his account books before him. He is discovered singing.*

AIR I. An old woman cloathed in gray

Through all the employments of life
Each neighbour abuses his brother;
Whore and rogue they call husband and wife:
All professions be-rogue one another.
The priest calls the lawyer a cheat,
The lawyer be-knaves the divine;
And the statesman, because he's so great,
Thinks his trade as honest as mine.

A lawyer is an honest employment, so is mine. Like me, too, he acts in a double capacity, both against rogues and for 'em; for 'tis but fitting that we should protect and encourage cheats, since we live by 'em. 10

SCENE II

Filch, his servant, enters.

FILCH. Sir, black Moll hath sent word her trial comes on in the afternoon, and she hopes you will order matters so as to bring her off.

PEACHUM. Why, she may plead her belly at worst; to my knowledge she hath taken care of that security. But as the wench is very active and industrious, you may satisfy her that I'll soften the evidence.

FILCH. Tom Gagg, sir, is found guilty. 20

PEACHUM. A lazy dog! When I took him the time before, I told him what he would come to if he did not mend his hand. This is death without reprieve. I may venture to book him. [*Writes.*] For Tom Gagg, forty pounds. Let Betty Sly know that

I'll save her from Transportation, for I can get more by her staying in England.

FILCH. Betty hath brought more goods into our lock to-year than any five of the gang; and in truth, 'tis a pity to lose so good a customer.

PEACHUM. If none of the gang take her off, she may, in the common course of business, live a twelve-month longer. I love to let women scape. A good sportsman always lets the hen-partridges fly, because the breed of the game depends upon them. Besides, here the law allows us no reward; there is nothing to be got by the death of women—except our wives.

FILCH. Without dispute, she is a fine woman! 'Twas to her I was obliged for my education, and (to say a bold word) she hath trained up more young fellows to the business than the gaming-table.

PEACHUM. Truly, Filch, thy observation is right. We and the surgeons are more beholden to women than all the professions besides.

AIR II. The bonny gray-eyed morn, &c.

FILCH. *'Tis woman that seduces all mankind,*
  By her we first were taught the wheedling arts:
 Her very eyes can cheat; when most she's kind,
  She tricks us of our money with our hearts.
 For her, like wolves by night we roam for prey,
  And practise ev'ry fraud to bribe her charms;
 For suits of love, like law, are won by pay,
  And beauty must be fee'd into our arms.

PEACHUM. But make haste to Newgate, boy, and let my friends know what I intend; for I love to make them easy one way or other.

FILCH. When a gentleman is long kept in suspense, penitence may break his spirit ever after. Besides, certainty gives a man a good air upon his trial, and makes him risk another without fear or scruple. But I'll away, for 'tis a pleasure to be the messenger of comfort to friends in affliction. [*He goes out.*]

25. *Transportation,* i.e., to the colonies, where criminals were often sent. Return to England would mean death.
27. *lock,* shop for the disposal of stolen goods.

SCENE III

PEACHUM [*Turning back to his book. One of his many sources of income is his reward for turning criminals over to the police after they are no longer useful to him*]. But 'tis now high time to look about me for a decent execution against next sessions. I hate a lazy rogue, by whom one can get nothing 'till he is hàng'd. A register of the gang. [*Reading.*] Crook-finger'd Jack. A year and a half in the service: let me see how much the stock owes to his industry; one, two, three, four, five gold watches, and seven silver ones. A mighty clean-handed fellow! sixteen snuff-boxes, five of them of true gold. Six dozen of handkerchiefs, four 10 silver-hilted swords, half a dozen of shirts, three tie-periwigs, and a piece of broad cloth. Considering these are only the fruits of his leisure hours, I don't know a prettier fellow, for no man alive hath a more engaging presence of mind upon the road. Wat Dreary, alias Brown Will, an irregular dog, who hath an under-hand way of disposing his goods. I'll try him only for a sessions or two longer upon his good behaviour. Harry Paddingdon, a poor petty-larceny rascal, without the least genius; that fellow, though he were to live six months, will never come to the gal-lows with any credit. Slippery Sam; he goes off the next 20 sessions, for the villain hath the impudence to have views of fol-lowing his trade as a tailor, which he calls an honest employment. Mat of the Mint; listed not above a month ago, a promising sturdy fellow, and diligent in his way; somewhat too bold and hasty, and may raise good contributions on the publick, if he does not cut himself short by murder. Tom Tipple, a guzzling soaking sot, who is always too drunk to stand himself, or to make others stand. A cart is absolutely necessary for him. Robin of Bagshot, alias Gorgon, alias Bluff Bob, alias Carbuncle, alias Bob Booty.

SCENE IV

Mrs. Peachum enters.

MRS. PEACHUM. What of Bob Booty, husband? I hope nothing bad hath betided him. You know, my dear, he's a favourite cus-tomer of mine. 'Twas he made me a present of this ring.

11. *tie-periwig,* a small wig of which the lower part was tied, distinguished from the full dress wig, which was much larger and fuller.

16. *sessions,* term of court.

18. *petty-larceny,* stealing goods worth less than one shilling. The penalty was whipping; so Peachum can 'hope for no reward from betraying him to a hangman.

PEACHUM. I have set his name down in the black-list, that's all my dear; he spends his life among women, and as soon as his money is gone, one or other of the ladies will hang him for the reward, and there's forty pound lost to us for-ever.

MRS. PEACHUM. You know, my dear, I never meddle in matters of death; I always leave those affairs to you. Women indeed are bitter bad judges in these cases, for they are so partial to 10 the brave that they think every man handsome who is going to the camp or the gallows.

AIR III. Cold and raw, &c.

If any wench Venus's girdle wear,
   Though she be never so ugly,
Lilies and roses will quickly appear,
   And her face look wondrous snuggly.
Beneath the left ear, so fit but a cord,
   (A rope so charming a zone is!)
The youth in his cart hath the air of a lord,
   And we cry, There dies an Adonis!   20

But really, husband, you should not be too hardhearted, for you never had a finer, braver set of men than at present. We have not had a murder among them all, these seven months. And truly, my dear, that is a great blessing.

PEACHUM. What a dickens is the woman always a whimpring about murder for? No gentleman is ever looked upon the worse for killing a man in his own defence; and if business cannot be carried on without it, what would you have a gentleman do?

MRS. PEACHUM. If I am in the wrong, my dear, you must excuse me, for nobody can help the frailty of an overscrupulous 30 conscience.

PEACHUM. Murder is as fashionable a crime as a man can be guilty of. How many fine gentlemen have we in Newgate every year, purely upon that article? If they have wherewithal to persuade the jury to bring it in manslaughter, what are they the worse for it? So, my dear, have done upon this subject. Was captain Macheath here this morning, for the banknotes he left with you last week?

MRS. PEACHUM. Yes, my dear; and though the bank hath stopt payment, he was so cheerful and so agreeable! Sure there is 40 not a finer gentleman upon the road than the captain! If he comes

from Bagshot at any reasonable hour he hath promised to make
one this evening with Polly, and me, and Bob Booty, at a party
of quadrille. Pray, my dear, is the captain rich?

PEACHUM. The captain keeps too good company ever to grow
rich. Marybone and the chocolate-houses are his undoing. The
man that proposes to get money by play should have the education of a fine gentleman, and be trained up to it from his youth.

MRS. PEACHUM. Really, I am sorry upon Polly's account the
captain hath not more discretion. What business hath he to   50
keep company with lords and gentlemen? he should leave them
to prey upon one another.

PEACHUM. Upon Polly's account! What, a plague, does the
woman mean?—Upon Polly's account!

MRS. PEACHUM. Captain Macheath is very fond of the girl.

PEACHUM. And what then?

MRS. PEACHUM. If I have any skill in the ways of women, I am
sure Polly thinks him a very pretty man.

PEACHUM. And what then? you would not be so mad to have
the wench marry him? Gamesters and highwaymen are gen-   60
erally very good to their whores, but they are very devils to their
wives.

MRS. PEACHUM. But if Polly should be in love, how should we
help her, or how can she help herself? Poor girl, I am in the utmost concern about her.

AIR IV. Why is your faithful slave disdain'd?

> *If love the virgin's heart invade,*
> *How, like a moth, the simple maid*
> *Still plays about the flame!*
> *If soon she be not made a wife,*
> *Her honour's singed, and then for life,*   70
> *She's—what I dare not name.*

PEACHUM. Look ye, wife. A handsome wench in our way of
business, is as profitable as at the bar of a Temple coffee-house,
who looks upon it as her livelihood to grant every liberty but
one. You see I would indulge the girl as far as prudently we can.
In any thing, but marriage! after that, my dear, how shall we be
safe? are we not then in her husband's power? for a husband hath
the absolute power over all a wife's secrets but her own. If the

42. *Bagshot*, heath near London where many robberies took place.
44. *quadrille*, a popular card game for four people.
46. *Marybone*, the most popular gambling resort of the time in London.

girl had the discretion of a court lady, who can have a dozen young fellows at her ear without complying with one, I 80 should not matter it; but Polly is tinder, and a spark will at once set her on a flame. Married! If the wench does not know her own profit, sure she knows her own pleasure better than to make herself a property! My daughter to me should be, like a court lady to a minister of state, a key to the whole gang. Married! If the affair is not already done, I'll terrify her from it, by the example of our neighbours.

MRS. PEACHUM. Mayhap, my dear, you may injure the girl. She loves to imitate the fine ladies, and she may only allow the captain liberties in the view of interest. 90

PEACHUM. But 'tis your duty, my dear, to warn the girl against her ruin, and to instruct her how to make the most of her beauty. I'll go to her this moment, and sift her. In the mean time, wife, rip out the coronets and marks of these dozen of cambric handkerchiefs, for I can dispose of them this afternoon to a chap in the city. [*He goes out hastily.*]

SCENE V

MRS. PEACHUM. Never was a man more out of the way in an argument, than my husband! Why must our Polly, forsooth, differ from her sex, and love only her husband? And why must our Polly's marriage, contrary to all observation, make her the less followed by other men? All men are thieves in love, and like a woman the better for being another's property.

AIR V. Of all the simple things we do, &c.

A maid is like the golden oar,
Which hath guineas intrinsical in't,
*Whose worth is never known, **before***
It is tried and imprest in the mint. 10
A wife's like a guinea in gold,
Stampt with the name of her spouse;
*Now here, now there; is bought, **or is sold;***
And is current in every house.

SCENE VI ·

Filch returns from his errand.

MRS. PEACHUM. Come hither, Filch. I am as fond of this child, as though my mind misgave me he were my own. He hath as fine

a hand at picking a pocket as a woman, and is as nimble-fingered
as a juggler. If an unlucky session does not cut the rope of thy
life, I pronounce, boy, thou wilt be a great man in history. Where
was your post last night, my boy?

FILCH. I plied at the opera, madam; and considering 'twas
neither dark nor rainy, so that there was no great hurry in getting chairs and coaches, made a tolerable hand on't. These seven
handkerchiefs, madam.   10

MRS. PEACHUM. Coloured ones, I see. They are of sure sale from
our ware-house at Redriff among the seamen.

FILCH. And this snuff-box.

MRS. PEACHUM. Set in gold! A pretty encouragement this to a
young beginner.

FILCH. I had a fair tug at a charming gold watch. Pox take the
tailors for making the fobs so deep and narrow! It stuck by the
way, and I was forced to make my escape under a coach. Really,
madam, I fear I shall be cut off in the flower of my youth, so that
every now and then (since I was pumpt) I have thoughts of   20
taking up and going to sea.

MRS. PEACHUM. You should go to Hockley in the hole, and to
Marybone, child, to learn valour. These are the schools that have
bred so many brave men. I thought, boy, by this time, thou hadst
lost fear as well as shame. Poor lad! how little does he know yet
of the Old Bailey! For the first fact I'll ensure thee from being
hanged; and going to sea, Filch, will come time enough upon a
sentence of transportation. But now, since you have nothing better to do, even go to your book, and learn your catechism; for
really a man makes but an ill figure in the ordinary's paper,   30
who cannot give a satisfactory answer to his questions. But, hark
you, my lad, don't tell me a lie; for you know I hate a liar. Do
you know of any thing that hath past between captain Macheath
and our Polly?

FILCH. I beg you, Madam, don't ask me: for I must either tell
a lie to you or to Miss Polly; for I promised her I would not tell.

MRS. PEACHUM. But when the honour of our family is concern'd—

FILCH. I shall lead a sad life with Miss Polly, if ever she come

20. *pumpt*, subjected to vigorous questioning by the police.

22. *Hockley in the hole*, a famous beer garden, much frequented by the
lower classes. Addison gives an account of it in *Spectator*, 436.

26. *Old Bailey*, the criminal court. There lived Jonathan Wild, who furnished Fielding material for a novel and was perhaps the model for Peachum.

30. *ordinary*, chaplain at Newgate.

to know that I told you. Besides, I would not willingly for- 40
feit my own honour by betraying any body.

MRS. PEACHUM. Yonder comes my husband and Polly. Come,
Filch, you shall go with me into my own room, and tell me the
whole story. I'll give thee a glass of a most delicious cordial that
I keep for my own drinking. [*They go out together.*]

SCENE VII

*Peachum and his daughter Polly enter. He has been trying to in-
struct her in wise conduct in love, but she prides herself on
her understanding of the world and her ability to take care of
herself.*

POLLY. I know as well as any of the fine ladies how to make the
most of my self and of my man too. A woman knows how to be
mercenary, though she hath never been in a court or at an assembly. We have it in our natures, papa. If I allow captain Macheath
some trifling liberties, I have this watch and other visible marks
of his favour to show for it. A girl who cannot grant some things,
and refuse what is most material, will make a poor hand of her
beauty, and soon be thrown upon the common.

AIR VI. What shall I do to show how much I love her?

> *Virgins are like the fair flower in its lustre,*
> *Which in the garden enamels the ground;* 10
> *Near it the bees in play flutter and cluster,*
> *And gaudy butterflies frolick around.*
> *But, when once pluck'd, 'tis no longer alluring,*
> *To Covent-garden 'tis sent, (as yet sweet),*
> *There fades, and shrinks, and grows past all enduring,*
> *Rots, stinks, and dies, and is trod under feet.*

PEACHUM. You know, Polly, I am not against your toying and
trifling with a customer in the way of business, or to get out a
secret, or so. But if I find out that you have played the fool and
are married, you jade you, I'll cut your throat, hussy. Now 20
you know my mind.

14. *Covent Garden*, flower and vegetable markets were there. It was
also a district frequented by prostitutes.

SCENE VIII

Mrs. Peachum rushes in in great anger at the news she has wormed out of Filch.

AIR VII. Oh London is a fine Town

MRS. PEACHUM.

> *Our Polly is a sad slut! nor heeds what we have taught her.*
> *I wonder any man alive will ever rear a daughter!*
> *For she must have both hoods and gowns, and hoops to swell her pride,*
> *With scarfs and stays, and gloves and lace; and she will have men beside;*
> *And when she's drest with care and cost, all-tempting, fine and gay.*
> *As men should serve a cowcumber, she flings herself away.*

You baggage! you hussy! you inconsiderate jade! had you been hanged, it would not have vexed me, for that might have been your misfortune; but to do such a mad thing by choice! The wench is married, husband.   10

PEACHUM. Married? the captain is a bold man, and will risk any thing for money; to be sure he believes her a fortune. Do you think your mother and I should have lived comfortably so long together, if ever we had been married? Baggage!

MRS. PEACHUM. I knew she was always a proud slut; and now the wench hath play'd the fool and married, because forsooth she would do like the gentry. Can you support the expence of a husband, hussy, in gaming, drinking and whoring? Have you money enough to carry on the daily quarrels of man and wife about who shall squander most? There are not many hus-   20
bands and wives, who can bear the charges of plaguing one another in a handsome way. If you must be married, could you introduce nobody into our family, but a highwayman! Why, thou foolish jade, thou wilt be as ill used, and as much neglected, as if thou hadst married a Lord!

PEACHUM. Let not your anger, my dear, break through the rules of decency, for the captain looks upon himself in the military capacity, as a gentleman by his profession. Besides what he hath already, I know he is in a fair way of getting, or of dying; and both these ways, let me tell you, are most excellent 30
chances for a wife. Tell me hussy, are you ruined, or no?

MRS. PEACHUM. With Polly's fortune, she might very well have gone off to a person of distinction. Yes, that you might, you pouting slut!

PEACHUM. What, is the wench dumb! Speak, or I'll make you plead by squeezing out an answer from you. Are you really bound wife to him, or are you only upon liking? [*Pinches her.*]

POLLY [*Screaming*]. Oh!

MRS. PEACHUM. How the mother is to be pitied who hath handsome daughters! Locks, bolts, bars, and lectures of morality 40 are nothing to them: they break through them all. They have as much pleasure in cheating a father and mother, as in cheating at cards.

PEACHUM. Why, Polly, I shall soon know if you are married, by Macheath's keeping from our house.

AIR VIII. Grim King of the Ghosts, &c.

POLLY. *Can love be controlled by advice?*
    Will Cupid our mothers obey?
Though my heart were as frozen as ice,
    At his flame 'twould have melted away.
When he kissed me so closely he prest, 50
    'Twas so sweet, that I must have complied:
So I thought it both safest and best
    To marry, for fear you should chide.

MRS. PEACHUM. Then all the hopes of our family are gone for ever and ever!

PEACHUM. And Macheath may hang his father and mother-in-law, in hope to get into their daughter's fortune.

POLLY. I did not marry him (as 'tis the fashion) coolly and deliberately for honour or money. But, I love him.

MRS. PEACHUM. Love him! worse and worse! I thought the 60 girl had been better bred. Oh husband! husband! her folly makes me mad! my head swims! I'm distracted! I can't support myself— Oh! [*Faints.*]

PEACHUM. See, wench, to what a condition you have reduced your poor mother! a glass of cordial, this instant. How the poor woman takes it to heart! [*Polly goes out, and returns with it.*] Ah, hussy, now this is the only comfort your mother has left!

POLLY. Give her another glass, sir; my Mamma drinks double the quantity whenever she is out of order. This, you see, fetches her. 70

MRS. PEACHUM. The girl shows such a readiness, and so much concern, that I could almost find in my heart to forgive her.

AIR IX. O Jenny, O Jenny, where hast thou been?

POLLY.
> *O Polly, you might have toyed and kissed.*
> *By keeping men off, you keep them on.*
> *But he so teased me,*
> *And he so pleased me,*
> *What I did, you must have done.*

MRS. PEACHUM. Not with a highway-man.—You sorry slut!

PEACHUM. A word with you, wife. 'Tis no new thing for a wench to take man without consent of Parents. You know 80 'tis the frailty of woman, my dear.

MRS. PEACHUM. Yes, indeed, the sex is frail. But the first time a woman is frail, she should be somewhat nice methinks, for then or never is the time to make her fortune. After that, she hath nothing to do but to guard herself from being found out, and she may do what she pleases.

PEACHUM. Make your self a little easy; I have a thought shall soon set all matters again to rights. Why so melancholy, Polly? since what is done cannot be undone, we must all endeavour to make the best of it. 90

MRS. PEACHUM. Well, Polly; as far as one woman can forgive another, I forgive thee.—Your father is too fond of you, hussy.

POLLY. Then all my sorrows are at an end.

MRS. PEACHUM. A mighty likely speech, in troth, for a wench who is just married!

AIR X. Thomas, I cannot, &c.

POLLY.
> *I, like a ship in storms, was tost;*
> *Yet afraid to put into land;*
> *For seized in the port the vessel's lost,*
> *Whose treasure is contreband.*
> *The waves are laid,*
> *My duty's paid.*
> *O joy beyond expression!*
> *Thus, safe a-shore,*
> *I ask no more,*
> *My all is in my possession.*

100

PEACHUM. I hear customers in t'other room; go, talk with 'em, Polly; but come to us again, as soon as they are gone.—But, hark ye, child, if 'tis the gentleman who was here yesterday about the repeating watch, say, you believe we can't get intelligence of it, till to-morrow. For I lent it to Suky Straddle, to make a 110 figure with to-night at a tavern in Drury-Lane. If t'other gentleman calls for the silver-hilted sword; you know beetle-browed Jemmy hath it on, and he doth not come from Tunbridge till Tuesday night; so that it cannot be had till then.

[*Polly goes out, leaving her father and mother to talk it over.*

SCENE IX

PEACHUM. Dear wife, be a little pacified. Don't let your passion run away with your senses. Polly, I grant you, hath done a rash thing.

MRS. PEACHUM. If she had had only an intrigue with the fellow, why the very best families have excused and huddled up a frailty of that sort. 'Tis marriage, husband, that makes it a blemish.

PEACHUM. But money, wife, is the true fuller's earth for reputations, there is not a spot or a stain but what it can take out. A rich rogue now-a-days is fit company for any gentleman; and the world, my dear, hath not such a contempt for roguery as 10 you imagine. I tell you, wife, I can make this match turn to our advantage.

MRS. PEACHUM. I am very sensible husband, that captain Macheath is worth money, but I am in doubt whether he hath not two or three wives already, and then if he should die in a session or two, Polly's dower would come into dispute.

PEACHUM. That, indeed, is a point which ought to be consider'd.

AIR XI. A soldier and a sailor

A fox may steal your hens, sir,
A whore your health and pence, sir,
Your daughter rob your chest, sir, 20
Your wife may steal your rest, sir,
    A thief your goods and plate.
But this is all but picking,

111. *Drury Lane*, another place of popular resort, much frequented by ladies of dubious reputation.

7. *fuller's earth*, a claylike earthy substance used in cleaning or thickening (fulling) cloth.

With rest, pence, chest and chicken;
It ever was decreed, sir,
If lawyer's hand is fee'd, sir,
He steals your whole estate.

The lawyers are bitter enemies to those in our way. They don't
care that any body should get a clandestine livelihood but themselves.   30

SCENE X

Polly reenters.

POLLY. 'Twas only Nimming Ned. He brought in a damask
window-curtain, a hoop-petticoat, a pair of silver candlesticks, a
perriwig, and one silk stocking, from the fire that happened last
night.

PEACHUM. There is not a fellow that is cleverer in his way, and
saves more goods out of the fire than Ned. But now, Polly, to
your affair; for matters must not be left as they art. You are married then, it seems?

POLLY. Yes, Sir.

PEACHUM. And how do you propose to live, child?   10

POLLY. Like other women, sir, upon the industry of my husband.

MRS. PEACHUM. What, is the wench turned fool? A highwayman's wife, like a soldier's, hath as little of his pay, as of his company.

PEACHUM. And had not you the common views of a gentlewoman in your marriage, Polly?

POLLY. I don't know what you mean, sir.

PEACHUM. Of a jointure, and of being a widow.

POLLY. But I love him, sir: how then could I have thoughts 20
of parting with him?

PEACHUM. Parting with him! Why, that is the whole scheme
and intention of all marriage-articles. The comfortable estate of
widowhood, is the only hope that keeps up a wife's spirits. Where
is the woman who would scruple to be a wife, if she had it in her
power to be a widow whenever she pleased? If you have any
views of this sort, Polly, I shall think the match not so very
unreasonable.

1. *Nimming*, thieving.

POLLY. How I dread to hear your advice! Yet I must beg you
to explain yourself.   30

PEACHUM. Secure what he hath got, have him peached the next
sessions, and then at once you are made a rich widow.

POLLY. What, murder the man I love! The blood runs cold at
my heart with the very thought of it.

PEACHUM. Fye, Polly! what hath murder to do in the affair?
Since the thing sooner or later must happen, I dare say, the captain himself would like that we should get the reward for his
death sooner than a stranger. Why, Polly, the captain knows,
that as 'tis his employment to rob, so 'tis ours to take robbers;
every man in his business. So that there is no malice in the   40
case.

MRS. PEACHUM. Ay, husband, now you have nicked the matter.
To have him peached is the only thing could ever make me forgive her.

AIR XII. Now ponder well, ye parents dear

POLLY.   *Oh, ponder well! be not severe;*
               So save a wretched wife!
               For on the rope that hangs my dear
               Depends poor Polly's life.

MRS. PEACHUM. But your duty to your parents, hussy, obliges
you to hang him. What would many a wife give for such   50
an opportunity!

POLLY. What is a jointure, what is widow-hood to me? I know
my heart. I cannot survive him.

AIR XIII. Le printemps rappelle aux armes

The turtle thus with plaintive crying,
   Her lover dying,
The turtle thus with plaintive crying
   Laments her dove.
Down she drops quite spent with sighing,
Paired in death, as paired in love.

Thus, sir, it will happen to your poor Polly.   60

MRS. PEACHUM. What, is the fool in love in earnest then? I hate
thee for being particular: why, wench, thou art a shame to thy
very sex.

POLLY. But hear me, mother.—If you ever loved—

MRS. PEACHUM. Those cursed play-books she reads have been her ruin. One word more, hussy, and I shall knock your brains 10 out, if you have any.

PEACHUM. Keep out of the way, Polly, for fear of mischief, and consider of what is proposed to you.

MRS. PEACHUM. Away, hussy. Hang your husband, and be 70 dutiful.

SCENE XI

Mrs. Peachum and Peachum come down to the front of the stage. Polly is left at the rear but listens closely to hear what they say.

MRS. PEACHUM. The thing, husband, must and shall be done. For the sake of intelligence we must take other measures, and have him peached the next Session without her consent. If she will not know her duty, we know ours.

PEACHUM [*Sentimentally*]. But really, my dear, it grieves one's heart to take off a great man. When I consider his personal brav-. ery, his fine stratagem, how much we have already got by him, and how much more we may get, methinks I can't find in my heart to have a hand in his death. I wish you could have made Polly undertake it.   10

MRS. PEACHUM. But in a case of necessity—our own lives are in danger.

PEACHUM. Then, indeed, we must comply with the customs of the world, and make gratitude give way to interest.—He shall be taken off.

MRS. PEACHUM. I'll undertake to manage Polly.

PEACHUM. And I'll prepare the matters for the Old Bailey.
[*They go out, and Polly comes down.*]

SCENE XII

POLLY. Now I'm a wretch, indeed.—Methinks I see him already in the cart, sweeter and more lovely than the nosegay in his hand! —I hear the crowd extolling his resolution and intrepidity!— What vollies of sighs are sent from the windows of Holborn, that so comely a youth should be brought to disgrace!—I see him at the tree! the whole circle are in tears!—Even butchers weep!—

2. *cart,* in which prisoners were carried to Holborn for execution.

Jack Ketch himself hesitates to perform his duty, and would be glad to lose his fee, by a reprieve. What then will become of Polly!—As yet I may inform him of their design, and aid him in his escape.—It shall be so.—But then he flies, absents him- 10 self, and I bar my self from his dear, dear conversation! that too will distract me.—If he keeps out of the way, my Papa and Mama may in time relent, and we may be happy.—If he stays, he is hanged, and then he is lost for ever!—He intended to lie concealed in my room, 'till the dusk of the evening: If they are abroad I'll this instant let him out, lest some accident should prevent him. [*She goes out and shortly returns with Macheath.*]

SCENE XIII

AIR XIV. Pretty Parrot, say, &c.

MACHEATH.   *Pretty Polly, say,*
  When I was away,
  Did your fancy never stray
  To some newer lover?
POLLY.   *Without disguise,*
  Heaving sighs,
  Doating eyes,
  My constant heart discover.
  Fondly let me loll!
MACHEATH.   *O pretty, pretty Poll.*   10

POLLY. And are *you* as fond as ever, my dear?
MACHEATH. Suspect my honour, my courage, suspect any thing but my love.—May my pistols miss fire, and my mare slip her shoulder while I am pursued, if I ever forsake thee!

POLLY. Nay, my dear, I have no reason to doubt you, for I find in the romance you lent me, none of the great heroes were ever false in love.

AIR XV. Pray, fair one, be kind

MACHEATH. ·   *My heart was so free,*
  It roved like the Bee,
  'Till Polly my passion requited;   20
  I sipt each flower,

7. *Jack Ketch,* the hangman, from the name of a notorious one who died in 1686.

I changed ev'ry hour,
But here ev'ry flower is united.

POLLY. Were you sentenced to transportation, sure, my dear,
you could not leave me behind you—could you?

MACHEATH. Is there any power, any force that could tear me
from thee? You might sooner tear a pension out of the hands of
a courtier, a fee from a lawyer, a pretty woman from a looking-
glass, or any woman from quadrille.—But to tear me from thee is
impossible!   30

AIR XVI. Over the hills and far away

Were I laid on Greenland's coast,
And in my arms embraced my lass;
Warm amidst eternal frost,
Too soon the half year's night would pass.
POLLY. *Were I sold on Indian soil.*
Soon as the burning day was closed,
I could mock the sultry toil,
When on my charmer's breast reposed.
MACHEATH. *And I would love you all the day,*
POLLY. *Every night would kiss and play,*   40
MACHEATH. *If with me you'd fondly stray*
POLLY. *Over the hills and far away.*

POLLY. Yes, I would go with thee. But oh!—how shall I speak
it? I must be torn from thee. We must part.

MACHEATH. How! Part!

POLLY. We must, we must.—My Papa and Mama are set against
thy life. They now, even now are in search after thee. They are
preparing evidence against thee. Thy life depends upon a moment.

AIR XVII. Gin thou were mine awn thing

O what pain it is to part!
Can I leave thee, can I leave thee?   50
O what pain it is to part!
Can thy Polly ever leave thee?
But lest death my love should thwart,
And bring thee to the fatal cart,
Thus I tear thee from my bleeding heart!
Fly hence, and let me leave thee.

One kiss and then—one kiss—begone—farewell.

MACHEATH. My hand, my heart, my dear, is so riveted to thine, that I cannot unloose my hold.

POLLY. But my Papa may intercept thee, and then I should   60 lose the very glimmering of hope. A few weeks, perhaps, may reconcile us all. Shall thy Polly hear from thee?

MACHEATH. Must I then go?

POLLY. And will not absence change your love?

MACHEATH. If you doubt it, let me stay—and be hanged.

POLLY. O how I fear! how I tremble!—Go—but when safety will give you leave, you will be sure to see me again; for 'till then Polly is wretched.

AIR XVIII. O the broom, &c.

MACHEATH.   *The miser thus a shilling sees,*
      Which he's obliged to pay,   70
  With sighs resigns it by degrees,
      And fears 'tis gone for aye.

POLLY.   *The boy thus, when his sparrow's flown,*
      The bird in silence eyes;
  But soon as out of sight 'tis gone,
      Whines, whimpers, sobs and cries.

[*They part sorrowfully from each other, she going out one door, he at the other, each looking back at the other as they sing.*

ACT II

SCENE I

A meeting of criminals in a tavern near Newgate Prison. Jemmy Twitcher, Crook-finger'd Jack, Wat Dreary, Robin of Bagshot, Nimming Ned, Henry Padington, Matt of the Mint, Ben Budge, and the rest of the Gang are seated at the table, with wine, brandy and tobacco.

BEN. But prythee, Matt, what is become of thy brother Tom? I have not seen him since my return from transportation.

MATT. Poor brother Tom had an accident this time twelvemonth, and so clever a made fellow he was, that I could not save him from those flaying rascals the surgeons; and now, poor man, he is among the otamys at Surgeon's Hall.

BEN. So it seems, his time was come.

JEMMY. But the present time is ours, and no body alive hath more. Why are the laws levelled at us? are we more dishonest than the rest of mankind? what we win, gentlemen, is our 10 own by the law of arms, and the right of conquest.

CROOK-FINGERED JACK. Where shall we find such another set of practical philosophers, who to a man are above the fear of death?

WAT. Sound men, and true!

ROBIN. Of tried courage, and indefatigable industry!

NED. Who is there here that would not die for his friend?

HARRY. Who is there here that would betray him for his interest?

MATT. Show me a gang of courtiers that can say as much.

BEN. We are for a just partition of the world, for every 20 man hath a right to enjoy life.

MATT. We retrench the superfluities of mankind. The world is avaritious, and I hate avarice. A covetous fellow, like a Jack-daw, steals what he was never made to enjoy, for the sake of hiding it. These are the robbers of mankind, for money was made for the free-hearted and generous, and where is the injury of taking from another, what he hath not the heart to make use of?

JEMMY. Our several stations for the day are fixt. Good luck attend us all. Fill the glasses.

AIR XIX. Fill ev'ry glass, &c.

MATT. *Fill ev'ry glass, for wine inspires us,* 30
   And fires us
  With courage, love and joy.
  Women and wine should life employ.
  Is there ought else on earth desirous?
CHORUS. *Fill ev'ry glass, &c.*

SCENE II

As they conclude their song, Macheath enters. He is intent on escaping from the danger disclosed to him by Polly in their scene together.

6. *otamys,* corruption of anatomies, skeletons.
9. *levelled,* directed.

MACHEATH. Gentlemen, well met. My heart hath been with you this hour; but an unexpected affair hath detained me. No ceremony, I beg you.

MATT. We were just breaking up to go upon duty. Am I to have the honour of taking the air with you, sir, this evening upon the heath? I drink a dram now and then with the stage-coachmen in the way of friendship and intelligence; and I know that about this time there will be passengers upon the western road, who are worth speaking with.

MACHEATH. I was to have been of that party—but—   10

MATT. But what, sir?

MACHEATH. Is there any man who suspects my courage?

MATT. We have all been witnesses of it.

MACHEATH. My honour and truth to the gang?

MATT. I'll be answerable for it.

MACHEATH. In the division of our booty, have I ever shown the least marks of avarice or injustice?

MATT. By these questions something seems to have ruffled you. Are any of us suspected?

MACHEATH. I have a fixt confidence, gentlemen, in you all,   20
as men of honour, and as such I value and respect you. Peachum is a man that is useful to us.

MATT. Is he about to play us any foul play? I'll shoot him through the head.

MACHEATH. I beg you, gentlemen, act with conduct and discretion. A pistol is your last resort.

MATT. He knows nothing of this meeting.

MACHEATH. Business cannot go on without him. He is a man who knows the world, and is a necessary agent to us. We have had a slight difference, and till it is accommodated I shall   30
be obliged to keep out of his way. Any private dispute of mine shall be of no ill consequence to my friends. You must continue to act under his direction, for the moment we break loose from him, our gang is ruined.

MATT. As a bawd to a whore, I grant you, he is to us of great convenience.

MACHEATH. Make him believe I have quitted the gang, which I can never do but with life. At our private quarters I will continue to meet you. A week or so will probably reconcile us.

MATT. Your instructions shall be observ'd. 'Tis now high   40
time for us to repair to our several duties; so till the evening, at our quarters in Moor-fields, we bid your farewell.

MACHEATH. I shall wish my self with you. Success attend you.
[*He sits down melancholy at the table.*]

AIR XX. March in *Rinaldo*, with drums and trumpets

MATT. *Let us take the road.*
  Hark! I hear the sound of coaches!
  The hour of attack approaches,
  To your arms, brave boys, and load.
  See the ball I hold!
  Let the chemists toil like asses,   50
  Our fire their fire surpasses,
  And turns all our lead to gold.

[*The gang ranged in the front of the stage, load their pistols,
and stick them under their girdles; then go off singing the
first part in chorus.*

SCENE III

MACHEATH. What a fool is a fond wench! Polly is most con-
foundedly bit.—I love the sex. And a man who loves money,
might as well be contented with one guinea, as I with one woman.
The town perhaps hath been as much obliged to me, for recruiting it with free-hearted ladies, as to any recruiting officer in the
army. If it were not for us and the other gentlemen of the sword,
Drury-lane would be uninhabited.

AIR XXI. Would you have a young virgin, &c.

If the heart of a man is deprest with cares,
The mist is dispelled when a woman appears;
Like the notes of a fiddle, she sweetly, sweetly 10
Raises the spirits, and charms our ears.
 Roses and lillies her cheeks disclose,
 But her ripe lips are more sweet than those.
  Press her,
  Caress her,
  With blisses,
  Her kisses
Dissolve us in pleasure, and soft repose.

2. *bit*, deceived.

I must have women. There is nothing unbends the mind like them.
Money is not so strong a cordial for the time.—Drawer.—   20
[*Enter Drawer.*] Is the Porter gone for all the ladies, according
to my directions?

DRAWER. I expect him back every minute. But you know, sir,
you sent him as far as Hockley in the Hole for three of the ladies,
for one in Vinegar Yard, and for the rest of them somewhere
about Lewkner's Lane. Sure some of them are below, for I hear
the bar bell. As they come I will show them up.—Coming, coming.

SCENE IV

*Mrs. Coaxer, Dolly Trull, Mrs. Vixen, Betty Doxy, Jenny Diver,
Mrs. Slammekin, Suky Tawdry, and Molly Brazen enter. They
are the female counterparts of the group who have just gone
out.*

MACHEATH. Dear Mrs. Coaxer, you are welcome. You look
charmingly to-day. I hope you don't want the repairs of quality,
and lay on paint.—Dolly Trull! kiss me, you slut; are you as
amorous as ever, hussy? You are always so taken up with stealing
hearts, that you don't allow your self time to steal any thing else.
—Ah Dolly, thou wilt ever be a coquette!—Mrs. Vixen, I'm
yours, I always loved a woman of wit and spirit; they make
charming mistresses, but plaguy wives.—Betty Doxy! come
hither, hussy. Do you drink as hard as ever? You had better stick
to good wholesome beer; for in troth, Betty, strong-waters   10
will in time ruin your constitution. You should leave those to your
betters.—What! and my pretty Jenny Diver too! As prim and
demure as ever! There is not any prude, though ever so high
bred, hath a more sanctified look, with a more mischievous heart.
Ah! thou art a dear artful hypocrite.—Mrs. Slammekin! as careless and genteel as ever! all you fine ladies, who know your own
beauty, affect an undress.—But see, here's Suky Tawdry come to
contradict what I was saying. Every thing she gets one way she
lays out upon her back. Why, Suky, you must keep at least a
dozen tally-men. Molly Brazen! [*She kisses him.*] That's well   20
done. I love a free-hearted wench. Thou hast a most agreeable
assurance, girl, and art as willing as a turtle.—But hark! I hear
music. The harper is at the door. If music be the food of Love,

20. *tally-men*, sellers of goods on the installment plan of payment.
23. *If music be* . . . the first line of *Twelfth Night*.

play on. E'er you seat your selves, ladies, what think you of a
dance? Come in. [*Enter harper.*] Play the French tune, that Mrs.
Slammekin was so fond of.

    [*A Dance à la ronde in the French manner; near the end of it
    this Song and Chorus.*

AIR XXII. Cotillon

    Youth's the season made for joys,
        Love is then our duty;
    She alone who that employs,
        Well deserves her beauty.   30
        Let's be gay,
        While we may,
    Beauty's a flower despised in decay.

CHORUS.   *Youth's the season, &c.*
    Let us drink and sport to-day,
    Ours is not to-morrow.
    Love with youth flies swift away,
    Age is nought but sorrow.
        Dance and sing,
        Time's on the wing,   40
    Life never knows the return of spring.

CHORUS.   *Let us drink, &c.*

MACHEATH. Now pray ladies, take your places. Here Fellow,
[*Pays the Harper.*] Bid the drawer bring us more wine. [*Exit
Harper.*] If any of the ladies choose gin, I hope they will be so
free to call for it.

JENNY. You look as if you meant me. Wine is strong enough
for me. Indeed, sir, I never drink strong-waters, but when I have
the colic.

MACHEATH. Just the excuse of the fine ladies! Why, a lady   50
of quality is never without the colic. I hope, Mrs. Coaxer, you
have had good success of late in your visits among the mercers.

COAXER. We have so many interlopers—Yet with industry, one
may still have a little picking. I carried a silver-flower'd lutestring
and a piece of black padesoy to Mr. Peachum's lock but last week.

VIXEN. There's Molly Brazen hath the ogle of a rattlesnake. She
rivetted a linen-draper's eye so fast upon her, that he was nicked
of three pieces of cambric before he could look off.

54. *lutestring*, lustring, a strong, lustrous silk fabric.
55. *padesoy*, a strong corded silk. Mrs. Coaxer is a shoplifter.

BRAZEN. O dear madam!—But sure nothing can come up to your handling of laces! And then you have such a sweet deluding tongue! To cheat a man is nothing; but the woman must have fine parts indeed who cheats a woman!

VIXEN. Lace, madam, lies in a small compass, and is of easy conveyance. But you are apt, madam, to think too well of your friends.

COAXER. If any woman hath more art than another, to be sure, 'tis Jenny Diver. Though her fellow be never so agreeable, she can pick his pocket as coolly, as if money were her only pleasure. Now that is a command of the passions uncommon in a woman!

JENNY. I never go to the tavern with a man, but in the view of business. I have other hours, and other sort of men for my pleasure. But had I your address, madam—

MACHEATH. Have done with your compliments, ladies; and drink about: You are not so fond of me, Jenny, as you use to be.

JENNY. 'Tis not convenient, sir, to show my fondness among so many rivals. 'Tis your own choice, and not the warmth of my inclination, that will determine you.

AIR XXIII. All in a misty morning

Before the barn-door crowing,
The cock by hens attended,
His eyes around him throwing,   80
Stands for a while suspended:
Then one he singles from the crew,
And cheers the happy hen;
With how do you do, and how do you do,
And how do you do again.

MACHEATH. Ah Jenny! thou art a dear slut.

TRULL. Pray, madam, were you ever in keeping?

TAWDRY. I hope, madam, I ha'nt been so long upon the town, but I have met with some good fortune as well as my neighbours.

TRULL. Pardon me, madam, I meant no harm by the question; 'twas only in the way of conversation.

TAWDRY. Indeed, madam, if I had not been a fool, I might have lived very handsomely with my last friend. But upon his missing five guineas, he turned me off. Now I never suspected he had counted them.

SLAMMEKIN. Who do you look upon, madam, as your best sort of keepers?

TRULL. That, madam, is thereafter as they be.

SLAMMEKIN. I, madam, was once kept by a Jew; and, bating their religion, to women they are a good sort of people.   100

TAWDRY. Now for my part, I own I like an old fellow: for we always make them pay for what they can't do.

VIXEN. A spruce prentice, let me tell you, ladies, is no ill thing, they bleed freely. I have sent at least two or three dozen of them, in my time, to the plantations.

JENNY. But to be sure, sir, with so much good fortune as you have had upon the road, you must be grown immensely rich.

MACHEATH. The road, indeed, hath done me justice, but the gaming-table hath been my ruin.

AIR XXIV. When once I lay with another man's wife

JENNY.   *The gamesters and lawyers are jugglers alike,*   110
      If they meddle your all is in danger:.
    Like gypsies, if once they can finger a souse,
    Your pockets they pick, and they pilfer your house,
      And give your estate to a stranger.

A man of courage should never put any thing to the risk, but his life. These are the tools of a man of honour. Cards and dice are only fit for cowardly cheats, who prey upon their friends. [*She takes up his Pistol. Tawdry takes up the other.*]   ·

TAWDRY. This, sir, is fitter for your hand. Besides your loss of money, 'tis a loss to the ladies. Gaming takes you off from   120 women. How fond could I be of you! but before company, 'tis ill bred.

MACHEATH. Wanton hussies!

JENNY. I must and will have a kiss to give my wine a zest. [*They take him about the neck, and make signs to Peachum and Constables; who rush in upon him.*]

SCENE V

PEACHUM. I seize you, sir, as my prisoner.

MACHEATH. Was this well done, Jenny?—Women are decoy ducks; who can trust them! Beasts, jades, jilts, harpies, furies, whores!

104. *bleed,* pay.
105. *to the plantations,* i.e. they have been transported for stealing to support the prostitutes.

PEACHUM. Your case, Mr. Macheath, is not particular. The greatest heroes have been ruined by women. But, to do them justice, I must own they are a pretty sort of creatures, if we could trust them. You must now, sir, take your leave of the ladies, and if they have a mind to make you a visit, they will be sure to find you at home. The gentleman, ladies, lodges in Newgate. Con- 10 stables, wait upon the captain to his lodgings.

AIR XXV. When first I laid siege to my Chloris

MACHEATH. *At the tree I shall suffer with pleasure,*
At the tree I shall suffer with pleasure,
Let me go where I will,
In all kinds of ill,
I shall find no such furies as these are.

PEACHUM. Ladies, I'll take care the reckoning shall be discharged. [*Exit Macheath, guarded with Peachum and constables.*
The women remain.]   20

SCENE VI

VIXEN. Look ye, Mrs. Jenny, though Mr. Peachum may have made a private bargain with you and Suky Tawdry for betraying the captain, as we were all assisting, we ought all to share alike.

COAXER. I think, Mr. Peachum, after so long an acquaintance, might have trusted me as well as Jenny Diver.

SLAMMEKIN. I am sure at least three men of his hanging, and in a year's time too, (if he did me justice) should be set down to my account.

TRULL. Mrs. Slammekin, that is not fair. For you know one of them was taken in bed with me.   10

JENNY. As far as a bowl of punch or a treat, I believe Mrs. Suky will join with me.—As for any thing else, ladies, you cannot in conscience expect it.

SLAMMEKIN. Dear madam—

TRULL. I would not for the world—

SLAMMEKIN. 'Tis impossible for me—

TRULL. As I hope to be sav'd, madam—

SLAMMEKIN. Nay, then I must stay here all night—

TRULL. Since you command me.

[*They go out with great ceremony.*

SCENE VII

NEWGATE. *The constables bring in Macheath to Lockit, the jailer, and his turnkeys.*

LOCKIT. Noble captain, you are welcome. You have not been a lodger of mine this year and half. You know the custom, sir. Garnish, captain, garnish. Hand me down those fetters there.

MACHEATH. Those, Mr. Lockit, seem to be the heaviest of the whole set. With your leave, I should like the further pair better.

LOCKIT. Look ye, captain, we know what is fittest for our prisoners. When a gentleman uses me with civility, I always do the best I can to please him.—Hand them down I say.—We have them of all prices, from one guinea to ten, and 'tis fitting every gentleman should please himself.   10

MACHEATH. I understand you, sir. [*Gives money.*] The fees here are so many, and so exorbitant, that few fortunes can bear the expence of getting off handsomly, or of dying like a gentleman.

LOCKIT. Those, I see, will fit the captain better.—Take down the further pair. Do but examine them, sir.—Never was better work.—How genteely they are made!—They will fit as easy as a glove, and the nicest man in England might not be asham'd to wear them. [*He puts on the chains.*] If I had the best gentleman in the land in my custody I could not equip him more hand- 20 somly. And so, sir—I now leave you to your private meditations.

[*He and the rest go out, leaving Macheath alone.*

SCENE VIII

AIR XXVI. Courtiers, courtiers think it no harm

MACHEATH. *Man may escape from rope and gun;*
　　　　Nay, some have out-lived the doctor's pill:
　　　　Who takes a woman must be undone,
　　　　That basilisk is sure to kill.
　　　　The fly that sips treacle is lost in the sweets,
　　　　So he that tastes woman, woman, woman,
　　　　He that tastes woman, ruin meets.

---

3. *garnish*, tip, customary when a prisoner entered jail. The necessity for a sizeable tip is made clear in the following lines.

To what a woful plight have I brought my self! Here must I (all
day long, 'till I am hanged) be confined to hear the reproaches
of a wench who lays her ruin at my door.—I am in the cus-   10
tody of her father, and to be sure if he knows of the matter, I
shall have a fine time on't betwixt this and my execution.—But I
promised the wench marriage.—What signifies a promise to a
woman? does not man in marriage itself promise a hundred things
that he never means to perform? Do all we can, women will believe us; for they look upon a promise as an excuse for following
their own inclinations.—But here comes Lucy, and I cannot get
from her—would I were deaf!

SCENE IX

Lucy enters, indignant and angry.

LUCY. You base man, you,—how can you look me in the face
after what hath past between us?—See here, perfidious wretch,
how I am forc'd to bear about the load of infamy you have laid
upon me—O Macheath! thou hast robbed me of my quiet—to
see thee tortured would give me pleasure.

AIR XXVII. A lovely lass to a friar came

Thus when a good huswife sees a rat
In her trap in the morning taken,
With pleasure her heart goes pit a pat,
In revenge for her loss of bacon.
Then she throws him   10
To the dog or cat,
To be worried, crushed and shaken.

MACHEATH. Have you no bowels, no tenderness, my dear Lucy,
to see a husband in these circumstances?
LUCY. A husband!
MACHEATH [*Intent on getting out of a bad situation*]. In ev'ry
respect but the form, and that, my dear, may be said over us at
any time.—Friends should not insist upon ceremonies. From a
man of honour, his word is as good as his bond.
LUCY. 'Tis the pleasure of all you fine men to insult the   20
women you have ruined.

AIR XXVIII. 'Twas when the sea was roaring

> *How cruel are the traitors,*
> *Who lie and swear in jest,*
> *To cheat unguarded creatures*
> *Of virtue, fame, and rest!*
> *Whoever steals a shilling,*
> *Thro' shame the guilt conceals:*
> *In love the perjured villain*
> *With boasts the theft reveals.*

MACHEATH. The very first opportunity, my dear, (have but 30
patience) you shall be my wife in whatever manner you please.

LUCY. Insinuating monster! And so you think I know nothing
of the affair of Miss Polly Peachum.—I could tear thy eyes out!

MACHEATH. Sure, Lucy, you can't be such a fool as to be jealous
of Polly!

LUCY. Are you not married to her, you brute, you?

MACHEATH [*Amused*]. Married! Very good. The wench gives it
out only to vex thee, and to ruin me in thy good opinion. 'Tis
true, I go to the house; I chat with the girl, I kiss her, I say a
thousand things to her (as all gentlemen do) that mean noth- 40
ing, to divert myself; and now the silly jade hath set it about that
I am married to her, to let me know what she would be at. Indeed, my dear Lucy, these violent passions may be of ill consequence to a woman in your condition.

LUCY. Come, come, captain, for all your assurance, you know
that Miss Polly hath put it out of your power to do me the justice
you promised me.

MACHEATH. A jealous woman believes every thing her passion
suggests. To convince you of my sincerity, if we can find the
ordinary, I shall have no scruples of making you my wife; 50
and I know the consequence of having two at a time.

LUCY. That you are only to be hanged, and so get rid of them
both.

MACHEATH. I am ready, my dear Lucy, to give you satisfaction
—if you think there is any in marriage.—What can a man of
honour say more?

LUCY. So then it seems you are not married to Miss Polly.

MACHEATH. You know, Lucy, the girl is prodigiously conceited.
No man can say a civil thing to her, but (like other fine ladies)
her vanity makes her think he's her own for ever and ever. 60

AIR XXIX. *The sun had loosed his weary teams*

> *The first time at the looking-glass*
> *The mother sets her daughter,*
> *The image strikes the smiling lass*
> *With self-love ever after.*
> *Each time she looks, she, fonder grown,*
> *Thinks every charm grows stronger:*
> *But alas, vain maid, all eyes but your own*
> *Can see you are not younger.*

When women consider their own beauties, they are all alike un-reasonable in their demands; for they expect their lovers 70 should like them as long as they like themselves.

LUCY. Yonder is my father—perhaps this way we may light upon the ordinary, who shall try if you will be as good as your word.—For I long to be made an honest woman.

SCENE X

Enter Peachum and Lockit with an Account-Book. They are discussing the division of the reward for the capture of Macheath.

LOCKIT. In this last affair, brother Peachum, we are agreed. You have consented to go halves in Macheath.

PEACHUM. We shall never fall out about an execution.—But as to that article, pray how stands our last year's account?

LOCKIT. If you will run your eye over it, you'll find 'tis fair and clearly stated.

PEACHUM. This long arrear of the government is very hard upon us! Can it be expected that we should hang our acquaintance for nothing, when our betters will hardly save theirs without be-ing paid for it. Unless the people in employment pay better, 10 I promise them for the future, I shall let other rogues live besides their own.

LOCKIT. Perhaps, brother, they are afraid these matters may be carried too far. We are treated too by them with contempt, as if our profession were not reputable.

PEACHUM. In one respect indeed, our employment may be reckoned dishonest, because, like great statesmen, we encourage those who betray their friends.

LOCKIT. Such language, brother, any where else, might turn to your prejudice. Learn to be more guarded, I beg you.   20

AIR XXX. How happy are we, &c.

When you censure the age,
Be cautious and sage,
Lest the courtiers offended should be:
If you mention vice or bribe,
'Tis so pat to all the tribe;
Each cries—That was levelled at me.

PEACHUM. Here's poor Ned Clincher's name, I see. Sure, brother Lockit, there was a little unfair proceeding in Ned's case: for he told me in the condemned hold, that for value received, you had promised him a Session or two longer without molestation.   30

LOCKIT. Mr. Peachum,—this is the first time my honour was ever called in question.

PEACHUM. Business is at an end—if once we act dishonourably.

LOCKIT. Who accuses me?

PEACHUM. You are warm, brother.

LOCKIT. He that attacks my honour, attacks my livelihood.— And this usage—sir—is not to be born.

PEACHUM. Since you provoke me to speak—I must tell you too, that Mrs. Coaxer charges you with defrauding her of her information-money, for the apprehending of curl-pated Hugh.   40 Indeed, indeed, brother, we must punctually pay our spies, or we shall have no information.

LOCKIT. Is this language to me, sirrah—who have saved you from the gallows, sirrah! [*They seize each other by the collar. For a moment it looks as if they would fight.*]

PEACHUM. If I am hanged, it shall be for ridding the world of an arrant rascal.

LOCKIT. This hand shall do the office of the halter you deserve, and throttle you—you dog!—

PEACHUM. Brother, brother,—we are both in the wrong—   50 we shall be both losers in the dispute—for you know we have it in our power to hang each other. You should not be so passionate.

LOCKIT. Nor you so provoking.

PEACHUM. 'Tis our mutual interest; 'tis for the interest of the world we should agree. If I said any thing, brother, to the prejudice of your character, I ask pardon.

LOCKIT. Brother Peachum—I can forgive as well as resent.— Give me your hand. Suspicion does not become a friend.

PEACHUM. I only meant to give you occasion to justify yourself: But I must now step home, for I expect the gentleman 60 about this snuff-box, that Filch nimmed two nights ago in the park. I appointed him at this hour. [*He goes out.*

SCENE XI

Lucy comes weeping to her father.

LOCKIT. Whence come you, hussy?

LUCY. My tears might answer that question.

LOCKIT. You have then been whimpering and fondling, like a spaniel, over that fellow that hath abused you.

LUCY. One can't help love; one can't cure it. 'Tis not in my power to obey you, and hate him.

LOCKIT. Learn to bear your husband's death like a reasonable woman. 'Tis not the fashion, now-a-days, so much as to affect sorrow upon these occasions. No woman would ever marry, if she had not the chance of mortality for a release. Act like a 10 woman of spirit, hussy, and thank your father for what he is doing.

AIR XXXI. Of a noble race was Shenkin

LUCY.
    Is then his fate decreed, sir,
      Such a man can I think of quitting?
    When first we met, so moves me yet,
      O see how my heart is splitting!

LOCKIT. Look ye, Lucy—there is no saving him.—So, I think, you must ev'n do like other widows—buy your self weeds, and be cheerful.

AIR XXXII.

    You'll think, e'er many days ensue,   20
      This sentence not severe;
    I hang your husband, child, 'tis true,
      But with him hang your care.
      Twang dang dillo dee.

Like a good wife, go moan over your dying husband. That, child, is your duty—consider girl, you can't have the man and the

4. *abused,* deceived.

money too—so make yourself as easy as you can by getting all
you can from him. [*He pushes her away from him and goes out.
She returns to Macheath.*

SCENE XII

LUCY. Though the ordinary was out of the way to day, I hope,
my dear, you will, upon the first opportunity, quiet my scruples—
[*Breaking down.*] Oh sir!—my father's hard heart is not to be
softened, and I am in the utmost despair.

MACHEATH. But if I could raise a small sum—would not twenty
guineas, think you, move him?—Of all the arguments in the way
of business, the perquisite is the most prevailing.—Your father's
perquisites for the escape of prisoners must amount to a considerable sum in the year. Money well timed, and properly applied, will do any thing.   10

AIR XXXIII. London Ladies

*If you at an office solicit your due,
    And would not have matters neglected;
You must quicken the clerk with the perquisite too,
    To do what his duty directed.
Or would you the frowns of a lady prevent,
    She too has this palpable failing,
The perquisite softens her into consent;
    That reason with all is prevailing.*

LUCY. What love or money can do shall be done: for all my   20
comfort depends upon your safety.

SCENE XIII

*Polly rushes frantically in and tries to embrace Macheath, who
tries to escape her.*

POLLY. Where is my dear husband?—Was a rope ever intended
for this neck!—O let me throw my arms about it, and throttle
thee with love!—Why dost thou turn away from me?—'Tis thy
Polly—'tis thy wife.

MACHEATH. Was ever such an unfortunate rascal as I am!

LUCY. Was there ever such another villain!

POLLY. O Macheath! was it for this we parted? Taken! Imprisoned! Tried! Hanged!—Cruel reflection! I'll stay with thee 'till death.—No force shall tear thy dear wife from thee now.— What means my love?—Not one kind word! not one kind 10 look! think what thy Polly suffers to see thee in this condition!

AIR XXXIV. *All in the downs, &c.*

Thus when the swallow, seeking prey,
Within the sash is closely pent,
His consort with bemoaning lay,
Without sits pining for th' event.
Her chatt'ring lovers all around her skim;
She heeds them not (poor bird) her soul's with him.

MACHEATH [*Aside*]. I must disown her. The wench is distracted.

LUCY. Am I then bilked of my virtue? Can I have no reparation? Sure men were born to lie, and women to believe them! O 20 villain! villain!

POLLY. Am I not thy wife?—Thy neglect of me, thy aversion to me too severely proves it.—Look on me.—Tell me, am I not thy wife?

LUCY. Perfidious wretch!

POLLY. Barbarous husband!

LUCY. Hadst thou been hanged five months ago, I had been happy.

POLLY. And I too.—If you had been kind to me 'till death, it would not have vexed me.—And that's no very unreasonable 30 request, (though from a wife) to a man who hath not above seven or eight days to live.

LUCY. Art thou then married to another? Hast thou two wives, monster?

MACHEATH. If women's tongues can cease for an answer— hear me.

LUCY. I won't.—Flesh and blood can't bear my usage.

POLLY. Shall I not claim my own? Justice bids me speak.

AIR XXXV. *Have you heard of a frolicksome ditty*

MACHEATH. *How happy could I be with either,*
Were t'other dear charmer away!   40
But while you thus teaze me together,
To neither a word will I say,
But tol de rol, &c.

POLLY. Sure, my dear, there ought to be some preference shown to a wife! At least she may claim the appearance of it. He must be distracted with his misfortunes, or he could not use me thus!

LUCY. O villain, villain! thou hast deceived me.—I could even inform against thee with pleasure. Not a prude wishes more heartily to have facts against her intimate acquaintance, than I now wish to have facts against thee. I would have her satis- 50 faction, and they should all out.

AIR XXXVI. Irish Trot

POLLY. *I'm bubbled.*
LUCY.   *I'm bubbled.*
POLLY. *Oh how I am troubled!*
LUCY. *Bamboozled, and bit!*
POLLY.   *My distresses are doubled.*
LUCY. *When you come to the tree, should the hangman refuse,*
     These fingers, with pleasure, could fasten the noose.
POLLY. *I'm bubbled, &c.*

MACHEATH. Be pacified, my dear Lucy.—This is all a fetch 60 of Polly's to make me desperate with you in case I get off. If I am hang'd, she would fain have the credit of being thought my widow.—Really, Polly, this is no time for a dispute of this sort; for whenever you are talking of marriage, I am thinking of hanging.

POLLY. And hast thou the heart to persist in disowning me?

MACHEATH. And hast thou the heart to persist in persuading me that I am married? Why, Polly, dost thou seek to aggravate my misfortunes?

LUCY [*On her dignity*]. Really, Miss Peachum, you but 70 expose yourself. Besides, 'tis barbarous in you to worry a gentleman in his circumstances.

AIR XXXVII

POLLY.   *Cease your funning;*
            Force or cunning
       Never shall my heart trepan.
         All these sallies
         Are but malice
      To seduce my constant man.
        'Tis most certain,
        By their flirting   80

51. *bubbled,* cheated.

Women oft have envy shown:
Pleased, to ruin
Others wooing;
Never happy in their own!

POLLY. Decency, madam, methinks might teach you to behave yourself with some reserve with the husband, while his wife is present.

MACHEATH. But seriously, Polly, this is carrying the joke a little too far.

LUCY. If you are determined, madam, to raise a disturbance 90 in the prison, I shall be obliged to send for the turnkey to shew you the door. I am sorry, madam, you force me to be so ill-bred.

POLLY. Give me leave to tell you, madam; these forward airs don't become you in the least, madam. And my duty, madam, obliges me to stay with my husband, madam.

AIR XXXVIII. Good-morrow, gossip Joan.

LUCY.   *Why how now, madam flirt?*
               If you thus must chatter,
               And are for flinging dirt,
               Let's try who best can spatter;
                         Madam flirt!   100
POLLY.   *Why how now, saucy jade;*
               Sure the wench is tipsy!
               How can you see me made   [*To him.*
               The scoff of such a gipsy?
                         Saucy jade!   [*To her.*

SCENE XIV

Peachum comes in. He is afraid for his daughter to be long with Macheath.

PEACHUM. Where's my wench? Ah hussy! hussy!—Come you home, you slut; and when your fellow is hanged, hang yourself, to make your family some amends.

POLLY. Dear, dear father, do not tear me from him—I must speak; I have more to say to him.—Oh! twist thy fetters about me, that he may not haul me from thee!

PEACHUM. Sure all women are alike! If ever they commit the folly, they are sure to commit another by exposing themselves.—Away.—Not a word more!—You are my prisoner now, hussy.

AIR XXXIX. Irish howl

POLLY.   *No power on earth can e'er divide*   10
        The knot that sacred love hath tied.
        When parents draw against our mind,
        The true-love's knot they faster bind.
        Oh, oh ray, oh Amborah—oh, oh, &c.
[*Holding Macheath, Peachum pulling her, and finally dragging her away.*]

SCENE XV

MACHEATH [*Determined to wriggle out of the difficulty*]. I am naturally compassionate, wife; so that I could not use the wench as she deserv'd; which made you at first suspect there was something in what she said.

LUCY. Indeed, my dear, I was strangely puzzled.

MACHEATH. If that had been the case, her father would never have brought me into this circumstance.—No, Lucy,—I had rather die than be false to thee.

LUCY. How happy am I, if you say this from your heart! For I love thee so, that I could sooner bear to see thee hanged   10 than in the arms of another.

MACHEATH. But couldst thou bear to see me hanged?

LUCY. O Macheath, I can never live to see that day.

MACHEATH. You see, Lucy, in the account of love you are in my debt; and you must now be convinced, that I rather choose to die than be another's.—Make me, if possible, love thee more, and let me owe my life to thee.—If you refuse to assist me, Peachum and your father will immediately put me beyond all means of escape.

LUCY. My father, I know, hath been drinking hard with the   20 prisoners: and I fancy he is now taking his nap in his own room.— If I can procure the keys, shall I go off with thee, my dear?

MACHEATH. If we are together, 'twill be impossible to lie conceal'd. As soon as the search begins to be a little cool, I will send to thee.—'Till then my heart is thy prisoner.

LUCY. Come then, my dear husband—owe thy life to me—and though you love me not—be grateful.—[*Hesitating.*] But that Polly runs in my head strangely.

MACHEATH. A moment of time may make us unhappy forever.

AIR XL. The Lass of Patie's Mill.

LUCY. *I like the fox shall grieve,* 30
Whose mate hath left her side,
Whom hounds, from morn to eve,
Chase o'er the country wide.
Where can my lover hide?
Where cheat the wary pack?
If love be not his guide,
He never will come back!

[*They go out.*

ACT III

SCENE I

Macheath has escaped as planned at the end of the last act. Lockit is certain that his daughter has assisted the highwayman and is trying to get a confession from her.

LOCKIT. To be sure, wench, you must have been aiding and abetting to help him to this escape.

LUCY. Sir, here hath been Peachum and his daughter Polly, and to be sure they know the ways of Newgate as well as if they had been born and bred in the place all their lives. Why must all your suspicion light upon me?

LOCKIT. Lucy, Lucy, I will have none of these shuffling answers.

LUCY. Well then—if I know any thing of him I wish I may be burnt!

LOCKIT. Keep your temper, Lucy, or I shall pronounce you 10 guilty.

LUCY. Keep yours, sir,—I do wish I may be burnt. I do.—And what can I say more to convince you?

LOCKIT [*Coming to practical issues*]. Did he tip handsomely?— How much did he come down with? Come hussy, don't cheat your father; and I shall not be angry with you.—Perhaps, you have made a better bargain with him than I could have done.— How much, my good girl?

LUCY. You know, sir, I am fond of him, and would have given money to have kept him with me. 20

LOCKIT. Ah, Lucy! thy education might have put thee more

upon thy guard; for a girl in the bar of an alehouse is always besieged.

LUCY. Dear sir, mention not my education—for 'twas to that I owe my ruin.

AIR XLI. *If love's a sweet passion, &c.*

When young at the bar you first taught me to score,
And bid me be free with my lips, and no more;
I was kissed by the parson, the squire, and the sot:
When the guest was departed, the kiss was forgot.
But his kiss was so sweet, and so closely he prest,　　30
That I languished and pined 'till I granted the rest.

If you can forgive me, sir, I will make a fair confession, for to be sure he hath been a most barbarous villain to me.

LOCKIT. And so you have let him escape, hussy—have you?

LUCY. When a woman loves; a kind look, a tender word can persuade her to any thing—and I could ask no other bribe.

LOCKIT. Thou wilt always be a vulgar slut, Lucy.—If you would not be looked upon as a fool, you should never do any thing but upon the foot of interest. Those that act otherwise are their own bubbles.　　40

LUCY. But love, sir, is a misfortune that may happen to the most discreet woman, and in love we are all fools alike.—Notwithstanding all he swore, I am now fully convinced that Polly Peachum is actually his wife.—Did I let him escape, (fool that I was!) to go to her?—Polly will wheedle her self into his money, and then Peachum will hang him, and cheat us both.

LOCKIT. So I am to be ruined, because, forsooth, you must be in love!—a very pretty excuse!

LUCY. I could murder that impudent happy strumpet:—I gave him his life, and that creature enjoys the sweets of it.—Un-　　50
grateful Macheath!

AIR XLII. South-sea ballad

My love is all madness and folly,
*　　Alone I lie,*
*　　Toss, tumble, and cry,*
What a happy creature is Polly!
Was e'er such a wretch as I!
With rage I redden like scarlet,
That my dear inconstant varlet,

Stark blind to my charms,
Is lost in the arms   60
Of that jilt, that inveigling harlot!
Stark blind to my charms,
Is lost in the arms
Of that jilt, that inveigling harlot!
This, this my resentment alarms.

LOCKIT. And so, after all this mischief, I must stay here to be entertain'd with your caterwauling, mistress puss!—Out of my sight, wanton strumpet! you shall fast and mortify yourself into reason, with now and then a little handsome discipline to bring you to your senses.—Go. [*He pushes her off.*]   70

SCENE II

LOCKIT. Peachum then intends to outwit me in this affair; but I'll be even with him.—The dog is leaky in his liquor, so I'll ply him that way, get the secret from him, and turn this affair to my own advantage.—Lions, wolves, and vultures don't live together in herds, droves or flocks.—Of all animals of prey, man is the only sociable one. Every one of us preys upon his neighbour, and yet we herd together.—Peachum is my companion, my friend.— According to the custom of the world, indeed, he may quote thousands of precedents for cheating me.—And shall not I make use of the privilege of friendship to make him a return?   10

AIR XLIII. Packington's pound

Thus gamesters united in friendship are found,
Though they know that their industry all is a cheat;
They flock to their prey at the dice-box's sound,
And join to promote one another's deceit.
    But if by mishap
    They fail of a chap,
To keep in their hands, they each other entrap.
Like pikes, lank with hunger, who miss of their ends,
They bite their companions, and prey on their friends.

Now, Peachum, you and I, like honest tradesmen, are to   20 have a fair trial which of us two can over-reach the other.— Lucy.—[*Enter Lucy.*] Are there any of Peachum's people now in the house?

LUCY. Filch, sir, is drinking a quartern of strong-waters in the next room with black Moll.

LOCKIT. Bid him come to me.

[*She goes out, and shortly thereafter Filch enters.*]

SCENE III

LOCKIT. Why, boy, thou lookest as if thou wert half starved; like a shotten herring.

FILCH. One had need have the constitution of a horse to go through the business.—Since the favourite child-getter was disabled by a mishap, I have picked up a little money by helping the ladies to a pregnancy against their being called down to sentence. —But if a man cannot get an honest livelihood any easier way, I am sure, 'tis what I can't undertake for another Session.

LOCKIT. Truly, if that great man should tip off, 'twould be an irreparable loss. The vigor and prowess of a knight-errant never saved half the ladies in distress that he hath done.—But, boy, can'st thou tell me where thy master is to be found?

FILCH. At his lock, sir, at the Crooked Billet.

LOCKIT. Very well.—I have nothing more with you. [*Exit Filch.*] I'll go to him there, for I have many important affairs to settle with him; and in the way of those transactions, I'll artfully get into his secret.—So that Macheath shall not remain a day longer out of my clutches.   [*He goes out.*]

SCENE IV

A GAMING-HOUSE. *Macheath, in a fine tarnished Coat, Ben Budge, and Mat of the Mint enter. They have been having no success in highway robbery.*

MACHEATH. I am sorry, gentlemen, the road was so barren of money. When my friends are in difficulties, I am always glad that my fortune can be serviceable to them. [*Gives them money.*] You see, gentlemen, I am not a mere court friend, who professes every thing and will do nothing.

---

2. *shotten*, a herring that has cast its spawn.
13. *lock*, a storehouse for stolen goods.

AIR XLIV. Lillibulero

The modes of the court so common are grown,
That a true friend can hardly be met;
Friendship for interest is but a loan,
Which they let out for what they can get.
'Tis true, you find 10
Some friends so kind,
Who will give you good counsel themselves to defend.
In sorrowful ditty,
They promise, they pity,
But shift you for money, from friend to friend.

But we, gentlemen, have still honour enough to break through the corruptions of the world.—And while I can serve you, you may command me.

BEN. It grieves my heart that so generous a man should be involved in such difficulties, as oblige him to live with such ill 20 company, and herd with gamesters.

MATT. See the partiality of mankind!—One man may steal a horse, better than another look over a hedge.—Of all mechanics, of all servile handicraftsmen, a gamester is the vilest. But yet, as many of the quality are of the profession, he is admitted amongst the politest company. I wonder we are not more respected.

MACHEATH. There will be deep play to-night at Marybone, and consequently money may be picked up upon the road. Meet me there, and I'll give you the hint who is worth setting.

MATT. The fellow with a brown coat with a narrow gold 30 binding, I am told, is never without money.

MACHEATH. What do you mean, Matt?—Sure you will not think of meddling with him!—He's a good honest kind of a fellow, and one of us.

BEN. To be sure, sir, we will put our selves under your direction.

MACHEATH. Have an eye upon the money-lenders.—A Rouleau, or two, would prove a pretty sort of an expedition. I hate extortion.

MATT. Those Rouleaus are very pretty things.—I hate your 40 bank bills—there is such a hazard in putting them off.

MACHEATH. There is a certain man of distinction, who in his time hath nicked me out of a great deal of the ready. He is in my

29. *setting*, waiting to rob.
37. *Rouleau*, a cylindrical packet of from twenty to fifty gold pieces.

cash, Ben;—I'll point him out to you this evening, and you shall
draw upon him for the debt.—The company are met; I hear the
dice-box in the other room. So, gentlemen, your servant. You'll
meet me at Marybone.

SCENE V

PEACHUM'S LOCK. *Peachum and Lockit are seated at a table with
wine, brandy, pipes and tobacco. Lockit has told Peachum
of Macheath's escape; now they are discussing other matters
of business.*

LOCKIT. The coronation account, brother Peachum, is of so
intricate a nature, that I believe it will never be settled. .
PEACHUM. It consists indeed of a great variety of articles.—It
was worth to our people, in fees of different kinds, above ten
instalments.—This is part of the account, brother, that lies open
before us.
LOCKIT. A lady's tail of rich brocade—that, I see, is disposed of.
PEACHUM. To Mrs. Diana Trapes, the tally-woman, and she
will make a good hand on't in shoes and slippers, to trick out
young ladies, upon their going into keeping.—   10
LOCKIT. But I don't see any article of the jewels.
PEACHUM. Those are so well known, that they must be sent
abroad.—You'll find them entered under the article of exportation.—As for the snuff-boxes, watches, swords, &c.—I thought it
best to enter them under their several heads.
LOCKIT. Seven and twenty women's pockets complete; with
the several things therein contained; all sealed, numbered, and
entered.
PEACHUM. But, brother, it is impossible for us now to enter
upon this affair.—We should have the whole day before us.—   20
Besides, the account of the last half year's plate is a book by it
self, which lies at the other office.
LOCKIT. Bring us then more liquor.—To-day shall be for pleasure—to-morrow for business.—Ah brother, those daughters of
ours are two slippery hussies.—Keep a watchful eye upon Polly,
and Macheath in a day or two shall be our own again.

1. *coronation account*, list of things stolen during the coronation of
George II, 1727.

AIR XLV. Down in the north country

LOCKIT. *What gudgeons are we men!*
Ev'ry woman's easy prey.
Though we have felt the hook, again
We bite, and they betray.   30

The bird that hath been trapped,
When he hears his calling mate,
To her he flies, again he's clapt
Within the wiry grate.

PEACHUM. But what signifies catching the bird, if your daughter Lucy will set open the door of the cage?

LOCKIT. If men were answerable for the follies and frailties of their wives and daughters, no friends could keep a good correspondence together for two days.—This is unkind of you, brother; for among good friends, what they say or do goes   40
for nothing.

[*Enter a Servant.*

SERVANT. Sir, here's Mrs. Diana Trapes wants to speak with you.

PEACHUM. Shall we admit her, brother Lockit?

LOCKIT. By all means—she's a good customer, and a fine-spoken woman—and a woman who drinks and talks so freely will enliven the conversation.

PEACHUM. Desire her to walk in.

[*Exit Servant. A moment later Mrs. Trapes enters.*

SCENE VI

PEACHUM. Dear Mrs. Dye, your servant—one may know by your kiss, that your gin is excellent.

TRAPES. I was always very curious in my liquors.

LOCKIT. There is no perfumed breath like it—I have been long acquainted with the flavour of those lips—han't I, Mrs. Dye?

TRAPES. Fill it up.—I take as large draughts of liquor, as I did of love.—I hate a flincher in either.

AIR XLVI. A shepherd kept sheep, &c.

In the days of my youth I could bill like a dove, fa, la, la, &c.
Like a sparrow at all times was ready for love, fa, la, la, &c.

3. *curious,* careful.

The life of all mortals in kissing should pass,   10
Lip to lip while we're young—then the lip to the glass, fa, la, &c.

But now, Mr. Peachum, to our business.—If you have blacks of
any kind, brought in of late; mantoes—velvet scarfs—petticoats—
let it be what it will—I am your chap—for all my ladies are very
fond of mourning.

PEACHUM. Why, look ye, Mrs. Dye—you deal so hard with us,
that we can afford to give the gentlemen, who venture their lives
for the goods, little or nothing.

TRAPES. The hard times oblige me to go very near in my dealing.—To be sure, of late years I have been a great sufferer   20
by the parliament.—Three thousand pounds would hardly make
me amends.—The act for destroying the Mint was a severe cut
upon our business.—'Till then, if a customer step: out of the way
—we knew where to have her.—No doubt you know Mrs. Coaxer
—there's a wench now ('till to-day) with a good suit of clothes
of mine upon her back, and I could never set eyes upon her for
three months together.—Since the act too against imprisonment
for small sums, my loss there too hath been very considerable,
and it must be so, when a lady can borrow a handsome petticoat,
or a clean gown, and I not have the least hank upon her!   30
And, o' my conscience, now-a-days most ladies take a delight in
cheating, when they can do it with safety.

PEACHUM. Madam, you had a handsome gold watch of us t'other
day for seven guineas.—Considering we must have our profit—
to a gentleman upon the road, a gold watch will be scarce worth
the taking.

TRAPES. Consider, Mr. Peachum, that watch was remarkable,
and not of very safe sale.—If you have any black velvet scarfs—
they are a handsome winter wear; and take with most gentlemen
who deal with my customers.—'Tis I that put the ladies upon   40
a good foot. 'Tis not youth or beauty that fixes their price. The
gentlemen always pay according to their dress, from half a crown
to two guineas; and yet those hussies make nothing of bilking of
me.—Then too, allowing for accidents.—I have eleven fine customers now down under the surgeon's hands,—what with fees
and other expences, there are great goings-out, and no comings-in,
and not a farthing to pay for at least a month's clothing.—We run
great risks—great risks indeed.

PEACHUM. As I remember, you said something just now of Mrs.
Coaxer.   50

22. *Mint*, in Southwark, a resort for criminals, destroyed in 1723.

TRAPES. Yes, sir.—To be sure I stripped her of a suit of my own clothes about two hours ago; and have left her as she should be, in her shift, with a lover of hers at my house. She called him up stairs, as he was going to Marybone in a hackney-coach.—And I hope, for her own sake and mine, she will perswade the captain to redeem her, for the captain is very generous to the ladies.

LOCKIT. What captain?

TRAPES. He thought I did not know him.—An intimate acquaintance of yours, Mr. Peachum—only captain Macheath—as fine as a Lord.   60

PEACHUM [*Excited*]. To-morrow, dear Mrs. Dye, you shall set your own price upon any of the goods you like—we have at least half a dozen velvet scarfs, and all at your service. Will you give me leave to make you a present of this suit of night-clothes for your own wearing?—But are you sure it is captain Macheath?

TRAPES. Though he thinks I have forgot him; nobody knows him better. I have taken a great deal of the captain's money in my time at second-hand, for he always loved to have his ladies well drest.

PEACHUM. Mr. Lockit and I have a little business with the   70 captain;—you understand me—and we will satisfy you for Mrs. Coaxer's debt.

LOCKIT. Depend upon it—we will deal like men of honour.

TRAPES. I don't enquire after your affairs—so whatever happens, I wash my hands on't.—It hath always been my maxim, that one friend should assist another.—But if you please—I'll take one of the scarfs home with me, 'tis always good to have something in hand.

SCENE VII

NEWGATE. *Lucy enters mournfully, bearing a bottle of poison.*

LUCY. Jealousy, rage, love and fear are at once tearing me to pieces. How I am weather-beaten and shatter'd with distress!

AIR XLVII. One evening having lost my way

I'm like a skiff on the ocean tost,
Now high, now low, with each billow born,
With her rudder broke, and her anchor lost,
Deserted and all forlorn.
While thus I lie rolling and tossing all night,

> *That Polly lies sporting on seas of delight!*
> *Revenge, revenge, revenge.*
> *Shall appease my restless sprite.*   10

I have the rats-bane ready.—I run no risk; for I can lay her death upon the gin, and so many die of that naturally that I shall never be call'd in question.—But say I were to be hanged—I never could be hang'd for any thing that would give me greater comfort, than the poisoning that slut.

    [*Enter Filch.*

FILCH. Madam, here's our Miss Polly come to wait upon you.

LUCY. Show her in.

SCENE VIII

Polly enters.

    LUCY. Dear madam, your servant.—I hope you will pardon my passion, when I was so happy to see you last.—I was so over-run with the spleen, that I was perfectly out of my self. And really when one hath the spleen, every thing is to be excus'd by a friend.

AIR XLVIII. Now Roger, I'll tell thee, because thou'rt my son

> *When a wife's in her pout,*
> *(As she's sometimes, no doubt)*
>   *The good husband as meek as a lamb,*
>   *Her vapours to still,*
>   *First grants her her will,*   10
> *And the quieting draught is a dram.*
> *Poor man! And the quieting draught is a dram.*

—I wish all our quarrels might have so comfortable a reconciliation.

    POLLY. I have no excuse for my own behaviour, madam, but my misfortunes.—And really, madam, I suffer too upon your account.

    LUCY. But, Miss Polly—in the way of friendship, will you give me leave to propose a glass of cordial to you?

    POLLY. Strong-waters are apt to give me the headache—I   20 hope, madam, you will excuse me.

LUCY. Not the greatest lady in the land could have better in her
closet, for her own private drinking.—You seem mighty low in
spirits, my dear.

POLLY. I am sorry, madam, my health will not allow me to
accept of your offer.—I should not have left you in the rude
manner I did when we met last, madam, had not my papa hauled
me away so unexpectedly.—I was indeed somewhat provoked,
and perhaps might use some expressions that were disrespectful.
—But really, madam, the captain treated me with so much   30
contempt and cruelty, that I deserved your pity, rather than your
resentment.

LUCY. But since his escape, no doubt all matters are made up
again.—Ah Polly! Polly! 'tis I am the unhappy wife; and he loves
you as if you were only his mistress.

POLLY. Sure, madam, you cannot think me so happy as to be
the object of your jealousy.—A man is always afraid of a woman
who loves him too well—so that I must expect to be neglected
and avoided.

LUCY. Then our cases, my dear Polly, are exactly alike.   40
Both of us indeed have been too fond.

AIR XLIX. O Bessy Bell, &c.

POLLY. *A curse attends that woman's love,*
        Who always would be pleasing.
LUCY.   *The pertness of the billing dove,*
        Like tickling, is but teasing.
POLLY. *What then in love can woman do?*
LUCY.   *If we grow fond they shun us.*
POLLY. *And when we fly them, they pursue:*
LUCY.   *But leave us when they've won us.*

LUCY. Love is so very whimsical in both sexes, that it is im-   50
possible to be lasting.—But my heart is particular, and contradicts
my own observation.

POLLY. But really, mistress Lucy, by his last behaviour, I think
I ought to envy you.—When I was forced from him, he did not
shew the least tenderness.—But perhaps he hath a heart not capable of it.

AIR L. Wou'd fate to me Belinda give

Among the men, coquets we find,
Who court by turns all woman-kind;

> *And we grant all their hearts desired,*
> *When they are flattered and admired.*   60

The coquets of both sexes are self-lovers, and that is a love no other whatever can dispossess. I fear, my dear Lucy, our husband is one of those.

LUCY. Away with these melancholy reflections,—indeed, my dear Polly, we are both of us a cup too low.—Let me prevail upon you, to accept of my offer.

AIR LI. Come, sweet lass

> *Come, sweet lass,*
> *Let's banish sorrow*
> *'Till to-morrow;*
> *Come sweet lass,*   70
> *Let's take a chirping glass.*
> *Wine can clear*
> *The vapours of despair;*
> *And make us light as air;*
> *Then drink, and banish care.*

I can't bear, child, to see you in such low spirits.—And I must persuade you to what I know will do you good.—I shall now soon be even with the hypocritical strumpet. [*Aside, as she goes out to prepare the drink.*]

SCENE IX

POLLY. All this wheedling of Lucy cannot be for nothing.—At this time too! when I know she hates me!—The dissembling of a woman is always the forerunner of mischief.—By pouring strong-waters down my throat, she think to pump some secrets out of me.—I'll be upon my guard, and won't taste a drop of her liquor, I'm resolv'd.

SCENE X

Lucy reenters with the cordial.

LUCY. Come, Miss Polly.

POLLY. Indeed, child, you have given yourself trouble to no purpose.—You must, my dear, excuse me.

LUCY. Really, Miss Polly, you are so squeamishly affected about taking a cup of strong-waters, as a lady before company. I vow, Polly, I shall take it monstrously ill if you refuse me.—Brandy and men (though women love them never so well) are always taken by us with some reluctance—unless 'tis in private.

POLLY. I protest, madam, it goes against me. [*Enter at the rear Macheath in the custody of Lockit, and accompanied by* 10 *Peachum.*] What do I see! Macheath again in custody!—Now every glimmering of happiness is lost. [*Drops the glass of liquor on the ground.*]

LUCY. Since things are thus, I'm glad the wench hath escaped: for by this event, 'tis plain, she was not happy enough to deserve to be poisoned.

SCENE XI

LOCKIT. Set your heart to rest, captain.—You have neither the chance of love or money for another escape—for you are ordered to be called down upon your trial immediately.

PEACHUM. Away, hussies!—This is not a time for a man to be hampered with his wives.—You see, the gentleman is in chains already.

LUCY. O husband, husband, my heart longed to see thee; but to see thee thus distracts me!

POLLY. Will not my dear husband look upon his Polly? Why hadst thou not flown to me for protection? with me thou 10 hadst been safe.

AIR LII. The last time I went o'er the moor

POLLY.	*Hither, dear husband, turn your eyes.*
LUCY.	*Bestow one glance to cheer me.*
POLLY.	*Think with that look, thy Polly dies.*
LUCY.	*O shun me not,—but hear me.*
POLLY.	*'Tis Polly sues.*
LUCY.	*'Tis Lucy speaks.*
POLLY.	*Is thus true love requited?*
LUCY.	*My heart is bursting.*
POLLY.	*Mine too breaks.*
LUCY.	*Must I,*
POLLY.	*Must I be slighted?*

20

MACHEATH. What would you have me say, ladies?—You see, this affair will soon be at an end, without my disobliging either of you.

PEACHUM. But the settling this point, Captain, might prevent a law-suit between your two widows.

AIR LIII. Tom Tinker's my true love, &c.

MACHEATH. *Which way shall I turn me—how can I decide?*
Wives, the day of our death, are as fond as a bride.
One wife is too much for most husbands to hear,   30
But two at a time there's no mortal can bear.
This way, and that way, and which way I will,
What would comfort the one, t'other wife would take ill.

POLLY. But if his own misfortunes have made him insensible to mine—a Father sure will be more compassionate.—Dear, dear sir, sink the material evidence, and bring him off at his tryal—Polly upon her knees begs it of you.

AIR LIV. I am a poor shepherd undone

When my hero in court appears,
And stands arraigned for his life,
Then think of poor Polly's tears;   40
For ah! poor Polly's his wife.
Like the sailor he holds up his hand,
Distrest on the dashing wave.
To die a dry death at land,
Is as bad as a watry grave.
And alas, poor Polly!
Alack, and well-a-day!
Before I was in love,
Oh! every month was May.

LUCY. If Peachum's heart is hardened; sure you, sir, will   50
have more compassion on a daughter.—I know the evidence is in your power.—How then can you be a tyrant to me? [*Kneeling.*]

AIR LV. Ianthe the lovely, &c.

When he holds up his hand arraigned for his life,
O think of your daughter, and think I'm his wife!

What are cannons, or bombs, or clashing of swords?
For death is more certain by witnesses words.
Then nail up their lips; that dread thunder allay;
And each month of my life will hereafter be May.

LOCKIT. Macheath's time is come, Lucy.—We know our 60
own affairs, therefore let us have no more whimpering or whining.

AIR LVI. A cobler there was, &c.

Our selves, like the Great, to secure a retreat,
When matters require it, must give up our gang:
   And good reason why,
   Or, instead of the fry,
   Ev'n Peachum and I,
Like poor petty rascals, might hang, hang;
Like poor petty rascals, might hang.

PEACHUM. Set your heart at rest, Polly.—Your husband is to
die to day.—Therefore, if you are not already provided, 'tis 70
high time to look about for another. There's comfort for you,
you slut.

LOCKIT. We are ready, sir, to conduct you to the Old Bailey.

AIR LVII. Bonny Dundee

MACHEATH. *The charge is prepared; the lawyers are met;*
   The judges all ranged (a terrible show!)
   I go, undismayed.—For death is a debt,
   A debt on demand.—So, take what I owe.
   Then, farewell, my love—dear charmers, adieu.
   Contented I die—'tis the better for you.
   Here ends all dispute the rest of our lives, 80
   For this way at once I please all my wives.

Now, Gentlemen, I am ready to attend you.
         [Peachum and Lockit take him out.

SCENE XII

POLLY. Follow them, Filch, to the court. And when the trial
is over, bring me a particular account of his behaviour, and of

every thing that happened.—You'll find me here with Miss Lucy. [*Exit Filch.*] But why is all this music?

LUCY. The prisoners, whose trials are put off till next Session, are diverting themselves.

POLLY. Sure there is nothing so charming as music! I'm fond of it to distraction—But alas!—now, all mirth seems an insult upon my affliction.—Let us retire, my dear Lucy, and indulge our sorrows.—The noisy crew, you see, are coming upon us.   10

[*They go mournfully out as a group of prisoners in chains enter and dance grotesquely.*

SCENE XIII

THE CONDEMNED HOLD. *Macheath is discovered in a melancholy posture.*

AIR LVIII. Happy groves

O cruel, cruel, cruel case!
Must I suffer this disgrace?

AIR LIX. Of all the girls that are so smart

Of all the friends in time of grief,
When threat'ning death looks grimmer,
Not one so sure can bring relief,
As this best friend a brimmer.   [*Drinks.*

AIR LX. Britons strike home

Since I must swing,—I scorn, I scorn to wince or whine.
                                                      [*Rises.*

AIR LXI. Chevy Chase

But now again my spirits sink;
I'll raise them high with wine.
                              [*Drinks a glass of wine.*

AIR LXII. To old Sir Simon the king

But valour the stronger grows,   10
The stronger liquor we're drinking.

And how can we feel our woes,
When we've lost the trouble of thinking?

[*Drinks.*

AIR LXIII. Joy to great Caesar

If thus—A man can die.
Much bolder with brandy.

[*Pours out a bumper of brandy.*

AIR LXIV. There was an old woman, &c.

So I drink off this bumper—And now I can stand the test,
And my comrades shall see, that I die as brave as the best.

[*Drinks.*

AIR LXV. Did you ever hear of a gallant sailor

But can I leave my pretty hussies,
Without one tear, or tender sigh?

AIR LXVI. Why are mine eyes still flowing

Their eyes, their lips, their busses   20
Recall my love—Ah must I die!

AIR LXVII. Green sleeves

Since laws were made for ev'ry degree,
To curb vice in others, as well as me,
I wonder we han't better company
   Upon Tyburn tree!
But gold from law can take out the sting;
And if rich men like us were to swing,
'Twould thin the land, such numbers to string
   Upon Tyburn tree!

[*A Jailor enters.*

JAILOR. Some friends of yours, Captain, desire to be ad- 30
mitted—I leave you together.
[*Enter Ben Budge and Mat of the Mint.*

SCENE XIV

MACHEATH. For my having broke prison, you see, gentlemen,
I am ordered immediate execution.—The sheriffs officers, I be-

lieve, are now at the door.—That Jemmy Twitcher should peach
me, I own surpriz'd me!—'Tis a plain proof that the world is all
alike, and that even our gang can no more trust one another than
other people. Therefore, I beg you, gentlemen, look well to your
selves, for in all probability you may live some months longer.

MAT. We are heartily sorry, captain, for your misfortune.—
But 'tis what we must all come to.

MACHEATH. Peachum and Lockit, you know, are infamous 10
scoundrels. Their lives are as much in your power, as yours are
in theirs—remember your dying friend!—'Tis my last request.
—Bring those villains to the gallows before you, and I am satisfied.

MAT. We'll do't.

[The Jailor enters again.

JAILOR. Miss Polly and Miss Lucy intreat a word with you.

MACHEATH. Gentlemen, adieu.

SCENE XV

Enter Lucy and Polly.

MACHEATH. My dear Lucy—my dear Polly—whatsoever hath
past between us, is now at an end.—If you are fond of marrying
again, the best advice I can give you, is to ship yourselves off for
the West-Indies, where you'll have a fair chance of getting a
husband a-piece; or by good luck, two or three, as you like best.

POLLY. How can I support this sight!

LUCY. There is nothing moves one so much as a great man in
distress.

AIR LXVIII. All you that must take a leap, &c.

LUCY.   *Would I might be hanged!*
POLLY.   *And I would so too!* 10
LUCY.   *To be hanged with you,*
POLLY.   *My dear, with you.*
MACHEATH. *O leave me to thought! I fear! I doubt!*
            I tremble! I droop!—See my courage is out.
                                [Turns up the empty bottle.
POLLY.   *No token of love?*
MACHEATH.   *See my courage is out.*
                                [Turns up the empty pot.

4. *the West Indies*, the scene of Gay's companion piece to this, *Polly.*

LUCY.   *No token of love?*
POLLY.   *Adieu.*
LUCY.   *Farewell.*
MACHEATH. *But hark! I hear the toll of the bell.*   20
CHORUS.   *Tol de rol lol, &c.*

JAILOR. Four women more, captain, with a child a-piece! See, here they come.

[*Enter women and children.*

MACHEATH. What—four wives more!—This is too much.— Here—tell the sheriff's officers I am ready.

[*Exit Macheath guarded.*

SCENE XVI

Enter Player and Beggar.

PLAYER. But honest friend, I hope you don't intend that Macheath shall be really executed.

BEGGAR. Most certainly, sir.—To make the piece perfect, I was for doing strict poetical justice.—Macheath is to be hanged; and for the other personages of the drama, the audience must have supposed they were all either hanged or transported.

PLAYER. Why then, friend, this is a down-right deep tragedy. The catastrophe is manifestly wrong, for an opera must end happily.

BEGGAR. Your objection, sir, is very just; and is easily re- 10 moved. For you must allow, that in this kind of drama, 'tis no matter how absurdly things are brought about—so—you rabble there—run and cry a reprieve—let the prisoner be brought back to his wives in triumph.

PLAYER. All this we must do, to comply with the taste of the town.

BEGGAR. Through the whole piece you may observe such a similitude of manners in high and low life, that it is difficult to determine whether (in the fashionable vices) the fine gentlemen imitate the gentlemen of the road, or the gentlemen of the 20 road the fine gentlemen.—Had the play remained, as I at first intended, it would have carried a most excellent moral. 'Twould have shown that the lower sort of people have their vices in a degree as well as the rich: and that they are punished for them.

SCENE XVII

To them Macheath with Rabble, &c.

MACHEATH. So, it seems, I am not left to my choice, but must have a wife at last.—Look ye, my dears, we will have no controversy now. Let us give this day to mirth, and I am sure she who thinks her self my wife will testify her joy by a dance.

ALL. Come, a dance—a dance.

MACHEATH. Ladies, I hope you will give me leave to present a partner to each of you. And (if I may without offence) for this time, I take Polly for mine.—And for life, you slut,—for we were really married.—As for the rest—But at present keep your own secret. [*To Polly.*] 10

A DANCE

AIR LXIX. Lumps of Pudding, &c.

Thus I stand like a Turk, with his doxies around;
From all sides their glances his passion confound;
For black, brown, and fair, his inconstancy burns,
And the different beauties subdue him by turns:
Each calls forth her charms, to provoke his desires:
Though willing to all; with but one he retires.
But think of this maxim, and put off your sorrow,
The wretch of to-day, may be happy to morrow.

CHORUS.　　　*But think of this maxim, &c.*

BURLESQUE DRAMA

THE METHODS of the writer of dramatic burlesque resemble those of the cartoonist, who is always careful to make clear the identity of his subject at the same time exaggerating certain characteristics which for one reason or another lend themselves to such treatment. The heavy underjaw and ferocious scowl of a Mussolini as they are sketched by the cartoonists correspond to the selection of, for instance, particularly sentimental or especially bombastic passages from popular plays which a dramatist is burlesquing. The dramatist cannot, of course, be content with the rather hasty and obvious touches of the cartoon. His exaggeration, which cannot be divorced from reality, is rather of ideas, emotions, traits of character than of mere physical characteristics, though at times he makes use of the latter. Obviously the greatest danger is that the subject may be so localized or so limited as to have no appeal or significance beyond a small group and a brief time. This is particularly true of the drama, where many fashions change rapidly, and what seems significant to one generation is forgotten by the next.

It is when the dramatist goes beyond superficialities of technique and has concerned himself with the follies and excesses of men as they are represented in the theater that he escapes such limitations of time and detail. In the *Critic* Sheridan is burlesquing the sentimental tragedy of his time. Like Buckingham's *Rehearsal* a century earlier, he makes fun of the absurdities of plot, the bombastic style, and the inconsistency of character that marked these plays that put all their stress on the display and development of sentiment. The play does much more than this, however. If it were concerned only with such things, it would be as dead today as the sentimental drama is, having at best only historical interest. He is concerned with states of mind rather than merely with theatrical fashions. His characters are alive quite apart from sentimental

533

drama. The first act is devoted to a discussion of the whole state of the theater, with its "log-rolling," its plagiarism (which had particular point since Sheridan himself was not free from charges of borrowing), its efforts to keep the press conciliated (and therefore the foibles of the press, particularly what we would now call the columnist), and its hangers-on. Nor is he partial; both authors and critics feel the sting of his lash. Indeed, so broad is the picture that he draws that the *Critic* becomes not only a burlesque but also, in a somewhat limited sense, a comedy of manners. It all is colored by the flashes of a gay and lively wit that still has power to interest and impress us after the local allusions are all forgotten.

Richard Brinsley Sheridan, unlike his great master, Congreve, was an Irishman educated in England. Born in Dublin in 1751, he was sent over to Harrow at the proper age and went on from there to Oxford. There his interest in drama found expression in a farce called *Jupiter*, a burlesque somewhat in the manner of the *Critic*. In 1773 he married Elizabeth Ann Linley, with whom he had eloped the preceding year, and settled down in London to that career which was to bring him fame and a quickly dissipated fortune. In 1775 he produced a comic opera *The Duenna* (with music by his father-in-law, one of the famous composers of the time) in the manner of *The Beggar's Opera*, and a farce reminiscent of Molière, *St. Patrick's Day, or the Scheming Lieutenant*. In the following year he became with his father-in-law owner of the Drury Lane Theater, one of the two great London theaters of the time and managed it so successfully that for many years it brought in handsome returns. For it Sheridan wrote his masterpieces: *The Rivals* (1775), *The School for Scandal* and *A Trip to Scarborough* (both in 1777), and *The Critic* (1779). At the end of the last decade of the century he took up his pen once more to adapt for his theater two plays by the popular German dramatist, Kotzebue.

In the meanwhile he had been elected to Parliament in 1780, where he served for the next thirty-two years, making a great name for himself as an orator, partly on account of a famous six-hour speech against Warren Hastings (friend of

Clive) in 1787 and for his earlier speeches in the defence of the American colonies. When he failed of re-election to Parliament in 1812 he was left without income and the last four years of his life were spent in a mad and not always successful attempt to escape the pursuit of his creditors. On his death in 1816 he was buried with great ceremony in Westminster Abbey.

He brings to a fitting close an era of drama at whose beginning stands Congreve. *The Rivals* and *The School for Scandal* are developments of the comedy of manners but they are lighter in tone, less serious and less general in their satire, less sharp and biting in their cynicism, less licentious than the comedies of Congreve and his contemporaries. *The Critic* is built solidly on the foundation laid early in the seventeenth century by Beaumont and Fletcher in *The Knight of the Burning Pestle* and later added to by Buckingham in *The Rehearsal* and Henry Fielding in *The Tragedy of Tragedies, or the Life and Death of Tom Thumb the Great.* One of the surest signs of the maturity of an art is its ability to make fun of itself, and no English dramatist has more capably made fun of his own medium than Sheridan did in *The Critic*.

SUGGESTED READINGS

Cambridge History of English Literature, VOL. XI. NEW YORK, 1914.
Nettleton, G. H., *English Drama of the Restoration and Eighteenth Century*. NEW YORK, 1932.
Nicoll, Allardyce, *History of Late Eighteenth Century Drama*. NEW YORK, 1927.
Rhodes, R. C., *Harlequin Sheridan*. LONDON, 1933.
Sheridan, R. B. *The Works* ED. BY R. C. RHODES. 3 VOLS. NEW YORK AND LONDON, 1929.

Beaumont, Francis and John Fletcher, *The Knight of the Burning Pestle*. MERMAID SERIES, VOL. 1. NEW YORK, [n. d.]
Fielding, Henry, *The Tragedy of Tragedies; or the Life and Death of Tom Thumb the Great*, ED. BY J. T. HILLHOUSE. LONDON, 1918.
Kaufman, George and Moss Hart, *Once in a Lifetime*. NEW YORK, 1930.
Shaw, G. B., *Fanny's First Play*. NEW YORK, 1911.
Villiers, George, Lord Buckingham, *The Rehearsal*. NEW YORK, 1910.

THE CRITIC, OR A TRAGEDY REHEARSED
by Richard Brinsley Sheridan

Characters

MR. DANGLE
MRS. DANGLE
MR. SNEER
SIR FRETFUL PLAGIARY
SIGNOR PASTICCIO RITORNELLO

HIS THREE DAUGHTERS
FRENCH INTERPRETER
MR. PUFF
THE UNDER PROMPTER

Characters in the Tragedy

SIR CHRISTOPHER HATTON
SIR WALTER RALEIGH
EARL OF LEICESTER
GOVERNOR OF TILBURY FORT
TILBURINA
HER CONFIDANTE
DON FEROLO WHISKERANDOS
JUSTICE
JUSTICE'S LADY
CONSTABLE

"TOM JENKINS"
BEEFEATER
LORD BURLEIGH
THE NIECES *of Sir Walter Raleigh and of Sir Christopher Hatton*
THE THAMES, *with his "Banks"*
TWO SENTINELS, CONSTABLES, ATTENDANTS, *etc.*

To Mrs. Greville

Madam,

In requesting your permission to address the following pages to you, which as they aim themselves to be critical, require every protection and allowance that approving taste or friendly prejudice can give them, I yet ventured to mention no other motive than the gratification of private friendship and esteem. Had I suggested a hope that your implied approbation would give a sanction to their defects, your particular reserve, and dislike to the reputation of critical taste, as well as of poetical talent, would have made you refuse the protection of your name to such a purpose. However, I am not so ungrateful as now to attempt to combat this disposition in you. I shall not here presume to argue that the present state of poetry claims and expects every assistance that taste and example can afford it: nor endeavour to prove that a fastidious concealment of the most elegant productions of judgement and fancy is an ill return for the possession of those endowments. Continue to deceive yourself in the idea that you are known only to be eminently admired and regarded for the valuable qualities that attach private friendships, and the graceful talents that adorn conversation. Enough of what you have written has stolen into full public notice to answer my purpose; and you will, perhaps, be the only person, conversant in elegant literature, who shall read this address and not perceive that by publishing your particular approbation of the following drama, I have a more interested object than to boast the true respect and regard with which

I have the honour to be, Madam,

Your very sincere
And obedient humble servant,

R. B. SHERIDAN.

PROLOGUE

By *the* HON. RICHARD FITZPATRICK

The sister Muses, whom these realms obey,
Who o'er the drama hold divided sway,
Sometimes, by evil counsellors, 'tis said,
Like earth-born potentates have been misled:
In those gay days of wickedness and wit,
When Villiers criticized what Dryden writ,
The tragic queen, to please a tasteless crowd,
Had learned to bellow, rant, and roar so loud,
That frightened Nature, her best friend before,
The blust'ring bedlam's company forswore.
Her comic sister, who had wit, 'tis true,
With all her merits, had her failings too;
And would sometimes in mirthful moments use
A style too flippant for a well-bred Muse.
Then female modesty abashed began
To seek the friendly refuge of the fan,

Awhile behind that slight entrenchment stood,
'Till driv'n from thence, she left the stage for good.
In our more pious, and far chaster times,
These sure no longer are the Muse's crimes!   20
But some complain that, former faults to shun,
The reformation to extremes has run.
The frantic hero's wild delirium past,
Now insipidity succeeds bombast;
So slow Melpomene's cold numbers creep,
Here dullness seems her drowsy court to keep,
And we are scarce awake, whilst you are fast asleep.
Thalia, once so ill-behaved and rude,
Reformed, is now become an arrant prude,
Retailing nightly to the yawning pit   30
The purest morals, undefiled by wit!
Our author offers in these motley scenes
A slight remonstrance to the drama's queens:
Nor let the goddesses be over-nice;
Free-spoken subjects give the best advice.
Although not quite a novice in his trade,
His cause to-night requires no common aid.
To this, a friendly, just, and pow'rful court,
I come ambassador to beg support.
Can he undaunted, brave the critic's rage?   40
In civil broils, with brother bards engage?
Hold forth their errors to the public eye,
Nay more, e'en newspapers themselves defy!
Say, must his single arm encounter all?
By numbers vanquished, e'en the brave may fall;
And though no leader should success distrust
Whose troops are willing, and whose cause is just;
To bid such hosts of angry foes defiance,
His chief dependence must be, YOUR ALLIANCE.

25. *Melpomene*, the muse of tragedy.
28. *Thalia*, the muse of comedy.

ACT I

SCENE I

MR. AND MRS. DANGLE ARE AT BREAKFAST. *Mr. Dangle is rustling through the newspapers looking for news of the theaters. He prides himself on being an authority on the subject of the stage and extends himself to make all possible "contacts."*

DANGLE [*Reading*]. 'Brutus to Lord North.' 'Letter the second on the State of the Army'—Pshaw! 'To the first L— dash D of the A— dash Y.'—'Genuine Extract of a Letter from St. Kitt's.'—'Coxheath Intelligence.'—'It is now confidently asserted that Sir Charles Hardy.'—Pshaw!—Nothing but about the fleet and the nation!—and I hate all politics but theatrical politics.—Where's the *Morning Chronicle?*

MRS. DANGLE. Yes, that's your *Gazette.*

DANGLE. So, here we have it.—*Theatrical intelligence extraordinary.*—We hear there is a new tragedy in rehearsal at Drury   10
Lane Theatre, called *The Spanish Armada*, said to be written by Mr. Puff, a gentleman well known in the theatrical world; if we may allow ourselves to give credit to the report of the performers, who, truth to say, are in general but indifferent judges, this piece abounds with the most striking and received beauties of modern composition.'—So! I am very glad my friend Puff's tragedy is in such forwardness.—Mrs. Dangle, my dear, you will be very glad to hear that Puff's tragedy—

MRS. DANGLE. Lord, Mr. Dangle, why will you plague me about such nonsense? Now the plays are begun I shall have no   20
peace. Isn't it sufficient to make yourself ridiculous by your passion for the theatre, without continually teasing me to join you? Why can't you ride your hobby-horse without desiring to place me on a pillion behind you, Mr. Dangle?

DANGLE. Nay, my dear, I was only going to read—

MRS. DANGLE [*Venting her fear of a French invasion, threatened in 1779*]. No, no; you will never read anything that's worth listening to:—you hate to hear about your country; there are letters every day with Roman signatures, demonstrating the certainty of an invasion, and proving that the nation is utterly undone.   30
But you never will read anything to entertain one.

DANGLE [*Insulted and scornful*]. What has a woman to do with politics, Mrs. Dangle?

MRS. DANGLE. And what have you to do with the theatre, Mr.

Dangle? Why should you affect the character of a critic? I have no patience with you! Haven't you made yourself the jest of all your acquaintance by your interference in matters where you have no business? Are not you called a theatrical quidnunc, and a mock Maecenas to second-hand authors?

DANGLE. True; my power with the managers is pretty no-   40
torious; but is it no credit to have applications from all quarters for my interest? From lords to recommend fiddlers, from ladies to get boxes, from authors to get answers, and from actors to get engagements.

MRS. DANGLE. Yes, truly; you have contrived to get a share in all the plague and trouble of theatrical property, without the profit, or even the credit of the abuse that attends it.

DANGLE. I am sure, Mrs. Dangle, you are no loser by it, however; *you* have all the advantages of it:—mightn't you, last winter, have had the reading of the new pantomime a fortnight pre-   50
vious to its performance? And doesn't Mr. Fosbrook let you take places for a play before it is advertised, and set you down for a box for every new piece through the season? And didn't my friend, Mr. Smatter, dedicate his last farce to you at my particular request, Mrs. Dangle?

MRS. DANGLE. Yes; but wasn't the farce damned, Mr. Dangle? And to be sure it is extremely pleasant to have one's house made the motley rendezvous of all the lackeys of literature—the very high 'change of trading authors and jobbing critics!—Yes, my drawing-room is an absolute register-office for candidate ac-   60
tors, and poets without character; then to be continually alarmed with misses and ma'ams piping hysteric changes on Juliets and Dorindas, Pollys and Ophelias; and the very furniture trembling at the probationary starts and unprovoked rants of would-be Richards and Hamlets! And what is worse than all, now that the manager has monopolized the Opera House, haven't we the signors and signoras calling here, sliding their smooth semibreves, and gargling glib divisions in their outlandish throats—with foreign emissaries and French spies, for aught I know, disguised like fiddlers and figure-dancers!   70

DANGLE. Mercy! Mrs. Dangle!

38. *quidnunc*, gossip.   39. *Maecenas*, a wealthy Roman, patron to Virgil.
59. *'change*, Stock Exchange.
66. *manager . . . Opera House*, Sheridan himself was manager of Drury Lane, and he and the manager of the other important theater in London at the time, Covent Garden, by their close cooperation exercised what amounted to a monopoly on London theaters. It caused much bitter satire.
67. *semibreve*, whole note.   68. *divisions*, variations, modulations.

MRS. DANGLE. And to employ yourself so idly at such an alarming crisis as this, too—when, if you had the least spirit, you would have been at the head of one of the Westminster associations—or trailing a volunteer pike in the Artillery Ground? But you—o' my conscience, I believe if the French were landed to-morrow your first inquiry would be, whether they had brought a theatrical troop with them.

DANGLE. Mrs. Dangle, it does not signify—I say the stage is 'the mirror of Nature,' and the actors are 'the abstract, and brief 80 chronicles of the time':—and pray, what can a man of sense study better? Besides, you will not easily persuade me that there is no credit or importance in being at the head of a band of critics, who take upon them to decide for the whole town, whose opinion and patronage all writers solicit, and whose recommendation no manager dares refuse!

MRS. DANGLE. Ridiculous! Both managers and authors of the least merit laugh at your pretensions. The Public is their Critic—without whose fair approbation they know no play can rest on the stage, and with whose applause they welcome such at- 90 tacks as yours, and laugh at the malice of them, where they can't at the wit.

DANGLE. Very well, madam—very well.

[Enter Servant.

SERVANT. Mr. Sneer, sir, to wait on you.

DANGLE. Oh, show Mr. Sneer up. [Exit Servant.] Plague on't, now we must appear loving and affectionate, or Sneer will hitch us into a story.

MRS. DANGLE. With all my heart; you can't be more ridiculous than you are.

DANGLE. You are enough to provoke—[Enter Mr. Sneer.] 100 Ha! my dear Sneer, I am vastly glad to see you. My dear, here's Mr. Sneer.

MRS. DANGLE. Good morning to you, sir.

DANGLE. Mrs. Dangle and I have been diverting ourselves with the papers. Pray, Sneer, won't you go to Drury Lane Theatre the first night of Puff's tragedy?

SNEER. Yes; but I suppose one shan't be able to get in, for on the first night of a new piece they always fill the house with orders to support it. But here, Dangle, I have brought you two pieces, one of which you must exert yourself to make the 110

74. *Westminster associations*, companies of militia.
80. *mirror of Nature, etc.*, phrases from *Hamlet*.

managers accept; I can tell you that, for 'tis written by a person
of consequence.

DANGLE. So! now my plagues are beginning.

SNEER. Aye, I am glad of it, for now you'll be happy. Why, my
dear Dangle, it is a pleasure to see how you enjoy your volunteer
fatigue, and your solicited solicitations.

DANGLE. It's a great trouble—yet, egad, it's pleasant too. Why,
sometimes of a morning, I have a dozen people call on me at
breakfast time, whose faces I never saw before, nor ever desire to
see again.   120

SNEER. That must be very pleasant indeed!

DANGLE. And not a week but I receive fifty letters, and not a
line in them about any business of my own.

SNEER. An amusing correspondence!

DANGLE [Reading]. 'Bursts into tears, and exit.' What, is this a
tragedy?

SNEER. No, that's a genteel comedy, not a translation—only
taken from the French; it is written in a style which they have
lately tried to run down; the true sentimental, and nothing ridiculous in it from the beginning to the end.   130

MRS. DANGLE. Well, if they had kept to that, I should not have
been such an enemy to the stage: there was some edification to
be got from those pieces, Mr. Sneer!

SNEER. I am quite of your opinion, Mrs. Dangle; the theatre, in
proper hands, might certainly be made the school of morality;
but now, I am sorry to say it, people seem to go there principally
for their entertainment.

MRS. DANGLE. It would have been more to the credit of the
managers to have kept it in the other line.

SNEER. Undoubtedly, madam, and hereafter perhaps to   140
have had it recorded, that in the midst of a luxurious and dissipated age, they preserved two houses in the capital, where the
conversation was always moral at least, if not entertaining!

DANGLE. Now, egad, I think the worst alteration is in the nicety
of the audience. No double entendre, no smart innuendo admitted; even Vanbrugh and Congreve obliged to undergo a
bungling reformation!

SNEER. Yes, and our prudery in this respect is just on a par
with the artificial bashfulness of a courtesan, who increases the
blush upon her cheek in an exact proportion to the diminu-   150
tion of her modesty.

142. *two houses*, Drury Lane and Covent Garden.

DANGLE. Sneer can't even give the public a good word!—But what have we here? This seems a very odd—

SNEER. Oh, that's a comedy, on a very new plan; replete with wit and mirth, yet of a most serious moral! You see it is called *The Reformed Housebreaker;* where by the mere force of humour, *housebreaking* is put into so ridiculous a light, that if the piece has its proper run, I have no doubt but that bolts and bars will be entirely useless by the end of the season.

DANGLE. Egad, this is new indeed!   160

SNEER. Yes; it is written by a particular friend of mine, who has discovered that the follies and foibles of society are subjects unworthy the notice of the Comic Muse, who should be taught to stoop only at the greater vices and blacker crimes of humanity —gibbeting capital offences in five acts and pillorying petty larcenies in two. In short, his idea is to dramatize the penal laws, and make the stage a court of ease to the Old Bailey.

DANGLE. It is truly moral.

[*Enter Servant.*

SERVANT. Sir Fretful Plagiary, sir.

DANGLE. Beg him to walk up.—[*Exit Servant.*] Now, Mrs.   170
Dangle, Sir Fretful Plagiary is an author to your own taste.

MRS. DANGLE. I confess he is a favourite of mine, because everybody else abuses him.

SNEER. Very much to the credit of your charity, madam, if not of your judgement.

DANGLE. But, egad, he allows no merit to any author but himself, that's the truth on't—though he's my friend.

SNEER. Never. He is as envious as an old maid verging on the desperation of six-and-thirty: and then the insidious humility with which he seduces you to give a free opinion on any of   180
his works, can be exceeded only by the petulant arrogance with which he is sure to reject your observations.

DANGLE. Very true, egad—though he's my friend.

SNEER. Then his affected contempt of all newspaper strictures; though, at the same time, he is the sorest man alive, and shrinks like scorched parchment from the fiery ordeal of true criticism: yet is he so covetous of popularity, that he had rather be abused than not mentioned at all.

DANGLE. There's no denying it—though he is my friend.

SNEER. You have read the tragedy he has just finished,   190
haven't you?

DANGLE. Oh, yes; he sent it to me yesterday.

SNEER. Well, and you think it execrable, don't you?

DANGLE. Why, between ourselves, egad, I must own—though he's my friend—that it is one of the most—[*He hears Sir Fretful approaching.*]—He's here [*Aside.*]—finished and most admirable perform—

SIR FRETFUL [*Without*]. Mr. Sneer with him, did you say?

[*Enter Sir Fretful. He is affected in manners, with a strong sense of his own greatness as a dramatist. Sneer and Dangle delight in baiting him.*

DANGLE. Ah, my dear friend!—Egad, we were just speaking of your tragedy. Admirable, Sir Fretful, admirable!   200

SNEER. You never did anything beyond it, Sir Fretful—never in your life.

SIR FRETFUL. You make me extremely happy; for without a compliment, my dear Sneer, there isn't a man in the world whose judgement I value as I do yours—and Mr. Dangle's.

MRS. DANGLE. They are only laughing at you, Sir Fretful; for it was but just now that—

DANGLE. Mrs. Dangle! Ah, Sir Fretful, you know Mrs. Dangle. My friend Sneer was rallying just now. He knows how she admires you, and—   210

SIR FRETFUL. O Lord, I am sure Mr. Sneer has more taste and sincerity than to—[*Aside.*] A damned double-faced fellow!

DANGLE. Yes, yes,—Sneer *will* jest—but a better-humoured—

SIR FRETFUL. Oh, I know—

DANGLE. He has a ready turn for ridicule—his wit costs him nothing.

SIR FRETFUL. No, egad,—[*Aside.*] or I should wonder how he came by it.

MRS. DANGLE. Because his jest is always at the expense of his friend.   220

DANGLE. But, Sir Fretful, have you sent your play to the managers yet?—or can I be of any service to you?

SIR FRETFUL. No, no, I thank you; I believe the piece had sufficient recommendation with it. I thank you, though—I sent it to the manager of Covent Garden Theatre this morning.

SNEER. I should have thought, now, that it might have been cast (as the actors call it) better at Drury Lane.

SIR FRETFUL. O Lud! no—never send a play there while I live—hark'ee! [*He whispers to Sneer. He is warning him that the manager is likely to steal his ideas for his own plays, a charge made against Sheridan.*]

SNEER. *Writes himself!*—I know he does—   230

SIR FRETFUL. I say nothing—I take away from no man's merit

—am hurt at no man's good fortune—I say nothing—But this I will say—through all my knowledge of life, I have observed—that there is not a passion so strongly rooted in the human heart as envy!

SNEER. I believe you have reason for what you say, indeed.

SIR FRETFUL. Besides, I can tell you it is not always so safe to leave a play in the hands of those who write themselves.

SNEER. What, they may steal from them, hey, my dear Plagiary? 240

SIR FRETFUL. Steal!—to be sure they may; and, egad, serve your best thoughts as gipsies do stolen children, disfigure them to make 'em pass for their own.

SNEER. But your present work is a sacrifice to Melpomene, and *he*, you know, never—

SIR FRETFUL. That's no security. A dexterous plagiarist may do anything. Why, sir, for aught I know, he might take out some of the best things in my ·tragedy and put them into his own comedy.

SNEER. That might be done, I dare be sworn. 250

SIR FRETFUL. And then, if such a person gives you the least hint or assistance, he is devilish apt to take the merit of the whole—

DANGLE. If it succeeds.

SIR FRETFUL. Aye,—but with regard to this piece, I think I can hit that gentleman, for I can safely swear he never read it.

SNEER. I'll tell you how you may hurt him more.

SIR FRETFUL. How?

SNEER. Swear he wrote it.

SIR FRETFUL. Plague on't now, Sneer, I shall take it ill. I believe you want to take away my character as an author! 260

SNEER. Then I am sure you ought to be very much obliged to me.

SIR FRETFUL. Hey!—Sir!—

DANGLE. Oh, you know, he never means what he says.

SIR FRETFUL. Sincerely then—you do like the piece?

SNEER. Wonderfully!

SIR FRETFUL. But come now, there must be something that you think might be mended, hey?—Mr. Dangle, has nothing struck you?

DANGLE. Why, faith, it is but an ungracious thing for the 270 most part to—

SIR FRETFUL. With most authors it is just so, indeed; they are in general strangely tenacious! But, for my part, I am never so well

244. *sacrifice* . . . , i.e., it is a tragedy.

pleased as when a judicious critic points out any defect to me; for what is the purpose of showing a work to a friend, if you don't mean to profit by his opinion?

SNEER. Very true. Why, then, though I seriously admire the piece upon the whole, yet there is one small objection; which, if you'll give me leave, I'll mention.

SIR FRETFUL. Sir, you can't oblige me more.   280

SNEER. I think it wants incident.

SIR FRETFUL. Good God!—you surprise me!—wants incident!

SNEER. Yes; I own I think the incidents are too few.

SIR FRETFUL. Good God! Believe me, Mr. Sneer, there is no person for whose judgement I have a more implicit deference. But I protest to you, Mr. Sneer, I am only apprehensive that the incidents are too crowded.—My dear Dangle, how does it strike you?

DANGLE. Really, I can't agree with my friend Sneer. I think the plot quite sufficient; and the four first acts by many degrees   290 the best I ever read or saw in my life. If I might venture to suggest anything, it is that the interest rather falls off in the fifth.

SIR FRETFUL. Rises, I believe you mean, sir.

DANGLE. No, I don't, upon my word.

SIR FRETFUL. Yes, yes, you do, upon my soul—it certainly don't fall off, I assure you. No, no, it don't fall off!

DANGLE. Now, Mrs. Dangle, didn't you say it struck you in the same light?

MRS. DANGLE. No, indeed, I did not—I did not see a fault in any part of the play from the beginning to the end.   300

SIR FRETFUL. Upon my soul, the women are the best judges after all!

MRS. DANGLE. Or if I made any objection, I am sure it was to nothing in the piece! but that I was afraid it was, on the whole, a little too long.

SIR FRETFUL. Pray, madam, do you speak as to duration of time; or do you mean that the story is tediously spun out?

MRS. DANGLE. O Lud! no. I speak only with reference to the usual length of acting plays.

SIR FRETFUL. Then I am very happy—very happy indeed   310 —because the play is a short play, a remarkably short play. I should not venture to differ with a lady on a point of taste; but, on these occasions, the watch, you know, is the critic.

MRS. DANGLE. Then, I suppose, it must have been Mr. Dangle's drawling manner of reading it to me.

SIR FRETFUL. Oh, if Mr. Dangle read it, that's quite another affair! But I assure you, Mrs. Dangle, the first evening you can spare me three hours and a half, I'll undertake to read you the whole from beginning to end, with the prologue and epilogue, and allow time for the music between the acts. 320

MRS. DANGLE. I hope to see it on the stage next.

DANGLE. Well, Sir Fretful, I wish you may be able to get rid as easily of the newspaper criticisms as you do of ours.

SIR FRETFUL. The *newspapers!* Sir, they are the most villanous—licentious—abominable—infernal—Not that I ever read them—No—I make it a rule never to look into a newspaper.

DANGLE. You are quite right, for it certainly must hurt an author of delicate feelings to see the liberties they take.

SIR FRETFUL. No!—quite the contrary; their abuse is, in fact, the best panegyric—I like it of all things. An author's reputation 330 is only in danger from their support.

SNEER. Why, that's true—and that attack now on you the other day—

SIR FRETFUL. What? where?

DANGLE. Aye, you mean in a paper of Thursday; it was completely ill-natured, to be sure.

SIR FRETFUL. Oh, so much the better. Ha! ha! ha! I wouldn't have it otherwise.

DANGLE. Certainly it is only to be laughed at; for—

SIR FRETFUL. You don't happen to recollect what the fel- 340 low said, do you?

SNEER. Pray, Dangle—Sir Fretful seems a little anxious—

SIR FRETFUL. O Lud, no!—anxious,—not I,—not the least.—I— But one may as well hear, you know.

DANGLE. Sneer, do *you* recollect?—[*Aside.*] Make out something.

SNEER [*To Dangle*]. I will.—Yes, yes, I remember perfectly.

SIR FRETFUL. Well, and pray now—not that it signifies—what might the gentleman say?

SNEER. Why, he roundly asserts that you have not the 350 slightest invention, or original genius whatever; though you are the greatest traducer of all other authors living.

SIR FRETFUL. Ha! ha! ha!—very good! [*His laugh grows shorter and more forced after each of Sneer's reports.*]

SNEER. That as to Comedy, you have not one idea of your own, he believes, even in your common-place book, where stray jokes and pilfered witticisms are kept with as much method as the ledger of the Lost-and-Stolen Office.

SIR FRETFUL. Ha! ha! ha!—very pleasant!

SNEER. Nay, that you are so unlucky as not to have the skill 360
even to *steal* with taste: but that you glean from the refuse of
obscure volumes, where more judicious plagiarists have been before you; so that the body of your work is a composition of
dregs and sediments—like a bad tavern's worst wine.

SIR FRETFUL. Ha! ha!

SNEER. In your more serious efforts, he says, your bombast
would be less intolerable, if the thoughts were ever suited to the
expression; but the homeliness of the sentiment stares through
the fantastic encumbrance of its fine language, like a clown in
one of the new uniforms!   370

SIR FRETFUL. Ha! ha!

SNEER. That your occasional tropes and flowers suit the general coarseness of your style, as tambour sprigs would a ground
of linsey-woolsey; while your imitations of Shakespeare resemble
the mimicry of Falstaff's page, and are about as near the
standard of the original.

SIR FRETFUL. Ha!—

SNEER. In short, that even the finest passages you steal are of no
service to you; for the poverty of your own language prevents
their assimilating; so that they lie on the surface like lumps of 380
marl on a barren moor, encumbering what it is not in their power
to fertilize!

SIR FRETFUL [*After great agitation*]. Now another person
would be vexed at this.

SNEER. Oh! but I wouldn't have told you, only to divert you.

SIR FRETFUL. I know it—I *am* diverted—ha! ha! ha!—not the
least invention! Ha! ha! ha! very good!—very good!

SNEER. Yes—no genius! Ha! ha! ha!

DANGLE. A severe rogue! ha! ha! ha! But you are quite 390
right, Sir Fretful, never to read such nonsense.

SIR FRETFUL. To be sure—for if there is anything to one's
praise, it is a foolish vanity to be gratified at it, and if it is abuse—
why one is always sure to hear of it from one damned good-
natured friend or another!

[*Enter Servant.*

SERVANT. Sir, there is an Italian gentleman with a French interpreter, and three young ladies, and a dozen musicians, who
say they are sent by Lady Rondeau and Mrs. Fuge.

DANGLE. Gadso! they come by appointment. Dear Mrs. Dangle,

373. *tambour sprigs*, etc., fine embroidery on a ground of coarse cloth
made of linen and wool or cotton and wool.
381. *marl*, a chalky clay deposit.

do let them know I'll see them directly.   400

MRS. DANGLE. You know, Mr. Dangle, I shan't understand a
word they say.

DANGLE. But you hear there's an interpreter.

MRS. DANGLE. Well, I'll try to endure their complaisance till
you come.   [*Exit.*

SERVANT. And Mr. Puff, sir, has sent word that the last rehearsal
is to be this morning, and that he'll call on you presently.

DANGLE. That's true—I shall certainly be at home. [*Exit Servant.*] Now, Sir Fretful, if you have a mind to have justice done
you in the way of answer—egad, Mr. Puff's your man.   410

SIR FRETFUL. Pshaw! sir, why should I wish to have it answered, when I tell you I am pleased at it?

DANGLE. True, I had forgot that. But I hope you are not fretted
at what Mr. Sneer—

SIR FRETFUL. Zounds! no, Mr. Dangle, don't I tell you these
things never fret me in the least.

DANGLE. Nay, I only thought—

SIR FRETFUL. And let me tell you, Mr. Dangle, 'tis damned af-
fronting in you to suppose that I am hurt, when I tell you I am
not.   420

SNEER. But why so warm, Sir Fretful?

SIR FRETFUL. Gad's life! Mr. Sneer, you are as absurd as Dangle;
how often must I repeat it to you, that nothing can vex me but
your supposing it possible for me to mind the damned nonsense
you have been repeating to me!—and let me tell you, if you
continue to believe this, you must mean to insult me, gentlemen
—and then your disrespect will affect me no more than the newspaper criticisms—and I shall treat it—with exactly the same calm
indifference and philosophic contempt—and so, your servant.
[*Exit, with a vain attempt at unruffled dignity.*]   430

SNEER. Ha! ha! ha! Poor Sir Fretful! Now will he go and vent
his philosophy in anonymous abuse of all modern critics and authors. But, Dangle, you must get your friend Puff to take me to
the rehearsal of his tragedy.

DANGLE. I'll answer for't, he'll thank you for desiring it. But
come and help me to judge of this musical family; they are
recommended by people of consequence, I assure you.

SNEER. I am at your disposal the whole morning—but I thought
you had been a decided critic in music, as well as in literature.

DANGLE. So I am—but I have a bad ear. I'faith, Sneer,   440
though, I am afraid we were a little too severe on Sir Fretful—
though he is my friend.

SNEER. Why, 'tis certain, that unnecessarily to mortify the vanity of any writer, is a cruelty which mere dullness never can deserve; but where a base and personal malignity usurps the place of literary emulation, the aggressor deserves neither quarter nor pity.

DANGLE. That's true, egad!—though he's my friend!

[*They go out together.*

SCENE II

A DRAWING ROOM IN THE DANGLE HOUSE. *Mrs. Dangle is surrounded by Signor Pasticcio Ritornello, his three daughters, a French "interpreter" who knows perhaps a dozen words of English, and several household servants who don't know quite what to make of all the racket.*

INTERPRETER. Je dis, madame, j'ai l'honneur *to introduce* et de vous demander votre protection pour le Signor Pasticcio Ritornello et pour sa charmante famille.

SIGNOR PASTICCIO. Ah! vossignoria, noi vi preghiamo di favorirci colla vostra protezione.

FIRST DAUGHTER. Vossignoria, fateci questa grazia.

SECOND DAUGHTER. Sì, signora.

INTERPRETER. Madame—*me interpret.* C'est-à-dire—*in English* —qu'ils vous prient de leur faire l'honneur—

MRS. DANGLE. I say again, gentlemen, I don't understand a   10 word you say.

SIGNOR PASTICCIO. Questo signore spiegherà.

INTERPRETER. Oui—*me interpret.* Nous avons les lettres de recommandation pour Monsieur Dangle de—

MRS. DANGLE. Upon my word, sir, I don't understand you.

SIGNOR PASTICCIO. La Contessa Rondeau è nostra padrona.

1. *Je dis, etc.,* I say, madame, I have the honour to introduce and to ask your protection for Signor Pasticcio Ritornello and his charming family.
4. *Vossignoria, etc.* your ladyship, we pray you to favor us with your protection.
Your ladyship, do this kindness.
Yes, my lady.
8. *C'est à dire,* that is to say . . . that they pray you to do them the honour . . .
12. *Questo* . . . , What does the lady say?
13. *Nous avons* . . . , We have letters of recommendation for Mr. Dangle of . . .
16. *La Contessa* . . . , The Countess Rondeau is our patroness.

THIRD DAUGHTER. Sì, padre, et Miladi Fuge.
INTERPRETER. Oh!—*me interpret*. Madame, ils disent—*in English*—qu'ils ont l'honneur d'être protégés de ces dames. *You understand?*   20
MRS. DANGLE. No, sir—no understand!
[*Enter Dangle and Sneer.*
INTERPRETER. Ah, voici Monsieur Dangle!
ALL ITALIANS. Ah! Signor Dangle! [*They turn to him with elaborate gestures. Mrs. Dangle breathes a sigh of relief.*]
MRS. DANGLE. Mr. Dangle, here are two very civil gentlemen trying to make themselves understood, and I don't know which is the interpreter.
DANGLE. Eh bien!
[*Interpreter and Signor Pasticcio speak together.*
INTERPRETER. Monsieur Dangle—le grand bruit de vos talens pour la critique, et de votre intérêt avec messieurs les directeurs à tous les théâtres—   ·   30
SIGNOR PASTICCIO. Vossignoria siete si famoso per la vostra conoscenza, e vostro interesse coi direttori da—
DANGLE. Egad, I think the interpreter is the hardest to be understood of the two!
SNEER. Why, I thought, Dangle, you had been an admirable linguist!
DANGLE. So I am, if they would not talk so damned fast.
SNEER. Well, I'll explain that—the less time we lose in hearing them the better—for that, I suppose, is what they are brought here for.   40
[*Sneer speaks to Signor Pasticcio. They sing trios, &c., Dangle beating out of time. Servant enters and whispers to Dangle.*
DANGLE. Show him up. [*Exit Servant.*] Bravo! admirable! bravissimo! admirabilissimo! Ah, Sneer! where will you find voices such as these in England?
SNEER. Not easily.
DANGLE. But Puff is coming. Signor and little signoras—obligatissimo!—Sposa Signora Danglena—Mrs. Dangle, shall I beg you to offer them some refreshments, and take their address in the next room.

17. *Sì . . .*, Yes, father, and Milady Fuge.
18. *Madame, ils disent . . .*, Madame, they say . . . that they have the honor to be protégés of these ladies.
28. *le grand bruit . . .*, the great fame of your talent for criticism and your influence with the managers of all the theaters . . .
31. *Vossignoria . . .*, the same, in Italian. 46. *Sposa*, wife.

[*Exit Mrs. Dangle with the Italians and interpreter cere-.*
moniously. Re-enter Servant.

SERVANT. Mr. Puff, sir!

DANGLE. My dear Puff!   50

[*Enter Puff. He is a journalist who prides himself on his*
vivid rhetoric.

PUFF. My dear Dangle, how is it with you?

DANGLE. Mr. Sneer, give me leave to introduce Mr. Puff to you.

PUFF. Mr. Sneer, is this? Sir, he is a gentleman whom I have
long panted for the honour of knowing—a gentleman whose
critical talents and transcendent judgement—

SNEER. Dear sir—

DANGLE. Nay, don't be modest, Sneer, my friend Puff only talks
to you in the style of his profession.

SNEER. His profession!

PUFF. Yes, sir; I make no secret of the trade I follow—   60
among friends and brother authors, Dangle knows I love to be
frank on the subject, and to advertise myself *viva voce.* I am, sir,
a practitioner in panegyric, or to speak more plainly—a professor of the art of puffing, at your service—or anybody else's.

SNEER. Sir, you are very obliging!—I believe, Mr. Puff, I have
often admired your talents in the daily prints.

PUFF. Yes, sir, I flatter myself I do as much business in that way
as any six of the fraternity in town. Devilish hard work all the
summer, friend Dangle! never worked harder! But, hark'ee—the
winter managers were a little sore, I believe.   70

DANGLE. No—I believe they took it all in good part.

PUFF. Aye! Then that must have been affectation in them; for,
egad, there were some of the attacks which there was no laughing
at!

SNEER. Aye, the humorous ones. But I should think, Mr. Puff,
that authors would in general be able to do this sort of work for
themselves.

PUFF. Why, yes—but in a clumsy way. Besides, we look on
that as an encroachment, and so take the opposite side. I dare
say now you conceive half the very civil paragraphs and ad-   80
vertisements you see, to be written by the parties concerned, or
their friends? No such thing. Nine out of ten, manufactured by
me in the way of business.

SNEER. Indeed!

PUFF. Even the auctioneers now—the auctioneers, I say, though
the rogues have lately got some credit for their language—not
an article of the merit theirs!—take them out of their pulpits, and

they are as dull as catalogues!—No, sir; 'twas I first enriched their style—'twas I first taught them to crowd their advertisements with panegyrical superlatives, each epithet rising above the 90 other—like the bidders in their own auction-rooms! From *me* they learned to inlay their phraseology with variegated chips of exotic metaphor: by *me*, too, their inventive faculties were called forth. Yes, sir, by *me* they were instructed to clothe ideal walls with gratuitous fruits—to insinuate obsequious rivulets into visionary groves—to teach courteous shrubs to nod their approbation of the grateful soil! or on emergencies to raise upstart oaks, where there never had been an acorn; to create a delightful vicinage without the assistance of a neighbour; or fix the temple of Hygeia in the fens of Lincolnshire! 100

DANGLE. I am sure you have done them infinite service; for now, when a gentleman is ruined, he parts with his house with some credit.

SNEER. Service! if they had any gratitude, they would erect a statue to him; they would figure him as a presiding Mercury, the god of traffic and fiction, with a hammer in his hand instead of a caduceus. But pray, Mr. Puff, what first put you on exercising your talents in this way?

PUFF. Egad, sir—sheer necessity—the proper parent of an art so nearly allied to invention: you must know, Mr. Sneer, 110 that from the first time I tried my hand at an advertisement my success was such, that for some time after I led a most extraordinary life indeed!

SNEER. How, pray?

PUFF. Sir, I supported myself two years entirely by my misfortunes.

SNEER. By your misfortunes?

PUFF. Yes, sir, assisted by long sickness, and other occasional disorders; and a very comfortable living I had of it.

SNEER. From sickness and misfortunes! You practised as a 120 doctor and an attorney at once?

PUFF. No, egad; both maladies and miseries were my own.

SNEER. Hey!—what the plague!

DANGLE. 'Tis true, i'faith.

PUFF [*Exposing one of the "rackets" of the time*]. Hark'ee! By advertisements—'To the charitable and humane!' and 'To those whom Providence hath blessed with affluence!'

100. *Hygeia*, the goddess of health. The fens of Lincolnshire were noted as breeding places for fevers.
107. *caduceus*, Mercury's wand, with serpents entwined.

SNEER. Oh, I understand you.

PUFF. And, in truth, I deserved what I got; for I suppose never man went through such a series of calamities in the same 130 space of time! Sir, I was five times made a bankrupt, and reduced from a state of affluence by a train of unavoidable misfortunes! Then, sir, though a very industrious tradesman, I was twice burnt out, and lost my little all, both times! I lived upon those fires a month. I soon after was confined by a most excruciating disorder, and lost the use of my limbs! That told very well; for I had the case strongly attested, and went about to collect the subscriptions myself.

DANGLE. Egad, I believe that was when you first called on me—

PUFF. In November last? Oh, no!—I was at that time a 140 close prisoner in the Marshalsea, for a debt benevolently contracted to serve a friend! I was afterwards twice tapped for a dropsy, which declined into a very profitable consumption! I was then reduced to—oh, no, then, I became a widow with six helpless children—after having had eleven husbands pressed, and being left every time eight months gone with child, and without money to get me into a hospital!

SNEER. And you bore all with patience, I make no doubt?

PUFF. Why, yes, though I made some occasional attempts at *felo de se;* but as I did not find those *rash actions* answer, 150 I left off killing myself very soon. Well, sir, at last, what with bankruptcies, fires, gouts, dropsies, imprisonments, and other valuable calamities, having got together a pretty handsome sum, I determined to quit a business which had always gone rather against my conscience, and in a more liberal way still to indulge my talents for fiction and embellishment, through my favourite channels of diurnal communication—and so, sir, you have my history.

SNEER. Most obligingly communicative indeed; and your confession, if published, might certainly serve the cause of true 160 charity, by rescuing the most useful channels of appeal to benevolence from the cant of imposition. But surely, Mr. Puff, there is no great *mystery* in your present profession?

PUFF. Mystery, sir! I will take upon me to say the matter was never scientifically treated, nor reduced to rule before.

SNEER. Reduced to rule?

PUFF. O Lud, sir, you are very ignorant, I am afraid. Yes, sir, puffing is of various sorts: the principal are: the puff direct—the puff preliminary—the puff collateral—the puff collusive, and the

150. *felo de se,* suicide.

puff oblique, or puff by implication. These all assume, as 170
circumstances require, the various forms of Letter to the Editor—
Occasional Anecdote—Impartial Critique—Observation from
Correspondent, or Advertisement from the Party.

sneer. The puff direct, I can conceive—

puff. Oh, yes, that's simple enough; for instance, a new comedy
or farce is to be produced at one of the theatres (though, by the
by, they don't bring out half what they ought to do): the author,
suppose Mr. Smatter, or Mr. Dapper—or any particular friend
of mine. Very well; the day before it is to be performed, I write
an account of the manner in which it was received: I have 180
the plot from the author, and only add—Characters strongly
drawn—highly coloured—hand of a master—fund of genuine
humour—mine of invention—neat dialogue—Attic salt! Then for
the performance—Mr. Dodd was astonishingly great in the character of Sir Harry! That universal and judicious actor, Mr.
Palmer, perhaps never appeared to more advantage than in the
Colonel; but it is not in the power of language to do justice to
Mr. King! Indeed, he more than merited those repeated bursts of
applause which he drew from a most brilliant and judicious audience! As to the scenery—The miraculous powers of Mr. de 190
Loutherbourg's pencil are universally acknowledged! In short,
we are at a loss which to admire most—the unrivalled genius of
the author, the great attention and liberality of the managers, the
wonderful abilities of the painter, or the incredible exertions of
all the performers!

sneer. That's pretty well indeed, sir.

puff. Oh, cool—quite cool—to what I sometimes do.

sneer. And do you think there are any who are influenced by
this?

puff. O Lud! yes, sir; the number of those who undergo 200
the fatigue of judging for themselves is very small indeed!

sneer. Well, sir—the puff preliminary?

puff. Oh, that, sir, does well in the form of a *caution*. In a matter of gallantry now—Sir Flimsy Gossamer wishes to be well
with Lady Fanny Fete. He applies to me—I open trenches for
him with a paragraph in the *Morning Post*:—It is recommended
to the beautiful and accomplished Lady F four stars F dash E to
be on her guard against that dangerous character, Sir F dash G;
who, however pleasing and insinuating his manners may be, is
certainly not remarkable for the *constancy of his attach-* 210

184. *Mr. Dodd, Mr. Palmer, Mr. King*, actors who played parts in the
Critic.

ments!—in italics. Here, you see, Sir Flimsy Gossamer is introduced to the particular notice of Lady Fanny—who, perhaps,
never thought of him before; she finds herself publicly cautioned
to avoid him, which naturally makes her desirous of seeing him;
the observation of their acquaintance causes a pretty kind of mutual embarrassment, this produces a sort of sympathy of interest
—which, if Sir Flimsy is unable to improve effectually, he at
least gains the credit of having their names mentioned together,
by a particular set, and in a particular way—which nine times
out of ten is the full accomplishment of modern gallantry.   220

DANGLE. Egad, Sneer, you will be quite an adept in the business.

PUFF. Now, sir, the puff collateral is much used as an append-
age to advertisements, and may take the form of anecdote.—
Yesterday, as the celebrated George Bon-Mot was sauntering
down St. James's Street, he met the lively Lady Mary Myrtle,
coming out of the Park—'Good God, Lady Mary, I'm surprised
to meet you in a white jacket, for I expected never to have seen
you but in a full-trimmed uniform and a light-horseman's cap!'
'Heavens, George, where could you have learned that?' 'Why,'
replied the wit, 'I just saw a print of you, in a new publica-   230
tion called the *Camp Magazine*, which, by the by, is a devilish
clever thing, and is sold at No. 3, on the right hand of the way,
two doors from the printing-office, the corner of Ivy Lane,
Paternoster Row, price only one shilling!'

SNEER. Very ingenious indeed!

PUFF. But the puff collusive is the newest of any; for it acts in
the disguise of determined hostility. It is much used by bold
booksellers and enterprising poets.—An indignant correspondent
observes, that the new poem called *Beelzebub's Cotillion, or Pro-
serpine's Fête Champêtre*, is one of the most unjustifiable   240
performances he ever read! The severity with which certain characters are handled is quite shocking! And as there are many descriptions in it too warmly coloured for female delicacy, the
shameful avidity with which this piece is bought by all people
of fashion is a reproach on the taste of the times, and a disgrace
to the delicacy of the age!—Here, you see, the two strongest
inducements are held forth: first, that nobody ought to read it;
and secondly, that everybody buys it; on the strength of which
the publisher boldly prints the tenth edition, before he had sold
ten of the first; and then establishes it by threatening himself   250
with the pillory, or absolutely indicting himself for *scan. mag.!*

251. *pillory*, punishment for improper publication. *scan. mag.*, scandalum
magnatum, i.e., slander of the peers.

DANGLE. Ha! ha! ha!—'gad, I know it is so.

PUFF. As to the puff oblique, or puff by implication, it is too various and extensive to be illustrated by an instance; it attracts in titles and presumes in patents; it lurks in the *limitation* of a subscription, and invites in the assurance of crowd and incommodation at public places; it delights to draw forth concealed merit, with a most disinterested assiduity; and sometimes wears a countenance of smiling censure and tender reproach. It has a wonderful memory for parliamentary debates, and will often give 260 the whole speech of a favoured member with the most flattering accuracy. But, above all, it is a great dealer in reports and suppositions. It has the earliest intelligence of intended preferments that will reflect *honour* on the *patrons;* and embryo promotions of modest gentlemen—who know nothing of the matter themselves. It can hint a ribbon for implied services, in the air of a common report; and with the carelessness of a casual paragraph, suggests officers into commands, to which they have no pretension but their wishes. This, sir, is the last principal class of the art of puffing—an art which I hope you will now agree with 270 me is of the highest dignity—yielding a tablature of benevolence and public spirit; befriending equally trade, gallantry, criticism, and politics: the applause of genius! the register of charity! the triumph of heroism! the self-defence of contractors! the fame of orators!—and the gazette of ministers!

SNEER. Sir, I am completely a convert both to the importance and ingenuity of your profession; and now, sir, there is but one thing which can possibly increase my respect for you, and that is, your permitting me to be present this morning at the rehearsal of your new trage— 280

PUFF. Hush, for Heaven's sake. *My* tragedy! Egad, Dangle, I take this very ill—you know how apprehensive I am of being known to be the author.

DANGLE. I'faith, I would not have told, but it's in the papers, and your name at length—in the *Morning Chronicle.*

PUFF. Ah! those damned editors never can keep a secret! Well, Mr. Sneer, no doubt you will do me great honour—I shall be infinitely happy—highly flattered—

DANGLE. I believe it must be near the time—shall we go together? 290

PUFF. No; it will not be yet this hour, for they are always late at that theatre: besides, I must meet you there, for I have some little matters here to send to the papers, and a few paragraphs to scribble before I go. [*Looking at memorandums.*] Here is 'A con-

scientious baker, on the subject of the army bread'; and 'A de-
tester of visible brick-work, in favour of the new-invented
stucco'; both in the style of Junius, and promised for to-morrow.
The Thames navigation too is at a stand. Miso-mad or Anti-shoal
must go to work again directly. Here too are some political
memorandums, I see; aye—To take Paul Jones, and get the 300
Indiamen out of the Shannon—reinforce Byron—compel the
Dutch to—so!—I must do that in the evening papers, or reserve
it for the *Morning Herald;* for I know that I have undertaken
to-morrow, besides, to establish the unanimity of the fleet in the
Public Advertiser, and to shoot Charles Fox in the *Morning Post.*
So, egad, I ha'n't a moment to lose!

DANGLE. Well!—we'll meet in the Green Room.

[*While Puff bustles officiously out at one side, Dangle and
Sneer, laughing at him, go out the other.*

ACT II

SCENE I

THE STAGE OF THE THEATER, *about an hour after the close of the
preceding act. Dangle, Puff, and Sneer come out before the
curtain.*

PUFF. No, no, sir; what Shakespeare says of actors may be
better applied to the purpose of plays; *they* ought to be "the abstract and brief chronicles of the times." Therefore when history,
and particularly the history of our own country, furnishes anything like a case in point, to the time in which an author writes,
if he knows his own interest he will take advantage of it; so, sir,
I call my tragedy *The Spanish Armada;* and have laid the scene
before Tilbury Fort.

SNEER. A most happy thought, certainly!

297. *Junius,* a celebrated but anonymous writer of letters criticizing current conditions and prominent figures. His identity has never been discovered.

300. *Paul Jones,* the American naval captain who harried British shipping
off the coast of Britain itself during the Revolution.

301. *Indiamen,* ships in the East Indies trade, tied up by Jones' ravages.
Byron, John Byron, vice-admiral of the Royal Navy, grandfather of the
poet.

305. *Fox,* Charles James Fox, one of the great political orators of the
time. Agreed with Burke in favoring the cause of the colonies.

DANGLE. Egad, it was—I told you so. But pray, now, I 10
don't understand how you have contrived to introduce any love
into it.

PUFF. Love! Oh, nothing so easy: for it is a received point
among poets, that where history gives you a good heroic outline
for a play, you may fill up with a little love at your own discretion: in doing which, nine times out of ten, you only make
up a deficiency in the private history of the times. Now I rather
think I have done this with some success.

SNEER. No scandal about Queen Elizabeth, I hope?

PUFF. O Lud! no, no. I only suppose the Governor of Til- 20
bury Fort's daughter to be in love with the son of the Spanish
admiral.

SNEER. Oh, is that all!

DANGLE. Excellent, i'faith! I see it at once. But won't this appear
rather improbable?

PUFF. To be sure it will—but what the plague! a play is not to
show occurrences that happen every day, but things just so
strange, that though they never *did*, they might happen.

SNEER. Certainly nothing is unnatural, that is not physically
impossible.   30

PUFF. Very true, and for that matter Don Ferolo Whiskerandos
—for that's the lover's name—might have been over here in the
train of the Spanish ambassador; or Tilburina, for that is the lady's
name, might have been in love with him, from having heard his
character, or seen his picture; or from knowing that he was the
last man in the world she ought to be in love with—or for any
other good female reason. However, sir, the fact is, that though
she is but a knight's daughter, egad! she is in love like any princess!

DANGLE. Poor young lady! I feel for her already! for I can 40
conceive how great the conflict must be between her passion and
her duty! her love for her country, and her love for Don Ferolo
Whiskerandos!

PUFF. Oh, amazing!—her poor susceptible heart is swayed to
and fro by contending passions, like—

[*Enter Under Prompter.*

UNDER PROMPTER. Sir, the scene is set, and everything is ready
to begin, if you please.

PUFF. 'Egad; then we'll lose no time.

UNDER PROMPTER. Though I believe, sir, you will find it very
short, for all the performers have profited by the kind per- 50
mission you granted them.

PUFF. Hey! what!

UNDER PROMPTER. You know, sir, you gave them leave to cut out or omit whatever they found heavy or unnecessary to the plot, and I must own they have taken very liberal advantage of your indulgence.

PUFF. Well, well. They are in general very good judges; and I know I am luxuriant.—Now, Mr. Hopkins, as soon as you please.

UNDER PROMPTER [To the music]. Gentlemen, will you play a few bars of something, just to— 60

PUFF. Aye, that 's right—for as we have the scenes and dresses, egad, we'll go to't, as if it was the first night's performance; but you need not mind stopping between the acts. [Exit Under Prompter. Orchestra play. Then the bell rings.] Soh! stand clear, gentlemen. Now you know there will be a cry of Down!—down! —hats off!—silence! Then up curtain, and let us see what our painters have done for us.

SCENE II

The curtain rises and they stand a bit to one side so that Puff can comment on the action of the play as it progresses. Two sentinels, apparently sound asleep, slouch on a bench before a backdrop representing the fort.

DANGLE. Tilbury Fort!—very fine indeed!

PUFF. Now, what do you think I open with?

SNEER. Faith, I can't guess.

PUFF. A clock. Hark! [Clock strikes.] I open with a clock striking, to beget an awful attention in the audience—it also marks the time, which is four o'clock in the morning, and saves a description of the rising sun, and a great deal about gilding the eastern hemisphere.

DANGLE. But pray, are the sentinels to be asleep?

PUFF. Fast as watchmen. 10

SNEER. Isn't that odd, though, at such an alarming crisis?

PUFF. To be sure it is, but smaller things must give way to a striking scene at the opening; that 's a rule. And the case is, that two great men are coming to this very spot to begin the piece; now, it is not to be supposed they would open their lips, if these fellows were watching them, so, egad, I must either have sent them off their posts, or set them asleep.

SNEER. Oh, that accounts for it! But tell us, who are these coming?

PUFF. These are they—Sir Walter Raleigh and Sir Christo- 20
pher Hatton. You'll know Sir Christopher by his turning out his
toes—famous, you know, for his dancing. I like to preserve all the
little traits of character.—Now attend.

[*Enter Sir Walter Raleigh and Sir Christopher Hatton.*

SIR CHRISTOPHER. True, gallant Raleigh!

DANGLE. What, they had been talking before?

PUFF. Oh, yes; all the way as they came along.—I beg pardon,
gentlemen [*to the actors*], but these are particular friends of
mine, whose remarks may be of great service to us. [*To Sneer
and Dangle.*] Don't mind interrupting them whenever anything
strikes you. 30

SIR CHRISTOPHER. True, gallant Raleigh!
But oh, thou champion of thy country's fame,
There *is* a question which I yet must ask;
A question which I never asked before—
What mean these mighty armaments?
This general muster? and this throng of chiefs?

SNEER. Pray, Mr. Puff, how came Sir Christopher Hatton never
to ask that question before?

PUFF. What, before the play began? how the plague could he?

DANGLE. That's true, i'faith! 40

PUFF. But you will hear what he thinks of the matter.

SIR CHRISTOPHER. Alas, my noble friend, when I behold
Yon tented plains in martial symmetry
Arrayed—when I count o'er yon glittering lines
Of crested warriors, where the proud steeds neigh,
And valour-breathing trumpet's shrill appeal
Responsive vibrates on my listening ear;
When virgin majesty herself I view,
Like her protecting Pallas veiled in steel,
With graceful confidence exhort to arms! 50
When briefly all I hear or see bears stamp
Of martial vigilance and stern defence,
I cannot but surmise—Forgive, my friend,
If the conjecture 's rash—I cannot but
Surmise—the State some danger apprehends!

20-21. *Sir Walter Raleigh*, one of the greatest of Elizabeth's favorites,
especially interested in colonizing the New World. *Sir Christopher Hatton*, Lord Chancellor to Elizabeth. His dancing was reported to please her
greatly.

SNEER. A very cautious conjecture that.

PUFF. Yes, that 's his character; not to give an opinion, but on secure grounds.—Now then.

SIR WALTER. Oh, most accomplished Christopher—

PUFF. He calls him by his Christian name, to show that they   60
are on the most familiar terms.

SIR WALTER. Oh, most accomplished Christopher, I find
  Thy stanch sagacity still tracks the future,
  In the fresh print of the o'ertaken past.

PUFF. Figurative!

SIR WALTER. Thy fears are just.

SIR CHRISTOPHER. But where? whence? when? and what
  The danger is—methinks I fain would learn.

SIR WALTER. You know, my friend, scarce two revolving suns
  And three revolving moons have closed their course,   70
  Since haughty Philip, in despite of peace,
  With hostile hand hath struck at England's trade.

SIR CHRISTOPHER. I know it well.

SIR WALTER. Philip, you know, is proud Iberia's king!

SIR CHRISTOPHER. He is.

SIR WALTER.   His subjects in base bigotry
  And Catholic oppression held,—while we,
  You know, the Protestant persuasion hold.

SIR CHRISTOPHER. We do.

SIR WALTER. You know, beside, his boasted armament,
  The famed Armada, by the Pope baptized,   80
  With purpose to invade these realms—

SIR CHRISTOPHER.   Is sailed,
  Our last advices so report.

SIR WALTER. While the Iberian admiral's chief hope,
  His darling son—

SIR CHRISTOPHER.   Ferolo Whiskerandos hight—

SIR WALTER. The same—by chance a prisoner hath been ta'en,
  And in this fort of Tilbury—

SIR CHRISTOPHER.   Is now
  Confined,—'tis true, and oft from yon tall turret's top
  I've marked the youthful Spaniard's haughty mien—
  Unconquered, though in chains.

SIR WALTER.   You also know—

DANGLE. Mr. Puff, as he *knows* all this, why does Sir Wal-   90
ter go on telling him?

PUFF. But the audience are not supposed to know anything of
the matter, are they?

SNEER. True, but I think you manage ill: for there certainly appears no reason why Sir Walter should be so communicative.

PUFF. 'Fore Gad, now, that is one of the most ungrateful observations I ever heard—for the less inducement he has to tell all this the more, I think, you ought to be obliged to him; for I am sure you'd know nothing of the matter without it.

DANGLE. That's very true, upon my word. 100

PUFF. But you will find he was *not* going on.

SIR CHRISTOPHER. Enough, enough,—'tis plain—and I no more
Am in amazement lost!—

PUFF. Here now, you see, Sir Christopher did not in fact ask any one question for his own information.

SNEER. No, indeed: his has been a most disinterested curiosity!

DANGLE. Really, I find we are very much obliged to them both.

PUFF. To be sure you are. Now then for the Commander-in-Chief, the Earl of Leicester; who, you know, was no favourite but of the Queen's—We left off—'in amazement lost!'— 110

SIR CHRISTOPHER. Am in amazement lost.—
• But see, where noble Leicester comes! supreme
In honours and command.

SIR WALTER.   And yet methinks,
At such a time, so perilous, so feared,
That staff might well become an abler grasp.

SIR CHRISTOPHER. And so, by Heaven! think I; but soft, he 's here!

PUFF. Aye, they envy him.

SNEER. But who are these with him?

PUFF. Oh! very valiant knights; one is the Governor of the fort, the other the Master of the Horse.—And now, I think, 120
you shall hear some better language: I was obliged to be plain and intelligible in the first scene, because there was so much matter of fact in it; but now, i'faith, you have trope, figure, and metaphor as plenty as noun-substantives.

[*Enter Earl of Leicester, the Governor, and others.*

LEICESTER. How 's this, my friends! is't thus your new-fledged zeal
And plumèd valour moulds in roosted sloth?
Why dimly glimmers that heroic flame,
Whose red'ning blaze, by patriot spirit fed,
Should be the beacon of a kindling realm?
Can the quick current of a patriot heart 130
Thus stagnate in a cold and weedy converse,
Or freeze in tideless inactivity?
No! rather let the fountain of your valour
Spring through each stream of enterprise,
Each petty channel of conducive daring,

Till the full torrent of your foaming wrath
O'erwhelm the flats of sunk hostility!

PUFF. There it is—followed up!

SIR WALTER. No more! the freshening breath of thy rebuke
Hath filled the swelling canvas of our souls!   140
And thus, though fate should cut the cable of
    [All take hands.
Our topmost hopes, in friendship's closing line
We'll grapple with despair, and if we fall,
We'll fall in Glory's wake!

LEICESTER. There spoke Old England's genius!
Then, are we all resolved?

ALL. We are—all resolved!

LEICESTER. To conquer—or be free?

ALL. To conquer, or be free!

LEICESTER. All?   150

ALL. All!

DANGLE. *Nem. con.* egad!

PUFF. Oh, yes, where they *do* agree on the stage, their unanimity is wonderful!

LEICESTER. Then let 's embrace—and now—

SNEER. What the plague, is he going to pray?

PUFF. Yes, hush!—in great emergencies there is nothing like a prayer!

LEICESTER. O mighty Mars!

DANGLE. But why should he pray to *Mars?*   160

PUFF. Hush!

LEICESTER.   If in thy homage bred,
Each point of discipline I've still observed;
Nor but by due promotion, and the right
Of service, to the rank of Major-General
Have risen; assist thy votary now!

GOVERNOR. Yet do not rise,—hear me!

MASTER. And me!

KNIGHT. And me!

SIR WALTER. And me!   170

SIR CHRISTOPHER. And me!

PUFF. Now, pray all together.

ALL. Behold thy votaries submissive beg,
That thou wilt deign to grant them all they ask;
Assist them to accomplish all their ends,

152. *Nem. con.,* nemine contradicente, with no dissenting votes.

And sanctify whatever means they use
To gain them! *[Exeunt.*

SNEER. A very orthodox quintetto!

PUFF. Vastly well, gentlemen.—Is that well managed or not?
Have you such a prayer as that on the stage? 180

SNEER. Not exactly.

LEICESTER [*To Puff*]. But, sir, you haven't settled how we are
to get off here.

PUFF. You could not go off kneeling, could you?

SIR WALTER [*To Puff*]. Oh, no, sir! impossible!

PUFF. It would have a good effect, i'faith, if you could exeunt
praying! Yes, and would vary the established mode of springing
off with a glance at the pit.

SNEER. Oh, never mind; so as you get them off, I'll answer for
it the audience won't care how. 190

PUFF. Well, then, repeat the last line standing, and go off the
old way.

ALL. And sanctify whatever means they use
To gain them.

DANGLE. Bravo! a fine exit.

SNEER. Stay a moment.—

[*The Sentinels get up.*
FIRST SENTINEL. All this shall to Lord Burleigh's ear.
SECOND SENTINEL. 'Tis meet it should. [*Exeunt Sentinels.*

DANGLE. Hey! why, I thought those fellows had been asleep?

PUFF. Only a pretence, there's the art of it; they were 200
spies of Lord Burleigh's.

SNEER. But isn't it odd, they were never taken notice of, not
even by the Commander-in-Chief?

PUFF. O Lud, sir, if people who want to listen, or overhear,
were not always connived at in a tragedy, there would be no
carrying on any plot in the world.

DANGLE. That's certain!

PUFF. But take care, my dear Dangle, the morning gun is going
to fire. [*Cannon fires.*]

DANGLE. Well, that will have a fine effect. 210

PUFF. I think so, and helps to realize the scene. [*Cannon twice.*]
What the plague!—*three* morning guns!—there never is but one!
—aye, this is always the way at the theatre—give these fellows

201. *Lord Burleigh,* William Cecil, Elizabeth's great Lord Treasurer and
one of her chief and wisest counsellors.

a good thing, and they never know when to have done with it.
You have no more cannon to fire?

PROMPTER [*From within*]. No, sir.

PUFF. Now, then, for soft music.

SNEER. Pray, what 's that for?

PUFF. It shows that Tilburina is coming; nothing introduces
you a heroine like soft music.—Here she comes.   220

DANGLE. And her confidant, I suppose?

PUFF. To be sure: here they are—inconsolable to the minuet
in *Ariadne!* [*Soft music.*]

    [*Enter Tilburina and Confidant.*

TILBURINA. Now has the whispering breath of gentle morn
  Bade Nature's voice and Nature's beauty rise;
  While orient Phœbus with unborrowed hues
  Clothes the waked loveliness which all night slept
  In heavenly drapery! Darkness is fled.
  Now flowers unfold their beauties to the sun,
  And blushing, kiss the beam he sends to wake them.   230
  The striped carnation and the guarded rose,
  The vulgar wallflower and smart gillyflower,
  The polyanthus mean—the dapper daisy,
  Sweet-william and sweet marjoram, and all
  The tribe of single and of double pinks!
  Now, too, the feathered warblers tune their notes
  Around, and charm the listening grove—The lark!
  The linnet! chaffinch! bullfinch! goldfinch! greenfinch!
  But oh, to me no joy can they afford!
  Nor rose, nor wallflower, nor smart gillyflower,   240
  Nor polyanthus mean, nor dapper daisy,
  Nor William sweet, nor marjoram—nor lark,
  Linnet, nor all the finches of the grove!

PUFF. Your white handkerchief, madam.

TILBURINA. I thought, sir, I wasn't to use that 'till 'heart-rending
woe.'

PUFF. Oh, yes, madam—at 'the finches of the grove,' if you
please.

TILBURINA.   Nor lark,   249
  Linnet, nor all the finches of the grove!   [*Weeps.*

PUFF. Vastly well, madam!

DANGLE. Vastly well, indeed!

TILBURINA. For, oh, too sure, heart-rending woe is now
  The lot of wretched Tilburina!

223. *Ariadne*, one of the popular Italian operas, with music by Handel.

DANGLE. Oh!—'tis too much.

SNEER. Oh!—it is, indeed.

CONFIDANT. Be comforted, sweet lady—for who knows
But Heaven has yet some milk-white day in store.

TILBURINA. Alas, my gentle Nora, 260
Thy tender youth as yet hath never mourned
Love's fatal dart. Else wouldst thou know, that when
The soul is sunk in comfortless despair,
It cannot taste of merriment.

DANGLE. That 's certain.

CONFIDANT. But see where your stern father comes;
It is not meet that he should find you thus.

PUFF. Hey, what the plague! what a cut is here!—why, what
is become of the description of her first meeting with Don Whiskerandos? his gallant behaviour in the sea fight, and the simile of
the canary bird? 270

TILBURINA. Indeed, sir, you'll find they will not be missed.

PUFF [Disappointed]. Very well.—Very well!

TILBURINA. The cue, ma'am, if you please.

CONFIDANT. It is not meet that he should find you thus.

TILBURINA. Thou counsel'st right, but 'tis no easy task
For barefaced grief to wear a mask of joy.
[Enter Governor.

GOVERNOR. How 's this—in tears?—O Tilburina, shame!
Is this a time for maudling tenderness,
And Cupid's baby woes?—hast thou not heard
That haughty Spain's Pope-consecrated fleet 280
Advances to our shores, while England's fate,
Like a clipped guinea, trembles in the scale!

TILBURINA. Then is the crisis of *my* fate at hand!
I see the fleet's approach—I see—

PUFF. Now pray, gentlemen, mind. This is one of the most
useful figures we tragedy writers have, by which a hero or heroine, in consideration of their being often obliged to overlook
things that *are* on the stage, is allowed to hear and see a number
of things that are not.

SNEER. Yes—a kind of poetical second-sight! 290

PUFF. Yes.—Now then, madam.

TILBURINA. I see their decks
Are cleared!—I see the signal made!
The line is formed!—a cable's length asunder!
I see the frigates stationed in the rear;
And now I hear the thunder of the guns!

I hear the victor's shouts—I also hear
The vanquished groan!—and now 'tis smoke—and now
I see the loose sails shiver in the wind!
I see—I see—what soon you'll see—   300
GOVERNOR. Hold, daughter! peace! this love hath turned thy brain:
The Spanish fleet thou *canst* not see—because
—It is not yet in sight!

DANGLE. Egad, though, the Governor seems to make no allowance for this poetical figure you talk of.

PUFF. No, a plain matter-of-fact man—that's his character.

TILBURINA. But will you then refuse his offer?
GOVERNOR. I must—I will—I can—I ought—I do.
TILBURINA. Think what a noble price.
GOVERNOR. No more—you urge in vain.   310
TILBURINA. His liberty is all he asks.

SNEER. All *who* asks, Mr. Puff? Who is—

PUFF. Egad, sir, I can't tell. Here has been such cutting and slashing, I don't know where they have got to myself.

TILBURINA. Indeed, sir, you will find it will connect very well.
—And your reward secure.

PUFF. Oh, if they hadn't been so devilish free with their cutting here, you would have found that Don Whiskerandos has been tampering for his liberty, and has persuaded Tilburina to make this proposal to her father. And now, pray observe the con-   320
ciseness with which the argument is conducted. Egad, the *pro* and *con* goes as smart as hits in a fencing match. It is indeed a sort of small-sword logic, which we have borrowed from the French.

TILBURINA. A retreat in Spain!
GOVERNOR. Outlawry here!
TILBURINA. Your daughter's prayer!
GOVERNOR. Your father's oath!
TILBURINA. My lover!
GOVERNOR. My country!
TILBURINA. Tilburina!   330
GOVERNOR. England!
TILBURINA. A title!
GOVERNOR. Honour!
TILBURINA. A pension!
GOVERNOR. Conscience!
TILBURINA. A thousand pounds!
GOVERNOR. Hah! thou hast touched me nearly!

PUFF. There, you see—she threw in *Tilburina*. Quick, parry carte with *England!* Hah! thrust in tierce *a title!*—parried by

338-339. *parry carte, etc.,* terms in fencing.

honour. Hah! *a pension* over the arm! put by by *conscience.* 340
Then flankonade with *a thousand pounds*—and a palpable hit,
egad!

TILBURINA.   Canst thou
Reject the *suppliant*, and the *daughter* too?
GOVERNOR. No more; I would not hear thee plead in vain,
The *father* softens—but the *governor*
Is fixed!   [*Exit.*

DANGLE. Aye, that antithesis of persons is a most established
figure.

TILBURINA. 'Tis well—hence, then, fond hopes, fond passion hence;
Duty, behold I am all over thine—   351
WHISKERANDOS [*Without*]. Where is my love—my—
TILBURINA. Ha!
WHISKERANDOS [*Entering*]. My beauteous enemy—

PUFF. Oh, dear, ma'am, you must start a great deal more than
that; consider you had just determined in favour of duty, when
in a moment the sound of his voice revives your passion, over-
throws your resolution, destroys your obedience. If you don't
express all that in your start you do nothing at all.
TILBURINA. Well, we'll try again!   360
DANGLE. Speaking from within has always a fine effect.
SNEER. Very.

WHISKERANDOS. My conquering Tilburina! How! is't thus
We meet? why are thy looks averse? what means
That falling tear—that frown of boding woe?
Ha! now indeed I am a prisoner!
Yes, now I feel the galling weight of these
Disgraceful chains—which, cruel Tilburina!
Thy doting captive gloried in before.—
But thou art false, and Whiskerandos is undone!   370
TILBURINA. Oh, no; how little dost thou know thy Tilburina!
WHISKERANDOS. Art thou then true? Begone cares, doubts, and fears,
I make you all a present to the winds;
And if the winds reject you—try the waves.

PUFF. The wind, you know, is the established receiver of all
stolen sighs, and cast-off griefs and apprehensions.

TILBURINA. Yet must we part?—stern duty seals our doom:
Though here I call yon conscious clouds to witness,
Could I pursue the bias of my soul,
All friends, all right of parents I'd disclaim,   380
And thou, my Whiskerandos, shouldst be father
And mother, brother, cousin, uncle, aunt,

And friend to me!

WHISKERANDOS. O matchless excellence!—and must we part?
Well, if—we must—we must—and in that case
The less is said the better.

PUFF. Hey day! here 's a cut! What, are all the mutual pro-
testations out?

TILBURINA. Now pray, sir, don't interrupt us just here, you ruin
our feelings.   390

PUFF. *Your* feelings!—but zounds, *my* feelings, ma'am!

SNEER. No; pray don't interrupt them.

WHISKERANDOS. One last embrace—

TILBURINA. Now—farewell, for ever.

WHISKERANDOS. For ever!

TILBURINA. Aye, for ever.   [*Going.*

PUFF. 'Sdeath and fury! Gad's life! sir! madam, if you go out
without the parting look, you might as well dance out. Here,
here!

CONFIDANT. But pray, sir, how am *I* to get off here?   400

PUFF. *You*, pshaw! what the devil signifies how *you* get off!
edge away at the top, or where you will. [*Pushes the Confidant
off.*] Now, ma'am, you see—

TILBURINA. We understand you, sir.

—Aye, for ever.

BOTH. Oh!—[*Turning back and exeunt. The curtain comes down.*

DANGLE. Oh, charming!

PUFF. Hey!—'tis pretty well, I believe: you see I don't attempt
to strike out anything new, but I take it I improve on the established modes.   410

SNEER. You do, indeed. But pray, is not Queen Elizabeth to
appear?

PUFF. No, not once—but she is to be talked of for ever; so that,
egad, you'll think a hundred times that she is on the point of coming in.

SNEER. Hang it, I think it 's a pity to keep *her* in the green room
all the night.

PUFF. Oh, no, that always has a fine effect—it keeps up expectation.

DANGLE. But are we not to have a battle?   420

PUFF. Yes, yes, you will have a battle at last, but, egad, it 's not
to be by land, but by sea—and that is the only quite new thing in
the piece.

402. *top*, back stage.

DANGLE. What, Drake at the Armada, hey?

PUFF. Yes, i'faith—fireships and all: then we shall end with the procession. Hey! that will do, I think?

SNEER. No doubt on't.

PUFF. Come, we must not lose time—so now for the *under-plot.*

SNEER. What the plague, have you another plot?   430

PUFF. O Lord, yes—ever while you live have two plots to your tragedy. The grand point in managing them is only to let your underplot have as little connexion with your main plot as possible. I flatter myself nothing can be more distinct than mine, for as in my chief plot the characters are all great people, I have laid my underplot in low life; and as the former is to end in deep distress, I make the other end as happy as a farce.—Now, Mr. Hopkins, as soon as you please.

[*Enter Under Prompter.*

UNDER PROMPTER. Sir, the carpenter says it is impossible you can go to the park scene yet.   440

PUFF. The park scene! No—I mean the description scene here, in the wood.

UNDER PROMPTER. Sir, the performers have cut it out.

PUFF. Cut it out!

UNDER PROMPTER. Yes, sir.

PUFF. What! the whole account of Queen Elizabeth?

UNDER PROMPTER. Yes, sir.

PUFF. And the description of her horse and sidesaddle?

UNDER PROMPTER. Yes, sir.

PUFF. So, so, this is very fine indeed! Mr. Hopkins, how the   450 plague could you suffer this?

HOPKINS [*From within*]. Sir, indeed the pruning-knife—

PUFF. The pruning-knife—zounds, the axe! why, here has been such lopping and topping, I shan't have the bare trunk of my play left presently. Very well, sir—the performers must do as they please, but upon my soul, I'll print it, every word.

SNEER. That I would, indeed.

PUFF. Very well, sir—then we must go on. Zounds! I would not have parted with the description of the horse! Well, sir, go on.—Sir, it was one of the finest and most laboured things.—   460 Very well, sir, let them go on.—There you had him and his accoutrements from the bit to the crupper.—Very well, sir, we must go to the park scene.

424. *Drake*, Sir Francis Drake, the great explorer and privateer (pirate to the Spanish).

UNDER PROMPTER. Sir, there is the point, the carpenters say that unless there is some business put in here before the drop, they shan't have time to clear away the fort, or sink Gravesend and the river.

PUFF. So! this is a pretty dilemma, truly!—Gentlemen, you must excuse me, these fellows will never be ready unless I go and look after them myself. 470

SNEER. Oh, dear sir, these little things will happen.

PUFF. To cut out this scene!—but I'll print it—egad, I'll print it, every word!

[They go out, with Puff gesticulating violently.

ACT III

SCENE I

BEFORE THE CURTAIN, *as in Scene 1 of Act II. Enter Puff, Sneer, and Dangle.*

PUFF. Well, we are ready—now then for the justices.
   [Curtain rises; Justices, Constables, &c., discovered.

SNEER. This, I suppose, is a sort of senate scene.

PUFF. To be sure—there has not been one yet.

DANGLE. It is the underplot, isn't it?

PUFF. Yes. What, gentlemen, do you mean to go at once to the discovery scene?

JUSTICE. If you please, sir.

PUFF. Oh, very well—hark'ee, I don't choose to say anything more, but i'faith, they have mangled my play in a most shocking manner! 10

DANGLE. It's a great pity!

PUFF. Now then, Mr. Justice, if you please.

JUSTICE. Are all the volunteers without?
CONSTABLE.   They are,
   Some ten in fetters, and some twenty drunk.
JUSTICE. Attends the youth, whose most opprobrious fame
   And clear convicted crimes have stamped him soldier?
CONSTABLE. He waits your pleasure; eager to repay
   The blest reprieve that sends him to the fields
   Of glory, there to raise his branded hand
   In honour's cause.
JUSTICE.   'Tis well—'tis Justice arms him! 20
   Oh! may he now defend his country's laws

With half the spirit he has broke them all!
  If 'tis your worship's pleasure, bid him enter.
CONSTABLE. I fly, the herald of your will.   [*Exit Constable.*

PUFF. Quick, sir!

SNEER. But, Mr. Puff, I think not only the Justice but the clown
seems to talk in as high a style as the first hero among them.

PUFF. Heaven forbid they should not in a free country! Sir,
I am not for making slavish distinctions, and giving all the fine
language to the upper sort of people.   30

DANGLE. That 's very noble in you indeed.

[*Enter Justice's Lady.*

PUFF. Now pray mark this scene.

LADY. Forgive this interruption, good my love;
  But as I just now passed a prisoner youth,
  Whom rude hands hither lead, strange bodings seized
  My fluttering heart, and to myself I said,
  An if our Tom had lived, he'd surely been
  This stripling's height!

JUSTICE. Ha! sure some powerful sympathy directs
  Us both—
       [*Enter Son and Constable.*   40

JUSTICE. What is thy name?

SON. My name 's Tom Jenkins—*alias*, have I none—
  Though orphaned, and without a friend!

JUSTICE. Thy parents?

SON. My father dwelt in Rochester, and was,
  As I have heard, a fishmonger—no more.

PUFF. What, sir, do you leave out the account of your birth,
parentage, and education?

SON. They have settled it so, sir, here.

PUFF. Oh! oh!   50

LADY. How loudly nature whispers at my heart!
  Had he no other name?

SON.   I've seen a bill
  Of his, signed *Tomkins*, creditor.

JUSTICE. This does indeed confirm each circumstance
  The gipsy told!—Prepare!

SON. I do.

JUSTICE. No orphan, nor without a friend, art thou—
  I am thy father, *here* 's thy mother, *there*
  Thy uncle—this thy first cousin, and those
  Are all your near relations!   60

MOTHER. O ecstasy of bliss!

SON. O most unlooked-for happiness!

JUSTICE. O wonderful event!

[*They faint alternately in each other's arms.*

PUFF. There, you see relationship, like murder, will out.

JUSTICE. Now let's revive—else were this joy too much!
But come—and we'll unfold the rest within,
And thou, my boy, must needs want rest and food.
Hence may each orphan hope, as chance directs,
To find a father—where he least expects!   [*Exeunt.*

PUFF. What do you think of that?   70

DANGLE. One of the finest discovery-scenes I ever saw. Why, this underplot would have made a tragedy itself.

SNEER. Aye, or a comedy either.

PUFF. And keeps quite clear, you see, of the other.

[*Enter Scenemen, taking away the seats.*

PUFF. The scene remains, does it?

SCENEMAN. Yes, sir.

PUFF. You are to leave one chair, you know. But it is always awkward in a tragedy to have you fellows coming in in your playhouse liveries to remove things. I wish that could be managed better.—So now for my mysterious yeoman.   80

[*Enter a Beefeater.*

BEEFEATER. Perdition catch my soul, but I do love thee.

SNEER. Haven't I heard that line before?

PUFF. No, I fancy not. Where, pray?

DANGLE. Yes, I think there is something like it in *Othello.*

PUFF. Gad! now you put me in mind on't, I believe there is; but that's of no consequence—all that can be said is, that two people happened to hit on the same thought—and Shakespeare made use of it first, that's all.

SNEER. Very true.

PUFF. Now, sir, your soliloquy—but speak more to the pit,   90 if you please—the soliloquy always to the pit—that's a rule.

BEEFEATER. Though hopeless love finds comfort in despair,
It never can endure a rival's bliss!
But soft—I am observed.   [*Exit Beefeater.*

DANGLE. That's a very short soliloquy.

PUFF. Yes, but it would have been a great deal longer if he had not been observed.

SNEER. A most sentimental Beefeater that, Mr. Puff.

81. *Beefeater,* a yeoman of the guard, attending on royalty.

PUFF. Hark'ee, I would not have you be too sure that he *is* a
Beefeater.   100
SNEER. What, a hero in disguise?
PUFF. No matter—I only give you a hint. But now for my
principal character. Here he comes—Lord Burleigh in person!
Pray, gentlemen, step this way—softly—I only hope the Lord
High Treasurer is perfect—if he is but perfect!

[*Enter Burleigh, goes slowly to a chair and sits.*

SNEER. Mr. Puff!
PUFF. Hush! vastly well, sir! vastly well! a most interesting
gravity!
DANGLE. What, isn't he to speak at all?
PUFF. Egad, I thought you'd ask me that—yes, it is a very   110
likely thing that a minister in his situation, with the whole affairs
of the nation on his head, should have time to talk!—but hush!
or you'll put him out.
SNEER. Put him out! how the plague can that be, if he's not
going to say anything?
PUFF. There's a reason! why his part is to *think*, and how the
plague do you imagine he can *think* if you keep talking?
DANGLE. That's very true, upon my word!

[*Burleigh comes forward, shakes his head, and exit.*

SNEER. He is very perfect, indeed. Now pray, what did he
mean by that?   120
PUFF. You don't take it?
SNEER. No; I don't, upon my soul.
PUFF. Why, by that shake of the head, he gave you to understand that even though they had more justice in their cause and
wisdom in their measures, yet, if there was not a greater spirit
shown on the part of the people; the country would at last fall a
sacrifice to the hostile ambition of the Spanish monarchy.
SNEER. The devil!—did he mean all that by shaking his head?
PUFF. Every word of it. If he shook his head as I taught him.
DANGLE. Ah! there certainly is a vast deal to be done on the   130
stage by dumb show, and expression of face, and a judicious author knows how much he may trust to it.
SNEER. Oh, here are some of our old acquaintance.

[*Enter Hatton and Raleigh.*

SIR CHRISTOPHER. *My* niece, and *your* niece too!
By Heaven! there's witchcraft in't—he could not else
Have gained their hearts.—But see where they approach,

Some horrid purpose lowering on their brows!

SIR WALTER. Let us withdraw and mark them.   [*They withdraw.*

SNEER. What is all this?

PUFF. Ah! here has been more pruning!—but the fact is,   140
these two young ladies are also in love with Don Whiskerandos.
Now, gentlemen, this scene goes entirely for what we call *situ-*
ation and *stage effect*, by which the greatest applause may be obtained, without the assistance of language, sentiment, or character:
pray mark!

[*Enter the two Nieces.*

FIRST NIECE. Ellena here!
    She is his scorn as much as I—that is
    Some comfort still!

PUFF. Oh, dear madam, you are not to say that to her face!—
aside, ma'am, *aside*. The whole scene is to be *aside*.   150

[*Both nieces address the subsequent asides directly to the audience, oblivious of each other's presence.*

FIRST NIECE. She is his scorn as much as I—that is
    Some comfort still!

SECOND NIECE. I know he prizes not Pollina's love,
    But Tilburina lords it o'er his heart.

FIRST NIECE. But see the proud destroyer of my peace.
    Revenge is all the good I've left.

SECOND NIECE. He comes, the false disturber of my quiet.
    Now vengeance do thy worst.—

[*Enter Whiskerandos.*

WHISKERANDOS. O hateful liberty—if thus in vain
    I seek my Tilburina!   160

BOTH NIECES. And ever shalt!

[*They rush toward him. Sir Christopher and Sir Walter come
forward.*

BOTH. Hold! we will avenge you.

WHISKERANDOS. Hold *you*—or see your nieces bleed.—

[*The two nieces draw their two daggers to strike Whiskerandos;
the two uncles at the instant, with their two swords drawn,
catch their two nieces' arms, and turn the points of their swords
to Whiskerandos, who immediately draws two daggers, and
holds them to the two nieces' bosoms.*

PUFF. There's situation for you! there's a heroic group! You
see the ladies can't stab Whiskerandos—he durst not strike them
for fear of their uncles—the uncles durst not kill him because of
their nieces. I have them all at a dead lock!—for every one of
them is afraid to let go first.

SNEER. Why, then, they must stand there for ever.

PUFF. So they would, if I hadn't a very fine contrivance 170
for't. Now mind—

[Enter Beefeater with his Halberd.

BEEFEATER. In the Queen's name I charge you all to drop
Your swords and daggers!
[They drop their swords and daggers.

SNEER. That is a contrivance, indeed.
PUFF. Aye—in the Queen's name.

SIR CHRISTOPHER. Come, niece!
SIR WALTER. Come, niece! *[Exeunt with the two nieces.*
WHISKERANDOS. What 's he, who bids us thus renounce our guard?
BEEFEATER. Thou must do more—renounce thy love!
WHISKERANDOS. Thou liest—base Beefeater!
BEEFEATER. Ha! Hell! the lie! 180
By Heaven, thou'st roused the lion in my heart!
Off, yeoman's habit!—base disguise! off! off!
[Discovers himself, by throwing off his upper dress, and appear-
ing in a very fine waistcoat.
Am I a Beefeater now?
Or beams my crest as terrible as when
In Biscay's Bay I took thy captive sloop?

PUFF. There, egad! he comes out to be the very captain of the
privateer who had taken Whiskerandos prisoner, and was himself an old lover of Tilburina's.
DANGLE. Admirably managed, indeed. 190
PUFF. Now, stand out of their way.

WHISKERANDOS. I thank thee, Fortune! that hast thus bestowed
A weapon to chastise this insolent. *[Takes up one of the swords.]*
BEEFEATER. I take thy challenge, Spaniard, and I thank
Thee, Fortune, too!—*[Takes up the other sword].*

DANGLE. That's excellently contrived!—it seems as if the two
uncles had left their swords on purpose for them.
PUFF. No, egad, they could not help leaving them.

WHISKERANDOS. Vengeance and Tilburina!
BEEFEATER. Exactly so.
[They fight, and after the usual number of wounds given, Whis-
kerandos falls.

WHISKERANDOS. Oh, cursed parry!—that last thrust in tierce 200
Was fatal!—Captain, thou hast fenced well!
And Whiskerandos quits this bustling scene
For all eter—

BEEFEATER.   —nity—he would have added, but stern death
Cut short his being, and the noun at once!

PUFF. Oh, my dear sir, you are too slow; now mind me. Sir,
shall I trouble you to die again?

WHISKERANDOS. And Whiskerandos quits this bustling scene
For all eter—

BEEFEATER.   —nity—he would have added—

PUFF. No, sir—that's not it—once more, if you please.

WHISKERANDOS. I wish, sir, you would practise this with-   210
out me. I can't stay dying here all night.

PUFF. Very well, we'll go over it by and by.—I must humour
these gentlemen!   [*Exit Whiskerandos.*

BEEFEATER. Farewell, brave Spaniard! and when next—

PUFF. Dear sir, you needn't speak that speech as the body has
walked off.

BEEFEATER. That's true, sir—then I'll join the fleet.

PUFF. If you please. [*Exit Beefeater.*] Now, who comes on?

[*Enter Governor, with his hair properly disordered.*
GOVERNOR. A hemisphere of evil planets reign!
And every planet sheds contagious frenzy!   220
My Spanish prisoner is slain! my daughter,
Meeting the dead corse borne along, has gone
Distract!   [*A loud flourish of trumpets.*
           But hark! I am summoned to the fort;
Perhaps the fleets have met! amazing crisis!
O Tilburina! from thy aged father's beard
Thou'st plucked the few brown hairs which time had left!
                                          [*Exit Governor.*

SNEER. Poor gentleman!

PUFF. Yes—and no one to blame but his daughter!

DANGLE. And the planets.

PUFF. True. Now enter Tilburina!   230

SNEER. Egad, the business comes on quick here.

PUFF. Yes, sir—now she comes in stark mad in white satin.

SNEER. Why in white satin?

PUFF. O Lord, sir, when a heroine goes mad she always goes
into white satin—don't she, Dangle?

DANGLE. Always—it's a rule.

PUFF. Yes—here it is. [*Looking at the book.*] 'Enter Tilburina
stark mad in white satin, and her confidant stark mad in white
linen.'

[*Enter Tilburina and Confidant mad, according to custom.*

SNEER. But what the deuce, is the confidant to be mad too?   240

PUFF. To be sure she is: the confidant is always to do whatever her mistress does; weep when she weeps, smile when she smiles, go mad when she goes mad. Now, madam confidant—but keep your madness in the background, if you please.

TILBURINA. The wind whistles—the moon rises—see,
They have killed my squirrel in his cage!
Is this a grasshopper!—Ha! no, it is my
Whiskerandos—you shall not keep him—
I know you have him in your pocket—
An oyster may be crossed in love!—Who says   250
A whale 's a bird?—Ha! did you call, my love?
He 's here! He 's there!—He 's everywhere!
Ah me! He 's nowhere!   [*Exit Tilburina.*

PUFF. There, do you ever desire to see anybody madder than that?

SNEER. Never, while I live!

PUFF. You observed how she mangled the metre?

DANGLE. Yes, egad, it was the first thing made me suspect she was out of her senses.

SNEER. And pray, what becomes of her?   260

PUFF. She is gone to throw herself into the sea, to be sure—and that brings us at once to the scene of action, and so to my catastrophe—my sea-fight, I mean.

SNEER. What, you bring that in at last?

PUFF. Yes, yes—you know my play is *called* the *Spanish Armada;* otherwise, egad, I have no occasion for the battle at all. Now, then, for my magnificence!—my battle!—my noise!—and my procession! You are all ready?

PROMPTER [*Within*]. Yes, sir.

PUFF. Is the Thames dressed?   270

[*Enter Thames with two Attendants.*

THAMES. Here I am, sir.

PUFF. Very well, indeed. See, gentlemen, there's a river for you! This is blending a little of the masque with my tragedy, a new fancy, you know, and very useful in my case: for as there *must be a procession,* I suppose Thames and all his tributary rivers to compliment Britannia with a fête in honour of the victory.

SNEER. But pray, who are these gentlemen in green with him?

PUFF. Those?—those are his banks.

SNEER. His banks?   280

PUFF. Yes, one crowned with alders and the other with a villa!
—you take the allusions? But hey! what the plague! you have
got both your banks on one side. Here, sir, come round. Ever
while you live, Thames, go between your banks. [*Bell rings.*]
There, soh! now for't! Stand aside, my dear friends!—away,
Thames!   [*Exit Thames between his banks.*

> [*Flourish of drums—trumpets—cannon, &c., &c. Scene
> changes to the sea—the fleets engage—the music plays
> 'Britons, strike home.'—Spanish fleet destroyed by fire-
> ships, &c.—English fleet advances—music plays 'Rule Bri-
> tannia.'—The procession of all the English rivers and their
> tributaries with their emblems, &c., begins with Handel's
> water music, ends with a chorus, to the march in 'Judas
> Maccabaeus.'—During this scene, Puff directs and applauds
> everything—then*

PUFF. Well, pretty well—but not quite perfect. So, ladies and
gentlemen, if you please, we'll rehearse this piece again to-
morrow.

CURTAIN DROPS

ROMANTIC TRAGEDY

THE TERM ROMANTIC has been used with so many different connotations in the drama that it is difficult now to give it exactness of meaning. In its broadest sense it has been used to distinguish the method of English drama from that of the "classical" Greeks. In this sense the term would include practically all English tragedy except Jonson's two Roman plays and a few other conscious attempts to write according to what were believed to be classical precepts. On the other hand, we have come to oppose romantic and realistic as methods of treating dramatic subjects. As in the case of romantic and realistic comedy we find that he who writes realistic tragedy is prone to examine closely the details of life as men and women live it here and now, while he who writes romantically is concerned with emotions, colored by the diffused glow of distance in time or place or both. In this sense the "classical" Greek drama is also romantic, as are *Hamlet*, Webster's *Duchess of Malfi*, or Fitch's *Beau Brummel*. A third and still more limited definition of romantic tragedy would confine it to plays dealing with love as the central motive, particularly love in conflict with misunderstanding or with hate. The emotional turmoil which then results becomes the chief concern of the dramatist. He is not at pains to make a thorough psychological analysis of the characters involved. He is content to show in broad strokes how tragic forces work out of such a situation. In *A Blot in the 'Scutcheon*, for instance, there is the element of family pride set in opposition to the youthful intensity, i.e., the rashness, of the young lovers. No particular attempt is made to build either Mildred or Mertoun into well-rounded, complete figures.

There are hazards for the dramatists. The emotion may degenerate into sentimentality unless the writer gives it balance by the application of wit or reason. Instead of a true dramatic conflict he may get only "passioning," the continued analysis

of his emotion by the character, a concern for the manifestations of his passion and its results on himself. *A Blot on the
'Scutcheon* has not escaped these dangers completely.

Romantic love has always been looked upon as a suitable
subject for comedy, but it may be said to have been introduced
to tragedy in English in *Romeo and Juliet*. Shakespeare was
unwilling, however, to let the simple love situation bear the
whole weight of the action; so he set it against the background
of a story of bloody and futile family antagonism. From then
on it became an increasingly popular and serious subject for
tragedy. By Browning's time there was no longer a feeling, as
there had once been, that love was hardly as worthy of treatment in tragedy as were the affairs of state or the workings of
other emotions like ambition or courage. After the vogue of
heroic and sentimental tragedy dramatists were quite ready to
accept the old maxim that it was love that made the world go
round, a point of view which lies tacitly behind a great deal
of modern drama.

Robert Browning was born in London in the year that R. B.
Sheridan failed of re-election to Parliament. He grew up in
the atmosphere of a cultivated and refined home, encouraged
to indulge his very early literary interests. He read widely,
early coming under the spell of Shelley's poetry. His education was rather informal; first under private tutors, later in
private schools, and still later in desultory attendance at the
University of London. His first poem, *Pauline*, was published
at his own cost in 1833. Then he went travelling in Russia and
Italy to broaden his contacts with life, and a year after his return published a second long poem, *Paracelsus* (1835), dealing
imaginatively with the career of the great medieval physician
and, as some insisted, mountebank.

At about this time he made the acquaintance of Macready,
one of the greatest tragic actors of the day, who persuaded
him to try his hand at writing for the theater. In the next few
years he made several attempts, among them *A Blot in the
'Scutcheon*, which appeared in 1843, but none of them was
especially popular. Popular taste was running more and more

to melodrama and saccharine sentimental drama such as was being written by Dion Boucicault.

Browning grew steadily in reputation as a poet, however, though in 1846 he was still less famous than Elizabeth Barrett with whom he eloped in that year. The story of this courtship has been told in our own time in the *Barretts of Wimpole Street*. Browning and his bride went to Italy, which became a second homeland for Browning and which he visited frequently even after the death of his wife in 1861. In the last years of his life he came to enjoy an effusive popularity, as uncritical as it was excited, which resulted in the formation of a great number of Browning societies and in the development of what amounted to a Browning cult.

The variety and extent of his work is astounding when one considers that so much of it is of high quality, though we would now deny that it is all so preeminent as his adorers liked to think. In an active creative life he tried his hand at almost every type of verse and many different subjects, from simple lyrics to paraphrases of Euripides' plays. He had a strong sense of the dramatic; that is evidenced fully by his "dramatic monologues." But it was dramatic in a special sense, in what might be called a descriptive, i.e., static, rather than narrative, i.e., active, sense. It was the drama of the individual soul's attempt to understand itself, as Browning himself indicated. That is interesting to read and analyze, but it is hardly the kind of conflict that can be externalized in action on the stage. There is much of this, particularly in Mildred's case, in *A Blot*, but here he can set her and her love against her brother and his sense of family honor, which provides enough movement for the play to be actable.

SUGGESTED READINGS

Cambridge History of English Literature. VOL. XIII. NEW YORK, 1917.
Chesterton, G. K., *Robert Browning.* NEW YORK, 1903.
Gleason, K. F., *The Dramatic Art of Robert Browning.* BOSTON, 1927.
Nicoll, Allardyce, *History of Early Nineteenth Century Drama.* NEW YORK, 1930.
Vaughan, C. E., *Types of Tragic Drama.* LONDON, 1908.

Coward, Noel, *Cavalcade*. NEW YORK, 1933.
Masefield, John, *Tristan and Isolt*. NEW YORK, 1927.
Millay, Edna St. Vincent, *The King's Henchman*. NEW YORK, 1927.
Otway, Thomas, *Venice Preserved*.
Shakespeare, William, *Romeo and Juliet*.
Shelley, P. B., *The Cenci*. NEW YORK, 1909.
Webster, John, *The Duchess of Malfi*. MERMAID SERIES. NEW YORK [n.d.]

A BLOT IN THE 'SCUTCHEON

by Robert Browning

Characters

THOROLD, LORD TRESHAM, *the head of the family and inordinately proud of its honorable pedigree*

MILDRED TRESHAM, *his fourteen year old sister, in love with Mertoun, whom she is secretly meeting*

AUSTIN TRESHAM, *Thorold's younger brother*

GUENDOLEN TRESHAM, *their cousin, engaged to marry Austin. She is lively and sharp-witted*

HENRY, EARL MERTOUN, *a young neighbor of the Treshams, also of a very old family*

GERARD, *a faithful retainer of the Treshams*

Other retainers of the Treshams

THE TIME *is the eighteenth century*

ACT I

SCENE I

THE INTERIOR OF A LODGE *in Lord Tresham's park. Many Retainers crowded at the window, supposed to command a view of the entrance to his mansion. Gerard, the warrener, his back to a table on which are flagons, etc.*

1ST RETAINER. Ay, do! push, friends, and then you'll push down me!
   —What for? Does any hear a runner's foot
Or a steed's trample or a coach-wheel's cry?
Is the Earl come or his least poursuivant?
But there's no breeding in a man of you
Save Gerard yonder: [*Making room.*] here's a half-place yet,
Old Gerard!

4. *poursuivant*, herald.

585

GERARD.   Save your courtesies, my friend.
Here is my place.

2ND RETAINER.   Now, Gerard, out with it!
What makes you sullen, this of all the days
I' the year? To-day that young rich bountiful,   10
Handsome Earl Mertoun, whom alone they match
With our Lord Tresham through the countryside,
Is coming here in utmost bravery
To ask our master's sister's hand?

GERARD.   What then?

2ND RETAINER. What then? Why, you, she speaks to, if she meets
Your worship, smiles on as you hold apart
The boughs to let her through her forest walks,
You, always favourite for your no-deserts,
You've heard, these three days, how Earl Mertoun sues
To lay his heart and house and broad lands too   20
At Lady Mildred's feet: and while we squeeze
Ourselves into a mousehole lest we miss
One congee of the least page in his train,
You sit o' one side—"there's the Earl," say I—
"What then?" say you!

3RD RETAINER.   I'll wager he has let
Both swans he tamed for Lady Mildred swim
Over the falls and gain the river!

GERARD.   Ralph,
Is not to-morrow my inspecting-day
For you and for your hawks?

4TH RETAINER.   Let Gerard be!
He's coarse-grained, like his carved black crossbow stock.   30
Ha, look now, while we squabble with him, look!
  [*They crowd more closely around the window as the*
     visitors begin to arrive.
Well done, now—is not this beginning, now,
To purpose?

1ST RETAINER. Our retainers look as fine—
That's comfort. Lord, how Richard holds himself
With his white staff! Will not a knave behind
Prick him upright?

4TH RETAINER.   He's only bowing, fool!
The Earl's man bent us lower by this much.

1ST RETAINER. That's comfort. Here's a very cavalcade!

3RD RETAINER. I don't see wherefore Richard, and his troop

    23. *congee*, a formal bow, originally at departure.

Of silk and silver varlets there, should find   40
Their perfumed selves so indispensable
On high days, holidays! Would it so disgrace
Our family, if I, for instance, stood—
In my right hand a cast of Swedish hawks,
A leash of greyhounds in my left?—

GERARD.   —With Hugh
  The logman for supporter, in his right
  The bill-hook, in his left the brushwood-shears!

3RD RETAINER. Out on you, crab! What next, what next? The
  Earl!

1ST RETAINER. Oh Walter, groom, our horses, do they match
  The Earl's? Alas, that first pair of the six—   50
  They paw the ground—Ah Walter! and that brute
  Just on his haunches by the wheel!

6TH RETAINER.   Ay—ay!
  You, Philip, are a special hand, I hear,
  At soups and sauces: what's a horse to you?
  D' ye mark that beast they've slid into the midst
  So cunningly?—then, Philip, mark this further;
  No leg has he to stand on!

1ST RETAINER.   No? That's comfort.

2ND RETAINER. Peace, Cook! The Earl descends. Well, Gerard, see
  The Earl at least! Come, there's a proper man,
  I hope! Why, Ralph, no falcon, Pole or Swede,   60
  Has got a starrier eye.

3RD RETAINER.   His eyes are blue:
  But leave my hawks alone!

4TH RETAINER.   So young, and yet
  So tall and shapely!

5TH RETAINER.   Here's Lord Tresham's self!
  There now—there's what a nobleman should be!
  He's older, graver, loftier, he's more like
  A House's head.

2ND RETAINER.   But you'd not have a boy
  —And what's the Earl beside?—possess too soon
  That stateliness?

1ST RETAINER.   Our master takes his hand—
  Richard and his white staff are on the move—
  Back fall our people—(tsh!—there's Timothy   70
  Sure to get tangled in his ribbon-ties,
  And Peter's cursed rosette's a-coming off!)

44. *cast*, pair.   45. *leash*, three.

—At last I see our lord's back and his friend's;
And the whole beautiful bright company
Close round them—in they go!
> [*Jumping down from the window-bench, and making for
> the table and its jugs.*

                        Good health, long life,
Great joy to our Lord Tresham and his House!

6TH RETAINER. My father drove his father first to court,
After his marriage day—ay, did he!

2ND RETAINER.   God bless
Lord Tresham, Lady Mildred, and the Earl!
Here, Gerard, reach your beaker!

GERARD.   Drink, my boys!   80
Don't mind me—all's not right about me—drink!

2ND RETAINER [*Aside*]. He's vexed, now, that he let the show
    escape!
> [*To Gerard.*] Remember that the Earl returns this way.

GERARD. That way?

2ND RETAINER.   Just so.

GERARD.   Then my way's here.
> [*Goes in the opposite direction.*

2ND RETAINER.   Old Gerard
Will die soon—mind, I said it! He was used
To care about the pitifullest thing
That touched the House's honour, not an eye
But his could see wherein: and on a cause
Of scarce a quarter this importance, Gerard
Fairly had fretted flesh and bone away   90
In cares that this was right, nor that was wrong,
Such point decorous, and such square by rule—
He knew such niceties, no herald more:
And now—you see his humour: die he will!

1ST RETAINER. God help him! Who's for the great servants'-hall
To hear what's going on inside? They'd follow
Lord Tresham into the saloon.

3RD RETAINER.   I!—

4TH RETAINER.   I!—
Leave Frank alone for catching, at the door,
Some hint of how the parley goes inside!
Prosperity to the great House once more!   100
Here's the last drop!

1ST RETAINER.   Have at you! Boys, hurrah!

SCENE II

A SALON IN THE MANSION. *Enter Lord Tresham, Lord Mertoun,*
Austin, and Guendolen.

TRESHAM. I welcome you, Lord Mertoun, yet once more,
   To this ancestral roof of mine. Your name
   —Noble among the noblest in itself,
   Yet taking in your person, fame avers,
   New price and lustre,—(as that gem you wear,
   Transmitted from a hundred knightly breasts,
   Fresh chased and set and fixed by its last lord,
   Seems to re-kindle at the core)—your name
   Would win you welcome!—
MERTOUN.   Thanks!
TRESHAM.   —But add to that,
   The worthiness and grace and dignity   10
   Of your proposal for uniting both
   Our Houses even closer than respect
   Unites them now—add these, and you must grant
   One favour more, nor that the least,—to think
   The welcome I should give;—'t is given! My lord,
   My only brother, Austin: he's the king's.
   Our cousin, Lady Guendolen—betrothed
   To Austin: all are yours.
MERTOUN.   I thank you—less
   For the expressed commendings which your seal,
   And only that, authenticates—forbids   20
   My putting from me . . . to my heart I take
   Your praise . . . but praise less claims my gratitude,
   Than the indulgent insight it implies
   Of what must needs be uppermost with one
   Who comes, like me, with the bare leave to ask,
   In weighed and measured unimpassioned words,
   A gift, which, if as calmly 't is denied,
   He must withdraw, content upon his cheek,
   Despair within his soul. That I dare ask
   Firmly, near boldly, near with confidence   30
   That gift, I have to thank you. Yes, Lord Tresham,
   I love your sister—as you'd have one love
   That lady . . . oh more, more I love her! Wealth,
   Rank, all the world thinks me, they're yours, you know,

16. *he's the king's*, he's in the army.

To hold or part with, at your choice—but grant
My true self, me without a rood of land,
A piece of gold, a name of yesterday,
Grant me that lady, and you . . . Death or life?

GUENDOLEN [*Apart to Austin*]. Why, this is loving, Austin!

AUSTIN.   He's so young!

GUENDOLEN. Young? Old enough, I think, to half surmise   40
He never had obtained an entrance here,
Were all this fear and trembling needed.

AUSTIN.   Hush!
He reddens.

GUENDOLEN.   Mark him, Austin; that's true love!
Ours must begin again.

TRESHAM.   .   We'll sit, my lord.
Ever with best desert goes diffidence.
I may speak plainly nor be misconceived.
That I am wholly satisfied with you
On this occasion, when a falcon's eye
Were dull compared with mine to search out faults,
Is somewhat. Mildred's hand is hers to give   50
Or to refuse.

MERTOUN.   But you, you grant my suit?
I have your word if hers?

TRESHAM.   My best of words
If hers encourage you. I hope it will.
Have you seen Lady Mildred, by the way?

MERTOUN [*Embarrassed*]. I . . . I . . . our two demesnes, re-
        member, touch;
I have been used to wander carelessly
After my stricken game: the heron roused
Deep in my woods, has trailed its broken wing
Thro' thicks and glades a mile in yours,—or else
Some eyass ill-reclaimed has taken flight   60
And lured me after her from tree to tree,
I marked not whither. I have come upon
The lady's wondrous beauty unaware,
And—and then . . . I have seen her.

GUENDOLEN [*Aside to Austin*].   Note that mode
Of faltering out that, when a lady passed,
He, having eyes, did see her! You had said—
"On such a day I scanned her, head to foot;
"Observed a red, where red should not have been,

36. *rood*, one fourth an acre.   60. *eyass*, a young bird.

"Outside her elbow; but was pleased enough
"Upon the whole." Let such irreverent talk 70
Be lessoned for the future!

TRESHAM.   What's to say
May be said briefly. She has never known
A mother's care; I stand for father too.
Her beauty is not strange to you, it seems—
You cannot know the good and tender heart,
Its girl's trust and its woman's constancy,
How pure yet passionate, how calm yet kind,
How grave yet joyous, how reserved yet free
As light where friends are—how imbued with lore
The world most prizes, yet the simplest, yet 80
The . . . one might know I talked of Mildred—thus
We brothers talk!

MERTOUN.   I thank you.

TRESHAM.   In a word,
Control's not for this lady; but her wish
To please me outstrips in its subtlety
My power of being pleased: herself creates
The want she means to satisfy. My heart
Prefers your suit to her as 't were its own.
Can I say more?

MERTOUN.   No more—thanks, thanks—no more!

TRESHAM. This matter then discussed . . .

MERTOUN.   —We'll waste no breath
On aught less precious. I'm beneath the roof 90
Which holds her: while I thought of that, my speech
To you would wander—as it must not do,
Since as you favour me I stand or fall.
I pray you suffer that I take my leave!

TRESHAM. With less regret 'tis suffered, that again
We meet, I hope, so shortly.

MERTOUN.   We? again?—
Ah, yes, forgive me—when shall . . . you will crown
Your goodness by forthwith apprising me
When . . . if . . . the lady will appoint a day
For me to wait on you—and her.

TRESHAM.   So soon 100
As I am made acquainted with her thoughts
On your proposal—howsoe'er they lean—
A messenger shall bring you the result.

MERTOUN. You cannot bind me more to you, my lord.

Farewell till we renew . . . I trust, renew
A converse ne'er to disunite again.

TRESHAM. So may it prove!

MERTOUN.   You, lady, you, sir, take
My humble salutation!

GUENDOLEN AND AUSTIN.   Thanks!

TRESHAM.   Within there!

> [*Servants enter. Tresham conducts Mertoun to the door.
> Meantime Austin remarks,*

                                                Well,

Here I have an advantage of the Earl,
Confess now! I'd not think that all was safe   110
Because my lady's brother stood my friend!
Why, he makes sure of her—"do you say, yes—
"She'll not say, no,"—what comes it to beside?
I should have prayed the brother, "speak this speech,
"For Heaven's sake urge this on her—put in this—
"Forget not, as you'd save me, t' other thing,—
"Then set down what she says, and how she looks,
"And if she smiles, and" (in an under breath)
"Only let her accept me, and do you
"And all the world refuse me, if you dare!"   120

GUENDOLEN. That way you'd take, friend Austin? What a shame
I was your cousin, tamely from the first
Your bride, and all this fervour's run to waste!
Do you know you speak sensibly to-day?
The Earl's a fool.

AUSTIN.   Here's Thorold. Tell him so!

TRESHAM [*Returning*]. Now, voices, voices! 'St! the lady's first!
How seems he?—seems he not . . . come, faith give fraud
The mercy-stroke whenever they engage!
Down with fraud, up with faith! How seems the Earl?
A name! a blazon! if you knew their worth,   130
As you will never! come—the Earl?

GUENDOLEN.   He's young.

TRESHAM. What's she? an infant save in heart and brain.
Young! Mildred is fourteen, remark! and you . . .
Austin, how old is she?

GUENDOLEN.   There's tact for you!
I meant that being young was good excuse
If one should tax him . . .

TRESHAM.   Well?

GUENDOLEN.   —With lacking wit.

TRESHAM. He lacked wit? Where might he lack wit, so please
    you?

GUENDOLEN. In standing straighter than the steward's rod
  And making you the tiresomest harangue,
  Instead of slipping over to my side   140
  And softly whispering in my ear, "Sweet lady,
  "Your cousin there will do me detriment
  "He little dreams of: he's absorbed, I see,
  "In my old name and fame—be sure he'll leave
  "My Mildred, when his best account of me
  "Is ended, in full confidence I wear
  "My grandsire's periwig down either cheek.
  "I'm lost unless your gentleness vouchsafes" . . .

TRESHAM. . . . "To give a best of best accounts, yourself,
  Of me and my demerits." You are right!   150
  He should have said what now I say for him.
  Yon golden creature, will you help us all?
  Here's Austin means to vouch for much, but you
  —You are . . . what Austin only knows! Come up,
  All three of us: she's in the library
  No doubt, for the day's wearing fast. Precede!

GUENDOLEN. Austin, how we must—!

TRESHAM.   Must what? Must speak truth,
  Malignant tongue! Detect one fault in him!
  I challenge you!

GUENDOLEN.   Witchcraft's a fault in him,
  For you're bewitched.

TRESHAM.   What's urgent we obtain   160
  Is, that she soon receive him—say, to-morrow—
  Next day at furthest.

GUENDOLEN.   Ne'er instruct me!

TRESHAM.   Come!
  —He's out of your good graces, since forsooth,
  He stood not as he'd carry us by storm
  With his perfections! You're for the composed
  Manly assured becoming confidence!
  —Get her to say, "to-morrow," and I'll give you . . .
  I'll give you black Urganda, to be spoiled
  With petting and snail-paces. Will you? Come!

SCENE III

MILDRED'S CHAMBER, *late in the evening of the same day. Conspicuous is a large stained glass window with a purple pane in the center. Guendolen is laughingly crying up the pedigree of Mildred's suitor. Mildred grows ill at ease as Guendolen delays her departure.*

GUENDOLEN. Now, Mildred, spare those pains. I have not left
    Our talkers in the library, and climbed
    The wearisome ascent to this your bower
    In company with you,—I have not dared . . .
    Nay, worked such prodigies as sparing you
    Lord Mertoun's pedigree before the flood,
    Which Thorold seemed in very act to tell
    —Or bringing Austin to pluck up that most
    Firm-rooted heresy—your suitor's eyes,
    He would maintain, were gray instead of blue—   10
    I think I brought him to contrition!—Well,
    I have not done such things, (all to deserve
    A minute's quiet cousin's talk with you,)
    To be dismissed so coolly.
MILDRED.   Guendolen!
    What have I done? what could suggest . . .
GUENDOLEN.   There, there!
    Do I not comprehend you'd be alone
    To throw those testimonies in a heap,
    Thorold's enlargings, Austin's brevities,
    With that poor silly heartless Guendolen's
    Ill-timed misplaced attempted smartnesses—   20
    And sift their sense out? now, I come to spare you
    Nearly a whole night's labour. Ask and have!
    Demand, be answered! Lack I ears and eyes?
    Am I perplexed which side of the rock-table
    The Conqueror dined on when he landed first,
    Lord Mertoun's ancestor was bidden take—
    The bow-hand or the arrow-hand's great meed?
    Mildred, the Earl has soft blue eyes!
MILDRED.   My brother—
    Did he . . . you said that he received him well?
GUENDOLEN. If I said only "well" I said not much.   30

27. *bow hand,* left hand, which holds the bow. *arrow hand,* right hand.

Oh, stay—which brother?

MILDRED.   Thorold! who—who else?

GUENDOLEN. Thorold (a secret) is too proud by half,—
  Nay, hear me out—with us he's even gentler
  Than we are with our birds. Of this great House
  The least retainer that e'er caught his glance
  Would die for him, real dying—no mere talk:
  And in the world, the court, if men would cite
  The perfect spirit of honour, Thorold's name
  Rises of its clear nature to their lips.
  But he should take men's homage, trust in it,   40
  And care no more about what drew it down.
  He has desert, and that, acknowledgment;
  Is he content?

MILDRED.   You wrong him, Guendolen.

GUENDOLEN. He's proud, confess; so proud with brooding o'er
  The light of his interminable line,
  An ancestry with men all paladins,
  And women all . . .

MILDRED [*Anxiously*]. Dear Guendolen, 't is late!
  When yonder purple pane the climbing moon
  Pierces, I know 't is midnight.

GUENDOLEN.   Well, that Thorold
  Should rise up from such musings, and receive   50
  One come audaciously to graft himself
  Into this peerless stock, yet find no flaw,
  No slightest spot in such an one . . .

MILDRED.   Who finds
  A spot in Mertoun?

GUENDOLEN.   Not your brother; therefore,
  Not the whole world.

MILDRED.   I am weary, Guendolen.
  Bear with me!

GUENDOLEN.   I am foolish.

MILDRED.   Oh no, kind!
  But I would rest.

GUENDOLEN.   Good night and rest to you!
  I said how gracefully his mantle lay
  Beneath the rings of his light hair?

MILDRED.   Brown hair.

GUENDOLEN. Brown? why, it *is* brown: how could you know
    that?   60

MILDRED. How? did not you—Oh, Austin 't was, declared

His hair was light, not brown—my head!—and look,
The moon-beam purpling the dark chamber! Sweet,
Good night!

GUENDOLEN.   Forgive me—sleep the soundlier for me!
                              [*Going, she turns suddenly.*
                                        Mildred!

Perdition! all's discovered! Thorold finds
—That the Earl's greatest of all grandmothers
Was grander daughter still—to that fair dame
Whose garter slipped down at the famous dance!   *Goes.*
MILDRED. Is she—can she be really gone at last?
My heart! I shall not reach the window. Needs   70
Must I have sinned much, so to suffer.

   [*She lifts the small lamp which is suspended before the Vir-
      gin's image in the window, and places it by the purple
      pane.*

                                    There!
   [*She returns to the seat in front, and meditates moodily on
      the complications of her life and love.*
Mildred and Mertoun! Mildred, with consent
Of all the world and Thorold, Mertoun's bride!
Too late! 'T is sweet to think of, sweeter still
To hope for, that this blessed end soothes up
The curse of the beginning; but I know
It comes too late: 't will sweetest be of all
To dream my soul away and die upon.
   [*A noise without.*
The voice! Oh why, why glided sin the snake
Into the paradise Heaven meant us both?   80
   [*The window opens softly. A low voice sings.*

*There's a woman like a dew-drop, she's so purer than the
   purest;
And her noble heart's the noblest, yes, and her sure faith's the
   surest:
And her eyes are dark and humid, like the depth on depth of
   lustre*

---

68. *garter . . . dance*, the traditional account of the founding of the order
of the Garter. At a ball the great King Edward III picked up a garter lost
by the Countess of Salisbury and in a gallant mood fastened it about his own
knee, silencing his grinning courtiers with the words, *Honi soit qui mal y
pense* (Shamed be he who evil thinks), which became the motto of the
order.

Hid i' the harebell, while her tresses, sunnier than the wild-grape cluster,

Gush in golden-tinted plenty down her neck's rose-misted marble:

Then her voice's music . . . call it the well's bubbling, the bird's warble!

[*A figure wrapped in a mantle appears at the window.*

And this woman says, "My days were sunless and my nights were moonless,

"Parched the pleasant April herbage, and the lark's heart's out-break tuneless,

"If you loved me not!" And I who—(ah, for words of flame!) adore her,

Who am mad to lay my spirit prostrate palpably before her—

[*He enters, approaches her seat, and bends over her.*

I may enter at her portal soon, as now her lattice takes me,   91

And by noontide as by midnight make her mine, as hers she makes me!

[*The Earl throws off his slouched hat and long cloak.*

My very heart sings, so I sing, Beloved!

MILDRED. Sit, Henry—do not take my hand!

MERTOUN.   'T is mine.

The meeting that appalled us both so much
Is ended.

MILDRED. What begins now?

MERTOUN.   Happiness
Such as the world contains not.

MILDRED.   That is it.

Our happiness would, as you say, exceed
The whole world's best of blisses: we—do we   100
Deserve that? Utter to your soul, what mine
Long since, Beloved, has grown used to hear,
Like a death-knell, so much regarded once,
And so familiar now; this will not be!

MERTOUN. Oh, Mildred, have I met your brother's face?
Compelled myself—if not to speak untruth,
Yet to disguise, to shun, to put aside
The truth, as—what had e'er prevailed on me
Save you, to venture? Have I gained at last

Your brother, the one scarer of your dreams,
And waking thoughts' sole apprehension too?   110
Does a new life, like a young sunrise, break
On the strange unrest of our night, confused
With rain and stormy flaw—and will you see
No dripping blossoms, no fire-tinted drops
On each live spray, no vapour steaming up,
And no expressless glory in the East?
When I am by you, to be ever by you,
When I have won you and may worship you,
Oh, Mildred, can you say "this will not be"?

MILDRED. Sin has surprised us, so will punishment.   120

MERTOUN. No—me alone, who sinned alone!

MILDRED.   The night
You likened our past life to—was it storm
Throughout to you then, Henry?

MERTOUN.   Of your life
I spoke—what am I, what my life, to waste
A thought about when you are by me?—you
It was, I said my folly called the storm
And pulled the night upon. 'T was day with me—
Perpetual dawn with me.

MILDRED.   Come what come will,
You have been happy: take my hand!

MERTOUN [After a pause].   How good   130
Your brother is! I figured him a cold—
Shall I say, haughty man?

MILDRED.   They told me all.
I know all.

MERTOUN.   It will soon be over.

MILDRED.   Over?
Oh, what is over? what must I live through
And say, "'t is over"? Is our meeting over?
Have I received in presence of them all
The partner of my guilty love—with brow
Trying to seem a maiden's brow—with lips
Which make believe that when they strive to form
Replies to you and tremble as they strive,
It is the nearest ever they approached   140
A stranger's . . . Henry, yours that stranger's . . . lip—
With cheek that looks a virgin's, and that is . . .
Ah, God, some prodigy of thine will stop
This planned piece of deliberate wickedness

In its birth even! some fierce leprous spot
Will mar the brow's dissimulating! I
Shall murmur no smooth speeches got by heart,
But, frenzied, pour forth all our woeful story,
The love, the shame, and the despair—with them
Round me aghast as round some cursed fount   150
That should spirt water, and spouts blood. I'll not
. . . Henry, you do not wish that I should draw
This vengeance down? I'll not affect a grace
That's gone from me—gone once, and gone for ever!

MERTOUN. Mildred, my honour is your own. I'll share
  Disgrace I cannot suffer by myself.
A word informs your brother I retract
This morning's offer; time will yet bring forth
Some better way of saving both of us.

MILDRED. I'll meet their faces, Henry!

MERTOUN.   When? to-morrow!   160
Get done with it!

MILDRED.   Oh, Henry, not to-morrow!
Next day! I never shall prepare my words
And looks and gestures sooner.—How you must
Despise me!

MERTOUN.   Mildred, break it if you choose,
A heart the love of you uplifted—still
Uplifts, thro' this protracted agony,
To heaven! but Mildred, answer me,—first pace
The chamber with me [*They walk up and down together.*]—
  once again—now, say
Calmly the part, the . . . what it is of me
You see contempt (for you did say contempt)   170
—Contempt for you in! I will pluck it off
And cast it from me!—but no—no, you'll not
Repeat that?—will you, Mildred, repeat that?

MILDRED. Dear Henry!

MERTOUN.   I was scarce a boy—e'en now
What am I more? And you were infantine
When first I met you; why, your hair fell loose
On either side! My fool's-cheek reddens now
Only in the recalling how it burned
That morn to see the shape of many a dream—
You know we boys are prodigal of charms   180
To her we dream of—I had heard of one,
Had dreamed of her, and I was close to her,

Might speak to her, might live and die her own,
Who knew? I spoke. Oh, Mildred, feel you not
That now, while I remember every glance
Of yours, each word of yours, with power to test
And weigh them in the diamond scales of pride,
Resolved the treasure of a first and last
Heart's love shall have been bartered at its worth,
—That now I think upon your purity 190
And utter ignorance of guilt—your own
Or other's guilt—the girlish undisguised
Delight at a strange novel prize—(I talk
A silly language, but interpret, you!)
If I, with fancy at its full, and reason
Scarce in its germ, enjoined you secrecy,
If you had pity on my passion, pity
On my protested sickness of the soul
To sit beside you, hear you breathe, and watch
Your eyelids and the eyes beneath—if you 200
Accorded gifts and knew not they were gifts—
If I grew mad at last with enterprise
And must behold my beauty in her bower
Or perish—(I was ignorant of even
My own desires—what then were you?) if sorrow—
Sin—if the end came—must I now renounce
My reason, blind myself to light, say truth
Is false and lie to God and my own soul?
Contempt were all of this!

MILDRED.   Do you believe.
    Or, Henry, I'll not wrong you—you believe 210
That I was ignorant. I scarce grieve o'er
The past. We'll love on; you will love me still.

MERTOUN. Oh, to love less what one has injured! Dove,
    Whose pinion I have rashly hurt, my breast—
Shall my heart's warmth not nurse thee into strength?
Flower I have crushed, shall I not care for thee?
Bloom o'er my crest, my fight-mark and device!
Mildred, I love you and you love me.

MILDRED.   Go!
    Be that your last word. I shall sleep to-night.

MERTOUN. This is not our last meeting?

MILDRED.   One night more. 220

MERTOUN. And then—think, then!

MILDRED.   Then, no sweet courtship-days,

No dawning consciousness of love for us,
No strange and palpitating births of sense
From words and looks, no innocent fears and hopes,
Reserves and confidences: morning's over!
MERTOUN. How else should love's perfected noontide follow?
All the dawn promised shall the day perform.
MILDRED. So may it be! but—
                    You are cautious, Love?
Are sure that unobserved you scaled the walls?
MERTOUN. Oh, trust me! Then our final meeting's fixed   230
To-morrow night?
MILDRED.   Farewell! Stay, Henry . . . wherefore?
His foot is on the yew-tree bough; the turf
Receives him; now the moonlight as he runs
Embraces him—but he must go—is gone.
Ah, once again he turns—thanks, thanks, my Love!
He's gone. Oh, I'll believe him every word!
I was so young, I loved him so, I had
No mother, God forgot me, and I fell.
There may be pardon yet: all's doubt beyond.
Surely the bitterness of death is past.   240

ACT II

THE LIBRARY, *the next morning. Enter Lord Tresham, hastily.*

TRESHAM. This way! In, Gerard, quick!
                    [*As Gerard enters, Tresham secures the door.*
                              Now speak! or, wait—
I'll bid you speak directly.   [*Seats himself.*
                    Now repeat
Firmly and circumstantially the tale
You just now told me; it eludes me; either
I did not listen, or the half is gone
Away from me. How long have you lived here?
Here in my house, your father kept our woods
Before you?
GERARD.   —As his father did, my lord.
I have been eating, sixty years almost,
Your bread.
TRESHAM.   Yes, yes. You ever were of all   10
The servants in my father's house, I know,
The trusted one. You'll speak the truth.

GERARD.   I'll speak
   God's truth. Night after night . . .
TRESHAM.   Since when?
GERARD.   At least
   A month—each midnight has some man access
   To Lady Mildred's chamber.
TRESHAM.   Tush, "access"—
   No wide words like "access" to me!
GERARD.   He runs
   Along the woodside, crosses to the South,
   Takes the left tree that ends the avenue . . .
TRESHAM. The last great yew-tree?
GERARD.   You might stand upon
   The main boughs like a platform. Then he . . .
TRESHAM.   Quick!   20
GERARD. Climbs up, and, where they lessen at the top,
   —I cannot see distinctly, but he throws,
   I think—for this I do not vouch—a line
   That reaches to the lady's casement—
TRESHAM.   —Which
   He enters not! Gerard, some wretched fool
   Dares pry into my sister's privacy!
   When such are young, it seems a precious thing
   To have approached,—to merely have approached,
   Got sight of, the abode of her they set
   Their frantic thoughts upon. He does not enter?   30
   Gerard?
GERARD.   There is a lamp that's full i' the midst,
   Under a red square in the painted glass
   Of Lady Mildred's . . .
TRESHAM.   Leave that name out! Well?
   That lamp?
GERARD.   —Is moved at midnight higher up
   To one pane—a small dark-blue pane; he waits
   For that among the boughs: at sight of that,
   I see him, plain as I see you, my lord,
   Open the lady's casement, enter there . . .
TRESHAM.—And stay?
GERARD.   An hour, two hours.
TRESHAM.   And this you saw
   Once?—twice?—quick!
GERARD.   Twenty times.
TRESHAM.   And what brings you   40

Under the yew-trees?
GERARD.   The first night I left
My range so far, to track the stranger stag
That broke the pale, I saw the man.
TRESHAM.   Yet sent
No cross-bow shaft through the marauder?
GERARD.   But
He came, my lord, the first time he was seen,
In a great moonlight, light as any day,
From Lady Mildred's chamber.
TRESHAM [*After a pause*].   You have no cause
—Who could have cause to do my sister wrong?
GERARD. Oh, my lord, only once—let me this once
Speak what is on my mind! Since first I noted   50
All this, I've groaned as if a fiery net
Plucked me this way and that—fire if I turned
To her, fire if I turned to you, and fire
If down I flung myself and strove to die.
The lady could not have been seven years old
When I was trusted to conduct her safe
Through the deer-herd to stroke the snow-white fawn
I brought to eat bread from her tiny hand
Within a month. She ever had a smile
To greet me with—she . . . if it could undo   60
What's done, to lop each limb from off this trunk . . .
All that is foolish talk, not fit for you—
I mean, I could not speak and bring her hurt
For Heaven's compelling. But when I was fixed
To hold my peace, each morsel of your food
Eaten beneath your roof, my birth-place too,
Choked me. I wish I had grown mad in doubts
What it behoved me do. This morn it seemed
Either I must confess to you, or die:
Now it is done, I seem the vilest worm   70
That crawls, to have betrayed my lady.
TRESHAM.   No—
No, Gerard!
GERARD.   Let me go!
TRESHAM.   A man, you say:
What man? Young? Not a vulgar hind? What dress?
GERARD. A slouched hat and a large dark foreign cloak
Wraps his whole form; even his face is hid;
But I should judge him young: no hind, be sure!

TRESHAM. Why?
GERARD.   He is ever armed: his sword projects
    Beneath the cloak.
TRESHAM.   Gerard—I will not say
    No word, no breath of this!
GERARD.   ·   Thanks, thanks, my lord!   [*Goes.*
TRESHAM [*Paces the room. After a pause*].   Oh,
        thought's absurd!—as with some monstrous fact   ·   80
    Which, when ill thoughts beset us, seems to give
    Merciful God that made the sun and stars,
    The waters and the green delights of earth,
    The lie! I apprehend the monstrous fact—
    Yet know the maker of all worlds is good,
    And yield my reason up, inadequate
    To reconcile what yet I do behold—
    Blasting my sense! There's cheerful day outside:
    This is my library, and this the chair
    My father used to sit in carelessly   90
    After his soldier-fashion, while I stood
    Between his knees to question him: and here
    Gerard our gray retainer,—as he says,
    Fed with our food, from sire to son, an age,—
    Has told a story—I am to believe!
    That Mildred . . . oh, no, no! both tales are true,
    Her pure cheek's story and the forester's!
    Would she, or could she, err—much less, confound
    All guilts of treachery, of craft, of . . . Heaven
    Keep me within its hand!—I will sit here   100
    Until thought settle and I see my course.
    Avert, oh God, only this woe from me!
        [*As he sinks his head between his arms on the table, Guen-
        dolen's voice is heard at the door.*
    Lord Tresham! [*She knocks.*] Is Lord Tresham there?
        [*Tresham, hastily turning, pulls down the first book above
        him and opens it.*
TRESHAM. Come in! [*She enters.*] Ha, Guendolen!—good morn-
        ing.
GUENDOLEN.   Nothing more?
TRESHAM. What should I say more?
GUENDOLEN.   Pleasant question! more?
    This more. Did I besiege poor Mildred's brain
    Last night till close on morning with "the Earl,"
    "The Earl"—whose worth did I asseverate

Till I am very fain to hope that . . . Thorold,
What is all this? You are not well!

TRESHAM.   Who, I?

You laugh at me.

GUENDOLEN.   Has what I'm fain to hope,
Arrived then? Does that huge tome show some blot
In the Earl's 'scutcheon come no longer back
Than Arthur's time?

TRESHAM.   When left you Mildred's chamber?

GUENDOLEN. Oh, late enough, I told you! The main thing
To ask is, how I left her chamber,—sure,
Content yourself, she'll grant this paragon
Of Earls no such ungracious . . .

TRESHAM [*Roughly*].   Send her here!

GUENDOLEN. Thorold?

TRESHAM.   I mean—acquaint her, Guendolen,
—But mildly!

GUENDOLEN.   Mildly?

TRESHAM.   Ah, you guessed aright!
I am not well: there is no hiding it.
But tell her I would see her at her leisure—
That is, at once! here in the library!
The passage in that old Italian book
We hunted for so long is found, say, found—
And if I let it slip again . . . you see,
That she must come—and instantly!

GUENDOLEN.   I'll die
Piecemeal, record that, if there have not gloomed
Some blot i' the 'scutcheon!

TRESHAM.   Go! or, Guendolen,
Be you at call,—with Austin, if you choose,—
In the adjoining gallery! There, go!   [*Guendolen goes.*
Another lesson to me! You might bid
A child disguise his heart's sore, and conduct
Some sly investigation point by point
With a smooth brow, as well as bid me catch
The inquisitorial cleverness some praise.
If you had told me yesterday, "There's one
"You needs must circumvent and practise with,
"Entrap by policies, if you would worm
"The truth out: and that one is—Mildred!" There,
There—reasoning is thrown away on it!
Prove she's unchaste . . . why, you may after prove

That she's a poisoner, traitress, what you will!
Where I can comprehend nought, nought's to say.
Or do, or think. Force on me but the first
Abomination,—then outpour all plagues,
And I shall ne'er make count of them.
    [*Enter Mildred.*

MILDRED.   What book
    Is it I wanted, Thorold? Guendolen
    Thought you were pale; you are not pale. That book?
    That's Latin surely. [*She leans over his shoulder.*]
TRESHAM.   Mildred, here's a line,   150
    (Don't lean on me: I'll English it for you)
    "Love conquers all things." What love conquers them?
    What love should you esteem—best love?
MILDRED.   True love.
TRESHAM. I mean, and should have said, whose love is best
    Of all that love or that profess to love?
MILDRED. The list's so long: there's father's, mother's, hus-
    band's . . .
TRESHAM. Mildred, I do believe a brother's love
    For a sole sister must exceed them all.
    For see now, only see! there's no alloy
    Of earth that creeps into the perfect'st gold   160
    Of other loves—no gratitude to claim;
    You never gave her life, not even aught
    That keeps life—never tended her, instructed,
    Enriched her—so, your love can claim no right
    O'er her save pure love's claim: that's what I call
    Freedom from earthliness. You'll never hope
    To be such friends, for instance, she and you,
    As when you hunted cowslips in the woods
    Or played together in the meadow hay.
    Oh, yes—with age, respect comes, and your worth   170
    Is felt, there's growing sympathy of tastes,
    There's ripened friendship, there's confirmed esteem:
    —Much head these make against the newcomer!
    The startling apparition, the strange youth—
    Whom one half-hour's conversing with, or, say,
    Mere gazing at, shall change (beyond all change
    This Ovid ever sang about) your soul
    . . . Her soul, that is,—the sister's soul! With her
    'T was winter yesterday; now, all is warmth,

The green leaf's springing and the turtle's voice,　　　　180
"Arise and come away!" Come whither?—far
Enough from the esteem, respect, and all
The brother's somewhat insignificant
Array of rights! All which he knows before,
Has calculated on so long ago!
I think such love, (apart from yours and mine,)
Contented with its little term of life,
Intending to retire betimes, aware
How soon the background must be place for it,
—I think, am sure, a brother's love exceeds　　　　190
All the world's love in its unworldliness.

MILDRED. What is this for?

TRESHAM.　　　　　　　　This, Mildred, is it for!
Or, no, I cannot go to it so soon!
That's one of many points my haste left out—
Each day, each hour throws forth its silk-slight film
Between the being tied to you by birth,
And you, until those slender threads compose
A web that shrouds her daily life of hopes
And fears and fancies, all her life, from yours:
So close you live and yet so far apart!　　　　200
And must I rend this web, tear up, break down
The sweet and palpitating mystery
That makes her sacred? You—for you I mean,
Shall I speak, shall I not speak?

MILDRED.　　　　　　　Speak!

TRESHAM.　　　　　　　　I will.
Is there a story men could—any man
Could tell of you, you would conceal from me?
I'll never think there's falsehood on that lip.
Say "There is no such story men could tell,"
And I'll believe you, though I disbelieve
The world—the world of better men than I,　　　　210
And women such as I suppose you. Speak!
[After a pause.] Not speak? Explain then! Clear it up then!
Move
Some of the miserable weight away
That presses lower than the grave! Not speak?
Some of the dead weight, Mildred! Ah, if I
Could bring myself to plainly make their charge

180. turtle, dove.

Against you! Must I, Mildred? Silent still?
[*After a pause.*] Is there a gallant that has night by night
Admittance to your chamber? [*After a pause.*] Then, his name!
Till now, I only had a thought for you: 220
But now,—his name!
MILDRED.   Thorold, do you devise
Fit expiation for my guilt, if fit
There be! 'T is nought to say that I'll endure
And bless you,—that my spirit yearns to purge
Her stains off in the fierce renewing fire:
But do not plunge me into other guilt!
Oh, guilt enough! I cannot tell his name.
TRESHAM. Then judge yourself! How should I act? Pronounce!
MILDRED. Oh, Thorold, you must never tempt me thus!
To die here in this chamber by that sword   230
Would seem like punishment: so should I glide,
Like an arch-cheat, into extremest bliss!
'T were easily arranged for me: but you—
What would become of you?
TRESHAM.   And what will now
Become of me? I'll hide your shame and mine
From every eye; the dead must heave their hearts
Under the marble of our chapel-floor;
They cannot rise and blast you. You may wed
Your paramour above our mother's tomb;
Our mother cannot move from 'neath your foot.   240
We too will somehow wear this one day out:
But with to-morrow hastens here—the Earl!
The youth without suspicion . . . face can come
From Heaven, and heart from . . . whence proceed such
     hearts?
I have despatched last night at your command
A missive bidding him present himself
To-morrow—here—thus much is said; the rest
Is understood as if 't were written down—
"His suit finds favour in your eyes." Now dictate
This morning's letter that shall countermand   250
Last night's—do dictate that!
MILDRED.   But, Thorold—if
I will receive him as I said?
TRESHAM [*Unable to believe his ears*]. The Earl?
MILDRED. I will receive him.
TRESHAM. [*Starting up*].   Ho there! Guendolen!

[Guendolen and Austin enter.
And, Austin, you are welcome, too! Look there!
The woman there!

AUSTIN AND GUENDOLEN. How? Mildred?

TRESHAM. Mildred once!
Now the receiver night by night, when sleep
Blesses the inmates of her father's house,
—I say, the soft sly wanton that receives
Her guilt's accomplice 'neath this roof which holds
You, Guendolen, you, Austin, and has held   260
A thousand Treshams—never one like her!
No lighter of the signal-lamp her quick
Foul breath near quenches in hot eagerness
To mix with breath as foul! no loosener
O' the lattice, practised in the stealthy tread,
The low voice and the noiseless come-and-go!
Not one composer of the bacchant's mien
Into—what you thought Mildred's, in a word!
Know her!

GUENDOLEN. Oh, Mildred, look to me, at least!
Thorold—she's dead, I'd say, but that she stands   270
Rigid as stone and whiter!

TRESHAM. You have heard . . .

GUENDOLEN. Too much! You must proceed no further.

MILDRED. Yes—
Proceed! All's truth. Go from me!

TRESHAM. All is truth,
She tells you! Well, you know, or ought to know,
All this I would forgive in her. I'd con
Each precept the harsh world enjoins, I'd take
Our ancestors' stern verdicts one by one,
I'd bind myself before them to exact
The prescribed vengeance—and one word of hers,
The sight of her, the bare least memory   280
Of Mildred, my one sister, my heart's pride
Above all prides, my all in all so long,
Would scatter every trace of my resolve.
What were it silently to waste away
And see her waste away from this day forth,
Two scathed things with leisure to repent,
And grow acquainted with the grave, and die
Tired out if not at peace, and be forgotten?
It were not so impossible to bear.

But this—that, fresh from last night's pledge renewed   290
Of love with the successful gallant there,
She calmly bids me help her to entice,
Inveigle an unconscious trusting youth
Who thinks her all that's chaste and good and pure,
—Invites me to betray him . . . who so fit
As honour's self to cover shame's arch-deed?
—That she'll receive Lord Mertoun—(her own phrase)—
This, who could bear? Why, you have heard of thieves,
Stabbers, the earth's disgrace, who yet have laughed,
"Talk not to me of torture—I'll betray   300
"No comrade I've pledged faith to!"—you have heard
Of wretched women—all but Mildreds—tied
By wild illicit ties to losels vile
You'd tempt them to forsake; and they'll reply
"Gold, friends, repute, I left for him, I find
"In him, why should I leave him then for gold,
"Repute or friends?"—and you have felt your heart
Respond to such poor outcasts of the world
As to so many friends; bad as you please,
You've felt they were God's men and women still,   310
So, not to be disowned by you. But she
That stands there, calmly gives her lover up
As means to wed the Earl that she may hide
Their intercourse the surelier: and, for this,
I curse her to her face before you all.
Shame hunt her from the earth! Then Heaven do right
To both! It hears me now—shall judge her then!

[*As Mildred faints and falls, Tresham rushes out.*

AUSTIN. Stay, Tresham, we'll accompany you!
GUENDOLEN.   We?
What, and leave Mildred? We? Why, where's my place
But by her side, and where yours but by mine?   320
Mildred—one word! Only look at me, then!
AUSTIN. No, Guendolen! I echo Thorold's voice.
She is unworthy to behold . . .
GUENDOLEN.   Us two?
If you spoke on reflection, and if I
Approved your speech—if you (to put the thing
At lowest) you the soldier, bound to make
The king's cause yours and fight for it, and throw
Regard to others of its right or wrong,

303. *losels*, good-for-nothings.

—If with a death-white woman you can help,
Let alone sister, let alone a Mildred,   330
You left her—or if I, her cousin, friend
This morning, playfellow but yesterday,
Who said, or thought at least a thousand times,
"I'd serve you if I could," should now face round
And say, "Ah, that's only to signify
"I'd serve you while you're fit to serve yourself:
"So long as fifty eyes await the turn
"Of yours to forestall its yet half-formed wish,
"I'll proffer my assistance you'll not need—
"When every tongue is praising you, I'll join   340
"The praisers' chorus—when you're hemmed about
"With lives between you and detraction—lives
"To be laid down if a rude voice, rash eye,
"Rough hand should violate the sacred ring
"Their worship throws about you,—then indeed,
"Who'll stand up for you stout as I?" If so
We said, and so we did,—not Mildred there
Would be unworthy to behold us both,
But we should be unworthy, both of us,
To be beheld by—by—your meanest dog,   350
Which, if that sword were broken in your face
Before a crowd, that badge torn off your breast,
And you cast out with hooting and contempt,
—Would push his way thro' all the hooters, gain
Your side, go off with you and all your shame
To the next ditch you choose to die in! Austin,
Do you love me? Here's Austin, Mildred,—here's
Your brother says he does not believe half—
No, nor half that—of all he heard! He says,
Look up and take his hand!
AUSTIN.   Look up and take   360
My hand, dear Mildred!
MILDRED.   I—I was so young!
Beside, I loved him, Thorold—and I had
No mother; God forgot me: so, I fell.
GUENDOLEN. Mildred!
MILDRED.   Require no further! Did I dream
That I could palliate what is done? All's true.
Now, punish me! A woman takes my hand?
Let go my hand! You do not know, I see.
I thought that Thorold told you.

GUENDOLEN. What is this?
Where start you to?
MILDRED. Oh, Austin, loosen me!
You heard the whole of it—your eyes were worse,   370
In their surprise, than Thorold's! Oh, unless
You stay to execute his sentence, loose
My hand! Has Thorold gone, and are you here?
GUENDOLEN. Here, Mildred, we two friends of yours will wait
Your bidding; be you silent, sleep or muse!
Only, when you shall want your bidding done,
How can we do it if we are not by?
Here's Austin waiting patiently your will!
One spirit to command, and one to love
And to believe in it and do its best,   380
Poor as that is, to help it—why, the world
Has been won many a time, its length and breadth,
By just such a beginning!
MILDRED. I believe
If once I threw my arms about your neck
And sunk my head upon your breast, that I
Should weep again.
GUENDOLEN. Let go her hand now, Austin!
Wait for me. Pace the gallery and think
On the world's seemings and realities,
Until I call you. [*Austin goes.*
MILDRED. No—I cannot weep.
No more tears from this brain—no sleep—no tears!   390
O Guendolen, I love you!
GUENDOLEN. Yes: and "love"
Is a short word that says so very much!
It says that you confide in me.
MILDRED. Confide!
GUENDOLEN. Your lover's name, then! I've so much to learn,
Ere I can work in your behalf!
MILDRED. My friend,
You know I cannot tell his name.
GUENDOLEN. At least
He is your lover? and you love him too?
MILDRED. Ah, do you ask me that?—but I am fallen
So low!
GUENDOLEN. You love him still, then?
MILDRED. My sole prop
Against the guilt that crushes me! I say,   400

Each night ere I lie down, "I was so young—
"I had no mother, and I loved him so!"
And then God seems indulgent, and I dare
Trust him my soul in sleep.
GUENDOLEN.   How could you let us
E'en talk to you about Lord Mertoun then?
MILDRED. There is a cloud around me.
GUENDOLEN.   But you said
You would receive his suit in spite of this?
MILDRED. I say there is a cloud . . .
GUENDOLEN.   No cloud to me!
Lord Mertoun and your lover are the same!
MILDRED. What maddest fancy . . .
GUENDOLEN [*Calling aloud*].   Austin! (spare your pains—   410
When I have got a truth, that truth I keep)—
MILDRED. By all you love, sweet Guendolen, forbear!
Have I confided in you . . .
GUENDOLEN.   Just for this!
Austin!—Oh, not to guess it at the first!
But I did guess it—that is, I divined,
Felt by an instinct how it was: why else
Should I pronounce you free from all that heap
Of sins which had been irredeemable?
I felt they were not yours—what other way
Than this, not yours? The secret's wholly mine!   420
MILDRED. If you would see me die before his face . . .
GUENDOLEN. I'd hold my peace! And if the Earl returns
To-night?
MILDRED.   Ah Heaven, he's lost!
GUENDOLEN.   I thought so. Austin!
    [*Enter Austin.*
Oh, where have you been hiding?
AUSTIN.   Thorold's gone,
I know not how, across the meadow-land.
I watched him till I lost him in the skirts
O' the beech-wood.
GUENDOLEN.   Gone? All thwarts us.
MILDRED.   Thorold too?
GUENDOLEN. I have thought. First lead this Mildred to her room.
Go on the other side; and then we'll seek
Your brother: and I'll tell you, by the way,   430
The greatest comfort in the world. You said
There was a clue to all. Remember, Sweet,

He said there was a clue! I hold it. Come!
> [*They go out, Guendolen and Austin supporting Mildred between them.*]

ACT III

SCENE I

THE END OF THE YEW-TREE AVENUE UNDER MILDRED'S WINDOW. *A light seen through a central red pane. Evening of the same day. Enter Tresham through the trees. He has been trying all day to blot out from his mind the guilty secret he has uncovered.*

Again here! But I cannot lose myself.
The heath—the orchard—I have traversed glades
And dells and bosky paths which used to lead
Into green wild-wood depths, bewildering
My boy's adventurous step. And now they tend
Hither or soon or late; the blackest shade
Breaks up, the thronged trunks of the trees ope wide,
And the dim turret I have fled from, fronts
Again my step; the very river put
Its arm about me and conducted me   10
To this detested spot. Why then, I'll shun
Their will no longer: do your will with me!
Oh, bitter! To have reared a towering scheme
Of happiness, and to behold it razed,
Were nothing: all men hope, and see their hopes
Frustrate, and grieve awhile, and hope anew.
But I . . . to hope that from a line like ours
No horrid prodigy like this would spring,
Were just as though I hoped that from these old
Confederates against the sovereign day,   20
Children of older and yet older sires,
Whose living coral berries dropped, as now
On me, on many a baron's surcoat once,
On many a beauty's wimple—would proceed
No poison-tree, to thrust, from hell its root,
Hither and thither its strange snaky arms.
Why came I here? What must I do? [*A bell strikes.*] A bell?

20. *confederates*, the trees which by their shade keep out the light of day.

Midnight! and 't is at midnight . . : Ah, I catch
—Woods, river, plains, I catch your meaning now,
And I obey you! Hist! This tree will serve.   30
    [He retires behind one of the trees. After a pause, enter Mer-
      toun cloaked as before.

MERTOUN. Not time! Beat out thy last voluptuous beat
Of hope and fear, my heart! I thought the clock
I' the chapel struck as I was pushing through
The ferns. And so I shall no more see rise
My love-star! Oh, no matter for the past!
So much the more delicious task to watch
Mildred revive: to pluck out, thorn by thorn,
All traces of the rough forbidden path
My rash love lured her to! Each day must see
Some fear of hers effaced, some hope renewed: 40
Then there will be surprises, unforeseen
Delights in store. I'll not regret the past.
    [The light is placed above in the purple pane.
And see, my signal rises, Mildred's star!
I never saw it lovelier than now
It rises for the last time. If it sets,
'T is that the re-assuring sun may dawn.
    [As he prepares to ascend the last tree of the avenue, Tresham
      arrests his arm.
Unhand me—peasant, by your grasp! Here's gold.
'T was a mad freak of mine. I said I'd pluck
A branch from the white-blossomed shrub beneath
The casement there. Take this, and hold your peace.   50
TRESHAM. Into the moonlight yonder, come with me!
Out of the shadow!
MERTOUN.   I am armed, fool!
TRESHAM.   Yes,
Or no? You'll come into the light, or no?
My hand is on your throat—refuse!—
MERTOUN.   That voice!
Where have I heard . . . no—that was mild and slow.
I'll come with you.   *[They advance.*
TRESHAM.   You're armed: that's well. Declare
Your name: who are you?
MERTOUN.   (Tresham!—she is lost!)
TRESHAM. Oh, silent? Do you know, you bear yourself
Exactly as, in curious dreams I've had
How felons, this wild earth is full of, look   60

When they're detected, still your kind has looked!
The bravo holds an assured countenance,
The thief is voluble and plausible,
But silently the slave of lust has crouched
When I have fancied it before a man.
Your name!

MERTOUN. I do conjure Lord Tresham—ay,
Kissing his foot, if so I might prevail—
That he for his own sake forbear to ask
My name! As heaven's above, his future weal   70
Or woe depends upon my silence! Vain!
I read your white inexorable face.
Know me, Lord Tresham!

  [*He throws off his disguises.*

TRESHAM.   Mertoun! [*After a pause.*] Draw now!
                                                        Hear me
MERTOUN
  But speak first!

TRESHAM.   Not one least word on your life!
Be sure that I will strangle in your throat
The least word that informs me how you live
And yet seem what you seem! No doubt 't was you
Taught Mildred still to keep that face and sin.
We should join hands in frantic sympathy
If you once taught me the unteachable,
Explained how you can live so, and so lie.   80
With God's help I retain, despite my sense,
The old belief—a life like yours is still
Impossible. Now draw!

MERTOUN.   Not for my sake,
Do I entreat a hearing—for your sake,
And most, for her sake!

TRESHAM.   Ha ha, what should I
Know of your ways? A miscreant like yourself,
How must one rouse his ire? A blow?—that's pride
No doubt, to him! One spurns him, does one not?
Or sets the foot upon his mouth, or spits
Into his face! Come! Which, or all of these?   90

MERTOUN. 'Twixt him and me and Mildred, Heaven be judge!
Can I avoid this? Have your will, my lord!

  [*He draws and, after a few passes, falls.*

TRESHAM [*Amazed*]. You are not hurt?

MERTOUN.   You'll hear me now!

TRESHAM.   But rise!

MERTOUN. Ah, Tresham, say I not "you'll hear me now!"
And what procures a man the right to speak
In his defence before his fellow man,
But—I suppose—the thought that presently
He may have leave to speak before his God
His whole defence?

TRESHAM.   Not hurt? It cannot be!   100
You made no effort to resist me. Where
Did my sword reach you? Why not have returned
My thrusts? Hurt where?

MERTOUN.   My lord—

TRESHAM [*Remorseful*].   How young he is!

MERTOUN. Lord Tresham, I am very young, and yet
I have entangled other lives with mine.
Do let me speak, and do believe my speech!
That when I die before you presently,—

TRESHAM. Can you stay here till I return with help?

MERTOUN. Oh, stay by me! When I was less than boy
I did you grievous wrong and knew it not—   110
Upon my honour, knew it not! Once known,
I could not find what seemed a better way
To right you than I took: my life—you feel
How less than nothing were the giving you
The life you've taken! But I thought my way
The better—only for your sake and hers:
And as you have decided otherwise,
Would I had an infinity of lives
To offer you! Now say—instruct me—think!
Can you, from the brief minutes I have left,   120
Eke out my reparation? Oh think—think!
For I must wring a partial—dare I say,
Forgiveness from you, ere I die?

TRESHAM.   I do
Forgive you.

MERTOUN.   Wait and ponder that great word!
Because, if you forgive me, I shall hope
To speak to you of—Mildred!

TRESHAM.   Mertoun, haste
And anger have undone us. 'Tis not you
Should tell me for a novelty you're young,
Thoughtless, unable to recall the past.
Be but your pardon ample as my own!

MERTOUN. Ah, Tresham, that a sword-stroke and a drop   130

Of blood or two, should bring all this about!
Why, 't was my very fear of you, my love
Of you—(what passion like a boy's for one
Like you?)—that ruined me! I dreamed of you—
You, all accomplished, courted everywhere,
The scholar and the gentleman. I burned
To knit myself to you: but I was young,
And your surpassing reputation kept me
So far aloof! Oh, wherefore all that love?
With less of love, my glorious yesterday   140
Of praise and gentlest words and kindest looks,
Had taken place perchance six months ago.
Even now, how happy we had been! And yet
I know the thought of this escaped you, Tresham!
Let me look up into your face; I feel
'T is changed above me: yet my eyes are glazed.
Where? where? [*As he endeavours to raise himself, his eye
    catches the lamp.*] Ah, Mildred! What will Mildred do?
Tresham, her life is bound up in the life
That's bleeding fast away! I'll live—must live,—
There, if you'll only turn me I shall live   150
And save her! Tresham—oh, had you but heard!
Had you but heard! What right was yours to set
The thoughtless foot upon her life and mine,
And then say, as we perish, "Had I thought,
"All had gone otherwise"? We've sinned and die:
Never you sin, Lord Tresham! for you'll die,
And God will judge you.

TRESHAM.   Yes, be satisfied!
    That process is begun.

MERTOUN.   And she sits there
Waiting for me! Now, say you this to her—
You, not another—say, I saw him die   160
As he breathed this, "I love her"—you don't know
What those three small words mean! Say; loving her
Lowers me down the bloody slope to death
With memories . . . I speak to her, not you,
Who had no pity, will have no remorse,
Perchance intend her . . . Die along with me,
Dear Mildred! 't is so easy, and you'll 'scape
So much unkindness! Can I lie at rest,
With rude speech spoken to you, ruder deeds
Done to you?—heartless men shall have my heart,   170

And I tied down with grave-clothes and the worm,
Aware, perhaps, of every blow—oh God!—
Upon those lips—yet of no power to tear
The felon stripe by stripe! Die, Mildred! Leave
Their honourable world to them! For God
We're good enough, though the world casts us out.
   [A whistle is heard.

TRESHAM. Ho, Gerard!
    *[Enter Gerard, Austin and Guendolen, with lights. They
    have been searching for Tresham since they learned the
    truth.*

            No one speak! You see what's done.
I cannot bear another voice.

MERTOUN.   There's light—
Light all about me, and I move to it,
Tresham, did I not tell you—did you not   180
Just promise to deliver words of mine
To Mildred?

TRESHAM.   I will bear those words to her.

MERTOUN. Now?

TRESHAM.   Now. Lift you the body, and leave me
The head.
    [As they have half raised Mertoun, he turns suddenly.

MERTOUN.   I knew they turned me: turn me not from her!
There! stay you! there!   *Dies.*

GUENDOLEN. *[After a pause].* Austin, remain you here
With Thorold until Gerard comes with help:
Then lead him to his chamber. I must go
To Mildred.

TRESHAM.   Guendolen, I hear each word
You utter. Did you hear him bid me give
His message? Did you hear my promise? I,   190
And only I, see Mildred.

GUENDOLEN.   She will die.

TRESHAM. Oh no, she will not die! I dare not hope
She'll die. What ground have you to think she'll die?
Why, Austin's with you!

AUSTIN.   Had we but arrived
Before you fought!

TRESHAM.   There was no fight at all.
He let me slaughter him—the boy! I'll trust
The body there to you and Gerard—thus!
Now bear him on before me.

AUSTIN.   Whither bear him?
TRESHAM. Oh, to my chamber! When we meet there next,
  We shall be friends.
        [*They bear out the body of Mertoun.*
                      Will she die, Guendolen?   100
GUENDOLEN. Where are you taking me?
TRESHAM.   He fell just here.
    Now answer me. Shall you in your whole life
    —You who have nought to do with Mertoun's fate,
    Now you have seen his breast upon the turf,
    Shall you e'er walk this way if you can help?
    When you and Austin wander arm-in-arm
    Through our ancestral grounds, will not a shade
    Be ever on the meadow and the waste—
    Another kind of shade than when the night
    Shuts the woodside with all its whispers up?   210
    But will you ever so forget his breast
    As carelessly to cross this bloody turf
    Under the black yew avenue? That's well!
    You turn your head: and I then?—
GUENDOLEN.   What is done
    Is done. My care is for the living. Thorold,
    Bear up against this burden: more remains
    To set the neck to!
TRESHAM.   Dear and ancient trees
    My fathers planted, and I loved so well!
    What have I done that, like some fabled crime
    Of yore, lets loose a Fury leading thus   220
    Her miserable dance amidst you all?
    Oh, never more for me shall winds intone
    With all your tops a vast antiphony,
    Demanding and responding in God's praise!
    Hers ye are now, not mine! Farewell—farewell!

                    SCENE II

MILDRED'S CHAMBER, *at the same time as the preceding scene.
Mildred alone, worried because Mertoun hasn't come.*

    He comes not! I have heard of those who seemed
    Resourceless in prosperity,—you thought
    Sorrow might slay them when she listed; yet
    Did they so gather up their diffused strength

At her first menace, that they bade her strike,
And stood and laughed her subtlest skill to scorn.
Oh, 't is not so with me! The first woe fell,
And the rest fall upon it, not on me:
Else should I bear that Henry comes not?—fails   10
Just this first night out of so many nights?
Loving is done with. Were he sitting now,
As so few hours since, on that seat, we'd love
No more—contrive no thousand happy ways
To hide love from the loveless, any more.
I think I might have urged some little point
In my defence, to Thorold; he was breathless
For the least hint of a defence: but no,
The first shame over, all that would might fall.
No Henry! Yet I merely sit and think
The morn's deed o'er and o'er. I must have crept   20
Out of myself. A Mildred that has lost
Her lover—oh, I dare not look upon
Such woe! I crouch away from it! 'T is she,
Mildred, will break her heart, not I! The world
Forsakes me: only Henry's left me—left?
When I have lost him, for he does not come,
And I sit stupidly . . . Oh Heaven, break up
This worse than anguish, this mad apathy,
By any means or any messenger!
TRESHAM (*Without*).   Mildred!
MILDRED. Come in! Heaven hears me!
       [*Enter Tresham.*] You? alone?   30
Oh, no more cursing!
TRESHAM.   Mildred, I must sit.
There—you sit!
MILDRED.   Say it, Thorold—do not look
The curse! deliver all you come to say!
What must become of me? Oh, speak that thought
Which makes your brow and cheeks so pale!
TRESHAM.   My thought?
MILDRED. All of it!
TRESHAM.   How we waded—years ago—
After those water-lilies, till the plash,
I know not how, surprised us; and you dared
Neither advance nor turn back: so, we stood
Laughing and crying until Gerard came—   40
Once safe upon the turf, the loudest too,

For once more reaching the relinquished prize!
How idle thoughts are, some men's, dying men's!
Mildred,—
MILDRED   You call me kindlier by my name
Than even yesterday: what is in that?
TRESHAM. It weighs so much upon my mind that I
This morning took an office not my own!
.I might . . . of course, I must be glad or grieved,
Content or not, at every little thing
That touches you. I may with a wrung heart   50
Even reprove you, Mildred; I did more:
Will you forgive me?
MILDRED.   Thorold? do you mock?
Or no . . . and yet you bid me . . . say that word!
TRESHAM. Forgive me, Mildred!—are you silent, Sweet?
MILDRED [Starting up]. Why does not Henry Mertoun come to-
      night?
Are you, too, silent? [Dashing his mantle aside, and pointing
      to his scabbard, which is empty.] Ah, this speaks for you!
You've murdered Henry Mertoun! Now proceed!
What is it I must pardon? This and all?
Well, I do pardon you—I think I do.
Thorold, how very wretched you must be!   60
TRESHAM. He bade me tell you . . .
MILDRED.   What I do forbid
Your utterance of! So much that you may tell
And will not—how you murdered him . . . but, no!
You'll tell me that he loved me, never more
Than bleeding out his life there: must I say
"Indeed," to that? Enough! I pardon you.
TRESHAM. You cannot, Mildred! for the harsh words, yes:
Of this last deed Another's judge; whose doom
I wait in doubt, despondency and fear.
MILDRED. Oh, true! There's nought for me to pardon! True!   70
You loose my soul of all its cares at once.
Death makes me sure of him forever! You
Tell me his last words? He shall tell me them,
And take my answer—not in words, but reading
Himself the heart I had to read him late,
Which death . . .
TRESHAM.   Death? You are dying too? Well said
Of Guendolen! I dared not hope you'd die:
But she was sure of it.

MILDRED.   Tell Guendolen
I loved her, and tell Austin . . .
TRESHAM.   Him you loved:
And me?
MILDRED. Ah, Thorold! Was't not rashly done   80
  To quench that blood, on fire with youth and hope
  And love of me—whom you loved too, and yet
  Suffered to sit here waiting his approach
  While you were slaying him? Oh, doubtlessly
  You let him speak his poor confused boy's-speech
  —Do his poor utmost to disarm your wrath
  And respite me!—you let him try to give
  The story of our love and ignorance,
  And the brief madness and the long despair—
  You let him plead all this, because your code   90
  Of honour bids you hear before you strike:
  But at the end, as he looked up for life
  Into your eyes—you struck him down!
TRESHAM.   No! No!
  Had I but heard him—had I let him speak
  Half the truth—less—had I looked long on him
  I had desisted! Why, as he lay there,
  The moon on his flushed cheek, I gathered all
  The story ere he told it: I saw through
  The troubled surface of his crime and yours
  A depth of purity immovable.   100
  Had I but glanced, where all seemed turbidest
  Had gleamed some inlet to the calm beneath;
  I would not glance: my punishment's at hand.
  There, Mildred, is the truth! and you—say on—
  You curse me?
MILDRED.   As I dare approach that Heaven
  Which has not bade a living thing despair,
  Which needs no code to keep its grace from stain,
  But bids the vilest worm that turns on it
  Desist and be forgiven,—I—forgive not,
  But bless you, Thorold, from my soul of souls!   110
                    [Falls on his neck.
  There! Do not think too much upon the past!
  The cloud that's broke was all the same a cloud
  While it stood up between my friend and you;
  You hurt him 'neath its shadow: but is that
  So past retrieve? I have his heart, you know;

I may dispose of it: I give it you!
It loves you as mine loves! Confirm me, Henry!   [*Dies*

TRESHAM. I wish thee joy, Beloved! I am glad
  In thy full gladness!

GUENDOLEN [*Without*]. Mildred! Tresham! [*Entering with*
  Austin.] Thorold,
  I could desist no longer. Ah, she swoons!   120
  That's well.

TRESHAM.   Oh, better far than that!

GUENDOLEN.   She's dead!
  Let me unlock her arms!

TRESHAM.   She threw them thus
  About my neck, and blessed me, and then died:
  You'll let them stay now, Guendolen!

AUSTIN.   Leave her
  And look to him! What ails you, Thorold?

GUENDOLEN.   White
  As she, and whiter! Austin! quick—this side!

AUSTIN. A froth is oozing through his clenched teeth;
  Both lips, where they're not bitten through, are black:
  Speak, dearest Thorold!   [*He supports Tresham.*

TRESHAM.   Something does weigh down
  My neck beside her weight: thanks: I should fall   130
  But for you, Austin, I believe!—there, there,
  'T will pass away soon!—ah,—I had forgotten:
  I am dying.

GUENDOLEN. Thorold—Thorold—why was this?

TRESHAM. I said, just as I drank the poison off,
  The earth would be no longer earth to me,
  The life out of all life was gone from me.
  There are blind ways provided, the foredone
  Heart-weary player in this pageant-world
  Drops out, by letting the main masque defile
  By the conspicuous portal: I am through—   140
  Just through!

GUENDOLEN.   Don't leave him, Austin! Death is close.

TRESHAM. Already Mildred's face is peacefuller.
  I see you, Austin—feel you: here's my hand,
  Put yours in it—you, Guendolen, yours too!
  You're lord and lady now—you're Treshams; name
  And fame are yours: you hold our 'scutcheon up.
  Austin, no blot on it! You see how blood
  Must wash one blot away: the first blot came

And the first blood came. To the vain world's eye
All's gules again: no care to the vain world,   150
From whence the red was drawn!
AUSTIN.   No blot shall come!
TRESHAM. I said that: yet it did come. Should it come,
    Vengeance is God's, not man's. Remember me!   [*Dies.*
GUENDOLEN [*Letting fall the pulseless arm*]. Ah, Thorold, we can
    but—remember you!

150. *gules*, heraldic term for red.

FARCE

FARCE IS MELODRAMA that has grown sophisticated and super-cilious of violence and too strenuous excitement. It has shaved off its black mustache, slicked down its hair, and joined the most polite circles of society, where it makes a great show of easy conversation and witty repartee. It still stresses action rather than character, but now the action is toned down, is polished, has no threat of really serious consequences such as loom up frequently in melodrama.

The word farce means stuffing, such as would be crammed into a sausage skin. How it came to have its present meaning we do not know for certain. It may have meant a type of entertainment pushed into another show (between the acts of a play, for instance) to give a spicy flavor to an otherwise serious program. Or it may have meant only a type of enter-tainment chock-full of jokes and witty scenes and dialogue. Whatever the case, it apparently grew up early, along side the religious plays, ever ready to offer comic relief to their pon-derous moralizing.

The line between farce and other types of comedy is diffi-cult to draw, for it must constantly be shifted. True farce, however, always puts its stress on the comic, or rather the absurd, the almost incredible situation, and lets characters fit into it as they will. The farceur is chiefly concerned with building up a succession of lively situations set forth, as in the comedy of manners, in lively dialogue. The more rapidly he can pile absurdity upon absurdity without completely alienat-ing our common sense, the more brilliantly successful he is.

The form is not, at its best, intellectually empty, however. For all its tomfoolery, it manages to strike a satiric note from time to time. It reaches out to left and to right, respecting no persons or things, frightened by no shibboleths, taking nothing seriously. So that in the end, by a rather back-handed method, the best of farce does involve commentary on life, if only by laughing at its superficialities and inconsistencies.

Oscar Wilde is another Irishman who distinguished himself in the writing of comedy. He was born into a prominent Dublin family on 16 October, 1854. In 1871 he went to Trinity College, Dublin and three years later to Oxford, where he distinguished himself in the field of humane letters. He left the University in 1878, after having had a trip to Greece with the great classical scholar, Mahaffy.

Like the University Wits three hundred years before, he came up to London intent on making a name for himself in literature. He soon achieved great notoriety by his fantastic dress and manners and by his exceedingly clever conversation. By 1881 he had become so prominent a figure that he was not only a regular subject for caricature in *Punch* but was also satirized by Gilbert and Sullivan in their opera *Patience* as Bunthorne, the poet who goes around striking the "aesthetic attitude." In the same year his first book of poems was published and received with great enthusiasm. From then on he enjoyed an extended season of popularity, giving series of lectures in England and America, writing several volumes of short stories and essays and finally producing a series of dramatic successes capped by the *Importance of Being Earnest*, which was produced on 14 February, 1895.

In that same year, however, all his prospects and achievements turned to dust and ashes. He sued the Marquis of Queensbury for criminal libel, lost the suit, and was himself accused of corrupting the son of the Marquis. At the first trial the jury disagreed as to his guilt, but on a second trial he was found guilty and sentenced to two years imprisonment. That resulted in two of his best known works, *De Profundis*, written while he was in prison, and *The Ballad of Reading Gaol*, revised after his release. He spent his last years on the Continent, and died in Paris on 30 November, 1900.

Though his affectations repelled many and the charges of immorality against him shocked more, there is no doubt that he was one of the wittiest men of his time. He had a great gift for facile epigram, often barbed so that even the thick-skinned might squirm. His comedies exemplify this trait, with their deft strokes that make for exceptionally clever dialogue which covers up the weaknesses or excesses of the plot.

SUGGESTED READINGS

Harris, Frank, *Oscar Wilde*. LONDON, 1924.
Ransome, Arthur, *Oscar Wilde, a Critical Study*. LONDON, 1913.
Smith, R. M., and H. G. Rhodes, *Types of Farce Comedy*. NEW YORK [n. d.]

Coward, Noël, *Design for Living*. NEW YORK AND LONDON, 1933.
Kaufman, G. S., and Marc Conelly, *Dulcy*. In H. L. Cohen. *Longer Plays by Modern Authors*. NEW YORK, 1922.
Shakespeare, William, *The Taming of the Shrew*.
——, *The Merry Wives of Windsor*.
Shaw, George Bernard, *Androcles and the Lion*. NEW YORK, 1914.

THE IMPORTANCE OF BEING EARNEST
by Oscar Wilde

Characters

JOHN WORTHING, J.P.

ALGERNON MONCRIEFF

REV. CANON CHASUBLE, D.D.

MERRIMAN (*Butler*)

LANE (*Manservant*)

LADY BRACKNELL

HON. GWENDOLEN FAIRFAX

CECILY CARDEW

MISS PRISM (*Governess*)

The Scenes of the Play

ACT I. *Algernon Moncrieff's Flat in Half-Moon Street, W.*

ACT II. *The Garden at the Manor House, Woolton.*

ACT III. *Drawing-Room of the Manor House, Woolton.*

TIME—*The Present*

PLACE—*London*

ACT I

SCENE.—*Morning-room in Algernon's flat in Half-Moon Street. The room is luxuriously and artistically furnished. The sound of a piano is heard in the adjoining room. Lane is arranging afternoon tea on the table, and after the music has ceased, Algernon enters.*

ALGERNON. Did you hear what I was playing, Lane?

LANE. I didn't think it polite to listen, sir.

ALGERNON. I'm sorry for that, for your sake. I don't play accurately—anyone can play accurately—but I play with wonderful expression. As far as the piano is concerned, sentiment is my forte. I keep science for Life.

LANE. Yes, sir.

ALGERNON. And, speaking of the science of Life, have you got the cucumber sandwiches cut for Lady Bracknell?

LANE. Yes, sir. [*Hands them on a salver.*] 10

ALGERNON [*Inspects them, takes two, and sits down on the sofa*]. Oh! . . . by the way, Lane, I see from your book that on Thursday night, when Lord Shoreman and Mr. Worthing were dining with me, eight bottles of champagne are entered as having been consumed.

LANE. Yes, sir; eight bottles and a pint.

ALGERNON. Why is it that at a bachelor's establishment the servants invariably drink the champagne? I ask merely for information.

LANE. I attribute it to the superior quality of the wine, sir. 20 I have often observed that in married households the champagne is rarely of a first-rate brand.

ALGERNON. Good Heavens! Is marriage so demoralizing as that?

LANE. I believe it *is* a very pleasant state, sir. I have had very little experience of it myself up to the present. I have only been married once. That was in consequence of a misunderstanding between myself and a young woman.

ALGERNON [*Languidly*]. I don't know that I am much interested in your family life, Lane.

LANE. No, sir; it is not a very interesting subject. I never 30 think of it myself.

ALGERNON. Very natural, I am sure. That will do, Lane, thank you.

LANE. Thank you, sir. [*Lane goes out.*]

ALGERNON. Lane's views on marriage seem somewhat lax. Really, if the lower orders don't set us a good example, what on earth is the use of them? They seem, as a class, to have absolutely no sense of moral responsibility.

[*Enter Lane.*

LANE. Mr. Ernest Worthing.

[*Enter Jack. Lane goes out.*

ALGERNON. How are you, my dear Ernest? What brings 40 you up to town?

JACK. Oh, pleasure, pleasure! What else should bring one anywhere? Eating as usual, I see, Algy!

ALGERNON [*Stiffly*]. I believe it is customary in good society to take some slight refreshment at five o'clock. Where have you been since last Thursday?

JACK [*Sitting down on the sofa*]. In the country.

ALGERNON. What on earth do you do there?

JACK [*Pulling off his gloves*]. When one is in town one amuses oneself. When one is in the country one amuses other people. 50 It is excessively boring.

ALGERNON. And who are the people you amuse?

JACK [*Airily*]. Oh, neighbours, neighbours.

ALGERNON. Got nice neighbours in your part of Shropshire?

JACK. Perfectly horrid! Never speak to one of them.

ALGERNON. How immensely you must amuse them! [*Goes over and takes sandwich.*] By the way, Shropshire is your county, is it not?

JACK. Eh? Shropshire? Yes, of course. Hallo! Why all these cups? Why cucumber sandwiches? Why such reckless ex- 60 travagance in one so young? Who is coming to tea?

ALGERNON. Oh! merely Aunt Augusta and Gwendolen.

JACK. How perfectly delightful!

ALGERNON. Yes, that is all very well; but I am afraid Aunt Augusta won't quite approve of your being here.

JACK. May I ask why?

ALGERNON. My dear fellow, the way you flirt with Gwendolen is perfectly disgraceful. It is almost as bad as the way Gwendolen flirts with you.

JACK. I am in love with Gwendolen. I have come up to 70 town expressly to propose to her.

ALGERNNON. I thought you had come up for pleasure. . . . I call that business.

JACK. How utterly unromantic you are!

ALGERNON. I really don't see anything romantic in proposing. It is very romantic to be in love. But there is nothing romantic about a definite proposal. Why, one may be accepted. One usually is, I believe. Then the excitement is all over. The very essence of romance is uncertainty. If ever I get married, I'll certainly try to forget the fact. 80

JACK. I have no doubt about that, dear Algy. The Divorce Court was specially invented for people whose memories are so curiously constituted.

ALGERNON. Oh! there is no use speculating on that subject. Divorces are made in Heaven—[*Jack puts out his hand to take a sandwich. Algernon at once interferes.*] Please don't touch the cucumber sandwiches. They are ordered specially for Aunt Augusta. [*Takes one and eats it.*]

JACK. Well, you have been eating them all the time.

ALGERNON. That is quite a different matter. She is my aunt. 90 [*Takes plate from below.*] Have some bread and butter. The bread and butter is for Gwendolen. Gwendolen is devoted to bread and butter.

JACK [*Advancing to table and helping himself*]. And very good bread and butter it is, too.

ALGERNON. Well, my dear fellow, you need not eat as if you were going to eat it all. You behave as if you were married to her already. You are not married to her already, and I don't think you ever will be.

JACK. Why on earth do you say that? 100

ALGERNON. Well, in the first place girls never marry the men they flirt with. Girls don't think it right.

JACK. Oh, that is nonsense!

ALGERNON. It isn't. It is a great truth. It accounts for the extraordinary number of bachelors that one sees all over the place. In the second place, I don't give my consent.

JACK. Your consent!

ALGERNON. My dear fellow, Gwendolen is my first cousin. And before I allow you to marry her, you will have to clear up the whole question of Cecily. [*Rings bell.*] 110

JACK. Cecily! What on earth do you mean? What do you mean, Algy, by Cecily? I don't know anyone of the name of Cecily.

[*Enter Lane.*

ALGERNON. Bring me that cigarette case Mr. Worthing left in the smoking-room the last time he dined here.

LANE. Yes, sir. [*Lane goes out.*]

JACK. Do you mean to say you have had my cigarette case all this time? I wish to goodness you had let me know. I have been writing frantic letters to Scotland Yard about it. I was very nearly offering a large reward. 120

ALGERNON. Well, I wish you would offer one. I happen to be more than usually hard up.

JACK. There is no good offering a large reward now that the thing is found.

[*Enter Lane with the cigarette case on a salver. Algernon takes it at once. Lane goes out.*

ALGERNON. I think that is rather mean of you, Ernest, I must say. [*Opens case and examines it.*] However, it makes no matter, for, now that I look at the inscription, I find that the thing isn't yours after all.

JACK. Of course it's mine. [*Moving to him.*] You have seen me with it a hundred times, and you have no right whatsoever 130 to read what is written inside. It is a very ungentlemanly thing to read a private cigarette case.

ALGERNON. Oh! it is absurd to have a hard-and-fast rule about what one should read and what one shouldn't. More than half of modern culture depends on what one shouldn't read.

JACK. I am quite aware of the fact, and I don't propose to discuss modern culture. It isn't the sort of thing one should talk of in private. I simply want my cigarette case back.

ALGERNON. Yes; but this isn't your cigarette case. This cigarette case is a present from someone of the name of Cecily, and   140 you said you didn't know anyone of that name.

JACK. Well, if you want to know, Cecily happens to be my aunt.

ALGERNON. Your aunt!

JACK. Yes. Charming old lady she is, too. Lives at Tunbridge Wells. Just give it back to me, Algy.

ALGERNON [*Retreating to-back of sofa*]. But why does she call herself little Cecily if she is your aunt and lives at Tunbridge Wells? [*Reading.*] "From little Cecily with her fondest love."

JACK [*Moving to sofa and kneeling upon it*]. My dear fel-   150 low, what on earth is there in that? Some aunts are tall, some aunts are not tall. That is a matter that surely an aunt may be allowed to decide for herself. You seem to think that every aunt should be exactly like your aunt! That is absurd! For Heaven's sake give me back my cigarette case. [*Follows Algernon round the room.*]

ALGERNON. Yes. But why does your aunt call you her uncle? "From little Cecily, with her fondest love to her dear Uncle Jack." There is no objection, I admit, to an aunt being a small aunt, but why an aunt, no matter what her size may be,   160 should call her own nephew her uncle, I can't quite make out. Besides, your name isn't Jack at all; it is Ernest.

JACK. It isn't Ernest; it's Jack.

ALGERNON. You have always told me it was Ernest. I have introduced you to everyone as Ernest. You answer to the name of Ernest. You look as if your name was Ernest. You are the most earnest looking person I ever saw in my life. It is perfectly absurd your saying that your name isn't Ernest. It's on your cards. Here is one of them. [*Taking it from case.*] "Mr. Ernest Worthing, B 4, The Albany." I'll keep this as a proof your   170 name is Ernest if ever you attempt to deny it to me, or to Gwendolen, or to anyone else. [*Puts the card in his pocket.*]

JACK. Well, my name is Ernest in town and Jack in the country, and the cigarette case was given to me in the country.

ALGERNON. Yes, but that does not account for the fact that your small Aunt Cecily, who lives at Tunbridge Wells, calls you her dear uncle. Come, old boy, you had much better have the thing out at once.

JACK. My dear Algy, you talk exactly as if you were a dentist. It is very vulgar to talk like a dentist when one isn't a dentist. 180 It produces a false impression.

ALGERNON. Well, that is exactly what dentists always do. Now, go on! Tell me the whole thing. I may mention that I have always suspected you of being a confirmed and secret Bunburyist; and I am quite sure of it now.

JACK. Bunburyist? What on earth do you mean by a Bunburyist?

ALGERNON. I'll reveal to you the meaning of that incomparable expression as soon as you are kind enough to inform me why you are Ernest in town and Jack in the country. 190

JACK. Well, produce my cigarette case first.

ALGERNON. Here it is. [*Hands cigarette case.*] Now produce your explanation, and pray make it improbable. [*Sits on sofa.*]

JACK. My dear fellow, there is nothing improbable about my explanation at all. In fact it's perfectly ordinary. Old Mr. Thomas Cardew, who adopted me when I was a little boy, made me in his will guardian to his grand-daughter, Miss Cecily Cardew. Cecily, who addresses me as her uncle from motives of respect that you could not possibly appreciate, lives at my place in the country under the charge of her admirable governess, Miss 200 Prism.

ALGERNON. Where is that place in the country, by the way?

JACK. That is nothing to you, dear boy. You are not going to be invited. . . . I may tell you candidly that the place is not in Shropshire.

ALGERNON. I suspected that, my dear fellow! I have Bunburyed all over Shropshire on two separate occasions. Now, go on. Why are you Ernest in town and Jack in the country?

JACK. My dear Algy, I don't know whether you will be able to understand my real motives. You are hardly serious enough. 210 When one is placed in the position of guardian, one has to adopt a very high moral tone on all subjects. It's one's duty to do so. And as a high moral tone can hardly be said to conduce very much to either one's health or one's happiness, in order to get up to town I have always pretended to have a younger brother of the name of Ernest, who lives in the Albany, and gets into the most dreadful scrapes. That, my dear Algy, is the whole truth pure and simple.

ALGERNON. The truth is rarely pure and never simple. Modern life would be very tedious if it were either, and modern literature a complete impossibility!

JACK. That wouldn't be at all a bad thing.

ALGERNON. Literary criticism is not your forte, my dear fellow. Don't try it. You should leave that to people who haven't been at a University. They do it so well in the daily papers. What you really are is a Bunburyist. I was quite right in saying you were a Bunburyist. You are one of the most advanced Bunburyists I know.

JACK. What on earth do you mean?

ALGERNON. You have invented a very useful younger brother called Ernest, in order that you may be able to come up to town as often as you like. I have invented an invaluable permanent invalid called Bunbury, in order that I may be able to go down into the country whenever I choose. Bunbury is perfectly invaluable. If it wasn't for Bunbury's extraordinary bad health, for instance, I wouldn't be able to dine with you at Willis's to-night, for I have been really engaged to Aunt Augusta for more than a week.

JACK. I haven't asked you to dine with me anywhere to-night.

ALGERNON. I know. You are absolutely careless about sending out invitations. It is very foolish of you. Nothing annoys people so much as not receiving invitations.

JACK. You had much better dine with your Aunt Augusta.

ALGERNON. I haven't the smallest intention of doing anything of the kind. To begin with, I dined there on Monday, and once a week is quite enough to dine with one's own relatives. In the second place, whenever I do dine there I am always treated as a member of the family, and sent down with either no woman at all, or two. In the third place, I know perfectly well whom she will place me next to, to-night. She will place me next Mary Farquhar, who always flirts with her own husband across the dinner-table. That is not very pleasant. Indeed, it is not even decent . . . and that sort of thing is enormously on the increase. The amount of women in London who flirt with their own husbands is perfectly scandalous. It looks so bad. It is simply washing one's clean linen in public. Besides, now that I know you to be a confirmed Bunburyist I naturally want to talk to you about Bunburying. I want to tell you the rules.

JACK. I'm not a Bunburyist at all. If Gwendolen accepts me,

I am going to kill my brother, indeed I think I'll kill him in any case. Cecily is a little too much interested in him. It is rather 260 a bore. So I am going to get rid of Ernest. And I strongly advise you to do the same with Mr. . . . with your invalid friend who has the absurd name.

ALGERNON. Nothing will induce me to part with Bunbury, and if you ever get married, which seems to me extremely problematic, you will be very glad to know Bunbury. A man who marries without knowing Bunbury has a very tedious time of it.

JACK. That is nonsense. If I marry a charming girl like Gwendolen, and she is the only girl I ever saw in my life that I would marry, I certainly won't want to know Bunbury. 270

ALGERNON. Then your wife will. You don't seem to realize, that in married life three is company and two is none.

JACK [Sententiously]. That, my dear young friend, is the theory that the corrupt French Drama has been propounding for the last fifty years.

ALGERNON. Yes; and that the happy English home has proved in half the time.

JACK. For heaven's sake, don't try to be cynical. It's perfectly easy to be cynical.

ALGERNON. My dear fellow, it isn't easy to be anything 280 now-a-days. There's such a lot of beastly competition about. [The sound of an electric bell is heard.] Ah! that must be Aunt Augusta. Only relatives, or creditors, ever ring in that Wagnerian manner. Now, if I get her out of the way for ten minutes, so that you can have an opportunity for proposing to Gwendolen, may I dine with you to-night at Willis's?

JACK. I suppose so, if you want to.

ALGERNON. Yes, but you must be serious about it. I hate people who are not serious about meals. It is so shallow of them.

[Enter Lane.

LANE. Lady Bracknell and Miss Fairfax. [Algernon goes 290 forward to meet them. Enter Lady Bracknell and Gwendolen.

LADY BRACKNELL. Good afternoon, dear Algernon, I hope you are behaving very well.

ALGERNON. I'm feeling very well, Aunt Augusta.

LADY BRACKNELL. That's not quite the same thing. In fact the two things rarely go together. [Sees Jack and bows to him with icy coldness.]

ALGERNON [To Gwendolen]. Dear me, you are smart!

GWENDOLEN. I am always smart! Aren't I, Mr. Worthing?

JACK. You're quite perfect, Miss Fairfax.

GWENDOLEN. Oh! I hope I am not that. It would leave no room for developments, and I intend to develop in *many direc-* 300 *tions.* [*Gwendolen and Jack sit down together in the corner.*]

LADY BRACKNELL. I'm sorry if we are a little late, Algernon, but I was obliged to call on dear Lady Harbury. I hadn't been there since her poor husband's death. I never saw a woman so altered; she looks quite twenty years younger. And now I'll have a cup of tea, and one of those nice cucumber sandwiches you promised me.

ALGERNON. Certainly, Aunt Augusta. [*Goes over to tea-table.*]

LADY BRACKNELL. Won't you come and sit here, Gwendolen?

GWENDOLEN. Thanks, mamma, I'm quite comfortable 310 where I am.

ALGERNON [*Picking up empty plate in horror*]. Good heavens! Lane! Why are there no cucumber sandwiches? I ordered them specially.

LANE [*Gravely*]. There were no cucumbers in the market this morning, sir. I went down twice.

ALGERNON. No cucumbers!

LANE. No, sir. Not even for ready money.

ALGERNON. That will do, Lane, thank you.

LANE. Thank you, sir. [*Goes out.*]   320

ALGERNON. I am greatly distressed, Aunt Augusta, about there being no cucumbers, not even for ready money.

LADY BRACKNELL. It really makes no matter, Algernon. I had some crumpets with Lady Harbury, who seems to me to be living entirely for pleasure now.

ALGERNON. I hear her hair has turned quite gold from grief.

LADY BRACKNELL. It certainly has changed its colour. From what cause I, of course, cannot say. [*Algernon crosses and hands tea.*] Thank you. I've quite a treat for you to-night, Algernon. I am going to send you down with Mary Farquhar. She is 330 such a nice woman, and so attentive to her husband. It's delightful to watch them.

ALGERNON. I am afraid, Aunt Augusta, I shall have to give up the pleasure of dining with you to-night after all.

LADY BRACKNELL [*Frowning*]. I hope not, Algernon. It would put my table completely out. Your uncle would have to dine upstairs. Fortunately he is accustomed to that.

ALGERNON. It is a great bore, and, I need hardly say, a terrible disappointment to me, but the fact is I have just had a telegram to say that my poor friend Bunbury is very ill again. [*Ex-* 340 *changes glances with Jack.*] They seem to think I should be with him.

LADY BRACKNELL. It is very strange. This Mr. Bunbury seems to suffer from curiously bad health.

ALGERNON. Yes; poor Bunbury is a dreadful invalid.

LADY BRACKNELL. Well, I must say, Algernon, that I think it is high time that Mr. Bunbury made up his mind whether he was going to live or to die. This shilly-shallying with the question is absurd. Nor do I in any way approve of the modern sympathy with invalids. I consider it morbid. Illness of any kind is 350 hardly a thing to be encouraged in others. Health is the primary duty of life. I am always telling that to your poor uncle, but he never seems to take much notice . . . as far as any improvement in his ailments goes. I should be much obliged if you would ask Mr. Bunbury, from me, to be kind enough not to have a relapse on Saturday, for I rely on you to arrange my music for me. It is my last reception and one wants something that will encourage conversation, particularly at the end of the season when every-one has practically said whatever they had to say, which, in most cases, was probably not much. 360

ALGERNON. I'll speak to Bunbury, Aunt Augusta, if he is still conscious, and I think I can promise you he'll be all right by Saturday. You see, if one plays good music, people don't listen, and if one plays bad music people don't talk. But I'll run over the programme I've drawn out, if you will kindly come into the next room for a moment.

LADY BRACKNELL. Thank you, Algernon. It is very thoughtful of you. [*Rising, and following Algernon.*] I'm sure the pro-gramme will be delightful, after a few expurgations. French songs I cannot possibly allow. People always seem to think that 370 they are improper, and either look shocked, which is vulgar, or laugh, which is worse. But German sounds a thoroughly respect-able language, and indeed, I believe is so. Gwendolen, you will accompany me.

GWENDOLEN. Certainly, mamma. [*Lady Bracknell and Algernon go into the music-room, Gwendolen remains behind.*]

JACK. Charming day it has been, Miss Fairfax.

GWENDOLEN. Pray don't talk to me about the weather, Mr. Worthing. Whenever people talk to me about the weather, I al-ways feel quite certain that they mean something else. And that makes me so nervous. 380

JACK. I do mean something else.

GWENDOLEN. I thought so. In fact, I am never wrong.

JACK. And I would like to be allowed to take advantage of Lady Bracknell's temporary absence. . . .

GWENDOLEN. I would certainly advise you to do so. Mamma has a way of coming back suddenly into a room that I have often had to speak to her about.

JACK [*Nervously*]. Miss Fairfax, ever since I met you I have admired you more than any girl . . . I have ever met since . . . I met you. 390

GWENDOLEN. Yes, I am quite aware of the fact. And I often wish that in public, at any rate, you had been more demonstrative. For me you have always had an irresistible fascination. Even before I met you I was far from indifferent to you. [*Jack looks at her in amazement.*] We live, as I hope you know, Mr. Worthing, in an age of ideals. The fact is constantly mentioned in the more expensive monthly magazines, and has reached the provincial pulpits I am told: and my ideal has always been to love some one of the name of Ernest. There is something in that name that inspires absolute confidence. The moment Algernon first mentioned 400 to me that he had a friend called Ernest, I knew I was destined to love you.

JACK. You really love me, Gwendolen?

GWENDOLEN. Passionately!

JACK. Darling! You don't know how happy you've made me.

GWENDOLEN. My own Ernest!

JACK. But you don't really mean to say that you couldn't love me if my name wasn't Ernest?

GWENDOLEN. But your name is Ernest.

JACK. Yes, I know it is. But supposing it was something 410 else? Do you mean to say you couldn't love me then?

GWENDOLEN [*Glibly*]. Ah! that is clearly a metaphysical speculation, and like most metaphysical speculations has very little reference at all to the actual facts of real life, as we know them.

JACK. Personally, darling, to speak quite candidly, I don't much care about the name of Ernest . . . I don't think that name suits me at all.

GWENDOLEN. It suits you perfectly. It is a divine name. It has a music of its own. It produces vibrations.

JACK. Well, really, Gwendolen, I must say that I think 420 there are lots of other much nicer names. I think Jack, for instance, a charming name.

GWENDOLEN. Jack? . . . No, there is very little music in the name Jack, if any at all, indeed. It does not thrill. It produces absolutely no vibrations. . . . I have known several Jacks, and they all, without exception, were more than usually plain. Besides, Jack is a notorious domesticity for John! And I pity any woman who is married to a man called John. She would probably never be allowed to know the entrancing pleasure of a single moment's solitude. The only really safe name is Ernest. 430

JACK. Gwendolen, I must get christened at once—I mean we must get married at once. There is no time to be lost.

GWENDOLEN. Married, Mr. Worthing?

JACK [*Astounded*]. Well . . . surely. You know that I love you, and you led me to believe, Miss Fairfax, that you were not absolutely indifferent to me.

GWENDOLEN. I adore you. But you haven't proposed to me yet. Nothing has been said at all about marriage. The subject has not even been touched on.

JACK. Well . . . may I propose to you now? 440

GWENDOLEN. I think it would be an admirable opportunity. And to spare you any possible disappointment, Mr. Worthing, I think it only fair to tell you quite frankly beforehand that I am fully determined to accept you.

JACK. Gwendolen!

GWENDOLEN. Yes, Mr. Worthing, what have you got to say to me?

JACK. You know what I have got to say to you.

GWENDOLEN. Yes, but you don't say it.

JACK. Gwendolen, will you marry me? [*Goes on his* 450 *knees.*]

GWENDOLEN. Of course I will, darling. How long you have been about it! I am afraid you have had very little experience in how to propose.

JACK. My own one, I have never loved anyone in the world but you.

GWENDOLEN. Yes, but men often propose for practice. I know my brother Gerald does. All my girl-friends tell me so. What wonderfully blue eyes you have, Ernest! They are quite, quite blue. I hope you will always look at me just like that, especially when there are other people present. 460

[*Enter Lady Bracknell. She is shocked.*

LADY BRACKNELL. Mr. Worthing! Rise, sir, from this semi-recumbent posture. It is most indecorous.

GWENDOLEN. Mamma! [*He tries to rise; she restrains him.*] I must beg you to retire. This is no place for you. Besides, Mr. Worthing has not quite finished yet.

LADY BRACKNELL. Finished what, may I ask?

GWENDOLEN. I am engaged to Mr. Worthing, mamma. [*They rise together.*]

LADY BRACKNELL. Pardon me, you are not engaged to anyone. When you do become engaged to some one, I, or your 470 father, should his health permit him, will inform you of the fact. An engagement should come on a young girl as a surprise, pleasant or unpleasant, as the case may be. It is hardly a matter that she could be allowed to arrange for herself. . . . And now I have a few questions to put to you, Mr. Worthing. While I am making these inquiries, you, Gwendolen, will wait for me below in the carriage.

GWENDOLEN [*Reproachfully*]. Mamma!

LADY BRACKNELL. In the carriage, Gwendolen! [*Gwendolen goes to the door. She and Jack blow kisses to each other behind Lady Bracknell's back. Lady Bracknell looks vaguely about as if she could not understand what the noise was. Finally turns round.*] Gwendolen, the carriage! 480

GWENDOLEN. Yes, mamma. [*Goes out, looking back at Jack.*

LADY BRACKNELL [*Sitting down*]. You can take a seat, Mr. Worthing. [*Looks in her pocket for note-book and pencil.*]

JACK. Thank you, Lady Bracknell, I prefer standing.

LADY BRACKNELL [*Pencil and note-book in hand*]. I feel bound to tell you that you are not down on my list of eligible young men, although I have the same list as the dear Duchess of Bolton has. We work together, in fact. However, I am quite ready to enter your name, should your answers be what a really affectionate mother requires. Do you smoke? 490

JACK. Well, yes, I must admit I smoke.

LADY BRACKNELL. I am glad to hear it. A man should always have an occupation of some kind. There are far too many idle men in London as it is. How old are you?

JACK. Twenty-nine.

LADY BRACKNELL. A very good age to be married at. I have always been of opinion that a man who desires to get married should know either everything or nothing. Which do you know?

JACK [*After some hesitation*]. I know nothing, Lady Bracknell.

LADY BRACKNELL. I am pleased to hear it. I do not approve 500 of anything that tampers with natural ignorance. Ignorance is like a delicate exotic fruit; touch it and the bloom is gone. The whole theory of modern education is radically unsound. Fortunately in England, at any rate, education produces no effect whatsoever. If it did, it would prove a serious danger to the upper classes, and probably lead to acts of violence in Grosvenor Square. What is your income?

JACK. Between seven and eight thousand a year.

LADY BRACKNELL [*Makes a note in her book*]. In land, or in investments?   510

JACK. In investments, chiefly.

LADY BRACKNELL. That is satisfactory. What between the duties expected of one during one's life-time, and the duties exacted from one after one's death, land has ceased to be either a profit or a pleasure. It gives one position, and prevents one from keeping it up. That's all that can be said about land.

JACK. I have a country house with some land, of course, attached to it, about fifteen hundred acres, I believe; but I don't depend on that for my real income. In fact, as far as I can make out, the poachers are the only people who make anything out 520 of it.

LADY BRACKNELL. A country house! How many bedrooms? Well, that point can be cleared up afterwards. You have a town house, I hope? A girl with a simple, unspoiled nature, like Gwendolen, could hardly be expected to reside in the country.

JACK. Well, I own a house in Belgrave Square, but it is let by the year to Lady Bloxham. Of course, I can get it back whenever I like, at six months' notice.

LADY BRACKNELL. Lady Bloxham? I don't know her.

JACK. Oh, she goes about very little. She is a lady con- 530 siderably advanced in years.

LADY BRACKNELL. Ah, now-a-days that is no guarantee of respectability of character. What number in Belgrave Square?

JACK. 149.

LADY BRACKNELL [*Shaking her head*]. The unfashionable side. I thought there was something. However, that could easily be altered.

JACK. Do you mean the fashion, or the side?

LADY BRACKNELL [*Sternly*]. Both, if necessary, I presume. What are your politics?   540

JACK. Well, I am afraid I really have none. I am a Liberal Unionist.

LADY BRACKNELL. Oh, they count as Tories. They dine with us. Or come in the evening, at any rate. Now to minor matters. Are your parents living?

JACK. I have lost both my parents.

LADY BRACKNELL. Both? . . . That seems like carelessness. Who was your father? He was evidently a man of some wealth. Was he born in what the Radical papers call the purple of commerce, or did he rise from the ranks of the aristocracy?   550

JACK. I am afraid I really don't know. The fact is, Lady Bracknell, I said I had lost my parents. It would be nearer the truth to say that my parents seem to have lost me . . . I don't actually know who I am by birth. I was . . . well, I was found.

LADY BRACKNELL. Found!

JACK. The late Mr. Thomas Cardew, an old gentleman of a very charitable and kindly disposition, found me, and gave me the name of Worthing, because he happened to have a first-class ticket for Worthing in his pocket at the time. Worthing is a place in Sussex. It is a seaside resort.   560

LADY BRACKNELL. Where did the charitable gentleman who had a first-class ticket for this seaside resort find you?

JACK [Gravely]. In a hand-bag.

LADY BRACKNELL. A hand-bag?

JACK [Very seriously]. Yes, Lady Bracknell. I was in a hand-bag—a somewhat large, black leather hand-bag, with handles to it—an ordinary hand-bag in fact.

LADY BRACKNELL. In what locality did this Mr. James, or Thomas, Cardew come across this ordinary hand-bag?

JACK. In the cloak-room at Victoria Station. It was given   570 to him in mistake for his own.

LADY BRACKNELL. The cloak-room at Victoria Station?

JACK. Yes. The Brighton line.

LADY BRACKNELL. The line is immaterial. Mr. Worthing, I confess I feel somewhat bewildered by what you have just told me. To be born, or at any rate bred, in a hand-bag, whether it had handles or not, seems to me to display a contempt for the ordinary decencies of family life that remind one of the worst excesses of the French Revolution. And I presume you know what that unfortunate movement led to? As for the particular   580 locality in which the hand-bag was found, a cloak-room at a railway station might serve to conceal a social indiscretion—has probably, indeed, been used for that purpose before now—but it could hardly be regarded as an assured basis for a recognized position in good society.

JACK. May I ask you then what you would advise me to do? I need hardly say I would do anything in the world to ensure Gwendolen's happiness.

LADY BRACKNELL. I would strongly advise you, Mr. Worthing,

to try and acquire some relations as soon as possible, and to   590
make a definite effort to produce at any rate one parent, of either
sex, before the season is quite over.

JACK. Well, I don't see how I could possibly manage to do that.
I can produce the hand-bag at any moment. It is in my dressing-
room at home. I really think that should satisfy you, Lady Bracknell.

LADY BRACKNELL. Me, sir! What has it to do with me? You can
hardly imagine that I and Lord Bracknell would dream of allowing our only daughter—a girl brought up with the utmost care—
to marry into a cloakroom, and form an alliance with a   600
parcel? Good morning, Mr. Worthing! [*Lady Bracknell sweeps
out in majestic indignation.*]

JACK. Good morning! [*Algernon, from the other room, strikes
up the Wedding March. Jack looks perfectly furious, and goes to
the door.*] For goodness' sake don't play that ghastly tune, Algy!
How idiotic you are!

[*The music stops, and Algernon enters cheerily.*]

ALGERNON. Didn't it go off all right, old boy? You don't mean
to say Gwendolen refused you? I know it is a way she has. She
is always refusing people. I think it is most ill-natured of her.

JACK. Oh, Gwendolen is as right as a trivet. As far as she is
concerned, we are engaged. Her mother is perfectly unbearable.
Never met such a Gorgon . . . I don't really know what a   610
Gorgon is like, but I am quite sure that Lady Bracknell is one. In
any case, she is a monster, without being a myth, which is rather
unfair. . . . I beg your pardon, Algy, I suppose I shouldn't talk
about your own aunt in that way before you.

ALGERNON. My dear boy, I love hearing my relations abused.
It is the only thing that makes me put up with them at all. Relations are simply a tedious pack of people, who haven't got the
remotest knowledge of how to live, nor the smallest instinct
about when to die.

JACK. Oh, that is nonsense!   620

ALGERNON. It isn't!

JACK. Well, I won't argue about the matter. You always want
to argue about things.

ALGERNON. That is exactly what things were originally made
for.

JACK. Upon my word, if I thought that, I'd shoot myself . . .
[*A pause.*] You don't think there is any chance of Gwendolen
becoming like her mother in about a hundred and fifty years, do
you, Algy?

ALGERNON. All women become like their mothers. That is 630
their tragedy. No man does. That's his.

JACK. Is that clever?

ALGERNON. It is perfectly phrased! and quite as true as any observation in civilized life should be.

JACK. I am sick to death of cleverness. Everybody is clever now-a-days. You can't go anywhere without meeting clever people. The thing has become an absolute public nuisance. I wish to goodness we had a few fools left.

ALGERNON. We have.

JACK. I should extremely like to meet them. What do they 640
talk about?

ALGERNON. The fools? Oh! about the clever people, of course.

JACK. What fools!

ALGERNON. By the way, did you tell Gwendolen the truth about your being Ernest in town, and Jack in the country?

JACK [*In a very patronising manner*]. My dear fellow, the truth isn't quite the sort of thing one tells to a nice, sweet, refined girl. What extraordinary ideas you have about the way to behave to a woman!

ALGERNON. The only way to behave to a woman is to 650
make love to her, if she is pretty, and to someone else if she is plain.

JACK. Oh, that is nonsense.

ALGERNON. What about your brother? What about the profligate Ernest?

JACK. Oh, before the end of the week I shall have got rid of him. I'll say he died in Paris of apoplexy. Lots of people die of apoplexy, quite suddenly, don't they?

ALGERNON. Yes, but it's hereditary, my dear fellow. It's a sort of thing that runs in families. You had much better say a 660
severe chill.

JACK. You are sure a severe chill isn't hereditary, or anything of that kind?

ALGERNON. Of course it isn't!

JACK. Very well, then. My poor brother Ernest is carried off suddenly in Paris, by a severe chill. That gets rid of him.

ALGERNON. But I thought you said that . . . Miss Cardew was a little too much interested in your poor brother Ernest? Won't she feel his loss a good deal?

JACK. Oh, that is all right. Cecily is not a silly, romantic 670
girl, I am glad to say. She has got a capital appetite, goes for long walks, and pays no attention at all to her lessons.

ALGERNON. I would rather like to see Cecily.

JACK. I will take very good care you never do. She is excessively pretty, and she is only just eighteen.

ALGERNON. Have you told Gwendolen yet that you have an excessively pretty ward who is only just eighteen?

JACK. Oh! one doesn't blurt these things out to people. Cecily and Gwendolen are perfectly certain to be extremely great friends. I'll bet you anything you like that half an hour after 680 they have met, they will be calling each other sister.

ALGERNON. Women only do that when they have called each other a lot of other things first. Now, my dear boy, if we want to get a good table at Willis's, we really must go and dress. Do you know it is nearly seven?

JACK [Irritably]. Oh! it always is nearly seven.

ALGERNON. Well, I'm hungry.

JACK. I never knew you when you weren't. . . .

ALGERNON. What shall we do after dinner? Go to a theatre?

JACK. Oh, no! I loathe listening. 690

ALGERNON. Well, let us go to the Club?

JACK. Oh, no! I hate talking.

ALGERNON. Well, we might trot round to the Empire at ten?

JACK. Oh, no! I can't bear looking at things. It is so silly.

ALGERNON. Well, what shall we do?

JACK. Nothing!

ALGERNON. It is awfully hard work doing nothing. However, I don't mind hard work where there is no definite object of any kind.

[Enter Lane.

LANE. Miss Fairfax. 700

[Enter Gwendolen. Lane goes out.

ALGERNON. Gwendolen, upon my word!

GWENDOLEN. Algy, kindly turn your back. I have something very particular to say to Mr. Worthing.

ALGERNON. Really, Gwendolen, I don't think I can allow this at all.

GWENDOLEN. Algy, you always adopt a strictly immoral attitude towards life. You are not quite old enough to do that. [Algernon retires to the fireplace.]

JACK. My own darling!

GWENDOLEN. Ernest, we may never be married. From the 710 expression on mamma's face I fear we never shall. Few parents now-a-days pay any regard to what their children say to them. The old-fashioned respect for the young is fast dying out. Whatever influence I ever had over mamma, I lost at the age of three. But although she may prevent us from becoming man and wife, and I may marry someone else, and marry often, nothing that she can possibly do can alter my eternal devotion to you.

JACK. Dear Gwendolen.

GWENDOLEN. The story of your romantic origin, as related to me by mamma, with unpleasing comments, has naturally 720 stirred the deeper fibres of my nature. Your Christian name has an irresistible fascination. The simplicity of your character makes you exquisitely incomprehensible to me. Your town address at the Albany I have. What is your address in the country?

JACK. The Manor House, Woolton, Hertfordshire. [*Algernon, who has been carefully listening, smiles to himself, and writes the address on his shirt-cuff. Then picks up the Railway Guide.*]

GWENDOLEN. There is a good postal service, I suppose? It may be necessary to do something desperate. That, of course, will require serious consideration. I will communicate with you daily.

JACK. My own one!

GWENDOLEN. How long do you remain in town? 730

JACK. Till Monday.

GWENDOLEN. Good! Algy, you may turn round now.

ALGERNON. Thanks, I've turned round already.

GWENDOLEN. You may also ring the bell.

JACK. You will let me see you to your carriage, my own darling?

GWENDOLEN. Certainly.

JACK [*To Lane, who now enters*]. I will see Miss Fairfax out.

LANE. Yes, sir. [*Jack and Gwendolen go off. Lane presents several letters on a salver to Algernon. It is to be surmised that* 740 *they are bills, as Algernon, after looking at the envelopes, tears them up.*]

ALGERNON. A glass of sherry, Lane.

LANE. Yes, sir.

ALGERNON. To-morrow, Lane, I'm going Bunburying.

LANE. Yes, sir.

ALGERNON. I shall probably not be back till Monday. You can put up my dress clothes, my smoking jacket, and all the Bunbury suits . . .

LANE. Yes, sir. [*Handing sherry.*] 750

ALGERNON. I hope to-morrow will be a fine day, Lane.

LANE. It never is, sir.

ALGERNON. Lane, you're a perfect pessimist.

LANE. I do my best to give satisfaction, sir.

[*Enter Jack. Lane goes off.*

JACK. There's a sensible, intellectual girl! the only girl I ever cared for in my life. [*Algernon is laughing immoderately.*] What on earth are you so amused at?

ALGERNON. Oh, I'm a little anxious about poor Bunbury, that's all.

JACK. If you don't take care, your friend Bunbury will get 760 you into a serious scrape some day.

ALGERNON. I love scrapes. They are the only things that are never serious.

JACK. Oh, that's nonsense, Algy. You never talk anything but nonsense.

ALGERNON. Nobody ever does. [*Jack looks indignantly at him, and leaves the room. Algernon lights a cigarette, reads his shirt-cuff, and smiles.*]

ACT II

SCENE.—*Garden at the Manor House, the morning of the next day. A flight of gray stone steps leads up to the house. The garden, an old-fashioned one, full of roses. Time of year, July. Basket chairs, and a table covered with books, are set under a large yew tree. Miss Prism discovered seated at the table. Cecily is at the back watering flowers.*

MISS PRISM [*Calling*]. Cecily, Cecily! Surely such a utilitarian occupation as the watering of flowers is rather Moulton's duty than yours? Especially at a moment when intellectual pleasures await you. Your German grammar is on the table. Pray open it at page fifteen. We will repeat yesterday's lesson.

CECILY [*Coming over very slowly*]. But I don't like German. It isn't at all a becoming language. I know perfectly well that I look quite plain after my German lesson.

MISS PRISM. Child, you know how anxious your guardian is that you should improve yourself in every way. He laid par- 10 ticular stress on your German, as he was leaving for town yesterday. Indeed, he always lays stress on your German when he is leaving for town.

CECILY. Dear Uncle Jack is so very serious! Sometimes he is so serious that I think he cannot be quite well.

MISS PRISM [*Drawing herself up*]. Your guardian enjoys the best of health, and his gravity of demeanour is especially to be commended in one so comparatively young as he is. I know no one who has a higher sense of duty and responsibility.

CECILY. I suppose that is why he often looks a little bored 20 when we three are together.

MISS PRISM. Cecily! I am surprised at you. Mr. Worthing has many troubles in his life. Idle merriment and triviality would be out of place in his conversation. You must remember his constant anxiety about that unfortunate young man, his brother.

CECILY. I wish Uncle Jack would allow that unfortunate young man, his brother, to come down here sometimes. We might have a good influence over him, Miss Prism. I am sure you certainly would. You know German, and geology, and things of that kind influence a man very much. [*Cecily begins to write in her* 30 *diary.*]

MISS PRISM [*Shaking her head*]. I do not think that even I could produce any effect on a character that, according to his own brother's admission, is irretrievably weak and vacillating. Indeed, I am not sure that I would desire to reclaim him. I am not in favour of this modern mania for turning bad people into good people at a moment's notice. As a man sows so let him reap. You must put away your diary, Cecily. I really don't see why you should keep a diary at all.

CECILY. I keep a diary in order to enter the wonderful se- 40 crets of my life. If I didn't write them down I should probably forget all about them.

MISS PRISM. Memory, my dear Cecily, is the diary that we all carry about with us.

CECILY. Yes, but it usually chronicles the things that have never happened, and couldn't possibly have happened. I believe that Memory is responsible for nearly all the three-volume novels that Mudie sends us.

MISS PRISM. Do not speak slightingly of the three-volume novel, Cecily. I wrote one myself in earlier days. 50

CECILY. Did you really, Miss Prism? How wonderfully clever you are! I hope it did not end happily? I don't like novels that end happily. They depress me so much.

MISS PRISM. The good ended happily, and the bad unhappily. That is what Fiction means.

CECILY. I suppose so. But it seems very unfair. And was your novel ever published?

MISS PRISM. Alas! no. The manuscript unfortunately was abandoned. I use the word in the sense of lost or mislaid. To your work, child, these speculations are profitless. 60

CECILY [*Smiling*]. But I see dear Dr. Chasuble coming up through the garden.

MISS PRISM [*Rising and advancing*]. Dr. Chasuble! This is indeed a pleasure.

[*Enter Canon Chasuble. He tries to be gallant in a pompous way.*

CHASUBLE. And how are we this morning? Miss Prism, you are, I trust, well?

CECILY. Miss Prism has just been complaining of a slight headache. I think it would do her so much good to have a short stroll with you in the park, Dr. Chasuble.

MISS PRISM. Cecily, I have not mentioned anything about 70 a headache.

CECILY. No, dear Miss Prism, I know that, but I felt instinctively that you had a headache. Indeed I was thinking about that, and not about my German lesson, when the Rector came in.

CHASUBLE. I hope, Cecily, you are not inattentive.

CECILY. Oh, I am afraid I am.

CHASUBLE. That is strange. Were I fortunate enough to be Miss Prism's pupil, I would hang upon her lips. [*Miss Prism glares.*] I spoke metaphorically.—My metaphor was drawn from bees. Ahem! Mr. Worthing, I suppose, has not returned from town 80 yet?

MISS PRISM. We do not expect him till Monday afternoon.

CHASUBLE. Ah yes, he usually likes to spend his Sunday in London. He is not one of those whose sole aim is enjoyment, as, by all accounts, that unfortunate young man, his brother, seems to be. But I must not disturb Egeria and her pupil any longer.

MISS PRISM. Egeria? My name is Lætitia, Doctor.

CHASUBLE [*Bowing*]. A classical allusion merely, drawn from the Pagan authors. I shall see you both no doubt at Evensong.

MISS PRISM. I think, dear Doctor, I will have a stroll with 90 you. I find I have a headache after all, and a walk might do it good.

CHASUBLE. With pleasure, Miss Prism, with pleasure. We might go as far as the schools and back.

MISS PRISM. That would be delightful. Cecily, you will read your Political Economy in my absence. The chapter on the Fall of the Rupee you may omit. It is somewhat too sensational. Even these metallic problems have their melodramatic side. [*Goes down the garden with Dr. Chasuble.*]

CECILY [*Picks up books and throws them back on table*]. Hor-

rid Political Economy! Horrid Geography! Horrid, horrid 100
German!

[*Enter Merriman with a card on a salver.*

MERRIMAN. Mr. Ernest Worthing has just driven over from the
station. He has brought his luggage with him.

CECILY [*Takes the card and reads it*]. "Mr. Ernest Worthing,
B 4 The Albany, W." Uncle Jack's brother! Did you tell him
Mr. Worthing was in town?

MERRIMAN. Yes, Miss. He seemed very much disappointed. I
mentioned that you and Miss Prism were in the garden. He said
he was anxious to speak to you privately for a moment.

CECILY. Ask Mr. Ernest Worthing to come here. I suppose 110
you had better talk to the housekeeper about a room for him.

MERRIMAN. Yes, Miss. [*Merriman goes off.*

CECILY. I have never met any really wicked person before. I
feel rather frightened. I am so afraid he will look just like everyone else.

[*Enter Algernon, very gay and debonnair.*
He does!

ALGERNON [*Raising his hat*]. You are my little cousin Cecily,
I'm sure.

CECILY. You are under some strange mistake. I am not little. In
fact, I am more than usually tall for my age. [*Algernon is* 120
rather taken aback.] But I am your cousin Cecily. You, I see from
your card, are Uncle Jack's brother, my cousin Ernest, my wicked
cousin Ernest.

ALGERNON. Oh! I am not really wicked at all, cousin Cecily.
You musn't think that I am wicked.

CECILY. If you are not, then you have certainly been deceiving
us all in a very inexcusable manner. I hope you have not been
leading a double life, pretending to be wicked and being really
good all the time. That would be hypocrisy.

ALGERNON [*Looks at her in amazement*]. Oh! of course I 130
have been rather reckless.

CECILY. I am glad to hear it.

ALGERNON. In fact, now you mention the subject, I have been
very bad in my own small way.

CECILY. I don't think you should be so proud of that, though
I am sure it must have been very pleasant.

ALGERNON. It is much pleasanter being here with you.

CECILY. I can't understand how you are here at all. Uncle Jack
won't be back till Monday afternoon.

ALGERNON. That is a great disappointment. I am obliged to   140
go up by the first train on Monday morning. I have a business
appointment that I am anxious . . . to miss.

CECILY. Couldn't you miss it anywhere but in London?

ALGERNON. No; the appointment is in London.

CECILY. Well, I know, of course, how important it is not to
keep a business engagement, if one wants to retain any sense of
the beauty of life, but still I think you had better wait till Uncle
Jack arrives. I know he wants to speak to you about your emigrating.

ALGERNON. About my what?   150

CECILY. Your emigrating. He has gone up to buy your outfit.

ALGERNON. I certainly wouldn't let Jack buy my outfit. He has
no taste in neckties at all.

CECILY. I don't think you will require neckties. Uncle Jack is
sending you to Australia.

ALGERNON. Australia! I'd sooner die.

CECILY. Well, he said at dinner on Wednesday night, that you
would have to choose between this world, the next world, and
Australia.

ALGERNON. Oh, well! The accounts I have received of   160
Australia and the next world, are not particularly encouraging.
This world is good enough for me, cousin Cecily.

CECILY. Yes, but are you good enough for it?

ALGERNON. I'm afraid I'm not that. That is why I want you to
reform me. You might make that your mission, if you don't mind,
cousin Cecily.

CECILY. I'm afraid I've not time, this afternoon.

ALGERNON. Well, would you mind my reforming myself this
afternoon?

CECILY. That is rather Quixotic of you. But I think you   170
should try.

ALGERNON. I will. I feel better already.

CECILY. You are looking a little worse.

ALGERNON. That is because I am hungry.

CECILY. How thoughtless of me. I should have remembered
that when one is going to lead an entirely new life, one requires
regular and wholesome meals. Won't you come in?

ALGERNON. Thank you. Might I have a button-hole first? I
never have any appetite unless I have a button-hole first.

CECILY. A Maréchal Niel? [*Picks up scissors.*]   180.

ALGERNON. No, I'd sooner have a pink rose.

CECILY. Why? [*Cuts a flower.*]

ALGERNON. Because you are like a pink rose, cousin Cecily.

CECILY. I don't think it can be right for you to talk to me like that. Miss Prism never says such things to me.

ALGERNON. Then Miss Prism is a short-sighted old lady. [*Cecily puts the rose in his button-hole.*] You are the prettiest girl I ever saw.

CECILY. Miss Prism says that all good looks are a snare.

ALGERNON. They are a snare that every sensible man would   190
like to be caught in.

CECILY. Oh! I don't think I would care to catch a sensible man. I shouldn't know what to talk to him about.

   [*They pass into the house. Miss Prism and Dr. Chasuble return.*]

MISS PRISM. You are too much alone, dear Dr. Chasuble. You should get married. A misanthrope I can understand—a womanthrope, never!

CHASUBLE [*With a scholar's shudder*]. Believe me, I do not deserve so neologistic a phrase. The precept as well as the practice of the Primitive Church was distinctly against matrimony.

MISS PRISM [*Sententiously*]. That is obviously the reason   200
why the Primitive Church has not lasted up to the present day. And you do not seem to realize, dear Doctor, that by persistently remaining single, a man converts himself into a permanent public temptation. Men should be careful; this very celibacy leads weaker vessels astray.

CHASUBLE. But is a man not equally attractive when married?

MISS PRISM. No married man is ever attractive except to his wife.

CHASUBLE. And often, I've been told, not even to her.

MISS PRISM. That depends on the intellectual sympathies   210
of the woman. Maturity can always be depended on. Ripeness can be trusted. Young women are green. [*Dr. Chasuble starts.*] I spoke horticulturally. My metaphor was drawn from fruits. But where is Cecily?

CHASUBLE. Perhaps she followed us to the schools.

   [*Enter Jack slowly from the back of the garden. He is dressed in the deepest mourning, with crape hat-band and black gloves.*

MISS PRISM. Mr. Worthing!

CHASUBLE. Mr. Worthing?

MISS PRISM. This is indeed a surprise. We did not look for you till Monday afternoon.

JACK [*Shakes Miss Prism's hand in a tragic manner*]. I have   220 returned sooner than I expected. Dr. Chasuble, I hope you are well?

CHASUBLE. Dear Mr. Worthing, I trust this garb of woe does not betoken some terrible calamity?

JACK. My brother.

MISS PRISM. More shameful debts and extravagance?

CHASUBLE. Still leading his life of pleasure?

JACK [Shaking his head]. Dead!

CHASUBLE. Your brother Ernest dead?

JACK. Quite dead. 230

MISS PRISM. What a lesson for him! I trust he will profit by it.

CHASUBLE. Mr. Worthing, I offer you my sincere condolence. You have at least the consolation of knowing that you were always the most generous and forgiving of brothers.

JACK. Poor Ernest! He had many faults, but it is a sad, sad blow.

CHASUBLE. Very sad indeed. Were you with him at the end?

JACK. No. He died abroad; in Paris, in fact. I had a telegram last night from the manager of the Grand Hotel.

CHASUBLE. Was the cause of death mentioned? 240

JACK. A severe chill, it seems.

MISS PRISM. As a man sows, so shall he reap.

CHASUBLE [Raising his hand]. Charity, dear Miss Prism, charity! None of us are perfect. I myself am peculiarly susceptible to draughts. Will the interment take place here?

JACK. No. He seems to have expressed a desire to be buried in Paris.

CHASUBLE. In Paris! [Shakes his head.] I fear that hardly points to any very serious state of mind at the last. You would no doubt wish me to make some slight allusion to this tragic domestic 250 affliction next Sunday. [Jack presses his hand convulsively.] My sermon on the meaning of the manna in the wilderness can be adapted to almost any occasion, joyful, or, as in the present case, distressing. [All sigh.] I have preached it at harvest celebrations, christenings, confirmations, on days of humiliation and festal days. The last time I delivered it was in the Cathedral, as a charity sermon on behalf of the Society for the Prevention of Discontentment among the Upper Orders. The Bishop, who was present, was much struck by some of the analogies I drew.

JACK. Ah, that reminds me, you mentioned christenings I 260 think, Dr. Chasuble? I suppose you know how to christen all right? [Dr. Chasuble looks astounded.] I mean, of course, you are continually christening, aren't you?

MISS PRISM. It is, I regret to say, one of the Rector's most constant duties in this parish. I have often spoken to the poorer classes on the subject. But they don't seem to know what thrift is.

CHASUBLE. But is there any particular infant in whom you are interested, Mr. Worthing? Your brother was, I believe, unmarried, was he not?

JACK. Oh, yes.   270

MISS PRISM [*Bitterly*]. People who live entirely for pleasure usually are.

JACK. But it is not for any child, dear Doctor. I am very fond of children. No! the fact is, I would like to be christened myself, this afternoon, if you have nothing better to do.

CHASUBLE. But surely, Mr. Worthing, you have been christened already?

JACK. I don't remember anything about it.

CHASUBLE. But have you any grave doubts on the subject?

JACK. I certainly intend to have. Of course, I don't know   280 if the thing would bother you in any way, or if you think I am a little too old now.

CHASUBLE. Not at all. The sprinkling, and, indeed, the immersion of adults is a perfectly canonical practice.

JACK. Immersion!

CHASUBLE. You need have no apprehensions. Sprinkling is all that is necessary, or indeed I think advisable. Our weather is so changeable. At what hour would you wish the ceremony performed?

JACK. Oh, I might trot around about five if that would   290 suit you.

CHASUBLE. Perfectly, perfectly! In fact I have two similar ceremonies to perform at that time. A case of twins that occurred recently in one of the outlying cottages on your own estate. Poor Jenkins the carter, a most hard-working man.

JACK. Oh! I don't see much fun in being christened along with other babies. It would be childish. Would half-past five do?

CHASUBLE. Admirably! Admirably! [*Takes out watch.*] And now, dear Mr. Worthing, I will not intrude any longer into a house of sorrow. I would merely beg you not to be too   300 much bowed down by grief. What seem to us bitter trials at the moment are often blessings in disguise.

MISS PRISM. This seems to me a blessing of an extremely obvious kind.

[*Enter Cecily from the house.*]

CECILY. Uncle Jack! Oh, I am pleased to see you back. But

what horrid clothes you have on! Do go and change them.

MISS PRISM. Cecily!

CHASUBLE. My child! my child! [*Cecily goes towards Jack; he kisses her brow in a melancholy manner.*]

CECILY. What is the matter, Uncle Jack? Do look happy! 310 You look as if you had a toothache and I have such a surprise for you. Who do you think is in the dining-room? Your brother!

JACK. Who?

CECILY. Your brother Ernest. He arrived about half an hour ago.

JACK. What nonsense! I haven't got a brother.

CECILY. Oh, don't say that. However badly he may have behaved to you in the past he is still your brother. You couldn't be so heartless as to disown him. I'll tell him to come out. And you will shake hands with him, won't you, Uncle Jack? [*Runs 320 back into the house.*]

CHASUBLE. These are very joyful tidings.

MISS PRISM. After we had all been resigned to his loss, his sudden return seems to me peculiarly distressing.

JACK. My brother is in the dining-room? I don't know what it all means. I think it is perfectly absurd.

[*Enter Algernon and Cecily hand in hand. They come slowly up to Jack.*

JACK. Good heavens! [*Motions Algernon away.*]

ALGERNON. Brother John, I have come down from town to tell you that I am very sorry for all the trouble I have given you, and that I intend to lead a better life in the future. [*Jack glares at 330 him and does not take his hand.*]

CECILY. Uncle Jack, you are not going to refuse your own brother's hand?

JACK. Nothing will induce me to take his hand. I think his coming down here disgraceful. He knows perfectly well why.

CECILY. Uncle Jack, do be nice. There is some good in everyone. Ernest has just been telling me about his poor invalid friend, Mr. Bunbury, whom he goes to visit so often. And surely there must be much good in one who is kind to an invalid, and leaves the pleasures of London to sit by a bed of pain. 340

JACK. Oh, he has been talking about Bunbury, has he?

CECILY. Yes, he has told me all about poor Mr. Bunbury, and his terrible state of health.

JACK. Bunbury! Well, I won't have him talk to you about Bunbury or about anything else. It is enough to drive one perfectly frantic.

ALGERNON. Of course I admit that the faults were all on my side. But I must say that I think that Brother John's coldness to me is peculiarly painful. I expected a more enthusiastic welcome, especially considering it is the first time I have come here. 350

CECILY. Uncle Jack, if you don't shake hands with Ernest I will never forgive you.

JACK. Never forgive me?

CECILY. Never, never, never!

JACK. Well, this is the last time I shall ever do it. [*Shakes hands with Algernon and glares.*]

CHASUBLE. It's pleasant, is it not, to see so perfect a reconciliation? I think we might leave the two brothers together.

MISS PRISM. Cecily, you will come with us.

CECILY. Certainly, Miss Prism. My little task of reconcili- 360 ation is over.

CHASUBLE. You have done a beautiful action to-day, dear child.

MISS PRISM. We must not be premature in our judgments.

CECILY. I feel very happy. [*They all go off.*]

JACK. You young scoundrel, Algy, you must get out of this place as soon as possible. I don't alow any Bunburying here. [*Enter Merriman.*]

MERRIMAN. I have put Mr. Ernest's things in the room next to yours, sir. I suppose that is all right?

JACK. What?

MERRIMAN. Mr. Ernest's luggage, sir. I have unpacked it 370 and put it in the room next to your own.

JACK. His luggage?

MERRIMAN. Yes, sir. Three portmanteaus, a dressing-case, two hat-boxes, and a large luncheon-basket.

ALGERNON. I am afraid I can't stay more than a week this time.

JACK. Merriman, order the dog-cart at once. Mr. Ernest has been suddenly called back to town.

MERRIMAN. Yes, sir. [*Goes back into the house.*]

ALGERNON. What a fearful liar you are, Jack. I have not 380 been called back to town at all.

JACK. Yes, you have.

ALGERNON. I haven't heard anyone call me.

JACK. Your duty as a gentleman calls you back.

ALGERNON. My duty as a gentleman has never interfered with my pleasures in the smallest degree.

JACK. I can quite understand that.

ALGERNON. Well, Cecily is a darling.

JACK. You are not to talk of Miss Cardew like that. I don't like it. 390

ALGERNON. Well, I don't like your clothes. You look perfectly ridiculous in them. Why on earth don't you go up and change? It is perfectly childish to be in deep mourning for a man who is actually staying for a whole week with you in your house as a guest. I call it grotesque.

JACK. You are certainly not staying with me for a whole week as a guest or anything else. You have got to leave . . . by the four-five train.

ALGERNON. I certainly won't leave you so long as you are in mourning. It would be most unfriendly. If I were in mourn- 400 ing you would stay with me, I suppose. I should think it very unkind if you didn't.

JACK. Well, will you go if I change my clothes?

ALGERNON. Yes, if you are not too long. I never saw anybody take so long to dress, and with such little result.

JACK. Well, at any rate, that is better than being always over-dressed as you are.

ALGERNON. If I am occasionally a little over-dressed, I make up for it by being always immensely over-educated.

JACK. Your vanity is ridiculous, your conduct an outrage, 410 and your presence in my garden utterly absurd. However, you have got to catch the four-five, and I hope you will have a pleasant journey back to town. This Bunburying, as you call it, has not been a great success for you. [*Goes into the house.*]

ALGERNON. I think it has been a great success. I'm in love with Cecily, and that is everything.

[*Enter Cecily at the back of the garden. She picks up the can and begins to water the flowers.*]

But I must see her before I go, and make arrangements for another Bunbury. Ah, there she is.

CECILY. Oh, I merely came back to water the roses. I 420 thought you were with Uncle Jack.

ALGERNON. He's gone to order the dog-cart for me.

CECILY. Oh, is he going to take you for a nice drive?

ALGERNON. He's going to send me away.

CECILY. Then have we got to part?

ALGERNON. I am afraid so. It's a very painful parting.

CECILY. It is always painful to part from people whom one has known for a very brief space of time. The absence of old friends one can endure with equanimity. But even a momentary separation from anyone to whom one has just been introduced is 430 almost unbearable.

ALGERNON. Thank you.

[*Enter Merriman.*

MERRIMAN. The dog-cart is at the door, sir. [*Algernon looks appealingly at Cecily.*]

CECILY. It can wait, Merriman . . . for : . . five minutes.

MERRIMAN. Yes, miss. [*Exit Merriman.*]

ALGERNON. I hope, Cecily, I shall not offend you if I state quite frankly and openly that you seem to me to be in every way the visible personification of absolute perfection.

CECILY. I think your frankness does you great credit, 440 Ernest. If you will allow me I will copy your remarks into my diary. [*Goes over to table and begins writing in diary.*]

ALGERNON. Do you really keep a diary? I'd give anything to look at it. May I?

CECILY. Oh, no. [*Puts her hand over it.*] You see, it is simply a very young girl's record of her own thoughts and impressions, and consequently meant for publication. When it appears in volume form I hope you will order a copy. But pray, Ernest, don't stop. I delight in taking down from dictation. I have reached "absolute perfection." You can go on. I am quite 450 ready for more.

ALGERNON [*Somewhat taken aback*]. Ahem! Ahem!

CECILY. Oh, don't cough, Ernest. When one is dictating one should speak fluently and not cough. Besides, I don't know how to spell a cough. [*Writes as Algernon speaks.*]

ALGERNON [*Speaking very rapidly*]. Cecily, ever since I first looked upon your wonderful and incomparable beauty, I have dared to love you wildly, passionately, devotedly, hopelessly.

CECILY. I don't think that you should tell me that you love me wildly, passionately, devotedly, hopelessly. Hopelessly doesn't 460 seem to make much sense, does it?

ALGERNON. Cecily!

[*Enter Merriman.*

MERRIMAN. The dog-cart is waiting, sir.

ALGERNON. Tell it to come round next week, at the same hour.

MERRIMAN [*Looks at Cecily, who makes no sign*]. Yes, sir. [*Merriman retires.*]

CECILY. Uncle Jack would be very much annoyed if he knew you were staying on till next week, at the same hour.

ALGERNON. Oh, I don't care about Jack. I don't care for anybody in the whole world but you. I love you, Cecily. You 470 will marry me, won't you?

CECILY. You silly you! Of course. Why, we have been engaged for the last three months.

ALGERNON. For the last three months?

CECILY. Yes, it will be exactly three months on Thursday.

ALGERNON. But how did we become engaged?

CECILY. Well, ever since dear Uncle Jack first confessed to us that he had a younger brother who was very wicked and bad, you of course have formed the chief topic of conversation between myself and Miss Prism. And of course a man who is 480 much talked about is always very attractive. One feels there must be something in him after all. I daresay it was foolish of me, but I fell in love with you, Ernest.

ALGERNON. Darling! And when was the engagement actually settled?

CECILY. On the 4th of February last. Worn out by your entire ignorance of my existence, I determined to end the matter one way or the other, and after a long struggle with myself I accepted you under this dear old tree here. The next day I bought this little ring in your name, and this is the little bangle 490 with the true lovers' knot I promised you always to wear.

ALGERNON. Did I give you this? It's very pretty, isn't it?

CECILY. Yes, you've wonderfully good taste, Ernest. It's the excuse I've always given for your leading such a bad life. And this is the box in which I keep all your dear letters. [Kneels at table, opens box, and produces letters tied up with blue ribbon.]

ALGERNON. My letters! But my own sweet Cecily, I have never written you any letters.

CECILY. You need hardly remind me of that, Ernest. I remember only too well that I was forced to write your letters for 500 you. I wrote always three times a week, and sometimes oftener.

ALGERNON. Oh, do let me read them, Cecily?

CECILY. Oh, I couldn't possibly. They would make you far too conceited. [Replaces box.] The three you wrote me after I had broken off the engagement are so beautiful, and so badly spelled, that even now I can hardly read them without crying a little.

ALGERNON. But was our engagement ever broken off?

CECILY. Of course it was. On the 22nd of last March. You can see the entry if you like. [Shows diary.] "To-day I broke off my engagement with Ernest. I feel it is better to do so. The 510 weather still continues charming."

ALGERNON. But why on earth did you break it off? What had I done? I had done nothing at all. Cecily, I am very much hurt indeed to hear you broke it off. Particularly when the weather was so charming.

CECILY. It would hardly have been a really serious engagement if it hadn't been broken off at least once. But I forgave you before the week was out.

ALGERNON [*Crossing to her, and kneeling*]. What a perfect angel you are, Cecily.   520

CECILY. You dear romantic boy. [*He kisses her, she puts her fingers through his hair.*] I hope your hair curls naturally, does it?

ALGERNON. Yes, darling, with a little help from others.

CECILY. I am so glad.

ALGERNON. You'll never break off our engagement again, Cecily?

CECILY. I don't think I could break it off now that I have actually met you. Besides, of course, there is the question of your name.

ALGERNON [*Nervously*]. Yes, of course.   530

CECILY. You must not laugh at me, darling, but it had always been a girlish dream of mine to love some one whose name was Ernest. [*Algernon rises, Cecily also.*] There is something in that name that seems to inspire absolute confidence. I pity any poor married woman whose husband is not called Ernest.

ALGERNON. But, my dear child, do you mean to say you could not love me if I had some other name?

CECILY. But what name?

ALGERNON. Oh, any name you like—Algernon, for instance. . . .

CECILY. But I don't like the name of Algernon.   540

ALGERNON. Well, my own dear, sweet, loving little darling, I really can't see why you should object to the name of Algernon. It is not at all a bad name. In fact, it is rather an aristocratic name. Half of the chaps who get into the Bankruptcy Court are called Algernon. But seriously, Cecily . . . [*Moving to her.*] . . . if my name was Algy, couldn't you love me?

CECILY [*Rising*]. I might respect you, Ernest, I might admire your character, but I fear that I should not be able to give you my undivided attention.

ALGERNON. Ahem! Cecily! [*Picking up hat.*] Your Rector   550 here is, I suppose, thoroughly experienced in the practice of all the rites and ceremonials of the church?

CECILY. Oh, yes. Dr. Chasuble is a most learned man. He has never written a single book, so you can imagine how much he knows.

ALGERNON. I must see him at once on a most important christening—I mean on most important business.

CECILY. Oh!

ALGERNON. I sha'n't be away more than half an hour.

CECILY. Considering that we have been engaged since Feb- 560
ruary the 14th, and that I only met you to-day for the first time, I
think it is rather hard that you should leave me for so long a
period as half an hour. Couldn't you make it twenty minutes?

ALGERNON. I'll be back in no time. [*Kisses her and rushes down
the garden.*]

CECILY. What an impetuous boy he is. I like his hair so much. I
must enter his proposal in my diary.

[*Enter Merriman.*

MERRIMAN. A Miss Fairfax has just called to see Mr. Worthing.
On very important business, Miss Fairfax states.

CECILY. Isn't Mr. Worthing in his library? 570

MERRIMAN. Mr. Worthing went over in the direction of the
Rectory some time ago.

CECILY. Pray ask the lady to come out here; Mr. Worthing is
sure to be back soon. And you can bring tea.

MERRIMAN. Yes, miss. [*Goes out.*]

CECILY. Miss Fairfax! I suppose one of the many good elderly
women who are associated with Uncle Jack in some of his philanthropic work in London. I don't quite like women who are
interested in philanthropic work. I think it is so forward of them.

[*Enter Merriman.*

MERRIMAN. Miss Fairfax. 580

[*Enter Gwendolen. Merriman goes out.*

CECILY [*Advancing to meet her*]. Pray let me introduce myself
to you. My name is Cecily Cardew.

GWENDOLEN. Cecily Cardew? [*Moving to her and shaking
hands.*] What a very sweet name! Something tells me that we are
going to be great friends. I like you already more than I can say.
My first impressions of people are never wrong.

CECILY. How nice of you to like me so much after we have
known each other such a comparatively short time. Pray sit down.

GWENDOLEN [*Still standing up*]. I may call you Cecily, may I
not? 590

CECILY. With pleasure!

GWENDOLEN. And you will always call me Gwendolen, won't
you?

CECILY. If you wish.

GWENDOLEN. Then that is all quite settled, is it not?

CECILY. I hope so. [*A pause. They both sit down together.*]

GWENDOLEN. Perhaps this might be a favorable opportunity for my mentioning who I am. My father is Lord Bracknell. You have never heard of papa, I suppose?

CECILY. I don't think so.   600

GWENDOLEN. Outside the family circle, papa, I am glad to say, is entirely unknown. I think that is quite as it should be. The home seems to me to be the proper sphere for the man. And certainly once a man begins to neglect his domestic duties he becomes painfully effeminate, does he not? And I don't like that. It makes men so very attractive. Cecily, mamma, whose views on education are remarkably strict, has brought me up to be extremely short-sighted; it is part of her system; so do you mind my looking at you through my glasses?

CECILY. Oh, not at all, Gwendolen. I am very fond of   610
being looked at.

GWENDOLEN [*After examining Cecily carefully through a lorgnette*]. You are here on a short visit, I suppose.

CECILY. Oh, no, I live here.

GWENDOLEN [*Severely*]. Really? Your mother, no doubt, or some female relative of advanced years, resides here also?

CECILY. Oh, no. I have no mother, nor, in fact, any relations.

GWENDOLEN. Indeed?

CECILY. My dear guardian, with the assistance of Miss Prism, has the arduous task of looking after me.   620

GWENDOLEN. Your guardian?

CECILY. Yes, I am Mr. Worthing's ward.

GWENDOLEN. Oh! It is strange he never mentioned to me that he had a ward. How secretive of him! He grows more interesting hourly. I am not sure, however, that the news inspires me with feelings of unmixed delight. [*Rising and going to her.*] I am very fond of you, Cecily; I have liked you ever since I met you. But I am bound to state that now that I know that you are Mr. Worthing's ward, I cannot help expressing a wish you were—well, just a little older than you seem to be—and not quite so   630
very alluring in appearance. In fact, if I may speak candidly—

CECILY. Pray do! I think that whenever one has anything unpleasant to say, one should always be quite candid.

GWENDOLEN. Well, to speak with perfect candour, Cecily, I wish that you were fully forty-two, and more than usually plain for your age. Ernest has a strong upright nature. He is the very soul of truth and honour. Disloyalty would be as impossible to him as deception. But even men of the noblest possible moral character are extremely susceptible to the influence of the physi-

cal charms of others. Modern, no less than Ancient History, 640
supplies us with many most painful examples of what I refer to.
If it were not so, indeed, History would be quite unreadable.

CECILY. I beg your pardon, Gwendolen, did you say Ernest?

GWENDOLEN. Yes.

CECILY. Oh, but it is not Mr. Ernest Worthing who is my
guardian. It is his brother—his elder brother.

GWENDOLEN [*Sitting down again*]. Ernest never mentioned to
me that he had a brother.

CECILY. I am sorry to say they have not been on good terms for
a long time. 650

GWENDOLEN. Ah! that accounts for it. And now that I think of
it I have never heard any man mention his brother. The subject
seems distasteful to most men. Cecily, you have lifted a load from
my mind. I was growing almost anxious. It would have been terrible if any cloud had come across a friendship like ours, would
it not? Of course you are quite, quite sure that it is not Mr.
Ernest Worthing who is your guardian?

CECILY. Quite sure. [*A pause.*] In fact, I am going to be his.

GWENDOLEN [*Enquiringly*]. I beg your pardon?

CECILY [*Rather shy and confidingly*]. Dearest Gwen- 660
dolen, there is no reason why I should make a secret of it to you.
Our little county newspaper is sure to chronicle the fact next
week. Mr. Ernest Worthing and I are engaged to be married.

GWENDOLEN [*Quite politely, rising.*] My darling Cecily, I think
there must be some slight error. Mr. Ernest Worthing is engaged
to me. The announcement will appear in the *Morning Post* on
Saturday at the latest.

CECILY [*Very politely, rising*]. I am afraid you must be under
some misconception. Ernest proposed to me exactly ten minutes
ago. [*Shows diary.*] 670

GWENDOLEN [*Examines diary through her lorgnette carefully*].
It is certainly very curious, for he asked me to be his wife yesterday afternoon at 5.30. If you would care to verify the incident,
pray do so. [*Produces diary of her own.*] I never travel without
my diary. One should always have something sensational to read
in the train. I am so sorry, dear Cecily, if it is any disappointment
to you, but I am afraid *I* have the prior claim.

CECILY. It would distress me more than I can tell you, dear
Gwendolen, if it caused you any mental or physical anguish, but
I feel bound to point out that since Ernest proposed to you 680
he clearly has changed his mind.

GWENDOLEN [*Meditatively*]. If the poor fellow has been entrapped into any foolish promise I shall consider it my duty to rescue him at once, and with a firm hand.

CECILY [*Thoughtfully and sadly*]. Whatever unfortunate entanglement my dear boy may have got into, I will never reproach him with it after we are married.

GWENDOLEN. Do you allude to me, Miss Cardew, as an entanglement? You are presumptuous. On an occasion of this kind it becomes more than a moral duty to speak one's mind. It becomes a pleasure.   690

CECILY. Do you suggest, Miss Fairfax, that I entrapped Ernest into an engagement? How dare you? This is no time for wearing the shallow mask of manners. When I see a spade I call it a spade.

GWENDOLEN [*Satirically*]. I am glad to say that I have never seen a spade. It is obvious that our social spheres have been widely different.

[*Enter Merriman, followed by the footman. He carries a salver, tablecloth, and plate-stand. Cecily is about to retort. The presence of the servants exercises a restraining influence, under which both girls chafe.*

MERRIMAN. Shall I lay tea here as usual, miss?

CECILY [*Sternly, in a calm voice*]. Yes, as usual. [*Merriman begins to clear and lay cloth. A long pause. Cecily and Gwendolen glare at each other.*]   700

GWENDOLEN. Are there many interesting walks in the vicinity, Miss Cardew?

CECILY. Oh, yes, a great many. From the top of one of the hills quite close one can see five counties.

GWENDOLEN. Five counties! I don't think I should like that. I hate crowds.

CECILY [*Sweetly*]. I suppose that is why you live in town? [*Gwendolen bites her lip, and beats her foot nervously with her parasol.*]   710

GWENDOLEN [*Looking round*]. Quite a well-kept garden this is, Miss Cardew.

CECILY. So glad you like it, Miss Fairfax.

GWENDOLEN. I had no idea there were any flowers in the country.

CECILY. Oh, flowers are as common here, Miss Fairfax, as people are in London.

GWENDOLEN. Personally I cannot understand how anybody manages to exist in the country, if anybody who is anybody does. The country always bores me to death.   720

CECILY. Ah! This is what the newspapers call agricultural depression, is it not? I believe the aristocracy are suffering very much from it just at present. It is almost an epidemic amongst them, I have been told. May I offer you some tea, Miss Fairfax?

GWENDOLEN [*With elaborate politeness*]. Thank you. [*Aside.*] Detestable girl! But I require tea!

CECILY [*Sweetly*]. Sugar?

GWENDOLEN [*Superciliously*]. No, thank you. Sugar is not fashionable any more. [*Cecily looks angrily at her, takes up the tongs and puts four lumps of sugar into the cup.*]   730

CECILY [*Severely*]. Cake or bread and butter?

GWENDOLEN [*In a bored manner*]. Bread and butter, please. Cake is rarely seen at the best houses nowadays.

CECILY [*Cuts a very large slice of cake, and puts it on the tray*]. Hand that to Miss Fairfax. [*Merriman does so, and goes out with footman. Gwendolen drinks the tea and makes a grimace. Puts down cup at once, reaches out her hand to the bread and butter, looks at it, and finds it is cake. Rises in indignation.*]

GWENDOLEN. You have filled my tea with lumps of sugar, and though I asked most distinctly for bread and butter, you have 740 given me cake. I am known for the gentleness of my disposition, and the extraordinary sweetness of my nature, but I warn you, Miss Cardew, you may go too far.

CECILY [*Rising*]. To save my poor, innocent, trusting boy from the machinations of any other girl there are no lengths to which would I not go.

GWENDOLEN. From the moment I saw you I distrusted you. I felt that you were false and deceitful. I am never deceived in such matters. My first impressions of people are invariably right.

CECILY. It seems to me, Miss Fairfax, that I am trespassing 750 on your valuable time. No doubt you have many other calls of a similar character to make in the neighbourhood.

[*Enter Jack.*

GWENDOLEN [*Catching sight of him*]. Ernest! My own Ernest!

JACK. Gwendolen! Darling! [*Offers to kiss her.*]

GWENDOLEN [*Drawing back*]. A moment! May I ask if you are engaged to be married to this young lady? [*Points to Cecily.*]

JACK [*Laughing*]. To dear little Cecily! Of course not! What could have put such an idea into your pretty little head?

GWENDOLEN. Thank you. You may. [*Offers her cheek.*]

CECILY [*Very sweetly*]. I knew there must be some misun- 760 derstanding, Miss Fairfax. The gentleman whose arm is at present around your waist is my dear guardian, Mr. John Worthing.

GWENDOLEN. I beg your pardon?

CECILY. This is Uncle Jack.

GWENDOLEN [*Receding*]. Jack! Oh!

[*Enter Algernon.*

CECILY. Here is Ernest.

ALGERNON [*Goes straight over to Cecily without noticing any-one else*]. My own love! [*Offers to kiss her.*]

CECILY [*Drawing back*]. A moment, Ernest! May I ask you—are you engaged to be married to this young lady?   770

ALGERNON [*Looking round*]. To what young lady? Good heavens! Gwendolen!

CECILY. Yes, to good heavens, Gwendolen, I mean to Gwendolen.

ALGERNON [*Laughing*]. Of course not! What could have put such an idea into your pretty little head?

CECILY. Thank you. [*Presenting her cheek to be kissed.*] You may. [*Algernon kisses her.*]

GWENDOLEN. I felt there was some slight error, Miss Cardew. The gentleman who is now embracing you is my cousin, Mr.   780 Algernon Moncrieff.

CECILY [*Breaking away from Algernon*]. Algernon Moncrieff! Oh! [*The two girls move towards each other and put their arms round each other's waists as if for protection.*]

CECILY. Are you called Algernon?

ALGERNON. I cannot deny it.

CECILY. Oh!

GWENDOLEN. Is your name really John?

JACK [*Standing rather proudly*]. I could deny it if I liked. I could deny anything if I liked. But my name certainly is   790 John. It has been John for years.

CECILY [*To Gwendolen*]. A gross deception has been practised on both of us.

GWENDOLEN. My poor wounded Cecily!

CECILY. My sweet, wronged Gwendolen!

GWENDOLEN [*Slowly and seriously*]. You will call me sister, will you not? [*They embrace. Jack and Algernon groan and walk up and down.*]

CECILY [*Rather brightly*]. There is just one question I would like to be allowed to ask my guardian.   800

GWENDOLEN. An admirable idea! Mr. Worthing, there is just one question I would like to be permitted to put to you. Where is your brother Ernest? We are both engaged to be married to your brother Ernest, so it is a matter of some importance to us to know where your brother Ernest is at present.

JACK [*Slowly and hesitatingly*]. Gwendolen—Cecily—it is very painful for me to be forced to speak the truth. It is the first time in my life that I have ever been reduced to such a painful position, and I am really quite inexperienced in doing anything of the kind. However I will tell you quite frankly that I have no 810 brother Ernest. I have no brother at all. I never had a brother in my life, and I certainly have not the smallest intention of ever having one in the future.

CECILY [*Surprised*]. No brother at all?

JACK [*Cheerily*]. None!

GWENDOLEN [*Severely*]. Had you never a brother of any kind?

JACK [*Pleasantly*]. Never. Not even of any kind.

GWENDOLEN. I am afraid it is quite clear, Cecily, that neither of us is engaged to be married to anyone.

CECILY. It is not a very pleasant position for a young girl 820 suddenly to find herself in. Is it?

GWENDOLEN. Let us go into the house. They will hardly venture to come after us there.

CECILY. No, men are so cowardly, aren't they? [*They retire into the house with scornful looks.*]

JACK. This ghastly state of things is what you call Bunburying, I suppose?

ALGERNON. Yes, and a perfectly wonderful Bunbury it is. The most wonderful Bunbury I have ever had in my life.

JACK. Well, you've no right whatsoever to Bunbury here. 830

ALGERNON. That is absurd. One has a right to Bunbury anywhere one chooses. Every serious Bunburyist knows that.

JACK. Serious Bunburyist! Good heavens!

ALGERNON. Well, one must be serious about something, if one wants to have any amusement in life. I happen to be serious about Bunburying. What on earth you are serious about I haven't got the remotest idea. About everything, I should fancy. You have such an absolutely trivial nature.

JACK. Well, the only small satisfaction I have in the whole of this wretched business is that your friend Bunbury is quite 840 exploded. You won't be able to run down to the country quite so often as you used to do, dear Algy. And a very good thing, too.

ALGERNON. Your brother is a little off colour, isn't he, dear Jack? You won't be able to disappear to London quite so frequently as your wicked custom was. And not a bad thing, either.

JACK. As for your conduct towards Miss Cardew, I must say that your taking in a sweet, simple, innocent girl like that is quite inexcusable. To say nothing of the fact that she is my ward.

ALGERNON. I can see no possible defence at all for your deceiving a brilliant, clever, thoroughly experienced young lady 850 like Miss Fairfax. To say nothing of the fact that she is my cousin.

JACK. I wanted to be engaged to Gwendolen, that is all. I love her.

ALGERNON. Well, I simply wanted to be engaged to Cecily. I adore her.

JACK. There is certainly no chance of your marrying Miss Cardew.

ALGERNON. I don't think there is much likelihood, Jack, of you and Miss Fairfax being united.

JACK. Well, that is no business of yours. 860

ALGERNON. If it was my business, I wouldn't talk about it. [Begins to eat muffins.] It is very vulgar to talk about one's business. Only people like stock-brokers do that, and then merely at dinner parties.

JACK. How you can sit there, calmly eating muffins, when we are in this horrible trouble, I can't make out. You seem to me to be perfectly heartless.

ALGERNON. Well, I can't eat muffins in an agitated manner. The butter would probably get on my cuffs. One should always eat muffins quite calmly. It is the only way to eat them. 870

JACK. I say it's perfectly heartless your eating muffins at all, under the circumstances.

ALGERNON. When I am in trouble, eating is the only thing that consoles me. Indeed, when I am in really great trouble, as anyone who knows me intimately will tell you, I refuse everything except food and drink. At the present moment I am eating muffins because I am unhappy. Besides, I am particularly fond of muffins. [Rising.]

JACK [Rising]. Well, that is no reason why you should eat them all in that greedy way. [Takes muffins from Algernon.] 880

ALGERNON [Offering tea-cake]. I wish you would have tea-cake instead. I don't like tea-cake.

JACK. Good heavens! I suppose a man may eat his own muffins in his own garden.

ALGERNON. But you have just said it was perfectly heartless to eat muffins.

JACK. I said it was perfectly heartless of you, under the circumstances. That is a very different thing.

ALGERNON. That may be. But the muffins are the same. [He seizes the muffin-dish from Jack.] 890

JACK. Algy, I wish to goodness you would go.

ALGERNON. You can't possibly ask me to go without having some dinner. It's absurd. I never go without my dinner. No one ever does, except vegetarians and people like that. Besides I have just made arrangements with Dr. Chasuble to be christened at a quarter to six under the name of Ernest.

JACK. My dear fellow, the sooner you give up that nonsense the better. I made arrangements this morning with Dr. Chasuble to be christened myself at 5.30, and I naturally will take the name of Ernest. Gwendolen would wish it. We can't both be chris- 900 tened Ernest. It's absurd. Besides, I have a perfect right to be christened if I like. There is no evidence at all that I ever have been christened by anybody. I should think it extremely probable I never was, and so does Dr. Chasuble. It is entirely different in your case. You have been christened already.

ALGERNON. Yes, but I have not been christened for years.

JACK. Yes, but you have been christened. That is the important thing.

ALGERNON. Quite so. So I know my constitution can stand it. If you are not quite sure about your ever having been christened, 910 I must say I think it rather dangerous your venturing on it now. It might make you very unwell. You can hardly have forgotten that someone very closely connected with you was very nearly carried off this week in Paris by a severe chill.

JACK. Yes, but you said yourself that a severe chill was not hereditary.

ALGERNON. It usedn't to be, I know—but I daresay it is now. Science is always making wonderful improvements in things.

JACK [*Picking up the muffin-dish*]. Oh, that is nonsense; you are always talking nonsense. 920

ALGERNON. Jack, you are at the muffins again! I wish you wouldn't. There are only two left. [*Takes them.*] I told you I was particularly fond of muffins.

JACK. But I hate tea-cake.

ALGERNON. Why on earth then do you allow tea-cake to be served up for your guests? What ideas you have of hospitality!

JACK. Algernon! I have already told you to go. I don't want you here. Why don't you go?

ALGERNON. I haven't quite finished my tea yet, and there is still one muffin left. [*Jack groans, and sinks into a chair.* 930 *Algernon still continues eating, as the curtain falls.*]

ACT III

SCENE.—*Morning-room at the Manor House shortly after the preceding scene. Gwendolen and Cecily are at the window, looking out into the garden.*

GWENDOLEN. The fact that they did not follow us at once into the house, as anyone else would have done, seems to me to show that they have some sense of shame left.

CECILY. They have been eating muffins. That looks like repentance.

GWENDOLEN [*After a pause*]. They don't seem to notice us at all. Couldn't you cough?

GWENDOLEN. They're looking at us. What effrontery!

CECILY. They're approaching. That's very forward of them.

GWENDOLEN. Let us preserve a dignified silence.   10

CECILY. Certainly. It's the only thing to do now.

[*Enter Jack, followed by Algernon. They whistle some dreadful popular air from a British opera.*

GWENDOLEN. This dignified silence seems to produce an unpleasant effect.

CECILY. A most distasteful one.

GWENDOLEN. But we will not be the first to speak.

CECILY. Certainly not.

GWENDOLEN. Mr. Worthing, I have something very particular to ask you. Much depends on your reply.

CECILY. Gwendolen, your common sense is invaluable. Mr. Moncrieff, kindly answer me the following question. Why   20 did you pretend to be my guardian's brother?

ALGERNON. In order that I might have an opportunity of meeting you.

CECILY [*To Gwendolen*]. That certainly seems a satisfactory explanation, does it not?

GWENDOLEN. Yes, dear, if you can believe him.

CECILY. I don't. But that does not affect the wonderful beauty of his answer.

GWENDOLEN. True. In matters of grave importance, style, not sincerity, is the vital thing. Mr. Worthing, what explanation   30 can you offer to me for pretending to have a brother? Was it in order that you might have an opportunity of coming up to town to see me as often as possible?

JACK. Can you doubt it, Miss Fairfax?

GWENDOLEN. I have the gravest doubts upon the subject. But I intend to crush them. This is not the moment for German scepticism. [*Moving to Cecily.*] Their explanations appear to be quite satisfactory, especially Mr. Worthing's. That seems to me to have the stamp of truth upon it.

CECILY. I am more than content with what Mr. Moncrieff 40 said. His voice alone inspires one with absolute credulity.

GWENDOLEN. Then you think we should forgive them?

CECILY. Yes. I mean no.

GWENDOLEN. True! I had forgotten. There are principles at stake that one cannot surrender. Which of us should tell them? The task is not a pleasant one.

CECILY. Could we not both speak at the same time?

GWENDOLEN. An excellent idea! I nearly always speak at the same time as other people. Will you take the time from me?

CECILY. Certainly. [*Gwendolen beats time with uplifted* 50 *finger.*]

GWENDOLEN AND CECILY [*Speaking together*]. Your Christian names are still an insuperable barrier. That is all!

JACK AND ALGERNON [*Speaking together*]. Our Christian names! Is that all? But we are going to be christened this afternoon.

GWENDOLEN [*To Jack*]. For my sake you are prepared to do this terrible thing?

JACK. I am.

CECILY [*To Algernon*]. To please me you are ready to face this fearful ordeal? 60

ALGERNON. I am!

GWENDOLEN. How absurd to talk of the equality of the sexes! Where questions of self-sacrifice are concerned, men are infinitely beyond us.

JACK. We are. [*Clasps hands with Algernon.*]

CECILY. They have moments of physical courage of which we women know absolutely nothing.

GWENDOLEN [*To Jack*]. Darling!

ALGERNON [*To Cecily*]. Darling! [*They fall into each other's arms. Enter Merriman. He coughs loudly, seeing the situation.*

MERRIMAN. Ahem! Ahem! Lady Bracknell! 70

JACK. Good heavens!

[*Enter Lady Bracknell. The couples separate in alarm. Exit Merriman.*

LADY BRACKNELL. Gwendolen! What does this mean?

GWENDOLEN. Merely that I am engaged to be married to Mr. Worthing, Mamma.

LADY BRACKNELL. Come here. Sit down. Sit down immediately. Hesitation of any kind is a sign of mental decay in the young, of physical weakness in the old. [*Turns to Jack.*] Apprised, sir, of my daughter's sudden flight by her trusty maid, whose confidence I purchased by means of a small coin, I followed her 80 at once by a luggage train. Her unhappy father is, I am glad to say, under the impression that she is attending a more than usually lengthy lecture by the University Extension Scheme on the Influence of a Permanent Income on Thought. I do not propose to undeceive him. Indeed I have never undeceived him on any question. I would consider it wrong. But of course, you will clearly understand that all communication between yourself and my daughter must cease immediately from this moment. On this point, as indeed on all points, I am firm.

JACK. I am engaged to be married to Gwendolen, Lady 90 Bracknell!

LADY BRACKNELL. You are nothing of the kind, sir. And now, as regards Algernon! . . . Algernon!

ALGERNON. Yes, Aunt Augusta.

LADY BRACKNELL. May I ask if it is in this house that your invalid friend Mr. Bunbury resides?

ALGERNON [*Stammering*]. Oh, no! Bunbury doesn't live here. Bunbury is somewhere else at present. In fact, Bunbury is dead.

LADY BRACKNELL. Dead! When did Mr. Bunbury die? His death must have been extremely sudden. 100

ALGERNON [*Airily*]. Oh, I killed Bunbury this afternoon. I mean poor Bunbury died this afternoon.

LADY BRACKNELL. What did he die of?

ALGERNON. Bunbury? Oh, he was quite exploded.

LADY BRACKNELL. Exploded! Was he the victim of a revolutionary outrage? I was not aware that Mr. Bunbury was interested in social legislation. If so, he is well punished for his morbidity.

ALGERNON. My dear Aunt Augusta, I mean he was found out! The doctors found out that Bunbury could not live, that is 110 what I mean—so Bunbury died.

LADY BRACKNELL. He seems to have had great confidence in the opinion of his physicians. I am glad, however, that he made up his mind at the last to some definite course of action, and acted under proper medical advice. And now that we have finally got rid of this Mr. Bunbury, may I ask, Mr. Worthing, who is that young person whose hand my nephew Algernon is now holding in what seems to me a peculiarly unnecessary manner?

JACK. That lady is Miss Cecily Cardew, my ward. [*Lady Bracknell bows coldly to Cecily.*] 　　　　　　　　　　　　　　120

ALGERNON. I am engaged to be married to Cecily, Aunt Augusta.

LADY BRACKNELL. I beg your pardon?

CECILY. Mr. Moncrieff and I are engaged to be married, Lady
Bracknell.

LADY BRACKNELL [*With a shiver, crossing to the sofa and sitting
down*]. I do not know whether there is anything peculiarly exciting in the air of this particular part of Hertfordshire, but the
number of engagements that go on seems to me considerably
above the proper average that statistics have laid down for our
guidance. I think some preliminary enquiry on my part 　　130
would not be out of place. Mr. Worthing, is Miss Cardew at all
connected with any of the larger railway stations in London? I
merely desire information. Until yesterday I had no idea that
there were any families or persons whose origin was a Terminus.
[*Jack looks perfectly furious, but restrains himself.*]

JACK [*In a clear, cold voice*]. Miss Cardew is the granddaugh-
ter of the late Mr. Thomas Cardew of 149, Belgrave Square, S.W.;
Gervase Park, Dorking, Surrey; and the Sporran, Fifeshire, N.B.

LADY BRACKNELL. That sounds not unsatisfactory. Three addresses always inspire confidence, even in tradesmen. But 　　140
what proof have I of their authenticity?

JACK. I have carefully preserved the Court Guide of the period.
They are open to your inspection, Lady Bracknell.

LADY BRACKNELL [*Grimly*]. I have known strange errors in that
publication.

JACK. Miss Cardew's family solicitors are Messrs. Markby,
Markby, and Markby.

LADY BRACKNELL. Markby, Markby, and Markby? A firm of
the very highest position in their profession. Indeed I am told that
one of the Mr. Markbys is occasionally to be seen at dinner 　　150
parties. So far I am satisfied.

JACK [*Very irritably*]. How extremely kind of you, Lady
Bracknell! I have also in my possession, you will be pleased to
hear, certificates of Miss Cardew's birth, baptism, whooping
cough, registration, vaccination, confirmation, and the measles;
both the German and the English variety.

LADY BRACKNELL. Ah! A life crowded with incident, I see;
though perhaps somewhat too exciting for a young girl. I am
not myself in favour of premature experiences. [*Rises, looks at
her watch.*] Gwendolen! the time approaches for our de- 　　160
parture. We have not a moment to lose. As a matter of form, Mr.

Worthing, I had better ask you if Miss Cardew has any little fortune?

JACK. Oh, about a hundred and thirty thousand pounds in the Funds. That is all. Good-bye, Lady Bracknell. So pleased to have seen you.

LADY BRACKNELL [*Sitting down again*]. A moment, Mr. Worthing. A hundred and thirty thousand pounds! And in the Funds! Miss Cardew seems to me a most attractive young lady, now that I look at her. Few girls of the present day have any really   170 solid qualities, any of the qualities that last, and improve with time. We live, I regret to say, in an age of surfaces. [*To Cecily.*] Come over here, dear. [*Cecily goes across.*] Pretty child! your dress is sadly simple, and your hair seems almost as Nature might have left it. But we can soon alter all that. A thoroughly experienced French maid produces a really marvellous result in a very brief space of time. I remember recommending one to young Lady Lancing, and after three months her own husband did not know her.

JACK [*Aside*]. And after six months nobody knew her.   180

LADY BRACKNELL [*Glares at Jack for a few moments. Then bends, with a practised smile, to Cecily*]. Kindly turn round, sweet child. [*Cicely turns completely round.*] No, the side view is what I want. [*Cecily presents her profile.*] Yes, quite as I expected. There are distinct social possibilities in your profile. The two weak points in our age are its want of principle and its want of profile. The chin a little higher, dear. Style largely depends on the way the chin is worn. They are worn very high, just at present. Algernon!

ALGERNON. Yes, Aunt Augusta!   190

LADY BRACKNELL. There are distinct social possibilities in Miss Cardew's profile.

ALGERNON. Cecily is the sweetest, dearest, prettiest girl in the whole world. And I don't care twopence about social possibilities.

LADY BRACKNELL. Never speak disrespectfully of society, Algernon. Only people who can't get into it do that. [*To Cecily.*] Dear child, of course you know that Algernon has nothing but his debts to depend upon. But I do not approve of mercenary marriages. When I married Lord Bracknell I had no fortune of any kind. But I never dreamed for a moment of allowing   200 that to stand in my way. Well, I suppose I must give my consent.

ALGERNON. Thank you, Aunt Augusta.

LADY BRACKNELL. Cecily, you may kiss me!

CECILY [*Kisses her*]. Thank you, Lady Bracknell.

LADY BRACKNELL. You may also address me as Aunt Augusta for the future.

CECILY. Thank you, Aunt Augusta.

LADY BRACKNELL. The marriage, I think, had better take place quite soon.

ALGERNON. Thank you, Aunt Augusta. 210

CECILY. Thank you, Aunt Augusta.

LADY BRACKNELL. To speak frankly, I am not in favour of long engagements. They give people the opportunity of finding out each other's character before marriage, which I think is never advisable.

JACK. I beg your pardon for interrupting you, Lady Bracknell, but this engagement is quite out of the question. I am Miss Cardew's guardian, and she cannot marry without my consent until she comes of age. That consent I absolutely decline to give.

LADY BRACKNELL. Upon what grounds, may I ask? Alger- 220 non is an extremely, I may almost say an ostentatiously, eligible young man. He has nothing, but he looks everything. What more can one desire?

JACK. It pains me very much to have to speak frankly to you, Lady Bracknell, about your nephew, but the fact is that I do not approve at all of his moral character. I suspect him of being untruthful. [*Algernon and Cecily look at him in indignant amazement.*]

LADY BRACKNELL. Untruthful! My nephew Algernon? Impossible! He is an Oxonian. 230

JACK. I fear there can be no possible doubt about the matter. This afternoon, during my temporary absence in London on an important question of romance, he obtained admission to my house by means of the false pretence of being my brother. Under an assumed name he drank, I've just been informed by my butler, an entire pint bottle of my Perrier-Jouet, Brut, '89; a wine I was specially reserving for myself. Continuing his disgraceful deception, he succeeded in the course of the afternoon in alienating the affections of my only ward. He subsequently stayed to tea, and devoured every single muffin. And what makes his conduct all the more heartless is, that he was perfectly well aware from 240 the first that I have no brother, that I never had a brother, and that I don't intend to have a brother, not even of any kind. I distinctly told him so myself yesterday afternoon.

LADY BRACKNELL. Ahem! Mr. Worthing, after careful consideration I have decided entirely to overlook my nephew's conduct to you.

JACK. That is very generous of you, Lady Bracknell. My own decision, however, is unalterable. I decline to give my consent.

LADY BRACKNELL [To Cecily]. Come here, sweet child. [Cecily goes over.] How old are you, dear? 250

CECILY. Well, I am really only eighteen, but I always admit to twenty when I go to evening parties.

LADY BRACKNELL. You are perfectly right in making some slight alteration. Indeed, no woman should ever be quite accurate about her age. It looks so calculating. . . . [In meditative manner.] Eighteen, but admitting to twenty at evening parties. Well, it will not be very long before you are of age and free from the restraints of tutelage. So I don't think your guardian's consent is, after all, a matter of any importance.

JACK. Pray excuse me, Lady Bracknell, for interrupting 260 you again, but it is only fair to tell you that according to the terms of her grandfather's will Miss Cardew does not come legally of age till she is thirty-five.

LADY BRACKNELL. That does not seem to me to be a grave objection. Thirty-five is a very attractive age. London society is full of women of the very highest birth who have, of their own free choice, remained thirty-five for years. Lady Dumbleton is an instance in point. To my own knowledge she has been thirty-five ever since she arrived at the age of forty, which was many years ago now. I see no reason why our dear Cecily should not be 270 even still more attractive at the age you mention than she is at present. There will be a large accumulation of property.

CECILY. Algy, could you wait for me till I was thirty-five?

ALGERNON. Of course I could, Cecily. You know I could.

CECILY. Yes, I felt it instinctively, but I couldn't wait all that time. I hate waiting even five minutes for anybody. It always makes me rather cross. I am not punctual myself, I know, but I do like punctuality in others, and waiting, even to be married, is quite out of the question.

ALGERNON. Then what is to be done, Cecily? 280

CECILY. I don't know, Mr. Moncrieff.

LADY BRACKNELL. My dear Mr. Worthing, as Miss Cardew states positively that she cannot wait till she is thirty-five—a remark which I am bound to say seems to me to show a somewhat impatient nature—I would beg of you to reconsider your decision.

JACK. But my dear Lady Bracknell, the matter is entirely in your own hands. The moment you consent to my marriage with Gwendolen, I will most gladly allow your nephew to form an alliance with my ward.

LADY BRACKNELL [*Rising and drawing herself up*]. You 290 must be quite aware that what you propose is out of the question.

JACK. Then a passionate celibacy is all that any of us can look forward to.

LADY BRACKNELL. That is not the destiny I propose for Gwendolen. Algernon, of course, can choose for himself. [*Pulls out her watch.*] Come, dear, [*Gwendolen rises*] we have already missed five, if not six, trains. To miss any more might expose us to comment on the platform.

[*Enter Dr. Chasuble.*]

CHASUBLE. Everything is quite ready for the christenings.

LADY BRACKNELL. The christenings, sir! Is not that some- 300 what premature?

CHASUBLE [*Looking rather puzzled, and pointing to Jack and Algernon*]. Both these gentlemen have expressed a desire for immediate baptism.

LADY BRACKNELL. At their age? The idea is grotesque and irreligious! Algernon, I forbid you to be baptised. I will not hear of such excesses. Lord Bracknell would be highly displeased if he learned that that was the way in which you wasted your time and money.

CHASUBLE. Am I to understand then that there are to be no 310 christenings at all this afternoon?

JACK. I don't think that, as things are now, it would be of much practical value to either of us, Dr. Chasuble.

CHASUBLE. I am grieved to hear such sentiments from you, Mr. Worthing. They savour of the heretical views of the Anabaptists, views that I have completely refuted in four of my unpublished sermons. However, as your present mood seems to be one peculiarly secular, I will return to the church at once. Indeed, I have just been informed by the pew-opener that for the last hour and a half Miss Prism has been waiting for me in the vestry. 320

LADY BRACKNELL [*Starting*]. Miss Prism! Did I hear you mention a Miss Prism?

CHASUBLE. Yes, Lady Bracknell. I am on my way to join her.

LADY BRACKNELL. Pray allow me to detain you for a moment. This matter may prove to be one of vital importance to Lord Bracknell and myself. Is this Miss Prism a female of repellent aspect, remotely connected with education?

CHASUBLE [*Somewhat indignantly*]. She is the most cultivated of ladies, and the very picture of respectability.

LADY BRACKNELL. It is obviously the same person. May I 330 ask what position she holds in your household?

CHASUBLE [*Severely*]. I am a celibate, madam.

JACK [*Interposing*]. Miss Prism, Lady Bracknell, has been for the last three years Miss Cardew's esteemed governess and valued companion.

LADY BRACKNELL. In spite of what I hear of her, I must see her at once. Let her be sent for.

CHASUBLE [*Looking off*]. She approaches; she is nigh.

[*Enter Miss Prism hurriedly.*

MISS PRISM. I was told you expected me in the vestry, dear Canon. I have been waiting for you there for an hour and three-quarters. [*Catches sight of Lady Bracknell, who has fixed her with a stony glare. Miss Prism grows pale and quails. She looks anxiously round as if desirous to escape.*]

LADY BRACKNELL [*In a severe, judicial voice*]. Prism! [*Miss Prism bows her head in shame.*] Come here, Prism! [*Miss Prism approaches in a humble manner.*] Prism! Where is that baby? [*General consternation. The Canon starts back in horror. Algernon and Jack pretend to be anxious to shield Cecily and Gwendolen from hearing the details of a terrible public scandal.*] Twent-eight years ago, Prism, you left Lord Bracknell's house, Number 104, Upper Grosvenor Street, in charge of a perambulator that contained a baby, of the male sex. You never returned. A few weeks later, through the elaborate investigations of the Metropolitan police, the perambulator was discovered at midnight, standing by itself in a remote corner of Bayswater. It contained the manuscript of a three-volume novel of more than usually revolting sentimentality. [*Miss Prism starts in involuntary indignation.*] But the baby was not there! [*Everyone looks at Miss Prism.*] Prism, where is that baby? [*A pause.*]

MISS PRISM. Lady Bracknell, I admit with shame that I do not know. I only wish I did. The plain facts of the case are these. On the morning of the day you mention, a day that is forever branded on my memory, I prepared as usual to take the baby out in its perambulator. I had also with me a somewhat old but capacious hand-bag in which I had intended to place the manuscript of a work of fiction that I had written during my few unoccupied hours. In a moment of mental abstraction, for which I never can forgive myself, I deposited the manuscript in the bassinette, and placed the baby in the hand-bag.

JACK [*Who has been listening attentively*]. But where did you deposit the hand-bag?

MISS PRISM. Do not ask me, Mr. Worthing.

JACK. Miss Prism, this is a matter of no small importance to me.

I insist on knowing where you deposited the hand-bag that contained that infant.

MISS PRISM. I left it in the cloak-room of one of the larger railway stations in London.

JACK. What railway station?

MISS PRISM [*Quite crushed*]. Victoria. The Brighton line. [*Sinks into a chair.*] 380

JACK. I must retire to my room for a moment. Gwendolen, wait here for me.

GWENDOLEN. If you are not too long, I will wait here for you all my life. [*Exit Jack in great excitement.*]

CHASUBLE. What do you think this means, Lady Bracknell?

LADY BRACKNELL. I dare not even suspect, Dr. Chasuble. I need hardly tell you that in families of high position strange coincidences are not supposed to occur. They are hardly considered the thing. [*Noises heard overhead as if someone was throwing trunks about. Everybody looks up.*] 390

CECILY. Uncle Jack seems strangely agitated.

CHASUBLE. Your guardian has a very emotional nature.

LADY BRACKNELL. This noise is extremely unpleasant. It sounds as if he was having an argument. I dislike arguments of any kind. They are always vulgar, and often convincing.

CHASUBLE [*Looking up*]. It has stopped now. [*The noise is redoubled.*]

LADY BRACKNELL. I wish he would arrive at some conclusion.

GWENDOLEN. This suspense is terrible. I hope it will last.

[*Enter Jack with a hand-bag of black leather in his hand.*]

JACK [*Rushing over to Miss Prism*]. Is this the hand-bag, 400 Miss Prism? Examine it carefully before you speak. The happiness of more than one life depends on your answer.

MISS PRISM [*Calmly*]. It seems to be mine. Yes, here is the injury it received through the upsetting of a Gower Street omnibus in younger and happier days. Here is the stain on the lining caused by the explosion of a temperance beverage, an incident that occurred at Leamington. And here, on the lock, are my initials. I had forgotten that in an extravagant mood I had had them placed there. The bag is undoubtedly mine. I am delighted to have it so unexpectedly restored to me. It has been a great in- 410 convenience being without it all these years.

JACK [*In a pathetic voice*]. Miss Prism, more is restored to you than this hand-bag. I was the baby you placed in it.

MISS PRISM [*Amazed*]. You?

JACK [*Embracing her*]. Yes . . . mother!

MISS PRISM [*Recoiling in indignant astonishment*]. Mr. Worthing! I am unmarried!

JACK. Unmarried! I do not deny that is a serious blow. But after all, who has the right to cast a stone against one who has suffered? Cannot repentance wipe out an act of folly? Why should there be one law for men and another for women? Mother, I forgive you. [*Tries to embrace her again.*]

MISS PRISM [*Still more indignant*]. Mr. Worthing, there is some error. [*Pointing to Lady Bracknell.*] There is the lady who can tell you who you really are.

JACK [*After a pause*]. Lady Bracknell, I hate to seem inquisitive, but would you kindly inform me who I am?

LADY BRACKNELL. I am afraid that the news I have to give you will not altogether please you. You are the son of my poor sister, Mrs. Moncrieff, and consequently Algernon's elder brother.

JACK. Algy's elder brother! Then I have a brother after all. I knew I had a brother! I always said I had a brother! Cecily,—how could you have ever doubted that I had a brother? [*Seizes hold of Algernon.*] Dr. Chasuble, my unfortunate brother. Miss Prism, my unfortunate brother. Gwendolen, my unfortunate brother. Algy, you young scoundrel, you will have to treat me with more respect in the future. You have never behaved to me like a brother in all your life.

ALGERNON. Well, not till to-day, old boy, I admit. I did my best, however, though I was out of practice. [*Shakes hands.*]

GWENDOLEN [*To Jack*]. My own! But what own are you? What is your Christian name, now that you have become someone else?

JACK. Good heavens! . . . I had quite forgotten that point. Your decision on the subject of my name is irrevocable, I suppose?

GWENDOLEN. I never change, except in my affections.

CECILY. What a noble nature you have, Gwendolen!

JACK. Then the question had better be cleared up at once. Aunt Augusta, a moment. At the time when Miss Prism left me in the hand-bag, had I been christened already?

LADY BRACKNELL. Every luxury that money could buy, including christening, had been lavished on you by your fond and doting parents.

JACK. Then I was christened! That is settled. Now, what name was I given? Let me know the worst.

LADY BRACKNELL. Being the eldest son you were naturally christened after your father.

JACK [*Irritably*]. Yes, but what was my father's Christian name?

LADY BRACKNELL [*Meditatively*]. I cannot at the present moment recall what the General's Christian name was. But I have no doubt he had one. He was eccentric, I admit. But only in later years. And that was the result of the Indian climate, and marriage, and indigestion, and other things of that kind. 460

JACK. Algy! Can't you recollect what our father's Christian name was?

ALGERNON. My dear boy, we were never even on speaking terms. He died before I was a year old.

JACK. His name would appear in the Army Lists of the period, I suppose, Aunt Augusta?

LADY BRACKNELL. The General was essentially a man of peace, except in his domestic life. But I have no doubt his name would appear in any military directory. 470

JACK. The Army Lists of the last forty years are here. These delightful records should have been my constant study. [*Rushes to bookcase and tears the books out.*] M. Generals . . . Mallam, Maxbohm, Magley, what ghastly names they have—Markby, Migsby, Mobbs, Moncrieff! Lieutenant 1840, Captain, Lieutenant-Colonel, Colonel, General 1869, Christian names, Ernest John. [*Puts book very quietly down and speaks quite calmly.*] I always told you, Gwendolen, my name was Ernest, didn't I? Well, it is Ernest after all. I mean it naturally is Ernest. 480

LADY BRACKNELL. Yes, I remember that the General was called Ernest. I knew I had some particular reason for disliking the name.

GWENDOLEN. Ernest! My own Ernest! I felt from the first that you could have no other name!

JACK. Gwendolen, it is a terrible thing for a man to find out suddenly that all his life he has been speaking nothing but the truth. Can you forgive me?

GWENDOLEN. I can. For I feel that you are sure to change.

JACK. My own one!

CHASUBLE [*To Miss Prism*]. Lætitia! [*Embraces her.*] 490

MISS PRISM [*Enthusiastically*]. Frederick! At last!

ALGERNON. Cecily! [*Embraces her.*] At last!

JACK. Gwendolen! [*Embraces her.*] At last!

LADY BRACKNELL. My nephew, you seem to be displaying signs of triviality.

JACK. On the contrary, Aunt Augusta, I've now realized for the first time in my life the vital Importance of Being Earnest.

[*The lovers stand in affectionate groups with Lady Bracknell looking disapprovingly on, as the Curtain falls.*

REALISTIC TRAGEDY

THE TERM REALISTIC may be defined in almost as many ways as romantic, but in the drama it may be taken to mean a type which draws on the present, presents people of our own time. It is more than subject matter which is involved, however; the method of treatment is important, too. Realistic tragedy adopts the "scientific" (as opposed to the "imaginative" or "fanciful") point of view. Life in it is viewed coldly, sometimes dispassionately, without any rich colorings to heighten effects and to produce an illusion of unreality in either scene or character. The stress is rather on the recreation of a scene which the audience will feel is an integral part of its own experience, and of characters who will seem to be such as we might meet in the run of any ordinary day's experiences.

Such drama is likely to be the product of an age of growing social consciousness. Such an age is often intolerant of the romantic point of view, mistakenly labelling it "escapist" or at least impractical and hence useless for artistic purposes. It attributes the existence of sordidness to maladjustments in society and often, though certainly not always, tries to use the drama as an instrument for social change. As a result, one of the besetting dangers of realistic drama is that it falls so deeply into didacticism that the true dramatic spirit is lost. A romantic play like *The Merchant of Venice* may have much to say incidentally as to the nature of justice. It may even have a great speech in which a distinction is made between mercy and the meticulous weighing of justice in the scales of the law. But no one who reads the play attentively or sees it well acted would say that it exists to point out the inadequacies of the law. On the other hand, a play like Galsworthy's *Justice*, a realistic tragedy, is concerned with the very real problem of the workings of justice in the various levels of society: the ease with which wealth can escape the consequences of its crimes while poverty is punished with what may often be undue severity.

The tendency to preach is in a sense a reversion to the older types of moral play, with characters no longer flesh and blood but only abstractions, now representing not the twelve cardinal virtues and the seven deadly sins, but social forces in conflict. It is to be seen most vividly in the so-called proletarian drama in our time, where drama becomes class conscious and is devoted to the purposes of propaganda. So too in the totalitarian states the stage comes to be a medium for the propagation of "right" doctrine, though then it is often highly romantic or sentimental. In this country we see the tendency to preach in such plays as George Sklar and Paul Peter's *Stevedore* and in John Wexley's *The Last Mile*, to take only two of many well known and popular examples. Quite aside from the abstract question as to how wise it is to use the arts as propaganda, in actual practice it often happens that such attempts produce only wooden types instead of individuals as characters, alienate the sympathies of the audience by a too relentless or obvious pounding away at the thesis of the drama, and obscure any true dramatic conflict by the desire to preach.

O'Neill has wisely skirted such pitfalls in his realistic tragedies. Even a play like *The Hairy Ape*, which might easily have emerged as a manifesto for the downtrodden workers, is rather a study of man's attempt to come to self-knowledge. That Yank never gets much beyond muddled groping, that he never finds meaning to life is his tragedy. Much there is, it is true, of the gulfs between classes, but the play can hardly be called an indictment of any particular class or a document in the class war.

That is even more true of *Anna Christie*, which does not exist to indict anything but rather to show in direct and unembellished terms how the lives of three people may interact upon each other and how forces beyond their control act upon them to bring about their tragedy. The play is realistic in its frank acceptance of the cheapness and sordidness of some aspects of life, but it is also realistic in its recognition of the qualities of character in Burke and Anna, qualities that make it possible for the two to make adjustments with some measure of mutual understanding and yet with some sense of the tragic realities of their position. O'Neill has been careful to insist that the play does not have a happy ending, and in such characters we get a sense of that heroic quality which is essential to true tragedy.

Eugene O'Neill has made himself the chief of American dramatists. His work has been characterized by a sound dramatic sense but also by an experimental spirit that has resulted in highly original plays. Not all his experiments have been successful, but they bear witness to his skill, his originality, and sometimes his intrepidity in the use of tricks and devices to achieve his ends.

He was born into a theatrical family in New York City in 1888, went to Princeton for a year but left to try his hand, as it turned out, at a variety of things, from a secretarial position in a mail-order house to tending a shipment of mules from Buenos Aires to South Africa. After some years of adventurous living, marked by many vicissitudes, he decided to write plays. He spent a year (1914–1915) at Harvard in Professor Baker's course in playwriting, went back to New York and in the next year became associated with the Provincetown Players, who produced his play, *Bound East for Cardiff*. Since that time he has written a large and varied number of plays, growing steadily in power and in thoughtfulness. His most important works have been *Beyond the Horizon* (1920), *Anna Christie* (1921), *The Emperor Jones* (1920), *Strange Interlude* (1928), and *Mourning Becomes Electra* (1931), and *Ah, Wilderness!* (1933).

SUGGESTED READINGS

Clark, Barrett H., *Eugene O'Neill*. NEW YORK, 1933.
Morgan, Arthur E., *Tendencies of Modern English Drama*. NEW YORK, 1924.
Quinn, Arthur H., *A History of the American Drama from the Civil War to the Present Day*, VOL. II. NEW YORK, 1936.

Fitch, Clyde, *The Truth*, in *Plays*, BOSTON, 1915.
Galsworthy, John, *Strife*, *Justice*, *The Silver Box*. NEW YORK, 1928.
Rice, Elmer, *Street Scene*. NEW YORK, 1929.
Shaw, G. B., *Widowers' Houses*. NEW YORK, 1916.
Sheriff, Robert C., *Journey's End*. NEW YORK, 1929.
Sherwood, Robert, *Petrified Forest*. NEW YORK, 1935.

ANNA CHRISTIE [1]

by Eugene O'Neill

Characters

JOHNNY-THE-PRIEST

TWO LONGSHOREMEN

A POSTMAN

LARRY, *the bartender*

CHRIS. CHRISTOPHERSON, *captain of the barge "Simeon Winthrop"*

MARTHY OWEN, *his mistress*

ANNA CHRISTOPHERSON, *his daughter*

THREE MEN *of a steamer's crew*

MAT BURKE, *a stoker*

JOHNSON, *deck-hand on the barge*

ACT I

SCENE.—*"Johnny-the-Priest's" saloon near South Street, New York City. The stage is divided into two sections, showing a small back room on the right. On the left, forward, of the barroom, a large window looking out on the street. Beyond it, the main entrance—a double swinging door. Farther back, another window. The bar runs from left to right nearly the whole length of the rear wall. In back of the bar, a small showcase displaying a few bottles of case goods, for which there is evidently little call. The remainder of the rear space in front of the large mirrors is occupied by half-barrels of cheap whiskey of the "nickel-a-shot" variety, from which the liquor is drawn by means of spigots. On the right is an open doorway leading to the back room. In the back room are four round wooden tables with five chairs grouped about each. In the rear, a family entrance opening on a side street.*

It is late afternoon of a day in fall.

As the curtain rises, Johnny is discovered. "Johnny-the-Priest" deserves his nickname. With his pale, thin, clean-shaven face, mild blue eyes and white hair, a cassock would seem more suited to him than the apron he wears. Neither his voice nor his general manner dispel this illusion which has made him a

[1] Reprinted by permission of Random House, Inc., New York.

personage of the water front. They are soft and bland. But beneath all his mildness one senses the man behind the mask— cynical, callous, hard as nails. He is lounging at ease behind the bar, a pair of spectacles on his nose, reading an evening paper.

Two longshoremen enter from the street, wearing their working aprons, the button of the union pinned conspicuously on the caps pulled sideways on their heads at an aggressive angle.

FIRST LONGSHOREMAN [*As they range themselves at the bar*]. Gimme a shock. Number Two. [*He tosses a coin on the bar.*]

SECOND LONGSHOREMAN. Same here. [*Johnny sets two glasses of barrel whiskey before them.*]

FIRST LONGSHOREMAN. Here's luck! [*The other nods. They gulp down their whiskey.*]

SECOND LONGSHOREMAN [*Putting money on the bar*]. Give us another.

FIRST LONGSHOREMAN. Gimme a scoop this time—lager and porter. I'm dry.   10

SECOND LONGSHOREMAN. Same here. [*Johnny draws the lager and porter and sets the big, foaming schooners before them. They drink down half the contents and start to talk together hurriedly in low tones. The door on the left is swung open and Larry enters. He is a boyish, red-cheeked, rather good-looking young fellow of twenty or so.*]

LARRY [*Nodding to Johnny—cheerily*]. Hello, boss.

JOHNNY. Hello, Larry. [*With a glance at his watch.*] Just on time. [*Larry goes to the right behind the bar, takes off his coat, and puts on an apron.*]   20

FIRST LONGSHOREMAN [*Abruptly*]. Let's drink up and get back to it. [*They finish their drinks and go out left. The Postman enters as they leave. He exchanges nods with Johnny and throws a letter on the bar.*]

THE POSTMAN. Addressed care of you, Johnny. Know him?

JOHNNY [*Picks up letter, adjusting his spectacles. Larry comes and peers over his shoulders. Johnny reads very slowly*]. Christopher Christopherson.

THE POSTMAN [*Helpfully*]. Square-head name.

LARRY. Old Chris—that's who.   30

JOHNNY. Oh, sure. I was forgetting Chris carried a hell of a name like that. Letters come here for him sometimes before. I remember now. Long time ago, though.

THE POSTMAN. It'll get to him all right then?

JOHNNY. Sure thing. He comes here whenever he's in port.

THE POSTMAN [*Turning to go*]. Sailor, eh?

JOHNNY [*With a grin*]. Captain of a coal barge.

THE POSTMAN [*Laughing*]. Some job! Well, s'long.

JOHNNY. S'long. I'll see he gets it. [*The Postman goes out. Johnny scrutinizes the letter.*] You got good eyes, Larry. 40 Where's it from?

LARRY [*After a glance*]. St. Paul. That'll be in Minnesota, I'm thinkin'. Looks like a woman's writing, too, the old divil!

JOHNNY. He's got a daughter somewheres out West, I think he told me once. [*He puts the letter on the cash register.*] Come to think of it, I ain't seen old Chris in a dog's age. [*Putting his overcoat on, he comes around the end of the bar.*] Guess I'll be gettin' home. See you tomorrow.

LARRY. Good-night to ye, boss. [*As Johnny goes toward the street door, it is pushed open and Christopher Christopherson 50 enters. He is a short, squat, broad-shouldered man of about fifty, with a round, weather-beaten, red face from which his light blue eyes peer short-sightedly, twinkling with a simple good humor. His large mouth, overhung by a thick, drooping, yellow mustache, is childishly self-willed and weak, of an obstinate kindliness. A thick neck is jammed like a post into the heavy trunk of his body. His arms with their big, hairy freckled hands, and his stumpy legs terminating in large flat feet, are awkwardly short and muscular. He walks with a clumsy, rolling gait. His voice, when not raised in a hollow boom, is toned down to a sly, 60 confidential half-whisper with something vaguely plaintive in its quality. He is dressed in a wrinkled, ill-fitting dark suit of shore clothes, and wears a faded cap of gray cloth over his mop of grizzled, blond hair. Just now his face beams with a too-blissful happiness, and he has evidently been drinking. He reaches his hand out to Johnny.*]

CHRIS. Hello Yohnny! Have a drink on me. Come on, Larry. Give us drink. Have one yourself. [*Putting his hand in his pocket.*] Ay gat money—plenty money.

JOHNNY [*Shakes Chris by the hand*]. Speak of the devil. 70 We was just talkin' about you.

LARRY [*Coming to the end of the bar*]. Hello, Chris. Put it there. [*They shake hands.*]

CHRIS [*Beaming*]. Give us drink.

JOHNNY [*With a grin*]. You got a half-snootful now. Where'd you get it?

CHRIS [*Grinning*]. Oder fallar on oder barge—Irish fallar—he gat bottle vhiskey and we drank it, yust us two. Dot vhiskey gat kick, by yingo! Ay yust come ashore. Give us drink, Larry. Ay vas little drunk, not much. Yust feel good, [*He laughs and commences to sing in a nasal, high-pitched quaver.*]

"My Yosephine, come board de ship. Long time Ay vait for you.
De moon, she shi-i-i-ine. She looka yust like you.
Tchee-tchee, tchee-tchee, tchee-tchee, tchee-tchee."

[*To the accompaniment of this last he waves his hand as if he were conducting an orchestra.*]

JOHNNY [*With a laugh*]. Same old Yosie, eh, Chris?

CHRIS. You don't know a good song when you hear him. Italian fallar on oder barge, he learn me dat. Give us drink. [*He throws change on the bar.*]

LARRY [*With a professional air*]. What's your pleasure, gentlemen?

JOHNNY. Small beer, Larry.

CHRIS. Vhiskey—Number Two.

LARRY [*As he gets their drinks*]. I'll take a cigar on you.

CHRIS [*Lifting his glass*]. Skoal! [*He drinks.*]

JOHNNY. Drink hearty.

CHRIS [*Immediately*]. Have oder drink.

JOHNNY. No. Some other time. Got to go home now. So you've just landed? Where are you in from this time?

CHRIS. Norfolk. Ve make slow voyage—dirty vedder—yust fog, fog, fog, all bloody time! [*There is an insistent ring from the doorbell at the family entrance in the back room. Chris gives a start—hurriedly.*] Ay go open, Larry. Ay forgat. It vas Marthy. She come with me. [*He goes into the back room.*]

LARRY [*With a chuckle*]. He's still got that same cow livin' with him, the old fool!

JOHNNY [*With a grin*]. A sport, Chris is. Well, I'll beat it home. S'long. [*He goes to the street door.*]

LARRY. So long, boss.

JOHNNY. Oh—don't forget to give him his letter.

LARRY. I won't. [*Johnny goes out. In the meantime, Chris has opened the family entrance door, admitting Marthy. She might be forty or fifty. Her jowly, mottled face, with its thick red nose, is streaked with interlacing purple veins. Her thick, gray hair is piled anyhow in a greasy mop on top of her round head. Her figure is flabby and fat; her breath comes in wheezy*] *gasps; she speaks in a loud, mannish voice, punctuated by explosions of hoarse laughter. But there still twinkles in her blood-shot blue eyes a youthful lust for life which hard usage has failed to stifle, a sense of humor, mocking, but good-tempered. She wears a man's cap, double-breasted man's jacket, and a grimy, cal-* 120 *ico skirt. Her bare feet are encased in a man's brogans several sizes too large for her, which gives her a shuffling, wobbly gait.*]

MARTHY [*Grumblingly*]. What yuh tryin' to do, Dutchy, keep me standin' out there all day? [*She comes forward and sits at the table in the right corner, front.*]

CHRIS [*Mollifyingly*]. Ay'm sorry, Marthy. Ay talk to Yohnny. Ay forgat. What you goin' take for drink?

MARTHY [*Appeased*]. Gimme a scoop of lager an' ale.

CHRIS. Ay go bring him back. [*He returns to the bar.*] Lager and ale for Marthy, Larry. Vhiskey for me. [*He throws* 130 *change on the bar.*]

LARRY. Right you are. [*Then remembering, he takes the letter from in back of the bar.*] Here's a letter for you—from St. Paul, Minnesota—and a lady's writin'. [*He grins.*]

CHRIS [*Quickly taking it*]. Oh, den it come from my daughter, Anna. She live dere. [*He turns the letter over in his hands uncertainly.*]Ay don't gat letter from Anna—must be a year.

LARRY [*Jokingly*]. That's a fine fairy tale to be tellin'—your daughter! Sure, I'll bet it's some bum.

CHRIS [*Soberly*]. No. Dis come from Anna. [*Engrossed by the letter in his hand, uncertainly.*] By golly, Ay tank Ay'm too drunk for read dis letter from Anna. Ay tank Ay sat down for a minute. You bring drinks in back room, Larry. [*He goes into the room on right.*]

MARTHY [*Angrily*]. Where's my lager an' ale, yuh big 140 stiff?

CHRIS [*Preoccupied*]. Larry bring him. [*He sits down opposite her. Larry brings in the drinks and sets them on the table. He and Marthy exchange nods of recognition. Larry stands looking at Chris curiously. Marthy takes a long draught of her schooner and heaves a huge sigh of satisfaction, wiping her mouth with the back of her hand. Chris stares at the letter for a moment—slowly opens it, and, squinting his eyes, commences to read laboriously, his lips moving as he spells out the words. As he reads his face lights up with an expression of mingled joy and bewilder-* 150 *ment.*]

LARRY. Good news?

MARTHY [*Her curiosity also aroused*]. What's that yuh got—a letter, fur Gawd's sake?

CHRIS [*Pauses for a moment, after finishing the letter, as if to let the news sink in—then suddenly pounds his fist on the table with happy excitement*]. Py yiminy! Yust tank, Anna say she's comin' here right avay! She gat sick on yob in St. Paul, she say. It's short letter, don't tal me much more'n dat. [*Beaming.*] Py golly, dat's good news all at one time for ole fallar! [*Then turning to Marthy, rather shamefacedly.*] You know, Marthy, Ay've tole you Ay don't see my Anna since she vas little gel in Sveden five year ole. 160

MARTHY. How old'll she be now?

CHRIS. She must be—lat me see—she must be twenty year ole, py Yo!

LARRY [*Surprised*]. You've not seen her in fifteen years?

CHRIS [*Suddenly growing somber—in a low tone*]. No. Ven she vas a little gel, Ay vas bo'sun on vindjammer. Ay never gat home only few time dem year. Ay'm fool sailor fallar. My voman—Anna's mother—she gat tired vait all time Sveden for me ven Ay don't never come. She come dis country, bring Anna, dey go out Minnesota, live with her cousins on farm. Den ven her mo'der die ven Ay vas on voyage, Ay tank it's better dem cousins keep Anna. Ay tank it's better Anna live on farm, den she don't know dat ole davil, sea, she don't know fader like me. 170

LARRY [*With a wink at Marthy*]. This girl, now, 'll be marryin' a sailor herself, likely. It's in the blood.

CHRIS [*Suddenly springing to his feet and smashing his fist on the table in a rage*]. No, py God! She don't do dat! 180

MARTHY [*Grasping her schooner hastily—angrily*]. Hey, look out, yuh nut! Wanta spill my suds for me?

LARRY [*Amazed*]. Oho, what's up with you? Ain't you a sailor yourself now, and always been?

CHRIS [*Slowly*]. Dat's yust vhy Ay say it. [*Forcing a smile.*] Sailor vas all right fallar, but not for marry gel. No. Ay know dat. Anna's mo'der, she know it, too.

LARRY [*As Chris remains sunk in gloomy reflection*]. When is your daughter comin'? Soon?

CHRIS [*Roused*]. Py yiminy, Ay forgat. [*Reads through the letter hurriedly.*] She say she come right avay, dat's all. 190

LARRY. She'll maybe be comin' here to look for you, I s'pose. [*He returns to the bar, whistling. Left alone with Marthy, who stares at him with a twinkle of malicious humor in her eyes, Chris suddenly becomes desperately ill-at-ease. He fidgets, then gets up hurriedly.*]

CHRIS. Ay gat speak with Larry. Ay be right back. [*Mollify-ingly.*] Ay bring you oder drink.

MARTHY [*Emptying her glass*]. Sure. That's me. [*As he retreats with the glass she guffaws after him derisively.*]   200

CHRIS [*To Larry in an alarmed whisper*]. Py yingo, Ay gat gat Marthy shore off barge before Anna come! Anna raise hell if she find dat out. Marthy raise hell, too, for go, py golly!

LARRY [*With a chuckle*]. Serve ye right, ye old divil—havin' a woman at your age!

CHRIS [*Scratching his head in a quandary*]. You tal me lie for tal Marthy, Larry, so's she gat off barge quick.

LARRY. She knows your daughter's comin'. Tell her to get the hell out of it.

CHRIS. No, Ay don't like make her feel bad.   210

LARRY. You're an old mush! Keep your girl away from the barge then. She'll likely want to stay ashore anyway. [*Curiously.*] What does she work at, your Anna?

CHRIS. She stay on dem cousins' farm 'till two year ago. Dan she gat yob nurse gel in St. Paul. [*Then shaking his head reso-lutely.*] But Ay don't vant for her gat yob now. Ay vant for her stay with me.

LARRY [*Scornfully*]. On a coal barge! She'll not like that, I'm thinkin'.

MARTHY [*Shouts from next room*]. Don't I get that bucket   220 o' suds, Dutchy?

CHRIS [*Startled—in apprehensive confusion*]. Yes, Ay come, Marthy.

LARRY [*Drawing the lager and ale, hands it to Chris—laughing*]. Now you're in for it! You'd better tell her straight to get out!

CHRIS [*Shaking in his boots*]. Py golly. [*He takes her drink in to Marthy and sits down at the table. She sips in silence. Larry moves quietly close to the partition to listen, grinning with ex-pectation. Chris seems on the verge of speaking, hesitates, gulps down his whiskey desperately as if seeking for courage. He   230 attempts to whistle a few bars of "Yosephine" with careless bra-vado, but the whistle peters out futilely. Marthy stares at him keenly, taking in his embarrassment with a malicious twinkle of amusement in her eye. Chris clears his throat.*] Marthy—

MARTHY [*Aggressively*]. Wha's that? [*Then, pretending to fly into a rage, her eyes enjoying Chris' misery.*] I'm wise to what's in back of your nut, Dutchy. Yuh want to git rid o' me, huh?—

now she's comin'. Gimme the bum's rush ashore, huh? Lemme
tell yuh, Dutchy, there ain't a square-head workin' on a boat man
enough to git away with that. Don't start nothin' yuh can't 240
finish!

CHRIS [*Miserably*]. Ay don't start nutting, Marthy.

MARTHY [*Glares at him for a second—then cannot control a
burst of laughter*]. Ho-ho! Yuh're a scream, Square-head—an
honest-ter-Gawd knockout! Ho-ho! [*She wheezes, panting for
breath.*]

CHRIS [*With childish pique*]. Ay don't see nutting for laugh
at.

MARTHY. Take a slant in the mirror and yuh'll see. Ho-ho!
[*Recovering from her mirth—chuckling, scornfully.*] A 250
square-head tryin' to kid Marthy Owen at this late day!—after
me campin' with barge men the last twenty years. I'm wise to the
game, up, down, and sideways. I ain't been born and dragged up
on the water front for nothin'. Think I'd make trouble, huh?
Not me! I'll pack up me duds an' beat it. I'm quittin' yuh, get me?
I'm tellin' yuh I'm sick of stickin' with yuh, and I'm leavin' yuh
flat, see? There's plenty of other guys on other barges waitin' for
me. Always was, I always found. [*She claps the astonished Chris
on the back.*] So cheer up, Dutchy! I'll be offen the barge before
she comes. You'll be rid o' me for good—and me o' you— 260
good riddance for both of us. Ho-ho!

CHRIS [*Seriously*]. Ay don' tank dat. You vas good gel, Marthy.

MARTHY [*Grinning*]. Good girl? Aw, can the bull! Well, yuh
treated me square, yuhself. So it's fifty-fifty. Nobody's sore at
nobody. We're still good frien's, huh? [*Larry returns to bar.*]

CHRIS [*Beaming now that he sees his troubles disappearing*].
Yes, py golly.

MARTHY. That's the talkin'! In all my time I tried never to split
with a guy with no hard feelin's. But what was yuh so scared
about—that I'd kick up a row? That ain't Marthy's way. 270
[*Scornfully.*] Think I'd break my heart to loose yuh? Commit
suicide, huh? Ho-ho! Gawd! The world's full o' men if that's
all I'd worry about! [*Then with a grin, after emptying her glass.*]
Blow me to another scoop, huh? I'll drink your kid's health for
yuh.

CHRIS [*Eagerly*]. Sure tang. Ay go gat him. [*He takes the two
glasses into the bar.*] Oder drink. Same for both.

LARRY [*Getting the drinks and putting them on the bar*]. She's
not such a bad lot, that one.

CHRIS [*Jovially*]. She's good gel, Ay tal you! Py golly, Ay 280 calabrate now! Give me vhiskey here at bar, too. [*He puts down money. Larry serves him.*] You have drink, Larry.

LARRY [*Virtuously*]. You know I never touch it.

CHRIS. You don't know what you miss. Skoal! [*He drinks—then begins to sing loudly.*]

"My Yosephine, come board de ship—"

[*He picks up the drinks for Marthy and himself and walks unsteadily into the back room, singing.*]

"De moon, she shi-i-i-ine. She looks yust like you.
Tchee-tchee, tchee-tchee, tchee-tchee, tchee-tchee." 290

MARTHY [*Grinning, hands to ears*]. Gawd!

CHRIS [*Sitting down*]. Ay'm good singer, yes? Ve drink, eh? Skoal! Ay calabrate! [*He drinks.*] Ay calabrate 'cause Anna's coming home. You know, Marthy, Ay never write for her to come, 'cause Ay tank Ay'm no good for her. But all time Ay hope like hell some day she vant for see me and den she come. And dat's vay it happen now, py yiminy! [*His face beaming.*] What you tank she look like, Marthy? Ay bet you she's fine, good, strong gel, pooty like hell! Living on farm made her like dat. And Ay bet you some day she marry good, steady land 300 fallar here in East, have home all her own, have kits—and dan Ay'm ole grandfader, py golly! And Ay go visit dem every time Ay gat in port near! [*Bursting with joy.*] By yiminy crickens, Ay calabrate dat! [*Shouts.*] Bring oder drink, Larry! [*He smashes his fist on the table with a bang.*]

LARRY [*Coming in from bar—irritably*]. Easy there! Don't be breakin' the table, you old goat!

CHRIS [*By way of reply, grins foolishly and begins to sing*].

"My Yosephine comes board de ship—"

MARTHY [*Touching Chris' arm persuasively*]. You're 310 soused to the ears, Dutchy. Go out and put a feed into you. It'll sober you up. [*Then as Chris shakes his head obstinately.*] Listen, yuh old nut! Yuh don't know what time your kid's liable to show up. Yuh want to be sober when she comes, don't yuh?

CHRIS [*Aroused—gets unsteadily to his feet*]. Py golly, yes.

LARRY. That's good sense for you. A good beef stew'll fix you. Go around the corner.

CHRIS. All right. Ay be back soon, Marthy. [*Chris goes through the bar and out the street door.*]

LARRY. He'll come round all right with some grub in him. 320

MARTHY. Sure. [*Larry goes back to the bar and resumes his newspaper. Marthy sips what is left of her schooner reflectively. There is the ring of the family entrance bell. Larry comes to the door and opens it a trifle—then, with a puzzled expression, pulls it wide. Anna Christopherson enters. She is a tall, blond, fully-developed girl of twenty, handsome after a large, Viking-daughter fashion but now run down in health and plainly showing all the outward evidences of belonging to the world's oldest profession. Her youthful face is already hard and cynical beneath its layer of make-up. Her clothes are the tawdry finery of peas-* 330 *ant stock turned prostitute. She comes and sinks wearily in a chair by the table, left front.*]

ANNA. Gimme a whiskey—ginger ale on the side. [*Then, as Larry turns to go, forcing a winning smile at him.*] And don't be stingy, baby.

LARRY [*Sarcastically*]. Shall I serve it in a pail?

ANNA [*With a hard laugh*]. That suits me down to the ground. [*Larry goes into the bar. The two women size each other up with frank stares. Larry comes back with the drink which he sets before Anna and returns to the bar again. Anna downs her* 340 *drink at a gulp. Then, after a moment, as the alcohol begins to rouse her, she turns to Marthy with a friendly smile.*] Gee, I needed that bad, all right, all right!

MARTHY [*Nodding her head sympathetically*]. Sure—yuh look all in. Been on a bat?

ANNA. No—travelling—a day and a half on the train. Had to sit up all night in the dirty coach, too. Gawd, I thought I'd never get here!

MARTHY [*With a start—looking at her intently*]. Where'd yuh come from, huh? 350

ANNA. St. Paul—out in Minnesota.

MARTHY [*Staring at her in amazement—slowly*]. So—yuh're— [*She suddenly burst out into hoarse, ironical laughter.*] Gawd!

ANNA. All the way from Minnesota, sure. [*Flaring up.*] What you laughing at? Me?

MARTHY [*Hastily*]. No, honest, kid. I was thinkin' of somethin' else.

ANNA [*Mollified—with a smile*]. Well, I wouldn't blame you, at that. Guess I do look rotten—yust out of the hospital two weeks. I'm going to have another 'ski. What d'you say? Have some- 360 thing on me?

MARTHY. Sure I will. T'anks. [*She calls.*] Hey, Larry! Little service! [*He comes in.*]

ANNA. Same for me.

MARTHY. Same here. [*Larry takes their glasses and goes out.*]

ANNA. Why don't you come sit over here, be sociable. I'm a dead stranger in this burg—and I ain't spoke a word with no one since day before yesterday.

MARTHY. Sure thing. [*She shuffles over to Anna's table and sits down opposite her. Larry brings the drinks and Anna pays* 370 *him.*]

ANNA. Skoal! Here's how! [*She drinks.*]

MARTHY. Here's luck! [*She takes a gulp from her schooner.*]

ANNA [*Taking a package of Sweet Caporal cigarettes from her bag*]. Let you smoke in here, won't they?

MARTHY [*Doubtfully*]. Sure. [*Then with evident anxiety.*] On'y trow it away if yuh hear someone comin'.

ANNA [*Lighting one and taking a deep inhale*]. Gee, they're fussy in this dump, ain't they? [*She puffs, staring at the table top. Marthy looks her over with a new penetrating interest, tak-* 380 *ing in every detail of her face. Anna suddenly becomes conscious of this appraising stare—resentfully.*] Ain't nothing wrong with me, is there? You're looking hard enough.

MARTHY [*Irritated by the other's tone—scornfully*]. Ain't got to look much. I got your number the minute you stepped in the door.

ANNA [*Her eyes narrowing*]. Ain't you smart! Well, I got yours, too, without no trouble. You're me forty years from now. That's you! [*She gives a hard little laugh.*]

MARTHY [*Angrily*]. Is that so? Well, I'll tell you straight, 390 kiddo, that Marthy Owen never—[*She catches herself up short— with a grin.*] What are you and me scrappin' over? Let's cut it out, huh? Me, I don't want no hard feelin's with no one. [*Ex- tending her hand.*] Shake and forget it, huh?

ANNA [*Shakes her hand gladly*]. Only too glad to. I ain't look- ing for trouble. Let's have 'nother. What d'you say?

MARTHY [*Shaking her head*]. Not for mine. I'm full up. And you—Had anythin' to eat lately?

ANNA [*After a moment's hesitation*]. Not since this morning on the train.   400

MARTHY. Then yuh better go easy on it, hadn't yuh?

ANNA [*After a moment's hesitation*]. Guess you're right. I got to meet someone, too. But my nerves is on edge after that rotten trip.

MARTHY. Yuh said yuh was just outa the hospital?

ANNA. Two weeks ago. [*Leaning over to Marthy confiden-*

tially]. The joint I was in out in St. Paul got raided. That was the start. The judge give all us girls thirty days. The others didn't seem to mind being in the cooler much. Some of 'em was used to it. But me, I couldn't stand it. It got my goat right—couldn't eat or sleep or nothing. I never could stand being caged up no- 410
wheres. I got good and sick and they had to send me to the hospital. It was nice there. I was sorry to leave it, honest!

MARTHY [*After a slight pause*]. Did yuh say yuh got to meet someone here?

ANNA. Yes. Oh, not what you mean. It's my Old Man I got to meet. Honest! It's funny, too. I ain't seen him since I was a kid—don't even know what he looks like—yust had a letter every now and then. This was always the only address he give me to write him back. He's a yanitor of some building here now—used to be a sailor. 420

MARTHY [*Astonished*]. Janitor!

ANNA. Sure. And I was thinking maybe, seeing he ain't never done a thing for me in my life, he might be willing to stake me to a room and eats till I get rested up. [*Wearily.*] Gee, I sure need that rest! I'm all knocked out. [*Then resignedly.*] But I ain't expecting much from him. Give you a kick when you're down, that's what all men do. [*With sudden passion.*] Men, I hate 'em—all of 'em! And I don't expect he'll turn out no better than the rest. [*Then with sudden interest.*] Say, do you hang out around this dump much? 430

MARTHY. Oh, off and on.

ANNA. Then maybe you know him—my Old Man—or at least seen him?

MARTHY. It ain't old Chris, is it?

ANNA. Old Chris?

MARTHY. Chris Christopherson, his full name is.

ANNA [*Excitedly*]. Yes, that's him! Anna Christopherson—that's my real name—only out there I called myself Anna Christie. So you know him, eh?

MARTHY [*Evasively*]. Seen him about for years.

ANNA. Say, what's he like, tell me, honest? 440

MARTHY. Oh, he's short and—

ANNA [*Impatiently*]. I don't care what he looks like. What kind is he?

MARTHY [*Earnestly*]. Well, yuh can bet your life, kid, he's as good an old guy as ever walked on two feet. That goes!

ANNA [*Pleased*]. I'm glad to hear it. Then you think's he'll stake me to that rest cure I'm after?

MARTHY [*Emphatically*]. Surest thing you know. [*Disgustedly*.]
But where'd yuh get the idea he was a janitor?

ANNA. He wrote me he was himself.   450

MARTHY. Well, he was lyin'. He ain't. He's captain of a barge—
five men under him.

ANNA [*Disgusted in her turn*]. A barge? What kind of a barge?

MARTHY. Coal mostly.

ANNA. A coal barge! [*With a harsh laugh.*] If that ain't a swell
job to find your long lost Old Man working at! Gee, I knew
something'd be bound to turn out wrong—always does with me.
That puts my idea of his giving me a rest on the bum.

MARTHY. What d'yuh mean?

ANNA. I s'pose he lives on the boat, don't he?   460

MARTHY. Sure. What about it? Can't you live on it too?

ANNA [*Scornfully*]. Me? On a dirty coal barge! What d'you
think I am?

MARTHY [*Resentfully*]. What d'yuh know about barges, huh?
Bet yuh ain't never seen one. That's what comes of his bringing
yuh up inland—away from the old devil sea—where yuh'd be
safe—Gawd! [*The irony of it strikes her sense of humor and she
laughs hoarsely.*]

ANNA [*Angrily*]. His bringing me up! Is that what he tells
people? I like his nerve! He let them cousins of my Old Woman's
keep me on their farm and work me to death like a dog.   470

MARTHY. Well, he's got queer notions on some things. I've
heard him say a farm was the best place for a kid.

ANNA. Sure. That's what he'd always answer back—and a lot of
crazy stuff about staying away from the sea—stuff I couldn't
make head or tail to. I thought he must be nutty.

MARTHY. He is on that one point. [*Casually.*] So yuh didn't fall
for life on the farm, huh?

ANNA. I should say not! The old man of the family, his wife,
and four sons—I had to slave for all of 'em. I was only a poor
relation, and they treated me worse than they dare treat a   480
hired girl. [*After a moment's hesitation—somberly.*] It was one of
the sons—the youngest—started me—when I was sixteen. After
that, I hated 'em so I'd killed 'em all if I'd stayed. So I run away—
to St. Paul.

MARTHY [*Who has been listening sympathetically*]. I've heard
Old Chris talkin' about your bein' a nurse girl out there. Was that
all a bluff yuh put up when yuh wrote him?

ANNA. Not on your life, it wasn't. It was true for two years. I
didn't go wrong all at one jump. Being a nurse girl was yust what

finished me. Taking care of other people's kids, always lis- 490
tening to their bawling and crying, caged in, when you're only a
kid yourself and want to go out and see things. At last I got the
chance—to get into that house. And you bet your life I took it!
[*Defiantly.*] And I ain't sorry neither. [*After a pause—with bitter
hatred.*] It was all men's fault—the whole business. It was men on
the farm ordering and beating me—and giving me the wrong
start. Then when I was a nurse, it was men again hanging around,
bothering me, trying to see what they could get. [*She gives a
hard laugh.*] And now it's men all the time. Gawd, I hate 'em all,
every mother's son of 'em! Don't you? 500

MARTHY. Oh, I dunno. There's good ones and bad ones, kid.
You've just had a run of bad luck with 'em, that's all. Your Old
Man, now—old Chris—he's a good one.

ANNA [*Skeptically*]. He'll have to show me.

MARTHY. Yuh kept right on writing him yuh was a nurse girl
still, even after yuh was in the house, didn't yuh?

ANNA. Sure. [*Cynically.*] Not that I think he'd care a darn.

MARTHY. Yuh're all wrong about him, kid. [*Earnestly.*] I know
Old Chris well for a long time. He's talked to me 'bout you lots
of times. He thinks the world o' you, honest he does. 510

ANNA. Aw, quit the kiddin'!

MARTHY. Honest! Only, he's a simple old guy, see? He's got
nutty notions. But he means well, honest. Listen to me, kid—[*She
is interrupted by the opening and shutting of the street door in
the bar and by hearing Chris's voice.*] Ssshh!

ANNA. What's up?

CHRIS [*Who has entered the bar. He seems considerably so-
bered up*]. Py golly, Larry, dat grub taste good. Marthy in back?

LARRY. Sure—and another tramp with her. [*Chris starts for the
entrance to the back room.*] 520

MARTHY [*To Anna in a hurried, nervous whisper*]. That's him
now. He's comin' in here. Brace up!

ANNA. Who? [*Chris opens the door.*]

MARTHY [*As if she were greeting him for the first time*]. Why
hello, Old Chris. [*Then before he can speak, she shuffles hurriedly
past him into the bar, beckoning him to follow her.*] Come here.
I wanta tell yuh somethin'. [*He goes out to her. She speaks hurriedly in a low voice.*] Listen! I'm goin' to beat it down to the
barge—pack up me duds and blow. That's her in there—your
Anna—just come—waitin' for yuh. Treat her right, see? 530
She's been sick. Well, s'long! [*She goes into the back room—to
Anna.*] S'long, kid. I gotta beat it now. See yuh later.

ANNA [*Nervously*]. So long. [*Martha goes quickly out of the family entrance.*]

LARRY [*Looking at the stupefied Chris curiously*]. Well, what's up now?

CHRIS [*Vaguely*]. Nutting—nutting. [*He stands before the door to the back room in an agony of embarrassed emotion—then he forces himself to a bold decision, pushes open the door and walks in. He stands there, casts a shy glance at Anna, whose bril-* 540 *liant clothes, and, to him, high-toned appearance, awe him terribly. He looks about him with pitiful nervousness as if to avoid the appraising look with which she takes in his face, his clothes, etc.— his voice seeming to plead for her forebearance.*] Anna!

ANNA [*Acutely embarrassed in her turn*]. Hello—father. She told me it was you. I yust got here a little while ago.

CHRIS [*Goes slowly over to her chair*]. It's good—for see you— after all dem years, Anna. [*He bends down over her. After an embarrassed struggle they manage to kiss each other.*]

ANNA [*A trace of genuine feeling in her voice*]. It's good to see you, too.

CHRIS [*Grasps her arms and looks into her face—then* 550 *overcome by a wave of fierce tenderness*]. Anna lilla! Anna lilla! [*Takes her in his arms.*]

ANNA [*Shrinks away from him, half-frightened*]. What's that— Swedish? I don't know it. [*Then as if seeking relief from the tension in a voluble chatter.*] Gee, I had an awful trip coming here. I'm all in. I had to sit up in the dirty coach all night— couldn't get no sleep, hardly—and then I had a hard job finding this place. I never been in New York before, you know, and—

CHRIS [*Who has been staring down at her face admiringly, not hearing what she says—impulsively*]. You know you vas 560 awful pooty gel, Anna? Ay bet all men see you fall in love with you, py yiminy!

ANNA [*Repelled—harshly*]. Cut it! You talk same as they all do.

CHRIS [*Hurt—humbly*]. Ain't no harm for your fader talk dat vay, Anna.

ANNA [*Forcing a short laugh*]. No.—Course not. Only—it's funny to see you and not remember nothing. You're like a stranger.

CHRIS [*Sadly*]. Ay s'pose. Ay never come home only few times ven you vas kit in Sveden. You don't remember dat? 570

ANNA. No. [*Resentfully.*] But why didn't you never come home them days? Why didn't you never come out West to see me?

CHRIS [*Slowly*]. Ay tank, after your mo'der die, ven Ay vas avay on voyage, it's better for you you don't never see me! [*He sinks down in the chair opposite her dejectedly—then turns to her—sadly.*] Ay don't know, Anna, vhy Ay never come home Sveden in ole year. Ay vant come home end of every voyage. Ay vant see your mo'der, your two bro'der before dey vas drowned, you ven you was born—but—Ay—don't go. Ay sign on oder ships—go South America, go Australia, go China, go every port all over world many times—but Ay never go aboard ship sail for Sveden. Ven Ay gat money for pay passage home as passenger den—[*He bows his head guiltily.*] Ay forgat and Ay spend all money. Ven Ay tank again, it's too late. [*He sighs.*] Ay don't know vhy but dat's vay with most sailor fallar, Anna. Dat ole davil sea make dem crazy fools with her dirty tricks. It's so.

ANNA [*Who has watched him keenly while he has been speaking—with a trace of scorn in her voice*]. Then you think the sea's to blame for everything, eh? Well, you're still workin' on it, ain't you, spite of all you used to write me about hating it. That dame vas here told me you was captain of a coal barge—and you wrote me you was yanitor of a building!

CHRIS [*Embarrassed but lying glibly*]. Oh, Ay work on land long time as yanitor. Yust short time ago Ay got dis yob cause Ay vas sick, need open air.

ANNA [*Skeptically*]. Sick? You? You'd never think it.

CHRIS. And, Anna, dis ain't real sailor yob. Dis ain't real boat on sea. She's yust ole tub—like piece of land with house on it dat float. Yob on her ain't sea yob. No. Ay don't gat yob on sea, Anna, if Ay die first. Ay swear dat, ven your mo'der die. Ay keep my word, py yingo!

ANNA [*Perplexed*]. Well, I can't see no difference. [*Dismissing the subject.*] Speaking of being sick, I been there myself—yust out of the hospital two weeks ago.

CHRIS [*Immediately all concern*]. You, Anna? Py golly! [*Anxiously.*] You feel better now, dough, don't you? You look little tired, dat's all!

ANNA [*Wearily*]. I am. Tired to death. I need a long rest and I don't see much chance of getting it.

CHRIS. What you mean, Anna?

ANNA. Well, when I made up my mind to come to see you, I thought you was a yanitor—that you'd have a place where, maybe, if you didn't mind having me, I could visit a while and rest up—till I felt able to get back on the job again.

CHRIS [*Eagerly*]. But Ay gat place, Anna—nice place. You rest all you want, py yiminy! You don't never have to vork as nurse gel no more. You stay with me, py golly!

ANNA [*Surprised and pleased by his eagerness—with a smile*]. Then you're really glad to see me—honest?

CHRIS [*Pressing one of her hands in both of his*]. Anna, Ay   620 like see you like hell, Ay tal you! And don't you talk no more about gatting yob. You stay with me. Ay don't see you for long time, you don't forgat dat. [*His voice trembles.*] Ay'm gatting ole. Ay gat no one in vorld but you.

ANNA [*Touched—embarrassed by this unfamiliar emotion*]. Thanks. It sounds good to hear someone—talk to me that way. Say, though—if you're so lonely—it's funny—why ain't you ever married again?

CHRIS [*Shaking his head emphatically—after a pause*]. Ay love your mo'der too much for ever do dat, Anna.   630

ANNA [*Impressed—slowly*]: I don't remember nothing about her. What was she like? Tell me.

CHRIS. Ay tal you all about everytang—and you tal me all tangs happen to you. But not here now. Dis ain't good place for young gel, anyway. Only no good sailor fallar come here for gat drunk. [*He gets to his feet quickly and picks up her bag.*] You come with me, Anna. You need lie down, gat rest.

ANNA [*Half rises to her feet, then sits down again*]. Where're you going?

CHRIS. Come. Ve gat on board.   640

ANNA [*Disappointedly*]. On board your barge, you mean? [*Dryly.*] Nix for mine! [*Then seeing his crestfallen look—forcing a smile.*] Do you think that's a good place for a young girl like me—a coal barge?

CHRIS [*Dully*]. Yes, Ay tank. [*He hesitates—then continues more and more pleadingly.*] You don't know how nice it's on barge, Anna. Tug come and ve gat towed out on voyage—yust water all around, and sun, and fresh air, and good grub for make you strong, healthy gel. You see many tangs you don't see before. You gat moonlight at night, maybe; see steamer pass;   650 see schooner make sail—see everythang that's pooty. You need take rest like dat. You work too hard for young gel already. You need vacation, yes!

ANNA [*Who has listened to him with a growing interest—with an uncertain laugh*]. It sounds good to hear you tell it. I'd sure like a trip on the water, all right. It's the barge .idea has me stopped. Well, I'll go down with you and have a look—and maybe I'll take a chance. Gee, I'd do anything once.

CHRIS [*Picks up her bag again*]. Ve go, eh?

ANNA. What's the rush? Wait a second. [*Forgetting the* 660 *situation for a moment, she relapses into the familiar form and flashes one of her winning trade smiles at him.*] Gee, I'm thirsty.

CHRIS [*Sets down her bag immediately—hastily*]. Ay'm sorry, Anna. What you tank you like for drink, eh?

ANNA [*Promptly*]. I'll take a—[*Then suddenly reminded—confusedly.*] I don't know. Whata they got here?

CHRIS [*With a grin*] Ay don't tank dey got much fancy drink for young gel in dis place, Anna. Yinger ale—sas'prilla, maybe.

ANNA [*Forcing a laugh herself*]. Make it sas, then.

CHRIS [*Coming up to her—with a wink*]. Ay tal you, Anna, ve calabrate, yes—dis one time because ve meet after so 670 many year. [*In a half whisper, embarrassedly.*] Dey gat good port wine, Anna. It's good for you, Ay tank—little bit—for give you appetite. It ain't strong, neider. One glass don't go to your head, Ay promise.

ANNA [*With a half hysterical laugh*]. All right. I'll take port.

CHRIS. Ay go gat him. [*He goes out to the bar. As soon as the door closes, Anna starts to her feet.*]

ANNA [*Picking up her bag—half-aloud—stammeringly*]. Gawd, I can't stand this! I better beat it. [*Then she lets her bag drop, stumbles over to her chair again, and covering her face with her hands, begins to sob.*]

LARRY [*Putting down his paper as Chris comes up—with a* 680 *grin*]. Well, who's the blond?

CHRIS [*Proudly*]. Dat vas Anna, Larry.

LARRY [*In amazement*]. Your daughter, Anna? [*Chris nods. Larry lets a long, low whistle escape him and turns away embarrassedly.*]

CHRIS. Don't you tank she vas pooty gel, Larry?

LARRY [*Rising to the occasion*]. Sure! A peach!

CHRIS. You bet you! Give me drink for take back—one port vine for Anna—she calabrate dis one time with me—and small beer for me.

LARRY [*As he gets the drinks*]. Small beer for you, eh? She's reformin' you already. 690

CHRIS [*Pleased*]. You bet! [*He takes the drinks. As she hears him coming, Anna hastily dries her eyes, tries to smile. Chris comes in and sets the drinks down on the table—stares at her for*] *a second anxiously—patting her hand.*] You look tired, Anna. Vell, Ay make you take good long rest now. [*Picking up his beer.*] Come, you drink vine. It put new life in you. [*She lifts her glass—she grins.*] Skoal, Anna! You know dat Svedish word?

ANNA. Skoal! [*Downing her port at a gulp like a drink of whiskey—her lips trembling.*] Skoal? Guess I know that word, all right, all right!

THE CURTAIN FALLS

ACT II

SCENE.—*Ten days later. The stern of the deeply-laden barge, "Simeon Winthrop," at anchor in the outer harbor of Provincetown, Mass. It is ten o'clock at night. Dense fog shrouds the barge on all sides, and she floats motionless on a calm. A lantern set up on an immense coil of thick hawser sheds a dull, filtering light on objects near it—the heavy steel bits for making fast the tow lines, etc. In the rear is the cabin, its misty windows glowing wanly with the light of a lamp inside. The chimney of the cabin stove rises a few feet above the roof. The doleful tolling of bells, on Long Point, on ships at anchor, breaks the silence at regular intervals.*

As the curtain rises, Anna is dicovered standing near the coil of rope on which the lantern is placed. She looks healthy, transformed, the natural color has come back to her face. She is staring out into the fog astern with an expression of awed wonder. She has on a black, oilskin coat, but wears no hat. The cabin door is pushed open and Chris appears. He is dressed in yellow oilskins—coat, pants, and sou'wester—and wears high sea-boots.

CHRIS [*The glare from the cabin still in his eyes, peers blinkingly astern*]. Anna! [*Receiving no reply, he calls again, this time with apparent apprehension.*] Anna!

ANNA [*With a start—making a gesture with her hand as if to impose silence—in a hushed whisper*]. Yes, here I am. What d'you want?

CHRIS [*Walks over to her—solicitously*]. Don't you come turn in, Anna? It's late—after four bells. It ain't good for you stay out here in fog, Ay tank.

ANNA. Why not? [*With a trace of strange exultation.*] I ¹⁰ love this fog! Honest! It's so—[*She hesitates, groping for a word.*]

—Funny and still. I feel as if I was—out of things altogether.

CHRIS [*Spitting disgustedly*]. Fog's vorst one of her dirty tricks, py yingo!

ANNA [*With a short laugh*]. Beefing about the sea again? I'm getting so's I love it, the little I've seen.

CHRIS [*Glancing at her moodily*]. Dat's foolish talk, Anna. You see her more, you don't talk dat vay. [*Then seeing her irritation, he hastily adopts a more cheerful tone.*] But Ay'm glad you like it on barge. Ay'm glad it makes you feel good again. [*With a placating grin.*] You like live like dis alone with ole fa'der, eh?

ANNA. Sure I do. Everything's been so different from anything I ever come across before. And now—this fog—Gee, I wouldn't have missed it for nothing. I never thought living on ships was so different from land. Gee, I'd yust love to work on it, honest I would, if I was a man. I don't wonder you always been a sailor.

CHRIS [*Vehemently*]. Ay ain't a sailor, Anna. And dis ain't real sea. You only see nice part. [*Then as she doesn't answer, he continues hopefully.*] Vell, fog lift in morning, Ay tank.

ANNA [*The exultation again in her voice*]. I love it! I don't give a rap if it never lifts! [*Chris fidgets from one foot to the other worriedly. Anna continues slowly, after a pause.*] It makes me feel clean—out here—'s if I'd taken a bath.

CHRIS [*After a pause*]. You better go in cabin—read book. Dat put you to sleep.

ANNA. I don't want to sleep. I want to stay out here—and think about things.

CHRIS [*Walks away from her toward the cabin—then comes back*]. You act funny tonight, Anna.

ANNA [*Her voice rising angrily*]. Say, what're you trying to do—make things rotten? You been kind as kind can be to me and I certainly appreciate it—only don't spoil it all now. [*Then, seeing the hurt expression on her father's face, she forces a smile.*] Lets talk of something else. Come. Sit down here. [*She points to the coil of rope.*]

CHRIS [*Sits down beside her with a sigh*]. It's gatting pooty late in night, Anna. Must be near five bells.

ANNA [*Interestedly*]. Five bells? What time is that?

CHRIS. Half past ten.

ANNA. Funny I don't know nothing about sea talk—but those cousins was always talking crops and that stuff. Gee, wasn't I sick of it—and of them!

CHRIS. You don't like live on farm, Anna?

ANNA. I've told you a hundred times I hated it. [*Decidedly.*] I'd rather have one drop of ocean than all the farms in the world! Honest! And you wouldn't like a farm, neither. Here's where you belong. [*She makes a sweeping gesture seaward.*] But not on a coal barge. You belong on a real ship, sailing all over the world.

CHRIS [*Moodily*]. Ay've done dat many year, Anna, when Ay vas damn fool. 60

ANNA [*Disgustedly*]. Oh, rats! [*After a pause she speaks musingly.*] Was the men in our family always sailors—as far back as you know about?

CHRIS [*Shortly*]. Yes. Damn fools! All men in our village on coast, Sveden, go to sea. Ain't nutting else for dem to do. My fa'der die on board ship in Indian Ocean. He's buried at sea. Ay don't never know him only little bit. Den my tree bro'der, older'n me, dey go on ships. Den Ay go, too. Den my mo'der she's left all 'lone. She die pooty quick after dat—all 'lone. Ve vas all 70 avay on voyage when she die. [*He pauses sadly.*] Two my bro'der dey gat lost on fishing boat same like your bro'ders vas drowned. My oder bro'der, he save money, give up sea, den he die home in bed. He's only one dat ole davil don't kill. [*Defiantly.*] But me, Ay bet you Ay die ashore in bed, too!

ANNA. Were all of 'em yust plain sailors?

CHRIS. Able body seaman, most of dem. [*With a certain pride.*] Dey vas all smart seaman, too—A one. [*Then after hesitating a moment—shyly.*] Ay vas bo'sun.

ANNA. Bo'sun? 80

CHRIS. Dat's kind of officer.

ANNA. Gee, that was fine. What does he do?

CHRIS [*After a second's hesitation, plunged into gloom again by his fear of her enthusiasm*]. Hard vork all time. It's rotten, Ay tal you, for go to sea. [*Determined to disgust her with sea life—volubly.*] Dey're all fool fallar, dem fallar in our family. Dey all vork rotten yob on sea for nutting, don't care nutting but yust gat big pay day in pocket, gat drunk, gat robbed, ship avay again on oder voyage. Dey don't come home. Dey don't do anytang like good man do. And dat ole davil, sea, sooner, later she 90 svallow dem up.

ANNA [*With excited laugh*]. Good sports, I'd call 'em. [*Then hastily.*] But say—listen—did all the women of the family marry sailors?

CHRIS [*Eagerly—seeing a chance to drive home his point*]. Yes —and it's bad on dem like hell vorst of all. Dey don't see deir men only once in long while. Dey set and vait all 'lone. And vhen deir boys grows up, go to sea, dey sit and vait some more. [*Vehemently.*] Any gel marry sailor, she's crazy fool! Your mo'der she tal you same tang if she vas alive. [*He relapses* 100 *into an attitude of somber brooding.*]

ANNA [*After a pause—dreamily*]. Funny! I do feel sort of— nutty, tonight. I feel old.

CHRIS [*Mystified*]. Ole?

ANNA. Sure—like I'd been living a long, long time—out here in the fog. [*Frowning perplexedly.*] I don't know how to tell you yust what I mean. It's like I'd come home after a long visit away some place. It all seems like I'd been here before lots of times—on boats—in this same fog. [*With a short laugh.*] You must think I'm off my base. 110

CHRIS [*Gruffly*]. Anybody feel funny dat vay in fog.

ANNA [*Persistently*]. But why d'you s'pose I feel so—so—like I'd found something I'd missed and been looking for—'s if this was the right place for me to fit in? And I seem to have forgot everything that's happened—like it didn't matter anymore. And I feel clean, somehow—like you feel yust after you've took a bath. And I feel happy for once—yes, honest!—happier than I ever been anywhere before! [*As Chris makes no comment but a heavy sigh, she continues wonderingly.*] It's nutty for me to feel that way, don't you think? 120

CHRIS [*A grim foreboding in his voice.*] Ay tank Ay'm damn fool for bring you on voyage, Anna.

ANNA [*Impressed by his tone.*] You talk—nutty tonight your-self. You act's if you was scared something was going to happen.

CHRIS. Only God know dat, Anna.

ANNA [*Half mockingly*]. Then it'll be Gawd's will, like the preachers say—what does happen.

CHRIS [*Starts to his feet with fierce protest*]. No! Dat ole davil, sea, she ain't God! [*In the pause of silence that comes after his defiance a hail in a man's husky, exhausted voice comes* 130 *faintly out of the fog to port.*] "Ahoy!" [*Chris gives a startled exclamation.*]

ANNA [*Jumping to her feet*]. What's that?

CHRIS [*Who has regained his composure—sheepishly*]. Py golly, dat scare me for minute. It's only some fallar hail, Anna— loose his course in fog. Must be fisherman's power boat. His en-gine break down, Ay guess. [*The "ahoy" comes again through the wall of fog, sounding much nearer this time. Chris goes over*

to the port bulwark.] Sound from dis side. She come in from
open sea. [*He holds his hands to his mouth, megaphone-*   140
fashion, and shouts back.] Ahoy, dere! Vhat's trouble?

THE VOICE [*This time sounding nearer but up forward toward
the bow*]. Heave a rope when we come alongside. [*Then irritably.*] Where are ye, ye scut?

CHRIS. Ay hear dem rowing. Dey come up by bow, Ay tank.
[*Then shouting out again.*] Dis vay!

THE VOICE. Right ye are! [*There is a muffled sound of oars in
oar-locks.*]

ANNA [*Half to herself—resentfully*]. Why don't that guy stay
where he belongs?   150

CHRIS [*Hurriedly*]. Ay go up bow. All hands asleep 'cepting fallar on vatch. Ay gat heave line to dat fallar. [*He picks up
a coil of rope and hurries off toward the bow. Anna walks back
toward the extreme stern as if she wanted to remain as much iso-
lated as possible. She turns her back on the proceedings and stares
out into the fog. The Voice is heard again shouting "Ahoy" and
Chris answering "Dis vay." Then there is a pause—the murmur
of excited voices—then the scuffling of feet. Chris appears from
around the cabin to port. He is supporting the limp form of a man
dressed in dungarees, holding one of the man's arms around*   160
*his neck. The deckhand, Johnson, a young, blond Swede, follows
him, helping along another exhausted man similar fashion. Anna
turns to look at them. Chris stops for a second—volubly.*] Anna!
You come help, vill you? You find vhiskey in cabin. Dese fallars
need drink for fix dem. Dey vas near dead.

ANNA [*Hurrying to him*]. Sure—but who are they? What's the
trouble?

CHRIS. Sailor fallars. Deir steamer gat wrecked. Dey been five
days in open boat—four fallars—only one left able stand up.
Come, Anna. [*She precedes him into the cabin, holding the*   170
*door open while he and Johnson carry in their burdens. The door
is shut, then opened again as Johnson comes out. Chris's voice
shouts after him.*] Go gat oder fallar, Yohnson.

JOHNSON. Yes, sir. [*He goes. The door is closed again. Mat
Burke stumbles in around the port side of the cabin. He moves
slowly, feeling his way uncertainly, keeping hold of the port
bulwark with his right hand to steady himself. He is stripped to
the waist, has on nothing but a pair of dirty dungaree pants. He
is a powerful, broad-chested six-footer, his face handsome in a
hard, rough, bold, defiant way. He is about thirty, in the full*   180
power of his heavy-muscled, immense strength. His dark eyes

are bloodshot and wild from sleeplessness. The muscles of his arms and shoulders are lumped in knots and bunches, the veins of his forearms stand out like blue cords. He finds his way to the coil of hawser and sits down on it facing the cabin, his back bowed, head in his hands, in an attitude of spent weariness.]

BURKE [*Talking aloud to himself*]. Row, ye divil! Row! [*Then lifting his head and looking about him.*] What's this tub? Well, we're safe anyway—with the help of God. [*He makes the sign of the cross mechanically. Johnson comes along the deck to* 190 *port, supporting the fourth man, who is babbling to himself incoherently. Burke glances at him disdainfully.*] Is it losing the small wits ye i ver had, ye are? Deck-scrubbing scut! [*They pass him and go into the cabin, leaving the door open. Burke sags forward wearily.*] I'm bate out—bate out entirely.

ANNA [*Comes out of the cabin with a tumbler quarter-full of whiskey in her hand. She gives a start when she sees Burke so near her, the light from the open door falling full on him. Then, overcoming what is evidently a feeling of repulsion, she comes up beside him*]. Here you are. Here's a drink for you. You need 200 it, I guess.

BURKE [*Lifting his head slowly—confusedly*]. Is it dreaming I am?

ANNA [*Half smiling*]. Drink it and you'll find it ain't no dream.

BURKE. To hell with the drink—but I'll take it just the same. [*He tosses it down.*] Aah! I'm needin' that—and 'tis fine stuff. [*Looking up at her with frank, grinning admiration.*] But 'twasn't the booze I meant when I said, was I dreaming. I thought you was some mermaid out of the sea come to torment me. [*He reaches out to feel of her arm.*] Aye, rale flesh and blood, 210 divil a less.

ANNA [*Coldly. Stepping back from him*]. Cut that.

BURKE. But tell me, isn't this a barge I'm on—or isn't it?

ANNA. Sure.

BURKE. And what is a fine handsome woman the like of you doing on this scow?

ANNA [*Coldly*]. Never you mind. [*Then half amused in spite of herself.*] Say, you're a great one, honest—starting in kidding right after what you been through.

BURKE [*Delighted—proudly*]. Ah, it was nothing—aisy for 220 a rale man with guts to him, the like of me. [*He laughs.*] All in the day's work, darlin'. [*Then, more seriously but still in a boastful tone, confidentially.*] But I won't be denying 'twas a damn narrow squeak. We'd all ought to be with Davy Jones at the bottom of the sea, be rights. And only for me, I'm telling you, and the great strength and guts is in me, we'd be being scoffed by the fishes this minute.

ANNA [*Contemptuously*]. Gee, you hate yourself, don't you? [*Then turning away from him indifferently.*] Well, you'd better come in and lie down. You must want to sleep.　　　230

BURKE [*Stung—rising unsteadily to his feet with chest out and head thrown back—resentfully*]. Lie down and sleep, is it? Divil a wink I'm after having for two days and nights and divil a bit I'm needing now. Let you not be thinking I'm the like of them three weak scuts come in the boat with me. I could lick the three of them sitting down with one hand tied behind me. They may be bate out, but I'm not—and I've been rowing the boat with them lying in the bottom not able to raise a hand for the last two days we was in it. [*Furiously, as he sees this is making no impression on her.*] And I can lick all hands on this tub, 　240 wan be wan, tired as I am!

ANNA [*Sarcastically*]. Gee, ain't you a hard guy! [*Then, with a trace of sympathy, as she notices him swaying from weakness.*] But never mind that fight talk. I'll take your word for all you've said. Go on and sit down out here, anyway, if I can't get you to come inside. [*He sits down weakly.*] You're all in, you might as well own up to it.

BURKE [*Fiercely*]. The hell I am.

ANNA [*Coldly*]. Well, be stubborn then for all I care. And I must say I don't care for your language. The men I know　250 don't pull that rough stuff when ladies are around.

BURKE [*Getting unsteadily to his feet again—in a rage*]. Ladies! Ho-ho! Divil mend you! Let you not be making game of me. What would ladies be doing on this bloody hulk? [*As Anna attempts to go to the cabin, he lurches into her path.*] Aisy, now! You're not the old Square-head's woman, I suppose you'll be telling me next—living in his cabin with him, no less! [*Seeing the cold, hostile expression on Anna's face, he suddenly changes his tone to one of boisterous joviality.*] But I do be thinking, iver since the first look my eyes took at you, that it's a fool you　260 are to be wasting yourself—a fine, handsome girl—on a stumpy runt of a man like that old Swede. There's too many strapping great lads on the sea would give their heart's blood for one kiss of you!

ANNA [*Scornfully*]. Lads like you, eh?

BURKE [*Grinning*]. Ye take the words out o' my mouth. I'm the proper lad for you, if it's meself do be saying it. [*With a quick movement he puts his arms about her waist.*] Whisht, now, me daisy! Himself's in the cabin. It's wan of your kisses I'm needing to take the tiredness from me bones. Wan kiss, now! [*He* 270 *presses her to him and attempts to kiss her.*]

ANNA [*Struggling fiercely*]. Leggo of me, you big mut! [*She pushes him away with all her might. Burke, weak and tottering, is caught off his guard. He is thrown down backward and, in falling, hits his head a hard thump against the bulwark. He lies there still, knocked out for the moment. Anna stands for a second, looking down at him frightenedly. Then she kneels down beside him and raises his head to her knee, staring into his face anxiously for some sign of life.*]

BURKE [*Stirring a bit—mutteringly*]. God stiffen it! [*He* 280 *opens his eyes and blinks up at her with vague wonder.*]

ANNA [*Letting his head sink back on the deck, rising to her feet with a sigh of relief*]. You're coming to all right, eh? Gee, I was scared for a moment I'd killed you.

BURKE [*With difficulty rising to a sitting position—scornfully*]. Killed, is it? It'd take more than a bit of a blow to crack my thick skull. [*Then looking at her with the most intense admiration.*] But, glory be, it's a power of strength is in them two fine arms of yours. There's not a man in the world can say the same as you, that he seen Mat Burke lying at his feet and him dead 290 to the world.

ANNA [*Rather remorsefully*]. Forget it. I'm sorry it happened, see? [*Burke rises and sits on bench. Then severely.*] Only you had no right to be getting fresh with me. Listen, now, and don't go getting any more wrong notions. I'm on this barge because I'm making a trip with my father. The captain's my father. Now you know.

BURKE. The old square—the old Swede, I mean?

ANNA. Yes.

BURKE [*Rising—peering at her face*]. Sure I might have 300 known it, if I wasn't a bloody fool from birth. Where else'd you get that fine yellow hair is like a golden crown on your head.

ANNA [*With an amused laugh*]. Say, nothing stops you, does it? [*Then attempting a severe tone again.*] But don't you think you ought to be apologizing for what you said and done yust a minute ago, instead of trying to kid me with that mush?

BURKE [*Indignantly*]. Mush! [*Then bending forward toward her with very intense earnestness.*] Indade and I will ask your pardon a thousand times—and on my knees, if ye like. I didn't mean a word of what I said or did. [*Resentful again* 310 *for a second.*] But divil a woman in all ports of the world has iver made a great fool of me that way before!

ANNA [*With amused sarcasm*]. I see. You mean you're a lady-killer and they all fall for you.

BURKE [*Offended. Passionately*]. Leave off your fooling! 'Tis that is after getting my back up at you. [*Earnestly.*] 'Tis no lie I'm telling you about the women. [*Ruefully.*] Though it's a great jackass I am to be mistaking you, even in anger, for the like of them cows on the waterfront is the only women I've met up with since I was growed to a man. [*As Anna shrinks away from him at this, he hurries on pleadingly.*] I'm a hard, rough man and I'm not fit, I'm thinking, to be kissing the shoe-soles of a fine, dacent girl the like of yourself. 'Tis only the ignorance of your kind made me see you wrong. So you'll forgive me, for the love of God, and let us be friends from this out. [*Passionately.*] I'm thinking I'd rather be friends with you than have my wish for anything else in the world. [*He holds out his hand to her shyly.*]

ANNA [*Looking queerly at him, perplexed and worried, but moved and pleased in spite of herself—takes his hand uncertainly*]. Sure.

BURKE [*With boyish delight*]. God bless you! [*In his excitement he squeezes her hand tight.*]

ANNA. Ouch!

BURKE [*Hastily dropping her hand—ruefully*]. Your pardon, Miss. 'Tis a clumsy ape I am. [*Then simply—glancing down his arm proudly.*] It's great power I have in my hand and arm, and I do be forgetting it at times.

ANNA [*Nursing her crushed hand and glancing at his arm, not without a trace of his own admiration*]. Gee, you're some strong, all right.

BURKE [*Delighted*]. It's no lie, and why shouldn't I be, with me shoveling a million tons of coal in the stokeholes of ships since I was a lad only. [*He pats the coil of hawser invitingly.*] Let you sit down, now, Miss, and I'll be telling you a bit of myself, and you'll be telling me a bit of yourself, and in an hour we'll be as old friends as if we was born in the same house. [*He pulls at her sleeve shyly.*] Sit down now, if you plaze.

ANNA [*With a half laugh*]. Well—[*She sits down.*] But we won't talk about me, see? You tell me about yourself and the wreck.

BURKE [*Flattered*]. I'll tell you, surely. But can I be asking you one question, Miss, has my head in a puzzle?

ANNA [*Guardedly*]. Well—I dunno—what is it?

BURKE. What is it you do when you're not taking a trip with the Old Man? For I'm thinking a fine girl the like of you ain't living always on this tub.

ANNA [*Uneasily*]. No—of course I ain't. [*She searches his face suspiciously, afraid there may be some hidden insinuation in his words. Seeing his simple frankness, she goes on confidently.*] 360 Well, I'll tell you. I'm a governess, see? I take care of kids for people and learn them things.

BURKE [*Impressed*]. A governess, is it? You must be smart, surely.

ANNA. But let's not talk about me. Tell me about the wreck, like you promised me you would.

BURKE [*Importantly*]. 'Twas this way, Miss. Two weeks out we ran into the divil's own storm, and she sprang wan hell of a leak up for'ard. The skipper was hoping to make Boston before another blow would finish her, but ten days back we met up 370 with another storm the like of the first, only worse. Four days we was in it with green seas raking over her from bow to stern. That was a terrible time, God help us. [*Proudly.*] And if it wasn't for me and my great strength, I'm telling you—and it's God's truth —there'd been mutiny itself in the stokehole. 'Twas me held them to it, with a kick to wan and a clout to another, and they not caring a damn for the engineers any more, but fearing a clout of my right arm more than they'd fear the sea itself. [*He glances at her anxiously, eager for her approval.*]

ANNA [*Concealing a smile—amused by his boyish boast-* 380 *ing*]. You did some hard work, didn't you?

BURKE [*Promptly*]. I did that! I'm a divil for sticking it out when them that's weak give up. But much good it did anyone! 'Twas a mad, fightin' scramble in the last seconds with each man for himself. I disremember how it come about, but there was the four of us in wan boat and when we was raised high on a great wave I took a look about and divil a sight there was of ship or men on top of the sea.

ANNA [*In a subdued voice*]. Then all the others was drowned?

BURKE. They was, surely. 390

ANNA [*With a shudder*]. What a terrible end!

BURKE [*Turns to her*]. A terrible end for the like of them swabs does live on land, maybe. But for the like of us does be roaming the seas, a good end, I'm telling you—quick and clane.

ANNA [*Struck by the word*]. Yes, clean. That's yust the word for—all of it—the way it makes me feel.

BURKE. The sea, you mean? [*Interestedly.*] I'm thinking you have a bit of it in your blood, too. Your Old Man wasn't only a barge rat—begging your pardon—all his life, by the cut of him.

ANNA. No, he was bo'sun on sailing ships for years. And all   400 the men on both sides of the family have gone to sea as far back as he remembers, he says. All the women have married sailors, too.

BURKE [*With intense satisfaction*]. Did they, now? They had spirit in them. It's only on the sea you'd find rale men with guts is fit to wed with fine, high-tempered girls [*Then he adds half-boldly*] the like of yourself.

ANNA [*With a laugh*]. There you go kiddin' again. [*Then seeing his hurt expression—quickly.*] But you was going to tell me about yourself. You're Irish, of course I can tell that.

BURKE [*Stoutly*]. Yes, thank God, though I've not seen a   410 sight of it in fifteen years or more.

ANNA [*Thoughtfully*]. Sailors never do go home hardly, do they? That's what my father was saying.

BURKE. He wasn't telling no lie. [*With sudden melancholy.*] It's a hard and lonesome life, the sea is. The only women you'd meet in the ports of the world who'd be willing to speak you a kind word isn't woman at all. You know the kind I mane, they're a poor, wicked lot, God forgive them. They're looking to steal the money from you only.

ANNA [*Her face averted—rising to her feet—agitatedly*].   420 I think—I guess I'd better see what's doing inside.

BURKE [*Afraid he has offended her—beseechingly*]. Don't go, I'm saying! Is it I've given you offence with my talk of the like of them? Don't heed it at all! I'm clumsy in my wits when it comes to talking proper with a girl the like of you. And why wouldn't I be? Since the day I left home for to go to sea punching coal, this is the first time I've had a word with a rale dacent woman. So don't turn your back on me now, and we beginning to be friends.

ANNA [*Turning to him again—forcing a smile*]. I'm not   430 sore at you, honest.

BURKE [*Gratefully*]. God bless you!

ANNA [*Changing the subject abruptly*]. But if you honestly think the sea's such a rotten life, why don't you get out of it?

BURKE [*Surprised*]. Work on land, is it? [*She nods. He spits scornfully.*] Digging spuds in the muck from dawn to dark, I suppose? [*Vehemently.*] I wasn't made for it, Miss.

ANNA [*With a laugh*]. I thought you'd say that.

BURKE [*Argumentatively*]. But there's good jobs and bad jobs

at sea, like there'd be on land. I'm thinking if it's in the stoke- 440
hole of a proper liner I was, I'd be able to have a little house and
be home to it wan week out of four. And I'm thinking that maybe
then I'd have the luck to find a fine dacent girl—the like of yourself, now—would be willing to wed with me.

ANNA [*Turning away from him with a short laugh—uneasily*].
Why sure. Why not?

BURKE [*Edging up close to her—exultantly*]. Then you think
a girl the like of yourself might maybe not mind the past at all
but only be seeing the good herself put in me?

ANNA [*In the same tone*]. Why, sure.   450

BURKE [*Passionately*]. She'd not be sorry for it, I'd take my
oath! 'Tis no more drinking and roving about I'd be doing then,
but giving my pay day into her hand and staying at home with
her as meek as a lamb each night of the week I'd be in port.

ANNA [*Moved in spite of herself and troubled by this half-con-
cealed proposal—with a forced laugh*]. All you got to do is find
the girl.

BURKE. I have found her!

ANNA [*Half-frightenedly—trying to laugh it off*]. You have?
When? I thought you was saying—   460

BURKE [*Boldly and forcefully*]. This night, [*Hanging his head
—humbly.*] If she'll be having me. [*Then raising his eyes to hers
—simply.*] 'Tis you I mean.

ANNA [*Is held by his eyes for a moment—then shrinks back
from him with a strange, broken laugh*]. Say—are you—going
crazy? Are you trying to kid me? Proposing—to me!—for
Gawd's sake!—on such short acquaintance? [*Chris comes out of
the cabin and stands staring blinkingly astern. When he makes
out Anna in such intimate proximity to this strange sailor, an
angry expression comes over his face.*]   470

BURKE [*Following her—with fierce, pleading insistence*]. I'm
telling you there's the will of God in it that brought me safe
through the storm and fog to the wan spot in the world where
you was! Think of that now, and isn't it queer?

CHRIS. Anna! [*He comes toward them, raging, his fists
clenched.*] Anna, you gat in cabin, you hear!

ANNA [*All her emotions immediately transformed into resentment at his bullying tone*]. Who d'you think you're talking to—
a slave?

CHRIS [*Hurt—his voice breaking—pleadingly*]. You need 480
gat rest, Anna. You gat sleep. [*She does not move. He turns on
Burke furiously.*] What you doing here, you sailor fallar? You

ain't sick like oders. You gat in fo'c's'tle. Dey give you bunk. [*Threateningly.*] You hurry, Ay tal you!

ANNA [*Impulsively*]. But he is sick. Look at him. He can hardly stand up.

BURKE [*Straightening and throwing out his chest—with a bold laugh*]. Is it giving me orders ye are, me bucko? Let you look out, then! With wan hand, weak as I am, I can break ye in two and fling the pieces over the side—and your crew after you. 490 [*Stopping abruptly.*] I was forgetting. You're her Old Man and I'd not raise a fist to you for the world. [*His knees sag, he wavers and seems about to fall. Anna utters an exclamation of alarm and hurries to his side.*]

ANNA [*Taking one of his arms over her shoulder*]. Come on in the cabin. You can have my bed if there ain't no other place.

BURKE [*With jubilant happiness—as they proceed toward the cabin*]. Glory be to God, is it holding my arm about your neck you are! Anna! Anna! Sure it's a sweet name is suited to you.

ANNA [*Guiding him carefully*]. Ssh! Sssh!   500

BURKE. Whisht, is it? Indade, and I'll not. I'll be roaring it out like a fog horn over the sea! You're the girl of the world and we'll be marrying soon and I don't care who knows it!

ANNA [*As she guides him through the cabin door*]. Ssshh! Never mind that talk. You go to sleep. [*They go out of sight in the cabin. Chris, who has been listening to Burke's last words with open-mouthed amazement stands looking after them helplessly.*]

CHRIS [*Turns suddenly and shakes his fist out at the sea—with bitter hatred*]. Dat's your dirty trick, damn ole davil, you! [*Then in a frenzy of rage.*] But, py God, you don't do dat! Not 510 while Ay'm living! No, py God, you don't!

THE CURTAIN FALLS

ACT III

SCENE.—*The interior of the cabin on the barge, "Simeon Winthrop" (at dock in Boston)—a narrow, low-ceilinged compartment the walls of which are painted a light brown with white trimmings. In the rear on the left, a door leading to the sleeping quarters. In the far left corner, a large locker-closet, painted white, on the door of which a mirror hangs on a nail. In the rear wall, two small square windows and a door opening out on the deck toward the stern. In the right wall, two more windows looking out on the port deck. White curtains, clean and stiff, are at the windows. A table with two cane-bottomed chairs stands in the center of the cabin. A dilapidated, wicker rocker, painted brown, is also by the table.*

It is afternoon of a sunny day about a week later. From the harbor and docks outside, muffled by the closed door and windows, comes the sound of steamers' whistles and the puffing snort of the donkey engines of some ship unloading nearby.

As the curtain rises, Chris and Anna are discovered. Anna is seated in the rocking-chair by the table, with a newspaper in her hands. She is not reading but staring straight in front of her. She looks unhappy, troubled, frowningly concentrated on her thoughts. Chris wanders about the room, casting quick, uneasy side glances at her face, then stopping to peer absent-mindedly out of the window. His attitude betrays an overwhelmingly, gloomy anxiety which has him on tenter hooks. He pretends to be engaged in setting things shipshape, but this occupation is confined to picking up some object, staring at it stupidly for a second, then aimlessly putting it down again. He clears his throat and starts to sing to himself in a low, doleful voice: "My Yosephine, come aboard de ship. Long time Ay vait for you."

ANNA [*Turning on him, sarcastically*]. I'm glad someone's feeling good. [*Wearily.*] Gee, I sure wish we was out of this dump and back in New York.

CHRIS [*With a sigh*]. Ay'm glad when ve sail again, too. [*Then, as she makes no comment, he goes on with a ponderous attempt at sarcasm.*] Ay don't see vhy you don't like Boston, dough. You have good time here, Ay tank. You go ashore all time, every day and night veek ve've been here. You go to movies, see show, gat all kinds fun— [*His eyes hard with hatred.*] All with that damn Irish fallar! ₁₀

ANNA [*With weary scorn*]. Oh, for heaven's sake, are you off on that again? Where's the harm in his taking me around? D'you want me to sit all day and night in this cabin with you—and knit? Ain't I got a right to have as good a time as I can?

CHRIS. It ain't right kind of fun—not with that fallar, no.

ANNA. I been back on board every night by eleven, ain't I? [*Then struck by some thought—looks at him with keen suspicion —with rising anger.*] Say, look here, what d'you mean by what you yust said?

CHRIS [*Hastily*]. Nutting by what Ay say, Anna. ₂₀

ANNA. You said "ain't right" and you said it funny. Say, listen here, you ain't trying to insinuate that there's something wrong between us, are you?

CHRIS [*Horrified*]. No, Anna! No, Ay svear to God, Ay never tank dat!

ANNA [*Mollified by his very evident sincerity—sitting down again*]. Well, don't you never think it neither if you want me ever to speak to you again. [*Angrily again.*] If I ever dreamt you thought that, I'd get the hell out of this barge so quick you couldn't see me for dust.   30

CHRIS [*Soothingly*]. Ay wouldn't never dream—[*Then, after a second's pause, reprovingly.*] You vas gatting learn to svear. Dat ain't nice for young gel, you tank?

ANNA [*With a faint trace of a smile*]. Excuse me. You ain't used to such language, I know. [*Mockingly.*] That's what your taking me to sea has done for me.

CHRIS [*Indignantly*]. No, it ain't me. It's dat damn sailor fallar learn you bad tangs.

ANNA. He ain't a sailor. He's a stoker.

CHRIS [*Forcibly*]. Dat vas million times vorse, Ay tal you!   40 Dem fallars dat vork below shoveling coal vas de dirtiest, rough gang of no-good fallars in vorld!

ANNA. I'd hate to hear you say that to Mat.

CHRIS. Oh, Ay tal him same tang. You don't gat it in head Ay'm scared of him yust 'cause he vas stronger'n Ay vas. [*Menacingly.*] You don't gat for fight with fists with dem fallars. Dere's oder vay for fix him.

ANNA [*Glancing at him with sudden alarm*]. What d'you mean?

CHRIS [*Sullenly*]. Nutting.

ANNA. You'd better not. I wouldn't start no trouble with   50 him if I was you. He might forget some time that you was old and my father—and then you'd be out of luck.

CHRIS [*With smouldering hatred*]. Vell, yust let him! Ay'm ole bird maybe, but Ay bet Ay show him trick or two.

ANNA [*Suddenly changing her tone—persuasively*]. Aw come on, be good. What's eating you, anyway? Don't you want no one to be nice to me except yourself?

CHRIS [*Placated—coming to her—eagerly*]. Yes, Ay do, Anna —only not fallar on sea. But Ay like for you marry steady fallar got good yob on land. You have little home in country all   60 your own—

ANNA [*Rising to her feet—brusquely*]. Oh, cut it out! [*Scornfully.*] Little home in the country! I wish you could have seen the little home in the country where you had me in jail till I was sixteen! [*With rising irritation.*] Some day you're going to get me so mad with that talk, I'm going to turn loose on you and tell you—a lot of things that'll open your eyes.

CHRIS [*Alarmed*]. Ay don't vant—

ANNA. I know you don't; but you keep on talking yust the same. 70

CHRIS. Ay don't talk no more den, Anna.

ANNA. Then promise me you'll cut out saying nasty things about Mat Burke every chance you get.

CHRIS [*Evasive and suspicious*]. Vhy? You like dat fallar—very much, Anna?

ANNA. Yes, I certainly do! He's a regular man, no matter what faults he's got. One of his fingers is worth all the hundreds of men I met out there—inland.

CHRIS [*His face darkening*]. Maybe you tank you love him den?

ANNA [*Defiantly*]. What of it if I do? 80

CHRIS [*Scowling and forcing out the words*]. Maybe—you tank you—marry him?

ANNA [*Shaking her head*]. No! [*Chris' face lights up with relief. Anna continues slowly, a trace of sadness in her voice.*] If I'd met him four years ago—or even two years ago—I'd have jumped at the chance, I tell you that straight. And I would now —only he's such a simple guy—a big kid—and I ain't got the heart to fool him. [*She breaks off suddenly*]. But don't never say again he ain't good enough for me. It's me ain't good enough for him.

CHRIS [*Snorts scornfully*]. Py yiminy, you go crazy, Ay 90 tank!

ANNA [*With a mournful laugh*]. Well, I been thinking I was myself the last few days. [*She goes and takes a shawl from a hook near the door and throws it over her shoulders.*] Guess I'll take a walk down to the end of the dock for a minute and see what's doing. I love to watch the ships passing. Mat'll be along before long, I guess. Tell him where I am, will you?

CHRIS [*Despondently*]. All right, Ay tal him. [*Anna goes out the doorway on the rear. Chris follows her out and stands on the deck outside for a moment looking after her. Then he* 100 *comes back inside and shuts the door. He stands looking out of the window—mutters—"Dirty ole davil, you." Then he goes to the table, sets the cloth straight mechanically, picks up the newspaper Anna has let fall to the floor and sits down in the rocking-chair. He stares at the paper for a while, then puts it on table,*] *holds his head in his hands and sighs drearily. The noise of a man's heavy footsteps comes from the deck outside and there is a loud knock on the door. Chris starts, makes a move as if to get up and go to the door, then thinks better of it and sits still. The knock is repeated—then as no answer is heard, the door is* 110 *flung open and Mat Burke appears. Chris scowls at the intruder and his hand instinctively goes back to the sheath knife on his hip. Burke is dressed up—wears a cheap blue suit, a striped cotton shirt with a black tie, and black shoes newly shined. His face is beaming with good humor.*]

BURKE [*As he sees Chris—in a jovial tone of mockery*]. Well, God bless who's here! [*He bends down and squeezes his huge form through the narrow doorway.*] And how is the world treating you this afternoon, Anna's father?

CHRIS [*Sullenly*]. Pooty goot—if it ain't for some fallars.   120

BURKE [*With a grin*]. Meaning me, do you? [*He laughs.*] Well, if you ain't the funny old crank of a man! [*Then soberly.*] Where's herself? [*Chris sits dumb, scowling, his eyes averted. Burke is irritated by this silence.*] Where's Anna, I'm after asking you?

CHRIS [*Hesitating—then grouchily*]. She go down end of dock.

BURKE. I'll be going down to her, then. But first I'm thinking I'll take this chance when we're alone to have a word with you. [*He sits down opposite Chris at the table and leans over toward him.*] And that word is soon said. I'm marrying your Anna   130 before this day is out, and you might as well make up your mind to it whether you like it or no.

CHRIS [*Glaring at him with hatred and forcing a scornful laugh*]. Ho-ho! Dat's easy for say!

BURKE. You mean I won't? [*Scornfully.*] Is it the like of yourself will stop me, are you thinking?

CHRIS. Yes, Ay stop it if it come to vorst.

BURKE [*With scornful pity*]. God help you!

CHRIS. But ain't no need for me do dat. Anna—

BURKE [*Smiling confidently*]. Is it Anna you think will   140 prevent me?

CHRIS. Yes.

BURKE. And I'm telling you she'll not. She knows I'm loving her, and she loves me the same, and I know it.

CHRIS. Ho-ho! She only have fun. She make big fool of you, dat's all.

BURKE [*Unshaken—pleasantly*]. That's a lie in your throat, divil mend you!

CHRIS. No, it ain't lie. She tal me yust before she go out she never marry fallar like you. 150

BURKE. I'll not believe it. 'Tis a great old liar you are, and a divil to be making a power of trouble if you had your way. But 'tis not trouble I'm looking for, and me sitting down here. [*Earnestly.*] Let us be talking it out now as man to man. You're her father, and wouldn't it be a shame for us to be at each other's throats like a pair of dogs, and I married with Anna. So out with the truth, man alive. What is it you're holding against me at all?

CHRIS [*A bit placated, in spite of himself, by Burke's evident sincerity—but puzzled and suspicious*]. Vell—Ay don't vant for Anna gat married. Listen, you fallar. Ay'm a ole man. Ay 160 don't see Anna for fifteen year. She vas all Ay gat in vorld. And now ven she come on first trip—you tank Ay vant her leave me 'lone again?

BURKE [*Heartily*]. Let you not be thinking I have no heart at all for the way you'd be feeling.

CHRIS [*Astonished and encouraged—trying to plead persuasively*]. Den you do right tang, eh? You ship avay again, leave Anna alone. [*Cajolingly.*] Big fallar like you dat's on sea, he don't need vife. He gat new gel in every port, you know dat.

BURKE [*Angry for a second*]. God stiffen you! [*Then 170 controlling himself—calmly.*] I'll not be giving you the lie on that. But divil take you, there's a time comes to every man, on sea or land, that isn't a born fool, when he's sick of the lot of them cows, and wearing his heart out to meet up with a fine dacent girl, and have a home to call his own and be rearing up children in it. 'Tis small use you're asking me to leave Anna. She's the wan woman of the world for me, and I can't live without her now, I'm thinking.

CHRIS. You forgat all about her in one week out of port, Ay bet you! 180

BURKE. You don't know the like I am. Death itself wouldn't make me forget her. So let you not be making talk to me about leaving her. I'll not, and be damned to you! It won't be so bad for you as you'd make out at all. She'll be living here in the States, and her married to me. And you'd be seeing her often so —a sight more often than ever you saw her the fifteen years she was growing up in the West. It's quare you'd be the one to be making great trouble about her leaving you when you never laid eyes on her once in all them years.

CHRIS [*Guiltily*]. Ay taught it vas better Anna stay avay, 190 grow up inland where she don't ever know ole davil, sea.

BURKE [*Scornfully*]. Is it blaming the sea for your troubles ye are again, God help you? Well, Anna knows it now. 'Twas in her blood, anyway.

CHRIS. And Ay don't vant she ever know no-good fallar on sea—

BURKE. She knows one now.

CHRIS [*Banging the table with his fist—furiously*]. Dat's yust it! Dat's yust what you are—no-good, sailor fallar! You tank Ay lat her life be made sorry by you like her mo'der's vas by me! No, Ay svear! She don't marry you if Ay gat kill you first! 200

BURKE [*Looks at him a moment, in astonishment—then laughing uproariously*]. Ho-ho! Glory be to God, it's bold talk you have for a stumpy runt of a man!

CHRIS [*Threateningly*]. Vell—you see!

BURKE [*With grinning defiance*]. I'll see, surely! I'll see myself and Anna married this day, I'm telling you! [*Then with contemptuous exasperation.*] It's quare fool's blather you have about the sea done this and the sea done that. You'd ought to be shamed to be saying the like, and you an old sailor yourself. 210 I'm after hearing a lot of it from you and a lot more that Anna's told me you do be saying to her, and I'm thinking it's a poor weak thing you are, and not a man at all!

CHRIS [*Darkly*]. You see if Ay'm man—maybe quicker'n you tank.

BURKE [*Contemptuously*]. Yerra, don't be boasting. I'm thinking 'tis out of your wits you've got with fright of the sea. You'd be wishing Anna married to a farmer, she told me. That'd be a swate match, surely! Would you have a fine girl the like of Anna lying down at nights with a muddy scut stinking of pigs and 220 dung? Or would you have her tied for life to the like of them skinny, shrivelled swabs does be working in cities?

CHRIS. Dat's lie, you fool!

BURKE. 'Tis not. 'Tis your own mad notions I'm after telling. But you know the truth in your heart, if great fear of the sea has made you a liar and coward itself. [*Pounding the table.*] The sea's the only life for a man with guts in him isn't afraid of his own shadow! 'Tis only on the sea he's free, and him roving the face of the world, seeing all things, and not giving a damn for saving up money, or stealing from your friends, or any of the 230 black tricks that a landlubber'd waste his life on. 'Twas yourself knew it once, and you a bo'sun for years.

CHRIS [*Sputtering with rage*]. You vas crazy fool, Ay tal you!

BURKE. You've swallowed the anchor. The sea give you a clout once knocked you down, and you're not man enough to get up for another, but lie there for the rest of your life howling bloody murder. [*Proudly.*] Isn't it myself the sea has nearly drowned, and me battered and bate till I was that close to hell I could hear the flames roaring, and never a groan out of me till the sea gave up and it seeing the great strength and guts of a man was 240 in me?

CHRIS [*Scornfully*]. Yes, you vas a hell of fallar, hear you tal it!

BURKE [*Angrily*]. You'd be calling me a liar once too often, me old bucko! Wasn't the whole story of it and my picture itself in the newspapers of Boston a week back? [*Looking Chris up and down belittlingly.*] Sure I'd like to see you in the best of your youth do the like of what I done in the storm and after. 'Tis a mad lunatic, screeching with fear, you'd be this minute.

CHRIS. Ho-ho! You vas young fool! In ole years when Ay vas on windyammer, Ay vas through hundred storms vorse'n 250 dat! Ships vas ships den—and men dat sail on dem vas real men. And now what you gat on steamers? You gat fallars on deck don't know ship from mudscow. [*With a meaning glance at Burke.*] And below deck you gat fallars yust know how for shovel coal—might yust as vell vork on coal vagon ashore!

BURKE [*Stung—angrily*]. Is it casting insults at the men in the stokehole ye are, ye old ape? God stiffen you! Wan of them is worth any ten stock-fish-swilling Square-heads ever shipped on a windbag!

CHRIS [*His face working with rage, his hand going back to 260 the sheath-knife on his hip*]. Irish svine, you!

BURKE [*Tauntingly*]. Don't ye like the Irish, ye old baboon? 'Tis that you're needing in your family, I'm telling you—an Irishman and a man of the stokehole—to put guts in it so that you'll not be having grandchildren would be fearful cowards and jackasses the like of yourself!

CHRIS [*Half rising from his chair—in a voice choked with rage*]. You look out!

BURKE [*Watching him intently—a mocking smile on his lips*]. And it's that you'll be having, no matter what you'll do to 270 prevent; for Anna and me'll be married this day, and no old fool the like of you will stop us when I've made up my mind.

CHRIS [*With a hoarse cry*]. You don't! [*He throws himself at Burke, knife in hand, knocking his chair over backwards. Burke springs to his feet quickly in time to meet the attack. He laughs with the pure love of battle. The old Swede is like a child in his hands. Burke does not strike or mistreat him in any way, but simply twists his right hand behind his back and forces the knife from his fingers. He throws the knife into a far corner of the room—tauntingly.]* 280

BURKE. Old men is getting childish shouldn't play with knifes. [*Holding the struggling Chris at arm's length—with a sudden rush of anger, drawing back his fist.*] I've half a mind to hit you a great clout will put sense in your square head. Kape off me now, I'm warning you! [*He gives Chris a push with the flat of his hand which sends the old Swede staggering back against the cabin wall, where he remains standing, panting heavily, his eyes fixed on Burke with hatred, as if he were only collecting strength to rush at him again.*]

BURKE [*Warningly*]. Now don't be coming at me again, 290 I'm saying, or I'll flatten you on the floor with a blow, if 'tis Anna's father you are itself! I've no patience left for you. [*Then with an amused laugh.*] Well, 'tis a bold old man you are just the same, and I'd never think it was in you to come tackling me alone. [*A shadow crosses the cabin windows. Both men start. Anna appears in the doorway.*]

ANNA [*With pleased surprise as she sees Burke*]. Hello, Mat. Are you here already? I was down—[*She stops, looking from one to the other, sensing immediately that something has happened.*] What's up? [*Then noticing the overturned chair—* 300 *in alarm.*] How'd that chair get knocked over? [*Turning on Burke reproachfully.*] You ain't been fighting with him, Mat—after you promised?

BURKE [*His old self again*]. I've not laid a hand on him, Anna. [*He goes and picks up the chair, then turning on the still questioning Anna—with a reassuring smile.*] Let you not be worried at all. 'Twas only a bit of an argument we was having to pass the time till you'd come.

ANNA. It must have been some argument when you got to throwing chairs. [*She turns on Chris.*] Why don't you say 310 something? What was it about?

CHRIS [*Relaxing at last—avoiding her eyes—sheepishly*]. Ve vas talking about ships and fallars on sea.

ANNA [*With a relieved smile*]. Oh—the old stuff, eh?

BURKE [*Suddenly seeming to come to a bold decision—with a defiant grin at Chris*]. He's not after telling you the whole of it. We was arguing about you mostly.

ANNA [*With a frown*]. About me?

BURKE. And we'll be finishing it out right here and now and in your presence if you're willing. [*He sits down at the left of* table.]

ANNA [*Uncertainly—looking from him to her father*]. Sure. Tell me what it's all about.

CHRIS [*Advancing toward the table—protesting to Burke*]. No! You don't do dat, you! You tal him you don't vant for hear him talk, Anna.

ANNA. But I do. I want this cleared up.

CHRIS [*Miserably afraid now*]. Vell, not now, anyvay. You vas going ashore, yes? You ain't got time—

ANNA [*Firmly*]. Yes, right here and now. [*She turns to Burke.*] You tell me, Mat, since he don't want to.

BURKE [*Draws a deep breath—then plunges in boldly*]. The whole of it's in a few words only. So's he'd make no mistake, and him hating the sight of me, I told him in his teeth I loved you. [*Passionately.*] And that's God truth, Anna, and well you know it!

CHRIS [*Scornfully—forcing a laugh*]. Ho-ho! He tal same tang to gel every port he go!

ANNA [*Shrinking from her father with repulsion—resentfully*]. Shut up, can't you? [*Then to Burke—feelingly.*] I know it's true, Mat. I don't mind what he says.

BURKE [*Humbly grateful*]. God bless you!

ANNA. And then what?

BURKE. And then—[*Hesitatingly.*] And then I said—[*He looks at her pleadingly.*] I said I was sure—I told him I thought you have a bit of love for me, too. [*Passionately.*] Say you do, Anna! Let you not destroy me entirely, for the love of God! [*He grasps both her hands in his two.*]

ANNA [*Deeply moved and troubled—forcing a trembling laugh*]. So you told him that, Mat? No wonder he was mad. [*Forcing out the words.*] Well, maybe it's true, Mat. Maybe I do. I been thinking and thinking—I didn't want to, Mat, I'll own up to that—I tried to cut it out—but—[*She laughs helplessly.*] I guess I can't help it anyhow. So I guess I do, Mat. [*Then with a sudden joyous defiance.*] Sure I do! What's the use of kidding myself different? Sure I love you, Mat!

CHRIS [*With a cry of pain*]. Anna! [*He sits crushed.*]

BURKE [*With a great depth of sincerity in his humble gratitude.*] God be praised!

ANNA [*Assertively*]. And I ain't never loved a man in my life before, you can always believe that—no matter what happens.

BURKE [*Goes over to her and puts his arms around her*]. Sure I do be believing ivery word you iver said or iver will say. And 'tis you and me will be having a grand, beautiful life together to the end of our days! [*He tries to kiss her. At first she turns away her head—then, overcome by a fierce impulse of passionate love, she takes his head in both her hands and holds his face close to hers, staring into his eyes. Then she kisses him full on the lips.*]

ANNA [*Pushing him away from her—forcing a broken laugh*]. Good-bye. [*She walks to the doorway in rear—stands with   370 her back toward them, looking out. Her shoulders quiver once or twice as if she were fighting back her sobs.*]

BURKE [*Too in the seventh heaven of bliss to get any correct interpretation of her word—with a laugh*]. Good-by, is it? The divil you say! I'll be coming back at you in a second for more of the same! [*To Chris who has quickened to instant attention at his daughter's good-by, and has looked back at her with a stirring of foolish hope in his eyes.*] Now, me old bucko, what'll you be saying? You heard the words from her own lips. Confess I've bate you. Own up like a man when you're bate fair and   380 square. And here's my hand to you—[*Holds out his hand.*] And let you take it and we'll shake and forget what's over and done, and be friends from this out.

CHRIS [*With implacable hatred*]. Ay don't shake hands with you fallar—not vhile Ay live!

BURKE [*Offended*]. The back of my hand to you then, if that suits you better. [*Growling.*] 'Tis a rotten bad loser you are, divil mend you!

CHRIS. Ay don't lose—[*Trying to be scornful and self-convincing.*] Anna say she like you little bit but you don't hear her   390 say she marry you, Ay bet. [*At the sound of her name Anna has turned round to them. Her face is composed and calm again, but it is the dead calm of despair.*]

BURKE [*Scornfully*]. No, and I wasn't hearing her say the sun is shining either.

CHRIS [*Doggedly*]. Dat's all right. She don't say it, yust same.

ANNA [*Quietly—coming forward to them*]. No, I didn't say it, Mat.

CHRIS [*Eagerly*]. Dere! You hear!

BURKE [*Misunderstanding her—with a grin*]. You're wait-   400 ing till you do be asked, you mane? Well, I'm asking you now. And we'll be married this day, with the help of God!

ANNA [*Gently*]. You heard what I said, Mat—after I kissed you?

BURKE [*Alarmed by something in her manner*]. No—I disre-member.

ANNA. I said good-by. [*Her voice trembling.*] That kiss was for good-by, Mat.

BURKE [*Terrified*]. What d'you mane?

ANNA. I can't marry you, Mat—and we've said good-by.   410 That's all.

CHRIS [*Unable to hold back his exultation*]. Ay know it! Ay know dat vas so!

BURKE [*Jumping to his feet—unable to believe his ears*]. Anna! Is it making game of me you'd be? 'Tis a quare time to joke with me, and don't be doing it, for the love of God.

ANNA [*Looking him in the eyes—steadily*]. D'you think I'd kid you now? No, I'm not joking, Mat. I mean what I said.

BURKE. Ye don't! Ye can't! 'Tis mad you are, I'm telling you!

ANNA [*Fixedly*]. No I'm not.   420

BURKE [*Desperately*]. But what's come over you so sudden? You was saying you loved me—

ANNA. I'll say that as often as you want me to. It's true.

BURKE [*Bewilderedly*]. Then why—what, in the divil's name —Oh, God help me, I can't make head or tail to it all!

ANNA. Because it's the best way out I can figure, Mat. [*Her voice catching.*] I been thinking it over and thinking it over day and night all week. Don't think it ain't hard on me, too, Mat.

BURKE. For the love of God, tell me then, what is it that's pre-venting you wedding me when the two of us has love? [*Sud-*   430 *denly getting an idea and pointing at Chris—exasperately.*] Is it giving heed to the like of that old fool ye are, and him hating me and filling your ears full of bloody lies against me?

CHRIS [*Getting to his feet—raging triumphantly before Anna has a chance to get in a word*]. Yes, Anna believe me, not you! She know her old fa'der don't lie like you.

ANNA [*Turning on her father angrily*]. You sit down, d'you hear? Where do you come in butting in and making things worse? You're like a devil, you are! [*Harshly.*] Good Lord, and I was beginning to like you, beginning to forget all I've got held   440 up against you!

CHRIS [*Crushed—feebly*]. You ain't got nutting for hold against me, Anna.

ANNA. Ain't I yust! Well, lemme tell you—[*She glances at Burke and stops abruptly.*] Say, Mat, I'm s'prised at you. You didn't think anything he'd said—

BURKE [*Glumly*]. Sure, what else would it be?

ANNA. Think I've ever paid any attention to all his crazy bull? Gee, you must take me for a five-year-old kid.

BURKE [*Puzzled and beginning to be irritated at her too*].   450 I don't know how to take you, with your saying this one minute and that the next.

ANNA. Well, he has nothing to do with it.

BURKE. Then what is it has? Tell me, and don't keep me waiting and sweating blood.

ANNA [*Resolutely*]. I can't tell you—and I won't. I got a good reason—and that's all you need to know. I can't marry you, that's all there is to it. [*Distractedly*]. So, for Gawd's sake, let's talk of something else.

BURKE. I'll not! [*Then fearfully.*] Is it married to someone   460 else you are—in the West maybe?

ANNA [*Vehemently*]. I should say not.

BURKE [*Regaining his courage*]. To the divil with all other reasons then. They don't matter with me at all. [*He gets to his feet confidently, assuming a masterful tone.*] I'm thinking you're the like of them women can't make up their mind till they're drove to it. Well, then, I'll make up your mind for you bloody quick. [*He takes her by the arms, grinning to soften his serious bullying.*] We've had enough of talk! Let you be going into your room now and be dressing in your best and we'll be going   470 ashore.

CHRIS [*Aroused—angrily*]. No, py God, she don't do that! [*Takes hold of her arm.*]

ANNA [*Who has listened to Burke in astonishment. She draws away from him, instinctively repelled by his tone, but not exactly sure if he is serious or not—a trace of resentment in her voice*]. Say, Where do you get that stuff?

BURKE [*Imperiously*]. Never mind, now! Let you go get dressed, I'm saying. [*Then turning to Chris.*] We'll be seeing who'll win in the end—me or you.   480

CHRIS [*To Anna—also in an authoritative tone*]. You stay right here, Anna, you hear! [*Anna stands looking from one to the other of them as if she thought they had both gone crazy. Then the expression of her face freezes into a hardened sneer of her experience.*]

BURKE [*Violently*]. She'll not! She'll do what I say! You've had your hold on her long enough. It's my turn now.

ANNA [*With a hard laugh*]. Your turn? Say, what am I, anyway?

BURKE. 'Tis not what you are, 'tis what you're going to be   490 this day—and that's wedded to me before night comes. Hurry up now with your dressing.

CHRIS [*Commandingly*]. You don't do one tang he say, Anna! [*Anna laughs mockingly.*]

BURKE. She will, so!

CHRIS. Ay tal you she don't! Ay'm her fa'der.

BURKE. She will in spite of you. She's taking my orders from this out, not yours.

ANNA [*Laughing again*]. Orders is good!

BURKE [*Turning to her impatiently*]. Hurry up now, and   500 shake a leg. We've no time to be wasting. [*Irritated as she doesn't move.*] Do you hear what I'm telling you?

CHRIS. You stay dere, Anna!

ANNA [*At the end of her patience—blazing out at them passionately*]. You can go to hell, both of you! [*There is something in her tone that makes them forget their quarrell and turn to her in a stunned amazement. Anna laughs wildly.*] You're just like all the rest of them—you two! Gawd, you'd think I was a piece of furniture! I'll show you! Sit down now! [*As they hesitate—furiously.*] Sit down and let me talk for a minute. You're all   510 wrong, see? Listen to me! I'm going to tell you something—and then I'm going to beat it. [*To Burke—with a harsh laugh.*] I'm going to tell you a funny story, so pay attention. [*Pointing to Chris.*] I've been meaning to turn it loose on him every time he'd get my goat with his bull about keeping me safe inland. I wasn't going to tell you, but you've forced me into it. What's the dif? It's all wrong anyway, and you might as well get cured that way as any other. [*With hard mocking.*] Only don't forget what you said a minute ago about it not mattering to you what other reason I got so long as I wasn't married to no one else.   520

BURKE [*Manfully*]. That's my word, and I'll stick to it!

ANNA [*Laughing bitterly*]. What a chance! You make me laugh, honest! Want to bet you will? Wait 'n see! [*She stands at the table rear, looking from one to the other of the two men with her hard, mocking smile. Then she begins, fighting to control her emotion and speak calmly.*] First thing is, I want to tell you two guys something. You was going on 's if one of you had got to own me. But nobody owns me, see?—'cepting myself. I'll do what I please and no man, I don't give a hoot who he is, can tell me what to do! I ain't asking either of you for a living. I can   530 make it myself—one way or other. I'm my own boss. So put that in your pipe and smoke it! You and your orders!

BURKE [*Protestingly*]. I wasn't meaning it that way at all and

well you know it. You've no call to be raising this rumpus with
me. [*Pointing to Chris.*] 'Tis him you've a right—

ANNA. I'm coming to him. But you—you did mean it that way,
too. You sounded—yust like all the rest. [*Hysterically.*] But,
damn it, shut up! Let me talk for a change!

BURKE. 'Tis quare, rough talk, that—for a dacent girl the like
of you!   540

ANNA [*With a hard laugh*]. Decent? Who told you I was?
[*Chris is sitting with bowed shoulders, his head in his hands. She
leans over in exasperation and shakes him violently by the shoulder.*] Don't go to sleep, Old man! Listen here, I'm talking to you
now!

CHRIS [*Straightening up and looking about as if he were seeking
a way to escape—with frightened foreboding in his voice*]. Ay
don't vant to hear it. You vas going out of head, Ay tank, Anna.

ANNA [*Violently*]. Well, living with you is enough to drive
anyone off their nut. Your bunk about the farm being so   550
fine! Didn't I write you year after year how rotten it was and
what a dirty slave them cousins made of me? What'd you care?
Nothing! Not even enough to come out and see me! That crazy
bull about wanting to keep me away from the sea don't go down
with me! You yust didn't want to be bothered with me! You're
like all the rest of 'em!

CHRIS [*Feebly*]. Anna! It ain't so—

ANNA [*Not heeding his interruption—revengefully*]. But one
thing I never wrote you. It was one of them cousins that you
think is such nice people—the youngest son—Paul—that   560
started me wrong. [*Loudly.*] It wasn't none of my fault. I hated
him worse'n hell and he knew it. But he was big and strong—
[*Pointing to Burke.*]—like you!

BURKE [*Half springing to his feet—his fists clenched*]. God
blarst it! [*He sinks slowly back in his chair again, the knuckles
showing white on his clenched hands, his face tense with the
effort to suppress his grief and rage.*]

CHRIS [*In a cry of horrified pain*]. Anna!

ANNA [*To him—seeming not to have heard their interruptions*].
That was why I run away from the farm. That was what   570
made me get a yob as a nurse girl in St. Paul. [*With a hard, mocking laugh.*] And you think that was a nice yob for a girl, too,
don't you? [*Sarcastically.*] With all them nice inland fellers yust
looking for a chance to marry me, I s'pose. Marry me? What a
chance! They wasn't looking for marrying. [*As Burke lets a
groan of fury escape him—desperately.*] I'm owning up to every-

thing fair and square. I was caged in, I tell you—yust like in yail
—taking care of other people's kids—listening to 'em bawling and
crying day and night—when I wanted to be out—and I was
lonesome—lonesome as hell! [*With a sudden weariness in* 580
her voice.] So I give up finally. What was the use? [*She stops
and looks at the two men. Both are motionless and silent. Chris
seems in a stupor of despair, his house of cards fallen about him.
Burke's face is livid with the rage that is eating him up, but he is
too stunned and bewildered yet to find a vent for it. The con-
demnation she feels in their silence goads Anna into a harsh
strident defiance.*] You don't say nothing—either of you—but
I know what you're thinking. You're like all the rest! [*To Chris
furiously.*] And who's to blame for it, me or you? If you'd even
acted like a man—if you'd even been a regular father and 590
had me with you—maybe things would be different!

CHRIS [*In agony*]. Don't talk dat vay, Anna! Ay go crazy! Ay
von't listen! [*Puts his hands over his ears.*]

ANNA [*Infuriated by his action—stridently*]. You will too listen!
[*She leans over and pulls his hands from his ears—with hysterical
rage.*] You—keeping me safe inland—I wasn't no nurse girl the
last two years—I lied when I wrote you—I was in a house, that's
what!—yes, that kind of a house—the kind sailors like you and
Mat goes to in port—and your nice inland men, too—and all
men, God damn 'em! I hate 'em! Hate 'em! Hate 'em! [*She* 600
*breaks into hysterical sobbing, throwing herself into the chair and
hiding her face in her hands on the table. The two men have
sprung to their feet.*]

CHRIS [*Whimpering like a child*]. Anna! Anna! It's lie! It's lie!
[*He stands wringing his hands together and begins to weep.*]

BURKE [*His whole great body tense like a spring—dully and
gropingly*]. So that's what's in it!

ANNA [*Raising her head at the sound of his voice—with extreme
mocking bitterness*]. I s'pose you remember your promise, Mat?
No other reason was to count with you so long as I wasn't 610
married already. So I s'pose you want me to get dressed and go
ashore, don't you? [*She laughs.*] Yes, you do!

BURKE [*On the verge of his outbreak—stammeringly*]. God
stiffen you!

ANNA [*Trying to keep her hard, bitter tone, but gradually letting a note of pitiful pleading creep in*]. I s'pose if I tried to tell
you I wasn't—that—no more, you'd believe me, wouldn't you?
Yes, you would! And if I told you that yust getting out in this
barge, and being on the sea had changed me and made me feel

different about things, 's if all I'd been through wasn't me   620
and didn't count and was yust like it never happened—you'd
laugh, wouldn't you? And you'd die laughing sure if I said that
meeting you that funny way that night in the fog, and afterwards seeing that you was straight goods stuck on me, had got
me to thinking for the first time, and I sized you up as a different
kind of man—a sea man as different from the ones on land as
water is from mud—and that was why I got stuck on you, too. I
wanted to marry you and fool you, but I couldn't. Don't you
see how I'd changed? I couldn't marry you with you believing
a lie—and I was shamed to tell you the truth—till the both   630
of you forced my hand, and I seen you was the same as all the
rest. And now, give me a bawling out and beat it, like I can tell
you're going to. [*She stops, looking at Burke. He is silent, his
face averted, his features beginning to work with fury. She pleads
passionately.*] Will you believe it if I tell you that loving you
has made me—clean? It's the straight goods, honest! [*Then as he
doesn't reply—bitterly.*] Like hell you will! You're like all the
rest!

BURKE [*Blazing out—turning on her in a perfect frenzy of rage
—his voice trembling with passion*]. The rest, is it? God's   640
curse on you! Clane, it is? You slut, you, I'll be killing you now!
[*He picks up the chair on which he has been sitting, and, swinging
it high over his shoulder, springs toward her. Chris rushes forward
with a cry of alarm, trying to ward off the blow from his daughter. Anna looks up into Burke's eyes with the fearlessness of
despair. Burke checks himself, the chair held in the air.*]

CHRIS [*Wildly*]. Stop, you crazy fool! You vant for murder
her!

ANNA [*Pushing her father away brusquely, her eyes still holding Burke's*]. Keep out of this, you! [*To Burke—dully.*]   650
Well, ain't you got the nerve to do it? Go ahead! I'll be thankful
to you, honest. I'm sick of the whole game.

BURKE [*Throwing the chair away into a corner of the room
—helplessly*]. I can't do it, God help me, and your two eyes looking at me. [*Furiously.*] Though I do be thinking I'd have a good
right to smash your skull like a rotten egg. Was there iver a
woman in the world had the rottenness in her that you have, and
was there iver a man the like of me was made the fool of the
world, and me thinking thoughts about you, and having great
love for you, and dreaming dreams of the fine life we'd have   660
when we'd be wedded! [*His voice high pitched in lamentation
that is like a keen.*] Yerra, God help me! I'm destroyed entirely

and my heart is broken in bits! I'm asking God Himself, was it for this he'd have me roaming the earth since I was a lad only, to come to black shame in the end, where I'd be giving a power of love to a woman is the same as others you'd meet in any hooker-shanty in port, with red gowns on them and paint on their grinning mugs, would be sleeping with any man for a dollar or two!

ANNA [*In a scream*]. Don't, Mat! For Gawd's sake! [*Then raging and pounding the table with her hands.*] Get out of 670 here! Leave me alone! Get out of here!

BURKE [*His anger rushing back on him*]. I'll be going, surely! And I'll be drinking sloos of whiskey will wash that black kiss of yours off my lips; and I'll be getting dead rotten drunk so I'll not remember if 'twas iver born you was at all; and I'll be shipping away on some boat will take me to the other end of the world where I'll never see your face again! [*He turns toward the door.*]

CHRIS [*Who has been standing in a stupor—suddenly grasping Burke by the arm—stupidly*]. No, you don't go. Ay tank 680 maybe it's better Anna marry you now.

BURKE [*Shaking Chris off—furiously*]. Lave go of me, ye old ape! Marry her, is it? I'd see her roasting in hell first! I'm shipping away out of this, I'm telling you! [*Pointing to Anna—passionately.*] And my curse on you and the curse of Almighty God and all the Saints! You've destroyed me this day and may you lie awake in the long nights, tormented with thoughts of Mat Burke and the great wrong you've done him!

ANNA [*In anguish*]. Mat! [*But he turns without another word and strides out of the doorway. Anna looks after him wildly, 690 starts to run after him, then hides her face in her outstretched arms, sobbing. Chris stands in a stupor, staring at the floor.*]

CHRIS [*After a pause, dully*]. Ay tank Ay go ashore too.

ANNA [*Looking up, wildly*]. Not after him! Let him go! Don't you dar.—

CHRIS [*Somberly*]. Ay go for gat drink.

ANNA [*With a harsh laugh*]. So I'm driving you to drink, too, eh? I s'pose you want to get drunk so's you can forget—like him?

CHRIS [*Bursting out angrily*]. Yes, Ay vant! You tank Ay like hear dem tangs. [*Breaking down—weeping.*] Ay tank you 700 vasn't dat kind of gel, Anna.

ANNA [*Mockingly*]. And I s'pose you want me to beat it, don't you? You don't want me here disgracing you, I s'pose?

CHRIS. No, you stay here! [*Goes over and pats her on the shoulder, tears running down his face.*] Ain't your fault, Anna, Ay know dat. [*She looks up at him, softened. He bursts into rage.*] It's dat ole davil, sea, do this to me. [*He shakes his fist at the door.*] It's her dirty tricks! It vas all right on barge with yust you and me. Den she bring dat Irish fallar in fog, she make you like him, she make you fight with me all time! If dat Irish fallar don't 710 never come, you don't never tal me dem tangs, Ay don't never know, and everytang's all right. [*He shakes his fist again.*] Dirty ole davil!

ANNA [*With spent weariness*]. Oh, what's the use? Go on ashore and get drunk.

CHRIS [*Goes into room on left and gets his cap. He goes to the door, silent and stupid—then turns*]. You vait here, Anna?

ANNA [*Dully*]. Maybe—and maybe not. Maybe I'll get drunk, too. Maybe I'll—But what the hell do you care what I do? Go on and beat it. [*Chris turns stupidly and goes out. Anna sits at* 720 *the table, staring straight in front of her.*]

THE CURTAIN FALLS

ACT IV

SCENE.—*Same as Act Three, about nine o'clock of a foggy night two days later. The whistles of steamers in the harbor can be heard. The cabin is lighted by a small lamp on the table. A suit case stands in the middle of the floor. Anna is sitting in the rocking chair. She wears a hat, is all dressed up as in Act One. Her face is pale, looks terribly tired and worn, as if the two days just past had been ones of suffering and sleepless nights. She stares before her despondently, her chin in her hands. There is a timid knock on the door in the rear. Anna jumps to her feet with a startled exclamation and looks toward the door with an expression of mingled hope and fear.*

ANNA [*Faintly*]. Come in. [*Then summoning her courage— more resolutely.*] Come in. [*The door is opened and Chris appears in the doorway. He is in a very bleary, bedraggled condition, suffering from the after effects of his drunk. A tin pail of foaming beer is in his hand. He comes forward, his eyes avoiding Anna's.*

CHRIS [*Mutters stupidly*]. It's foggy.

ANNA [*Looking him over with contempt*]. So you come back at last, did you? You're a fine looking sight! [*Then jeeringly.*]

I thought you'd beaten it for good on account of the disgrace I'd brought on you. 10

CHRIS [*Wincing—faintly*]. Don't say dat, Anna, please! [*He sits in a chair by the table, setting down the can of beer, holding his head in his hands.*]

ANNA [*Looks at him with a certain sympathy*]. What's the trouble? Feeling sick?

CHRIS [*Dully*]. Inside my head feel sick.

ANNA. Well, what d'you expect after being soused for two days? [*Resentfully.*] It serves you right. A fine thing—you leaving me alone on this barge all that time!

CHRIS [*Humbly*]. Ay'm sorry, Anna. 20

ANNA [*Scornfully*]. Sorry!

CHRIS. But Ay'm not sick inside my head the vay you mean. Ay'm sick from tank too much about you, about me.

ANNA. And how about me? D'you suppose I ain't been thinking too?

CHRIS. Ay'm sorry, Anna. [*He sees her bag and gives a start.*] You pack your bag, Anna? You vas going—?

ANNA [*Forcibly*]. Yes, I was going right back to what you think.

CHRIS. Anna! 30

ANNA. I went ashore to get a train for New York. I'd been waiting and waiting 'till I was sick of it. Then I changed my mind and decided not to go today. But I'm going first thing tomorrow, so it'll all be the same in the end.

CHRIS [*Raising his head—pleadingly*]. No you never do dat, Anna!

ANNA [*With a sneer*]. Why not, I'd like to know?

CHRIS. You don't never gat to do—dat vay—no more, Ay tal you. Ay fix dat up all right.

ANNA [*Suspiciously*]. Fix up what? 40

CHRIS [*Not seeming to have heard her question—sadly*]. You vas vaiting, you say? You vasn't vaiting for me, Ay bet?

ANNA [*Callously*]. You'd win.

CHRIS. For dat Irish fallar?

ANNA [*Defiantly*]. Yes—if you want to know! [*Then with a forlorn laugh.*] If he did come back it'd only be 'cause he wanted to beat me up or kill me, I suppose. But even if he did, I'd rather have him come than not show up at all. I wouldn't care what he did.

CHRIS. Ay guess it's true you vas in love with him all right. 50

ANNA. You guess!

CHRIS [*Turning to her earnestly*]. And Ay'm sorry for you like hell he don't come, Anna!

ANNA [*Softened*]. Seems to me you've changed your tune a lot.

CHRIS. Ay've been tanking, and Ay guess it vas all my fault—all bad tangs dat happen to you. [*Pleadingly.*] You try for not hate me, Anna. Ay'm crazy ole fool, dat's all.

ANNA. Who said I hated you?

CHRIS. Ay'm sorry for everytang Ay do wrong for you, 60 Anna. Ay vant for you be happy all rest of your life for make up! It makes you happy marry dat Irish fallar, Ay vant it, too.

ANNA [*Dully*]. Well, there ain't no chance. But I'm glad you think different about it, anyway.

CHRIS [*Supplicatingly*]. And you tank—maybe—you forgive me sometime?

ANNA [*With a wan smile*]. I'll forgive you right now.

CHRIS [*Seizing her hand and kissing it—brokenly*]. Anna lilla! Anna lilla! 70

ANNA [*Touched but a bit embarrassed*]. Don't bawl about it. There ain't nothing to forgive, anyway. It ain't your fault, and it ain't mine, and it ain't his neither. We're all poor nuts, and things happen, and we yust get mixed in wrong, that's all.

CHRIS [*Eagerly*]. You say right tang, Anna, py golly! It ain't nobody's fault! [*Shaking his fist.*] It's dat ole davil, sea!

ANNA [*With an exasperated laugh*]. Gee, won't you ever can that stuff? [*Chris relapses into injured silence. After a pause Anna continues curiously.*] You said a minute ago you'd fixed something up—about me. What was it? 80

CHRIS [*After a hesitating pause*]. Ay'm shipping avay on sea again, Anna.

ANNA [*Astounded*]. You're—what?

CHRIS. Ay sign on steamer sail tomorrow. Ay gat my ole yob—bo'sun. [*Anna stares at him. As he goes on, a bitter smile comes over her face.*] Ay tank dat's best tang for you. Ay only bring you bad luck, Ay tank. Ay make your mo'der's life sorry. Ay don't vant make yours dat vay, but Ay do yust same. Dat ole davil, sea, she make me Yonah man ain't no good for nobody. And I tank now it ain't no use fight with sea. No man dat 90 live going to beat her, py yingo!

ANNA [*With a laugh of helpless bitterness*]. So that's how you've fixed me, is it?

CHRIS. Yes, Ay tank if dat ole davil gat me back she leave you alone den.

ANNA [*Bitterly*]. But, for Gawd's sake, don't you see, you're doing the same thing you've always done? Don't you see—? [*But she sees the look of obsessed stubbornness on her father's face and gives it up helplessly.*] But what's the use of talking. You ain't right, that's what. I'll never blame you for nothing no 100 more. But how you could figure out that was fixing me—!

CHRIS. Dat ain't all. Ay gat dem fallars in steamship office to pay you all money coming to me every month vhile Ay'm avay.

ANNA [*With a hard laugh*]. Thanks. But I guess I won't be hard up for no small change.

CHRIS [*Hurt—humbly*]. It ain't much, Ay know, but it's plenty for keep you so you never gat go back—

ANNA [*Shortly*]. Shut up, will you? We'll talk about it later, see?

CHRIS [*After a pause—ingratiatingly*]. You like Ay go 110 ashore look for dat Irish fallar, Anna?

ANNA [*Angrily*]. Not much! Think I want to drag him back?

CHRIS [*After a pause—uncomfortably*]. Py golly, dat booze don't go vell. Give me fever, Ay tank. Ay feel hot like hell. [*He takes off his coat and lets it drop on the floor. There is a loud thud.*]

ANNA [*With a start*]. What you got in your pocket, for Pete's sake—a ton of lead? [*She reaches down, takes the coat and pulls out a revolver—looks from it to him in amazement.*] A gun? What were you doing with this?

CHRIS [*Sheepishly*]. Ay forgat. Ain't nutting. Ain't loaded, 120 anyway.

ANNA [*Breaking it open to make sure—then closing it again—looking at him suspiciously*]. That ain't telling me why you got it?

CHRIS [*Sheepishly*]. Ay'm ole fool. Ay gat it vhen Ay go ashore first. Ay tank den it's all fault of dat Irish fallar.

ANNA [*With a shudder*]. Say, you're crazier than I thought. I never dreamt you'd go that far.

CHRIS [*Quickly*]. Ay don't. Ay gat better sense right avay. Ay don't never buy bullets even. It ain't his fault, Ay know. 130

ANNA [*Still suspicious of him*]. Well, I'll take care of this for a while, loaded or not. [*She puts it in the drawer of table and closes the drawer.*]

CHRIS [*Placatingly*]. Throw it overboard if you vant. Ay don't care. [*Then after a pause.*] Py golly, Ay tank Ay go lie down. Ay feel sick. [*Anna takes a magazine from the table. Chris hesitates by her chair.*] Ve talk again before Ay go, yes?

ANNA [*Dully*]. Where's this ship going to?

CHRIS. Cape Town. Dat's in South Africa. She's British steamer called Londonderry. [*He stands hesitatingly—finally blurts* 140 *out.*] Anna—you forgive me sure?

ANNA [*Wearily*]. Sure I do. You ain't to blame. You're yust—what you are—like me.

CHRIS [*Pleadingly*]. Den—you lat me kiss you again once?

ANNA [*Raising her face—forcing a wan smile*]. Sure. No hard feelings.

CHRIS [*Kisses her—brokenly*]. Anna lilla! Ay—[*He fights for words to express himself, but finds none—miserably—with a sob.*] Ay can't say it. Good-night, Anna.

ANNA. Good-night. [*He picks up the can of beer and goes* 150 *slowly into the room on left, his shoulders bowed, his head sunk forward dejectedly. He closes the door after him. Anna turns over the pages of the magazine, trying desperately to banish her thoughts by looking at the pictures. This fails to distract her, and flinging the magazine back on the table, she springs to her feet and walks about the cabin distractedly, clenching and unclenching her hands. She speaks aloud to herself in a tense, trembling voice.*] Gawd, I can't stand this much longer! What am I waiting for anyway?—like a damn fool! [*She laughs helplessly, then checks herself abruptly, as she hears the sound of heavy footsteps* 160 *on the deck outside. She appears to recognize these and her face lights up with joy. She gasps:*] Mat! [*A strange terror seems suddenly to seize her. She rushes to the table, takes the revolver out of the drawer and crouches down in the corner, left, behind the cupboard. A moment later the door is flung open and Mat Burke appears in the doorway. He is in bad shape—his clothes torn and dirty, covered with sawdust as if he had been grovelling or sleeping on barroom floors. There is a red bruise on his forehead over one of his eyes, another over one cheekbone, his knuckles are skinned and raw—plain evidence of the fighting he has been* 170 *through on his "bat." His eyes are bloodshot and heavy-lidded, his face has a bloated look. But beyond these appearances—the results of heavy drinking—there is an expression in his eyes of wild mental turmoil, of impotent animal rage baffled by its own abject misery.*]

BURKE [*Peers blinkingly about the cabin—hoarsely*]. Let you not be hiding from me, whoever's here—though 'tis well you know I'd have a right to come back and murder you. [*He stops to listen. Hearing no sound, he closes the door behind him and comes forward to the table. He throws himself into the* 180 *rocking-chair—despondently.*] There's no one here, I'm thinking, and 'tis a great fool I am to be coming. [*With a sort of dumb, uncomprehending anguish.*] Yerra, Mat Burke, 'tis a great jackass you've become and what's got into you at all, at all? She's gone out of this long ago, I'm telling you, and you'll never see her face again. [*Anna stands up, hesitating, struggling between joy and fear. Burke's eyes fall on Anna's bag. He leans over to examine it.*] What's this? [*Joyfully.*] It's hers. She's not gone! But where is she? Ashore? [*Darkly.*] What would she be doing ashore on this rotten night? [*His face suddenly convulsed with grief* 190 *and rage.*] 'Tis that, is it? Oh, God's curse on her! [*Raging.*] I'll wait 'till she comes and choke her dirty life out. [*Anna starts, her face grows hard. She steps into the room, the revolver in her right hand by her side.*]

ANNA [*In a cold hard tone*]. What are you doing here?

BURKE [*Wheeling about with a terrified gasp*]. Glory be to God! [*They remain motionless and silent for a moment, holding each other's eyes.*]

ANNA [*In the same hard voice*]. Well, can't you talk?

BURKE [*Trying to fall into an easy, careless tone*]. You've 200 a year's growth scared out of me, coming at me so sudden and me thinking I was alone.

ANNA. You've got your nerve butting in here without knocking or nothing. What d'you want?

BURKE [*Airily*]. Oh, nothing much. I was wanting to have a last word with you, that's all. [*He moves a step toward her.*]

ANNA [*Sharply—raising the revolver in her hand*]. Careful now! Don't try getting too close. I heard what you said you'd do to me.

BURKE [*Noticing the revolver for the first time*]. Is it murdering me you'd be now, God forgive you? [*Then with a con-* 210 *temptuous laugh.*] Or is it thinking I'd be frightened by that old tin whistle? [*He walks straight for her.*]

ANNA [*Wildly*]. Look out, I tell you!

BURKE [*Who has come so close that the revolver is almost touching his chest*]. Let you shoot, then! [*Then with sudden wild grief.*] Let you shoot, then! I'm saying, and be done with it! Let you end me with a shot and I'll be thanking you, for it's a rotten dog's life I've lived the past two days since I've known what you are, 'til I'm after wishing I was never born at all!

ANNA [*Overcome—letting the revolver drop to the floor,* 220 *as if her fingers had no strength to hold it—hysterically*]. What d'you want coming here? Why don't you beat it? Go on. [*She passes him and sinks down in the rocking-chair.*]

BURKE [*Following her—mournfully*]. 'Tis right you'd be asking

why I did come. [*Then angrily*.] 'Tis because 'tis a great weak
fool of the world I am, and me tormented with the wickedness
you'd told of yourself, and drinking oceans of booze that'd make
me forget. Forget? Divil a word I'd forget, and your face grinning always in front of my eyes, awake or asleep, 'till I do be
thinking a madhouse is the proper place for me.   230

ANNA [*Glancing at his hands and face—scornfully*]. You look
like you ought to be put away some place. Wonder you wasn't
pulled in. You been scrapping, too, ain't you?

BURKE. I have—with every scut would take off his coat to me!
[*Fiercely*.] And each time I'd be hitting one a clout in the mug,
it wasn't his face I'd be seeing at all, but yours, and me wanting
to drive you a blow would knock you out of the world where
I wouldn't be seeing or thinking more of you.

ANNA [*Her lips trembling pitifully*]. Thanks!

BURKE [*Walking up and down—distractedly*]. That's right,   240
make game of me! Oh, I'm a great coward surely, to be coming
back to speak with you at all. You've a right to laugh at me.

ANNA. I ain't laughing at you, Mat.

BURKE [*Unheeding*]. You to be what you are, and me to be
Mat Burke, and me to be drove back to look at you again! 'Tis
black shame is on me!

ANNA [*Resentfully*]. Then get out. No one's holding you!

BURKE [*Bewilderedly*]. And me to listen to that talk from a
woman like you and be frightened to close her mouth with a slap!
Oh, God help me, I'm a yellow coward for all men to spit at!   250
[*Then furiously*.] But I'll not be getting out of this 'till I've had
me word. [*Raising his fist threateningly*.] And let you look out
how you'd drive me! [*Letting his fist fall helplessly*.] Don't be
angry now! I'm raving like a real lunatic, I'm thinking, and the
sorrow you put on me has my brains drownded in grief. [*Suddenly bending down to her and grasping her arm intensely*.] Tell
me it's a lie, I'm saying! That's what I'm after coming to hear
you say.

ANNA [*Dully*]. A lie? What?

BURKE [*With passionate entreaty*]. All the badness you   260
told me two days back. Sure it must be a lie! You was only making
game of me, wasn't you? Tell me 'twas a lie, Anna, and I'll be
saying prayers of thanks on my two knees to the Almighty God!

ANNA [*Terribly shaken—faintly*]. I can't, Mat. [*As he turns
away—imploringly*.] Oh, Mat, won't you see that no matter
what I was I ain't that any more? Why, listen! I packed up my bag

this afternoon and went ashore. I'd been waiting here all alone
for two days, thinking maybe you'd come back—thinking maybe
you'd think over all I'd said—and maybe—oh, I don't know what
I was hoping! But I was afraid to even go out of the cabin   270
for a second, honest—afraid you might come and not find me here.
Then I gave up hope when you didn't show up and I went to the
railroad station. I was going to New York. I was going back—

BURKE [*Hoarsely*]. God's curse on you!

ANNA. Listen, Mat! You hadn't come, and I'd gave up hope.
But—in the station—I couldn't go. I'd bought my ticket and
everything. [*She takes the ticket from her dress and tries to hold
it before his eyes.*] But I got to thinking about you—and I couldn't
take the train—I couldn't! So I come back here—to wait some
more. Oh, Mat, don't you see I've changed? Can't you for-   280
give what's dead and gone—and forget it?

BURKE [*Turning on her—overcome by rage again*]. Forget, is
it? I'll not forget 'til my dying day, I'm telling you, and me tormented with thoughts. [*In a frenzy.*] Oh, I'm wishing I had wan
of them fornenst me this minute and I'd beat him with my fists
'till he'd be a bloody corpse! I'm wishing the whole lot of them
will roast in hell 'til the Judgment Day—and yourself along with
them, for you're as bad as they are.

ANNA [*Shuddering*]. Mat! [*Then after a pause—in a voice of
dead, stony calm.*] Well, you've had your say. Now you   290
better beat it.

BURKE [*Starts slowly for the door—hesitates—then after a
pause*]. And what'll you be doing?

ANNA. What difference does it make to you?

BURKE. I'm asking you!

ANNA [*In the same tone*]. My bag's packed and I got my ticket.
I'll go to New York tomorrow.

BURKE [*Helplessly*]. You mean—you'll be doing the same again?

ANNA [*Stonily*]. Yes.

BURKE [*In anguish*]. You'll not! Don't torment me with   300
that talk! 'Tis a she-divil you are, sent to drive me mad entirely!

ANNA [*Her voice breaking*]. Oh, for Gawd's sake, Mat, leave
me alone! Go away! Don't you see I'm licked? Why d'you want
to keep on kicking me?

BURKE [*Indignantly*]. And don't you deserve the worst I'd say,
God forgive you?

ANNA. All right. Maybe I do. But don't rub it in. Why ain't
you done what you said you was going to? Why ain't you got

that ship was going to take you to the other side of the earth
where you'd never see me again?   310

BURKE. I have.

ANNA [*Startled*]. What—then you're going—honest?

BURKE. I signed on today at noon, drunk as I was—and she's
sailing tomorrow.

ANNA. And where's she going to?

BURKE. Cape Town.

ANNA [*The memory of having heard that name a little while
before coming to her—with a start, confusedly*]. Cape Town?
Where's that? Far away?

BURKE. 'Tis at the end of Africa. That's far for you.   320

ANNA [*Forcing a laugh*]. You're keeping your word all right,
ain't you? [*After a slight pause—curiously.*] What's the boat's
name?

BURKE. The Londonderry.

ANNA [*It suddenly comes to her that this is the same ship her
father is sailing on*]. The Londonderry! It's the same—Oh, this is
too much! [*With a wild ironical laughter.*] Ha-ha-ha!

BURKE. What's up with you now?

ANNA. Ha-ha-ha! It's funny, funny! I'll die laughing!

BURKE [*Irritated*]. Laughing at what?   330

ANNA. It's a secret. You'll know soon enough. It's funny. [*Controlling herself—after a pause—cynically.*] What kind of a place
is this Cape Town? Plenty of dames there, I suppose?

BURKE. To hell with them! That I may never see another woman
to my dying hour!

ANNA. That's what you say now, but I'll bet that by the time
you get there you'll have forgot all about me and start in talking
the same old bull you talked to me the first one you meet.

BURKE [*Offended*]. I'll not, then! God mend you, is it making
me out to be the like of yourself you are, and you taking up   340
with this one and that all the years of your life?

ANNA [*Angrily assertive*]. Yes, that's yust what I do mean!
You been doing the same thing all your life, picking up a new
girl in every port. How're you any better than I was?

BURKE [*Thoroughly exasperated*]. Is it no shame you have at
all? I'm a fool to be wasting talk on you and you hardened in
badness. I'll go out of this and lave you alone forever. [*He starts
for the door—then stops to turn on her furiously.*] And I suppose
'tis the same lies you told them all before that you told to me?

ANNA [*Indignantly*]. That's a lie! I never did!   350

BURKE [*Miserably*]. You'd be saying that anyway.

ANNA [*Forcibly, with growing intensity*]. Are you trying to accuse me of being in love—really in love—with them?

BURKE. I'm thinking you were, surely.

ANNA [*Furiously, as if this were the last insult—advancing on him threateningly*]. You mutt, you! I've stood enough from you! Don't you dare. [*With scornful bitterness.*] Love 'em! Oh, my Gawd! You damn thick-head! Love 'em? [*Savagely.*] I hated 'em, I tell you! Hated 'em, hated 'em! And may Gawd strike me dead this minute and my mother, too, if she was alive, if I ain't   360 telling you the honest truth!

BURKE [*Immensely pleased by her vehemence—a light beginning to break over his face—but still uncertain, torn between doubt and the desire to believe—helplessly*]. If I could only be believing you now!

ANNA [*Distractedly*]. Oh, what's the use? What's the use of me talking? What's the use of anything? [*Pleadingly.*] Oh, Mat, you mustn't think that for a second! You mustn't! Think all the other bad about me you want to, and I won't kick, cause you've a right to. But don't think that! [*On the point of tears.*] I   370 couldn't bear it! It'd be yust too much to know you was going away where I'd never see you again—thinking that about me!

BURKE [*After an inward struggle—tensely—forcing out the words with difficulty*]. If I was believing—that you'd never had love for any other man in the world but me—I could be forgetting the rest, maybe.

ANNA [*With a cry of joy*]. Mat!

BURKE [*Slowly*]. If 'tis truth you're after telling, I'd have a right, maybe, to believe you'd changed—and that I'd changed you myself 'til the thing you'd been all your life wouldn't be   380 you any more at all.

ANNA [*Hanging on his words—breathlessly*]. Oh, Mat! That's what I been trying to tell you all along!

BURKE [*Simply*]. For I've a power of strength in me to lead men the way I want, and women too, maybe, and I'm thinking I'd change you to a new woman entirely, so I'd never know, or you either, what kind of woman you'd been in the past at all.

ANNA. Yes, you could, Mat! I know you could!

BURKE. And I'm thinking 'twasn't your fault, maybe, but having that old ape for a father that left you to grow up alone, made   390 you what you was. And if I could be believing 'tis only me you—

ANNA [*Distractedly*]. You got to believe it, Mat! What can I do? I'll do anything, anything you want to prove I'm not lying.

BURKE [*Suddenly seems to have a solution. He feels in the*

pocket of his coat and grasps something—solemnly]. Would you be willing to swear an oath, now—a terrible, fearful oath would send your soul to the divils in hell if you was lying?

ANNA [*Eagerly*]. Sure, I'll swear, Mat—on anything!

BURKE [*Takes a small, cheap old crucifix from his pocket and holds it up for her to see*]. Will you swear on this?   400

ANNA [*Reaching out for it*]. Yes. Sure I will. Give it to me.

BURKE [*Holding it away*]. 'Tis a cross was given me by my mother, God rest her soul. [*He makes the sign of the cross mechanically.*] I was a lad only, and she told me to keep it by me if I'd be waking or sleeping and never lose it, and it'd bring me luck. She died soon after. But I'm after keeping it with me from that day to this, and I'm telling you there's great power in it, and 'tis great bad luck it's saved me from and me roaming the seas, and I having it tied round my neck when my last ship sunk, and it bringing me safe to land when the others went to their   410 death. [*Very earnestly.*] And I'm warning you now, if you'd swear an oath on this, 'tis my old woman herself will be looking down from Hiven above, and praying Almighty God and the Saints to put a great curse on you if she'd hear you swearing a lie!

ANNA [*Awed by his manner—superstitiously*]. I wouldn't have the nerve—honest—if it was a lie. But it's the truth and I ain't scared to swear. Give it to me.

BURKE [*Handing it to her—almost frightenedly, as if he feared for her safety*]. Be careful what you'd swear, I'm saying.   420

ANNA [*Holding the cross gingerly*]. Well—what do you want me to swear? You say it.

BURKE. Swear I'm the only man in the world iver you felt love for.

ANNA [*Looking into his eyes steadily*]. I swear it.

BURKE. And that you'll be forgetting from this day all the badness you've done and never do the like of it again.

ANNA [*Forcibly*]. I swear it! I swear it by God!

BURKE. And may the blackest curse of God strike you if you're lying. Say it now!   430

ANNA. And may the blackest curse of God strike me if I'm lying!

BURKE [*With a stupendous sigh*]. Oh, glory be to God, I'm after believing you now! [*He takes the cross from her hand, his face beaming with joy, and puts it back in his pocket. He puts his arm about her waist and is about to kiss her when he stops, appalled by some terrible doubt.*]

ANNA [*Alarmed*]. What's the matter with you?

BURKE [*With a sudden fierce questioning*]. Is it Catholic ye are? 440

ANNA [*Confused*]. No. Why?

BURKE [*Filled with a sort of bewildered foreboding*]. Oh, God, help me! [*With a dark glance of suspicion at her.*] There's some divil's trickery in it, to be swearing an oath on a Catholic cross and you wan of the others.

ANNA [*Distractedly*]. Oh, Mat, don't you believe me?

BURKE [*Miserably*]. If it isn't a Catholic you are—

ANNA. I ain't nothing. What's the difference? Didn't you hear me swear?

BURKE [*Passionately*]. Oh, I'd a right to stay away from 450 you—but I couldn't! I was loving you in spite of it all and wanting to be with you, God forgive me, no matter what you are. I'd go mad if I'd not have you! I'd be killing the world—[*He seizes her in his arms and kisses her fiercely.*]

ANNA [*With a gasp of joy*]. Mat!

BURKE [*Suddenly holding her away from him and staring into her eyes as if to probe into her soul—slowly*]. If your oath is no proper oath at all, I'll have to be taking your naked word for it and have you anyway, I'm thinking—I'm needing you that bad!

ANNA [*Hurt—reproachfully*]. Mat! I swore, didn't I? 460

BURKE [*Defiantly, as if challenging fate*]. Oath or no oath, 'tis no matter. We'll be wedded in the morning, with the help of God. [*Still more defiantly.*] We'll be happy now, the two of us, in spite of the divil! [*He crushes her to him and kisses her again. The door on the left is opened and Chris appears in the doorway. He stands blinking at them. At first the old expression of hatred of Burke comes into his eyes instinctively. Then a look of resignation and relief takes its place. His face lights up with a sudden happy thought. He turns back into the bedroom—reappears immediately with the tin can of beer in his hand—grinning.*] 470

CHRIS. Ve have a drink on this, py golly! [*They break away from each other with startled exclamations.*]

BURKE [*Explosively*]. God stiffen it! [*He takes a step towards Chris threateningly.*]

ANNA [*Happily—to her father*]. That's the way to talk! [*With a laugh.*] And say, it's about time for you and Mat to kiss and make up. You're going to be shipmates on the Londonderry, did you know it?

BURKE [*Astounded*]. Shipmates—Has himself—

CHRIS [*Equally astounded*]. Ay vas bo'sun on her. 480

BURKE. The divil! [*Then angrily.*] You'd be going back to sea and leaving her alone, would you?

ANNA [*Quickly*]. It's all right, Mat. That's where he belongs, and I want him to go. You got to go, too; we'll need the money. [*With a laugh, as she gets the glasses.*] And as for me being alone, that runs in the family, and I'll get used to it. [*Pouring out their glasses.*] I'll get a little house somewhere and I'll make a regular place for you two to come back to,—wait and see. And now you drink up and be friends.

BURKE [*Happily—but still a bit resentful against the old* 490 *man*]. Sure! [*Clinking his glass against Chris'.*] Here's luck to you! [*He drinks.*]

CHRIS [*Subdued—his face melancholy*]. Skoal. [*He drinks.*]

BURKE [*To Anna, with a wink*]. You'll not be lonesome long. I'll see to that, with the help of God. 'Tis himself here will be having a grandchild to ride on his foot, I'm telling you!

ANNA [*Turning away in embarrassment*]. Quit the kidding, now. [*She picks up her bag and goes into the room on left. As soon as she is gone Burke relapses into an attitude of gloomy thought. Chris stares at his beer absent-mindedly. Finally* 500 *Burke turns on him.*]

BURKE. Is it any religion at all you have, you and your Anna?

CHRIS [*Surprised*]. Vhy yes, ve vas Lutheran in ole country.

BURKE [*Horrified*]. Luthers, is it? [*Then with a grim resignation, slowly, aloud to himself.*] Well, I'm damned then surely. Yerra, what's the difference? 'Tis the will of God, anyway.

CHRIS [*Moodily preoccupied with his own thoughts—speaks with somber premonition as Anna re-enters from the left*]. It's funny. It's queer, yes—you and me shipping on same boat dat vay. It ain't right. Ay don't know—it's dat funny vay ole davil sea 510 do her vorst dirty tricks, yes. It's so. [*He gets up and goes back and, opening the door, stares out into the darkness.*]

BURKE [*Nodding his head in gloomy acquiescence—with a great sigh*]. I'm fearing maybe you have the right of it for once, divil take you.

ANNA [*Forcing a laugh*]. Gee, Mat, you ain't agreeing with him, are you? [*She comes forward and puts her arm about his shoulder —with a determined gaiety.*] Aw say, what's the matter? Cut out the gloom. We're all fixed now, ain't we? Me and you? [*Pours out more beer into his glass and fills one for herself—slaps* 520 *him on the back.*] Come on! Here's to the sea, no matter what! Be a game sport and drink to that! Come on! [*She gulps down her glass. Burke banishes his superstitious premonitions with a defiant jerk of his head, grins up at her, and drinks to her toast.*]

CHRIS [*Looking out into the night—lost in his somber pre-occupation—shakes his head and mutters*]. Fog, fog, fog, all bloody time. You can't see where you vas going, no. Only dat ole davil, sea—she knows! [*The two stare at him. From the harbor comes the muffled, mournful wail of steamers' whistles.*]

THE CURTAIN FALLS

GENERAL INDEX

749